Lecture Notes in Artificial Intelligence   10383

Subseries of Lecture Notes in Computer Science

More information about this series at http://www.springer.com/series/1244

Herman Geuvers · Matthew England
Osman Hasan · Florian Rabe
Olaf Teschke (Eds.)

Intelligent Computer Mathematics

10th International Conference, CICM 2017
Edinburgh, UK, July 17–21, 2017
Proceedings

 Springer

Editors
Herman Geuvers ⓘ
Radboud University
Nijmegen
The Netherlands

Matthew England ⓘ
Coventry University
Coventry
UK

Osman Hasan ⓘ
National University of Sciences
  and Technology
Islamabad
Pakistan

Florian Rabe
Jacobs University Bremen
Bremen
Germany

Olaf Teschke
FIZ Karlsruhe
Berlin
Germany

ISSN 0302-9743   ISSN 1611-3349 (electronic)
Lecture Notes in Artificial Intelligence
ISBN 978-3-319-62074-9   ISBN 978-3-319-62075-6 (eBook)
DOI 10.1007/978-3-319-62075-6

Library of Congress Control Number: 2017944318

LNCS Sublibrary: SL7 – Artificial Intelligence

Printed on acid-free paper

This Springer imprint is published by Springer Nature
The registered company is Springer International Publishing AG
The registered company address is: Gewerbestrasse 11, 6330 Cham, Switzerland

Preface

This volume contains the papers presented at CICM 2017: the 10th Conference on Intelligent Computer Mathematics held during July 17–21, 2017 in Edinburgh.

Mathematics is "the queen of the sciences" (Friedrich Gauss), and "the language with which God has written the universe" (Galileo Galilei). This language is at the same time flexible enough to describe a wide variety of complex phenomena and rigorous enough to be verified in detail based on a small set of assumptions. But the collection of mathematical knowledge is exploding, and it can no longer be handled by the paradigmatic "pencil and paper" approach: Each year there are 120,000 new articles and some proofs are so large and complicated that human verification has become infeasible.

The Conference on Intelligent Computer Mathematics (CICM) offers a venue for discussing and developing ways of involving computers in the process of "doing mathematics" in the broadest sense. The conference is the result of merging three independent meetings with considerable overlap: Calculemus (integration of deduction and symbolic calculation), Mathematical Knowledge Management (MKM), and Digital Mathematical Libraries (DML). CICM has been held annually since 2008, with previous meetings in Birmingham (UK 2008), Grand Bend (Canada 2009), Paris (France 2010), Bertinoro (Italy 2011), Bremen (Germany 2012), Bath (UK 2013), Coimbra (Portugal 2014), Washington, DC (USA 2015), and Białystok (Poland 2016). As in previous years, we had several tracks: Calculemus, Digital Mathematics Libraries (DML), and Mathematical Knowledge Management (MKM), which mirror the three main communities that form CICM, and a track on "Systems and Projects."

The papers accepted to these four tracks form the content of these proceedings. CICM 2017 had invited talks by Alan Bundy (University of Edinburgh), Grant Olney Passmore (University of Cambridge), and Przemysław Chojecki (Polish Academy of Sciences). Additionally, the conference had two workshops, a doctoral mentoring program, and an informal track for presenting work in progress; the proceedings of these events are published with CEUR-WS. The program of the meeting, as well as additional materials, is available at http://cicm-conference.org/2017/.

The track structure of CICM provides a framework for organizing the conference. The Calculemus track examines the integration of symbolic computation and mechanized reasoning. The Digital Mathematics Libraries track deals with math-aware technologies, standards, algorithms, and processes. The Mathematical Knowledge Management track is concerned with all aspects of managing mathematical knowledge in informal, semi-formal, and formal settings. The Systems and Projects track contains descriptions of systems and relevant projects, both of which are key to a research topic where theory and practice interact on explicitly represented knowledge.

This year, CICM had 40 submissions. Each submission received at least three reviews. The reviewing included a response period, in which authors could clarify points raised by the reviewers. This made for a highly productive round of deliberations before the final decisions were taken. In the end, the Program Committees of the tracks decided to accept 24 papers for these proceedings.

The Program Committee work for the tracks was managed using the EasyChair system. This year we used the multi-track facility provided by EasyChair. This made track assignments, reviewing, and dealing with conflicts of interest very flexible. The fact that we had five chairs – the general chair and four track chairs – together with excellent conflict management made transparent and safe handling of submissions authored or co-authored by the track chairs very easy. As in previous years, several workshops and informal programs were organized in conjunction with CICM 2017. This year these were:

- The CICM Doctoral Program, providing a dedicated forum for PhD students to present their on-going or planned research and receive feedback, advice, and suggestions from a dedicated research advisory board.
- The CICM Work-in-Progress Session, a forum for the presentation of original work not yet in a suitable form for communication as a formal paper.
- MathUI 2017: 12th Workshop on Mathematical User Interfaces, an international workshop to discuss how users can be best supported when doing/ learning/searching for/interacting with mathematics using a computer. MathUI was organized by Andrea Kohlhase, University of Applied Sciences Neu-Ulm, Germany, and Marco Pollanen, Trent University Peterborough, Ontario Canada.
- The 28th OpenMath Workshop. OpenMath is a language for exchanging mathematical formulae across applications (such as computer algebra systems and theorem provers). The workshop was organized by James Davenport, the University of Bath, and Michael Kohlhase, FAU Erlangen-Nürnberg, Germany

The conference was organized at the University of Edinburgh. We heart-fully thank the University of Edinburgh for the hospitality, and in particular we thank the local organizers, Jacques Fleuriot and Suzanne Perry, for all their good work.

May 2017

Herman Geuvers
Matthew England
Osman Hasan
Florian Rabe
Olaf Teschke

Organization

CICM 2017 Organizing Committee

General Program Chair

Herman Geuvers   Radboud University, The Netherlands

Conference Chair

Jacques Fleuriot   University of Edinburgh, UK

Calculemus Track Chair

Matthew England   Coventry University, UK

DML Track Chair

Olaf Teschke   FIZ Karlsruhe, Germany

MKM Track Chair

Florian Rabe   Jacobs University Bremen, Germany

Systems and Projects Chair

Osman Hasan   National University of Sciences and Technology, Pakistan

Workshops Chair

Petros Papapanagiotou   University of Edinburgh, UK

Doctoral Programme Chair

Adnan Rashid   National University of Sciences and Technology, Pakistan

Publicity Chair

Serge Autexier   DFKI Bremen, Germany

CICM Steering Committee

Volker Sorge (Secretary)
Wolfgang Windsteiger (Calculemus representative)
Petr Sojka (DML representative)
Adam Naumowicz (MKM representative)
William Farmer (Treasurer)

Michael Kohlhase (Outgoing PC chair)
Herman Geuvers (Incoming PC chair)

Program Committee

Waqar Ahmed	National University of Sciences and Technology, Pakistan
Rob Arthan	Queen Mary University of London, UK
Thierry Bouche	Université Grenoble Alpes, France
Jacques Carette	McMaster University, Canada
James H. Davenport	University of Bath, UK
Gabriel Dos Reis	Texas A&M University, USA
Catherine Dubois	École National Supérieure d'Informatique pour l'Industrie et l'Entreprise, France
Matthew England	Coventry University, UK
Madalina Erascu	Institute e-Austria Timisoara and West University of Timisoara, Romania
William Farmer	McMaster University, Canada
Herman Geuvers	Radboud University Nijmegen, The Netherlands
Osman Hasan	National University of Sciences and Technology, Pakistan
Paul Jackson	University of Edinburgh, UK
Mateja Jamnik	University of Cambridge, UK
P. Jansson	Chalmers University of Technology and University of Gothenburg, Sweden
Dejan Jovanović	SRI International, USA
Cezary Kaliszyk	University of Innsbruck, Austria
Manfred Kerber	University of Birmingham, UK
Michael Kohlhase	FAU Erlangen Nürnberg, Germany
Thomas Koprucki	Weierstrass Institute for Applied Analysis and Stochastics (WIAS), Germany
Laura Kovacs	Vienna University of Technology, Austria
Temur Kutsia	RISC, Johannes Kepler University Linz, Austria
Alexander Maletzky	RISC, Johannes Kepler University Linz, Austria
Adam Naumowicz	Institute of Informatics, University of Bialystok, Poland
Michael Norrish	NICTA, Australia
Florian Rabe	Jacobs University Bremen, Germany
Renaud Rioboo	École National Supérieure d'Informatique pour l'Industrie et l'Entreprise, France
Jiří Rákosník	Institute of Mathematics of the Czech Academy of Sciences, Czech Republic
Claudio Sacerdoti Coen	University of Bologna, Italy
Alan Sexton	University of Birmingham, UK
Muhammad Umair Siddique	McMaster University, Canada
Geoff Sutcliffe	University of Miami, USA
Sofiene Tahar	Concordia University, Canada
Olaf Teschke	FIZ Karlsruhe, Germany

Nicolas Thiery	Université Paris Sud, France
Josef Urban	Czech Technical University in Prague, Czech Republic
Stephen Watt	University of Waterloo, Canada
Richard Zanibbi	Rochester Institute of Technology, USA

Additional Reviewers

Brown, Chad	Harrison, John	Robillard, Simon
Carette, Jacques	Mukherjee, Rajdeep	Wiedijk, Freek
Ebner, Gabriel	Müller, Fabian	
Gauthier, Thibault	Pak, Karol	

Invited Papers

Reformation: A Generic Algorithm for Repairing Faulty Logical Theories

Alan Bundy

University of Edinburgh, Edinburgh, UK
May 16, 2017

We are interested in how reasoning failures can trigger representational change. Moreover, we focus on *conceptual* changes, i.e., not just the addition or deletion of axioms in a fixed logical theory, but changes in the *language* in which the axioms are expressed. We present the *Reformation* algorithm to repair the language of faulty, first-order theories.

Typical language changes include: the splitting of a function (or predicate) into two functions (or predicates); the merging of two distinct functions (or predicates) into one; and the change of the arity of a function (or predicate), e.g., by removing or adding one or more arguments.

The reasoning failures we consider take two forms: that a false conjecture has been proved; or that a true conjecture cannot be proved.

The key idea is to analyse the use of the unification algorithm during these proofs (or failed proof attempts) to suggest possible repairs to the language of the theory. We have developed a non-standard version of the first-order unification algorithm in which some of its steps are paired: each step leading to failure is paired with one leading to success. If one of these steps is triggered during a unification application, Reformation suggests one or more signature repairs that will cause the dual step to be triggered instead. The hypothesis is that:

> *Reformation systematically generates reversible repairs to faulty, first-order theories.*

We will illustrate the application of Reformation to a range of examples and state some of its theoretical properties.

Many of the repairs that Reformation suggests are intuitively plausible and result in an acceptable refinement of the theory's language. These language repairs complement the more usual axiom deletions and additions that are traditionally used in belief revision and abduction. Reformation repairs provide a way in which an axiom is not totally lost, but has its meaning evolved. We are currently exploring how to combine our language-changing repairs with the axiom addition/deletion ones.

Reformation was initially implemented in the context of SL resolution proofs using first-order clauses. It can be adapted to any inference mechanism that uses a unification algorithm. For instance, we also have implementations for multi-sortedfirst-order logic and for a description logic.

The research reported in this paper was supported by EPSRC grant EP/N014758/1.

Formal Verification of Financial Algorithms, Progress and Prospects

Grant Olney Passmore

Aesthetic Integration, London and Clare Hall,
University of Cambridge, England, UK
grant.passmore@cl.cam.ac.uk

Abstract. Many deep issues plaguing today's financial markets are symptoms of a fundamental problem: The complexity of algorithms underlying modern finance has significantly outpaced the power of traditional tools used to design and regulate them. At Aesthetic Integration, we've pioneered the use of formal verification for analysing the safety and fairness of financial algorithms. With a focus on financial infrastructure (e.g., the matching logics of exchanges and dark pools), we'll describe the landscape, and illustrate our Imandra formal verification system on a number of real-world examples. We'll sketch many open problems and future directions along the way.

DeepAlgebra - An Outline of a Program

Przemysław Chojecki[1,2]

[1] Polish Academy of Sciences, Warsaw, Poland
pchojecki@impan.pl
[2] University of Oxford, Oxford, UK
http://pchojecki.impan.pl

Abstract. We outline a program in the area of formalization of mathematics to automate theorem proving in algebra and algebraic geometry. We propose a construction of a dictionary between automated theorem provers and (La)TeX exploiting syntactic parsers. We describe its application to a repository of human-written facts and definitions in algebraic geometry (The Stacks Project). We use deep learning techniques.

Contents

DeepAlgebra - An Outline of a Program

Przemysław Chojecki[1,2]([⊠])

[1] Polish Academy of Sciences, Warsaw, Poland
pchojecki@impan.pl
[2] University of Oxford, Oxford, UK
http://pchojecki.impan.pl

Abstract. We outline a program in the area of formalization of mathematics to automate theorem proving in algebra and algebraic geometry. We propose a construction of a dictionary between automated theorem provers and (La)TeX exploiting syntactic parsers. We describe its application to a repository of human-written facts and definitions in algebraic geometry (The Stacks Project). We use deep learning techniques.

1 Introduction

Mathematics is a basis for the modern world. Not just simple mathematics, but also complex proofs underpin current breakthroughs in technology and science. Much of the physics depends on mathematical proofs. Proofs in mathematics itself are ubiquitous and many new mathematical theorems are proved daily. This leads to a specialization and a loss of a global picture for most of mathematicians. The formalization of mathematics started taking place to circumvent this difficulty and make sure that modern mathematics stands on firm grounds (cf. [8]).

The largest single piece of formalized mathematics to this day is a proof of the Feit-Thompson Odd Order Theorem, done by collaborative efforts of 15 mathematicians over a period of six years [7]. The proof itself which spans 250 pages of mathematics was formalized into more than 150,000 lines of code with roughly 4,000 definitions and 13,000 theorems. The research group developed along the way many reusable libraries in the COQ proof assistant [5].

It is obvious that if the project of formalizing mathematics is to be completed, it has to proceed much faster and use more effectively human power - especially if we want to use machines for proving new theorems. In [1] authors name two main bottlenecks:

(1) lack of automated methods for formalization (*autoformalization*);
(2) lack of strong automated methods to fill in the gaps in already formalized human-written proofs.

Date: October 3, 2016.

These ideas were conceived while the author was a research fellow at the University of Oxford. We thank Wojciech Zaremba (OpenAI) for pointing us to [1] which triggered writing this article and Maciej Zdanowicz (University of Warsaw) for numerous discussions which helped the author clarify his ideas.

H. Geuvers et al. (Eds.): CICM 2017, LNAI 10383, pp. 1–8, 2017.
DOI: 10.1007/978-3-319-62075-6_1

A basis for the research in [1], where the authors deal with the second bottleneck, is Mizar Mathematical Library (MML) which contains over 50,000 lemmas. The authors have used deep learning methods to select premises for the automatic theorem proving and automatically prove as many theorems as possible using at each step all previous theorems and proofs. To some extent this solves (2), though much more optimization work is needed to attain level of human effectiveness.

In this work, we focus on the first bottleneck. We propose a program to automate a formalization of large parts of modern algebraic geometry using deep learning techniques run on well-chosen repositories of human-written mathematical facts (The Stacks Project [17]). The main problem is the construction of a dictionary between human-written proofs in (La)TeX and Interactive Theorem Provers. Here we outline our program and lay a theoretical basis for it. We report on our progress on implementing it in subsequent papers and in [6]. Our main theoretical input is to use syntactic parsers run on The Stacks Project to correctly translate [17] into COQ, and then use hammers to verify its validity in COQ/E, and possibly reprove some of it by automated methods. Eventually this approach should lead to proving new theorems in algebraic geometry purely by machines.

As the last remark in the introduction, we notice that the formalization of mathematics and automatic theorem proving is important, because it can be viewed as a toy model for a harder problem, namely constructing an AI with an ability to write a self-correcting code (this is listed as one of the special projects in OpenAI project, see [13]). We believe that bringing theorem proving by AI to the human-level is a necessary step (and a very important one) towards tackling this harder problem.

2   The Stacks Project

Algebraic geometry is one of the pillars of modern mathematics. Its main object of study is algebraic varieties (vanishing loci of sets of polynomials) and maps between them. It builds upon standard algebra and study of rings and modules, and as such is highly symbolic. Because of that, we believe it is easier to formalize it rather than more analytic parts of mathematics where reasoning is more ad hoc and proofs can use tricky approximations, which seem hard to teach to a computer. On the other hand, the problem with algebraic geometry is the level of abstraction and the amount of terms which one needs to formulate the problems correctly.

When trying to formalize human-written proofs with a goal of training neural networks on them, one has to be sure that proofs are correct in the first place. In other words, one has to choose sources well. Mathematicians often write proofs in informal ways, leaving gaps to readers which are assumed to be experts in a given field as well.

That is why we propose as our training source the Stacks Project [17]. This is a repository of facts and theorems in algebra and algebraic geometry, which starts from the basic material and goes up to the current developments in the field. It is still actively developed with the help of dozens of volunteers and currently contains 509,794 lines of code and 5,347 pages (as we write).

Its huge advantage is that it is completely self-contained. There are no references to outside sources. Every fact is proved and can be traced to the axioms introduced at the beginning. The only problem for our goal is that it is written by humans and for humans.

3   Dictionary

In order to formalize this amount of mathematics (and go beyond it) one needs to automate the process. We remind a reader that our goal is to develop an AI which could prove new theorems in algebraic geometry by itself. To do that, one firstly needs to translate the source (The Stacks project in our case) to one of **Interactive Theorem Provers** (ITPs) such as COQ [5] or Mizar [2,12][1], and then use an **Automatic Theorem Prover** (ATP), for example E [14,15][2], together perhaps with some deep learning techniques to facilitate proving more complex theorems.

The first step of our DeepAlgebra program is to construct a **dictionary** between (La)TeX files and COQ/Mizar, which would translate .tex files into ITPs and vice versa. While one direction is relatively easy (ITP to .tex) as one can use fairly simple, hard-coded language, the other direction is much less trivial. This is due to the fact to which we have alluded before, that human-written mathematics happens in general to be informal with many gaps left to readers. Computer needs to be taught which sentences and words can be ignored as informal discussions and which are crucial to on-going proofs, as mathematical papers are not constructed in the form of "theorem, proof, theorem, proof", but often contains a valuable discussion outside of it.

The other problem is to correctly implement the abstraction in the form of Types (COQ). Algebra tends to use many words for the same thing and correctly storing it is crucial. For example computer needs to know that a "reduced scheme of finite type over a field" is the same thing as an "algebraic variety", while both characterizations give slightly different perspectives.

When trying to formalize The Stacks Project, most of these problems do not appear (or are easier) as the text itself is written in the form of definitions, followed by lemmas, followed by theorems. Thus translating .tex file into COQ in this case needs much less work than with the general mathematical paper[3], and we shall report on our progress elsewhere. However this does not solve the general problem, which is needed in order to formalize current mathematical work. General mathematical papers tend to be worse structured with respect to machines.

---

[1] Other standard ITPs include HOL (Light), Isabelle and ACL2.
[2] Other standard ATPs include Vampyre, Z3 and JProver.
[3] Partly because of the clear dependancy graph of definitions and theorems used in the Stacks Project, cf. section Hammers.

Let us observe that one can divide dictionaries into two categories:

(1) **automated**, where no human-help is needed to make a translation between (La)TeX and ITPs;
(2) **semi-automated**, which are assisted by a human, to correct mistakes and fill in the gaps in human-written proofs, which could not be filled by a computer.

One of general goals in the field of **Automated Reasoning in Large Theories** (ARLT) [19] should be creating a perfect automated dictionary, which translates .tex files to COQ/Mizar without information losses[4]. Nevertheless for our purposes of formalizing The Stacks Project semi-automated dictionary would be enough and is much easier to construct.

We remark that the problem of constructing a dictionary does not appear when one starts with already formalized proofs like Mizar Mathematical Library (as in [1]). This however is very limited and in the end one needs to find ways to automatically formalize human-written proofs to keep up with the developments of modern mathematics and eventually surpass it using AI. Despite many efforts to optimize ITPs/ATPs and their theorem proving capabilities, there are currently no dictionaries existing.

4   Building a Dictionary

Creating a dictionary in the above sense can be viewed as a **Natural Language Processing** (NLP) problem, where one tries to pass between human-written mathematics and ITPs. This approach offers plethora of methods to choose from. We present one which we plan to implement.

For us a **Type** is an abstract mathematical term (e.g. "group"), while a **variable** is an object of certain Type (e.g. in a sentence "Let G be a group" G is a variable of Type "group"). By **relation** we mean a first order logical sentence involving Types and variables. By a **library** we will mean an already constructed repository of defined objects and proven formalized theorems (in COQ), which can be used to prove new theorems. By an **environment** we mean a statement of a lemma or a theorem, or a proof (so any piece in (La)TeX in a form of \begin{} ... \end{}). This terminology is consistent with COQ.

Method: We build a dictionary by using a syntactic parser to identify Types and variables together with relations between them, which we then transfer directly to COQ. Issues which usually arise in machine translations like idioms or complex grammar, rarely appear in mathematical texts, hence a syntactic parser together with hard-coded translation of certain phrases (and environments) is enough to build a dictionary.

---

[4] Of course ARLT does not necessarily mean mathematics and thus in different scientific disciplines by a dictionary we mean a (semi)-automated way of passing between human-written science and according formal verificators.

Implementation: When analysing a .tex file we differentiate between (mathematical) English text and formulas occuring most commonly between dollar signs. Processing formulas from (La)TeX to COQ is relatively easy - apart from complicated diagrams which have to be split into direct formulas[5] - we can basically rewrite (La)TeX code into COQ one to one (i.e. a rule-based approach to machine translation).

The real problem is putting a text into COQ. A typical mathematical sentence will look like "A has property P, because B". In order to put it into COQ, we have to identify Types and variables (what kind of objects we are considering; here A can be either a Type or a variable), then identify logical dependencies (Type of A determined by B implies P). The actual verification of a sentence in COQ is the next step with which we deal in the next section. Building a dictionary amounts to translating .tex file into COQ before verifying it formally.

In a mathematical sentence we first identify objects between dollar signs and nouns as potential Types and variables. This can be done using a modified version of spacy.io [16][6] where one treats any $...$ expressions with no operators ($=$, $<$, $>$, etc.) as words (and not formulas). Spacy.io gives a clear syntax decomposition and a parse tree (a dependency graph of a sentence). We look at nouns and $...$ objects and analyse which objects are already defined (as Types or variables) and which objects are not; this is done by a direct check with the library of terms we are maintaining. We conclude that those which are not known to our COQ library are being defined right now. From the syntax analysis done by spacy.io we get what is defined by what - we obtain a dependency graph of nouns (objects) defined by other nouns (objects) together with accompanying adjectives (properties). Verbs seem to not play a role in COQ and are only needed to indicate a dependence relation ("A has property P"), which we have already exploited through a syntactic parser.

In a basic sentence like "Let X be a reduced scheme.", spacy.io tells us that "reduced" is a property of a "scheme" and X refers to "be" which points to "scheme". Thus we define X as variable of Type "reduced scheme", which itself is a sub-Type of Type "scheme".

We remark that one has to distinguish between defining new variables (like X) and Types (like "reduced scheme"). A priori it seems natural to define any $...$ as a variable and any unidentified nouns as Types[7]. This should give correct output most of the time. However for a more tricky example consider an adjective "p-adic", mostly written in this way; here p does not define a new variable but is a part of an adjective. Fortunately in a sentence "Let X be a p-adic scheme" the word "p-adic" is correctly seen by spacy.io as an adjective related

---

[5] Instead of a diagram we will have a bunch of sentences of the form "$f : X \to Y$ is a morphism such that...".

[6] To be precise - we need a syntactic parser for syntax analysis; recently Google went open-source with its syntactic parser SyntaxNet and implemented it into TensorFlow [18]; spacy.io builds upon this Natural Language Understanding tool.

[7] One has to be careful with non-technical terms, but in the worst case they can also be defined as separate Types. The way out is to only start adding new Types/variables once DeepAlgebra finds a "Let ... be" expression or a similar one.

to "scheme". Thus the solution seems to be looking only for words classified as nouns by spacy.io, when looking for variables and Types.

A different problem to deal with is to interpret side remarks in mathematical texts which give some new perspective on a problem but does not necessarily give any input into proofs. The way to overcome it is to ignore any sentences which do not contain "triggers" like "Let ... be", "because", "since", "thus", $...$, etc. or actually ignore everything outside of a rigid structure Lemma, Proof, Theorem, Proof - this can be done with the Stacks Project. Another difficulty is to transfer whole environments (Theorem, Lemma, Proof, etc.) from .tex to COQ, but this is relatively simple as COQ uses the same environments as ordinary mathematical texts thus this can be hard-coded.

Once the translation into COQ is done we want to verify whether the sentence is valid; in our first example we want to conclude that B implies P. This is done in COQ using E and we discuss it in the next section. This takes place purely in COQ as we have formalized everything at this stage.

5   Hammers

Creating a dictionary is only the first step in automatic theorem proving - it allows to amass training material for an AI (neural networks). The next step is to actually perform an automated reasoning. Recent years show some activity in this area. The main activity concerned recreating some of the already formalized mathematics by using certain premises (lemmas/theorems). In DeepAlgebra project we will apply these already established techniques to the Stacks Project, after we formalize it using our dictionary. We quickly survey most up-to-date techniques in automatic theorem proving.

The main way to pass between ITPs and ATPs is by the way of **hammers**, which are proof assistant tools employing external ATPs to automatically find proofs of user given set of conjectures. Their main components are: lemmas (premises) selection which have high probability to be relevant to the set of conjectures, a translation between an ITP logic to a simpler ATP system, and then trials to prove the theorem by using combinations of existing theorems and search strategies[8].

Hammers are especially effective when one deals with ARLTs and have to juggle with hundreds of axioms and definitions. Their main goal is to make theorem proving more effective. For a general overview see [3]; a hammer for COQ is described in [4] and for Mizar in [11].

In the recent work [1] authors develop a deep learning hammer for Mizar and E prover. This is the very first use of deep learning techniques in theorem proving and already shows good results. We infer that similar techniques can be used in constructing a (semi)-automated dictionary. One of the keys to use machine learning in ITPs is constructing a dependency graph of definitions/theorems (cf. [9,10]). Thanks to its structure the Stacks Project has an easy to construct

---

[8] We should mention also a proof reconstruction module which translates a proof found by an ATP back to an ITP, so that it is accepted formally by an ITP as valid.

dependancy graph of its definitions, lemmas and theorems, which can be easily searched and hopefully also easily translated into COQ/Mizar, as we argued in the previous section. The easily accessible structure of the Stacks Project allows us to hope that one can recreate large parts of its content building on well-chosen premises selected at the beginning. This poses a natural problem in the spirit of recreating contents of COQ or Mizar Libraries (solved to some extent in [1]). The next step is to go beyond the Stacks Project and prove entirely new theorems, not previously proved by humans.

6   Summary

In this text we have outlined a program for possible formalization of large parts of algebraic geometry. Our plan can be summarized in the following steps:

(1) Construct an (semi-)automated dictionary between (La)TeX and Interactive Theorem Provers, by exploiting existing syntactic parsers.
(2) Formalize The Stacks Project using this dictionary (and verify its correctness along the way).
(3) Use automatic theorem provers with The Stacks Project as the input to prove new theorems in algebraic geometry and/or fill in gaps in [17].

We will report the progress on the implementation of this program in subsequent papers.

References

1. Alemi, A., Chollet, F., Irving, G., Szegedy, C., Urban, J.: DeepMath - deep sequence models for premise selection. arXiv:1606.04442
2. Bancerek, G., Byliński, C., Grabowski, A., Korniłowicz, A., Matuszewski, R., Naumowicz, A., Pąk, K., Urban, J.: Mizar: state-of-the-art and beyond. In: Kerber, M., Carette, J., Kaliszyk, C., Rabe, F., Sorge, V. (eds.) CICM 2015. LNCS (LNAI), vol. 9150, pp. 261–279. Springer, Cham (2015). doi:10.1007/978-3-319-20615-8_17
3. Blanchette, J., Kaliszyk, C., Paulson, L., Urban, J.: Hammering towards QED. J. Formalized Reasoning 9(1), 101–148 (2016). doi:10.6092/issn.1972-5787/4593. http://jfr.unibo.it/article/view/4593
4. Czajka, L., Kaliszyk, C.: Goal translation for a hammer for COQ (Extended Abstract). In: HaTT (2016)
5. COQ proof assistant. https://coq.inria.fr
6. DeepAlgebra. https://przchojecki.github.io/deepalgebra/
7. Gonthier, G., et al.: A machine-checked proof of the odd order theorem. In: Blazy, S., Paulin-Mohring, C., Pichardie, D. (eds.) ITP 2013. LNCS, vol. 7998, pp. 163–179. Springer, Heidelberg (2013). doi:10.1007/978-3-642-39634-2_14
8. Hales, T.: Developments in Formal Proofs. Seminaire Bourbaki 1086.abs/1408.6474
9. Heras, J., Komendantskaya, E.: Proof-pattern search in COQ/SSReflect. In: Proceedings of the 6th COQ workshop (2014)

10. Heras, J., Komendantskaya, E.: HoTT formalisation in COQ: dependency graphs and ML4PG. arXiv:1403.2531
11. Kaliszyk, C., Urban, J.: MizAR 40 for Mizar 40. J. Autom. Reasoning **55**(3), 245–256 (2015). doi:10.1007/s10817-015-9330-8
12. Mizar. http://mizar.org
13. OpenAI, Special projects. https://openai.com/blog/special-projects/
14. Schulz, S.: E - A Brainiac theorem prover. AI Commun. **15**(2–3), 111–126 (2002)
15. Schulz, S.: System description: E 1.8. In: McMillan, K., Middeldorp, A., Voronkov, A. (eds.) LPAR 2013. LNCS, vol. 8312, pp. 735–743. Springer, Heidelberg (2013). doi:10.1007/978-3-642-45221-5_49
16. https://spacy.io
17. The stacks project. http://stacks.math.columbia.edu
18. SyntaxNet. https://www.tensorflow.org/versions/r0.9/tutorials/syntaxnet/index.html
19. Urban, J., Vyskočil, J.: Theorem proving in large formal mathematics as an emerging AI field. In: Bonacina, M.P., Stickel, M.E. (eds.) Automated Reasoning and Mathematics. LNCS, vol. 7788, pp. 240–257. Springer, Heidelberg (2013). doi:10.1007/978-3-642-36675-8_13

Formalizing Mathematical Knowledge as a Biform Theory Graph: A Case Study

Jacques Carette$^{(\boxtimes)}$ and William M. Farmer$^{(\boxtimes)}$

Computing and Software, McMaster University, Hamilton, Canada
{carette,wmfarmer}@mcmaster.ca
http://www.cas.mcmaster.ca/~carette
http://imps.mcmaster.ca/wmfarmer

Abstract. A *biform theory* is a combination of an axiomatic theory and an algorithmic theory that supports the integration of reasoning and computation. These are ideal for formalizing algorithms that manipulate mathematical expressions. A *theory graph* is a network of *theories* connected by meaning-preserving *theory morphisms* that map the formulas of one theory to the formulas of another theory. Theory graphs are in turn well suited for formalizing mathematical knowledge at the most convenient level of abstraction using the most convenient vocabulary. We are interested in the problem of whether a body of mathematical knowledge can be effectively formalized as a theory graph of biform theories. As a test case, we look at the graph of theories encoding natural number arithmetic. We used two different formalisms to do this, which we describe and compare. The first is realized in $\mathrm{CTT_{uqe}}$, a version of Church's type theory with quotation and evaluation, and the second is realized in Agda, a dependently typed programming language.

1 Introduction

There are many methods for encoding mathematical knowledge. The two most prevalent are the *axiomatic* and the *algorithmic*. The axiomatic method, famously employed by Euclid in his *Elements* circa 300 BCE, encodes a body of knowledge as an *axiomatic theory* composed of a language and a set of *axioms* expressed in that language. The axioms are assumptions about the *concepts* of the language and the logical consequences of the axioms are the *facts* about the concepts. The algorithmic method in contrast uses an *algorithmic theory*, composed of a language and a set of *algorithms* that perform symbolic computations over the expressions of the language. Each algorithm procedurally encodes its input/output relation. For example, an algorithm that symbolically adds expressions that represent rational numbers encodes the addition function $+ : \mathbb{Q} \times \mathbb{Q} \to \mathbb{Q}$ over the rational numbers.

A complex body of mathematical knowledge comprises many different theories; these can be captured by the *little theories method* [10] as a *theory graph* [13]

This research was supported by NSERC.

H. Geuvers et al. (Eds.): CICM 2017, LNAI 10383, pp. 9–24, 2017.
DOI: 10.1007/978-3-319-62075-6_2

consisting of theories as nodes and theory morphisms as directed edges. A theory morphism is a meaning-preserving mapping from the formulas of one theory to the formulas of another. The theories serve as abstract mathematical models and the morphisms serve as information conduits that enable definitions and theorems to be transported from one theory to another [2]. A theory graph enables mathematical knowledge to be formalized at the most convenient level of abstraction using the most convenient vocabulary. Moreover, the structure of a theory graph provides the means to access relevant concepts and facts (c&f), reduce the duplication of c&f, and enable c&f to be interpreted in multiple ways.

The axiomatic method is the basis for formalizing mathematical knowledge in proof assistants and logical frameworks. Although many proof assistants support the little theories method to some extent, very few provide the means to explicitly build theory graphs. Notable exceptions are the IMPS theorem proving system [11] and the MMT module system for mathematical theories [16].

Computer algebra systems on the other hand are based on algorithmic theories, which are not usually organized as a graph. An exception is the Axiom system [12] in which a network of abstract and concrete algorithmic theories are represented by Axiom categories and domains, respectively. Algorithmic theories are challenging to fully formalize because a specification of a symbolic algorithm that encodes a mathematical function requires the ability to talk about the relationship between syntax and semantics.

Axiomatic and algorithmic knowledge complement each other, and both are needed. A *biform theory* [4,5] combines both, and furthermore supports the integration of reasoning and computation. We argue in [4] that biform theories are needed to build *high-level theories* analogous to high-level programming languages. Biform theories are challenging to formalize for the same reasons that algorithmic theories are challenging to formalize.

We are interested in the problem of whether the little theories method can be applied to biform theories. That is, can a body of mathematical knowledge be effectively formalized as a theory graph of biform theories? We use a graph (of biform theories) encoding natural number arithmetic as a test case. We describe two different formalizations, and compare the results. The first formalization is realized using the global approach in $\mathrm{CTT_{uqe}}$ [9], a variant of $\mathrm{CTT_{qe}}$ [7,8], a version of Church's type theory with quotation and evaluation, while the second is realized using the local approach in Agda [14,15], a dependently typed programming language. This dual formalization, contrasting the two approaches, forms the core of our contribution; each formalization has some smaller contributions, some of which may be of independent interest.

The rest of the paper is organized as follows. The notion of a biform theory is defined and discussed in Sect. 2. The theories that encode natural number arithmetic are presented in Sect. 3. The $\mathrm{CTT_{uqe}}$ formalization is discussed in Sect. 4, and the Agda version in Sect. 5. These two are presented in full in Appendices A and B of [3]. Section 6 compares the two formalizations. The paper ends with conclusions and future work in Sect. 7.

The authors are grateful to the reviewers for their comments and suggestions.

2   Biform Theories

Let $\mathcal{E}$ be a set of expressions and $f : \mathcal{E}^n \to \mathcal{E}$ be an n-ary function where $n \geq 1$. A *transformer for* f is an algorithm that implements f. Transformers manipulate expressions e in various ways: simple ones build bigger expressions from pieces, select components of e, or check whether e satisfies some syntactic property. More sophisticated transformers manipulate expressions in a mathematically meaningful way. We call these kinds of transformers *syntax-based mathematical algorithms (SBMAs)* [6]. Examples include algorithms that apply arithmetic operations to numerals, factor polynomials, transpose matrices, and symbolically differentiate expressions with variables. The *computational behavior* of a transformer is the relationship between its input and output expressions. When the transformer is an SBMA, its *mathematical meaning* is the relationship between the mathematical meanings of its input and output expressions.

A *biform theory* T is a triple (L, Π, Γ) where L is a language of some underlying logic, Π is a set of transformers for functions over expressions of L, and Γ is a set of formulas of L. L is generated from a set of symbols that include, e.g., types and constants. Each symbol is the name for a concept of T. The transformers in Π are for functions represented by symbols of L. The members of Γ are the *axioms* of T. They specify the concepts of T including the computational behaviors of transformers and the mathematical meanings of SBMAs. The underlying logic provides the semantic foundation for T. We say T is an *axiomatic theory* if Π is empty and an *algorithmic theory* if Γ is empty.

Expressing a biform theory in the underlying logic requires infrastructure for reasoning about expressions manipulated by the transformers as syntactic entities. The infrastructure provides a basis for *metareasoning with reflection* [7]. There are two main approaches for obtaining this infrastructure [6]. The *local approach* is to produce a deep embedding of a sublanguage L' of L that include all the expressions manipulated by the transformers of Π. The deep embedding consists of (1) an inductive type of *syntactic values* that represent the syntactic structures of the expressions in L', (2) an *informal quotation operator* that maps the expressions in L' to syntactic values, and (3) a *formal evaluation operator* that maps syntactic values to the values of the expressions in L' that they represent. The *global approach* is to replace the underlying logic of L with a logic such as that of [7] that has (1) an inductive type of *syntactic values* for all the expressions in L, (2) a *global formal quotation operator*, and (3) a *global formal evaluation operator*.

There are several ways, in a proof assistant, to construct a transformer π for $f : \mathcal{E}^n \to \mathcal{E}$. The simplest is to define f as a lambda abstraction A_f, and then π computes the value $f(e_1, \ldots, e_n)$ by reducing $A_f(e_1, \ldots, e_n)$ using β-reduction (and possibly other transformations such as δ-reduction, etc.). Another method is to specify the computational behavior of f by axioms, and then π can be implemented as a tactic that applies the axioms to $f(e_1, \ldots, e_n)$ as, e.g., rewrite rules or conditional rewrite rules. Finally, the computational behavior or mathematical meaning of f can be specified by axioms, and then π can be a program which satisfies these axioms; this program can operate on either internal or external data structures representing the expressions $e_1, \ldots, e_n$.

3   Natural Number Arithmetic: A Test Case

Figure 1 shows a theory graph composed of biform theories encoding natural number arithmetic. We start with eight axiomatic theories (seven in first-order logic (FOL) and one in simple type theory (STT)) and then add a variety of useful transformers in the appropriate theories. These eight are chosen because they fit together closely and have simple axiomatizations. Of the first-order theories, BT1 and BT5 are theories of 0 and S (which denotes the successor function); BT2 and BT6 are theories of 0, S, and $+$; and BT3, BT4, and BT7 are theories of 0, S, $+$, and $*$. Several other biform theories could be added to this graph, most notably Skolem arithmetic, the complete theory of 0, S, and $*$, which has a very complicated axiomatization [17]. The details of each theory is given below.

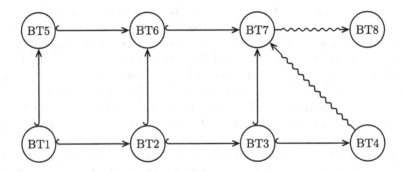

Fig. 1. Biform theory graph test case

Figure 1 shows the morphisms that connect these theories. The $\hookrightarrow$ arrows denote strict theory inclusions. The morphism from BT4 to BT7 is the identity mapping. It is meaning-preserving since each axiom of BT4 is a theorem of BT7. In particular, A7 follows from the induction schema A10. The theory morphism from BT7 to BT8 is interlogical since their logics are different. It is defined by the mapping of 0, S, $+$, $*$ to 0_ι, $S_{\iota \to \iota}$, $+_{\iota \to \iota \to \iota}$, $*_{\iota \to \iota \to \iota}$, respectively, where $+_{\iota \to \iota \to \iota}$ and $*_{\iota \to \iota \to \iota}$ are defined constants in BT8. It is meaning-preserving since A1–A6 and the instances of the induction schema A10 map to theorems of BT8.

We have formalized this biform theory graph in two ways: the first in $\mathrm{CTT}_{\mathrm{uqe}}$ using the global approach and the second in Agda using the local approach. These are discussed in the next two sections, while the full details are given in Appendices A and B of [3]. A "conventional" mathematical presentation of the theories would be as follows.

Biform Theory 1 (BT1: Simple Theory of 0 and S)
Logic: FOL. *Constants*: 0 (0-ary), S (unary).
Axioms:
    A1. $S(x) \neq 0$.
    A2. $S(x) = S(y) \supset x = y$.
Properties: incomplete, undecidable.
Transformers: Recognizer for the formulas of the theory.

Biform Theory 2 (BT2: Simple Theory of 0, S, and $+$)
Extends BT1.
Logic: FOL. *Constants*: $+$ (binary, infix).
Axioms:
    A3. $x + 0 = x$.
    A4. $x + S(y) = S(x + y)$.
Properties: incomplete, undecidable.
Transformers: Recognizer for the formulas of the theory and algorithm for adding natural numbers as binary numerals.

Biform Theory 3 (BT3: Simple Theory of 0, S, $+$, and $*$)
Extends BT2.
Logic: FOL. *Constants*: $*$ (binary, infix).
Axioms:
    A5. $x * 0 = 0$.
    A6. $x * S(y) = (x * y) + x$.
Properties: incomplete, undecidable.
Transformers: Recognizer for the formulas of the theory and algorithm for multiplying natural numbers as binary numerals.

Biform Theory 4 (BT4: Robinson Arithmetic (Q))
Extends BT3.
Logic: FOL.
Axioms:
    A7. $x = 0 \vee \exists y . S(y) = x$.
Properties: essentially incomplete, essentially undecidable.

Biform Theory 5 (BT5: Complete Theory of 0 and S)
Extends BT1.
Logic: FOL.
Axioms:
    A8. $(A(0) \wedge \forall x . (A(x) \supset A(S(x)))) \supset \forall x . A(x)$
    where A is any formula of BT5 in which x is not bound and $A(t)$ is the result
    of replacing each free occurrence of x in A with the term t.
Properties: complete, decidable.
Transformers: Generator for instances of the theory's induction schema and decision procedure for the theory.

Biform Theory 6 (BT6: Presburger Arithmetic)
Extends BT2 and BT5.
Logic: FOL.
Axioms:
   A9. $(A(0) \wedge \forall x \, . \, (A(x) \supset A(S(x)))) \supset \forall x \, . \, A(x)$
   where A is any formula of BT6 in which x is not bound and $A(t)$ is the result
   of replacing each free occurrence of x in A with the term t.
Properties: complete, decidable.
Transformers: Generator for instances of the theory's induction schema and
decision procedure for the theory.

Biform Theory 7 (BT7: First-Order Peano Arithmetic)
Extends BT3 and BT6.
Logic: FOL.
Axioms:
   A10. $(A(0) \wedge \forall x \, . \, (A(x) \supset A(S(x)))) \supset \forall x \, . \, A(x)$
   where A is any formula of BT7 in which x is not bound and $A(t)$ is the result
   of replacing each free occurrence of x in A with the term t.
Properties: essentially incomplete, essentially decidable.
Transformers: Generator for instances of the theory's induction schema.

Biform Theory 8 (BT8: Higher-Order Peano Arithmetic)
Logic: STT. *Types*: ι. *Constants*: 0_ι, $S_{\iota \to \iota}$.
Axioms:
   A11. $S_{\iota \to \iota}(x_\iota) \neq 0_\iota$.
   A12. $S_{\iota \to \iota}(x_\iota) = S_{\iota \to \iota}(y_\iota) \supset x_\iota = y_\iota$.
   A13. $(p_{\iota \to o}(0) \wedge \forall x_\iota \, . \, (p_{\iota \to o}(x_\iota) \supset p_{\iota \to o}(S(x_\iota)))) \supset \forall x_\iota \, . \, p_{\iota \to o}(x_\iota)$.
Properties: essentially incomplete, essentially decidable, categorical for standard
models.

It is important to note that axioms A8, A9 and A10 are all different since
they are over different languages; in particular, **BT6** adds $+$ to the language of
BT5, and **BT7** adds $*$ to the language of **BT6**.

4   Study 1: Test Case Formalized in CTT$_{\mathrm{uqe}}$

CTT$_{\mathrm{uqe}}$ supports the global approach for metareasoning with reflection. CTT$_{\mathrm{uqe}}$
contains (1) a logical base type ϵ that is an inductive type of syntactic values called *constructions* which are expressions of type ϵ, (2) a global quotation
operator $\ulcorner \cdot \urcorner$ that maps each expression $\mathbf{A}_\alpha$ of CTT$_{\mathrm{uqe}}$ to a construction that represents the syntactic structure of $\mathbf{A}_\alpha$, and (3) a typed global evaluation operator
$\llbracket \cdot \rrbracket_\alpha$ that maps each construction $\mathbf{B}_\epsilon$ of CTT$_{\mathrm{uqe}}$ representing an expression $\mathbf{A}_\alpha$
of type α to an expression whose value is the same as $\mathbf{A}_\alpha$. See [9] for details.
   A *biform theory* of CTT$_{\mathrm{uqe}}$ is a triple (L, Π, Γ) where L is a language generated by a set of base types and constants of CTT$_{\mathrm{uqe}}$, Π is a set of transformers
over expressions of L, and Γ is a set of formulas of L. Each transformer is for a
constant in L whose type has the form $\epsilon \to \cdots \to \epsilon$. We present biform theories

in $\mathrm{CTT_{uqe}}$ as a set of base types, constants, axioms, transformers, and theorems. The base types are divided into primitive and defined base types. A defined base type is declared by a formula that equates the base type to a nonempty subset of some type of L. Similarly, the constants are divided into primitive and defined constants. A defined constant $\mathbf{c}_\alpha$ is declared by an equation $\mathbf{c}_\alpha = \mathbf{A}_\alpha$ where $\mathbf{A}_\alpha$ is a defined expression.

The biform theory graph test case given in Sect. 3 is formalized in $\mathrm{CTT_{uqe}}$ as a theory graph of eight $\mathrm{CTT_{uqe}}$ theories as shown in Appendix A of [3]. Since $\mathrm{CTT_{uqe}}$ is not currently implemented, it is not possible to give the transformers as implemented algorithms. Instead we described their intended behavior.

We will concentrate our discussion on BT6 (given below). We have not included the following components of BT6 (that should be in BT6 according to its definition in Sect. 3) that are redundant or are subsumed by other components: Constants BT5-DEC-PROC$_{\epsilon \to \epsilon}$, IS-FO-BT1$_{\epsilon \to \epsilon}$, and IS-FO-BT1-ABS$_{\epsilon \to \epsilon}$; axioms 27 and 28; and transformers π_1, π_2, π_{11}, π_{12}, and π_{13}. See [9] for details.

BT6 has the usual constants $(0_\iota, S_{\iota \to \iota}, \text{ and } +_{\iota \to \iota \to \iota})$ and axioms (axioms 1–4 and 29) of Presburger arithmetic. Axiom 29 is the direct formalization of A9, the induction schema for Presburger arithmetic, stated in Sect. 3. It is expressed as a single universal formula in $\mathrm{CTT_{uqe}}$ that ranges over constructions representing function abstractions of the form $\lambda\, \mathbf{x}_\iota\, .\, \mathbf{A}_o$. These constructions are identified by the transformers π_{15} and π_{16} for the defined constant IS-FO-BT2-ABS$_{\epsilon \to \epsilon}$. π_{15} works by accessing data about variables, constants, and other subexpressions stored in the data structure for an expression, while π_{16} works by expanding the definition of IS-FO-BT2-ABS$_{\epsilon \to \epsilon}$. π_{15} is sound if the definition expansion mechanism is sound. Showing the soundness of π_{14} would require a formal verification of the implementation of the data structure for expressions. Of course, the results of π_{14} could be checked using π_{16}.

This biform theory has a defined constant $\mathrm{bnat}_{\iota \to \iota \to \iota}$ with the usual base 2 notation for expressing natural numbers in a binary form. There is a constant BPLUS$_{\epsilon \to \epsilon \to \epsilon}$ specified by axioms 5–15 for adding quotations of these natural numbers in binary form. BPLUS$_{\epsilon \to \epsilon \to \epsilon}$ is implemented by transformers π_3 and π_4. π_3 is some efficient algorithm implemented outside of $\mathrm{CTT_{uqe}}$, and π_4 is an algorithm that uses axioms 5–15 as conditional rewrite rules. π_4 is sound if the rewriting mechanism is sound. Showing the soundness of π_3 would require a formal verification of its program. The meaning formula for BPLUS$_{\epsilon \to \epsilon \to \epsilon}$, theorem 3, follows from axioms 5–15.

This biform theory also has a transformer π_{14} for BT6-DEC-PROC$_{\epsilon \to \epsilon}$ that implements an efficient decision procedure for the first-order formulas of the theory that is specified by axiom 30. The first-order formulas of the theory are identified by the transformers π_5 and π_6 for the defined constant IS-FO-BT2$_{\epsilon \to \epsilon}$ that are analogous to the transformers π_{15} and π_{16} for IS-FO-BT2-ABS$_{\epsilon \to \epsilon}$.

Biform Theory 6 (BT6: Presburger Arithmetic)

Primitive Base Types

1. ι (type of natural numbers).

Primitive Constants

1. 0_ι.
2. $S_{\iota \to \iota}$.
3. $+_{\iota \to \iota \to \iota}$ (infix).
4. $\text{BPLUS}_{\epsilon \to \epsilon \to \epsilon}$ (infix).
6. $\text{BT6-DEC-PROC}_{\epsilon \to \epsilon}$.

Defined Constants (selected)

1. $1_\iota = S\,0_\iota$.
3. $\text{bnat}_{\iota \to \iota \to \iota} = \lambda\, x_\iota \,.\, \lambda\, y_\iota \,.\, ((x_\iota + x_\iota) + y_\iota)$.
   Notational definition:
   $$(0)_2 = \text{bnat}\,0_\iota\,0_\iota.$$
   $$(1)_2 = \text{bnat}\,0_\iota\,1_\iota.$$
   $$(a_1 \cdots a_n 0)_2 = \text{bnat}\,(a_1 \cdots a_n)_2\,0_\iota \quad \text{where each } a_i \text{ is } 0 \text{ or } 1.$$
   $$(a_1 \cdots a_n 1)_2 = \text{bnat}\,(a_1 \cdots a_n)_2\,1_\iota \quad \text{where each } a_i \text{ is } 0 \text{ or } 1.$$

4. $\text{is-bnum}_{\epsilon \to o} = I\,f_{\epsilon \to o}\,.\,\forall\, u_\epsilon \,.\,(f_{\epsilon \to \epsilon}\,u_\epsilon \equiv$
   $\exists\, v_\epsilon \,.\,\exists\, w_\epsilon \,.\,(u_\epsilon = \ulcorner \text{bnat} \lfloor v_\epsilon \rfloor \lfloor w_\epsilon \rfloor \urcorner \wedge$
   $(v_\epsilon = \ulcorner 0_\iota \urcorner \vee f_{\epsilon \to \epsilon}\,v_\epsilon) \wedge (w_\epsilon = \ulcorner 0_\iota \urcorner \vee w_\epsilon = \ulcorner 1_\iota \urcorner)))$. (Notation of the
   form $\ulcorner \cdots \lfloor \cdot \rfloor \cdots \urcorner$ represents a quasiquotation; see [6] for details.)

5. $\text{IS-FO-BT2}_{\epsilon \to \epsilon} = \lambda\, x_\epsilon \,.\, \mathbf{B}_\epsilon$ where $\mathbf{B}_\epsilon$ is a complex expression such that
   $(\lambda\, x_\epsilon \,.\, \mathbf{B}_\epsilon) \ulcorner \mathbf{A}_\alpha \urcorner$ equals $\ulcorner T_o \urcorner$ [$\ulcorner F_o \urcorner$] if $\mathbf{A}_\alpha$ is [not] a term or formula of
   first-order logic with equality whose variables are of type ι and whose
   nonlogical constants are members of $\{0_\iota, S_{\iota \to \iota}, +_{\iota \to \iota \to \iota}\}$.

7. $\text{IS-FO-BT2-ABS}_{\epsilon \to \epsilon} =$
   $\lambda\, x_\epsilon \,.\, (\text{if } (\text{is-abs}_{\epsilon \to o}\,x_\epsilon)\,(\text{IS-FO-BT2}_{\epsilon \to \epsilon}\,(\text{abs-body}_{\epsilon \to \epsilon}\,x_\epsilon))\,\ulcorner F_o \urcorner)$.

Axioms

1. $S\,x_\iota \neq 0_\iota$.
2. $S\,x_\iota = S\,y_\iota \supset x_\iota = y_\iota$.
3. $x_\iota + 0_\iota = x_\iota$.
4. $x_\iota + S\,y_\iota = S\,(x_\iota + y_\iota)$.
5. $\text{is-bnum}\,u_\epsilon \supset u_\epsilon\,\text{BPLUS}\,\ulcorner (0)_2 \urcorner = u_\epsilon$.

   $\vdots$

15. $(\text{is-bnum}\,u_\epsilon \wedge \text{is-bnum}\,v_\epsilon) \supset$
    $\ulcorner \text{bnat} \lfloor u_\epsilon \rfloor 1_\iota \urcorner\,\text{BPLUS}\,\ulcorner \text{bnat} \lfloor v_\epsilon \rfloor 1_\iota \urcorner =$
    $\ulcorner \text{bnat} \lfloor (u_\epsilon\,\text{BPLUS}\,v_\epsilon)\,\text{BPLUS}\,\ulcorner (1)_2 \urcorner \rfloor 0_\iota \urcorner$.

29. Induction Schema for S and $+$
    $\forall\, f_\epsilon \,.\,((\text{is-expr}^{\iota \to o}_{\epsilon \to o}\,f_\epsilon \wedge [\text{IS-FO-BT2-ABS}_{\epsilon \to \epsilon}\,f_\epsilon]_o) \supset$
    $(([\![f_\epsilon]\!]_{\iota \to o}\,0_\iota \wedge (\forall\, x_\iota \,.\, [\![f_\epsilon]\!]_{\iota \to o}\,x_\iota \supset [\![f_\epsilon]\!]_{\iota \to o}\,(S\,x_\iota))) \supset \forall\, x_\iota \,.\, [\![f_\epsilon]\!]_{\iota \to o}\,x_\iota))$.

30. Meaning formula for $\text{BT6-DEC-PROC}_{\epsilon \to \epsilon}$.
    $\forall\, u_\epsilon \,.\,((\text{is-expr}^o_{\epsilon \to o}\,u_\epsilon \wedge \text{is-closed}_{\epsilon \to o}\,u_\epsilon \wedge [\text{IS-FO-BT2}_{\epsilon \to \epsilon}\,u_\epsilon]_o) \supset$
    $((\text{BT6-DEC-PROC}_{\epsilon \to \epsilon}\,u_\epsilon = \ulcorner T_o \urcorner \vee \text{BT6-DEC-PROC}_{\epsilon \to \epsilon}\,u_\epsilon = \ulcorner F_o \urcorner) \wedge$
    $[\text{BT6-DEC-PROC}_{\epsilon \to \epsilon}\,u_\epsilon]_o = [\![u_\epsilon]\!]_o))$.

Transformers

3. π_3 for BPLUS$_{\epsilon\to\epsilon\to\epsilon}$ is an efficient program that satisfies Axioms 5–15.
4. π_4 for BPLUS$_{\epsilon\to\epsilon\to\epsilon}$ uses Axioms 5–15 as conditional rewrite rules.
5. π_5 for IS-FO-BT2$_{\epsilon\to\epsilon}$ is an efficient program that accesses the data stored in the data structures that represent expressions.
6. π_6 for IS-FO-BT2$_{\epsilon\to\epsilon}$ uses the definition of IS-FO-BT2$_{\epsilon\to\epsilon}$.
14. π_{14} for BT6-DEC-PROC$_{\epsilon\to\epsilon\to\epsilon}$ is an efficient decision procedure that satisfies Axiom 30.
15. π_{15} for IS-FO-BT2-ABS$_{\epsilon\to\epsilon}$ is an efficient program that accesses the data stored in the data structures that represent expressions.
16. π_{16} for IS-FO-BT2-ABS$_{\epsilon\to\epsilon}$ uses the definition of IS-FO-BT2-ABS$_{\epsilon\to\epsilon}$.

Theorems (selected)

3. Meaning formula for BPLUS$_{\epsilon\to\epsilon\to\epsilon}$
$$\forall u_\epsilon \,.\, \forall v_\epsilon \,.\, ((\text{is-bnum } u_\epsilon \wedge \text{is-bnum } v_\epsilon) \supset$$
$$(\text{is-bnum } (u_\epsilon \text{ BPLUS } v_\epsilon) \wedge \quad (\llbracket u_\epsilon \text{ BPLUS } v_\epsilon \rrbracket_\iota = \llbracket u_\epsilon \rrbracket_\iota + \llbracket v_\epsilon \rrbracket_\iota))).$$

5   Study 2: Test Case Formalized in Agda

As our goal is to, in part, compare the global approach and the local approach, the formalization in Agda [15,18] eschews the use of its reflection capabilities[1]. Thus this formalization replaces the global type ϵ (of CTT$_{\text{uqe}}$) by a *set* of inductive types, one for each of the biform theories. This is still reflection, just hand-rolled. We also need to express formulas in FOL (as syntax), so we need a type for that as well. To be more modular, this is done as a type for first-order logic (with equality) over any ground language. We display some illustrative samples here; the full code is available in Appendix B of [3].

An abstract theory is modeled as a *record*. For example, we have BT$_1$:

```
record BT₁ : Set₁ where
    field
        nat : Set₀
        Z : nat
        S : nat → nat
        S≠Z : ∀ x → ¬ (S x ≡ Z)
        inj : ∀ x y → S x ≡ S y → x ≡ y

    One : nat
    One = S Z
```

For simplicity, we will take the built-in type $\mathbb{N}$, defined as an inductive type, as the *syntax* for natural numbers, which is also the syntax associated to the theory BT$_1$. Whereas in CTT$_{\text{uqe}}$ there is a global evaluation, here we also need

---

[1] As of early 2017, there is no official publication describing these features outside of the Agda documentation, but see [20,21].

to define evaluation explicitly (a subscript is used to indicate which theory it belongs to).

$$[\![\_]\!]_1 : \mathbb{N} \to \mathsf{nat}$$
$$[\![\ 0\ ]\!]_1 = \mathsf{Z}$$
$$[\![\ \mathsf{suc}\ x\ ]\!]_1 = \mathsf{S}\ [\![\ x\ ]\!]_1$$

The accompanying code furthermore proves some basic coherence theorems which are elided here. We make two further definitions which will be explained in more detail below.

nat-lang : GroundLanguage nat
nat-lang $=$ record { Lang $= \lambda\ X \to \mathbb{NX}$ (Carrier X)
           ; value $= \lambda\ \{V\} \to$ val $\{V\}$ }
where
    val : $\{V : \mathsf{DT}\} \to \mathbb{NX}$ (Carrier V) $\to$ (Carrier $V \to$ nat) $\to$ nat
    val z $env = \mathsf{Z}$
    val $\{V\}$ (s e) $env = \mathsf{S}$ (val $\{V\}$ e env)
    val (v x) $env = env\ x$

module fo$_1$ = FOL nat-lang

We can also demonstrate that the natural numbers are a model:

$\mathbb{N}$-is-T1 : BT$_1$
$\mathbb{N}$-is-T1 $=$ record { nat $= \mathbb{N}$; Z $= 0$; S $=$ suc
   ; S$\neq$Z $= \lambda\ x \to \lambda$ () ; inj $= \lambda$ { x .x refl $\to$ refl } }

One of the languages needed is an extension of the naturals which allows variables:

data $\mathbb{NX}$ (Var : Set$_0$) : Set$_0$ where
    z : $\mathbb{NX}$ Var
    s : $\mathbb{NX}$ Var $\to$ $\mathbb{NX}$ Var
    v : Var $\to$ $\mathbb{NX}$ Var

But where the informal description in Sect. 3 can get away with saying "Logic: FOL" and "Transformers: Recognizers for the formulas of the theory", here we need to be very explicit. To do so, we need to define some language infrastructure.

One of the important concepts is that of a *language with variables*, in other words a language with a reasonable definition of substitution. This requires *variables* to come from a type which has the structure of a decidable setoid (from the Agda library DecSetoid, and denoted **DT** below).

A language, expressed as an inductive type, is closed, i.e., cannot be extended. If a language does not have variables, we cannot add them. One solution is to deal with *contexts* as first-class citizens. While that is likely the best long-term solution, here we have gone with something simpler: create another language which does, and show that its variable-free fragment is equivalent to the original. As that aspect of our development is straightforward, albeit tedious, we elide it.

As we are concerned with statements in first-order logic over a variety of languages, it makes sense to modularize this aspect somewhat. Note that, as we are building syntax via inductive types, we can either build these as functors and then use a fixpoint combinator to tie the knot, or we can just bite the bullet and make one large definition. For now, we chose the latter. We do parametrize over a *ground language with variables*. In turn, this is defined as a type parametrized by a decidable setoid along with an evaluation function into some type T.

```
record GroundLanguage (T : Set₀) : Set₁ where
   open DecSetoid using (Carrier)
   field
      Lang : DT → Set₀
      value : {V : DT} → Lang V → (Carrier V → T) → T
```

A logic over a language (with variables), is then also a parametrized type as well as a parametrized interpretation into types. The definition is almost the same, except that a ground language interprets into T and a logic into $\mathsf{Set_0}$.

```
record LogicOverL (T : Set₀) (L : GroundLanguage T) : Set₁ where
   open DecSetoid using (Carrier)
   field
      Logic : DT → Set₀
      ⟦_⟧_ : ∀ {V} → Logic V → (Carrier V → T) → Set₀
```

The definition of first logic is then straightforward.

```
module FOL {T : Set₀} (L : GroundLanguage T) where
   open DecSetoid using (Carrier)
   open GroundLanguage L

   data FOL (V : DT) : Set where
      tt : FOL V
      ff : FOL V
      _and_ : FOL V → FOL V → FOL V
      _or_ : FOL V → FOL V → FOL V
      not : FOL V → FOL V
      _⊃_ : FOL V → FOL V → FOL V
      _==_ : Lang V → Lang V → FOL V
      all : Carrier V → FOL V → FOL V
      exist : Carrier V → FOL V → FOL V

   override : {V : DT} → (Carrier V → T) → Carrier V → T → (Carrier V → T)
   override {V} f x t y with DecSetoid._≟_ V y x
   ... | yes _ = t
   ... | no _ = f y
```

We can also prove that **FOL** is a logic over L by providing an interpretation. Of course, as we are modeling classical logic into a constructive logic, we have to use

a double-negation embedding. We also choose to interpret the logic's equality
$\_==\_$ as *propositional equality*, but we could make that choice a parameter as
well.

LoL-FOL : LogicOverL T L
LoL-FOL = record { Logic = FOL ; $[\![\_]\!]\_$ = interp }
   where
      interp : {Var : DT} → FOL Var → (Carrier Var → T) → Set$_0$
      interp tt env = $\top$
      interp ff env = $\bot$
      interp (e and f) env = interp e env × interp f env
      interp (e or f) env = ¬ ¬ (interp e env ⊎ interp f env)
      interp (not e) env = ¬ (interp e env)
      interp (e ⊃ f) env = (interp e env) → (interp f env)
      interp (x == y) env = value x env ≡ value y env
      interp {V} (all x p) env = $\forall$ z → interp p (override {V} env x z)
      interp {V} (exist x p) env = ¬ ¬ (Σ T (λ t → interp p (override {V} env x t)))

With the appropriate infrastructure in place, it is now possible to define BT_6
from the theories it extends.

record BT$_6$ {t_1 : BT$_1$} (t_2 : BT$_2$ t_1) (t_5 : BT$_5$ t_1) : Set$_1$ where
   open VarLangs using (XV; x)
   open DecSetoid using (Carrier)
   open BT$_2$ t_2 public
   open fo$_2$ using (FOL; tt; ff; LoL-FOL; $\_$and$\_$; all)
   open LogicOverL LoL-FOL

   field
      induct : (e : FOL XV) →
         $[\![$ e $]\!]$ (λ { x → $[\![$ 0 $]\!]_1$ }) →
         ($\forall$ y → $[\![$ e $]\!]$ (λ {x → y}) → $[\![$ e $]\!]$ (λ {x → S y})) →
         $\forall$ y → $[\![$ e $]\!]$ (λ {x → y})
   postulate
      decide : $\forall$ {W} → (Carrier W → nat) → FOL W → FOL NoVars
      meaning-decide : {W : DT} (env : Carrier W → nat) → (env' : $\bot$ → nat) →
      (e : FOL W) →
      let res = decide env e in
      (res ≡ tt ⊎ res ≡ ff) × ($[\![$ e $]\!]$ env) ≃ ($[\![$ res $]\!]$ env')

While Sect. 4 presents the *flattened* theory, here we need only define what is new
over the extended theory, namely an induction schema, a decision procedure and
its meaning formula.

Here is a guide to understanding the above definition: (1) XV is a (decidable)
type with a single inhabitant, x. (2) All fields of BT$_2$ are made publicly visible
for BT$_6$. (3) The language of first-order logic **PredL** over t_2 (and some of its
constructors) is also made visible. (4) (λ {x → y}) denotes a substitution for the
single variable x. (5) ≃ denotes *type equivalence*.

We represent numerals as vectors (of length at least 1) of binary digits.

```
data BinDigit : Set where zero one : BinDigit
data BNum : Set where
    bn : {n : ℕ} → Vec BinDigit (suc n) → BNum
```

This then allows a straightforward implementation of **bplus** to add numerals. It is then possible to *prove* that the meaning function for **bplus** is a theorem.

bplus-is-+ : $\forall\ x\ y \rightarrow$ [[bplus $x\ y$]]$_2$ ≡ [[x]]$_2$ + [[y]]$_2$

6   Comparison of the Two Formalizations

As expected, we were able to formalize this network of theories using both methods. Neither are fully complete; both are missing the actual decision procedures (which would be large undertakings). In particular,

- The CTT$_{uqe}$ formalization is missing the definition of the language recognizers, as well as the full assurance of being mechanically checked. It has no "implementation" of any transformers.
- The Agda version implements evaluation but not substitution — which means that the induction statement in BT5–BT7 are not quite the same as in CTT$_{uqe}$; the models will be the same however. It also does not implement any theory morphisms, as record definitions are not first-class in Agda.

More importantly, because of our (explicit) choice to contrast the global and local approaches, each version uses different infrastructure to reason about syntax.

- CTT$_{uqe}$ has a built-in inductive type of "all syntax", along with quotation and evaluation operators for the entire language of expressions.
- In the local approach, a new inductive type for each new "language" (the numerals, the numerals with plus, the numerals with plus and times, all three of these augmented with variables, first order logic, binary digits, binary numerals) has to be created. For many of these, a variety of traversals (folds) have to be implemented "by hand" even though the recursion patterns are obvious, at least to humans. Some of these are evaluation operators (one per language). There is no formal quotation operator.

The Agda version has a number of extra features: some transformers (such as for **bplus** and **btimes**) are implemented. Furthermore, the *meaning formula* for **bplus** is shown to be a theorem. A variety of coherence theorems are also shown, to gain confidence that the theories really are the ones we want.

It is worth remarking that defining the language of first-order formulas is complicated in *both* versions. This has been noticed before by people doing programming language meta-theory with proof assistants: encoding languages, especially languages with binders (such as FOL) along with traversals and basic reasoning can be very tedious [1].

The most notable differences in the two formalizations are:

1. Because FOL is classical, but Agda's host logic is constructive, a double-negation embedding was needed.
2. The use of *type equivalence* instead of boolean equality for verifying that the interpretation of a formula of FOL and the results of the decision procedure are "the same".
3. Borrowing the notion of *contractibility* from HoTT [19], to encode *definite description*.
4. Extending the decision procedure to *closeable* terms (by providing an explicit, total valuation) instead of restricting to closed terms.

The first is basically forced upon us by Agda: it has no Prop type (unlike Coq), and so we do not know a priori that all interpretations of first-order formulas are actually 0-types. The second is an active design decision: the infrastructure required to define the meaning of *closed* which is useful in a constructive setting is quite complex[2]. We believe the third is novel. The fourth point requires deeper investigating.

7 Conclusion

We have proposed a biform theory graph test case composed of eight theories that encode natural number arithmetic and include a variety of useful transformers. We have formalized this test case (as a set of biform theories and theory morphisms) in CTT$_{\text{uqe}}$ using the global approach (for metareasoning with reflection) and in Agda using the local approach. In both cases, we have produced substantial partial formalizations that indicate that full formalizations could be obtained with additional work.

Our results show that, by providing a built-in global infrastructure, the global approach has a significant advantage over the local approach. The local approach is burdened by the necessity to define an infrastructure — consisting of an inductive type and an evaluation operator for the type — for every set of expressions manipulated by a transformer. In general, new local infrastructures must be created each time a new theory is added to the theory graph. On the other hand, the global approach employs an infrastructure — consisting of an inductive type, a quotation operator, and an evaluation operator — for the entire set of expressions in the logic. This single infrastructure is used for every theory in the theory graph.

We recommend that future research is directed toward making the global approach for metareasoning with reflection into a practical method for formalizing biform theories. This can be done by developing and implementing logics such as CTT$_{\text{qe}}$ [7,8] and CTT$_{\text{uqe}}$ [9] and by adding global infrastructures to proof systems such as Agda and Coq (see [20,21] for work in this direction).

---

[2] It would require us to define *paths* in terms, bound and free variables along paths, quantification over paths, etc.

References

1. Aydemir, B.E., et al.: Mechanized metatheory for the masses: the POPLMARK challenge. In: Hurd, J., Melham, T. (eds.) TPHOLs 2005. LNCS, vol. 3603, pp. 50–65. Springer, Heidelberg (2005). doi:10.1007/11541868_4
2. Barwise, J., Seligman, J., Flow, I.: The Logic of Distributed Systems. Tracts in Computer Science, vol. 44. Cambridge University Press, Cambridge (1997)
3. Carette, J., Farmer, W.M.: Formalizing mathematical knowledge as a biform theory graph: a case study. arXiv:1704.02253 (2017)
4. Carette, J., Farmer, W.M.: High-level theories. In: Autexier, S., Campbell, J., Rubio, J., Sorge, V., Suzuki, M., Wiedijk, F. (eds.) CICM 2008. LNCS, vol. 5144, pp. 232–245. Springer, Heidelberg (2008). doi:10.1007/978-3-540-85110-3_19
5. Farmer, W.M.: Biform theories in Chiron. In: Kauers, M., Kerber, M., Miner, R., Windsteiger, W. (eds.) Calculemus/MKM -2007. LNCS, vol. 4573, pp. 66–79. Springer, Heidelberg (2007). doi:10.1007/978-3-540-73086-6_6
6. Farmer, W.M.: The formalization of syntax-based mathematical algorithms using quotation and evaluation. In: Carette, J., Aspinall, D., Lange, C., Sojka, P., Windsteiger, W. (eds.) CICM 2013. LNCS, vol. 7961, pp. 35–50. Springer, Heidelberg (2013). doi:10.1007/978-3-642-39320-4_3
7. Farmer, W.M.: Incorporating quotation and evaluation into church's type theory. Computing Research Repository (CoRR) abs/1612.02785, p. 72 (2016)
8. Farmer, W.M.: Incorporating quotation and evaluation into church's type theory: syntax and semantics. In: Kohlhase, M., Johansson, M., Miller, B., de Moura, L., Tompa, F. (eds.) CICM 2016. LNCS, vol. 9791, pp. 83–98. Springer, Cham (2016). doi:10.1007/978-3-319-42547-4_7
9. Farmer, W.M.: Theory morphisms in church's type theory with quotation and evaluation. Computing Research Repository (CoRR) abs/1703.02117, p. 15 (2017)
10. Farmer, W.M., Guttman, J.D., Javier Thayer, F.: Little theories. In: Kapur, D. (ed.) CADE 1992. LNCS, vol. 607, pp. 567–581. Springer, Heidelberg (1992). doi:10. 1007/3-540-55602-8_192
11. Farmer, W.M., Guttman, J.D., Thayer, F.J.: IMPS: an interactive mathematical proof system. J. Autom. Reasoning **11**, 213–248 (1993)
12. Jenks, R.D., Sutor, R.S.: Axiom: The Scientific Computation System. Springer, Heidelberg (1992)
13. Kohlhase, M.: Mathematical knowledge management: transcending the one-brain-barrier with theory graphs. Eur. Math. Soc. (EMS) Newslett. **92**, 22–27 (2014)
14. Norell, U.: Towards a practical programming language based on dependent type theory. Ph.D. thesis, Chalmers University of Technology (2007)
15. Norell, U.: Dependently typed programming in Agda. In: Kennedy, A., Ahmed, A. (eds.) Proceedings of TLDI 2009, pp. 1–2. ACM (2009)
16. Rabe, F., Kohlhase, M.: A scalable model system. Inf. Comput. **230**, 1–54 (2013)
17. Smoryński, C.: Logical Number Theory I: An Introduction. Springer, Heidelberg (1991)
18. Agda Team: Agda wiki. http://wiki.portal.chalmers.se/agda/pmwiki.php. Accessed 15 May 2017

19. The Univalent Foundations Theory Program: Homotopy Type Theory: Univalent Foundations of Mathematics. Institute for Advanced Study (2013). https://homotopytypetheory.org/book

20. van der Walt, P.: Reflection in Agda. Master's thesis, Universiteit Utrecht, (2012). https://dspace.library.uu.nl/handle/1874/256628

21. Walt, P., Swierstra, W.: Engineering proof by reflection in Agda. In: Hinze, R. (ed.) IFL 2012. LNCS, vol. 8241, pp. 157–173. Springer, Heidelberg (2013). doi:10.1007/978-3-642-41582-1_10

The Formalization of Vickrey Auctions: A Comparison of Two Approaches in Isabelle and Theorema

Alexander Maletzky and Wolfgang Windsteiger[(✉)]

Research Institute for Symbolic Computation (RISC),
Johannes Kepler University Linz (JKU), 4232 Hagenberg, Austria
{alexander.maletzky,wolfgang.windsteiger}@risc.jku.at

Abstract. In earlier work presented at CICM, four theorem provers (Isabelle, Mizar, Hets/CASL/TPTP, and Theorema) were compared based on a case study in theoretical economics, the formalization of the landmark Theorem of Vickrey in auction theory. At the time of this comparison the Theorema system was in a state of transition: The original Theorema system (Theorema 1) had been shut down by the Theorema group and the successor system Theorema 2.0 was just about to be launched. Theorema 2.0 participated in the competition, but only parts of the system were ready for use. In particular, the new reasoning engines had not been set up, so that some of the results in the system comparison had to be extrapolated from experience we had with Theorema 1. In this paper, we now want to compare a complete formalization of Vickrey's Theorem in Theorema 2.0 with the original formalization in Isabelle. On the one hand, we compare the mathematical setup of the two theories and, on the other hand, we also give an overview on statistical indicators, such as number of auxiliary lemmas and the total number of proof steps needed for all proofs in the theory. Last but not least, we present a shorter version of proof of the main theorem in Isabelle.

1 Introduction

The Theorem of Vickrey [13] formulates a key property of so-called *second-price auctions*. In this setting, one considers $n \in \mathbb{N}$ bidders participating in the auction of a single indivisible good. Each bidder submits a sealed bid, a bidder with the highest bid wins, and she has to pay the price given by the maximum of the remaining bids.

The Theorem of Vickrey provides a bidding strategy for participants in a second-price auction, namely it says, informally speaking, that *truthful bidding*, i.e. bidding the true valuation of the good, is a *weakly dominant strategy* for every participant, i.e. for each bidder the payoff is greater or equal to the payoff resulting from a different bid, and that truthful bidding is also *efficient*, i.e. it is guaranteed that the winner is a bidder with maximal valuation of the good.

A. Maletzky—The research was funded by the Austrian Science Fund (FWF): P 29498-N31.

© Springer International Publishing AG 2017
H. Geuvers et al. (Eds.): CICM 2017, LNAI 10383, pp. 25–39, 2017.
DOI: 10.1007/978-3-319-62075-6_3

As part of an effort to implement an auction theory toolbox [5], which should assist auction designers in the formal verification of properties of the auction mechanisms they design, four proof assistant systems of different nature (Isabelle [11,14], Mizar [1,4], Hets/CASL/TPTP [9,10,12], and Theorema [15]) were compared with respect to their suitability as a common platform for the auction theory toolbox [6]. At the time of publication the formalization in Isabelle was complete, whereas the Theorema formalization only contained the formulation of the theorem and all necessary definitions. Due to the complete redesign and reimplementation of the Theorema system at that time, the proofs were still missing and, in particular, the intermediate lemmas and their proofs were not yet known. The assessment of Theorema 2.0 in this comparison was therefore based on one hand on the user-interface, which allowed to judge the effort needed by a user to formulate the desired statements and the quality in which input and output of the system are presented to a user, and on the other hand on experience we had with the proving mechanisms in the predecessor system Theorema 1. The main motivations for the current paper are to close the gap of the missing formalization in Theorema 2.0 and to demonstrate the suitability of Theorema 2.0 as a platform for future formalization projects.

The definitions of the basic auction theory concepts follow the informal introduction given in [6], which is in turn based on influential auction theory literature [7,8]. We then compare the Theorema formalization to the known formalization in Isabelle, which was the basis for the original assessment in [6]. We concentrate on differences and similarities in the *structure of the formalization* and in *technical details* concerning the formalization approaches chosen in the two systems. Moreover, *a new proof in Isabelle* is given based on the automatically generated proof of the main theorem in Theorema 2.0.

2   The Two Systems: A User's Point of View

In this section we want to sketch briefly how a task of "formalizing some part of mathematics" is carried out typically in the two systems Theorema and Isabelle. Theorema 2.0 provides a user interface based on Mathematica technology, for its details we refer to [2], for examples see the screenshots in Fig. 3. When it comes to proving, Theorema is designed as a multi-method system, i.e., it provides various proving methods that can be selected by the user depending on the application domain. Typically, a *method* consists of a collection of inference rules and a strategy to apply the rules in order to generate a complete proof in a fully automated fashion. One of the main improvements in Theorema 2.0 is the easy customization of pre-defined prove-methods[1]. Each inference rule can be deactivated by a single mouse-click and rule-priorities can easily be adjusted via

---

[1] It should be noted that not all methods that were implemented in Theorema 1 are already available in Theorema 2.0. The standard method available, which was used also in the current formalization, is a natural-deduction-like prover for first-order predicate logic with certain enhancements for Theorema-specific language constructs.

drop-down menues in the Theorema-GUI. The primary goal in the Theorema system is to provide well-curated default settings such that the fully automated proofs appear as if written by a well-trained mathematician.

In order to prove a formula G w. r. t. a knowledge base K the user has to just mark the formula G in the notebook, select all formulas that constitute K by mouse-click in the Theorema-GUI, and configure the prove method if necessary. All the rest is then done fully automatically, the resulting proof object is stored in a separate file, and a link to a human-readable presentation of the proof is put into the notebook. The proof search may fail when no applicable inference rule is available anymore, when a predefined search-depth is reached, or when a pre-defined search-time is exhausted. A valuable feature in case of a failed proof is the possibility to inspect failing proofs in order to come up with an improved setup for the next prove-run. By reading a failed proof one often gets the idea, which additional lemma in the knowledge base would help the prover to succeed (or at least to proceed further). Other possibilities to improve the setup include the activation/deactivation of certain inference rules (in order to prevent the prover from running into an undesired path) and the modification of rule-priorities (in order to force the prover into a desired path). This phase of fiddling with the prover setup is interactive, sometimes non-trivial, and very similar to what a mathematician is faced when doing proofs with pencil and paper (searching for auxiliary knowledge, changing one's prove strategy, etc.). A typical approach for getting started with a proof is to let it run with small search-depth and low search-time with only definitions in the knowledge base. The proof will probably fail. Then inspect the failing proof and draw conclusions for an improved setup. If things go well, increase search-depth and search-time.

Proving in Isabelle proceeds interactively, meaning that every step in a proof must be written down explicitly by the user. One of the main differences to Theorema (at least at the moment) is that these steps can be huge: one single application of a powerful proof method like *metis* could potentially solve goals that need dozens of steps in Theorema. In that sense, proving in Isabelle could also be regarded (semi-)automatic: the user outlines the main structure of the proof and then, for each remaining subgoal, invokes tools like Sledgehammer for automatically finding relevant facts from the background theory together with suitable proof methods that close the respective subgoals. We refer to [14] for a more thorough exposition of working with Isabelle.

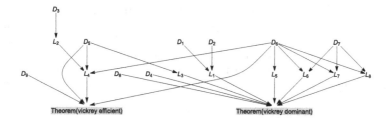

Fig. 1. The dependency graph of the formalization in Theorema.

3   The Two Formalizations: A Structural Comparison

3.1   The Content of the Formalizations

Figure 1 shows the structure of the entire theory developed in Theorema.[2] The labels in the graph stand for individual formulas (D_i are definitions, L_i are Lemmas) and an edge $F \to G$ in the graph means 'formula F is needed in the proof of formula G'.

In Theorema we use natural numbers $1, \ldots, n$ for the participants in the auction. We then define the basic auction theory concepts *bids*, *valuations*, *payments*, and *allocations* as n-tuples of numbers (Def. D_1–D_3). In fact, a bid (valuation, payment) tuple b (v, p) contains non-negative numbers, where b_i (v_i, p_i) represents participant i's bid (valuation, payment) of the good. An allocation tuple x contains exactly one 1 and otherwise 0, where $x_i = 1$ means that participant i gets the good. Given a valuation v, an allocation x, and a payment p, participant i's *payoff* (Def. D_4) is then just $v_i x_i - p_i$, i.e. if she gets the good it is the difference of her valuation and the payment, if she does not get the good the payoff is 0.

For truthful bidding we have to use valuations as bids, hence we need a property stating that a valuation is always also permitted as a bid (Lemma L_1 in Fig. 1).[3] Then we show from the definition of allocations that the good cannot be assigned to more than one bidder (Lemma L_2). Next we define the basic ingredients of a second-price auction, such as the *outcome of a second-price auction* and the *participant i being winner (or loser) in a second-price auction* (Def. D_5–D_7). Figure 1 displays nicely that the two statements in the main theorem are not proved directly from the definitions, but we introduce one layer of intermediate lemmas (L_3–L_8), from which the theorems are then proved. The proofs of the lemmas in this layer only need the definitions of the concepts involved, with the only exception being Lemma L_4, which states that in a second-price auction there can be at most one winner. The proof of this statement needs Lemma L_2 in addition to the definitions of a second-price auction and an auction-winner. The proof of the first part of Vickrey's theorem, truthful

---

[2] Theorema knowledge archives, which will be an efficient way of storing Theorema formalizations for later use in a structured hierarchical build-up of theories, are not yet available in the current release of Theorema 2.0. Currently, the formalization of Vickrey's Theorem is written in one Mathematica/Theorema notebook containing the statement of all pieces of formalized maths (definitions, lemmas, and theorems). A proof in Theorema 2.0 is represented in a data-structure called *proof object*, which contains the information about all logical steps the proof consists of. Proof objects and additional statistics about the proof run and user and system settings are stored in separate files. The Theorema formalization thus consists of the Theorema notebook together with its accompanying files, the current formalization being available for download in zip-format from the Theorema homepage at www.risc.jku.at/research/theorema/software/Vickrey.zip.

[3] This lemma could be omitted also, the four steps of its proof could as well be done in an extra branch of the proof of the main theorem. We rather see it as a means to structure the theory.

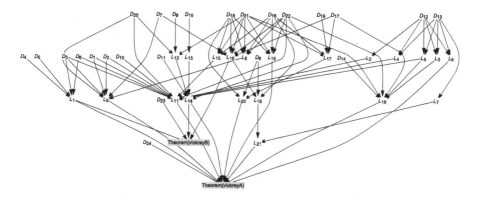

Fig. 2. The dependency graph of the formalization in Isabelle.

bidding being a weakly dominant strategy, uses above-mentioned Lemma L_1, another auxiliary Lemma L_3 (every participant in a second-price auction either wins or loses), and the 4 key Lemmas L_5 to L_8, which encapsulate knowledge about payments and allocations in case of modified bids. Lemmas L_5 and L_6 cover the cases where participant i wins with bid b_i and wins/loses with a modified bid a. Lemmas L_7 and L_8 are their counterparts for the case when i loses with bid b_i. The second part of the theorem, efficiency of truthful bidding in a second-price auction, only needs aforementioned Lemma L_4 and some definitions.

The formalization in Isabelle we used for our comparison is the one obtained from the web-page of the ForMaRE project.[4] It was created with Isabelle2013 and unfortunately contains some auxiliary lemmas whose proofs are not valid in the current version of Isabelle any more.[5] A vastly improved version of the formalization, which is concerned with the more general class of *combinatorial Vickrey-Clarke-Groves* auctions, is contained in the Archive of Formal Proofs (AFP) [3] and thus guaranteed to work in the current version of Isabelle. However, the AFP-version does not include the formulation of Vickrey's theorem that is the subject of the Theorema formalization, thus, it is not suitable as a reference for our present comparison.

The structure of the formalization in Isabelle, shown in Fig. 2, roughly resembles that of the formalization in Theorema: after proving some general facts about the maximum of functions over (finite) sets in theory `Maximum.thy`, and about vectors of real numbers in `Vectors.thy` (which does not have a counterpart in Theorema), the authors first introduce a couple of general concepts related to single-good auctions (e. g. valuations, allocations, bids, etc.) in theory `SingleGoodAuction.thy`. From this theory, the only lemma, that is needed later on in the proofs of the two main theorems, is Lemma L_1; this lemma exactly corresponds to Lemma L_1 in the Theorema formalization. Next comes the core theory of the whole formalization: `SecondPriceAuction.thy` states the property of being a second-price auction in terms of the vectors of bids and payments and

---

[4] www.cs.bham.ac.uk/research/projects/formare/code/auction-theory/isabelle/.
[5] The proofs of the important theorems are still fine, though.

in addition introduces various other auxiliary notions (e. g. winners and losers of second-price auctions, as in Theorema). Furthermore, the authors prove several lemmas, for instance that second-price auctions result in non-negative payments for all participants (L_{11}), that every second-price auction is also a single-good auction (L_{14}), what the payoffs of the winner and the losers, respectively, are, and, most importantly, what the payoff of the winner is if she deviates from her valuation (L_{21}). Finally, theory `Vickrey.thy` contains the statements and proofs of the two main theorems about weakly dominant strategies (Theorem *vickreyA*) and efficiency (Theorem *vickreyB*) in second-price auctions; the definitions of weakly dominant strategies and efficiency are put into a separate theory `SingleGoodAuctionProperties.thy`.

Still, there are also some essential structural differences between the formalizations in Theorema and in Isabelle. First, as already indicated above, the latter one includes theories about vectors of real numbers and about properties of the maximum of functions over sets. One of these properties, which features a key role in the proof of *vickreyA* about weak dominance, is the obvious fact that changing the value of a function f at x does not change the maximum of that function f over the set A, provided that $x \notin A$. In Theorema, in contrast, this property is not stated as a formula on the object level, but on the meta level in a specific set of simplification rules for 'max', which is a built-in construct in the Theorema language. For more details, we refer to Sect. 4.

The second main difference is that the ultimate goal of the authors of the formalization in Isabelle apparently not only was to prove the two Vickrey-theorems, but to build up an auction theory toolbox that aims at formally checking properties of various—potentially complex—types of auctions. Hence, their formalization not only consists of definitions and results used in the proofs of the two theorems, but also many other definitions, lemmas and theorems that are needed elsewhere. Moreover, several of the definitions/lemmas that *are* needed are stated in a more general form than actually required. For instance, the definition of an equilibrium in weakly-dominant strategies is given for arbitrary classes of single-good auctions in Isabelle, whereas in Theorema it is restricted to second-price auctions. This is the main reason why the dependency graph of the Isabelle formalization, shown in Fig. 2, is considerably more complex than that of the Theorema formalization shown in Fig. 1, although the former already omits all definitions and lemmas irrelevant for the two main theorems.

Furthermore, a minor structural difference is that the four crucial lemmas L_5–L_8 in the Theorema formalization do not have analogues in Isabelle. Instead, the four cases in the proof of *vickreyA* they correspond to are proved directly, without making use of any lemmas of this kind.

3.2   The Size of the Formalizations

In [6] the 'de Bruijn factor', i.e. the formalization size divided by the size of an informal TeX-source, measured after stripping comments and xz-compression, was used as criterion for the complexity/effort of the formalization. Theorema has already been exempted from that part of the comparison at that time due to the formalization missing the proofs. Still now with all proofs available, we do not think that measuring a Theorema formalization in terms of megabytes is the appropriate thing to do. Proofs are generated automatically including all the formatting of formulas and their nice appearance in the user front-end (including e. g. hyperlinks, tooltips, etc.). Since they need not be typed manually, their length in terms of kilo- or megabytes is irrelevant. Rather, a much more accurate measure for the effort to read and understand a proof is its size in terms of *proof steps*.[6] In Theorema there is a quite natural notion of proof step, it is one application of a proof rule. It should be mentioned, however, that not every proof rule needs to correspond to exactly one inference rule in classical logic. Theorema allows also specialized proof rules, which might combine several elementary inferences into a more complex step, or might involve rather complex computations in the background. Still, proof rules in Theorema are designed according to the principle that one step in a proof should be just as big that it can be perceived easily by a reader of a certain target audience. In the case of Vickrey auctions, we use a *standard predicate logic prover* enhanced with *a few special rules* dealing with *tuple operations* and the *maximum function*, hence targeting an audience that is familiar with the basic rules of logic, tuples and maximum, not more.

The entire formalization of Vickrey's Theorem in Theorema consists of 10 proofs with a total number of 171 proof steps. The most involved one is the proof of the first part of the theorem (truthful bidding is a weakly dominant strategy) with 41 steps.[7] Although the second part of the theorem (efficiency of truthful bidding in a second-price auction) is pretty straight-forward when given informally, it is interesting that the formal proof still needs 20 steps, ranking it as the fourth-biggest of all proofs.

The whole formalization in Isabelle consists of 247 proof steps in total. Note, however, that in Sect. 6 we illustrate how this number can be decreased to 185 by modeling the proof of *vickreyA* exactly after the proof of the corresponding theorem in Theorema. Counting proof steps in Isabelle is somewhat tricky, especially if the proofs are written in the Isar language: it is not clear how to count individual statements, whether to count them as one proof step, several steps, or not at all. For instance, one could argue that the combination '**unfolding** ⟨*defs*⟩ **by** *simp*', which unfolds definitions of constants in the current goal and then proves it by simplification, counts as two proof steps; the same effect, however, could also be achieved by simply writing '**by** (*simp add:* ⟨*defs*⟩)', which would reasonably only count as one single proof step. Keeping these considerations in

---

[6] The number of steps is no measure for the effort needed to generate the proof, since the steps are generated automatically.

[7] To get a feeling, how big a 41-step proof is: Theorema's proof display with natural-language proof explanation consumes ample space because the explanation of every proof step starts in a new line and every formula is printed nicely 2D-formatted in a separate line (see a sample screen-shot of a proof in Fig. 4). In this format the proof is approximately 5 pages. Its fully automated generation took 110 s on a standard laptop (4 cores 2.20 GHz each), 106 s for proof generation plus 4 s for subsequent simplification of the generated proof.

mind, it is obvious that there are many different ways of counting proof steps in Isabelle/Isar, and we do not claim that the counting schema we employed to arrive at the aforementioned 247 steps is the best one. Still, we believe that it is the *fairest* one for comparing proofs in Isabelle to proofs in Theorema. Roughly, every occurrence of **fix**, **assume**, **obtain**, **have**, **define**, **unfolding**, **qed**, **next** counts as 1 step; every occurrence of *of*, *OF* etc. counts as 1 step, too; and every occurrence of **proof**, **apply** and **by** counts as n steps, where n is the number of proof methods passed as arguments. Hence, even powerful proof methods like *auto*, *metis* etc. only count as 1 step, although simulating their behavior in Theorema would require lots of steps there.

4   The Two Formalizations: A Technical Comparison

Besides the structural differences between the two formalizations related to the different degrees of generality as discussed in the previous section, there are some technical differences—and similarities—as well.

A *second-price auction* is some mechanism that, given the number of participants n and the bids b, results in an allocation x of the good and a payment p. In Theorema, we decided to model the participants as natural numbers 1 to n with the effect that bids, valuations, allocations, and payments can be modeled as n-tuples of numbers, which are a built-in construct in Theorema. For $1 \leq i \leq n$ the ith entry of such a tuple is then just the bid/valuation/allocation/payment of participant i. The key property of *being a second-price auction outcome* is modeled in Theorema as a 4-ary predicate `secondPriceAuction` on bids b, allocations x, payments p, and the number of participants n, where `secondPriceAuction[b, x, p, n]` expresses that x and p satisfy the properties of a second-price auction for given b and n. The concepts 'being winner/loser in a second-price auction', 'being a weakly dominant strategy in a second-price auction', and 'being an efficient allocation' are also formulated as predicates on the respective tuples.

In contrast, the formalization in Isabelle makes heavy use of *sets*. More concretely, a general single-good auction in Isabelle is defined as a 4-tuple (N, b, x, p) consisting of the set of participants N, their bids b, the allocation x and the payment p, where bids, allocations, and payments are given as functions from type *nat* to type *real*.[8] Special kinds of auctions, like second-price auctions, are then simply modeled as the sets containing precisely those tuples with the desired

---

[8] Note that the authors of the formalization in Isabelle introduced a type-synonym 'vectors' for such function types, which corresponds exactly to what tuples are in Theorema. We want to emphasize, however, that the choice of tuples in Theorema is not system-enforced, it is more a matter of taste. The mathematical representation of the objects to be studied in Theorema can be chosen freely. In general, using built-in structures (like tuples) has the advantage of getting system support in computation and proving. Using non-built structures (like functions as done in Isabelle) would require to prove auxiliary knowledge about these entities. This knowledge would then be part of the formalization, like the knowledge about 'maximum' in the Isabelle formalization.

properties—but these properties are now given as 4-ary *relations* (i.e. functions whose result type is *bool*). So, in the end, sets and relations are mixed somewhat randomly, which in our opinion is counter-intuitive and occasionally leads to confusion. Instead, using relations exclusively would perhaps be more 'natural' and probably even fit better into the context of higher-order logic. Nevertheless, we shall emphasize that all this is largely a matter of taste; in the end, the difference between sets and relations boils down to a mere technicality that does not have a major impact on the formalization.

In Isabelle, the set of participants is not fixed to $\{1, \ldots, n\}$, but can be completely arbitrary (as long as it is finite and contains at least two elements). This is obviously more general, but we do not see any immediate advantage of it. After all, it is absolutely irrelevant for auction theory *what* the participants are, as long as one knows *how many* there are. Besides the fact that allocations in Theorema are modeled as tuples and in Isabelle as functions, they differ between the two formalizations in another respect: the definition of allocations in Isabelle in principle allows for *divisible* goods, as the values of an allocation are only required to be non-negative and to sum up to 1. Only the definition of second-price auctions incorporates the condition that allocations must allocate the good to one single participant. In Theorema, allocations need to have this property from the very beginning, making it slightly more difficult to reuse definitions and results from the existing formalization in potential future treatments of other kinds of auctions.

Another technical difference is related to the definition of *losers* of second-price auctions: in Theorema, the definition of a loser (i.e. a participant who is not awarded the good) explicitly requires that her bid be not the *unique* maximum among all bids, but at most the *tied* maximum. In other words: according to the formalization in Theorema, participant i is a loser iff her allocation and payment are both 0, and if additionally the tuple of bids b satisfies $b_i \leq \max(b_{i\leftarrow})$, where b_i is the tuple b at position i, and $b_{i\leftarrow}$ is the tuple b with position i deleted. However, this condition turns out to be redundant, since it automatically follows from the fact that in a second-price auction, by definition, one participant *with the highest bid* must be the winner, and all other participants must be losers. The formalization in Isabelle omits said condition and anything equivalent to it in the definition of losers and instead proves it as an auxiliary lemma.

Usually, it is tacitly assumed that at least two bidders participate in the auction, because otherwise the definition of the price as 'the maximum of the remaining bids' does not make sense. In a formal approach, of course, this assumption has to be made explicit. In [6] it has been suggested as an alternative to overcome this problem by defining $\max(\emptyset) := 0$. We do not consider this a viable choice because it is both unnatural and impractical, because it would mean that in case of only one participant in the auction, the good would be given away for free. Rather, we think that the common way of handling a second-price auction is to define the outcome in the special case of only one participant in a different way without referring to 'the maximum of the remaining bids'.

In the current state of the Theorema formalization, the assumption $n > 1$ is still omitted, and the prover does not yet check the side-condition $|t| > 0$ when it encounters an expression such as max$[t]$. We consider this an open issue in the current formalization in Theorema, but it does not affect the principal feasibility of the presented approach. Since 'max' is a built-in construct of the Theorema language, we do not define 'max' as part of the auction formalization (as in Isabelle), rather we rely on available computation and reasoning rules for expressions involving 'max'. The Theorema computation engine already contained algorithms for operations on concrete tuples and, of course, in these algorithms all necessary side-conditions are really checked, e. g. the expression max$[\langle\rangle]$ does not evaluate. As a generalization, we provide also *symbolic algorithms* on tuples, e. g. $(t_{i \leftarrow x})_i = x$, and the Theorema reasoning engine uses these algorithms in order to simplify expressions. In the case of maximum, these algorithms are then required to check $|t| > 0$ as soon as they encounter an expression max$[t]$ with symbolic t. In order to do this, the computation engine needs access to the current knowledge base in case the computation occurs as part of a proof.

5   The Two Proofs of the Main Theorem

Figure 3 shows the formulation of Vickrey's Theorem in the Theorema language. Roughly, it says, that for all[9] $n \in \mathbb{N}$, for all valuations v, allocations x, and payments p

1. using the valuations as bids is an `equilibriumWeaklyDominantStrategy` and
2. if the auction outcome with these bids conforms to the rules of a second-price auction then the allocation is `efficient`.

We want to concentrate on the first part of the theorem. Here b constitutes a *weakly dominant strategy* w.r.t. v and n iff b is a bid-tuple of length n, v is a valuation-tuple of length n, and for all $i = 1, \ldots, n$ and for all ..., see the definition of `equilibriumWeaklyDominantStrategy` in Fig. 3. The main part of this definition expresses that if i bids differently from b_i the payoff does not increase.

During the first phase of the proof, the universal quantifiers are eliminated. After expanding the definition of `equilibriumWeaklyDominantStrategy` we are left with three branches. The first two (v being a bid-tuple of length n and a valuation-tuple of length n, respectively) are trivial, the third one corresponds

---

[9] The universal quantifier for n is not visible locally, neither in the theorem nor in the definitions, because we use a 'global universal quantifier' $\underset{n \in \mathbb{N}}{\forall}$ at the beginning of the document. This mechanism in Theorema 2.0 is explained in detail in [2]. The Theorema language is untyped. Quantifiers range over all objects that can be expressed in the Theorema language, i.e. sets, tuples, and various kinds of numbers available in Mathematica. There are special ranges with limited domain, such as $i = 1, \ldots, n$ for finite integer fragments. The domain can also be restricted using conditions. All what is needed in the current formalization is essentially first-order.

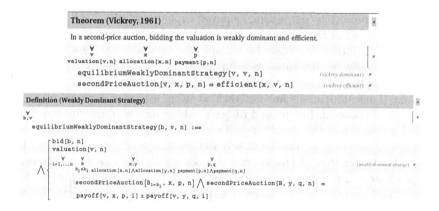

Fig. 3. The main theorem and the required definitions in Theorema.

to the main part of the definition of `equilibriumWeaklyDominantStrategy`. Essentially by Lemma L_3, the two formulas

$$\text{secondPriceAuctionWinner}[B, y, q, i] \vee \text{secondPriceAuctionLoser}[B, y, q, i] \quad (1)$$

$$\text{secondPriceAuctionWinner}[B_{i \leftarrow v_i}, \bar{x}, \bar{p}, i] \vee \text{secondPriceAuctionLoser}[B_{i \leftarrow v_i}, \bar{x}, \bar{p}, i] \quad (2)$$

are derived. In (1) B represents an arbitrary bid, whereas in (2) $B_{i \leftarrow v_i}$ represents the bid B with v_i at position i. Now the disjunction (1) gives rise to a case distinction 'i wins with an arbitrary bid' vs. 'i loses with an arbitrary bid'. In each branch then the disjunction (2) initiates a case distinction 'i wins when bidding her valuation' vs. 'i loses when bidding her valuation'. Note that the order in which (1) and (2) enter the knowledge base is random. Theorema first distinguishes cases based on (1). Both in Isabelle and in the pencil-and-paper proof in [6] the cases when bidding her valuation are treated first. However, all proofs end up with the same four cases. In order to get an impression how a Theorema proof actually looks, we refer to the screen-shot in Fig. 4. The part of the proof displayed there corresponds to the case i loses with an arbitrary bid but wins when bidding her valuation. We see that this branch relies on Lemma *lose-win* (L_7) and then succeeds by basic rewriting. The remaining three branches proceed analogously making use of Lemmas L_5, L_6, and L_8, respectively.

In the Isabelle formalization the proof of *vickreyA* is not very complicated, but lengthy. It starts by introducing the necessary objects, like an arbitrary, but fixed participant i and two vectors of bids (where in one case participant i bids arbitrarily, and in the other case she bids exactly her valuation of the good), and proving a couple of simple properties of these objects. Then comes the key step of the proof: the case distinction depending on whether i is allocated the good if she bids her valuation or not, analogous the hand-written proof in [6]. Here it is worth noting that Lemma L_{15} is used in order to infer that a participant loses if she is not assigned the good, i.e. that $x(i) \neq 1$ implies $x(i) = 0$; this means that L_{15} roughly corresponds to Lemma L_3 in Theorema. The first case, where i wins, proceeds by expressing i's payoff explicitly in terms of her valuation and the maximum of the remaining bids and by showing that this quantity is certainly non-negative, whereas the second case proceeds by showing that i's payoff is 0. Finally, in either case two further cases are distinguished depending on whether i wins with her alternative bid, yielding the same four cases as in Theorema. These four cases are not tackled using separate lemmas analogous to L_5–L_8 in Theorema, but proved directly taking into account the previously obtained properties of the payoff of participant i if she bids her valuation.

All in all, the proof in Isabelle closely follows the proof presented in [6]. It is considerably longer than the hand-crafted proof mainly because a lot of intermediate proof steps are required for inferring simple facts about bids, allocations, payments and payoffs that are more or less obvious, and hence omitted in [6].

6   A New Proof of *vickreyA* in Isabelle

The Isabelle proof of Vickrey's theorem is considerably longer than the corresponding proof in Theorema (even if one counts all the lemmas that are not proved separately in Isabelle, like L_5–L_8). This lead to the idea of translating the Theorema proof to Isabelle, to see whether the Isabelle formalization could perhaps be shortened; and indeed, with moderate effort we managed to reconstruct the Theorema proof almost one-to-one in Isabelle. Of course, we did not start completely from scratch but built upon the existing formalization as much as possible, which also necessitated a couple of new definitions and lemmas for establishing the connection to results that we wanted to reuse in our proof. In particular, we introduced new definitions of *winners* and *losers* that exactly resemble the definitions in the Theorema formalization, and we also proved another general result about the maximum of a function over a set, namely

```
lemma remaining-maximum-le-maximum:
  fixes A::"'a set"
    and f::"'a ⇒'b::linorder"
    and a::'a and b::'b
  assumes "card A > 1"
  shows "maximum (A - {a}) f ≤ maximum A (f(a := b))"
```

This lemma states that when removing an arbitrary element a from a set A, the maximum of a function f over that new set is certainly not larger than over the original set, even if f attains a different value at a. Stating and proving *remaining-maximum-le-maximum* was inspired by the formalization in Theorema where, however, the analogue of this lemma is not stated on the theory level, but instead on the reasoning level as a special inference rule.

Summarizing, the new proof of *vickreyA* depends on two additional definitions and seven additional lemmas. If the original proof of the theorem was replaced by the new one and all lemmas not needed any more were removed, the total number of proof steps would drop by 25% from 247 to 185, which is only slightly more than the 171 steps in Theorema.

```
next
  assume lose1: "spa-loser N b y q i"
  from cases2 show ?thesis
  proof
    assume win2: "spa-winner N (b(i := v i)) x p i"
    from lose1 card-N have "∀y' q' a. spa-winner N (b(i := a)) y' q' i ⟶
                                    (q i = 0 ∧ y i = 0 ∧ y' i = 1 ∧ a - q' i ≥ 0)"
      using lose-win by auto
    hence "q i = 0 ∧ y i = 0 ∧ x i = 1 ∧ v i - p i ≥ 0" using win2 by auto
    hence "q i = 0" and "y i = 0" and "x i = 1" and "v i - p i ≥ 0" by simp_all
    show ?thesis unfolding payoff-def
    proof -
      from ‹q i = 0› ‹y i = 0› ‹x i = 1›
        show "v i * y i - q i ≤ v i * x i - p i"
        proof (simp del: diff-ge-0-iff-ge)
          from ‹v i - p i ≥ 0› show "v i - p i ≥ 0" .
        qed
    qed
  next ...
qed
```

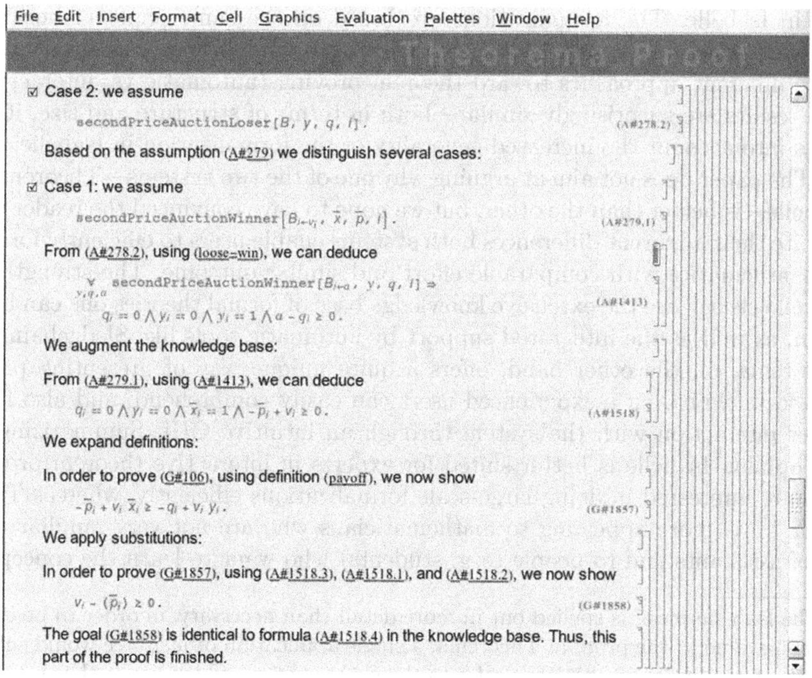

Fig. 4. An Isabelle proof and a Theorema proof side by side.

In Fig. 4 we show the part of the proof, where participant i is assumed to lose with some arbitrary bid and wins when bidding her valuation, in both systems.[10] In the Isabelle proof, q and y denote the payment- and allocation vectors, respectively, if i bids arbitrarily, whereas p and x denote the payment- and allocation vectors, respectively, if i bids her valuation; v is the vector of valuations, and b is some arbitrary vector of bids. *cases2* is a local fact corresponding to $A\#279$ in the Theorema-proof (it expresses that i either wins for loses if she bids her valuation). The full new proof, together with the original proof and all auxiliary concepts from the original formalization the proof depends upon, is available online.[11] It works in Isabelle2016-1. For the Theorema proof, it should be noted that the proof is displayed using Mathematica notebook technology. It employs lots of interactive GUI-features that are hard to resemble in print, e. g. all formula labels[12] are actually hyperlinks that jump to the point where the formula has been introduced, labels have tooltips that show the entire formula when hovered above, and the interface shows a schematic clickable tree representation of the proof, that allows easy navigation through a proof. For the details we refer to [2].

7   Conclusion and Future Work

We presented two formalizations of Vickrey's theorem, one in Theorema and one in Isabelle. The formalizations are based on the same paper elaboration, but were done independently of each other in two different proof assistants, with quite different approaches toward theorem proving (automatic vs. interactive). The results are surprisingly similar—both in terms of structure and size, if one takes into account the increased generality of the formalization in Isabelle.

The paper does not aim at arguing why one of the two systems—Theorema or Isabelle—is better than the other, but we hope to have convinced the reader that despite their apparent differences both systems enable users to efficiently formalize mathematics with comparable effort and similar outcome. The strengths of Isabelle clearly are the extensive knowledge base of formal theories one can build upon, as well as the integrated support by automatic tools like Sledgehammer. Theorema, on the other hand, offers a quite unique way of presenting proofs in a form that even inexperienced users can easily comprehend, and also facilitates interaction with the system through an intuitive GUI. Summarizing, in our opinion Isabelle is better suited for experts in interactive theorem proving who are interested in doing large-scale formalizations efficiently, whereas Theorema 2.0 is more appealing to mathematicians who are not very familiar with proof assistants and to people (e. g. students) who want to learn the concept of

---

[10] The Isabelle proof is spelled out in more detail than necessary, in order to be easily comparable to the proof in Theorema; a single application of *fastforce* would suffice. The aforementioned 185 steps refer to the short version, which is not shown here.

[11] www.risc.jku.at/people/amaletzk/Vickrey.zip.

[12] Definitions, lemmas, and theorems have user-defined labels. Formulas that are generated automatically during a proof have system-generated labels, where $A\#\ldots$ and $G\#\ldots$ refer to assumptions and goals, respectively.

mathematical proof, thanks to its intuitive handling and natural-style presentation of formal content. Of course, Theorema also claims for itself to enable large-scale undertakings.

As for current and future work, we have already mentioned the need for a more sophisticated means for checking side-conditions in symbolic tuple computations. The development of Theorema archives to have the possibility to efficiently store structured formalizations in Theorema language also deserves high priority.

References

1. Bancerek, G., Byliński, C., Grabowski, A., Korniłowicz, A., Matuszewski, R., Naumowicz, A., Pąk, K., Urban, J.: Mizar: state-of-the-art and beyond. In: Kerber, M., Carette, J., Kaliszyk, C., Rabe, F., Sorge, V. (eds.) CICM 2015. LNCS, vol. 9150, pp. 261–279. Springer, Cham (2015). doi:10.1007/978-3-319-20615-8_17
2. Buchberger, B., Jebelean, T., Kutsia, T., Maletzky, A., Windsteiger, W.: Theorema 2.0: computer-assisted natural-style mathematics. JFR $9(1)$, 149–185 (2016)
3. Caminati, M.B., Kerber, M., Lange, C., Rowat, C.: VCG - Combinatorial Vickrey-Clarke-Groves Auctions. Archive of Formal Proofs, April 2015
4. Grabowski, A., Korniłowicz, A., Naumowicz, A.: Mizar in a nutshell. J. Formal. Reason. $3(2)$, 153–245 (2010)
5. Kerber, M., Lange, C., Rowat, C., Windsteiger, W.: Developing an auction theory toolbox. In: Kerber, M., Lange, C., Rowat, C. (eds.) AISB 2013, pp. 1–4 (2013). Proceedings available online. http://www.cs.bham.ac.uk/research/projects/forma re/events/aisb2013/proceedings.php
6. Lange, C., Caminati, M.B., Kerber, M., Mossakowski, T., Rowat, C., Wenzel, M., Windsteiger, W.: A qualitative comparison of the suitability of four theorem provers for basic auction theory. In: Carette, J., Aspinall, D., Lange, C., Sojka, P., Windsteiger, W. (eds.) CICM 2013. LNCS, vol. 7961, pp. 200–215. Springer, Heidelberg (2013). doi:10.1007/978-3-642-39320-4_13
7. Maskin, E.: The unity of auction theory. J. Econ. Lit. $42(4)$, 1102–1115 (2004)
8. Milgrom, P.: Putting Auction Theory to Work. Cambridge University Press, Cambridge (2004)
9. Mossakowski, T., Haxthausen, A.E., Sannella, D., Tarlecki, A.: CASL - the common algebraic specification language. In: Bjørner, D., Henson, M.C. (eds.) Logics of Specification Languages. Monographs in Theoretical Computer Science, pp. 241–298. Springer, Heidelberg (2008)
10. Mossakowski, T., Maeder, C., Codescu, M.: Hets user guide. Technical report. version 0.98, DFKI Bremen (2013)
11. Paulson, L.C.: Isabelle: the next 700 theorem provers. In: Odifreddi, P. (ed.) Logic and Computer Science, pp. 361–386. Academic Press (1990)
12. Sutcliffe, G.: The TPTP problem library and associated infrastructure: the FOF and CNF parts, v3.5.0. J. Autom. Reason. $43(4)$, 337–362 (2009)
13. Vickrey, W.: Counterspeculation, auctions, and competitive sealed tenders. J. Financ. **XVI**, 8–37 (1961)
14. Wenzel, M.: Isabelle/Isar Reference Manual (2017)
15. Windsteiger, W.: Theorema 2.0: a graphical user interface for a mathematical assistant system. In: Kaliszyk, C., Lueth, C. (eds.) Proceedings of the 10th International Workshop UITP. EPTCS, vol. 118, pp. 72–82. Open Publishing Association (2012). doi10.4204/EPTCS.118.5. http://arxiv.org/abs/1307.1945v1

Automatically Proving Equivalence
by Type-Safe Reflection

Franck Slama and Edwin Brady[✉]

University of St Andrews, St Andrews, Scotland, UK
{fs39,ecb10}@st-andrews.ac.uk

Abstract. One difficulty with reasoning and programming with dependent types is that proof obligations arise naturally once programs become even moderately sized. For example, implementing an adder for binary numbers indexed over their natural number equivalents naturally leads to proof obligations for equalities of expressions over natural numbers. The need for these equality proofs comes, in intensional type theories, from the fact that the propositional equality enables us to prove as equal terms that are not judgementally equal, which means that the typechecker can't always obtain equalities by reduction. As far as possible, we would like to solve such proof obligations automatically. In this paper, we show one way to automate these proofs by reflection in the dependently typed programming language Idris. We show how defining reflected terms indexed by the original Idris expression allows us to construct and manipulate proofs. We build a hierarchy of tactics for proving equivalences in semi-groups, monoids, commutative monoids, groups, commutative groups, semi-rings and rings. We also show how each tactic reuses those from simpler structures, thus avoiding duplication of code and proofs.

Keywords: Proof automation · Equivalence · Equality · Proof by reflection · Correct-by-construction software · Type-driven development

1 Introduction

Proofs assistants like Coq [1] and programming languages like Agda [17] and Idris [3] are based on Intensional Type Theories that contain two notions of equality: propositional equality, that can be manipulated in the language, and judgemental (or definitional) equality. Propositional equality corresponds to the mathematical notion: this is a proposition that can be assumed, negated, proved or disproved. Since in type theory, propositions are types [13], the proposition that two elements x and y are equal corresponds to a type. If x and y are of type a, then the type $Id_a(x, y)$ represents the proposition "x is equal to y". If this type is inhabited, then x is said to be provably equal to y. Thus, Id is a type family (parameterised by the type a) indexed over two elements of a, giving $\text{Id}\ (a : \text{Type}) : a \to a \to \text{Type}$. For convenience, we write $(\text{Id}_a\ x\ y)$ as $(x =_a y)$.

Judgemental equality, on the other hand, is a primitive concept of the type theory. Whether or not two expressions are judgementally equal is a matter of

© Springer International Publishing AG 2017
H. Geuvers et al. (Eds.): CICM 2017, LNAI 10383, pp. 40–55, 2017.
DOI: 10.1007/978-3-319-62075-6_4

evaluating the definitions. For example, if $f : \mathbb{N} \rightarrow \mathbb{N}$ is defined by $f\ x := x + 2$, then $f\ 5$ is definitionally equal to 7. Definitional equality entails unfolding of functions and reductions, until no more reduction can be performed. We denote the definitional equality by $\equiv$.

Judgemental equality is included in propositional equality because what is equal by definition is provably equal. This is accomplished by giving a constructor for the type $Id(a, a)$ and no constructor when "a is not b". In these theories, Id is therefore implemented with the following type with one constructor:

```
data Id : a → a → Type where
    Refl : (x : a) → Id x x
```

The only way for $(Id_a\ x\ y)$ to be inhabited is therefore that x and y are equal by definition. In this case, the constructor `Refl` helps to create a proof of this equality: (`Refl x`) is precisely the proof which says that $x =_a x$. Here, we are using the notation of Idris, where unbound variables like `a` in the definition of `Id` are *implicitly* quantified, as a concise programming notation.

The propositional equality does not only contain the judgemental equality, however, because a principle of induction is associated with each inductive type. If `T` is an inductive type with a constant constructor and a recursive constructor, i.e., `T = 1 + T`, defined in Idris as:

```
data T : Type where
  T0 : T
  T1 : T → T
```

then we have the following induction principle for `T`:
$T\_ind : \forall P : T \rightarrow Type,\ (P\ T0) \rightarrow (\forall t : T,\ P\ t \rightarrow P\ (T1\ t)) \rightarrow (\forall t : T,\ P\ t)$.

For example, we can prove that $n + 0 = n$ for all n by induction on the $Nat\ n$, even if $n + 0 \not\equiv n$ with the usual definition of $+$, recursive on its first argument. So, the axiom of induction means the type $Id_a(x, y)$ contains not only the canonical form `Refl`, but also those added by inductive principles. There are therefore things which are *provably* equal, but not *definitionally* equal. Proving equalities is therefore in these theories something which isn't automatically decidable by the type-checker in the general case.

1.1   Motivating Example: Verified Binary Arithmetic

Proving that one term is equal to another is common in formal verification, and proof obligations arise naturally in dependently typed programming when indexing types over values in order to capture some logical properties. To demonstrate this, we revisit an example from previous work [2] which shows how proof obligations arise when a type is indexed by natural numbers. Our goal is to implement a verified library of binary numbers. To ensure functional correctness, we define the types `Bit` and `Binary` indexed over the value they represent (expressed as a natural number):

```
data Bit : Nat → Type where
     b0 : Bit Z
     b1 : Bit (S Z)

data Binary : (width : Nat) → (value : Nat) → Type where
     zero : Binary Z Z
     (#) : Binary w v → Bit bit → Binary (S w) (bit + 2 * v)
```

We will write a function to add two binary numbers. To do so, we begin with an auxiliary function, which adds three bits (the third is a carry bit), and produces the two bits of the result, where the first is the more significant bit:

```
addBit : Bit x → Bit y → Bit c → (bX ** (bY **
         (Bit bX, Bit bY, c + x + y = bY + 2 * bX)))
addBit b0 b0 b0 = (_ ** (_ ** (b0, b0, Refl)))
addBit b0 b0 b1 = (_ ** (_ ** (b0, b1, Refl)))
{- ... remaining cases follow the same pattern ... -}
```

The syntax (n ** t) denotes a *dependent pair*, where the type of the second argument t can refer to the first argument n. So, we can read this type as: "there exists a number bX, and a number bY, such that we have two bits Bit bX and Bit bY and the sum of the input bits c, x and y equals bY + 2 * bX." For example, on the second line, which corresponds to the computation $0_2 + 0_2 + 1_2 = (01)_2$, the function produces this bits b0 and b1, and a proof that $0 + 0 + 1 = 1 + (2 \times 0)$.

We then define the function adc that adds two binary numbers and a carry bit. This works for two binary numbers with the same number of bits, and produces a result with one more bit. We would like to write:

```
adc : Binary w x → Binary w y → Bit c → Binary (S w) (c + x + y)
adc zero zero carry = zero # carry
adc (numx # bX) (numy # bY) carry
  = let (vCarry0 ** (vLsb ** (carry0, lsb, _)))
            = addBit bX bY carry in
        adc numx numy carry0 # lsb
```

Unfortunately, this definition is rejected because the types do not match for both patterns. For the second case, the expected index is:
    ((c + (bit2 + (v1 + (v1 + 0)))) + (bit + (v + (v + 0))))
while we're trying to provide a term indexed over:
    vLsb + (((vCarry0 + v1) + v) + (((vCarry0 + v1) + v) + 0)).

The definition of adc we have given would behave correctly, and it has *provably* the expected type, but it does not have it *immediately* or *judgementally*: after full reductions the expected and provided types are still different. To make the previous definition acceptable, we need to solve two proof obligations adc_lemma_1 and adc_lemma_2 which demand proofs of equality between the two types. For example, using a proof script:

```
adc_lemma_2 = proof {
    intros;
```

```
    rewrite sym (plusZeroRightNeutral x);
    [...]
    rewrite (plusAssociative c (plus bit0 (plus v v)) bit1);
    rewrite plusCommutative bit1 (plus v v);
    [...]
    rewrite (plusAssociative (plus (plus x v) v1) (plus x v) v1);
    trivial;
}
```

Such proofs consist of a potentially long sequence of rewriting steps, each using one of the properties: neutral element, commutativity, associativity. Without some automation, this sequence of rewritings must be done by the programmer. Not only is this time consuming, but a small change in the definition may lead to a different proof obligation, thus invalidating the proof. A minor change in the datatype, or the definition of addBit or adc will require us to do a new proof, and thus, without support from the machine, these proofs could become the everyday routine in any dependently-typed language. It is worth mentioning that even without using dependent types, these proof obligations for equalities happen very frequently during the formal certification of most applications.

Our handwritten proof adc_lemma_2 uses only the existence of a neutral element, and the associativity and commutativity of + on Nat. Thus, we're rewriting a term by using the properties of a commutative monoid. With the right choice of combinators [4] such proofs could be made much simpler, but we would like a generic prover for commutative monoids to find a proof automatically.

1.2   Our Contributions

Provers for some algebraic structures have already been implemented for various proof assistants, including Coq [12] and Agda[1]. In this paper, we describe an implementation[2] of an automatic prover for equalities in a *hierarchy* of algebraic structures, including monoids, groups and rings (all potentially commutative), for the Idris language, making the following contributions:

1. We present a type-safe reflection mechanism (Sect. 2.3), where the reflected terms are indexed over the concrete terms, providing a direct way to extract proofs and guaranteeing that the reflected term is a sound representation.
2. The normalisation procedures are implemented by following a correct by construction approach (Sect. 2.4), instead of proving the correctness afterwards with auxiliary lemmas.
3. We develop a *hierarchy* of tactics where each tactic reuses the rewriting machinery of the structure from which it inherits. For example, simplifying neutral elements is implemented only at the monoid level, and reused at other levels. It is challenging to reuse the prover of a less expressive structure; for example, using the monoid prover to build the group prover is tricky because

---

[1] http://wiki.portal.chalmers.se/agda%5C?n=Libraries.UsingTheRingSolver.
[2] The implementation of our hierarchy of tactics can be found online at https://github.com/FranckS/RingIdris/Provers.

we lose the ability to express negations $(-x)$ and subtractions $(x - y)$. We present encodings (Sect. 2.6) to overcome this problem.

The principal novelty is in using *type-safe reflection*. Working by reflection for implementing tactics has been done several times, including the implementation of a ring solver for Coq, but without the type-safety and correctness-by-construction. We compare our approach with other implementations in Sect. 3.

2   A Hierarchy of Provers

We aim to build a prover not only for equalities on Nat, List, or any specific type, but for generic datatypes and properties. Using the right abstraction, we can generate proofs of equalities for many datatypes *at once* by implementing a generic hierarchy of provers for semi-groups, monoids, commutative-monoids, groups, commutative-groups, semi-rings and rings. The properties of an algebraic structure are expressed in an interface (an interface in Idris is similar to a type class in Haskell). This interface will extend the interface from which it inherits; for example, Group extends Monoid. This leads to a hierarchy of interfaces, with one tactic for each. At every level of the hierarchy, we will be able to work on any type, as long as there is a corresponding implementation of the interface.

2.1   Proving Equivalences Instead of Equalities

With some additional effort, we can produce a collection of tactics for proving *equivalences*, rather than only equalities. The machinery is very similar and we gain another degree of genericity, with the freedom of choosing the equivalence relation (which can be the usual equality). The user can define their own notion of equivalence, as long as they provide the proofs of the properties of the relevant algebraic structure. Let's call c the *carrier* type, i.e., the type on which we want to prove equivalences. The equivalence relation on c has the following profile $(\simeq) : c \to c \to Type$[3], and must be reflexive, symmetric and transitive.

Our tactics need to be able to test this equivalence between elements of the underlying set, that is a way of testing equivalence of constants. We therefore define a notion of Set[4], which requires the definition of the equivalence relation and an equivalence test set_eq. All the interfaces representing the algebraic structures will later extend Set:

```
interface Set c where
    (≃) : c → c → Type
    refl : (x : c) → x ≃ x
    sym : {x, y : c} → (x ≃ y) → (y ≃ x)
    trans : {x, y, z : c} → (x ≃ y) → (y ≃ z) → (x ≃ z)
    set_eq : (x : c) → (y : c) → Maybe (x ≃ y)
```

---

[3] This Type would be a Prop in systems, like Coq, that make a distinction between the world of computations and the world of logical statements.

[4] This notion of set is a way to talk about the carrier type and an equivalence relation, sometimes called Setoid.

To prove propositional equalities, the user instantiates ($\simeq$) with the built-in (=) when implementing Set. Note that ($\simeq$) is only weakly decidable in the sense that set_eq only produces a proof when the two elements are equivalent, but it doesn't produce a proof of dis-equivalence when they are different, instead producing the value Nothing. Our goal is only to generate proofs of equivalence, not to produce counter-examples. There is no tactic associated with Set, since we have no operations or properties associated to this structure. Equivalences in a Set are "syntactic equivalences" and can be proven with refl[5].

Working with equivalences instead of equalities brings one complication : the proofs of correctness that we produce by hand cannot use Idris' "rewrite" mechanism, which enables rewriting of a subterm by another one, provided that the two subterms are propositionally equal. This is a classical problem of working within a setoid, which can be mitigated by programming language support for rewriting terms in setoids. However, Idris is not equipped with any such support. For this reason, we define the following lemma, using the methods of the Set interface:

eq_preserves_eq : $\{c : \text{Type}\} \to \{\text{Set } c\} \to (x : c) \to (y : c) \to (c1 : c) \to (c2 : c) \to (x \simeq c1) \to (y \simeq c2) \to (c1 \simeq c2) \to (x \simeq y)$.

This lemma says that the equivalence preserves the equivalence, which means that in order to prove $x \simeq y$, we can prove a smaller problem $c1 \simeq c2$, provided that $x \simeq c1$ and that $y \simeq c2$. We will use this lemma extensively.

2.2   Hierarchy of Interfaces

We describe operations, constants and properties of each algebraic structure in an interface. The first algebraic theory is Magma, which is a structure built on top of Set that adds Plus operation, and no specific properties:

```
interface Set c => Magma c where
    + : c → c → c
```

This code means that a type c (for *carrier*) is a Magma if it is already a Set (i.e., it is equipped with the equivalence relation $\simeq$ and the equivalence test set_eq), and if it has a + operation. In fact, there is an additional requirement that will apply to all operations (in this case, the + operation), which is that they need to be "compatible" with the equivalence relation, which is expressed by the following axiom for +:

Plus_preserves_equiv : $\{c : \text{Type}\} \to \{\text{Magma } c\} \to \{c1 : c\} \to \{c2 : c\} \to \{c1' : c\} \to \{c2' : c\} \to (c1 \simeq c1') \to (c2 \simeq c2') \to ((c1 + c2) \simeq (c1' + c2'))$

We have this requirement because we support any equivalence relation. The user is free to define the equivalence relation of their choice, but it should be compatible with the operations that they are using. As with Set, there is no tactic for Magma, because there is no property; all equivalences are again syntactic equivalences, and can thus be proven by refl.

---

[5] refl is not to be confused with Refl, the constructor of =, but when ($\simeq$) is instantiated with the equality =, refl is implemented by Refl. Therefore, refl of the interface Set is a generalisation of Refl.

A semi-group is a magma (i.e., it still has a `Plus` operation), but moreover it has the property of associativity for this operation.

```
interface Magma c => SemiGroup c where
  Plus_assoc : (c1 : c) → (c2 : c) → (c3 : c) →
               ((c1 + c2) + c3 ≃ c1 + (c2 + c3))
```

Examples of magma are `Nat` equipped with addition, and `List` with concatenation. Next, a monoid is a semi-group with the property of neutral element for a distinguished element called `Zero`.

```
interface SemiGroup c => Monoid c where
  Zero : c
  Plus_neutral_1 : (c1 : c) → (Zero + c1 ≃ c1)
  Plus_neutral_2 : (c1 : c) → (c1 + Zero ≃ c1)
```

The hierarchy of interfaces continues with `Group`:

```
interface Monoid c => Group c where
  Minus : c → c → c
  Neg : c → c
  Minus_simpl : (c1 : c) → (c2 : c) → Minus c1 c2 ≃ c1 + (Neg c2)
  Plus_inverse : (c1 : c) → (c1 + (Neg c1) ≃ Zero,
                            (Neg c1) + c1 ≃ Zero)
```

The notion of group uses two new operations (`Neg` and `Minus`), but `Minus` can be simplified with $+$ and `Neg`. The important property of a group is that every element `c1` must admit `Neg c1` as inverse element for $+$. For reasons of space, we elide the remaining details of the hierarchy.

2.3 Type-Safe Reflection

When proving an equivalence $x \simeq y$, the universally-quantified variables are abstracted and they become part of the context. Our tactics normalise both sides of the "potential equivalence" $x \simeq y$, and compare the results by syntactic equivalence. The difficulty is that the normalisation function needs to consider variables, constants and operators. For this reason, we work by reflection, which allows us to work on syntax instead of values. We define one type of reflected terms for each algebraic structure. The novelty is not the use of reflected terms, but the use of a type-safe reflection mechanism where we index the reflected terms by the concrete value that they represent. Each of these datatype is parametrised over a type c, which is the type on which we want to prove equalities (the *carrier* type). It is also indexed over an implementation of the corresponding interface for c (we usually call it p, because it behaves as a *proof* telling that the structure c has the desired properties), indexed over a context of abstracted variables (a vector Γ of n elements of type c). Most importantly, it is indexed over a value of type c, which is the concrete value being encoded.

A magma is equipped with one operation, addition. Thus, to reflect terms in a magma we express constants, variables, and addition:

```
data ExprMa : Magma c → (Vect n c) → c → Type where
  ConstMa : (p : Magma c) → (Γ:Vect n c) → (c1:c) → ExprMa p Γ c1
  PlusMa : {p : Magma c} → {Γ:Vect n c} → {c1:c} → {c2:c}
          → ExprMa p Γ c1 → ExprMa p Γ c2 → ExprMa p Γ (c1+c2)
  VarMa : (p:Magma c) → (Γ:Vect n c)
          → (i:Fin n) → ExprMa p Γ (index i Γ)
```

For an expression e_x : ExprMa Γ x, we say that e_x denotes the value x in the context Γ. When an expression is a variable (VarMa _ Γ i), the denoted value is the corresponding variable in the context, i.e., (index i Γ). The expression (ConstMa _ Γ k) denotes the constant k in any context Γ. Finally, if e_x is an expression encoding the concrete value x, and e_y is an expression encoding the concrete value y, then the expression PlusMa e_x e_y denotes the concrete value $(x + y)$. Because the reflected terms embed their corresponding inputs, they are guaranteed to be sound representations. This is a *local* approach to syntax representation [11] in that the reflected representation will *only* represent terms in a magma.

There are no additional operations in semi-groups or monoids, so the reflected datatypes have the same shape as that for magma. However, the datatype for reflected terms in groups introduces two new constructors for Neg and Minus:

```
data ExprG : Group c → (Vect n c) → c → Type where
  ConstG : (p : Group c) → (Γ:Vect n c) → (c1:c) → ExprG p Γ c1
  PlusG : {p : Group c} → {Γ:Vect n c} → {c1:c} → {c2:c}
         → ExprG p Γ c1 → ExprG p Γ c2 → ExprG p Γ (c1+c2)
  MinusG : {p : Group c} → {Γ:Vect n c} → {c1:c} → {c2:c}
         → ExprG p Γ c1 → ExprG p Γ c2 → ExprG p Γ (Minus c1 c2)
  NegG : {p : Group c} → {Γ:Vect n c} → {c1:c}
        → ExprG p Γ c1 → ExprG p Γ (Neg c1)
  VarG : (p : Group c) → (Γ:Vect n c)
        → (i:Fin n) → ExprG p Γ (index i Γ)
```

The index of type c (the value encoded by an expression) is always expressed by using the lookup function index and the available operations in the implementation p, which for a group are +, Minus and Neg.

2.4   A Correct-by-Construction Approach

We take a *correct-by-construction* approach to implementing normalisation, which means that no additional proof will be required after defining normalisation. The normalisation function norm produces a new expression, and a proof that it has the same interpretation as the original. This will be enforced by the fact that all the datatypes for reflected terms (ExprMa, ExprG, ExprR, etc.) are indexed over the concrete value: a term of type Expr Γ x is the encoding of the concrete value x in the context Γ. For each structure, the type of norm has the following form:

norm : Expr Γ x → $(x'$ ** (Expr Γ x', $x \simeq x'$))

Every instance of **norm** produces a dependent pair: the new concrete value x', and a pair made of an **Expr** Γ x' which is the new encoded term indexed over the new concrete value we have just produced, and a proof that old and new concrete values x and x' are equivalent. This proof of $x \simeq y$ is the crucial component which allows us to automatically produce proofs of equivalences.

We will explain how to implement the tactic for **Group** specifically, and the other structures are implemented similarly. The equivalence we are trying to prove is $x \simeq y$, where x and y are elements of the type c, which implements a group. The reflected term for x is denoted e_x, and has type **ExprG** p Γ x, which means that e_x is guaranteed to be the encoding of x. Similarly, y, is encoded by e_y, and its type is indexed by the value y. Evaluating **norm** on e_x produces the normal form $e_{x'}$ of type **ExprG** p Γ x' and a proof p_x of $x \simeq x'$. Similarly, for e_y, it produces the normal form $e_{y'}$ of type **ExprG** p Γ y' and a proof p_y of $y \simeq y'$. It now suffices to compare the normal forms $e_{x'}$ and $e_{y'}$ using a syntactic equivalence test **ExprG_eq**, because once everything is in normal form, being equivalent is just a matter of being syntactically equivalent.

```
exprG_eq : {c:Type} → {n:Nat} → (p:Group c) → (Γ:Vect n c)
           → {x' : c} → {y' : c}
           → (ex' : ExprG p Γ x') → (ey' : ExprG p Γ y')
           → Maybe(x' ≃ y')
```

This syntactical equivalence test checks if the two input terms ex' and ey' are *syntactically* the same, and if they do, it directly builds a proof of equivalence between their indices $x' \simeq y'$, which is what we need, because we can use it with the two equivalences $x \simeq x'$ and $y \simeq y'$ that we already have, in order to get the desired proof of $x \simeq y$ with **eq_preserves_eq**. We put all of this together in a function **buildProofGroup**:

```
buildProofGroup:(p:Group c) → {Γ:Vect n c} → {x : c} → {y : c}
   → {x':c} → {y':c} → (ExprG p Γ x') → (ExprG p Γ y')
   → (x ≃ x') → (y ≃ y') → (Maybe (x ≃ y))
buildProofGroup p ex' ey' px py with (exprG_eq p ex' ey')
    buildProofGroup p ex' ey' px py | Just ex'_equiv_ey' =
              Just(eq_preserves_eq x y x' y' px py ex'_equiv_ey')
    buildProofGroup p ex' ey' px py | Nothing = Nothing
```

The arguments of type **ExprG** p Γ x' and **ExprG** p Γ y' are the normalised reflected left and right hand sides of the equivalence, which respectively represent the value x' and y'. This function also expects proofs of $x \simeq x'$ and of $y \simeq y'$, which are built by the normalisation process.

Finally, the main function which tries to prove the equivalence $x \simeq y$ has to normalise the two reflected terms encoding the left and the right hand side, and use the function **buildProof** to compose the two proofs:

```
groupDecideEq : (p:Group c) → {Γ:Vect n c} → {x : c} → {y : c}
           → (ExprG p Γ x) → (ExprG p Γ y) → Maybe (x ≃ y)
groupDecideEq p ex ey =
```

```
let (x' ** (ex', px)) = groupNormalise p ex in
let (y' ** (ey', py)) = groupNormalise p ey in
            buildProofGroup p ex' ey' px py
```

It remains to define the function `groupNormalise`, which is an instance of `norm` for groups:

```
groupNormalise:{c:Type} → {n:Nat} → (p:Group c) → {Γ:Vect n c}
      → {x:c} → (ExprG p Γ x) → (x' ** (ExprG p Γ x', x ≃ x'))
```

Each algebraic structure is equipped with a function for reducing reflected terms to their normal form. The algebraic theories which concern us admit a canonical representative[6] for any element, a property which we use to decide equalities. Without this property, it would be more complicated to decide equivalence without brute-forcing a series of rewritings, that would have no termination guarantee.

The normalisation function has more work to do for structures with many axioms (commutative-monoids, groups, commutative-groups, semi-rings and rings), than for the simpler structures (semi-groups and monoids). In the next section, we describe the normalisation process.

2.5   Normalisation Functions

We describe the normal form for rings, which is our most sophisticated structure. The input to the normalisation function is an expression with sums, products, constants and variables belonging to an ordered set V of variables. In short, the normalisation function takes in input a polynomial of multiple variables. As output, it produces a normal form representing the same polynomial. Therefore, we need a canonical representation of polynomials. There are several possibilities, but we choose classical mathematical conventions: the polynomial will be completely developed, i.e., the distributivity of $*$ over $+$ will be applied until it cannot be applied further. This is a simple but effective approach: the benefit of simplicity is that we can directly produce a proof of equivalence between the new and old concrete values during normalisation. Because the polynomial is completely developed, at the toplevel, it is a sum:

$$P = \sum_{i=1}^{a} (\prod_{j=1}^{b} Monomial_i^j) \text{ where } Monomial_i^j = C_i^j * \prod_{k=1}^{c} Var_{i,k}^j$$

with C_i^j a constant, and $Var_{i,k}^j$ one of the variable that belong to V.

It may be surprising that the normal form is a sum of product of monomials, and not directly a sum of monomials. This is because a monomial is a product of a constant C_i^j (e.g. 5) and of a product of variables (e.g. $x * y * z$). For example, $5 * (x * (y * z))$ is a monomial. Now let's consider the term $(5 * (x * (y * z))) * (4 * (z * z))$. This term is not a monomial, but we could be tempted to simplify it into

---

[6] It only holds for "pure" algebraic structures, i.e., in the absence of additional axioms.

the monomial $20 * (x * (y * (z * (z * z))))$. However, that would assume that the product is always commutative, which is not the case for *every* ring. Therefore, after development, the polynomial is a sum of *product of monomials*, and not directly a sum of monomials. The only rearrangement that can and needs to be done towards the multiplication is to check if two constants are consecutive in a product, and if so, to replace them by the constant that represents their product.

However, because $+$ is always commutative in a ring, the different products of monomials themselves can be rearranged in different ways in this sum. This will be done at the lower level for commutative groups if we can provide an ordering on products of monomials. This ordering will be defined by using an ordering on monomials, called `isBefore_mon`, which looks at the order of variables for comparing two monomials $Monomial_i^j$ and $Monomial_{i'}^{j'}$.

$$Monomial_i^j = C_i^j * (Var_{i,1}^j * \prod_{k=2}^{c} Var_{i,k}^j) \text{ and}$$

$$Monomial_{i'}^{j'} = C_{i'}^{j'} * (Var_{i',1}^{j'} * \prod_{k=2}^{c'} Var_{i',k}^{j'})$$

The order between these two monomials is decided by looking at the order between the variables $Var_{i,1}^j$ and $Var_{i',1}^{j'}$. If both monomials start with the same variable, we continue by inspecting the remaining variables. If one of the two monomials has fewer variables, that one comes first.

We can now build the order on *product of monomials*, named `isBefore`. Given two products of monomials $Prod_i$ and $Prod_{i'}$ we need to decide which one comes first. We will use the order `isBefore_mon` on the first monomials of these two products. If it says that $Monomial_i^1$ comes before $Monomial_{i'}^1$, then we decide that $Prod_i$ comes before $Prod_{i'}$. Conversely, if $Monomial_{i'}^1$ comes first, then $Prod_{i'}$ comes first. However, if $Monomial_i^1$ and $Monomial_{i'}^1$ have exactly the same position in the order, then we continue by inspecting the remaining monomials recursively. As previously, if one of the two products has fewer monomials than the other, then that one comes first.

Additionally, we use the following conventions when deciding on a normal form:

- The top-level sum of the polynomial is in right-associative form:
  $prodMon_1 + (prodMon_2 + (prodMon_3 + (... + prodMon_a)))$
- All the products that we have (the products of monomials and the products of variables), are written in right-associative form.
- We simplify as much as possible with constants. This includes simplifying addition with zero and multiplication with the constants zero and one, doing the computations between two nearby constants, etc...
- We simplify the sum of an expression e and its inverse $-e$ to zero.

2.6   Reusing the Provers

A novelty of our work is that instead of building a prover for a specific algebraic structure, we have built a hierarchy of provers. Each prover reuses components of the others so that the simplifications are not duplicated at different levels: normalisation of each structure uses as much as possible the normalisation function of the structure from which it inherits. For example, normalisation on monoids reuses normalisation on semi-groups so that it does not have to deal with associativity. In this case, the datatype reflecting terms in semi-groups has the same expressive power as that for monoids, so a term in a monoid can be transformed directly into a corresponding term of a semi-group. However, there is a difficulty with groups and monoids: if normalisation for groups uses the normalisation for monoids, we will have to encode negations somehow, which can't be directly expressed in a monoid. Therefore, we develop some specific encodings.

The idea is that we encode negations as variables, and let the monoid prover consider them as ordinary variables. To achieve this, we use the following datatype that helps us distinguish between a variable and the encoding of a negation:

```
data Variable:{c:Type} → {n:Nat} → (Vect n c) → c → Type where
  RealVariable : (Γ:Vect n c) →
                 (i:Fin n) → Variable Γ (index i Γ)
  EncodingNeg : (Γ:Vect n c) →
                 (i:Fin n) → Variable Γ (Neg (index i Γ))
```

We only need to encode negations of variables, as we can simplify the negation of a constant into a constant. Also, there cannot be a negation of something different non-atomic (i.e. a term that is not a variable or a constant), because normalisation of groups has systematically propagated Neg inside the parentheses, following simplification[7] $-(a + b) = -b + -a$.

All the constructors for variables now take a Variable as parameter, instead of taking directly an element of (Fin n). That gives the following, for groups:

```
    VarG : (p:Group c) → {Γ:Vect n c} → {val:c}
         → (Variable Γ val) → ExprG p Γ val
```

Thanks to this encoding, we can now transform an ExprG from the group level to an ExprMo at the monoid level. A constant (ConstG p Γ c1) is transformed into the corresponding constant (ConstMo _ Γ c1), a PlusG into the corresponding PlusMo, a variable into the same variable, the negation of a constant into the resulting constant, and finally the negation of a variable i into a (VarMo _ (EncodingNeg Γ i)).

We use a similar technique for converting an expression from the ring level to the commutative-group level, where we encode the product of monomials, because the product is not defined at the commutative-group level. That enables

---

[7] Note that we have to be careful and not simplify it to $(-a)+(-b)$ as it would assume that $+$ is commutative.

the function of normalisation for rings to benefit from the normalisation function for commutative-groups.

2.7   Automatic Reflection

We have built an automatic reflection mechanism which enables the machine to build reflected terms. This is not essential to our approach, but it simplifies the usage of the tactics by removing the need to write long encodings by hand. To do so, we used Idris' reflection mechanism, which enables pattern matching on syntax, rather than on constructors. While we omit the full details due to space constraints, reflecting values involves defining functions of the following form:

```
%reflection reflectGroup : (p : Group c) → (Γ : Vect n c) →
                           (x : c) → (Γ' ** ExprG p (Γ ++ Γ') x)
```

The %reflection annotation means that Idris treats this as a compile time function on *syntax*. Given a value of type c, in some context Γ, it constructs a reflected expression in an extended context Γ ++ Γ'. The context contains references to subexpressions which are not themselves representable by ExprG.

3   Related Work

Coq's ring solver [12], like ours, is implemented using proof-by-reflection techniques, but without the guarantees obtained with our type-safe reflection mechanism, and without the correct-by-construction approach: first, they define the normalisation of terms, then they prove correctness of the normalisation with an external lemma: $\forall$ (e1 e2 : Expr), beq_{Expr} (norm e1) (norm e2) = $true$ → reify e1 $\simeq$ reify e2. This needs a reify function, which we do not need. Furthermore, Coq's prover deals with rings and semi-rings (commutative or not), but not with any of the intermediate structures (semi-group, monoid, group, etc.). However, their implementation has better performances due to the use of sparse normal form and more optimised algorithms. Our automatic reflection was written with Idris reflection mechanism which allows pattern matching on syntax, and their automatic reflection is programmed in Ltac [7], a proof dedicated and untyped meta-language for the writing of automations. More recently, the Mtac extension [18] provides a typed language for implementing proof automation.

As well as the ring solver, Coq also provides the Omega solver [6], which solves a goal in Presburger arithmetic (i.e. a universally quantified formula made of equations and inequations), and a field [9] decision procedure for real numbers, which plugs to Coq's ring prover after simplification of the multiplicative inverses. Agda's reflection mechanism[8] gives access to a representation of the current goal (that is, the required type) at a particular point in a program. This allows various proof automations to be done in Agda [14,15].

---

[8] http://wiki.portal.chalmers.se/agda/pmwiki.php?n=ReferenceManual.Reflection.

Proofs by reflection has been intensively studied [5,16], but without anything similar to the type-safe reflection that we have presented here. If we leave the ground of nice mathematical structures, one can decide to work with arbitrary rewriting rules, but in the general case there isn't a complete decision procedure for such systems, because there is usually no normal form. This is where deduction modulo [8,10] and proof search heuristics start.

4 Results, Conclusions and Future Work

We have implemented a generic solution to the initial problem of index mismatch (Sect. 1.1) when using indexed types. This solution takes the form of a hierarchy of provers for equivalences in algebraic structures. These provers are generic in several ways: they work for many algebraic structures (semi-group, monoid, commutative monoid, group, commutative group, ring and semi-ring); for any type that behaves as one of these structures; and, for any equivalence relation on this type. The implementation is modular and each prover reuses the prover of the structure from which it inherits. These provers can automatically prove equivalences between terms, so the user need not prove obligations by hand, like adc_lemma_2. Thus, these provers enable the user to focus on the interesting proofs that requires specific knowledge and creativity, instead of routine, automatable, lemmas.

Our correct-by-construction method involved the design of a type-safe reflection mechanism where reflected terms are indexed over concrete inputs, and from which we are able to extract proofs directly. Unlike Coq's and Agda's ring provers, we do not have the duplication that arise when separating the computational content from the proof of correctness. Instead, construction of the proof is done step by step, following the construction of the normalised terms. In addition to avoiding redundancy, this simplifies the proof generation considerably. This development shows that if dependent types effectively bring some new problems, they are also very expressive tools for building correct-by-construction software where the development is *driven by the types*.

This work can be extended to build new provers for less common algebraic structures and for more specific structures. For example, regular expressions form a "pre semi-ring" with some extra axioms. We will refactor the semi-ring level with the creation of the intermediate structure of pre semi-ring, that will not necessary have the property that 0 is an annihilator element for the product. Then, we could build a specific prover for regular expressions, that would use the normalisation function of the pre semi-ring level and that would only have to deal with the specific properties of regular expressions: the neutral element $\varnothing$ for the concatenation of languages is also a neutral element for the product of languages, the idempotence of the addition of languages, and the rules of simplifications for the new Kleene star operation.

Acknowledgements. We thank the anonymous reviewers and Jacques Carette for their insightful comments on an earlier draft. We are also grateful for the support of the Scottish Informatics and Computer Science Alliance (SICSA) and EPSRC grant EP/N024222/1.

References

1. Bertot, Y., Castéran, P.: Interactive Theorem Proving and Program Development - Coq'Art: The Calculus of Inductive Constructions. Texts in Theoretical Computer Science. An EATCS Series. Springer, Heidelberg (2004)
2. Brady, E.: Constructing correct circuits: verification of functional aspects of hardware specifications with dependent types. In: Trends in Functional Programming (TFP 2007) (2007)
3. Brady, E.: Idris, a general-purpose dependently typed programming language: design and implementation. J. Funct. Program. **23**, 552–593 (2013)
4. Carette, J., O'Connor, R.: Theory presentation combinators. In: Jeuring, J., Campbell, J.A., Carette, J., Reis, G., Sojka, P., Wenzel, M., Sorge, V. (eds.) CICM 2012. LNCS, vol. 7362, pp. 202–215. Springer, Heidelberg (2012). doi:10.1007/978-3-642-31374-5_14
5. Chlipala, A.: Certified Programming with Dependent Types - A Pragmatic Introduction to the Coq Proof Assistant. MIT Press, Cambridge (2013)
6. Crégut, P.: Une procédure de décision reflexive pour un fragment de l'arithmétique de Presburger. In: Journées Francophones des Langages Applicatifs (2004)
7. Delahaye, D.: A proof dedicated meta-language. Electr. Notes Theor. Comput. Sci. **70**(2), 96–109 (2002)
8. Delahaye, D., Doligez, D., Gilbert, F., Halmagrand, P., Hermant, O.: Zenon Modulo: when achilles outruns the tortoise using deduction modulo. In: McMillan, K., Middeldorp, A., Voronkov, A. (eds.) LPAR 2013. LNCS, vol. 8312, pp. 274–290. Springer, Heidelberg (2013). doi:10.1007/978-3-642-45221-5_20
9. Delahaye, D., Mayero, M.: Field, une procédure de décision pour les nombres réels en Coq. In: Castéran, P. (ed.) Journées francophones des langages applicatifs (JFLA'01), pp. 33–48. Collection Didactique, INRIA (2001)
10. Dowek, G., Hardin, T., Kirchner, C.: Theorem proving modulo. J. Autom. Reasoning **31**(1), 33–72 (2003). http://dx.doi.org/10.1023/A:1027357912519
11. Farmer, W.M.: The formalization of syntax-based mathematical algorithms using quotation and evaluation. In: Carette, J., Aspinall, D., Lange, C., Sojka, P., Windsteiger, W. (eds.) CICM 2013. LNCS, vol. 7961, pp. 35–50. Springer, Heidelberg (2013). doi:10.1007/978-3-642-39320-4_3
12. Gregoire, B., Mahboubi, A.: Proving equalities in a commutative ring done right in Coq. In: Theorem Proving in Higher Order Logics (TPHOLS 2005), pp. 98–113 (2005)
13. Howard, W.: The formulae-as-types notion of construction. In: Seldin, J., Hindley, J. (eds.) To H.B. Curry: Essays on Combinatory Logic, Lambda Calculus, and Formalism. Academic Press, London (1980)
14. Kokke, P., Swierstra, W.: Auto in Agda – programming proof search using reflection. In: 12th International Conference on Mathematics of Program Construction, MPC 2015, pp. 276–301 (2015)
15. Lindblad, F., Benke, M.: A tool for automated theorem proving in Agda. In: Filliâtre, J.-C., Paulin-Mohring, C., Werner, B. (eds.) TYPES 2004. LNCS, vol. 3839, pp. 154–169. Springer, Heidelberg (2006). doi:10.1007/11617990_10

16. Malecha, G., Chlipala, A., Braibant, T.: Compositional computational reflection. In: 5th International Conference on Interactive Theorem Proving, ITP 2014, pp. 374–389 (2014)
17. Norell, U.: Towards a practical programming language based on dependent type theory. Ph.D. thesis, Chalmers University of Technology (2007)
18. Ziliani, B., Dreyer, D., Krishnaswami, N.R., Nanevski, A., Vafeiadis, V.: Mtac: a monad for typed tactic programming in Coq. In: ACM SIGPLAN International Conference on Functional Programming, ICFP 2013, pp. 87–100 (2013)

The Global Digital Mathematics Library and the International Mathematical Knowledge Trust

Patrick D.F. Ion[1(✉)] and Stephen M. Watt[2]

[1] AMS, University of Michigan, Ann Arbor, MI, USA
pion@umich.edu
[2] Faculty of Mathematics, University of Waterloo, Waterloo, ON, Canada
smwatt@uwaterloo.ca

Abstract. We recall some of the reasons why we want and do not yet have a Global Digital Mathematics Library (GDML), both before and after the setting up of a GDML WG at the Seoul 2014 ICM. The recent founding of an International Mathematical Knowledge Trust (IMKT) in Waterloo ON, Canada is an important move in the right direction. The IMKT's form and initial efforts will be described, with attention to why the project is the way it is.

1 Introduction and History

It's been suggested that vignettes from history help to emphasize the way that members of the mathematics community have long wished better access to more of the world's mathematics. We have before mentioned G. Peano [Peano:1894], E. Schröder [Schröder:1897] and pasigraphy, then Georg Valentin's comprehensive bibliography [Ion:2016].

A World Library has long been a dream. Here let us remind ourselves of the long story of the Great Library of Alexandria in the Mouseion founded ca. 323 BCE by Ptolemy, a lieutenant of Alexander the Great, after the conquest of Egypt in 332 BCE; but it was gone during the Roman era in Egypt.[1] Perhaps it burned in 48 BCE during Julius Caesar's siege of the city of Alexandria; perhaps it remained around, but reduced, until some time after 391 CE, when the Christian Emperor Theodosius issued a decree that officially outlawed pagan practices. The details of the history are naturally complex, but it seems clear that the Biblioteca Alexandrina once housed as many as three quarters of a million books and scrolls, and was associated with some of the ancient world's most influential mathematicians. Archimedes (287-212 BCE) spent much time at the Mouseion. Eratosthenes (276-195 BCE) created the eponymous sieve for finding prime numbers; he also deduced the earth was spherical and measured its circumference to within about one per

---

[1] Most of the ancient dates are to be taken as approximate at best, and much of the material can be found at [Mouseion].

H. Geuvers et al. (Eds.): CICM 2017, LNAI 10383, pp. 56–69, 2017.
DOI: 10.1007/978-3-319-62075-6_5

cent of the present measurement[2]. Apollonius (262-190 BCE) studied conic sections. Aristarchus of Samos (310-230 BCE) proved heliocentricity (i.e. not geocentricity) which influenced Copernicus. Hero (ca. 10 CE-70 CE) is known for Heron's formula for the triangle's area as well as for his amazing mechanical inventions. Hypatia, the daughter of Theon, the last director of the Mouseion and a brilliant mathematician was lynched by a rabble in 415 CE. There is now a new Bibliotheca Alexandrina [Bibliotheca Alexandrina][3]. One can only hope it lasts as long and makes such distinguished contributions to mathematics, science and culture as the ancient one did.

An important point here is that it seems in the internet culture remarkably easy to follow some trains of thought concerning history, but that corresponding meanderings for mathematics are not as easy by any means, although, often enough, much more available than they were half a century ago. We'd like that changed. Furthermore, the reported results of mathematics that one collects from elsewhere, such as the internet library, need to be well formulated and correct in a clear system. The little story above nowhere near meets those standards.

A World Digital Library has long been a dream and dates back at least to Vannevar Bush's [Bush, Vannevar:bio] imagined Memex from 1945 [Bush:1945]. We have recently sketched the history from then to roughly the present in more than one place: [Ion:2016, Watt:2016]. For the current purpose let us note the resolution of the International Mathematical Union (IMU) [IMU:2006]. A little later we have held, with the support of the Alfred P. Sloan Foundation [Sloan], a 2012 symposium on *The Future World Heritage Digital Mathematics Library* [NAS:2012] and the thorough National Research Council report in 2014 by Ingrid Daubechies et al. [NRC/USA:2014]. More recent personal views include those of J. Pitman and C. Lynch [Pitman & Lynch:2014] and Thierry Bouche [Bouche:2008, Bouche:2014].

There has been a change in our society and in the activity of the mathematical profession as a result of the widespread introduction of computing machinery. Modern mathematicians do communicate differently in our digital age. Until very recently the dominant technology for persistent communications has been printing. The businesses built up to provide printing and distribution services have controlled, with the collaboration of the leadership of the profession, the production of the literature we depend on. Being published in print was the ultimate goal for many a scientist, and, of course, without distribution there is no contribution to knowledge.

Thus the way to accumulate knowledge publicly, as opposed to within the understanding of an individual or team of individuals, was to aggregate

---

[2] At least as remarked in a lecture by Cédric Villani [Villani:2014] or by Carl Sagan [Sagan:2015]. Of course, the scholarship required to justify this fully would be considerable and we cannot provide a reference for it presently. He is alleged to have arrived at a circumference of 40,000 km versus NASA's current value of 40,030. These items illustrate the variety of sources a GDML needs to take into account, as well as how easy it may be for some to get interesting material.

[3] A scholarly work on these matters is *Life And Fate Of The Ancient Library Of Alexandria* by Mostafa El-Abbadi, who was a moving force behind the new Library and died in 2017 [El-Abbadi:1986, El-Abbadi:2017].

collections of printed artifacts in libraries. Ideally scholars would visit such libraries, or local libraries would be held near places at which they worked. Cataloging and access tools, such as printed bibliographies, were then developed. We see the digital avatars of this printed material in PDFs and other electronic document forms, and online catalogs now with linking through the World Wide Web. So there is a whole system now again dominated by commercial publishing that looks rather like a virtual image, with some enhancements, of the traditional publication and distribution of science from the last century or so. The copyright laws, and the odd notions going by the phrase 'intellectual property', arose in connection with such a business environment.

Of course, there's material that has been in print or penned manuscript that is in library collections and elsewhere that it will be a shame to lose. That should be digitized, collected and curated. For mathematics, whose results once proven are supposed to persist as truths (recognizing as we do nowadays that the underlying inference systems have to be preserved as well) this would seem obvious. Although the progress of mathematics is not entirely a matter of influential figures, even if we tend to name results after people, a recent example of interest, in direct connection with representation of mathematical knowledge, is that of notebook of Alan Turing's, which has recently come to light, with his *"Notes on Notation"* [Turing:1942]. Though mathematics as a subject is dependent on access to its literature, older documents are perhaps less valuable than is sometimes the case for other subjects. A recent *cri de coeur* for attention to the preservation of earlier material is nonetheless something that we need to pay attention to [Griffin:2017].

What seem to be changing us is the newer forms of scientific communication over electronic networks and the capability of individual authors to create documents of high technical sophistication themselves. For instance, mathematical authors not only do create, say using TeX, their documents involving the penalty copy of formulas that it used to cost so much extra in typesetting, they are asked by commercial publishers to do so as a cost-saving measure. This has advantages for the authors as well in providing a direct responsibility for the correctness of what is circulated.

But it does also mean that the nature of publication is changed. Many services that used to be provided by publishers are again the author's responsibilities. The culmination today of that change is the World Wide Web and the opportunities it offers for circulation of knowledge in forms different from print representations. Furthermore, now that much of the literature, especially the new part, is in digital form computers can be used to facilitate access, and also by treating the literature as data to analyze what we have in new ways. It's not just that modern technology can realize much of the dream of Paul Otlet's Mundaneum [Rayward:1975,Spiegel:2011] which was begun using large card catalogues.

The forms of document are changing since they are not limited by printing requirements. Color and visual complexity are comparatively easy to achieve, as are moving images and documents responsive to reader input which can be especially useful in education. The literature analysis aspect mentioned above has brought to the fore the developing notion of Mathematical Knowledge Management. In fact, that is likely ultimately to be the big change in a Global Digital Mathematical Library. A GDML is not be just a digital form of a collection of documents and manuscripts, it has to become a managed collection of mathematical knowledge, the nature of which is itself changing as the notions of proof and mathematical semantics evolve. That is how the International Mathematical Knowledge Trust got its name.

2   GDML Activity to Mar 2017

Ingrid Daubechies ended her term as President of the International Mathematical Union at the 2014 International Congress of Mathematicians in Seoul. There she convened a working group to consider the actions necessary to move the prospects for a Global Digital Mathematics Library (GDML[4]) forward. This followed a panel session at the ICM [Seoul DML Panel]. The IMU Working Group resolved to create a not-for-profit organization, the International Mathematical Knowledge Trust (IMKT).

2.1   The Working Group

The GDML WG has worked hard and did not, like some earlier efforts in this area, give up when little happened fast. For instance, it conducted about 100 telcon meetings[5]. These were occasions for strategizing the approach to grant proposal writing and discussions of details of many possible suggestions. They ranged from forms of governance to technical aspects of projects leading to a digital library. The telcons all have minutes held on the WG's private wiki (powered by Wikipedia's MediaWiki).

The GDML wiki, employing MediaWiki software, also hosts various drafts documents connected with the WG's discussions and has about 200 pages. This figure is only mentioned as an indication of the WG's activity level. The drafts are often enough early attempts that were later superseded but helped a lot in analyzing situations, or explanatory pieces about WG member positions, suggestions or ideas. As such they are not finished documents, which means the wiki has been kept private. However, it has been used to make the work of the WG more persistent, along with DropBox files and even GitHub.

2.2   MediaWiki Dangers

An example of the complications that occur when you decide to use modern technologies like wikis to enhance your communications can be given in the

---

[4] This is not the Geometry Description Markup Language invented to enable description of events at the CERN Large Hadron Collider. However, that GDML certainly has a relationship with the capture of mathematical meaning, as does SVG for two-dimensional geometry.

[5] A telephone bridge has been kindly provided by Wolfram Research.

essentially toy context of the GDML WG involving about a dozen persons. When you think of trying to put together a GDML for the whole world then there are many more scenarios of difficulty you need to try to prepare for and mitigate. As the complexity goes up so do the resources required to deal with them. That is in part how simple services do in fact often cost a lot of money.

One of the dangers that results from use of MediaWiki for a support system for a small group is that MediaWiki installations can be the target of spammers. They use them to generate click traffic that produces revenue through, say, Google Ads. The GDML WG wiki is carefully restricted in its access. Only explicitly registered users can actually edit pages, only explicitly registered users can read anything except the splash page, and only special administrator users can create new users. This is naturally hardly what you want for a publicly useful wiki, where at least the general web user should be able to read the pages or otherwise it isn't public information. An example of a world-read but very restricted other access is the one used in revising the Mathematics Subject Classification to MSC2010 [MSC2010:MediaWiki]. The only persons to edit pages were editorial staff at Mathematical Reviews and Zentralblatt, but all could see the changes to the MSC as they were being proposed. The control of access to a MediaWiki installation is configured in a PHP file usually in a standard location within a site. An upgrade to the version of MediaWiki, which was done by the site's ISP, did not preserve the cascade of rules that controlled access carefully.

The result was that for a couple of days the site behaved like a typical public wiki allowing new users to create new identities and write pages. This is after all the sort of behavior that a public wiki trying to organize a community should exhibit. Spammers know this and write scripts that create users, and provide a couple of junk pages for each user with almost plausible text on them, including links within the pages to sites for whom they are providing SEO (Search Engine Optimization) services. If the wiki is constantly being patrolled by its community, or by attentive administrators with clever bots, then unusual activity can be detected and reacted to by blocking and denying users and domains that seem nefarious.

As it was, in the case of MSC2010, in the course of about 4 days about 10,000 spurious users were created with about 20,000 associated pages. These users and pages did not interact with, or otherwise damage the usual business of MSC2010. However, the traffic caused by the linking activity for SEO purposes did make it look as though there was a great deal of new interest in MSC. Eventually, the activity generated caused the traffic limit for the site to be exceeded and the ISP's servers stopped answering queries. This was noted by the administrators of the online Encyclopedia of Mathematics who asked msc2010.org about the fact that the links they provided to background information on MSC codes were now often not working correctly. This led to the discovery of the malfeasance mentioned and to the not inconsiderable work needed to clean up the spammers work after reinstituting the intended access control.

It seems that this weakness in the access control mechanisms of wikis is a known problem, and the tools for combating the problem are only now being developed. There's an obvious sense in which open public goods are at risk of being co-opted or misused. A fortiori, developing a GDML is going to turn up other such difficulties. One area that the profession may need to be taking a lot more seriously in the digital world is likely to be the matter of authentication, authority and provenance trails.

2.3 Organized Outreach

The GDML WG also mounted outreach activities to encourage the mathematical community to support the idea of a GDML and to contribute initiatives. A successful one on *Mathematical Information in the Digital Age of Science* was held at the JMM 2016 [JMM:2016]. A list of some goals that seemed to people there to be sensible [Watt:2016] does also serve to illustrate the range of topics that naturally play into trying to produce a GDML. There are, of course, more as well:

1. Determining whether a result is known, where the answer is hoped to be positive so the result can be used. Here, proofs, examples, counter-examples, applications, and so on would be desired.
2. Determining whether a result is known, where the answer is hoped to be negative thus confirming a discovery or avoiding unintentional duplication.
3. Accelerating the advancement of mathematics, both for itself and for science and technology.
4. Organizing knowledge to accelerate the learning of mathematics.
5. Enhancing collaboration.
6. Making existing tools more powerful.

More ambitious goals included:

1. Certifying (machine validation) of all mathematical knowledge.
2. Serving as a mathematical assistant, or as a teacher.
3. Identifying holes in our mathematical knowledge.
4. Generating conjectures.
5. Reflection—refactoring or reformulating mathematics for elegance or ease of application.
6. Expanding the mathematical capacity of humanity.

In addition, with Wolfram Research and the Fields Institute, the GDML WG was an organizer of a Semantic Capture Language Workshop (SCLW) held at the Fields Institute February 2016 [Fields:2016]. A White Paper promised as a result from the workshop was finally produced and videos of almost all the lectures there are also available on the Fields site. There is also there a long documentary [Fields:docu] of the workshop with many interviews of participants. The consensus about the desirable ultimate goals of a GDML resulting from the workshop can be seen as even more ambitious:

1. The library should contain the full mathematical literature (peer-reviewed research mathematics), including all published versions of each work. It has been estimated that more than 200,000 theorems are proved each year, which is a very large amount of mathematics, though small in relation to other corpuses treated today, such as medical records.
2. The library should be able to cope with all major systems for computer mathematics, not only symbolic computation systems and theorem provers, but also systems like LaTeX and MathML processors needed to process the documents.
3. All formulas (terms, statements) in the mathematics should be usable in various computer systems for doing mathematics.
4. All algorithms in the mathematics should be available in an executable form.
5. All structures in the mathematics should be made explicit. For example, links between articles, references within the articles, and the substructure of proofs (like scopes of variables and assumptions) are all to be explicit.
6. All mathematics should be available in a fully verified form, with verification to the highest possible standards.
7. The relation between the human- and machine-readable forms (including the fully verified form) of the mathematics should be clear and explicit.
8. The library should be fully accessible to the whole world, making the intellectual property rights of everything fully explicit and aiming for maximal availability.

3   IMKT, Its Draft Charter and Founding

In May 2016, the IMU's CEIC (Committee on Electronic Information and Communication) endorsed a Charter for an IMKT suggested by the WG. This has to be understood as a "guiding document" not a legally binding one. It is naturally important grist to the mill of the lawyers who will oversee the founding.

After many tentative approaches at different levels, founding IMKT was finally formally proposed to the Alfred P. Sloan Foundation as a project to support. It was funded in mid-December 2016. Letters of support that were added to the proposal in the final stage from a wide range of organizations show that part of the community has begun to get our message: software (NAG, MapleSoft), bibliography (EuDML, zbMATH), institutes (Fields, Waterloo).

The work of the GDML WG was mentioned twice in the international organ of the IMU: [IMU-Net 77:May 2016], Sloan funding [IMU-Net 81:January 2017].

3.1   An Initial Corpus for GDML

In addition, IMKT has to concern itself with starting to aggregate access to the corpus of known mathematics and the new mathematics that is being developed. The CEIC, and thus its GDML WG, have had contact with the important [arXiv.org] project, based at the Cornell Library. There is also a Chinese project with some similarity to arXiv, namely [MathSciDoc] based on Tsinghua University and a community of Chinese mathematicians [ICCM]. Mathematics is a large category (21.9%) within arXiv, and fast growing (26.4% present submissions). Most arXiv subjects are "mathematics heavy" in any case.

The other natural groups with whom to seek cooperation are the European digital math library project [EuDML, Project Euclid]. Finally [HathiTrust] is another potential partner, but after initial favorable contacts (in Michigan) this has yet to be pursued further.

A final, and clearly current, strain of research in handling the scientific literature is machine learning. For mathematics this is already the matter of a large grant from Sloan to D. Blei and C. Lafferty [Lafferty & Blei: 2016] and we can look forward to the results. Another group with whom the GDML is in contact is also preparing a grant submission in this area. The IMKT will naturally welcome any good results coming out of this research, but will concentrate its own efforts elsewhere since these are developments that are underway and can expect results only in the longer term.

3.2 IMKT Initiatives

Sloan also expects that an incipient IMKT be promoting initiatives that are clearly activities building toward parts of an eventual GDML. Therefore the IMKT proposal foresaw four specific projects that progress would be made on.

Special Function Concordance: This initiative was announced to the OPSFA community in January 2017 [OP SF NET: 2017]. A first meeting involving stakeholders in the field, representing NIST's DLMF [DLMF] and DRMF [DRMF], INRIA's DDMF [DDMF], Maplesoft [Maple], Mathematica [Mathematica] and NAG [NAG], as well as other academics, was held even before the good news of funding from Sloan. The effort to broaden and mobilize the community working on this continues. It can be seen as an initial attempt to clarify the semantics of an area of mathematical research commonly considered well understood and of technological importance. This may be a baby step toward developing a semantic capture language as mentioned in the title of the Fields Institute workshop, but it promises to be something that can be useful to practical users of mathematics anyway.

FAbstracts: FAbstracts stands for Formal Abstracts and is a project envisaged by Tom Hales. The idea is to work out how to start by capturing more of the semantics of mathematical papers in a formal way and to use the organizational capacities offered by computers for this, without proceeding to try and provide full computer-checked formal proofs. Full machine-supported formal proofs, as carried out by Hales and an international team of collaborators for the Kepler Conjecture, or by Georges Gonthier and collaborators for the Feit-Thompson Theorem, are big projects. They require much work and lead to changes in proof argument structures that need to be developed.

FAbstracts will work with theorem statements and summary assertions about the mathematical content of an article. These assertions may even turn out to be wrong, but the important goal is the capture of a formal record of the key results of an item of the literature. This formal abstract can then be handled by programs looking for similarities and overlaps or possible implications between results. Once possible relationships are identified, for instance, then there may be an incentive to expand the level of formalization of a given item.

An essential part of FAbstracts is the intention to work out how to share and compare results in formalizing material. Typically, different teams may use different logical software bases, as in the cases of HOL Light and Coq for the two big achievements just mentioned. Though there have been comparisons and cross-walk efforts between systems before, there's a lot more experience to be gained by trying examples.

Harmonisation in the Formal Area: The proponents of several formal systems, meeting as they did at the Fields SCLW, expressed their willingness in principle to try and figure out the similarities and differences in their formalizations of some basic theorems in, say, Coq, HOL Light and Mizar, or even HoTT. Promoting this activity will be pursued.

Bibliographic ngram Work: This sort of simple statistical exploration of the mathematical literature is made more difficult than for ordinary text by the presence of the formulas of our subject. It does offer some easier opportunities for involvement of researchers since NLP has been widely developed, just not for mathematical texts. Furthermore it may be important enough to interest the important secondary sources in mathematics such as Mathematical Reviews [MathSciNet,zbMATH], who have already shown interest.

3.3 IMKT Governance Development

Ultimately the long-term goal of the GDML WG and of the new trust being set up is as follows:

> The purpose of the International Mathematical Knowledge Trust, IMKT, is to establish a mathematical knowledge commons — a public resource consisting of mathematical knowledge represented in non-proprietary, machine-readable formats and an international network of knowledge providers, information systems, and semantic services based on it, that is, a global digital mathematical library.

In practice, we have to begin by setting up a legal entity. It was, perhaps fortuitously for international connections, decided to set up in Waterloo ON, Canada, where PI Stephen Watt is Dean of the Faculty of Mathematics and Computer Science with over 8,000 students [Waterloo Math]. Canadian Federal Law was chosen as the legal home, and Canadian charitable status will be sought. Under the present law it is not mandatory, but it is recommended that IMKT have about 25% Canadian residents on the governing Board. There will also be a Scientific Advisory Board (SAB). It is the "Members" of a Trust who elect the Board of Directors, and the important questions are who they are, and how they are created. There must be voting Members, and one can have non-voting ones too. The Directors on the governing Board lay out the criteria for membership, and a renewal procedure is recommended. We shall choose to have voting Members be the Board, SAB, and others invited. Non-voting Members can be other individuals, and possibly societies.

A retained lawyer started drafting by-laws in March 2017. With those finalized we shall found the trust with a skeleton crew for the Directors on the Board of Governors (BG) and Trust Members (the grant PIs and a couple of others) and get charitable status.

At a phone meeting, the initial Board of Governors will decide on invitations for new Members and Directors. They will begin to appoint additional GB and SAB members as they agree to serve. One consideration that will be built into the by-laws is whatever is necessary to have relationships with subsidiaries or associated organizations elsewhere that allow donations and payments with favorable tax statuses. There are constraints to be met in setting up boards for a non-profit with an avowed intention of doing public good internationally. The board members need to be experienced but have also to be representative of the community to be served. In this case, they clearly must be from international backgrounds with ties over the world, to be diverse in points of view and to show no gender bias. These things are a matter of common sense but were also explicitly mentioned by our funders, and are not trivial to satisfy simultaneously in as small a population sample as the boards represent.

In addition, certain expertise, such as with non-profit legal and accounting issues, and management of projects such as those IMKT is intended to pursue, ought to be represented. One ends up making lists of persons known and annotating them with characteristics such as feeling for the science, feeling for the technologies that will be involved, experience in management or governance, nationality or locations of employment, or perceived relationships with possible patronage. The judgements such annotations are based upon are necessarily personal ones (though each person will be able to offer justifications for them) and made on the basis of limited information. Such lists are hardly the basis for an algorithm or in any way suitable for publication. Indeed, the persons you may obviously find desirable for your boards may well be unable or unwilling to serve for reasons you cannot know.

The current aim is for a "legally valid" Board to be in place by end of April 2017. Then we should have a credible Scientific Board, but with vacancies, by the end of June 2017. There will eventually be ca. 6–9 persons on the Board of Governors, with 2 or 3 Canadian residents. The Board of Governors must also appoint other Members who will make up the Scientific Advisory Board to a full complement of 12–15 depending on the acceptances of invitations to serve. Further election of Members and appointments to Boards will continue until full complements are achieved. The necessary meetings will be further telcons with some business carried out by e-mail, as foreseen in the Bylaws.

The IMKT will send reports to the Sloan Foundation and to the IMU EC, although it is not dependent on the IMU but just shares some of its goals.

4 Prognosis

The IMKT will be founded, and it will work toward spreading the ideas of cooperation to achieve a GDML. We should see other regional mathematical Knowledge Trusts formed. There will come a wider awareness of what well-organized mathematical knowledge resources can bring to both rich and poor communities. With better communication about how our subject's knowledge can be managed there will be a chance that it will not be lost to most, as could happen for plausible commercial reasons. If the mathematical community can organize a little better it can hope to avoid duplication of effort where it's not needed, and to achieve more. To a perhaps surprising extent many of the problems in implementing a GDML are social ones, though there are intellectual problems enough in trying to be clearer on what mathematical knowledge is, clear enough to make machinery to help us with it. There's certainly a lot to be done and a lot relevant going on.

References

[arXiv.org] Cornell University Library. https://arXiv.org

[Bibliotheca Alexandrina] The New Library of Alexandria Website. http://www.bibalex.org/en/Page/About

[Bouche:2008] Bouche, T.: Towards a digital mathematics library? A French pedestrian overview, Preprint. http://citeseerx.ist.psu.edu/viewdoc/summary?doi=10.1.1.399.9488

[Bouche:2014] Bouche, T.: Scripta Manent: The digital mathematics library as of 2014. Not. Am. Math. Soc. **61**, 1085–1088 (2014). http://www.ams.org/notices/201409/rnoti-p1085.pdf

[Bush, Vannevar:bio] Bush, V.: Wikipedia. https://en.wikipedia.org/wiki/Vannevar_Bush

[Bush:1945] Memex: Wikipedia. https://en.wikipedia.org/wiki/Memex

[Copeland:2017] Copeland, J.: Alan Turing's lost notebook. OUPblog, 18 February 2017. https://blog.oup.com/2017/02/alan-turing-lost-notebook/. Also LMS Newsletter, p. 22, April 2017 http://newsletter.lms.ac.uk/wp-content/uploads/2017/03/April-2017-proofs_for-web_3.pdf

[DDMF] Dynamic Dictionary of Mathematical Functions: INRIA. http://ddmf.msr-inria.inria.fr/1.9.1/ddmf

[DLMF] Digital Library of Mathematical Functions: NIST. http://dlmf.nist.gov, https://www.nist.gov

[DRMF] Digital Repository of Mathematical Formulae: NIST, GitHub. https://github.com/DRMF, https://www.nist.gov, https://github.com

[El-Abbadi:1986] El-Abbadi, M.: Life and fate of the ancient library of Alexandria, notices and Google book. http://www.mutayninh. com/life-and-fate-of-the-ancient-library-of-alexandria.pdf, https://books.google.it/books/about/Life_and_Fate_of_ the_Ancient_Library_of.html?hl=it&id=r6u-AAAACAAJ

[El-Abbadi:2017] Guyer, J.: Mostafa el-Abbadi, 88, Champion of Alexandria's Resurrected Library, Dies. NY Times Article, 28 February 2017. https://www.nytimes.com/2017/02/28/world/ middleeast/mostafa-el-abbadi-great-library-of-alexandria. html?_r=0

[Encyclopedia] Encyclopedia of Mathematics Website. https://www. encyclopediaofmath.org/

[EuDML] The European Digital Mathematics Library Website. https://eudml.org/

[Fields:2016] Semantic Representation of Mathematical Knowledge Workshop; Videos. http://www.fields.utoronto.ca/ programs/scientific/15-16/semantic/, http://www.fields. utoronto.ca/video-archive/event/2053

[Fields:docu] Excerpts from Video Documentary Towards a Semantic Language of Mathematics, Full Form. https://www. youtube.com/watch?v=HOtpVU4-FMc&feature=youtu. be, urlhttps://youtu.be/psSyM1zp82k

[Griffin:2017] Griffin, E.: Rescue old data before it's too late. Nature **545**, 267, 18 May 2017. doi:10.1038/545267a

[HathiTrust] HathiTrust Digital Library Website. https://hathitrust.org

[ICCM] International Consortium of Chinese Mathematicians Website. http://iccm.ymsc.tsinghua.edu.cn

[IMU:2006] Digital Mathematics Library: A Vision for the Future. International Mathematical Union (2006). http://www. mathunion.org/fileadmin/CEIC/Publications/dml_vision. pdf

[IMU-Net 77:May 2016] Editorial: Towards a Global Digital Mathematical Library. IMU-Net 77, May 2016. http://www.mathunion.org/ fileadmin/imu-net/pdfs/2016/IMU-Net-77.pdf

[IMU-Net 81:January 2017] Sloan Funding in CEIC Notes. IMU-Net 81, January 2017. http://www.mathunion.org/fileadmin/imu-net/pdfs/ 2017/IMU-Net-81.pdf

[Ion:2016] Ion, Patrick: The effort to realize a global digital mathematics library. In: Greuel, Gert-Martin, Koch, Thorsten, Paule, Peter, Sommese, Andrew (eds.) ICMS 2016. LNCS, vol. 9725, pp. 458–466. Springer, Cham (2016). doi:10.1007/ 978-3-319-42432-3_59

[JMM:2016] AMS: Special Session on Mathematical Information in the Digital Age of Science, Seattle, 6–7 January 2016. http://jointmathematicsmeetings.org/meetings/ national/jmm2016/2181_program_ss65.html

[Lafferty & Blei: 2016] Lafferty, C., Blei, D.: Grant by Alfred P. Sloan Foundation: to accelerate scientific discovery by using statistical machine learning to enable advanced search of mathematical literature. http://sloan.org/grant-detail/6703

[Maple] Maple (Version 15) Website. http://www.maplesoft.com

[Mathematica] Wolfram Mathematica (Version 11.1) Website. http://www.wolfram.com/mathematica/

[MathSciDoc] MathSciDoc, An Archive for Mathematicians Website. http://archive.ymsc.tsinghua.edu.cn

[MathSciNet] MathSciNet Website: American Mathematical Society. https://ams.org/mathscinet/

[Mouseion] The Mouseion Revisited Website. http://www.ldolphin.org/mouseion.html

[MSC2010:MediaWiki] http://msc2010.org/mscwiki/

[NAG] Numerical Algorithms Group Website. http://www.nag.com

[NAS:2012] Symposium Wiki on The Future World Heritage Digital Mathematics Library. National Academy of Sciences (2012). http://ada00.math.uni-bielefeld.de/mediawiki-1.18.1/index.php/Main_Page

[NRC/USA:2014] Developing a 21st Century Global Library for Mathematics Research. The National Academies Press (2014)

[OP SF NET: 2017] OP SF NET, vol. 24, no. 1, 15 January 2017. http://math.nist.gov/opsf/nl241.pdf

[Peano:1894] Peano, G. (1858–1932): Formulaire de mathématiques. t. I-V.Turin, Bocca frères, Ch. Clausen, pp. 1894–1908. Archived Book https://archive.org/details/formulairedesmat00pean

[Pitman & Lynch:2014] Pitman, J., Lynch, C.: Planning a 21st century global library for mathematics research. Not. Am. Math. Soc. **61**, 776–777 (2014). http://www.stat.berkeley.edu/~pitman/publications/planning_wdml.pdf

[Project Euclid] Project Euclid Website. Cornell University Library. https://projecteuclid.org

[Rayward:1975] Rayward, W.B.: The Universe of Information: the Work of Paul Otlet for Documentation and International Organisation. All-Union Institute for Scientific and Technical Information [VINITI] for the International Federation for Documentation. Moscow, p. 239 (1975). http://lib.ugent.be/fulltxt/handle/1854/3989/otlet-universeofinformation.pdf

[Sagan:2015] Saga, C.: Flat Earthers Hate the PROOF Given by Eratosthenes of a Spherical Earth Website Video. https://www.youtube.com/watch?v=h4AjYgjhwdw

[Schröder:1897] Schröder, E.: Über Pasigraphie, ihren gegenwärtigen Stand und die pasigraphische Bewegung in Italien, Verhandlungen des ersten Internationalen Mathematiker-Kongresses in Zürich vom 9. bis, pp. 147–162, 11 August 1897. English translation in The Monist **9**, 44–62 (1899) (Corrigenda p. 320). Original. http://www.mathunion.org/ICM/ICM1897/Main/icm1897.0147.0162.ocr.pdf

[Seoul DML Panel] Seoul ICM 2014 Panel on Digital Mathematical Libraries; Video. https://www.youtube.com/watch?v=OERXmv2oIyU

[Sloan] The Alfred P. Sloan Foundation, New York, NY 10111 Website. https://sloan.org

[Spiegel:2011] Internet Visionary Paul Otlet: Networked Knowledge, Decades Before Google, by Meike Laaff in Der Spiegel International, 22 July 2011. http://www.spiegel.de/international/world/internet-visionary-paul-otlet-networked-knowledge-decades-before-google-a-775951.html, http://www.spiegel.de/netzwelt/web/netzvisionaer-paul-otlet-googles-genialer-urahn-a-768312.html

[Turing:1942] Turing, A.: The reform of mathematical notation and phraseology. Unpublished manuscript from ca. 1942. Turing Archive as Auction lot http://www.turingarchive.org/browse.php/C/12, http://www.bonhams.com/auctions/22795/lot/1/

[Villani:2014] Villani, C.: Hamilton Lecture at Trinity College Dublin video, from minute 11:20. https://www.youtube.com/watch?v=aKfTI_CMiX4

[Waterloo Math] Faculty of Mathematics and Computer Science, University of Waterloo, Waterloo, ON, Canada. https://uwaterloo.ca/math/

[Watt:2016] Watt, S.M.: How to build a global digital mathematics library. In: 18th International Symposium on Symbolic and Numeric Algorithms for Scientific Computing, SYNASC 2016. http://synasc.ro/2016/invited-speakers-2/stephan-watt/index.html

[zbMATH] Website. http://www.zentralblatt-math.org/zbmath/

The New Numdam Platform

Thierry Bouche and Olivier Labbe[(⊠)]

Mathdoc (UMS 5638) University of Grenoble Alpes,
Mathdoc, 38000 Grenoble, France
{thierry.bouche,olivier.labbe}@univ-grenoble-alpes.fr

*This paper is dedicated to the memory of
Claude Goutorbe (1952–2016).*

Abstract. The Numdam French digital mathematics library has now
been in operation for more than 15 years with no major upgrade. It holds
more than 57000 documents either scanned or born digital (spanning over
one million pages). The information system has been recently completely
redesigned. In this article, we present the new Numdam ecosystem. A
metadata factory is used to store metadata from a variety of sources,
normalize it under JATS (articles) or BITS (books) XML formats, and
enhance it through manual editing or automated agents (tagging math
formulas, matching to external databases and interlinking, etc.). The
data model supports the main types of documents currently expected
to populate the DML: journals, seminars, conference proceedings, multivolume works, books, book parts, doctoral theses. All documents are in
collections that can belong to one or more corpus. The workflow has been
simplified and allows easy deployment on test and production web sites.
A platform holds all the data in one place, can generate multiple web
sites, each with a different view on the data, and provides an OAI-PMH
server to the outside world. Finally, the article presents future plans to
create a DML-ready platform based on the new Numdam platform.

1 Introduction

The Numdam programme [4] was launched at the very beginning of this century. It started at Cellule Mathdoc as a pilot digitization project of 5 serials
with the goal to provide digital preservation and wide access to our mathematical heritage. The paper collections were borrowed from publishers or libraries,
the digitization itself was outsourced. At that time, it was also considered to
outsource the online posting as Mathdoc felt it had little resources to manage it.
However, while the collections were under development, Claude Goutorbe tested
the possibility to build a web site on top of Numdam metadata based on the
EDBM technology that he had developed for the first web site of the Zentralblatt MATH database. EDBM (supposedly an acronym for *European database
manager*) is basically an indexing engine, with a library for searching, extended

---

This article is available at Zenodo via https://dx.doi.org/10.5281/zenodo.581405.

© Springer International Publishing AG 2017
H. Geuvers et al. (Eds.): CICM 2017, LNAI 10383, pp. 70–82, 2017.
DOI: 10.1007/978-3-319-62075-6_6

progressively with services written in Python. As it appeared very rapidly that this was going to work pretty well, and enabled us to keep access free to the Numdam content by avoiding external costs, the Numdam web site was open to the public back in 2002, based on an evolution of EDBM.

Numdam has evolved to become the French digital mathematics library, with more than 1 million pages acquired from a number of sources (our own digitization amounts to about 70% of the content, partnering publishers provide born digital files and metadata for the recent articles). Last year, the web site and associated tools such as the OAI-PMH server were still based on the 15 years old EDBM. Also, a custom internal XML format was used to store metadata, meant to capture the metadata we collected for the first digitized series, with some extensions added along the way, but still designed exclusively for articles published in journals. This became more and more troublesome as we were adding different content types such as books or theses.

For instance, when Numdam participated in the EuDML project [5], we had to convert our metadata to the EuDML metadata schema [6] based on the NLM Journal Archiving and Interchange Tag Suite (JATS), and set-up a separate OAI-PMH server [19] in order to expose Numdam content to the EuDML harvester.

Work on a full redesign of the Numdam hosting and dissemination platform has started a couple of years ago, initially led by the late Claude Goutorbe, now by the second author. An entirely new workflow has been built, with components dedicated to specific tasks and communication protocols between them. These components have now been released and are used in production. The Numdam web site [18] is running the new software since February 2017.

This article presents the new Numdam ecosystem: its architecture, the concept of a platform and its advantages to enable the construction of a larger virtual library, and the software engineering practices applied to this project to improve quality and prepare future changes.

2   Numdam Architecture

The overall Numdam architecture is presented in Fig. 1.

2.1   The Metadata Factory

A separate application, the metadata factory, shown on Fig. 2, imports and enhances metadata in the overall system. Documents from a variety of sources (digitized by Mathdoc, by other partners, or born digital documents) are all ingested in the metadata factory. A web interface allows manual modification of any metadata snippet (see Fig. 3). A number of services that enhance metadata can also be launched selectively on a range of items. The metadata factory software is based on eXistdb, which is a native XML database system [7], with editing templates adapted to our use of JATS and BITS.

This is where we perform the Extract Transform Load (ETL) steps (see, e.g. [22]). In our case, this means that for each ingested item, the XML is either

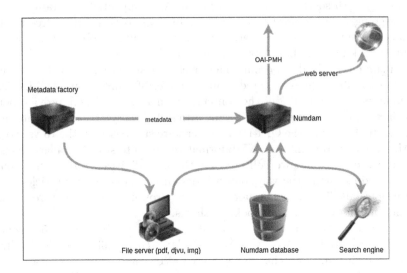

Fig. 1. Numdam platform architecture.

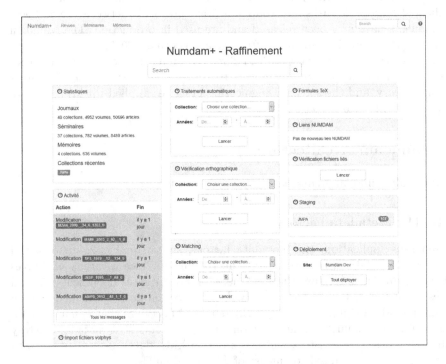

Fig. 2. The metadata factory dashboard.

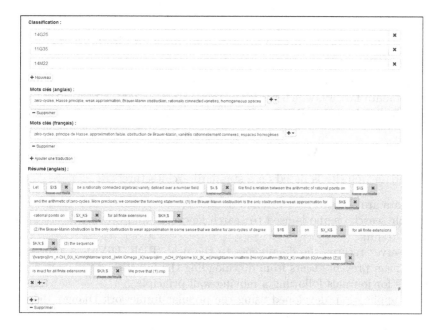

Fig. 3. The metadata factory: editing XML metadata.

loaded without change if it is tagged according to the new internal format (based on JATS for journal articles [16], and BITS for books [17]), or transformed on the fly to that format if it is tagged under our legacy custom DTD. For metadata coming from publishers, we typically perform transformations to JATS before ingestion.

An anti-pattern is a common structure or set of actions that initially looks like an appropriate and effective solution, but leads you eventually into trouble [15]. As noted by Ken Farmer in his list of ETL anti-patterns [8], a single program must not be used to perform all the steps. Therefore, we developed and use separate automated agents to enhance metadata:

- we use a spell checker in order to find OCR or typing errors in metadata such as titles or author names.
- we have a routine to correct some usual orthotypographical mistakes such as abusive capitalization or wrong spacing.
- we have separate routines to look up external databases such as EuDML, MathSciNet or zbMATH in order to provide deep interlinking for our articles or citations,
- we generate LaTeX driver files that produce the PDF full texts with cover pages.
- as we input all mathematical formulas as LaTeX, they are converted on the fly to MathML and stored in the XML file next to the TeX code,

- we also have a number of programs looking up our metadata for possible problems or errors (such as a relation from errata without backward relation. . .).

In this way, all the ingestion, manual or automated enhancements are managed in the metadata factory, which holds our reference metadata, which is fed to the public web site through a REST API.

2.2   The Numdam Web Site

The Numdam web site is based on a standard architecture:

- metadata are stored in a relational database,
- the Solr search engine is used to search keywords and provide facets in the search results,
- a file server returns the documents to the user (PDF, DjVu). A protection mechanism prevents users from downloading the full text of the most recent articles for journals following a moving wall principle,
- a web application, developed using the popular framework Django, displays the Numdam web pages in a browser interface,
- an OAI-PMH server exports metadata in multiple formats: the mandatory simple oai-dc, eudlm-article2 and eudml-book2 EuDML formats for much more details, and gallica (which exposes journal-level metadata in oai-dc).

The legacy Numdam (see Fig. 4) was based on a custom made search engine in the past. All metadata was stored in a PostgreSQL database with a structure modelled on our legacy (journal-only) DTD. All dynamical pages were produced on the fly as a result of a search query: The search and browsing interfaces, as well as the items' short and long record display pages were generated as a response to a search query. The data returned by the database was assembled (and transformed with XSLT) in order to build the page content. We didn't have a metadata factory but metadata was prepared using various scripts and manual editing yielding a collection of XML files that were ingested and indexed by EDBM. EDBM also created special indexes for features that were not implemented in the XML files (such as reverse citations, links to citing items from a cited item, etc.). We also had a special trouble coming from the fact that the content managing system SPIP [24] was used for the static web pages at www. numdam.org. The dynamic part of the web site had to mimick SPIP pages and menus, with hard coded links to SPIP articles. As SPIP and EDBM didn't manage some features the same way (like, for instance, bilingualism: cookies in the cas of SPIP, parameters in the case of EDBM), this could lead to a quite uneven user experience such as launching a search query in the English interface and ending up in a page written in French.

The new search engine is based on the Lucene search library. Communication with the Lucene engine is based on standards like XML, JSON and HTTP. Solr follows the NoSQL (Not only SQL) movement : the data stores are non-relational and therefore do not require fixed table schemas. They avoid join operations to

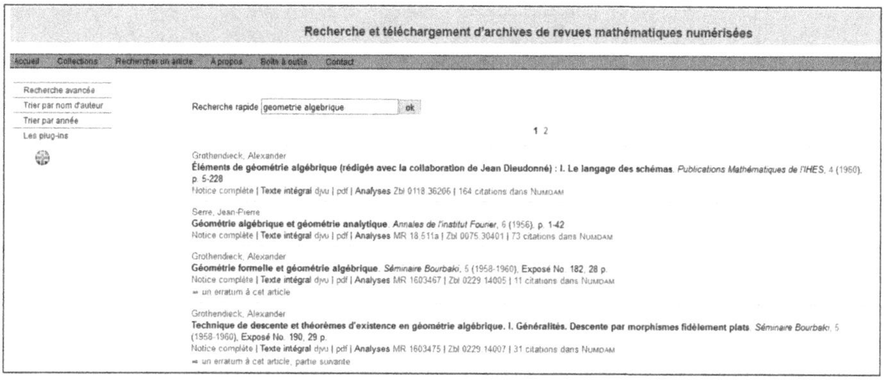

Fig. 4. The old Numdam web site.

retrieve documents, improving the search operation for complex queries. Solr brings additional benefits, such as faceting, spell checking, similar item search, hit highlighting and free text search. XSLT (EXtensible Stylesheet Language) was used to transform the model into XHTML, which was fine when user interactions were few and pages did not react to the environment, like the size of the browser window. The Model-View-Controller (MVC) design pattern [10] is now applied to separate the view from the user interactions, which are more important today with search facets used to filter search results. Graphic designers can now focus on the ergonomics of the web site, and can provide an adaptive view that reacts to the size of the window.

For a user, the Numdam interface looks like a common one for a digital library: menus allow navigation across collections, search fields let you specify search keywords, and facets let you quickly narrow the search results (see Fig. 4). In the past, Numdam objects were built to model a journal. Hacks had to be put in place to support memoirs and doctoral theses. The fact that we now have native support for other document types than journal articles has been used to have a different item page layout (aka landing page) depending on the item type (books or theses, edited books, chapters in edited books...). We are also experimenting with a specific browsing interface for books, ordered as in library shelves by author, year, title.

All the content is now organized in three major document types: journal article, single book, and multiple volume book. In Numdam, we have composed our objects into tree structures to represent a part-whole hierarchy, thus following the Composite design pattern in Object-Oriented software [10].

Figure 5 shows the objects used in our model:

- leaf: journal article or book part,
- container: journal issue, book (including monograph and edited book),
- collection: journal, book series, multivolume work.

As a collection is a composite, it can be embedded in a larger collection. For example, the Séminaire Bourbaki is a collection available in Numdam that

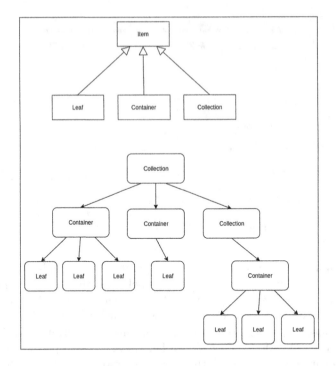

Fig. 5. Part-whole hierarchy.

happens to have been published in different venues over time (including Springer Lecture Notes in Mathematics, SMF's *Astérisque* series). A subset of this collection is thus part of the *Astérisque* collection, whose other volumes are currently being digitized and will soon be added to Numdam.

2.3   Mathematical Formulas

The handling of mathematical formulas has been improved thanks to the new system. In the previous Numdam system, we encoded metadata using an XML DTD that didn't know anything about mathematical content. As a result, we stored TEX math encoding (with dollars) as text strings (with special XML characters escaped). Thus the math in Numdam, although a reference math library, was not handled as such, and not very much exploitable as math knowledge. We did tag formulas as math and convert most of them to MathML when we generated JATS XML to be ingested in EuDML, but we could not exploit this on our own site!

Now the metadata factory automatically detects LATEX math environments while editing text blocks that may contain it (such as title, abstract, keyword...). The JATS XML superstructure identifying formulas is added, and the MathML alternative to the TEX code is added. Team members without computational skills can now use the metadata factory, edit mathematical formulas and

Abstract   Résumé

Let X be a rationally connected algebraic variety, defined over a number field k. We find a relation between the arithmetic of rational points on X and the arithmetic of zero-cycles. More precisely, we consider the following statements: (1) the Brauer-Manin obstruction is the only obstruction to weak approximation for K-rational points on X_K for all finite extensions K/k; (2) the Brauer-Manin obstruction is the only obstruction to weak approximation in some sense that we define for zero-cycles of degree 1 on X_K for all finite extensions K/k; (3) the sequence

$$\varprojlim_n CH_0\left(X_K\right)/n \to \prod_{w\in\Omega_K} \varprojlim_n CH_0''\left(X_{K_w}\right)/n \to \mathrm{Hom}\left(\mathrm{Br}\left(X_K\right),\mathbb{Q}/\mathbb{Z}\right)$$

is exact for all finite extensions K/k. We prove that (1) implies (2), and that (2) and (3) are equivalent. We also prove a similar implication for the Hasse principle. As an application, we prove the exactness of the sequence above for smooth compactifications of certain homogeneous spaces of linear algebraic groups.

Fig. 6. Mathematical formulas in graphical form.

Abstract   Résumé

Let X be a rationally connected algebraic variety, defined over a number field $k.$ We find a relation between the arithmetic of rational points on X and the arithmetic of zero-cycles. More precisely, we consider the following statements: (1) the Brauer-Manin obstruction is the only obstruction to weak approximation for K-rational points on X_K for all finite extensions $K/k;$ (2) the Brauer-Manin obstruction is the only obstruction to weak approximation in some sense that we define for zero-cycles of degree 1 on X_K for all finite extensions $K/k;$ (3) the sequence `\[\varprojlim _n CH_0(X_K)/n\rightarrow \prod _{w\in \Omega _K}\varprojlim _nCH_0^{\prime }(X_{K_w})/n\rightarrow \mathrm {Hom}(\mathrm {Br}(X_K),\mathbb {Q}/\mathbb {Z})\]` is exact for all finite extensions $K/k.$ We prove that (1) implies (2), and that (2) and (3) are equivalent. We also prove a similar implication for the Hasse principle. As an application, we prove the exactness of the sequence above for smooth compactifications of certain homogeneous spaces of linear algebraic groups.

Fig. 7. TEX source code of the formulas.

immediately preview the graphical form. Automated tests have been written to verify the validity of the TEX source code in all the articles stored in Numdam. We were able to detect and fix a little less than 100 issues. The improvement in the mathematical formulas handling allowed us to set additional goals and support mathematical formulas in references.

By default, mathematical formulas are displayed in graphical form using MathJax from MathML (see Fig. 6). A switch, easily accessible in all page headers, lets you display the TEX source code of the formulas for accessibility or copy-pasting (see Fig. 7).

These changes allow us to be fully embedded in the network of DMLs as we are now able to serve MathML (and, in fact, some other math-specific goodies such as mathematical subject classification codes) and full EuDML compliant metadata through our OAI-PMH server.

3   Numdam Platform

The new Numdam has been designed so that the same platform can generate multiple sites, all of them using the same data (PDF, DjVu, images, metadata, search engine). The industry platform definition is used here: "a set of assets organized in a common structure from which a company can efficiently develop and produce a stream of derivative products" [11].

The platform development was initially started in order to provide Mathdoc with a versatile tool for storing and delivering documents that we host like the Numdam collections, as well as some companion collections that will be added to the Numdam web site as "associated libraries".

An important feature of the platform is that it is very easy to update the platform content through its REST API, and the new system supports incremental updates (at the granularity of journal issue or single book), which will simplify a lot the online posting workflow as the (non-technical) people using the metadata factory can check their editing on a test web site until they are happy with it, then switch the validated items to the public web site. This is in strong contrast with the previous EDBM-based system where a large global index had to be recomputed from scratch for each modification.

We are also currently working on an extension to the platform that will replace the current farm of EDBM-powered Cedram web sites (where we have one overall web site with a global search engine, and one web site for each journal with a specific layout and web design, see [3]). As each journal publishes regularly content indepedant from each other, the possibility to add or remove articles while preparing new issues will be of great value to our staff.

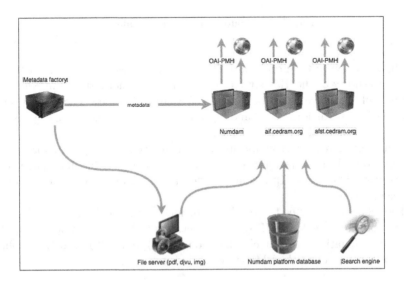

Fig. 8. The New Numdam platform: multisite.

Figure 8 shows 3 sites: numdam.org and 2 journal's web sites (aif.cedram.org and afst.cedram.org) that can be based on the same platform. The 3 sites can be hosted on the same physical server, or they can be cloned on separate virtual machines if needed, to improve performance.

An advantage of such an architecture is that bibliographical data can be collated and curated in only one place. Harvesting the metadata gathered by Mathdoc in a bigger virtual library is facilitated. As we have much better quality control on our metadata and native support to serve full math-aware metadata, the Numdam platform helps furthering the DML objective, this time using the DML definition of the "virtual library of all mathematical texts available digitally, both retrodigitized and born digital" [2]. As all document types envisioned to form the DML are natively supported by the platform, it can also serve to run a large DML system for content delivery, with content harvested through OAI-PMH or other means, this is a goal we intend to pursue in a near future.

In order to make the new Numdam platform successful, we had to prepare the change. The first step was to realize that Numdam was not just a software application, but an information system: a "Formal, sociotechnical, organizational system designed to collect, process, store, and distribute information" [20]. An information system has four components: technology, structure, people and process. Designing an information system requires to consider each component, not just new features or new technologies.

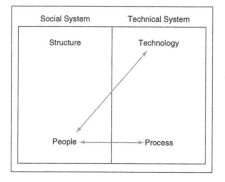

Fig. 9. Second-order change.

In the case of Numdam, a second-order change was anticipated. In a second-order change, the technology and processes evolve, and the people who perform the processes are affected by the change [20] (see Fig. 9). The objective was not only to replace the technology to automate some tasks or to use a more modular and modern technology, but also to involve a different set of people. The change was anticipated, and attention was paid to the ease of use of the interface. The metadata factory dashboard displays tasks that can be launched from the web interface, the status of these tasks, and lets you edit any metadata. The interface is now meant to be used by non-technical people. As a result of this second-order change, metadata are now updated more efficiently. They can be detected quickly and corrected before publication, by team members without computational skills.

To ensure that the interface of both the metadata factory and the Numdam web site were intuitive, an agile methodology, based on the SCRUM development process [23] was followed. Features were delivered on a regular basis and presented to the users. This iterative approach allowed us to implement the most important features first and to collaborate with the users regularly, thus following one of the principles of the Agile manifesto [1] where "customer" collaboration is valued over contract negotiation. Re-writing Numdam was also an opportunity to introduce some of the software engineering best practices. Test-driven development (TDD), where test cases are created before the code is written, helps prevent defects much more efficiently than many other forms of testing [14]. Continuous delivery, in particular deployment automation, reduces the delivery cycle time, and hence gets bug fixes to users faster [12]. This practice enabled us to deploy the source code and all the data (binary files, metadata) to test or production servers easily. In addition, it fostered the development team to submit and deploy the changes frequently, thus iterative development became natural. These software engineering best practices not only improve the software quality, but will also enable us to deliver multiple sites (Numdam, Cedram). The architecture will also make it easier to develop more APIs as the need for them appears, e.g. in the context of an international coordination of a global DML such as envisioned by the International Mathematical Knowledge Trust (IMKT, see [13]).

4   Conclusion

The new Numdam platform, publicly available since early 2017, was designed with a standard architecture (database, search engine, file server, OAI-PMH server, web applications developed with a popular framework). Some of the software engineering best practices were applied which make the source easier to maintain, and the model easier to extend. This platform will enable us to efficiently develop and produce a stream of derivative web sites. The next objective is to support the Cedram family of journals and to add associated collections to Numdam: Gallica-math [9] and Orsay mathematical publications [21] for a start. These collections are currently being posted with *ad hoc* unmaintained applications, and will benefit of much more visibility once integrated into the Numdam platform. Moreover they will be easily contributed to any DML harvester, thus enlarging the rich content already available in, e.g. EuDML.

In this sense, we view the platform as an enabling device to contribute more content to the global DML: We will be able to host in the same system, with the same quality metadata and a versatile format supporting all document types, more collections, including those from institutions that do not have the capacity to properly make them visible and interoperable to the other DML projects (or, in the case of very large generic digital libraries such as Gallica, the Digital Library of the French National Library, that would not allocate resources to a math-only project such as curating mathematical metadata),

Another application of the platform will be to create a DML web site much larger than those already existing. The goal is to create a larger virtual library, by harvesting metadata from other digital libraries, with much more detailed metadata than was available in the mini-DML [2], and a much larger coverage. This will require to set up an OAI-PMH harvester using the REST API in order to populate that instance of the platform.

We do believe that the architecture of the platform will make it easy to build such a virtual library, and to evolve with new APIs and innovative services on top of its holdings in order to keep pace with advances in the DML.

References

1. Beck, K., Beedle, M., van Bennekum, A., Cockburn, A., Cunningham, W., Fowler, M., Grenning, J., Highsmith, J., Hunt, A., Jeffries, R., Kern, J., Marick, B., Martin, R.C., Mellor, S., Schwaber, K., Sutherland, J., Thomas, D.: Manifesto for agile software development (2001). http://www.agilemanifesto.org/
2. Bouche, T.: Introducing the mini-DML project. In: Becker, H., Stange, K., Wegner, B. (eds.) New Developments in Electronic Publishing, AMS/SMM Special Session, Houston, ECM4 Satellite Conference, Stockholm, June 2004, pp. 19–29. FIZ Karlsruhe/Zentralblatt MATH (2005). http://www.emis.de/proceedings/Stockholm2004/bouche.pdf
3. Bouche, T.: CEDRICS: when CEDRAM meets tralics. In: Sojka, P. (ed.) Towards Digital Mathematics Library, DML 2008 Workshop, Birmingham, UK, 27 July 2008, pp. 3–15. Masaryk University, Brno (2008). http://dml.cz/dmlcz/702544
4. Bouche, T.: Toward a digital mathematics library? In: Borwein, J.M., Rocha, E.M., Rodrigues, J.F. (eds.) Communicating Mathematics in the Digital Era, pp. 47–73. AK Peters, November 2008. https://hal.archives-ouvertes.fr/hal-00347682
5. Bouche, T.: Reviving the free public scientific library in the digital age? the EuDML project. In: Kaiser, K., Krantz, S., Wegner, B. (eds.) Topics and Issues in Electronic Publishing, Proceedings of the AMS Special Session on Topics and Issues in Electronic Publishing at 2013 Joint Mathematics Meetings, San Diego, USA, 9–10 January 2013, pp. 57–80. FIZ Karlsruhe (2013). http://www.emis.de/proceedings/TIEP2013/05bouche.pdf
6. Bouche, T., Goutorbe, C., Jorda, J.P., Jost, M.: The EuDML metadata schema: version 1.0. In: Towards a Digital Mathematics Library, Bertinoro, Italy, 20–21 July 2011, pp. 45–61. Masaryk University Press (2011). http://eudml.org/doc/221288
7. Solutions, E.: eXistdb, an Open Source native XML database. Full online documentation at http://exist-db.org
8. Farmer, K.: Data Warehouse ETL for Data Scientists. http://www.ken-far.com/2011/03/data-warehouse-etl-for-data-scientists.html
9. Gallica-Math, a front-end to some mathematical content from Gallica. http://sites.mathdoc.fr/JMPA/
10. Gamma, E., Helm, R., Johnson, R., Vlissides, J.: Design Patterns: Elements of Reusable Object-oriented Software. Addison-Wesley Longman Publishing Co. Inc., Boston (1995)
11. Gawer, A., Cusumano, M.A.: Industry platforms and ecosystem innovation. J. Prod. Innov. Manage **31**(3), 417–433 (2014)
12. Humble, J., Farley, D.: Continuous Delivery: Reliable Software Releases Through Build, Test, and Deployment Automation, 1st edn. Addison-Wesley Professional, Boston (2010)
13. Ion, P.D.F., Watt, S.M.: The global digital mathematics library and the international mathematical knowledge trust. In: Geuvers, H., England, M., Hasan, O., Rabe, F., Teschke, O. (eds.) CICM 2017. LNCS(LNAI), vol. 10383, pp. 56–69. Springer, Cham (2017)

14. Jones, C.: Software Engineering Best Practices, 1st edn. McGraw-Hill Inc., New York (2010)
15. Koenig, A.: Patterns and antipatterns. JOOP **8**(1), 46–48 (1995)
16. National Center for Biotechnology Information: Journal archiving and interchange tag library, NISO JATS, August 2012. Full online documentation at http://jats.nlm.nih.gov/1.0/
17. National Center for Biotechnology Information: Book interchange tag suite (BITS), August 2016. Full online documentation at https://jats.nlm.nih.gov/extensions/bits/
18. Numdam, The French Digital Mathematical Library. http://www.numdam.org/
19. Open Archives Initiative: Protocol for Metadata Harvesting, documentation at http://www.openarchives.org/OAI/2.0/openarchivesprotocol.htm
20. Piccoli, G.: Information Systems for Managers: Texts and Cases, 1st edn. Wiley Publishing, New York (2007)
21. Publications Mathématiques d'Orsay. http://sites.mathdoc.fr/PMO/
22. SAS: ETL: What it is and why it matters. https://www.sas.com/en_us/insights/data-management/what-is-etl.html
23. Schwaber, K.: Scrum development process. In: Proceedings of the 10th Annual ACM Conference on Object Oriented Programming Systems, Languages, and Applications (OOPSLA), pp. 117–134 (1995)
24. SPIP, a publishing system for the Internet, see https://www.spip.net/en_rubrique25.html

Classification of Alignments Between Concepts of Formal Mathematical Systems

Dennis Müller[1]($\boxtimes$), Thibault Gauthier[2]($\boxtimes$), Cezary Kaliszyk[2]($\boxtimes$),
Michael Kohlhase[1]($\boxtimes$), and Florian Rabe[3]($\boxtimes$)

[1] FAU Erlangen-Nürnberg, Erlangen, Germany
d.mueller@kwarc.info, michael.kohlhase@fau.de
[2] University of Innsbruck, Innsbruck, Austria
{thibault.gauthier,cezary.kaliszyk}@uibk.ac.at
[3] Jacobs University, Bremen, Germany
f.rabe@jacobs-university.de

Abstract. Mathematical knowledge is publicly available in dozens of different formats and languages, ranging from informal (e.g. Wikipedia) to formal corpora (e.g., Mizar). Despite an enormous amount of overlap between these corpora, only few machine-actionable connections exist. We speak of *alignment* if the same concept occurs in different libraries, possibly with slightly different names, notations, or formal definitions. Leveraging these alignments creates a huge potential for knowledge sharing and transfer, e.g., integrating theorem provers or reusing services across systems. Notably, even imperfect alignments, i.e. concepts that are *very similar* rather than identical, can often play very important roles. Specifically, in machine learning techniques for theorem proving and in automation techniques that use these, they allow learning-reasoning based automation for theorem provers to take inspiration from proofs from different formal proof libraries or semi-formal libraries even if the latter is based on a different mathematical foundation. We present a classification of alignments and design a simple format for describing alignments, as well as an infrastructure for sharing them. We propose these as a centralized standard for the community. Finally, we present an initial collection of $\approx$12000 alignments from the different kinds of mathematical corpora, including proof assistant libraries and semi-formal corpora as a public resource.

1 Introduction

Motivation. The sciences are increasingly collecting and curating their knowledge systematically in machine-processable corpora. For example, in biology many important corpora take the form of ontologies, e.g., as collected on Bio-Portal. These corpora typically overlap substantially, and much recent work has focused on integrating them. A central problem here is to find *alignments*: pairs (a_1, a_2) of identifiers from different corpora that describe the same concept, giving rise to *ontology matching* [ESC07].

© Springer International Publishing AG 2017
H. Geuvers et al. (Eds.): CICM 2017, LNAI 10383, pp. 83–98, 2017.
DOI: 10.1007/978-3-319-62075-6_7

In the certification of programs and proofs, the ontology matching problem is most apparent when trying to use multiple reasoning systems together. For example, Wiedijk [Wie06] explored a single theorem (and its proof) across 17 proof assistants implicitly generating alignments between the concepts present in the theorem's statement and proof. The Why3 system [BFMP11] maintains a set of translations into different reasoning systems for discharging proof obligations. Each translation must manually code individual alignments of elementary concepts such as integers or lists in order to fully utilize the respective system's automation potential. But automating the generation and use of alignments, which would be necessary to scale up such efforts, is challenging because the knowledge involves rigorous notations, definitions, and properties, which leads to very diverse corpora with complex alignment options. This makes it very difficult to determine if an alignment is *perfect* (we will attempt to define this notion in the next section), or to predict whether an *imperfect* alignment will work just as well or not at all.

Alignment use cases. Many practical services are enabled by alignments:

- Simultaneous browsing of multiple corpora. This is already enabled (so far for a limited number of corpora) by our system presented in Sect. 4.
- Imperfect alignments can be used to search for a single query expression in multiple corpora at once. This has been demonstrated in the Whelp search engine [AGC+04] where Coq and Matita shared the URI syntax with the basic Calculus of Constructions constants aligned, as well as by the MathWebSearch engine [KR14].
- Statistical analogies extracted from large formal libraries combined with imperfect alignments can be used to create new conjectures and thus to automatically explore a logical corpus [GKU16]. This complements the more classical conjecturing and theory exploration mechanisms.
- Automated reasoning services can make use of alignments to provide more precise proof recommendations. The quality of the HOL(y)Hammer proof advice for HOL Light can be improved from 30% to 40% by using the imperfect alignments to HOL4 [GK15].
- Translations between systems. [KK13] uses more than 70 manually discovered alignments between HOL Light and Isabelle/HOL to obtain translated theorems that talk about target system constants and types. Note, that it is not necessary for the translation for the definitions of the concepts to be the same. It is enough if the same properties are provable or if they yield the same computational behavior. Consider the real numbers: In some HOL proof assistants they are defined using Cauchy sequences, while others use Dedekind cuts. The two structures share all the relevant real number properties. However, they disagree with respect to irrelevant properties, e.g., in the construction of the former usually a canonical Cauchy sequence for each real number is introduced. Despite this minor difference, we can use such an alignment in a logical translation [KK13].

– Refactoring of proof assistant corpora. Aligning concepts across versions of the same proof corpus combined with statement normalization and consistent name hashing allowed discovering 39 symbols with equivalent definitions [KU15] in the Flyspeck development [H+15].

Automatic search for alignments. Finding alignments, preferably automatically, has proved extremely difficult in general. There are three reasons for this: the conceptual differences between logical corpora found in proof assistants, computational corpora containing algorithms from computer algebra systems, narrative corpora that consists of semi-formal descriptions from wiki-related tools; the diversity of the underlying formal languages and tools; and the differences between the organization of the knowledge in the corpora.

Recently, the second and third authors have developed heuristic methods for automatically finding alignments [GK14] targeted at integrating logical corpora, which we integrate into our developments in Sect. 2. Independently, Deyan Ginev built a library [GC14] of about 50,000 alignments between narrative corpora including Wikipedia, Wolfram Mathworld, PlanetMath and the SMGloM semantic multilingual glossary for mathematics. For this, the NNexus system indexes the corpora and applies clustering algorithms to discover concepts.

Related Work. Alignments between computational corpora occur in bridges between the run time systems of programming languages. Alignments between logical and computational corpora are used in proof assistants with code generation such as Isabelle [WPN08] and Coq [Coq15]. Here functions defined in the logic are aligned with their implementations in the programming language in order to generate fast executable code from formalizations.

The dominant methods for integrating logical corpora so far have focused on truth-preserving translations between the underlying knowledge representation languages. For example, [KS10] translates from Isabelle/HOL to Isabelle/ZF. [KW10] translates from HOL Light to Coq, [OS06] to Isabelle/HOL, and [NSM01] to Nuprl. Older versions of Matita [ACTZ06] were able to read Coq compiled theory files. [CHK+11] build a library of translations between different logics.

However, most translations are not alignment-aware, i.e., it is not guaranteed that a_1 will be translated to a_2 even if the alignment is known. This is because a_1 and a_2 may be subtly incompatible so that a direct translation may even lead to inconsistency or ill-typed results. [OS06] was — to the authors knowledge — the first that could be parametrized by a set of alignments. The OpenTheory framework [Hur09] provides a number of higher-order logic concept alignments. In [KR16], the fourth and fifth author discuss the corpus integration problem and conclude that alignments are of utmost practical importance. Indeed, corpus integration can succeed with only alignment data even if no logic translation is possible. Conversely, logic translations contribute little to corpus integration without alignment data.

Contribution and Overview. Our contribution is three-fold.

·

First, we present a phenomenological study of alignments between proof assistant corpora, as well as with mathematical corpora in Sect. 2. We show a number of imperfect alignments and show how this can be used to benefit knowledge transfer. Second, we propose a standard for storing and sharing alignments (see Sect. 4), we cover the central ingredient – global identifiers based on MMT URIs [RK13] – in Sect. 3. Every symbol is assigned a unique way to access it across corpora and across logics. The URIs are used both in the system and to give several examples from logical and computational corpora in [MGK+17].

Most corpora are developed and maintained by separate, often disjoint communities. That makes it difficult for researchers to utilize alignments because no public resource exists for jointly building a large collection of alignments. Therefore we have started such a resource in form of a central repository as our third contribution—it is public, and we invite all researchers to contribute their alignments. We seeded our repository with the alignment sets mentioned above. Moreover, we are hosting a web-server that allows for conveniently querying for all symbols aligned with a given symbol, currently including ≈12000 alignments between proof assistant libraries and 22 alignments to semi-formal corpora (transitive closure not included). We describe this standard and infrastructure in Sect. 4.

2   Types of Alignments

Let us assume two corpora C_1, C_2 with underlying foundational logics F_1, F_2. We examine examples for how two concepts a_i from C_i can be aligned. Importantly, we allow for the case where a_1 and a_2 represent the same abstract mathematical concept without there being a direct, rigorous translation between them.

The types of alignments in this section are purely phenomenological in nature: they exemplify the difficulty of the problem and provide benchmarks for rigorous definitions. While some types are relatively straightforward, others are so difficult that giving a rigorous definitions remains an open problem. This is because alignments ideally legitimize translations from F_1 to F_2 that replace a_1 with a_2. But in many situations these translations, while possible in principle, are much more difficult than simply replacing one symbol with another. The alignment types below are roughly ordered by increasing difficulty of this translation.

Perfect Alignment. If a_1 and a_2 are logically equivalent (modulo a translation ϕ between F_1 and F_2 that is fixed in the context), we speak of a perfect alignment. More precisely, all formal properties (type, definition, axioms) of a_1 carry over to a_2 and vice versa. Typical examples are primitive types and their associated operations. Consider:

$$\texttt{Nat}_1 : \texttt{Type} \qquad \texttt{Nat}_2 : \texttt{Type}$$

then translations between C_1 and C_2 can simply interchange a_1 and a_2.

The above example is deceptively simple for two reasons. Firstly, it hides the problem that F_1 and F_2 do not necessarily share the symbol $\texttt{Type}$. Therefore, we need to assume that there are symbols $\mathtt{Type}_1$ and $\mathtt{Type}_2$, which have been already aligned (perfectly). Such alignments are crucial for all fundamental constructors that occur in the types and characteristic theorems of the symbols we want to align such as $\mathtt{Type}$, $\rightarrow$, $\mathtt{bool}$, $\wedge$, etc. These alignments can be handled with the same methodology as discussed here. Therefore, here and below, we assume we have such alignments and simply use the same fundamental constructors for F_1 and F_2.

Secondly, it ignores that we usually want (and can reasonably expect) only certain formal properties to carry over, namely those in the *interface theory* in the sense of [KR16]—i.e. those properties that are still meaningful after abstracting away from the specific foundational logics F_i. For example, in [MGK+17] we give many perfect alignments between symbols that use different but equivalent definitions.

Alignment up to Argument Order. Two function symbols can be perfectly aligned except that their arguments must be reordered when translating.

The most common example is function composition, whose arguments may be given in application order $(f \circ g)$ or in diagram order $(f; g)$. Another example is given

$$\mathtt{contains}_1 : (T : \mathtt{Type}) \rightarrow \mathtt{SubSet}\, T \rightarrow T \rightarrow \mathtt{bool}$$
$$\mathtt{in}_2 : (T : \mathtt{Type}) \rightarrow \mathtt{T} \rightarrow \mathtt{SubSet}\, T \rightarrow \mathtt{bool}$$

Here the expressions $\mathtt{contains}_1(T, A, x)$ and $\mathtt{in}_2(T, x, A)$ can be translated to each other.

Alignment up to Determined Arguments. The perfect alignment of two function symbols may be broken because they have different types even though they agree in most of their properties. This often occurs when F_1 uses a more fine-granular type system than F_2, which requires additional arguments.

Examples are untyped and typed (polymorphic, homogeneous) equality: The former is binary, while the latter is ternary

$$\mathtt{eq}_1 : \mathtt{Set} \rightarrow \mathtt{Set} \rightarrow \mathtt{bool}$$
$$\mathtt{eq}_2 : (T : \mathtt{Type}) \rightarrow T \rightarrow T \rightarrow \mathtt{bool}.$$

The types can be aligned, if we apply $\varphi(\mathtt{Set})$ to $\mathtt{eq}_2$. Similar examples arise between simply- and dependently-typed foundations, where symbols in the latter take additional arguments.

These additional arguments are uniquely determined by the values of the other arguments, and a translation from C_1 to C_2 can drop them, whereas the reverse translations must infer them – but F_1 usually has functionality for that (e.g. the type parameter of polymorphic equality is usually uniquely determined).

The additional arguments can also be proofs, used for example to represent partial functions as total functions, such as a binary and a ternary division operator

$$\text{div}_1 : \text{Real} \to \text{Real} \to \text{Real}$$
$$\text{div}_2 : \text{Real} \to (d : \text{Real}) \to \vdash d \neq 0 \to \text{Real}$$

Here inferring the third argument is undecidable in general, and it is unique only in the presence of proof irrelevance.

Alignment up to Totality of Functions. The functions a_1 and a_2 can be aligned everywhere where both are defined. This often happens since it is often convenient to represent partial functions as total ones by assigning values to all arguments. The most common example is division. div_1 might both have the type $\text{Real} \to \text{Real} \to \text{Real}$ with $x \, \text{div}_1 \, 0$ undefined and $x \, \text{div}_2 \, 0 = 0$.

Here a translation from C_1 to C_2 can always replace div_1 with div_2. The reverse translation can usually replace div_2 with div_1 but not always. In translation-worthy data-expressions, it is typically sound; in formulas, it can easily be unsound because theorems about div_2 might not require the restriction to non-zero denominators.

Alignment for Certain Arguments. Two function symbols may be aligned only for certain arguments. This occurs if a_1 has a smaller domain than a_2.

The most fundamental case is the function type constructor $\to$ itself. For example, $\to_1$ may be first-order in F_1 and $\to_2$ higher-order in F_2. Thus, a translation from C_1 to C_2 can replace $\to_1$ with $\to_2$, whereas the reverse translation must be partial.

Another important class of examples is given by subtyping (or the lack thereof). For example, we could have

$$\text{plus}_1 : \text{Nat} \to \text{Nat} \to \text{Nat}$$
$$\text{plus}_2 : \text{Real} \to \text{Real} \to \text{Real}.$$

Alignment up to Associativity. An associative binary function (either logically associative or notationally right- or left-associative) can be defined as a flexary function, i.e., a function taking an arbitrarily long sequence of arguments. In this case, translations must fold or unfold the argument sequence. For example

$$\text{plus}_1 : \text{Nat} \to \text{Nat} \to \text{Nat} \qquad \text{plus}_2 : \text{List Nat} \to \text{Nat}.$$

All of the above types of alignments allow us to translate expressions between our corpora by modifying the lists of arguments the respective symbols are applied to, even if not always in a straight-forward way. The following types of alignments are more abstract, and any translation along them might be more dependent on the specifics of the symbols under consideration.

Contextual Alignments. Two symbols may be aligned only in certain contexts. For example, the complex numbers are represented as pairs of real numbers in some proof assistant libraries and as an inductive data type in others. Then only selected occurrences of pairs of real numbers can be aligned with the complex numbers.

Alignment with a Set of Declarations. Here a single declaration in C_1 is aligned with a set of declarations in C_2. An example is a conjunction a_1 in C_1 of axioms aligned with a set of single axioms in C_2. More generally, the conjunction of a set of C_1-statements may be equivalent to the conjunction of a set of C_2-statements.

Here translations are much more involved and may require aggregation or projection operators.

Alignment between the Internal and External Perspective on Theories. When reasoning about complex objects in a proof assistant (such as algebraic structures, or types with comparison) it is convenient to express them as theories that combine the actual type with operations on it or even properties of such operations. The different proof assistants often have incompatible mechanisms of expressing such theories including type classes, records and functors, with the additional distinction whether they are first-class objects or not.

We define the crucial difference for alignments here only by example. We speak of the internal perspective if we use a theory like

$$\texttt{theory Magma}_1 = \{u_1 : \texttt{Type}, \circ_1 : u_1 \to u_1 \to u_1\}$$

and of the external perspective if we use operations like

$$\texttt{Magma}_2 : \texttt{Type}, \ u_2 : \texttt{Magma}_2 \to \texttt{Type},$$
$$\circ_2 : (G : \texttt{Magma}) \to u_2\, G \to u_2\, G \to u_2\, G$$

Here we have a non-trivial, systematic translation from C_1 to C_2. A reverse may also be possible, depending on the details of F_1.

Corpus-Foundation Alignment. Orthogonal to all of the above, we have to consider alignments, where a symbol is primitive in one system but defined in another. More concretely, a_1 can be built-into F_1 whereas a_2 is defined in F_2. This is common for corpora based on significantly different foundations, as each foundation is likely to select different primitives. Therefore, it mostly occurs for the most basic concepts. For example, the boolean connectives, integers and strings are defined in some systems but primitive in others, as in some foundations they may not be easy to define.

The corpus-foundation alignments can be reduced to previously considered cases if we follow the "foundations-as-theories" approach [KR16], where the foundations themselves are represented in an appropriate logical framework. Then a_1 is simply an identifier in the corpus of foundations of the framework F_1.

Opaque Alignments. The above alignments focused on logical corpora, partially because logical corpora allow for precise and mechanizable treatment of logical equivalence. Indeed, alignments from a logical into a computational or narrative corpus tend to be opaque: Whether and in what way the aligned symbols correspond to each other is not (or not easily) machine-understandable. For example, if a_2 refers to a function in a programming language library, that functions specification may be implicit or given only informally. Even worse, if a_2 is a wiki article, it may be subject to constant revision.

Nonetheless, such alignments are immensely useful in practice and should not be discarded. Therefore, we speak of opaque alignments if a_2 refers to a symbol whose semantics is unclear to machines.

Probabilistic Alignments. Orthogonal to all of the above, the correctness of an alignment may be known only to some degree of certainty. In that case, we speak of probabilistic alignments. These occur in particular when machine-learning techniques are used to find large sets of alignments automatically. This is critical in practice to handle the existing large corpora.

The problem of probabilistically estimating the similarity of concepts in different corpora was studied before in [GK14]. We briefly restate the relevant aspects in our setting. Let T_i be the set of toplevel expressions occurring in C_i, e.g., the types of all constants and the formulas of all theorems. We assume a fixed set F of alignments, covering in particular the foundational concepts in F_1 and F_2.

Definition 1. *The pattern $P(f)$ of an expression f is obtained by normalizing f to $N(f)$ and abstracting over all occurrences of concepts that are not in F, resulting in $P(f) = \lambda c_1 \ldots c_n. N(f)$. If two formulas $f \in T_1$ and $g \in T_2$ have α-equivalent patterns $\lambda d_1 \ldots d_m. N(g)$ and $\lambda e_1 \ldots e_m. N(h)$, we define their induced alignments by $I(f,g) = \{(d_1, e_1), \ldots, (d_m, e_m)\}$. We write $J(p)$ for the union of all $I(f,g)$ with $P(f) =_\alpha P(g) =_\alpha p$.*

Example 1. For the formula $\forall x.\ x = 2 \cdot \pi \Rightarrow cos(x) = 0$ with F not covering the concepts 2, π, 0, and cos, and using a normal form N that exploits the commutativity of equality, we get the pattern $\lambda c_1\ c_2\ c_3\ c_4.\ \forall x.\ x = c_1 \cdot c_2 \Rightarrow c_3 = c_4(x)$.

Let $a_1, \ldots, a_n$ be the set of all alignments in any $J(p)$. We first calculate an initial vector containing the similarities sim_i for each a_i by

$$sim_i = \sum_{\{p \mid a_i \in J(p)\}} \frac{1}{ln(2 + card\ \{\ f \mid P(f) = p\ \})}$$

Intuitively, an alignment has a high similarity value if it was produced by a large number of rare patterns.

Secondly, we iteratively transform this vector until its values stabilize. The idea behind this dynamical system is that the similarity score of an alignment should depend on the quality of its co-induced alignments. Each iteration step consists of two parts: we multiply the vector with the matrix

$$cor_{kl} = card\ \{\ (f,g) \mid a_k \in I(f,g) \wedge a_l \in I(f,g)\ \}$$

which measures the correlation between a_k and a_l, and then (in order to ensure convergence and squash all values into the interval $[0; 1]$) apply the function $x \mapsto \frac{x}{x+1}$ to each component.

3   Global Identifiers

An essential requirement for relating logical corpora is standardizing the identifiers so that each identifier in the corpus can be uniquely referenced. It is
desirable to use a uniform naming schema so that the syntax and semantics of
identifiers can be understood and implemented as generically as possible. Therefore, we use MMT URIs [RK13], which have been specifically designed for that
purpose.

3.1   General Structure

Syntax. MMT URIs are triples of the form

NAMESPACE ? MODULE ? SYMBOL

The namespace part is a URI that serve as globally unique root identifiers
of corpora, e.g. http://mathhub.info/MyLogic/MyLibrary. It is not necessary
(although often useful) for namespaces to also be URLs, i.e., a reference to a
physical location. But even if they are URLs, we do not specify what resource
dereferencing should return. Note that because MMT URIs use ? as a separator,
MODULE ? SYMBOL is the query part of the URI, which makes it easy to implement
dereferencing in practice.[1]

The module and symbol parts of an MMT URI are logically meaningful
names defined in the corpus: The module is the container (e.g., a signature,
functor, theory, class, etc.) and the symbol is a name inside the module (of a
type, constant, axiom, theorem etc.). Both module and symbol name may consist
of multiple/-separated segments to allow for nested modules and qualified symbol
names.

MMT URIs allow arbitrary Unicode characters. However, ? and /, which
MMT URIs use as delimiters, as well as any character not legal in URIs must
be escaped using the %-encoding. We refer to RFC 3986/7 for details.

3.2   Namespace Organization

MMT URIs standardize the syntax of the identifiers, but they still allow a lot of
freedom how to assign URIs to the concepts in a specific corpus. This assignment
is straightforward in principle—after all we only have to make sure that every
concept has a unique URI. However, as we will see below, the structure of a
corpus can pose some subtle issues that must be addressed carefully. Therefore,
we quickly discuss commonly used corpus structures and how these can be used
to form URIs systematically.

The common structuring feature of corpora is usually a directory tree. The
leaves of this tree are files and contain modules. Moreover, each corpus usually

---

[1] For simplicity in the remaining part of the paper we will not give complete HTTP
links, but rather use single keyword abbreviations. Complete names of logics and
modules are given in the online service.

has a certain root namespace. However, systems differ in how they subdivide a corpus into namespaces.

We distinguish the following cases:

- **flat** structure: All files share the same namespace regardless of their physical location in the directory tree. This naming schema is most well-known from SML. In this case, we can use the root namespace as the fixed namespace for all concepts in the corpus.
- **directory-based** structure: The namespace of a module is formed by concatenating the root namespace with the path to the directory containing it. There are two subcases regarding the treatment of the file name:
  - **files-as-modules**: Each file contains exactly one module, whose name is that of the file without the file name extension. The name of the module may be repeated *explicit*ly in the file or may be left *implicit*. Files as explicitly named modules is most well-known as the convention of Java.
  - **irrelevant file names**: The file name is irrelevant, i.e., the grouping of modules into files within the same directory is arbitrary. In particular, a file can contain multiple modules.
- **file-based** structure: The namespace of a module is formed by concatenating the root namespace of the corpus with the path to the file containing it.

3.3   URIs for Selected Proof Assistants

Using the principles defined above, we have developed MMT URI formation principles for some important proof assistants: **PVS** [ORS92], **Coq** [Coq15], and **Matita**, use directory-based namespaces, while **HOL4**, **Mizar** have one flat namespace. All of the systems define some kind of named, theory-like structure (e.g. articles in **Mizar**), which can be used for the module components. If modules are nested, we get module multi-part identifiers which are segmented by slashes. All modules declare symbols, whose names can directly be used in the symbol parts of the MMT URIs. If a symbol name N is declared multiple times in the same module (due to overloading), we use two-level names of the form N/i where i numbers all declarations of N in that module (starting at 1).

The exception to this are the HOL systems, in particular **HOL Light**, which does not have an obvious MMT URI formation principle because it does not maintain all its identifiers itself—instead it relies on the OCaml toplevel to store the assigned values. We use directory-based namespaces with files-as-modules. For constants and types introduced by a module we add the prefixes `const/` and `type/`respectively. If a file contains OCaml modules, we use their names to form multi-segment module names. Accordingly, if symbols result from OCaml structures, we form multi-segment symbol names. This has the effect that HOL Light URIs are formed in exactly the same way as for Coq. The other HOL systems can be treated similarly.

For informal collections of mathematical knowledge like Wikipedia, we can usually adopt similar measures. We interpret Wikipedia as having a flat namespace http://en.wikipedia.org/wiki, obtain modules via the files-as-models regime, and use the anchors of editable fragments as symbol names. Thus the statement of uniqueness of identity element and inverses in the Wikipedia article on groups would have the MMT URI https://en.wikipedia.org/wiki?Group_(mathematics)?Uniqueness_of_identity_element_and_inverses.

Details of the various definitions can be found in [MGK+17, PRA].

4   A Standard and Database for Alignments

Based on the observations of the previous sections, we now define a standard for alignments. Because many of the alignment types described in Sect. 2 are very difficult to handle rigorously and additional alignment types may be discovered in the future, we opt for a very simple and flexible definition.

Concretely, we use the following formal grammar for collections of alignments:

Collection	::=	(Comment | NSDef | Alignment)*
Comment	::=	// String
NSDef	::=	namespace String URI
Alignment	::=	URI URI (String = "String")*

Our definition aims at practicality, especially considering the typical case where researchers exchange and manipulate large collections of alignments. Therefore, our grammar allows for comments and for the introduction of short namespace definitions that abbreviate long namespaces. Our grammar represents each individual alignment as a pair of two URIs with arbitrary additional data stored as a list of key-value pairs.

The additional data in alignments makes our standard extensible: any user can standardize individual keys in order to define specific types of alignments. For example, for alignments up to argument order, we can add a key for giving the argument order. Moreover, this can be used to annotate metadata such as provenance or system versions.

In the sequel, we standardize some individual keys and use them to implement the most important alignment types from Sect. 2. In all definitions below, we assume that a_1 and a_2 are the aligned symbols.

Definition 2. *The key* direction *has the possible values* forward, backward, *and* both. *Its presence legitimizes, respectively, the translation that replaces every occurrence of a_1 with a_2, its inverse, or both.*

Alignments with direction key subsume the alignment types of perfect alignments (where the direction is both) and the unidirectional types of alignment up to totality of functions or up to associativity, and alignment for certain arguments. The absence of this key indicates those alignment types where no symbol-to-symbol translation is possible, in particular opaque alignments.

Definition 3. *The key* arguments *has values of the form* $(r_1, s_1) \ldots (r_k, s_k)$ *where the r_i and s_i are natural numbers. Its presence legitimizes the translation of $a_1(x_1, \ldots, x_m)$ to $a_2(y_1, \ldots, y_n)$ where each y_k is defined by*

– *if $k = s_i$ for some i: the recursive translation of x_{r_i}*
– *otherwise: inferred from the context.*

Alignments with **arguments** key subsume the alignment types of alignments up to argument order and of alignment up to determined arguments.

Example 2. We obtain the following argument alignments for some of the examples from Sect. 2:

$$\text{Nat}_1 \text{ Nat}_2 \text{ direction} = \text{``both''}$$
$$\text{eq}_1 \text{ eq}_2 \text{ arguments} = \text{``}(1,2)(2,3)\text{''}$$
$$\text{contains}_1 \text{ in}_2 \text{ arguments} = \text{``}(1,1)(2,3)(3,2)\text{''}$$

Finally, we standardize a key for probabilistic alignments:

Definition 4. *The key* similarity *has values that are real numbers in* $[0;1]$. *If used together with other keys like* direction *and* arguments, *it represents a certainty score for the correctness of the corresponding translation. If absent, its value can be assumed to be 1 indicating perfect certainty.*

We have implemented alignments in the MMT system [Rab13]. Moreover, we have created a public repository [PRA] and seeded it with a number of alignments (currently ≈12000) including the ones mentioned in this paper, the README of this repository furthermore describes the syntax for alignments above as well as the URI schemata for several proof assistants. The MMT system can be used to parse and serve all these alignments, implement the transitive closure, and (if possible) translate expressions according to alignments. Available alignments are shown in the MMT browser.

As an example service, we have started building an alignment-based math dictionary collecting formal and informal resources.[2] For this we extend the above grammar by the following:

$$\text{Alignment} \quad ::= \quad \text{String URI (String} = \text{''String'')}^*$$

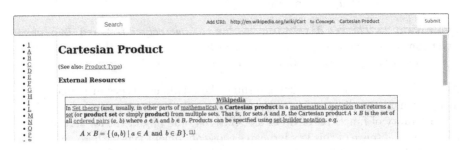

Fig. 1. The alignment-based dictionary—external resources

---

[2] https://mathhub.info/mh/mmt/:concepts?page=About.

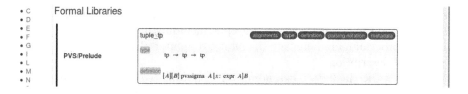

Fig. 2. The alignment-based dictionary—formal resources

This assigns a mathematical concept (identified by the string) to a formal or informal resource (identified by the URI). The dictionary uses the above public repository, so additions to the latter will be added to the former. We have imported the ≈50,000 conceptual alignments from [GC14], although we chose not to add them to the dictionary yet, since the majority of them are (due to the different intention behind the conceptual mappings in Nnexus) dubious, highly contextual or otherwise undesirable.

Each entry in the dictionary shows snippets from select online resources if available (Fig. 1), lists the associated formal statements (Fig. 2) and available alignments between them (Fig. 3), and allows for conveniently adding new individual URIs to concept entries as well as new formal alignments (Figs. 1 and 4 respectively).

Fig. 3. The alignment-based dictionary—available alignments

Fig. 4. The alignment based dictionary—field for adding alignments

5 Conclusion

We have motivated and proposed a standard for aligning mathematical corpora. We presented examples of alignments between logical, computational, and semi-formal corpora and classified the different examples. The presented MMT-based system for sharing such alignments has been preloaded with thousands of alignments between the various kinds of concepts, including proof assistant types and constants, programming language (including computer algebra) algorithms, and semi-formal descriptions.

Future work includes extending the automated discovery of alignments [GK14] to foundations other than HOL. Our main focus was on the logical corpora, but we expect to be able to find much more opaque alignments. We invite the community to use the service. Finally we plan to integrate the use of the alignments database in the various mathematical knowledge management systems. In particular, we want to relate our methods and the alignment database to the tool chain for ontology alignment, e.g. the Alignment API [DESTdS11] or the work on logic-independent formalization of alignments in DOL [CMK14].

Acknowledgements. We were supported by the German Science Foundation (DFG) under grants KO 2428/13-1 and RA-1872/3-1, the Austrian Science Fund (FWF) grant P26201, and the ERC starting grant no. 714034 *SMART*.

References

[ACTZ06] Asperti, A., Coen, C.S., Tassi, E., Zacchiroli, S.: Crafting a proof assistant. In: Altenkirch, T., McBride, C. (eds.) TYPES 2006. LNCS, vol. 4502, pp. 18–32. Springer, Heidelberg (2007). doi:10.1007/978-3-540-74464-1_2

[AGC+04] Asperti, A., Guidi, F., Coen, C.S., Tassi, E., Zacchiroli, S.: A content based mathematical search engine: Whelp. In: Filliâtre, J.-C., Paulin-Mohring, C., Werner, B. (eds.) TYPES 2004. LNCS, vol. 3839, pp. 17–32. Springer, Heidelberg (2006). doi:10.1007/11617990_2

[BFMP11] Bobot, F., Filliâtre, J., Marché, C., Paskevich, A.: Why3: shepherd your herd of provers. In: Boogie 2011: First International Workshop on Intermediate Verification Languages, pp. 53–64 (2011)

[CHK+11] Codescu, M., Horozal, F., Kohlhase, M., Mossakowski, T., Rabe, F.: Project abstract: logic atlas and integrator (LATIN). In: Davenport, J.H., Farmer, W.M., Urban, J., Rabe, F. (eds.) CICM 2011. LNCS, vol. 6824, pp. 289–291. Springer, Heidelberg (2011). doi:10.1007/978-3-642-22673-1_24

[CMK14] Codescu, M., Mossakowski, T., Kutz, O.: A categorical approach to ontology alignment. In: Proceedings of the 9th International Conference on Ontology Matching, pp. 1–12. CEUR-WS.org (2014)

[Coq15] Coq Development Team: The Coq Proof Assistant: Reference Manual. Technical report, INRIA (2015)

[DESTdS11] David, J., Euzenat, J., Scharffe, F., Trojahn dos Santos, C.: The alignment API 4.0. Semant. Web **2**(1), 3–10 (2011)

[ESC07] Euzenat, J., Shvaiko, P.: Ontology Matching. Springer, Heidelberg (2007)

[GC14] Ginev, D., Corneli, J.: Nnexus reloaded. In: Watt, et al. (eds.) [WDS+14], pp. 423–426

[GK14] Gauthier, T., Kaliszyk, C.: Matching concepts across HOL libraries. In: Watt, S.M., Davenport, J.H., Sexton, A.P., Sojka, P., Urban, J. (eds.) CICM 2014. LNCS, vol. 8543, pp. 267–281. Springer, Cham (2014). doi:10.1007/978-3-319-08434-3_20

[GK15]   Gauthier, T., Kaliszyk, C.: Sharing HOL4 and HOL Light proof knowl-
          edge. In: Davis, M., Fehnker, A., McIver, A., Voronkov, A. (eds.) LPAR
          2015. LNCS, vol. 9450, pp. 372–386. Springer, Heidelberg (2015). doi:10.
          1007/978-3-662-48899-7_26
[GKU16]   Gauthier, T., Kaliszyk, C., Urban, J.: Initial experiments with statistical
          conjecturing over large formal corpora. In: Kohlhase, A., et al. (eds.)
          Work in Progress at CICM 2016. CEUR, vol. 1785, pp. 219–228. CEUR-
          WS.org (2016)
[H+15]   Hales, T.C., et al.: A formal proof of the Kepler conjecture. CoRR,
          abs/1501.02155 (2015)
[Hur09]   Hurd, J.: OpenTheory: package management for higher order logic theo-
          ries. In: Reis, G.D., Théry, L. (eds.) Programming Languages for Mech-
          anized Mathematics Systems, pp. 31–37. ACM (2009)
[KK13]   Kaliszyk, C., Krauss, A.: Scalable LCF-style proof translation. In: Blazy,
          S., Paulin-Mohring, C., Pichardie, D. (eds.) ITP 2013. LNCS, vol. 7998,
          pp. 51–66. Springer, Heidelberg (2013). doi:10.1007/978-3-642-39634-2_7
[KR14]   Kaliszyk, C., Rabe, F.: Towards knowledge management for HOL light.
          In: Watt, et al. (eds.) [WDS+14], pp. 357–372
[KR16]   Kohlhase, M., Rabe, F.: QED reloaded: towards a pluralistic formal
          library of mathematical knowledge. J. Formalized Reason. **9**(1), 201–234
          (2016)
[KS10]   Krauss, A., Schropp, A.: A mechanized translation from higher-order
          logic to set theory. In: Kaufmann, M., Paulson, L.C. (eds.) ITP 2010.
          LNCS, vol. 6172, pp. 323–338. Springer, Heidelberg (2010). doi:10.1007/
          978-3-642-14052-5_23
[KU15]   Kaliszyk, C., Urban, J.: HOL(y)Hammer: online ATP service for HOL
          light. Math. Comput. Sci. **9**(1), 5–22 (2015)
[KW10]   Keller, C., Werner, B.: Importing HOL light into Coq. In: Kaufmann, M.,
          Paulson, L.C. (eds.) ITP 2010. LNCS, vol. 6172, pp. 307–322. Springer,
          Heidelberg (2010). doi:10.1007/978-3-642-14052-5_22
[MGK+17] Müller, D., Gauthier, T., Kaliszyk, C., Kohlhase, M., Rabe, F.: Classifi-
          cation of alignments between concepts of formal mathematical systems.
          Technical report (2017)
[NSM01]   Naumov, P., Stehr, M.-O., Meseguer, J.: The HOL/NuPRL proof trans-
          lator – A practical approach to formal interoperability. In: Boulton,
          R.J., Jackson, P.B. (eds.) TPHOLs 2001. LNCS, vol. 2152, pp. 329–345.
          Springer, Heidelberg (2001). doi:10.1007/3-540-44755-5_23
[ORS92]   Owre, S., Rushby, J.M., Shankar, N.: PVS: a prototype verification sys-
          tem. In: Kapur, D. (ed.) CADE 1992. LNCS, vol. 607, pp. 748–752.
          Springer, Heidelberg (1992). doi:10.1007/3-540-55602-8_217
[OS06]   Obua, S., Skalberg, S.: Importing HOL into Isabelle/HOL. In: Furbach,
          U., Shankar, N. (eds.) IJCAR 2006. LNCS, vol. 4130, pp. 298–302.
          Springer, Heidelberg (2006). doi:10.1007/11814771_27
[PRA]   Public repository for alignments. https://gl.mathhub.info/alignments/
          Public
[Rab13]   Rabe, F.: The MMT API: a generic MKM system. In: Carette, J.,
          Aspinall, D., Lange, C., Sojka, P., Windsteiger, W. (eds.) CICM 2013.
          LNCS, vol. 7961, pp. 339–343. Springer, Heidelberg (2013). doi:10.1007/
          978-3-642-39320-4_25
[RK13]   Rabe, F., Kohlhase, M.: A scalable module system. Inf. Comput. **230**(1),
          1–54 (2013)

[WDS+14] Watt, S.M., Davenport, J.H., Sexton, A.P., Sojka, P., Urban, J. (eds.): CICM 2014. LNCS, vol. 8543. Springer, Cham (2014)

[Wie06] Wiedijk, F. (ed.): The Seventeen Provers of the World. LNCS (LNAI), vol. 3600. Springer, Heidelberg (2006)

[WPN08] Wenzel, M., Paulson, L.C., Nipkow, T.: The Isabelle framework. In: Mohamed, O.A., Muñoz, C., Tahar, S. (eds.) TPHOLs 2008. LNCS, vol. 5170, pp. 33–38. Springer, Heidelberg (2008). doi:10.1007/978-3-540-71067-7_7

Software Citations, Information Systems, and Beyond

Michael Kohlhase[1] and Wolfram Sperber[2]([✉])

[1] Friedrich-Alexander Universität Erlangen-Nürnberg,
Martenstr. 3, 91058 Erlangen, Germany
michael.kohlhase@fau.de
[2] FIZ Karlsruhe/zbMATH, Franklinstr. 11, 10587 Berlin, Germany
wolfram@zbmath.org

Abstract. Even though software plays an ever-increasing role in today's research and engineering processes, the scholarly publication process has not quite caught up with this. In particular, referencing and citing software remains problematic. Citations for publications are well-standardized but don't immediately apply to software as, for instance, (*a*) software information is extremely heterogeneous, (*b*) software code is not persistent, and (*c*) the level of software information is often too coarse-granular.

Current initiatives try to solve (*a*) by postulating "landing pages" for software that aggregate standardized meta-data and can be used as targets for citations and (*b*) by version-specific sub-landing pages. However no information services that provide such landing pages currently exist, making these proposals ineffective in practice.

After an overview of the state-of-the-art, we propose to use swMATH's information system for mathematical software as a source of landing pages, show an approach for version-specific sub-pages, and discuss approaches to cope with problem (*c*) (granularity).

1 Introduction

Today's scientific digital libraries contain publications and (increasingly) the accompanying research data to make results reproducible by the scientific community. As much of the data and the results are created using scientific software, that is also increasingly considered as "research data" worth conserving and referencing itself. Therefore, detailed and persistent information about software is needed in scholarly processes and the archival publication record. For the first, we need software information services, for the latter, we need good practices for software citations. Citations for publications are well-standardized but don't immediately apply to software as, e.g.,

(a) *Software information is extremely heterogeneous*: it is distributed over web pages, manuals, scientific articles, generated system documentations, developer mailing lists, etc. This creates problems for software citations as it is unclear – i.e. there is no accepted best practice – which of the various information resources to cite as a substitute for the software itself.

© Springer International Publishing AG 2017
H. Geuvers et al. (Eds.): CICM 2017, LNAI 10383, pp. 99–114, 2017.
DOI: 10.1007/978-3-319-62075-6_8

(b) *Software systems and code are not persistent*: the software itself and the information pertaining to it are usually released in discrete versions or are continuously updated in revision control systems. Some citation-relevant information is version-specific, other pertains to the software per se and is therefore static. Again, there are no established standards for identifying software versions or revisions and how to integrate this information into citations. Moreover, new versions often supersede the old ones, so accessing old versions or revisions can be difficult.

(c) *The level of software information is often too coarse-granular*: we need to know which exact series of instructions or API functions were involved in producing a certain result to be reproducible.

These problems are generally recognized by the scholarly community, and there are a variety of initiatives that try to solve them. By and large, these initiatives have identified the problems and have proposed principles for dealing with them. For instance by stipulating "landing pages" for software that aggregate standardized meta-data and can be used as the targets for citations. While proposals abound of what (meta)-data such landing pages should contain, no public resources that provide such landing pages currently exist, making these proposals ineffective in practice.

In this paper we analyze the state of the art of and proposals for software citations and information systems (for mathematical software), derive requirements, and show how they can be met in existing systems, using our own swMATH system [swMath] which automatically aggregates information on mathematical software systems from the scientific literature and web information sources and the OpenDreamKit API theories [CICM1616] as examples.

In Sect. 2 the state of the art in software citations is previewed. In Sect. 3 we present the swMATH system and we show how it can be used to provide software object identifiers (SOI) – akin to document object identifiers (DOI) – and aggregated landing pages above; this addresses (*a*). Section 3.2 presents an extension of swMATH to include software versions (micro-archives of version-specific software information) to address (*b*). The pages in the micro-archives can be used to provide versioned SOIs and landing pages. Finally, in Sect. 4 we sketch how we can extend the ideas before to finer-grained citations of API functions to solve (*c*). Section 5 concludes the paper.

2 Approaches and Principles for Referencing and Citing Software

We will now review the current discussion of software information and citations. We will pay particular attention to math software, persistence/versions (*b*), and granularity (*c*) issues.

2.1 Mathematical Software Information on the Web

The landscape of software and software information in the Web is heterogeneous. Information on software exists in the following kinds of venues.

Websites. The analogon of publications for software are their websites. For mathematical software we estimate that 2/3 of the software products run their own websites, see [Chr+17]. The websites contain the software code (if it is open), manuals and documentations, APIs, information of legal rights, programming languages used, and context information, e.g., programming languages, software dependencies, test data, etc. Software websites are usually updated for new versions, and thus contain a mixture of general information about the software product and the current version (code, manuals and documentations, APIs, etc.). Distinguishing both categories is not always possible, but relevant for software citations. A further difficulty for processing information of the websites is that the websites are designed individually and have no common structure or metadata. The visibility in the Web for small and non-prominent software packages is a problem: finding new or specialized software is difficult for potential users.

Repositories have been established as community-driven focal points for accessing and archiving of software products. Often they collect and contain software products in a certain language or environment. Repositories trace back to activities of communities and are more prominent than websites of a single software. Moreover, they define rules and (proprietary) standards for the software listed in the repositories. Often they provide also a version management, e.g., CRAN [CRAN] as well as links to the mathematical background.

Portals and Directories restrict themselves to general information about a software, sometimes they cover also information about the current version but manual updating of the versions is expensive. Software portals and directories support the users finding relevant software. Mathematical software portals are focused on the content and its mathematical background, not on technical details.

Further Relevant Resources. Services like the OEIS [Inc] or cloud computing are based on mathematical software. Journals specialized to software play a pioneering role for evaluating software. Programming languages and environments, e.g., R for statistics [CRAN], define the base for software development in special mathematical domains, benchmarks are essential for the evaluation of performance, web archives are relevant for long-term storing.

2.2   The FORCE11 Software Citation Principles

The Software Citation Group of the FORCE11 Initiative [FORCE11] – a large community of scholars, librarians, archivists, publishers and research funders that aim to help facilitate the change toward improved knowledge creation and sharing – has analyzed the state of the art of software citations, has worked out the needs to software information resulting from different use cases, and has discussed the basics of software citations. It has formulated its findings as **Software Citation Principles** (SCPs) [SDK], six requirements for citing of software:

SCP1. Importance of Software: Software is a legitimate and citable product of research [...]

SCP2. Credit and Attribution: Software citations should facilitate giving scholarly credit and normative and legal attribution to all contributors to the software [...]

SCP3. Unique Identification: A software citation should include a method for identification that is machine actionable, globally unique, interoperable, [...]

SCP4. Persistence: Unique identifiers and meta-data describing the software and its disposition should persist [...]

SCP5. Accessibility: Software citations should facilitate access to the software itself and to its associated meta-data, documentation, data, and other materials necessary for both humans and machines [...]

SCP6. Specificity: Software citations should facilitate identification of, and access to, the specific version of software that was used. [...]

[SDK] goes on to point out that the development of a citation standard is not an isolated problem but essentially connected with maintaining of software and cannot solved without developing concepts for documentation and long-term archiving of software.

2.3   Some Consequences: Persistent Identifiers and Landing Pages

The huge amount of distributed information on the Web requires methods for persistent identification. There are many concepts and schemes for persistent identifiers, e.g., PURLs [PURL], URNs [URN], DOIs [DOI], and (for persons) ORCIDs [ORCID]. Moreover, publishers, libraries, and also the reviewing databases zbMATH [ZBM], MathSciNet [Ame] have own unique identifiers for their data.

SCP6 (specificity) distinguishes between general information about software and another for versions. So, **SCP3** (unique identification), requires unique identifiers for both the general information on software which we group to software product and on versions. Of course, software products and versions are closely related and overlapping. The relationship between software products and versions should be part of the meta-information on software, especially if the general information and the information about the versions are distributed.

SCP5 refers to the persistence of software information. The SCPs do not require that the software code must be persistent. This is the role of **software landing pages** introduced in [SDK] – i.e. web pages that contain meta-information about software. The main idea is that meta-information about software should be persistently available and citable – similar to bibliographic records of publications. Meta-data of publications are more or less standardized. Meta-data of software are more complex, cover information about software code but also about implementation, content, technical and legal data, context, etc. Meta-data of software are also strongly influenced from different use cases, for details see below.

So, in a nutshell landing pages provide persistent meta-information about (changing) software. But [SDK] does not define the content of the landing pages and the meta-data on them. To remedy this shortcoming and make the idea practical we propose to use the meta-data vocabulary of the CodeMeta project, see [CM], for software landing pages.

2.4 CodeMeta Meta-data for Landing Pages

Some aspects of meta-information of software have been discussed in the CodeMeta project. Basing on analysis of the common information of big software archives, a set of widely used meta-data fields for a machine-readable exchange format of software meta-data has been selected. Currently CodeMeta lists more than 40 meta-data fields encoded in JSON-LD describing relevant features of a software product and its versions and the developing parties (persons and institutions, called agents in CodeMeta).

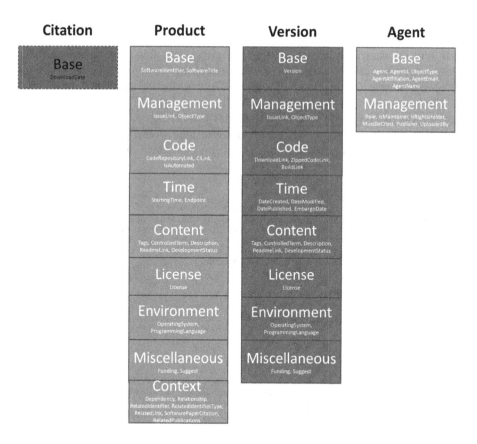

Fig. 1. CodeMeta meta-data and extensions

We use the concepts from the SCPs to give an overview over the fields in Fig. 1: The citation block on the left gives the meta-data that is specific to the citation, here only the reference date of the software. The second block concentrates on the software product itself. The version block specializes the meta-data that may change between versions (see **SCP6**), and finally the agent block is motivated by **SCP2**.

2.5   Software Citations

[SDK] also gives a recommendation for software citations in publications:

We recommend that all text citation styles support the following: (a) a label indicating that this is software, e.g., [Software], potentially with more information such as [Software: Source Code], [Software: Executable], or [Software: Container], and (b) support for version information, e.g., Version 1.8.7.

This proposal – while somewhat unspecific – significantly improves current practice of software citations in publications: The objects are uniquely defined as software and information about the version is given. We note that all information except the software type is already present in the CodeMeta meta-data set – which is the reason we propose it as the basis for software citations and landing pages.

The mathematical community typically uses TEX [CTAN], its bibliography add-on BibTEX, and increasingly BibLATEX [Leh10] for managing citations and creating references. BibLATEX provides citations formats for different object types, but unfortunately not for objects of type "software" or "software version" up to now.

```
                              @software{MIPLIB10,
@softwareversion{MIPLIB10:5,     developers = {Bixby, Robert E. and Boyd, E.A. and
   crossref = {MIPLIB10},                   Koch, Thorsten and Rehfeld, Daniel},
   version = {5},                title = {MIPLIB 2010 − the Mixed Integer Programming LIBrary},
   urldate = {2012−03−27}}       swmath = {4067},
                                 url = {http://miplib.zib.de}}
```

---

1   An Example

A reference to software MIPLIB [1].

References

1. Bixby, Robert E. (Developer), Boyd, E.A. (Developer), Indovina, R.R. (Developer), Koch, Thorsten (Developer), Rehfeldt, Daniel (Developer): MIPLIB 2010 – the Mixed Integer Programming LIBrary [software], Software Object Identifier, e.g., `http://swmath.org/software/4067`, version 5, [software version], Software Version Object Identifier, e.g., `http://miplib.zib.de`

Fig. 2. An example for software citation

To remedy this we have extended the BibLaTeX version with the biber [Biber] backend by new entry types software and software version and corresponding meta-data schemes (by introducing field, especially for the typing, the role of agents or the dates for uploading and downloading). Figure 2 shows the source and result of a BibLaTeX software citation. Note that we utilize the BibTeX/BibLaTeX crossref directive to avoid duplicating information. According to **SCP2** we have special "author-type" keys for the various agent roles in the CodeMeta meta-data set.

3   Persistent Identifiers, Landing Pages, and Versions in swMATH

The ideas formulated above can serve as a "requirement specification" for software citation metadata, and the BibTeX extension is an implementation of those. The main problem is that there are no public, comprehensive resources (software information systems) of landing pages that aggregate the kind of meta-information about software products and their versions either manually (software directories) or automatically (software information systems). For mathematical software, the situation is better: we have the swMATH [swMath] portal which supplies aggregated meta-data for more than 13,000 mathematical software systems. We will use swMATH in the following as an exemplar for a software information system.

3.1   The swMATH Information System for Mathematical Software

swMATH contains more than 18,000 records, each representing a software product with a unique identifier. swMATH is based on the more than 130,000 articles in the zbMATH publications database referring to mathematical software. The biggest challenge for a service like swMATH is to recognize these references. In many cases, only a name is mentioned, while a version or an explicit label as software is missing. swMATH tackles this with simple heuristics, by scanning titles, abstracts, as well as references of publications to detect typical terms – such as "solver", "program", or simply "software" – in combination with a name. After new candidates have been detected, they are checked manually to ensure high data quality. As part of this manual intervention step, additional meta-data, such as the URL of a software is added. Later on, websites are periodically checked and outdated URLs are removed or replaced. In case there is no permanent link that points to a website, the URLs of a corresponding repository record or a publication is used instead.

Another important feature for our analysis is the publication list for every software on swMATH. Each article in this list is annotated with its publication year. The publications can be sorted chronologically or by the number of citations an article has received. In swMATH, publications also serve as source for additional information, such as related software and the keyword cloud shown in every record (see Fig. 3).

Fig. 3. The swMATH (landing) page for MIPLIB

Summarizing, the original approach of swMATH bases on an analysis of software citations in the mathematical literature. This indirect method provides
statements especially about the mathematical background, the acceptance and

applications of a software but not about versions, technical details and integrability of software. Therefore swMATH tries to extend the information about software by integrating and linking further resources.

3.2 The Wayback Machine and Micro-archives for Software Versions

Web archives, e.g., the Internet Archive with the Wayback Machine [WB], periodically scan trusted websites. The Wayback Machine gives users the opportunity to nominate their websites for archiving and provides an overview page for each URL which documents the number of scans and the date of the scans. This is an interesting feature especially for software. It helps to avoid the so-called "reference rot", links leading to nowhere or significantly modified resources. The problem of reference rot was addressed in the Hiberlink project [HL] which has created a macro-archive of scholarly publications – also from sources like the WayBack Machine – and has defined versioned links (hiberlinks), see [Kle+14].

The set of all scans provides a comprehensive – nearly complete – overview about the development of a software product. Crucially, it provides also information about different software versions.

This allows to create **micro-archives** for a mathematical software based on the timed scans of the websites by the Wayback Machine. This idea was developed into an swMATH extension by Helge Holzmann [HSR16]. He used the swMATH software URLs as seed list and analyzed and grouped the stored scans of the websites in the Internet Machine (Fig. 4).

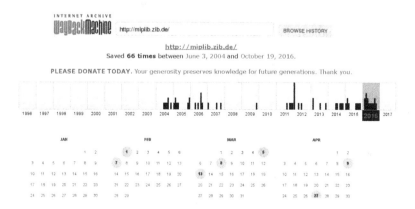

Fig. 4. The Wayback machine page for the software MIPLIB

The information on each scan of a website representing the development stage of the software at a certain date – in other words: a certain version – can be uniformly classified, in particular with respect to

- Software name and version
- Documentation, manual
- Software code
- Developers
- Contact
- License information and legal rights
- Environment and programming languages, technical parameters
- Citation recommendation
- APIs
- Further data, e.g., publications or the development of a software, test data, benchmarks, etc.

This classification scheme constitutes an additional uniform structure for software metadata, which can be aggregated into a secondary link page for the software information and represents a **landing page for a particular version** of the software product. It contains links to meta-data descriptions for the objects – if existing – in the classes and/or also direct links to the objects. The micro-archives are defined as the link pages and the linked resources in the Wayback Machine.

The concept of micro-archives is flexible. Meta-data schemes can be involved but they are not a necessary requirement. In a first attempt, the documents on the websites are classified by their document formats. This simple method is only a first approach, we plan to use more enhanced tools, e.g., machine learning, for classification. In essence, the scans of a website together form a web archive for the software which can be analyzed to distinguish the general from version-specific information. With this we can create landing pages not only for the software product, but also for its versions (Fig. 5).

One current handicap for software is the missing standardization, completeness, specification, and semantification of information on the websites of software, e.g., missing information about APIs or the availability of source code. But this information is relevant for the applicability, integrability, and further development of software. The problem of enrichment of software information is addressed in Sect. 4.

3.3 Software Citations with swMATH Landing Pages

We observe that the swMATH pages and micro-archives are suitable candidates for landing pages in software citations: they are

1. *comprehensive*: all mathematical software mentioned in the literature have a swMATH page, even if they do not have a web page (recall, that is 1/3 of the systems). The swMATH pages combine the direct information about a software resulting from the micro-archives and the indirect information about a software coming from the literature.
2. *informative*: they aggregate information even if the software website does not have it (e.g. the publication lists, word clouds, and authors).

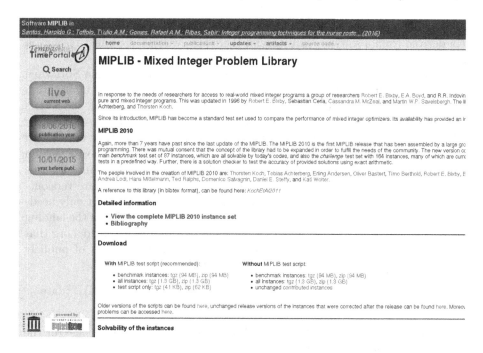

Fig. 5. Cutout of a micro-archive for the software MIPLIB

3. *persistent* and *specific*: they provide persistent identifiers and URLs (see also Sect. 3.4 below).
4. *low-maintenance*: analyzing publications and websites can be processed widely automated.

Therefore swMATH has added links to the overview page of a software in the Wayback Machine and from each publication to the corresponding version of software. If the version is not explicitly referenced in a publication, the micro-archive is assigned to a paper by comparing the publication dates of the paper and the software versions.

Their main shortcoming is that they are optimized to be human-readable and do not currently offer access to the CodeMeta meta-data in a machine-oriented way. This can be easily remedied by a suitable web service that does as the swMATH database has (most of) the relevant information.

3.4 Persistent Identifiers for Software Products and Software Versions in swMATH

In analogy to the DOIs we propose to use the swMATH identifiers (natural numbers: the mathematical software products are consecutively numbered as they become known to the system) as principal components for **Software Object Identifiers** (SOI) for a software product. Concretely, we propose to use identifiers of the form swMATH:4607 as SOIs; this allows to add different collections of software landing pages under other prefixes – e.g. for a software information system derived from a software directory; if there are overlaps, a conflict resolution mechanism could be established.

For the respective versions of the software product we can define **Software Version Object Identifiers** (SVOIs) accordingly. As the general information about the software product and a special version are closely related, the SVOIs reference the corresponding SOI. Thus it seems to be natural to design the SOIVs as a two stage identifier which concatenates the SOI and the notation of the version. As separator can be used for example the '/' symbol. So for version 5 of the MIPLIB package from Fig. 2, we would get the SVOI swMATH:4607/5; this would avoid separate identifiers for the software product and software version.

Note that the swMATH SOI for a mathematical software product only needs to be prefixed by http://swmath.org/software/ to obtain the URL of the landing page. Thus swMATH directly acts as a catalogue service like http://doi.org that is often used to hyperlink DOI-based citations. With the concept of publicly accessible SOIs software citations could be simplified to

⟨Agent⟩ (⟨role⟩): ⟨Software Title⟩, ⟨Version⟩, [software], [⟨SVOI⟩], ⟨date of the version⟩

as all other information can be obtained from the software landing page (or the corresponding meta-data web service).

We are currently experimenting with web services on top of swMATH, which allow to generate BibLATEX entries of the form described above directly for any SOI/SVOI in the swMATH database.

Of course, other software information services could define also similar name conventions for SOIs and SVOIs which could be maintained by a trusted institution, e.g., by the DOI service of TIB.

4   Fine-Grained References for Software Libraries and Open-API-Systems

The discussion above concentrated on software products, i.e. software systems that can be described adequately as a monolithical entity without discernable sub-systems. This is inadequate for many mathematical software systems, including (a) software libraries like the NumPy library [NPy] in Python which supplies a set of interface functions to be used for numerical computations in Python programs or (b) computer algebra systems like GAP [GAP], Sage [Sage], or Mathematica. Systems like the latter provide a programming interface that gives access to a set of API functions. In the case of Sage, this is the Python language, for GAP and Mathematica, these are system-specific languages. Note that even proprietary libraries and systems make the specifications of the APIs public, therefore we collectively speak of **open-API** systems. This class also contains programs like Office suites and CAD programs.

For open-API systems, we often want to reference specific API functions rather than the whole systems. Reasons range from reproducibility of scholarly results – e.g., how exactly did we convert the input data in MatLab – to discussing unexpected behaviors of particular API functions of open-API systems.

In analogy to the landing pages for software products we discussed above, we would need landing pages with meta-data for individual API functions. The most immediate way to do this is to reference a specific fragment of the manual, e.g., the documentation of `CharacteristicPolynomial` in GAP (see Fig. 6). But this approach does not satisfy the SCP principles discussed above. The first problem is that for instance **SCP3** calls for unique identifiers. The most obvious choice for this would be the manual and the function name but in software with method overloading (for instance GAP) this is ambiguous. Moreover most manuals do not use the function name as document fragment identifiers. In the case of the GAP manual the nearest anchor is https://www.gap-system.org/Manuals/doc/ref/chap24.html#X87FA0A727CDB060B. One wonders whether this generated anchor is persistent over versions.

Manual pages usually give the **functional "meta-data" for API functions:**

(i) the function name,
(ii) the call pattern; i.e. arguments, possibly argument and return type, and
(iii) a natural language description of the result to be expected and – if applicable – any side effects.

But there is no standardized and machine-actionable way of accessing these.

▸ `CharacteristicPolynomial(` [*F, E,*]*mat*[, *ind*] `)`   (attribute)

For a square matrix *mat*, `CharacteristicPolynomial` returns the *characteristic polynomial* of *mat*, that is, the `StandardAssociate` (56.5-5) of the determinant of the matrix *mat* - X · I, where X is an indeterminate and I is the appropriate identity matrix.

If fields *F* and *E* are given, then *F* must be a subfield of *E*, and *mat* must have entries in *E*. Then `CharacteristicPolynomial` returns the characteristic polynomial of the *F*-linear mapping induced by *mat* on the underlying *E*-vector space of *mat*. In this case, the characteristic polynomial is computed using `BlownUpMat` (24.13-3) for the field extension of E/F generated by the default field. Thus, if F = E, the result is the same as for the one argument version.

The returned polynomials are expressed in the indeterminate number *ind*. If *ind* is not given, it defaults to 1.

Fig. 6. The documentation of `CharacteristicFunction` in GAP

In the OpenDreamKit [ODK] project we have extended the idea of referencing API functions to a machine-understandable level. The goal of the OpenDreamKit is to develop a framework for virtual research environments for computational mathematics building on existing open-source systems like GAP, Sage, LMFDB, PARI-GP, and Jupyter. The integration of these systems requires a semantic description of their APIs, so that the respective object constructors and functions can be related to each other. Therefore we generate system-API-specific

OMDoc/MMT Content Dictionaries that contain the functional API meta-data in form of (*i*) symbol name, (*ii*) type, and (*iii*) CMP (commented mathematical property; a natural language description of the symbol meaning). We currently have ca. 350 generated CDs for the GAP system with an order of magnitude more classes and methods, and have recently added about the same amount of CDs for Sage. These CDs describe the system APIs in a uniform fashion and are keyed by function/constructor/class/- and category name. From this we can not only generate uniform human-oriented "landing pages" directly in the MMT system [Rab13], but we can also develop machine-oriented services that export linked open data about the system APIs, web services that generate BibTeX databases, and translation systems that make systems interoperable by aligning their APIs.

5   Conclusion and Future Work

We have discussed the problem of software citations in the special case of mathematical software. Based on the six "software citation principles" and the idea of software landing pages put forward by the FORCE11 group, we have proposed the CodeMeta meta-data vocabulary for landing pages and shown that the information in the swMATH software portal is sufficient to generate landing pages and persistent software identifiers for mathematical software. We have experimented with two extensions of this swMATH-based approach.

(i) micro-archives as collections of version-specific landing pages to combat the specificity requirement and
(ii) generated content dictionaries for referencing the API functions to alleviate the granularity restrictions of only dealing with whole software products.

Even though the swMATH portal limits itself to mathematical software, since it mainly relies on the zbMATH corpus for aggregating, the document-based aggregation method is not limited to mathematical software and could be extended given a suitably complete corpus (e.g., the Cornell ePrint arXiv, Num-Dam, PubMed or the back files of a large scientific publishing house). Given these considerations, we are confident that the ideas exposed here can be ported to major parts of the scholarly literature. As so often is the case (e.g., MathML was the first XML format standardized by the W3C) Mathematics (and Mathematical Knowledge Management) can play the role of a front-runner in scientific publication infrastructure.

Acknowledgements. We gratefully acknowledge fruitful discussions with Hagen Chrapary, Wolfgang Dalitz, Helge Holzmann, Heinz Kröger, Fabian Müller, Winfried Neun, and Olaf Teschke on software citations and the contributions of Paul-Olivier Dehaye, Alexander Konovalov, Marcus Pfeiffer, Nicolas Thierry, in the generation of OpenDreamKit content dictionaries. Finally, we acknowledge funding the of the research campus MODAL for the swMATH project and EU funding for the Open-DreamKit project in the Horizon 2020 framework under grant 676541.

References

[Biber]   Biber - a BibTeX replacement for users of BibLATEX. https://www.ctan.org/pkg/biber. Accessed 29 Mar 2017

[Chr+17] Chrapary, H., et al.: Design, concepts, and the state of the art of the swMATH service. Math. Comput. Sci (2017). doi:10.1007/s11786-017-0305-5

[CICM1616] Dehaye, P.-O., et al.: Interoperability in the OpenDreamKit project: the math-in-the-middle approach. In: Kohlhase, M., Johansson, M., Miller, B., de Moura, L., Tompa, F. (eds.) CICM 2016. LNCS, vol. 9791, pp. 117–131. Springer, Cham (2016). doi:10.1007/978-3-319-42547-4_9. https://github.com/OpenDreamKit/OpenDreamKit/blob/master/WP6/CICM2016/published.pdf

[CM]   CodeMeta: CodeMeta focuses on metadata and discovery systems for software citation and attribution. https://github.com/codemeta/codemeta/blob/master/codemeta-concepts.md. Accessed 29 Mar 2017

[CRAN]   The comprehensive R archive network. https://cran.rprojectorg/. Accessed 29 Mar 2017

[CTAN]   CTAN the comprehensive TEX archive network. http://ctan.org. Accessed 11 Dec 2012

[DOI]   DOI. https://www.doi.org/. Accessed 29 Mar 2017

[FORCE11] FORCE11-the future of research communications and e-scholarship. https://www.force11.org/. Accessed 29 Mar 2017

[GAP]   The GAP Group: GAP– groups, algorithms, and programming. http://www.gap-system.org. Accessed 30 Aug 2016

[HL]   Biberlink. http://hiberlink.org. Accessed 12 Mar 2017

[HSR16]   Holzmann, H., Sperber, W., Runnwerth, M.: Archiving software surrogates on the web for future reference. In: Fuhr, N., Kovács, L., Risse, T., Nejdl, W. (eds.) TPDL 2016. LNCS, vol. 9819, pp. 215–226. Springer, Cham (2016). doi:10.1007/978-3-319-43997-6_17

[Inc]   OEIS Foundation Inc., ed. The on-line encyclopedia of integer sequences. http://oeis.org. Accessed 28 May 2013

[Kle+14] Klein, M., et al.: Scholarly context not found: one in five articles suffers from reference rot. In: PLOS One (2014). doi:10.1371/journal.pone.0115253

[Leh10]   Lehmann, P.: The *biblatex* package. Technical report. CTAN: Comprehensive TEX Archive Network (2010). http://ctan.org/pkg/biblatex

[NPy]   NumPy. http://www.numpy.org/. Accessed 29 Mar 2017

[ODK]   OpenDreamKit open digital research environment toolkit for the advancement of mathematics. http://opendreamkit.org. Accessed 21 May 2015

[ORCID]   ORCID. https://orcid.org/. Accessed 29 Mar 2017

[PURL]   PURL Administration. https://archive.org/services/purl/. Accessed 29 Mar 2017

[Rab13]   Rabe, F.: The MMT API: a generic MKM system. In: Carette, J., Aspinall, D., Lange, C., Sojka, P., Windsteiger, W. (eds.) CICM 2013. LNCS, vol. 7961, pp. 339–343. Springer, Heidelberg (2013). doi:10.1007/978-3-642-39320-4_25. ISBN: 978-3-642-39319-8

[Sage]   The Sage Developers: SageMath, the Sage mathematics software system. http://www.sagemath.org. Accessed 30 Sep 2016

[SDK] Smith, A.M., Katz, D.S., Niemeyer, K.E.: FORCE11 software citation working group. Software Citation Principles (2016). https://peerj.com/preprints/2169/

[swMath] swMath an information system for mathemtical Software. http://www.swmath.org. Accessed 29 Mar 2017

[URN] Persistent identifier. http://www.persistent-identifier.de/. Accessed 29 Mar 2017

[WB] Internet archive wayback machine. https://archive.org/web/. Accessed 29 Mar 2017

[ZBM] zbMATH. http://www.zbmath.org. Accessed 12 Nov 2012

[Ame] The American Mathematical Society: MathSciNet mathematical reviews on the net. http://www.ams.org/mathscinet/

Semantic Preserving Bijective Mappings of Mathematical Formulae Between Document Preparation Systems and Computer Algebra Systems

Howard S. Cohl[1]([⊠]), Moritz Schubotz[2], Abdou Youssef[3],
André Greiner-Petter[4], Jürgen Gerhard[5], Bonita V. Saunders[1],
Marjorie A. McClain[1], Joon Bang[6], and Kevin Chen[6]

[1] Applied and Computational Mathematics Division, NIST, Gaithersburg, MD, USA
{howard.cohl,bonita.saunders,marjorie.mcclain}@nist.gov
[2] Department of Computer and Information Science, University of Konstanz,
Konstanz, Germany
moritz.schubotz@uni-konstanz.de
[3] Department of Computer Science, GWU, Washington DC, USA
ayoussef@gwu.edu
[4] DSIMG, Technische Universität, Berlin, Germany
andre.greiner-petter@t-online.de
[5] Maplesoft, Waterloo, ON, Canada
jgerhard@maplesoft.com
[6] Poolesville High School, Poolesville, MD, USA
joonb3@gmail.com, kchen1250@gmail.com

Abstract. Document preparation systems like LaTeX offer the ability to render mathematical expressions as one would write these on paper. Using LaTeX, LaTeXML, and tools generated for use in the National Institute of Standards (NIST) Digital Library of Mathematical Functions, semantically enhanced mathematical LaTeX markup (semantic LaTeX) is achieved by using a semantic macro set. Computer algebra systems (CAS) such as Maple and Mathematica use alternative markup to represent mathematical expressions. By taking advantage of Youssef's Part-of-Math tagger and CAS internal representations, we develop algorithms to translate mathematical expressions represented in semantic LaTeX to corresponding CAS representations and vice versa. We have also developed tools for translating the entire Wolfram Encoding Continued Fraction Knowledge and University of Antwerp Continued Fractions for Special Functions datasets, for use in the NIST Digital Repository of Mathematical Formulae. The overall goal of these efforts is to provide semantically enriched standard conforming MathML representations to the public for formulae in digital mathematics libraries. These representations include presentation MathML, content MathML, generic LaTeX, semantic LaTeX, and now CAS representations as well.

© Springer International Publishing AG 2017
H. Geuvers et al. (Eds.): CICM 2017, LNAI 10383, pp. 115–131, 2017.
DOI: 10.1007/978-3-319-62075-6_9

1   Problem and Current State

Scientists often use document preparation systems (DPS) to write scientific papers. The well-known DPS LaTeX has become a de-facto standard for writing mathematics papers. On the other hand, scientists working with formulae which occur in their research often need to evaluate special or numerical values, create figures, diagrams and tables. One often uses computer algebra systems (CAS), programs which provide tools for symbolic and numerical computation of mathematical expressions. DPS such as LaTeX, try to render mathematical expressions as accurately as possible and give the opportunity for customization of the layout of mathematical expressions. Alternatively, CAS represent expressions for use in symbolic computation with secondary focus on the layout of the expressions. This difference in format is a common obstacle for scientific workflows.

For example, consider the Euler-Mascheroni (Euler) constant represented by γ. Since generic LaTeX [3] does not provide any semantic information, the LaTeX representation of this mathematical constant is just the command for the Greek letter \gamma. Maple[1] and Mathematica, well-known CAS, represent the Euler constant γ with gamma and EulerGamma respectively. Scientists writing scientific papers, who use CAS often need to be aware of representations in both DPS and CAS. Often different CAS have different capabilities, which implies that scientists might need to know several CAS representations for mathematical symbols, functions, operators, etc. One also needs to be aware when CAS do not support direct translation. We refer to CAS translation as either the forward or backward translation respectively as DPS source to CAS source or vise-versa. For instance, the CAS representation of the number $e \approx 2.71828$ (the base of the natural logarithm) in Mathematica is E, whereas in Maple there is no directly translated symbol. In Maple, one needs to evaluate the exponential function at one via exp(1) to reproduce its value.

For a scientist, γ and e might represent something altogether different from these constants, such as a variable, function, distribution, vector, etc. In these cases, it would need to be translated in a different way. In order to avoid these kinds of semantic ambiguities (as well as for other reasons), Bruce Miller at NIST, developing for the Digital Library of Mathematical Functions (DLMF) (special functions and orthogonal polynomials of classical analysis) project, has created a set of semantic LaTeX macros [11,13]. Extensions and 'simplifications' have been provided by the Digital Repository of Mathematical Formulae (DRMF) project. We refer to this extended set of semantic LaTeX macros as the DLMF/DRMF macro set, and the mathematical LaTeX which uses this semantic macro set as semantic LaTeX.

---

[1] The mention of specific products, trademarks, or brand names is for purposes of identification only. Such mention is not to be interpreted in any way as an endorsement or certification of such products or brands by the National Institute of Standards and Technology, nor does it imply that the products so identified are necessarily the best available for the purpose. All trademarks mentioned herein belong to their respective owners.

Existing tools which attempt to achieve CAS translations include import/ export for LaTeX expressions (such as [10, 15]), as well as for MathML. CAS functions such as these, mostly provide only presentation translation in LaTeX and do not provide semantic solutions or workarounds to hidden problems such as subtle differences in CAS function definitions. These differences may also include differences in domains or complex branch cuts of multivalued functions. To fill this lack of knowledge in the CAS translation process, one needs to provide additional information in the DPS source itself and to create interactive documents with references to definitions, theorems and other representations of mathematical expressions. Our approach in this paper, is to develop independent tools for translation between different CAS and semantic LaTeX representations for mathematical expressions. We provide detailed information about CAS translation and warn about the existence of known differences in definitions, domains and branch cuts. For the DRMF, we have decided to focus on CAS translation between the semantic LaTeX representations of classical analysis and internal CAS representations for Maple and Mathematica.

1.1   A CAS, Generic and Semantic LaTeX Representation Example

An example of a mathematical expression is $P_n^{(\alpha,\beta)}(\cos(a\Theta))$ where $P_n^{(\alpha,\beta)}$ is the Jacobi polynomial [5, (18.5.7)]. Table 1 illustrates several DPS and CAS representations for this mathematical expression. Translating the generic LaTeX representation is difficult (see [3]) since the semantic context of the P is obscured. If it represents a special function, one needs to ascertain which function it represents, because there are many examples of standard functions in classical analysis which are given by a P. The semantic LaTeX representation of this mathematical expression encapsulates the mostly-unambiguous semantic meaning of the mathematical expression. This facilitates translation between it and CAS representations. We use the first scan of the Part-of-Math (POM) tagger [19] to facilitate translation between semantic LaTeX and CAS representations.

Table 1. DPS and CAS representations for Jacobi polynomial expression

Different Systems	Different Representations
Generic LaTeX	`P_n^{(\alpha,\beta)}(\cos(a\Theta))`
semantic LaTeX	`\JacobiP{\alpha}{\beta}{n}@{\cos@{a\Theta}}`
Maple	`JacobiP(n,alpha,beta,cos(a*Theta))`
Mathematica	`JacobiP[n,\[Alpha],\[Beta],Cos[a \[CapitalTheta]]]`

2   The Part-of-Math Tagger

There are different approaches for interpreting LaTeX. There exist several parsers for LaTeX, for instance `texvcjs`, which is a part of Mathoid [18]. There is also

LATEXML [12,13] which processes LATEX. There is also an alternative grammar developed by Ginev [7]. A new approach has been developed [19] which is not a fully fledged grammar but only extracts POM from math LATEX. The purpose of the POM is to extract semantic information from mathematics in LATEX. The tagger works in several stages (termed *scans*) and interacts with several machine learning (ML) based algorithms.

Given an input LATEX math document, the first scan of the tagger examines terms and groups them into sub-expressions when indicated. For instance \frac{1}{2} is a sub-expression of numerator and denominator. A term is, in the sense of Backus-Naur form, a pre-defined non-terminal expression and can represent LATEX macros, environments, reserved symbols (such as the LATEX line break command \\) or numerical or alphanumerical expressions. Sub-expressions and terms get tagged due the first scan of the tagger, with two separate tag categories: (1) definite tags (such as *operation, function, exponent,* etc.) that the tagger is certain of; and tags which consist of alternative and tentative features which include alternative roles and meanings. These second category of tags are drawn from a specific knowledge base which has been collected for the tagger. Tagged terms are called math terms. Math terms are rarely distinct at this stage and often have multiple features.

Scans 2 and 3 are expected to be completed in the next 2 years. These involve some natural language processing (NLP) algorithms as well as ML-based algorithms [14,17]. Those scans will: (1) select the right features from among the alternative features identified in the first scan; (2) disambiguate the terms; and (3) group subsequences of terms into unambiguous sub-expressions and tag them, thus deriving definite mostly-unambiguous semantics of math terms and expressions. The NLP/ML algorithms include math topic modeling, math context modeling, math document classification (into various standard areas of math), and definition-harvesting algorithms.

Specifically, to narrow down the role/meaning of a math term, it helps to know which area of mathematics the input document is in. This calls for a *math-document classifier*. Furthermore, knowing the topic, which is more specific than the area of the document, will shed even more light on the math terms. Even more targeted is the notion of *context* which, if properly formulated, will take the POM tagger a long way in narrowing down the tag choices.

In [19], Youssef defines a new notion of a math-term's context, which involves several components, such as (1) the area and topic of the term's document; (2) the document-provided definitions; (3) the topic model and theme class of the term's *neighborhood* in the document; (4) the actual mathematical expression containing the term; as well as (5) a small number of natural language sentences surrounding the mathematical expression. Parts of this context are the textual definitions and explanations of terms and notations which can be present or absent from the input document. These can also be near the target terms or far and distributed from them. The NLP/ML-based algorithms for the 2nd and 3rd scans of the tagger will model and track the term's contexts, and will harvest definitions and explanations and associate them with the target terms.

3 Semantic LATEX to CAS Translation

We have used a mathematical language parser (MLP) as an interface for the above-described first scan of the POM tagger to build syntax trees of mathematical expressions in LATEX and provide CAS translations from semantic LATEX to CAS representations. The MLP provides all functionality to interact with the results of the POM tagger. We extended the general information of each term to its CAS representation, links to definitions on the DLMF/DRMF websites, as well as the corresponding CAS websites. We also add information about domains, position of branch cuts and further explanations if necessary. Since the multiple scans of the POM tagger are still a work in progress, our CAS translation is based on the first scan (see Sect. 2). Figure 1 shows the syntax tree corresponding to the LATEX expression \sqrt[3]{x^3} + \frac{y}{2}; note that 'x' and '3' in 'x^3' are not treated (in Fig. 1) as siblings (i.e., children of '^') because the first scan of the tagger does not recognize this hierarchy (but it will be rectified in POM Scans 2 and 3). The general CAS translation process translates each node without changing the hierarchy of the tree recursively. With this approach, we are able to translate nested function calls.

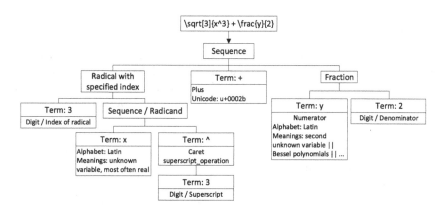

Fig. 1. Syntax tree of $\sqrt[3]{x^3} + \frac{y}{2}$ produced by the first scan of the POM tagger.

The syntax tree obtained by the first POM scan depends on the known terms of the tagger. Although the tagger's first scan tags macros if those macros' definition are provided to it, it is currently agnostic of the DLMF/DRMF macros. Therefore, as it currently stands, the first scan of the tagger extracts, but does not recognize/tag DLMF/DRMF macros as hierarchical structures, but rather treats those macros as sequences of terms. The syntax tree in Fig. 2 was created by the tagger for our Jacobi polynomial example in Sect. 1.1. The tagger extracts expressions enclosed between open and closed curly braces {...} which we refer to as *delimited balanced expressions*. The given argument is a sub-expression and produces another hierarchical tree structure.

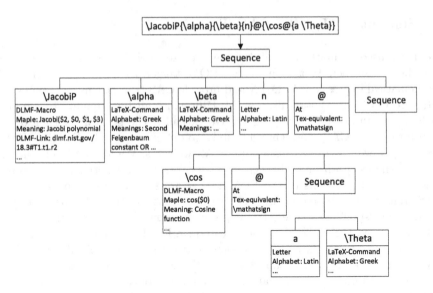

Fig. 2. Syntax tree for Jacobi polynomial expression generated by the first POM scan.

3.1 Implementation

CAS translations for DLMF/DRMF macros are stored in CSV files, to make them easy to edit. Besides that, CAS translations for Greek letters and mathematical constants are stored separately in JSON files. In addition to the DLMF/DRMF macro set, generic LaTeX also provides built-in commands for mathematical functions, such as \frac or \sqrt. CAS translations for these macros are defined in another JSON file.

Since the POM tagger assumes the existence of special formatted lexicon files to extract information for unknown commands, the CSV files containing CAS translation information has to be converted into lexicon files. Table 2 shows a part of the lexicon entry for the DLMF/DRMF macro \sin@@{z}[2]. Translations to CAS are realized by patterns with placeholders. The symbol $i indicates the i-th variable or parameter of the macro.

Table 2. A lexicon entry.

DLMF	\sin@@z
DLMF-Link	dlmf.nist.gov/4.14#E1
Maple	sin($0)
Mathematica	Sin[$0]

Our CAS translation process is structured recursively. A CAS translation of a node will be delegated to a specialized class for certain kinds of nodes. Even though our CAS translation process assumes semantic LaTeX with DLMF/DRMF macros, we sometimes allow for extra information obtained from

---

[2] The usage of multiple @ symbols in Miller's LaTeX macro set provides capability for alternative presentations, such as $\sin(z)$ and $\sin z$ for one and two @ symbols respectively.

generic LATEX expressions. For instance, we distinguish between the following cases: (1) a Latin letter is used for an elementary constant; (2) a generic LATEX command (such as the LATEX command for a Greek letter) is used for an elementary constant. In both cases, the program checks if there are known DLMF/DRMF macros to represent the constant in semantic LATEX. If so, we inform the user of the DLMF/DRMF macro for the constant, but the Latin letter or LATEX command is not translated.

There are currently only three known Latin letters where this occurs, the imaginary unit i, Euler's number e, and Catalan's constant C. If one wants to translate the Latin letter to the constant, then one needs to use the designated macro. In these three cases they are `\iunit`, `\expe` and `\CatalansConstant`. Examples of LATEX commands which may represent elementary constants are π and α which are often used to represent the ratio of a circle's circumference to its diameter, and the fine-structure constant respectively which are `\cpi` and `\finestructure`. Hence, Latin and Greek letters will be always translated as Latin and Greek letters respectively.

The program consists of two executable JAR files. One organizes the transformation from CSV files to lexicon files, while the other translates the generated syntax tree to a CAS representation. Figure 3 describes the CAS translation process. The program currently supports forward CAS translations for Maple and Mathematica.

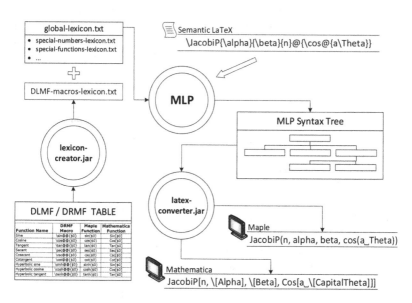

Fig. 3. Flow diagram for translation between semantic LATEX and a CAS representations. The MLP is the only interface to the POM tagger and provides all functionality for interaction with the results of the POM tagger (such as analyzing the syntax tree and extracting information from the lexicon.)

4   Maple to Semantic LaTeX Translation

Maple has its own syntax and programming language, and users interact with Maple by entering commands and expressions in Maple syntax. For example, the mathematical expression $\int_0^\infty (\pi + \sin(2x))/x^2\,dx$, would be entered in Maple as

$$\texttt{int((Pi+sin(2*x))/x\textasciicircum 2, x=0..infinity)}. \tag{1}$$

In the sequel, we will refer to Maple syntax such as the syntactically correct format (1) as (i) the 1D Maple representation. Maple also provides a (ii) 2D representation (whose internal format is similar to MATHML), and its display is similar to the LaTeX rendering of the mathematical expression. In addition, Maple uses two internal representations (iii) Maple_DAG, and (iv) Inert_Form representation. Note that, even though DAG commonly refers to the general graph theoretic/generic data structure, *directed acyclic graph*, in Maple it has become synonymous with "Maple internal data structure," whether it actually represents a DAG or not.

In our translation from Maple to semantic LaTeX, only the Maple 1D and Inert_Fo- rm representations are used. Programmatic access to the Maple kernel (its internal data structures/commands) from other programming languages such as Java or C is possible through a published application programming interface (API) called OpenMaple [8, Sect. 14.3]. The OpenMaple Java API is used in this project. Some of the functionality used includes (1) parsing a string in 1D representation and converting it to its Maple_DAG and Inert_Form representations (see below); (2) accessing elements of Maple's internal data structures; (3) performing manipulations on Maple data structures in the Maple kernel.

Mathematical expressions in Maple are internally represented as Maple_DAG representations. Figure 4 illustrates the Maple_DAG representation of the 1D Maple expression (1). The variable x is stored only once in memory, and all three occurrences of it refer to the same Maple object. This type of common subexpression reuse is the reason why Maple data structures are organized as DAGs and not as trees. In addition to mathematical expressions, Maple also has a variety of other data structures (e.g., sets, lists, arrays, vectors, matrices, tables, procedures, modules). The structure of a Maple_DAG is in the form $\boxed{Header}\boxed{Data_1}\cdots\boxed{Data_n}$. *Header* encodes both the type and

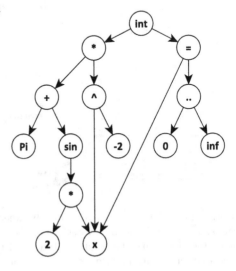

Fig. 4. Example Maple_DAG for (1).

the length n of the `Maple_DAG` and $Data_1, \ldots, Data_n$ are `Maple_DAGs` (see [8, Appendix A.3]).

For this project, another tree-like representation that closely mirrors the internal `Maple_DAG` representation (and can be accessed more easily through the OpenMaple Java API) was chosen, the `Inert_Form`. The `Inert_Form` is given by nested function calls of the form `_Inert_XXX` $(Data_1, \ldots, Data_n)$, where `XXX` is a type tag (see [8, Appendix A.3]), and $Data_1, \ldots, Data_n$ can themselves be `Inert_Forms`. In Maple, the `Inert_Form` representation can be obtained via the command `ToInert`. For example, the `Inert_Form` representation of the Maple expression (1) is

```
_Inert_FUNCTION( _Inert_NAME("Int"), _Inert_EXPSEQ(_Inert_PROD( _Inert_SUM( _Inert_NAME("Pi"),
_Inert_FUNCTION( _Inert_NAME("sin"), _Inert_EXPSEQ( _Inert_PROD(_Inert_NAME("x"),
_Inert_INTPOS(2))))), _Inert_POWER( _Inert_NAME("x"), _Inert_INTNEG(2)))
_Inert_EQUATION( _Inert_NAME("x"), _Inert_RANGE( _Inert_INTPOS(0),_Inert_NAME("infinity"))))))).
```

In order to facilitate access to the `Inert_Form` from the OpenMaple Java API, the `Inert_Form` is converted to a **nested list** representation (Fig. 5), where the first element of each (sub)-list is an `_Inert_XXX` tag. For example, the Maple equation `x=0..infinity` which contains the integration bounds (which is a sub-`Maple_DAG` of Maple expression (1)), is as follows in the **nested list** representation of the `Inert_Form`:

```
[_Inert_EQUATION, [_Inert_NAME, "x"], [_Inert_RANGE, [_Inert_INTPOS, 0], [_Inert_NAME, "infinity"]]].
```

4.1 Implementation

Our CAS translation engine enters the `1D` `Maple` representation via the Open-Maple API for Java [9] and converts the previously described `Inert_Form` to a **nested list** representation. For Maple expressions, the **nested list** has a tree structure. We have organized the backward translation in a similar fashion to the forward translation (see Sect. 3).

Since Maple automatically tries to simplify input expressions, we implemented some additional changes to prevent such simplifications and changes to the input expression. We would prefer that the representation of a translated expression remain as similar as possible to the input expression. This facilitates user comprehension, as well as the debugging process, of the CAS translation. Maple's internal representation presents obstacles when trying to keep an internal expression in the syntactical form of the input expression. For instance, Maple performs automatic (1) simplification of input expressions; (2) representation of radicals as powers with fractional exponents (e.g., `\sqrt[5]{x^3}` represented as `x^{3/5}`); (3) representation of negative terms as positive terms multiplied by `-1` (since Maple's internal structure has no primitives for negation or subtraction); and (4) representation of division by a term as a multiplication of that term raised to a negative power (since Maple's internal structure has no primitives for division).

To prevent automatic simplifications in Maple, one can enclose input expressions between single quotes '...', also known as **unevaluation quotes**. This does

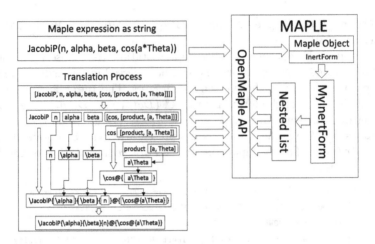

Fig. 5. The program flow diagram explains the translation from Maple to semantic LATEX. The input string is parsed into a Maple object and Maple procedures create a new internal form of the object and builds a **nested list** from this new form. The CAS translation process assembles the semantic LATEX expression by translating each element recursively.

not prevent arithmetic simplifications but does prevent all other simplifications to the input expression. For instance, if we have input `sin(Pi)+2-1`, then the output is 1; and if we have input `'sin(Pi)+2-1'`, then the output is `sin(Pi)+1`. By using unevaluation quotes, Maple does not convert a radical to a power with fractional exponents, and the internal representation remains an unevaluated `sqrt` (for square roots) or `root` (for higher order radicals). Maple automatically represents a negative term such as `-a` by a product `a*(-1)`. To resolve this we first switch the order of the terms so that constants are in front, e.g., `(-1)*a`, and then check if the leading constant is positive or negative. If it is negative, we remove the multiplication and insert a negative sign in front of the term.

Maple's rendering engine only changes negative powers to fractions if the power is a ratio of integers, otherwise it keeps the exponent representation. We only translate terms with negative integer exponents to fractions, and otherwise retain the internal exponent representation. For this purpose, we perform a preprocessing step (in Maple) that introduces a new `DIVIDE` element in the tree representation. For instance, without the `DIVIDE` element the input `(1/(x+3))^(-I)` produces `\left((3+x)^{-1}\right)^{-\iunit}`, and with the `DIVIDE` element it produces `\left(\frac{1}{3+x}\right)^{-\iunit}`.

Using the above described manipulations, a typical translated expression is very similar to the input expression. As an example, without any of the techniques above, the input expression `cos(Pi*2)/sqrt((3*beta)/4-3*I)` would be automatically simplified and changed internally, and the resulting semantic LATEX would be `2\idot(3\idot\beta+12\idot\iunit\idot(-1))^{-\frac{1}{2}}`.[3] With unevaluation quotes, the CAS translation produces

`\cos@{\cpi\idot2}\idot\left(\sqrt{\beta\idot\frac34+\iunit\idot(-3)}\right)^{-1}`.

Furthermore, with our improvements for subtractions, we translate the radicand to `\frac{3}{4}\idot\beta-3\idot\iunit`, and with the `DIVIDE` element, we translate the base with exponent `-1` as a fraction, and our translated expression is

`\frac{\cos@{2\idot\cpi}}{\sqrt{\frac{3}{4}\idot\beta-3\idot\iunit}}`,

which is very similar to the input expression.

5   Translation of the Maple/Mathematica CFSF/eCF datasets

We have developed Python tools to convert the Maple *Continued Fractions for Special Functions* (CFSF) formulae dataset [2]. This dataset is connected with the book *Handbook of Continued Fractions for Special Functions* (2008) [4] into semantic LaTeX. Using this semantic LaTeX we generate MediaWiki Wikitext for seeding in the DRMF. The Maple source for CFSF formulae is distributed in many

Table 3. Example CFSF statement

```
create( 'contfrac',
  label = "EF.exp.sfrac.01",
  booklabel = "11.1.2",
  dlmflabel = "4.9.3",
  front = 1,
  begin = [[2*z, 2-z], [z^2/6, 1]],
  general = [[(1/(4*(2*m-3)*(2*m-1)))*z^2,1]],
  function = exp,
  lhs = exp(z),
  category = "S-fraction"
):
```

.mpl files which are stored in a hierarchical directory substructure. The Maple source for CFSF formulae consists of `create` statements (e.g., Table 3) which contain a sequence of fields describing the details of the formula. The fields are: `type`, `category`, `constraints`, `begin`, `factor`, `front`, `parameters`, `booklabel`, `dlmflabel`, `function`, `lhs`, `even`, `odd`, and `general`.

For the example create statement in Table 3, we generate the semantic LaTeX:

`\expe^{z}=1+\frac{2z}{2-z}\subplus\frac{\frac{z^{2}}{6}}{1}\subplus`
`\CFK{m}{3}{\infty}@@{\frac{1}{4\left(2m-3\right)\left(2m-1\right)}z^{2}}{1}`,

which when rendered by `pdflatex` produces the formula

$$e^z = 1 + \cfrac{2z}{2-z} \,{\atop+}\, \cfrac{\frac{z^2}{6}}{1} \,{\atop+}\, \mathop{\mathrm{K}}_{m=3}^{\infty} \left(\frac{\frac{1}{4(2m-3)(2m-1)}z^2}{1} \cdot \right) \tag{2}$$

---

[3] `\idot` is our semantic LaTeX macro which represents multiplication without any corresponding presentation appearance.

The **type** field, which is the first argument of the **create** statement, represents its 0th field. (For the example in Table 3, **type=contfrac**). All fields except **category**, **parameters**, and **function** are used for conversion (although they contain potentially useful semantic information). After each field has been translated to semantic LaTeX, they are assembled together. For instance, **front** is joined with **begin**, which based on **type**, is determined to be a list of fractions joined together by **subplus** symbols. Finally **general** is merged with a **subplus**.

We operate on two external dictionaries. Dict. 1 stores every unique Maple symbol/function occurring in the CFSF dataset as well as their semantic LaTeX representations. These are stored as string arrays to denote positions of function arguments. Dict. 2 provides necessary information to convert our substructure of directories which contain the .mlp files, as well as their contents to generate sections and subsections in the produced LaTeX file.

Our translation starts with a tokenization process which searches for occurrences of key symbols/characters (e.g., mathematical operators, parentheses, spaces) within a given Maple representation and splits the string on those terms. This produces a list of tokens. We categorize into three types of tokens: (1) **normal** (operands, numbers, variables, etc.); (2) **operator** (addition, subtraction, negative sign, etc.); and (3) **function call** (those functions which are called). After tokenization, each token is parsed and translated to semantic LaTeX, and then re-assembled as follows. When encountering a **normal** token, we check that it is defined as having a translation in Dict. 1. If so, the token is swapped with the corresponding LaTeX macro. When encoutering an **operator** token, it is identified as either unary/binary, or as **enclosure** (i.e., parenthesis, square bracket, or curly brace). If **operator** is unary, the token after **operator** is used to generate the LaTeX representation. Binary **operator** is handled similarly, but instead uses preceding and following terms. If left **enclosure** is found, a flag is set until a matching **enclosure** is caught, and then the contents between matching **enclosures** are rebuilt (following the order of operations). If **function call** is encountered (listed in the Dict. 1), then we search for the corresponding delimiter. Function arguments are extracted by comparing with the Maple function (in Dict. 1), and then translated and used to replace dummy arguments. Finally, the newly built expression replaces the tokens from the original **function call** for the discovered delimiter. We translate 252 CFSF formulae from 55 files located in 10 subdirectories. This corresponds to an output semantic LaTeX file with 10 sections and 55 subsections.

We have also developed code to translate the Wolfram *Encoding Continued Fraction Knowledge* (eCF) dataset [6,16] to semantic LaTeX. We create Dict. 3, which contains a list of corresponding Mathematica functions/semantic LaTeX. An example statement from the eCF dataset is

```
ConditionalExpression[E^z==1+(2*z)/(2-z+z^2/(6*(1+Inactive[ContinuedFractionK]
[z^2/(4*(1+2*k)*(3+2*k)),1,{k,1,Infinity}])))),Element[z,Complexes]].
```

Our code produces the following semantic LaTeX

```
\expe^{z}=1+\frac{2z}{2-z+\frac{z^{2}}{6\left(1+\CFK{k}{1}{\infty}
@@{\frac{z^{2}}{4\left(1+2k\right)\left(3+2k\right)}}{1}\right)}}.
```

This produces the following rendered formula

$$e^z = 1 + \cfrac{2z}{2 - z + \cfrac{z^2}{6\left(1 + \mathop{\mathrm{K}}_{k=1}^{\infty}\left(\frac{\frac{z^2}{4(1+2k)(3+2k)}}{1}\right)\right)}}.$$

We input the eCF Mathematica dataset from a single Identities.m file and process every Mathematica expression as follows. For each Mathematica expression, (1) we identify all Mathematica function occurences; (2) extract its arguments; (3) and rebuild the corresponding semantic LaTeX expression from Dict. 3. During extraction, the program identifies the location of the function within a formula and searches until it finds a left bracket, indicating the beginning of a Mathematica function. Our splitting process is able to recognize recursive macro calls (matching fence symbols). We translate 1365 Mathematica eCF formulae.

6   Evaluation

Here, we describe our approach for validating the correctness of our mappings, as well as discuss the performance of our system obtained on a hand crafted test set.

One validation approach is to take advantage of numerical evaluation using software tools such as the DLMF Standard Reference Tables (DLMF Tables) [1], CAS, and software libraries[4]. These tools provide numerical evaluation for special functions with their own unique features. One can validate forward CAS translations by comparing numerical values in CAS to ground truth values.

Another validation approach is to use mathematical relations between different functions. For instance, if we forward translate two functions separately, one could determine if the relation between the two translated functions remains valid. One example relation is for the Jacobi elliptic functions sn, cn, dn, and the complete elliptic integral K [5, Table 22.4.3], namely $\mathrm{sn}(z + K(k), k) = \mathrm{cn}(z, k)/\mathrm{dn}(z, k)$, where $z \in \mathbb{C}$, and $k \in (0, 1)$. In the limit as $k \to 0$, this relation produces $\sin\left(z + \frac{\pi}{2}\right) = \cos z$, where $z \in \mathbb{C}$. The DLMF provides relations such as these for many special functions. An alternative relation is particularly helpful to validate CAS translations with different positions of branch cuts, namely the relation between the parabolic cylinder function U and the modified Bessel function of the second kind [5, (12.7.10)] $U(0, z) = \sqrt{z/(2\pi)}K_{1/4}(\frac{1}{4}z^2)$, where $z \in \mathbb{C}$. Note that z^2 is no longer on the principal branch of the modified Bessel function of the second kind when $\mathrm{ph}(z) \in (\frac{\pi}{2}, \pi)$, but a CAS would still compute values on the principal branch. Therefore, a CAS translation from \BesselK{\frac{1}{4}}@{\frac{1}{4}z^2} to BesselK(1/4,(1/4)*z^2) is incorrect if $\mathrm{ph}(z) \in (\frac{\pi}{2}, \pi)$, even though the equation is true in that domain. In order for the CAS to verify the formula in that domain, it must use [5, (10.34.4)]

---

[4] See for instance: http://dlmf.nist.gov/software.

for the function on the right-hand side. Other validation tests may not be able to identify a problem with this CAS translation.

One obstacle for such relations are the limitations of ever-improving CAS simplification functions. Define the formula difference, as the difference between the left- and right-hand sides of a mathematical formula. CAS simplify for the Jacobi elliptic/trigonometric relation should produce 0, but might have more difficulties with the parabolic cylinder function relation. However, CAS simplify functions work more effectively on round trip tests.

6.1   Round Trip Tests

One of the main techniques we use to validate CAS translations are round trip tests which take advantage of CAS simplification functions. Since we have developed CAS translations between semantic LaTeX ↔ Maple, round trip tests are evaluated in Maple. Maple's simplification function is called `simplify`. Two expressions are symbolically equivalent, if `simplify` returns zero for the formula difference. On the other hand, it is not possible to disprove the equivalence of the expressions when the function returns something different to zero.

Our round trip tests start either from a valid semantic LaTeX expression or from a valid Maple expression. A CAS translation from the start representation to the other representation and back again is called one cycle. A round trip reaches a fixed point, when the string representation is identical to its previous string representation. The round trip test concludes when it reaches a fixed point in both representations. Additionally, we test if the fixed point representation in Maple is symbolically equivalent to the input representation by simplifying the differences between both of these with the Maple simplify function. Since there is no mathematical equivalence tester for LaTeX expressions (neither generic nor semantic LaTeX), we manually verify LaTeX representations for our test cases by rendering the LaTeX.

As shown in Sect. 4.1, prior to backward translation, in round trip testing, there will be differences between input and output Maple representations. After adapting these changes, and assuming the functions exist in both semantic LaTeX and CAS,

Table 4. A round trip test reach a fixed point.

step	semantic LaTeX/Maple representations
0	\frac{\cos@{a\Theta}}{2}
1	(cos(a*Theta))/(2)
2	\frac{1}{2}\idot\cos@{a\idot\Theta}
3	(1)/(2)*cos(a*Theta)

the round trip test should reach a fixed point. In fact, we reached a fixed point in semantic LaTeX after one cycle and in Maple after $1\frac{1}{2}$ cycles (see Table 4 for an example) for most of the cases we tried. If the input representation is already identical to Maple's representation, then the fixed point will be reached after at most a half cycle.

One example exception is for CAS translations which introduce additional function compositions on arguments. For instance, Legendre's incomplete elliptic integrals [5, (19.2.4–7)] are defined with the amplitude ϕ in the first argument, while Maple's implementation takes the trigonometric sine of the amplitude as the first argument. For instance, one has the CAS translations `\EllIntF@{\phi}{k}` $\mapsto$ `EllipticF(sin(phi),k)`, and `\EllIntF@{\asin@{z}}{k}` $\leftarrow$ `EllipticF(z,k)`. These CAS translations produce an infinite chain of sine and inverse sine function calls. Because round trip tests prevent simplification during the translation process (see Sect. 4.1), Maple is not used to simplify the chain until the round trip test is concluded.

6.2   Summary of Evaluation Techniques

Equivalence tests for special function relations are able to verify relations in CAS as well as identify hidden problems such as differences in branch cuts and CAS limitations. We use the simplify method to test equivalences. For the relations in Sect. 6, CAS simplify for the Jacobi elliptic function example yields 0. Furthermore, a spectrum of real, complex, and complex conjugate numerical values for z and $k \in (0,1)$ the formula difference converges to zero for an increasing precision. If simplification returns something other than zero, we can test the equivalence for specific values. For the Bessel function relation, the formula difference for $z = 1+i$ converges to zero for increasing precision, but does not converge to zero if $z = -1 + i$. However, using analytic continuation [5, (10.34.4)], it does converges to zero. Clearly, the numerical evaluation test is also able to locate branch cut issues in the CAS translation. Furthermore, this provides a very powerful debugging method for our translation as well as for CAS functionality. This was demonstrated by discovering an overall sign error in DLMF equation [5, (14.5.14)].

Round trip tests are also useful for identifying syntax errors in the semantic LaTeX since the CAS translation then fails. The simplification procedure is improved for round trip tests, because it only needs to simplify similar expressions with identical function calls. However, this approach is not able to identify hidden problems that a CAS translation might need to resolve in order to be correct, if the round trip test has not reached a fixed point. Other than with the round trip test approach, we have not discovered any automated tests for backward CAS translations. We have evaluated 37 round trip test cases which produce a fixed point, similar to that given in Table 4. These use formulae from the DLMF/DRMF and produce a difference of the left- and right-hand sides equaling 0.

We have created a test dataset[5] of 4,165 semantic LaTeX formulae, extracted from the DLMF. We translated each test case to a representation in Maple and used Maple's simplify function on the formula difference to verify that the translated formulae remain valid. Our forward translation tool (Sect. 3) was able to translate 2,232 (approx. 53.59%) test cases and verify 477 of these. Preconversion improved the effectiveness of simplify and were used to convert the translated expression to a different form before simplification of the formula difference. We used conversions to exponential and hypergeometric form and expanded the translated expression. Pre-conversion increased the number of formulae verified to 662 and 1,570 test cases were translated but not verified. The remaining 1,933 test cases were not translated, because they contain

---

[5] We are planning to make the dataset available from http://drmf.wmflabs.org.

DLMF/DRMF macros without a known translation to Maple (987 cases), such as the q-hypergeometric function [5, (17.4.1)] (in 58 cases), or an error appeared during the translation or verification process (639 cases). Furthermore, 316 cases were ignored, because they did not contain enough semantic information to provide a translation or the test case was not a relation. It is interesting to note that we were able to enhance the semantics of 74 Wronskian relations by rewriting the macro so that it included the variable that derivatives are taken with respect to as a parameter. A similar semantic enhancement is possible for another 186 formulae where the potentially ambiguous prime notation "'" is used for derivatives.

Acknowledgements. We are indebted to Wikimedia Labs, the XSEDE project, Springer-Verlag, the California Institute of Technology, and Maplesoft for their contributions and continued support. We would also like to thank Eric Weisstein for supplying the Wolfram eCF dataset, Annie Cuyt, Franky Backeljauw, and Stefan Becuwe for supplying the University of Antwerp CFSF Maple dataset, and Adri Olde Daalhuis for discussions related to complex multivalued functions.

References

1. DLMF Standard Reference Tables. http://dlmftables.uantwerpen.be/. Joint project of NIST ACMD and U. Antwerp's CMA Group, Seen June 2017
2. Backeljauw, F., Cuyt, A.: Algorithm 895: a continued fractions package for special functions. Trans. Math. Softw. **36**(3), Art. 15, 20 (2009). Association for Computing Machinery
3. Cohl, H.S., Schubotz, M., McClain, M.A., Saunders, B.V., Zou, C.Y., Mohammed, A.S., Danoff, A.A.: Growing the digital repository of mathematical formulae with generic LaTeX sources. In: Kerber, M., Carette, J., Kaliszyk, C., Rabe, F., Sorge, V. (eds.) CICM 2015. LNCS, vol. 9150, pp. 280–287. Springer, Cham (2015). doi:10.1007/978-3-319-20615-8_18
4. Cuyt, A., Petersen, V.B., Verdonk, B., Waadeland, H., Jones, W.B.: Handbook of Continued Fractions for Special Functions. Springer, New York (2008). With contributions by Franky Backeljauw and Catherine Bonan-Hamada, Verified numerical output by Stefan Becuwe and Cuyt
5. Olver, F.W.J., Olde Daalhuis, A.B., Lozier, D.W., Schneider, B.I., Boisvert, R.F., Clark, C.W., Miller, B.R., Saunders, B.V. (eds.) NIST Digital Library of Mathematical Functions. http://dlmf.nist.gov/. Release 1.0.15 of 01 June 2017
6. Weisstein, E.: eCF Encoding Continued Fraction Knowledge in Computational Form. http://www.wolfram.com/broadcast/video.php?c=385&v=1342. Seen June 2017
7. Ginev, D.: LaTeXML-Plugin-MathSyntax. https://github.com/dginev/LaTeXML-Plugin-MathSyntax/. Seen June 2017
8. Bernardin, L., Chin, P., DeMarco, P., Geddes, K.O., Hare, D.E.G., Heal, K.M., Labahn, G., May, J.P., McCarron, J., Monagan, M.B., Ohashi, D., Vorkoetter, S.M.: Maple Programming Guide. Maplesoft, a division of Waterloo Maple Inc. (2016)
9. Maplesoft. OpenMaple API, Seen March 2017. https://www.maplesoft.com/support/help/Maple/view.aspx?path=OpenMaple. Since Maple 9, Seen June 2017
10. Maplesoft. Produce output suitable for LaTeX2e. http://www.maplesoft.com/support/help/Maple/view.aspx?path=latex. Since version Maple 18

11. Miller, B.R.: Drafting DLMF Content Dictionaries. Talk presented at the Open-Math Workshop of the 9th Conference on Intelligent Computer Mathematics, CICM 2016 (2016)
12. Miller, B.R.: LaTeXML: A LaTeX to XML converter. http://dlmf.nist.gov/LaTeXML/. Seen June 2017
13. Miller, B.R., Youssef, A.: Technical aspects of the digital library of mathematical functions. Ann. Math. Artif. Intell. **38**(1–3), 121–136 (2003)
14. Pagel, R., Schubotz, M.: Mathematical language processing project. In: CICM Workshops. CEUR Workshop Proceedings, vol. 1186. CEUR-WS.org (2014)
15. Wolfram Research. Generating and Importing TeX. https://reference.wolfram.com/language/tutorial/GeneratingAndImportingTeX.html
16. S. Wolfram. Computational Knowledge of Continued Fractions. http://blog.wolframalpha.com/2013/05/16/computational-knowledge-of-continued-fractions. Seen June 2017
17. Schubotz, M., Grigoriev, A., Cohl, H.S., Meuschke, N., Gipp, B., Youssef, A., Leich, M., Markl, V.: Semantification of identifiers in mathematics for better math information retrieval. In: The 39th Annual ACM Special Interest Group on Information Retrieval, Pisa, Tuscany, Italy (2016)
18. Schubotz, M., Wicke, G.: Mathoid: robust, scalable, fast and accessible math rendering for wikipedia. In: Watt, S.M., Davenport, J.H., Sexton, A.P., Sojka, P., Urban, J. (eds.) CICM 2014. LNCS, vol. 8543, pp. 224–235. Springer, Cham (2014). doi:10.1007/978-3-319-08434-3_17
19. Youssef, A.: Part-of-math tagging and applications. Submitted to the 10th Conference on Intelligent Computer Mathematics (CICM 2017), Edinburgh, Scotland, July 2017

Towards Mathematical AI via a Model of the Content and Process of Mathematical Question and Answer Dialogues

Joseph Corneli[1]($\boxtimes$), Ursula Martin[2], Dave Murray-Rust[1], and Alison Pease[3]

[1] University of Edinburgh, Edinburgh, UK
joseph.corneli@ed.ac.uk
[2] University of Oxford, Oxford, UK
[3] University of Dundee, Dundee, UK

Abstract. This paper outlines a strategy for building semantically meaningful representations and carrying out effective reasoning in technical knowledge domains such as mathematics. Our central assertion is that the semi-structured Q&A format, as used on the popular Stack Exchange network of websites, exposes domain knowledge in a form that is already reasonably close to the structured knowledge formats that computers can reason about. The knowledge in question is not only facts – but discursive, dialectical, argument for purposes of proof and pedagogy. We therefore assert that modelling the Q&A process computationally provides a route to domain understanding that is compatible with the day-to-day practices of mathematicians and students. This position is supported by a small case study that analyses one question from Mathoverflow in detail, using concepts from argumentation theory. A programme of future work, including a rigorous evaluation strategy, is then advanced.

Keywords: Q&A · Argumentation · Mathematics

1 Introduction

In this paper, we outline a computational approach to modelling mathematical dialogues, and show how it can be used to model *Q&A dialogues* in particular. We argue that a strongly empirical approach – along these lines – can support the development of robust, knowledge-rich, mathematical artificial intelligence. Mathematical dialogues convey the processes through which new mathematics is created and existing mathematics is taught. We claim that mathematical question and answer (Q&A) dialogues are a practically and theoretically important subclass. In particular, there is now a large corpus of mathematical questions, answers, and accompanying discussion available in online Q&A forums.

The Q&A forums that we consider here are "social machines" – defined by Tim Berners-Lee to be a class of systems "in which the people do the creative work and the machine does the administration" [4]. Question-and-answer

© Springer International Publishing AG 2017
H. Geuvers et al. (Eds.): CICM 2017, LNAI 10383, pp. 132–146, 2017.
DOI: 10.1007/978-3-319-62075-6_10

websites differ from other popular social machine formats, like general purpose forums, wikis, and mailing lists – with which they nevertheless share some features – in the relatively explicit semantics that they support (and require).

This has to do with both content and form. The Stack Exchange network of Q&A sites has a network-wide norm of focusing on questions whose answers are not primarily opinion-based: in other words, questions which have answers that can be considered "right" or "wrong," or that can otherwise be compared with each other in objective (as opposed to purely subjective) terms. Stack Exchange sites treat a wide range of technical and non-technical subjects, ranging from computer programming, to travel, to advice on academic careers, the internal logic of science fiction universes, and beyond. It has two specialist sites devoted to mathematics: Mathoverflow, for research-level Q&A (often dealing with new, open, conjectures, and for which background approximately equivalent to a strong mathematics degree is a minimum barrier to entry), and math.stackexchange.com, which focuses on non-research mathematics (e.g., at school, university, or postgraduate level). Whereas a mailing list, for example, would permit more open-ended discussions, the questions discussed on these websites tend to have right and wrong answers, and the discussion focuses on exposition of the correct answer (or answers).

Technical Q&A often embody knowledge about "how to" as well as "what is." In this regard, Q&A is similar to computer programming [38] – and it is no coincidence that the most popular site on the Stack Exchange subject is devoted to programming concepts. As a commentary on the medium and its affordances, it is useful to note that, by number of questions, the math.stackexchange.com website is the second-most popular site in the Stack Exchange network.[1]

Mathematical Q&A has some interesting things in common with other kinds of mathematical discussions, such as the discussions that take place among professional mathematicians working on a paper together, or among novice problem-solvers leading to personally-new insights. Both these types of dialogues have been studied extensively – in some cases using online discussions as a ready source of data [3, 31, 35, 37].

Proof dialogues often contain Q&A sub-dialogues: for example, a discussant may state "I'm sorry, I don't understand what you did in this part of the proof" or "I don't understand why this works, but it seems to." Similarly, Q&A dialogues contain elements of *mathematical argumentation*, typically sufficient to convince the querent and subsequent readers. Following Walton [42], Aberdein has outlined a range of purposes that "proof" may serve: inquiry, persuasion, information seeking, deliberation, negotiation, and debate [1]. Q&A dialogues seem to serve many similar purposes. Martin and Pease [26] developed an empirically-founded typology of questions on Mathoverflow (expanding on Mendes and Milic-Frayling's earlier study [28]). The three popular types of questions observed were "Is it true that... ?", "What is this?", and "Could I have an example please?" (we summarise this earlier work in more detail below).

---

[1] http://stackexchange.com/sites#questions.

We support our case for a strongly empirical approach to mathematical AI by building a proof-of-concept model of a Q&A dialogue, using a technique from argumentation theory [5] with suitable adaptations for the mathematics domain. We have stated the motivations for this approach elsewhere [27], and demonstrated its overall salience [32]. In brief, we show in [32] that it is possible to build meaningful computational models of proof dialogue. However, this earlier work dealt with the high-level logic of argument structure. Here we demonstrate extensions that provide a much more detailed model. We will summarise the relevant background below, and in our small proof-of-concept case study, introduce enough formalism to walk through an example in detail. The outline of the paper is as follows.

- We present a brief overview of relevant background in Sect. 2.
- Section 3 develops the main case study.
- Section 4 offers discussion and an outline of future work.

2   Background

2.1   Overview

The approach we take in this paper is grounded in a part of argumentation research called *Inference Anchoring Theory* (IAT), which was designed to model the inferential structure of dialogues, by connecting statements with their logical import [5]. In a recent paper we have described a broadly IAT-inspired theory that uses a constrained set of rules called a *dialogue game* to model mathematical discourse [32]. The specific set of rules were adapted from Lakatos's *Proofs and Refutations* [21]. The "Lakatos game" developed in [32] is a formalised approximation of the "informal logic" that people use when arguing about concepts on the way to a shared proof. The dialogue game shows which assertions are being used to support or to argue against a given conjecture, and it shows when assertions are in conflict with each other. This leads to a sociologically interesting, but rather atypical, idea of a proof as a developing set of mutually coherent statements that support a given conjecture, and that have yet to be successfully refuted. This conception of proof is at odds with the way mathematicians (and, especially, formal mathematicians) would describe proofs, i.e., that proofs are derivations from axioms by way of valid inference rules. Philosophers of mathematics have expressed doubt as to whether mathematical worldviews as different as these can be brought into alignment with each other in a routine way [39]. Nevertheless, mathematics has a logical structure, embodied in its theories and objects, which is typically not subject to debate. For instance, two numbers are either co-prime, or not. Accordingly, we have been developing a new strategy for representing mathematical discussions, in which 'The Cayley graph of group G', for example, is modelled as an object; the relationship between the proposition P and the proposition 'P is difficult to prove' is made explicit; and in which Lakatos-style conjectures, refutations, and repair are modelled. We call this framework *IAT+Content* or IATC. *Inferential structure*, like `implies`, describes statements about pieces of *mathematical content*; meta-level *reasoning*

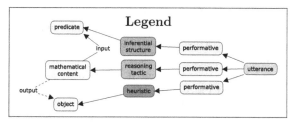

tactics, like `goal` or `auxiliary`, are used to strategise proof development; *heuristics* guide the proof or manipulate content. New nodes are brought into being in connection with IAT-style *performatives* labelled `agree`, `assert`, `challenge`, `define`, `query`, `retract`, and `suggest`. The Legend at right provides a schematic summary of the features of IATC.

While the proto-language is not complete (and not yet implemented, like the work in [32]), we hope to show that it can be used to model real-world mathematical dialogues. In the current paper, we focus on Q&A dialogues. These were summarised above; some further detail on this specific domain follows.

2.2   Q&A

The strategies used by Mathoverflow "contributors [to] communicate and collaborate to solve new mathematical 'micro-problems' online" have been studied previously [40], and a typology of collaborative acts was proposed: 1. *provide information*; 2. *clarify the question*; 3. *critique an answer*; 4. *revise an answer*; 5. *extend an answer*. The study focused on understanding, quantitatively, how these different activities contributed to answer quality. Some more specific activities within this framework are noted in an example,[2] e.g., 1→ referencing a related Q&A post, which IATC might model as an '`auxiliary`' problem; 2→ stating that the question is harder than the related post, which IATC would model with a (reversed) '`easy`' heuristic value judgement. This framework is useful as a high-level check on the completeness of IATC.

The difficulty of questions in math.stackexchange.com has been studied [24]. However, this was done, not primarily by examining the content of questions, but by devising a "competition-based" score that estimates a given question's difficulty using the estimated expertise of discussion participants (learned via a Bayesian model). In particular: "the expertise score of the best answerer is higher than that of the asker as well as all other answerers." Then, the difficulty of a question is estimated to be "higher than the expertise score of asker u_a, but lower than that of the best answerer u_b." These authors defer a detailed analysis of question content to future work.

Mathoverflow. Related work by some of us examined the production of mathematics on Mathoverflow [26]. A typology of questions was developed, as follows:

---

[2] http://mathoverflow.net/q/12732.

- **Conjecture 36%** — asks if a mathematical statement is true. May ask directly "Is it true that" or ask under what circumstances a statement is true. (This corresponds to the purpose of 'inquiry' noted by Walton.)
- **What is this 28%** — describes a mathematical object or phenomenon and asks what is known about it. (This also corresponds to 'inquiry'.)
- **Example 14%** — asks for examples of a phenomenon or an object with particular properties. (This may be 'inquiry' or 'information seeking'.)
- **Formula 5%** — ask for an explicit formula or computation technique.
- **Different proof 5%** — asks if there is an alternative to a known proof. In particular, since our sample concerns the field of group theory, a number of questions concern whether a certain result can be proved without recourse to the classification of finite simple groups.
- **Reference 4%** — asks for a reference for something the questioner believes to be already documented in the literature.
- **Perplexed 3%** — ask for help in understanding a phenomenon or difficulty. A typical question in this area might concern why accounts from two different sources (for example Wikipedia and a published paper) seem to contradict each other.
- **Motivation 3%** — asks for motivation or background. A typical question might ask why something is true or interesting, or has been approached historically in a particular way.
- **Other 2%** — closed by moderators as out of scope, duplicates, etc.

Answers are also examined, although in less detail. Responses typically present information known to the respondent, and readily checked by other users, but not necessarily assumed to be known by them. Some specific findings:

- **Existing research literature 56%** — over half of the questions in the sample refer to existing literature
- **Errors 37%** — many questions (and answers) contain errors; these are acknowledged politely, and corrected when pointed out.
- **Examples 34%** — the use of specific examples gives some evidence of broadly "Lakatosian" reasoning (i.e., per [21]).

3   Case Study

In this section we will use the IATC formalism to analyse one example Q&A dialogue in detail.[3] We quote the text of this dialogue verbatim, and present the analysis graphically. We selected one of the questions from Mathoverflow that was part of the sample described above: the example was classed as an "Is it true that. . . ?" question; examples and references are supplied. As they appear on the site, both the specific question and the top-rated answer are quite succinct. Below, we will replay the conversation in order. As we will see, most of the interesting argumentation takes place in comments.

---

[3] http://mathoverflow.net/q/34044.

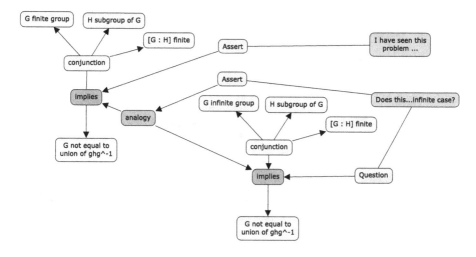

Fig. 1. Original question, diagrammed

(Original question, 18:05) I have seen this problem, that if G is a finite group and H is a proper subgroup of G with finite index then $G \neq \bigcup_{g \in G} ghg^{-1}$. Does this remain true for the infinite case also. [$\to$ Fig. 1]

The first follow-up comment to be submitted observes that this question doesn't quite make sense as written, and suggests a correction.

(First comment on question, 18:15) There's something I don't understand here: do you perhaps mean gHg^{-1} instead of ghg^{-1}? [$\to$ Fig. 2]

Meanwhile, it seems an answer was already being composed, since the following text appeared on the site one minute after the above clarification.[4]

(Answer, 18:16) Not in general. Every matrix in $\mathrm{GL}_2(\mathbf{C})$ is conjugate to an invertible upper triangular matrix (use eigenvectors), and the invertible upper triangular matrices are a proper subgroup. [$\to$ Fig. 3]

Even though an answer has been given, suggestions for fine-tuning the question continue in the comments.

(Second comment on question, 18:20) Yes, the statement is out of focus: gHg^{-1} is intended (and "infinite index case"). The natural starting point is to ask whether the proof for finite index breaks down. [$\to$ Fig. 4]

Quite a lot happens in the foregoing short comment. A change in the problem's set of hypotheses is suggested. The analogy to the known "inspiring" theorem for

---

[4] At this point, the discussion becomes multi-threaded, since comments can now attach to the answer as well.

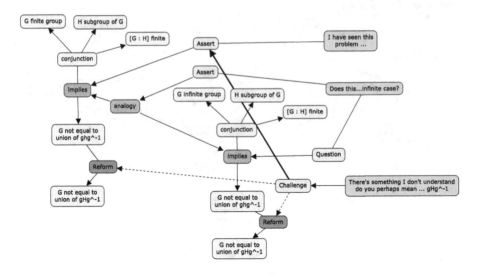

Fig. 2. First comment on question, diagrammed

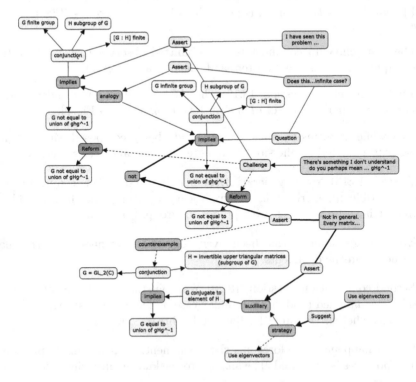

Fig. 3. Answer, diagrammed

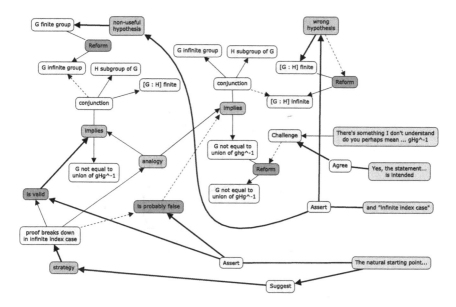

Fig. 4. Second comment on question, diagrammed

finite groups is deemed not particularly relevant, and its hypotheses are changed as well. This then suggests a strategy for proving the (revised) problem. (*NB.*, to save room, in the diagram that follows, we have elided some of the structure that accumulated earlier: the earlier nodes and links are still assumed.)

In the following comment, both the foregoing refinements and the earlier proposed answer are taken into account.

> (Third comment on question, 18:24) If G is a finite group then all its subgroups have finite index. What the statement should say is that if H is a proper finite index subset of G then $G \neq \cup_{g \in G} gHg^{-1}$ (the case of infinite G readily reduces to the case of finite G). As Keith shows, this is not always true for subgroups of infinite index. [$\rightarrow$ Fig. 5]

Here, the earlier assertion that $[G : H]$ is the "wrong hypothesis" is challenged. Essentially, this comment is looking for the most precise way to phrase the problem statement. "$[G : H]$ finite" is not wrong, but necessary if we want the implication to hold. The counterexample of invertible upper triangular matrices – "Keith's counterexample", diagrammed in Fig. 3 – does indeed have infinite index in $GL_2(\mathbf{C})$.[5] It is not, therefore, precisely a counterexample to the three-part conjunction in that diagram that it appears to refute; it does

---

[5] Intuitively, upper-triangular 2×2 matrices have one element that is zero, so the subgroup has one codimension in $GL_2(\mathbf{C})$, namely, a copy of $\mathbf{C}$. The fact that the index is infinite follows (but an algebraic proof is also straightforward). For an example of an infinite group and a subgroup with finite index, consider $\mathbf{Z}$ and $2\mathbf{Z}$: in this case, the group is equal to the union of cosets.

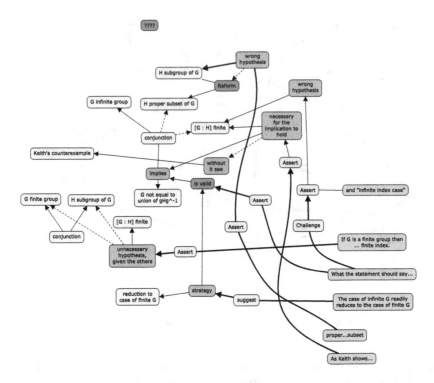

Fig. 5. Third comment on question, diagrammed

serve as a counterexample to the revised three-part conjunction in Fig. 4. One should keep in mind that the statement "not in general" that prefaces the answer was addressed not to the specific conjunction in Fig. 3, but instead to the OP's considerably more vague question "Does this remain true for the infinite case also?" Once the question has been clarified by other contributors, the logic of the answer works.

Subsequent to this, further terminological issues arise in comments on the answer, which again have to do with understanding exactly what is being asked, e.g., adding another condition of "discreteness" to the conjunction, for an answer with an even more "finite feel." New examples are proposed, both with reference to the literature and by straightforward adaptation of the answer already presented. In addition, four alternative answers are supplied, without attracting further comment (but with argumentation provided "in advance", so to speak). We will not draw diagrams for this material, because the illustrative presentation above is sufficient for our current purposes.

4   Discussion and Future Work

The case study that was examined above shows both the basic promise of the argument-theoretic approach to modelling mathematics, and some of the difficulties that would have to be overcome in 'scaling up' this approach. Bundy argues that the right representation is the key to successful reasoning [6, p. 16]. While both representation and reasoning are crucial (and, for 'functional inference', it is important to be strategic about representations *of* reasoning) in a material sense, the logically-prior step is that of building the representation. One alternative to hand-coding is to search for catalogues of existing data, and more specifically, of reasoning, that have already been represented in some preliminary and readily digestible form. Learning from text was a key part of IBM's approach in building the version of Watson that competed in *Jeopardy* [11]. The Austin-based company, Cycorp, known for its large hand-coded AI system, also emphasises learning from documents in more recent work [34]. More broadly, "Knowledge Extraction from Text" is a well-known domain of computing research (with workshops running since 2013). The requirements for knowledge extraction from mathematical text, in particular, are being worked out in specialist efforts in linguistics and NLP [8,10,13] (and see in particular the survey in [14]).

Issues associated with mining Wikipedia and scientific literature have been explored (e.g., [7,16,17]) with successful scientific and technical proofs-of-concept at various scales. The technical issues associated with mining mathematical literature are increasingly well-understood [29] – and implementation work is ongoing.[6] *Argument mining* is, however, a relatively new area [22,33]. In the current state of the art, discourse structure may have to be laboriously hand-coded.[7] We may be aided in our specific pursuit by the fact that much of mathematics is relatively "formulaic." For example, the first 100 most frequent schematic constructions (like "let X be a Y") were shown to cover half of the sentences on the detailed but mathematically informal ProofWiki website [18].

Even so, as we've seen in our case study, modelling mathematical arguments is far from a trivial task. The initially quite simple language of '`implies`' and '`analogy`' from Fig. 1 is complemented by a range of much more complex relations in Fig. 5, like '`necessary for the implication to hold`'. The 'Reform' relation has been applied to individual pieces of mathematical content, but in some cases the relevant transformations would have to happen on the graph of statements, for example, if we were to specify the '`analogy`' between two problem statements; reasoning from analogy can be complicated [25,36]. The precise representations need to be worked out; and, as indicated above, we also want our representations to be capable of simulating the reasoning evolved in an effective manner.

Looking to the future, given a suitably-represented knowledge base of mathematical facts from whatever source, one interesting line for research (with a Q&A feel) would build on the work of Nuamah et al. [30], who describe a strategy for automatically assembling the answers to queries when the answers are not directly stored in the database. As a simple example, it may be the case that there is no prerecorded answer to the following question:

---

[6] https://www.authorea.com/users/5713/articles/51708-understanding-a-dataset-arxiv-org/_show_article.

[7] https://research.googleblog.com/2017/05/coarse-discourse-dataset-for.html.

Does the country x that has the highest GDP per capita (GDP/c) out of all countries in South America have a higher GDP/c than the country y that has the highest GDP/c out of all countries in Africa?

Nevertheless the answer may be computed from information that is available in the database (namely, GDP/c for all countries, together with the association of countries to continents). We assert that at a high level the logic of 'functional inference from heterogenous data' would be similar if the data was not CIA Fact Book-style, but, instead, mathematical facts – or, indeed, facts about mathematical arguments.

Broadly, the proposal that we suggest pursues the slow refinement of mathematical knowledge from knowledge about mathematical arguments. We can compare and contrast this with a famous proposal in the computer mathematics community, the QED manifesto [2]. This proposed "a project to build a computer system that effectively represents all important mathematical knowledge and techniques." We agree with this general aim. However, the QED manifesto relied on the idea of "the use of strict formality in the internal representation of knowledge and the use of mechanical methods to check proofs of the correctness of all entries in the system." If relied on as the only method, formal mathematics may be a premature optimisation. More specifically, before achieving full formality, it may be necessary to be 'capable of being in uncertainties' [20, p. 193]. Later reassessments of the QED proposal [15,43] have had to deal with the fact that, by in large, it has not worked out as hoped.

In this paper, we have been inspired by the observation that Q&A is *both* a useful source *of* explicitly represented reasoning, *and* a useful (i.e., 'effective') modality *for* developing additional explicit reasonings. Q&A is a popular way for humans to learn from each other – including, in particular, about technical subjects like mathematics and computer programming. There are large existing 'traces' of Q&A dialogues available online, and many users actively engaging with these dialogues on a daily basis (both as querents and respondents). Q&A dialogues are, accordingly, a likely source of explicit knowledge – and they are, also, if our ansatz is correct, a potential modality for automated knowledge-building that could realise Turing's vision of machines that 'converse with each other to sharpen their wits' [41]. Naturally, dialogues between humans and automated agents/agencies would be a potential application. Systems like this could support activities ranging from automatic tutoring to mixed initiative proof and program-construction.

Argumentation techniques for agent research are surveyed in [9]. This work should be compared with Ganesalingam and Gowers's natural-language generating automated problem solver [12]. The kinds of natural language that are employed in Q&A dialogues is quite different from that employed in the textbook problems that are the focus of [12]. Nevertheless, at the level our proof-of-concept illustration above, we seem to have a good handle on the semantics of mathematical dialogues, and we should be able to support textbook reasoning as a special case. It should also be possible to map dialogue semantics to a theorem proving system (an LCF-inspired system like the one used by Ganesalingam and Gowers, would be one starting point but others should be considered as well).

Lastly, to evaluate systems working in this area – whether driven by argumentation, agents, theorem proving, simple machine learning heuristics, some combination, or by some other approach entirely – we propose the simple knowledge-based computational benchmarking task SEMATCH, which is defined as follows. This challenge problem requires a system to match existing *questions* and *answers* selected from the Stack Exchange network. This can be solved in suitably-blinded forward and backward directions (Q↦A or A↦Q); that is, the program that is being tested will be presented with a sample of questions and answers, and will not be told which question matches which answer: it will then try to recover that information by reasoning about the sample's content. Accordingly, SEMATCH can be applied to routinely evaluate heuristics, without necessarily requiring a system that is capable of generating new answers or new questions. As a benchmarking problem for programs that reason about natural language, one could compare SEMATCH with the Winograd Schema Challenge [23], which is similarly open-ended as to methods of solution. However, the Winograd Schema Challenge currently requires expert intervention to generate new test questions, which follow a certain prescribed form. In the case of SEMATCH, a large corpus of ground-truthed data exists. Additional benchmarks related to the same ground-truthed data can be straightforwardly devised, e.g., to correctly sort the answers to a given question in order of empirical user ratings, based on their contents. Ultimately, after workouts with evaluation metrics like this, along with generative experiments, a system may be devised that can answer specific sets of domain problems correctly, and have its answers validated by human experts.

Acknowledgements. Martin and Corneli were support by Martin's EPSRC fellowship award "The Social Machine of Mathematics" (EP/K040251/1); Murray-Rust was supported by "SOCIAM - the theory and practice of Social Machines" (EP/J017728/2).

References

1. Aberdein, A.: The informal logic of mathematical proof. In: van Kerkhove, B., van Bendegem, J.P., (eds.) Perspectives on Mathematical Practices: Bringing Together Philosophy of Mathematics, Sociology of Mathematics, and Mathematics Education. Logic, Epistemology, and the Unity of Science, vol. 5, pp. 135–151. Springer, Netherlands (2007)
2. Anonymous: the QED manifesto. In: Bundy, A. (ed.) CADE 1994. LNCS(LNAI), vol. 814, pp. 238–251. Springer, Heidelberg (1994). doi:10.1007/3-540-58156-1_17
3. Barany, M.: '[B]ut this is blog maths and we're free to make up conventions as we go along': Polymath1 and the modalities of 'massively collaborative mathematics'. In: Proceedings of the 6th International Symposium on Wikis and Open Collaboration. ACM (2010)
4. Berners-Lee, T., Fischetti, M.: Weaving the Web: The original design and ultimate destiny of the World Wide Web by its inventor. Harper Information (2000)

5. Budzynska, K., Janier, M., Reed, C., Saint-Dizier, P., Stede, M., Yaskorska, O.: A model for processing illocutionary structures and argumentation in debates. In: Proceedings of the Ninth International Conference on Language Resources and Evaluation (LREC 2014), Reykjavik, Iceland, 26–31 May 2014, pp. 917–924 (2014)
6. Bundy, A.: The interaction of representation and reasoning. Proc. Roy. Soc. Lond. A: Math. Phys. Eng. Sci. **469**(2157) (2013)
7. Buscaldi, D., Rosso, P.: Mining knowledge from Wikipedia for the question answering task. In: Proceedings of the International Conference on Language Resources and Evaluation, pp. 727–730 (2006)
8. Caprotti, O., Saludes, J.: The GF mathematical grammar library: from openmath to natural languages. In: Joint Proceedings of the 24th Workshop on OpenMath and the 7th Workshop on Mathematical User Interfaces (MathUI), p. 49. Citeseer (2012)
9. Carrera, Á., Iglesias, C.A.: A systematic review of argumentation techniques for multi-agent systems research. Artif. Intell. Rev. **44**(4), 509–535 (2015)
10. Cramer, M., Koepke, P., Schröder, B.: Parsing and disambiguation of symbolic mathematics in the naproche system. In: Davenport, J.H., Farmer, W.M., Urban, J., Rabe, F. (eds.) CICM 2011. LNCS, vol. 6824, pp. 180–195. Springer, Heidelberg (2011). doi:10.1007/978-3-642-22673-1_13
11. Ferrucci, D., et al.: Building Watson: an overview of the DeepQA project. AI Mag. **31**(3), 59–79 (2010)
12. Ganesalingam, M., Gowers, W.: A fully automatic theorem prover with human-style output. J. Autom. Reason, 1–39 (2016)
13. Ganesalingam, M.: The Language of Mathematics. Springer, Heidelberg (2013)
14. Ginev, D.: The structure of mathematical expressions. Master's thesis, Jacobs University, Bremen, Germany (2011)
15. Harrison, J., Urban, J., Wiedijk, F.: Preface: Twenty years of the QED manifesto. J. Formalized Reason. **9**(1), 1–2 (2016)
16. Hu, Y., Wan, X.: Mining and Analyzing the Future Works in Scientific Articles. CoRR abs/1507.02140 (2015)
17. Juršič, M., Cestnik, B., Urbančič, T., Lavrač, N.: Cross-domain literature mining: finding bridging concepts with crossbee. In: Proceedings of the 3rd International Conference on Computational Creativity, pp. 33–40 (2012)
18. Kaliszyk, C., Urban, J., Vyskočil, J., Geuvers, H.: Developing corpus-based translation methods between informal and formal mathematics [Poster of [19]]. http://cl-informatik.uibk.ac.at/cek/docs/14/ckjuvhg-cicm14-poster.pdf
19. Kaliszyk, C., Urban, J., Vyskočil, J., Geuvers, H.: Developing corpus-based translation methods between informal and formal mathematics: project description. In: Watt, S.M., Davenport, J.H., Sexton, A.P., Sojka, P., Urban, J. (eds.) CICM 2014. LNCS, vol. 8543, pp. 435–439. Springer, Cham (2014). doi:10.1007/978-3-319-08434-3_34
20. Keats, J.: To George and Tom Keats. In: Rollins, H.E. (ed.) The Letters of John Keats, vol. 1, pp. 191–194. Cambridge University Press, Cambridge (1958)
21. Lakatos, I.: Proofs and Refutations: The Logic of Mathematical Discovery. Cambridge University Press, Cambridge ([1976] 2015)
22. Lawrence, J., Reed, C., Allen, C., McAlister, S., Ravenscroft, A., Bourget, D.: Mining arguments from 19th century philosophical texts using topic based modelling. In: Proceedings of the First Workshop on Argumentation Mining, pp. 79–87. Citeseer (2014)

23. Levesque, H., Davis, E., Morgenstern, L.: The winograd schema challenge. In: Brewka, G., Eiter, T., McIlraith, S.A. (eds.) Proceedings of the Thirteenth International Conference on the Principles of Knowledge Representation and Reasoning. AAAI Press (2012)

24. Liu, J., Wang, Q., Lin, C.Y., Hon, H.W.: Question difficulty estimation in community question answering services. In: Proceedings of the 2013 Conference on Empirical Methods in Natural Language Processing, pp. 85–90. Association for Computational Linguistics (2013)

25. Macagno, F., Walton, D.: Argument from analogy in law, the classical tradition, and recent theories. Philos. Rhetoric **42**(2), 154–182 (2009)

26. Martin, U., Pease, A.: What does mathoverflow tell us about the production of mathematics? In: SOHUMAN, 2nd International Workshop on Social Media for Crowdsourcing and Human Computation, at ACM Web Science 1, Paris, May 2013

27. Martin, U., Pease, A., Corneli, J.: Bootstrapping the next generation of mathematical social machines. In: Kuper, L., Atkey, B. (eds.) Off the Beaten Track Workshop at POPL, UPMC Paris, 21 January 2017. ACM (2017)

28. Mendes Rodrigues, E., Milic-Frayling, N.: Socializing or knowledge sharing?: characterizing social intent in community question answering. In: Proceedings of the 18th ACM Conference on Information and Knowledge Management, pp. 1127–1136. ACM (2009)

29. Miller, B.R.: Strategies for Parallel Markup. CoRR abs/1507.00524 (2015)

30. Nuamah, K., Bundy, A., Lucas, C.: Functional inferences over heterogeneous data. In: Ortiz, M., Schlobach, S. (eds.) RR 2016. LNCS, vol. 9898, pp. 159–166. Springer, Cham (2016). doi:10.1007/978-3-319-45276-0_12

31. Pease, A., Martin, U.: Seventy four minutes of mathematics: An analysis of the third Mini-Polymath project. In: Proceedings of AISB/IACAP 2012, Symposium on Mathematical Practice and Cognition II (2012)

32. Pease, A., Lawrence, J., Budzynska, K., Corneli, J., Reed, C.: Lakatos-style collaborative mathematics through dialectical, structured and abstract argumentation. Artif. Intell. **246**, 181–219 (2017)

33. Peldszus, A., Stede, M.: From argument diagrams to argumentation mining in texts: A survey. Int. J. Cogn. Inf. Nat. Intell. (IJCINI) **7**(1), 1–31 (2013)

34. Schneider, D., Witbrock, M.J.: Semantic construction grammar: bridging the NL/Logic divide. In: Proceedings of the 24th International Conference on World Wide Web, pp. 673–678. ACM (2015)

35. Schoenfeld, A.H.: Mathematical Problem Solving. Academic Press (1985)

36. Sowa, J.F., Majumdar, A.K.: Analogical reasoning. In: Ganter, B., Moor, A., Lex, W. (eds.) ICCS-ConceptStruct 2003. LNCS, vol. 2746, pp. 16–36. Springer, Heidelberg (2003). doi:10.1007/978-3-540-45091-7_2

37. Stahl, G.: Group Cognition: Computer Support for Building Collaborative Knowledge. MIT Press, Cambridge (2006)

38. Sussman, G.J.: Why programming is a good medium for expressing poorly understood and sloppily formulated ideas. In: OOPSLA 2005: Companion to the 20th Annual ACM SIGPLAN Conference on Object-Oriented Programming, Systems, Languages, and Applications, p. 6. ACM (2005)

39. Tanswell, F.: A problem with the dependence of informal proofs on formal proofs. Philosophia Mathematica **23**(3), 295 (2015)

40. Tausczik, Y.R., Kittur, A., Kraut, R.E.: Collaborative problem solving: a study of mathoverflow. In: Proceedings of the 17th ACM Conference on Computer Supported Cooperative Work & Social Computing, CSCW 2014, pp. 355–367. ACM, New York (2014)
41. Turing, A.M.: Intelligent machinery, a heretical theory. Philosophia Math. 4(3), 256–260 ([1951] 1996)
42. Walton, D.: How can logic best be applied to arguments? Logic J. IGPL 5(4), 603–614 (1997)
43. Wiedijk, F.: The QED manifesto revisited. Stud. Logic, Grammar Rhetoric 10(23), 121–133 (2007)

Theory Morphisms in Church's Type Theory with Quotation and Evaluation

William M. Farmer[(✉)]

Computing and Software, McMaster University, Hamilton, Canada
wmfarmer@mcmaster.ca
http://imps.mcmaster.ca/wmfarmer

Abstract. CTT$_{qe}$ is a version of Church's type theory with global quotation and evaluation operators that is engineered to reason about the interplay of syntax and semantics and to formalize syntax-based mathematical algorithms. CTT$_{uqe}$ is a variant of CTT$_{qe}$ that admits undefined expressions, partial functions, and multiple base types of individuals. It is better suited than CTT$_{qe}$ as a logic for building networks of theories connected by theory morphisms. This paper presents the syntax and semantics of CTT$_{uqe}$, defines a notion of a theory morphism from one CTT$_{uqe}$ theory to another, and gives two simple examples involving monoids that illustrate the use of theory morphisms in CTT$_{uqe}$.

1 Introduction

A *syntax-based mathematical algorithm (SBMA)*, such as a symbolic differentiation algorithm, manipulates mathematical expressions in a mathematically meaningful way. Reasoning about SBMAs requires reasoning about the relationship between how the expressions are manipulated and what the manipulations mean mathematically. We argue in [6] that a logic with quotation and evaluation would provide a global infrastructure for formalizing SBMAs and reasoning about the interplay of syntax and semantics that is embodied in them.

Quotation is a mechanism for referring to a syntactic value (e.g., a syntax tree) that represents the syntactic structure of an expression, while *evaluation* is a mechanism for referring to the value of the expression that a syntactic value represents. Incorporating quotation and evaluation into a traditional logic like first-order logic or simple type theory is tricky; there are several challenging problems that the logic engineer must overcome [6,7]. CTT$_{qe}$ [7,8] is a version of Church's type theory with global quotation and evaluation operators inspired by the quote and eval operators in the Lisp programming language. We show in [7] that formula schemas and meaning formulas for SBMAs can be expressed in CTT$_{qe}$ using quotation and evaluation and that such schemas and meaning formulas can be instantiated and proved within the proof system for CTT$_{qe}$.

The *little theories method* [9] is an approach for understanding and organizing mathematical knowledge as a *theory graph* [12] consisting of axiomatic *theories* as

---

This research was supported by NSERC.

H. Geuvers et al. (Eds.): CICM 2017, LNAI 10383, pp. 147–162, 2017.
DOI: 10.1007/978-3-319-62075-6_11

nodes and *theory morphisms*[1] as directed edges. A theory consists of a *language* of expressions that denote mathematical values and a set of *axioms* that express in the language assumptions about the values. A theory morphism is a meaning-preserving mapping from the formulas of one theory to the formulas of another theory. Theory morphisms serve as information conduits that enable definitions and theorems to be passed from an abstract theory to many other more concrete theories.

A *biform theory* [2] is a combination of an axiomatic theory and an algorithmic theory (a collection of algorithms that perform symbolic computations). It consists of a *language* L generated from a set of *symbols*, a set of *transformers*, and a set of *axioms*. The expressions of L denote mathematical values that include syntactic values representing the expressions of L. The transformers are SBMAs and other algorithms that implement functions on the expressions of L and are represented by symbols of L. The axioms are formulas of L that express properties about the symbols and transformers of the biform theory. Unlike traditional logics, CTT_{qe} is well suited for formalizing biform theories. Can the little theories method be applied to biform theories formalized in CTT_{qe}? This would require a definition of a theory morphism for CTT_{qe} theories.

Defining a notion of a theory morphism in a logic with quotation is not as straightforward as in a logic without quotation due to the following problem:

Constant Interpretation Problem. Let T_1 and T_2 be theories in a logic with a quotation operator $\ulcorner \cdot \urcorner$. If a theory morphism Φ from T_1 to T_2 interprets two distinct constants c and c' in T_1 by a single constant d in T_2, then Φ would map the true formula $\ulcorner c \urcorner \neq \ulcorner c' \urcorner$ of T_1 to the false formula $\ulcorner d \urcorner \neq \ulcorner d \urcorner$ of T_2, and hence Φ would not be meaning preserving. Similarly, if Φ interprets c as an expression e in T_2 that is not a constant, then Φ would map a true formula like $\text{is-constant}(\ulcorner c \urcorner)$ to the false formula $\text{is-constant}(\ulcorner e \urcorner)$.

This paper defines a notion of a theory morphism that overcomes this problem in CTT_{uqe}, a variant of CTT_{qe} that admits undefined expressions, partial functions, and multiple base types of individuals. CTT_{uqe} merges the machinery for quotation and evaluation found in CTT_{qe} [7] with the machinery for undefinedness found in $\mathcal{Q}_0^{\text{u}}$ [5]. Like CTT_{qe} and $\mathcal{Q}_0^{\text{u}}$, CTT_{uqe} is based on $\mathcal{Q}_0$ [1], Peter Andrews' elegant version of Church's type theory. See [7] for references related to CTT_{uqe}.

CTT_{uqe} is better suited than CTT_{qe} as a logic for the little theories method for two reasons. First, it is often convenient for a theory morphism from T_1 to T_2 to interpret different kinds of values by values of different types. Since CTT_{qe} contains only one base type of individuals, ι, all individuals in a theory T_1 must be interpreted by values of the same type in T_2. Allowing multiple base types of individuals in CTT_{uqe} eliminates this restriction. Second, it is often useful to interpret a type α in T_1 by a subset of the denotation of a type β in T_2. As shown in [3], this naturally leads to partial functions on the type β. CTT_{uqe} has

---

[1] Theory morphisms are also known as *immersions, realizations, theory interpretations, translations,* and *views.*

built-in support for partial functions and undefinedness based on the traditional approach to undefinedness [4]; CTT_{qe} has no such built-in support.[2]

The rest of the paper is organized as follows. The syntax and semantics of CTT_{uqe} are presented in Sects. 2 and 3. The notion of a theory morphism in CTT_{uqe} is defined in Sect. 4. Section 5 contains two simple examples of theory morphisms in CTT_{uqe} involving monoids. The paper concludes in Sect. 6 with a summary of the paper's results and some brief remarks about constructing theory morphisms in an implementation of CTT_{uqe} and about future work.

The syntax and semantics of CTT_{uqe} are presented as briefly as possible. The reader should consult [5,7] for a more in-depth discussion on the ideas underlying the syntax and semantics in CTT_{uqe}. Due to limited space, a proof system is not given in this paper for CTT_{uqe}. A proof system for CTT_{uqe} can be straightforwardly derived by merging the proof systems for CTT_{qe} [7] and Q_0^u [5].

2   Syntax

The syntax of CTT_{uqe} is the same as the syntax of CTT_{qe} [7] except that (1) the types include denumerably many base types of individuals instead of just the single ι type, (2) the expressions include conditional expressions, and (3) the logical constants include constants for definite description and exclude is-expr$_{\epsilon \to o}$— which we will see is not needed since all constructions are "proper" in CTT_{uqe}.

2.1   Types

Let $\mathcal{B}$ be a denumerable set of symbols that contains o and ϵ. A *type* of CTT_{uqe} is a string of symbols defined inductively by the following formation rules:

1. *Base type:* If $\alpha \in \mathcal{B}$, then α is a type.
2. *Function type:* If α and β are types, then $(\alpha \to \beta)$ is a type.

Let $\mathcal{T}$ denote the set of types of CTT_{uqe}. o and ϵ are the *logical base types* of CTT_{uqe}. $\alpha, \beta, \gamma, \ldots$ are syntactic variables ranging over types. When there is no loss of meaning, matching pairs of parentheses in types may be omitted. We assume that function type formation associates to the right so that a type of the form $(\alpha \to (\beta \to \gamma))$ may be written as $\alpha \to \beta \to \gamma$.

2.2   Expressions

A *typed symbol* is a symbol with a subscript from $\mathcal{T}$. Let $\mathcal{V}$ be a set of typed symbols such that $\mathcal{V}$ contains denumerably many typed symbols with subscript α for each $\alpha \in \mathcal{T}$. A *variable of type α* of CTT_{uqe} is a member of $\mathcal{V}$ with subscript α.

---

[2] A logic without support for partial functions and undefinedness—such as CTT_{qe} or the logic of HOL [10]—can interpret α by a type β' that is isomorphic to a subset of β. However, this approach is more complicated and farther from standard mathematics practice than interpreting α directly by a subset of β.

$\mathbf{f}_\alpha, \mathbf{g}_\alpha, \mathbf{h}_\alpha, \mathbf{u}_\alpha, \mathbf{v}_\alpha, \mathbf{w}_\alpha, \mathbf{x}_\alpha, \mathbf{y}_\alpha, \mathbf{z}_\alpha, \ldots$ are syntactic variables ranging over variables of type α. We will assume that $f_\alpha, g_\alpha, h_\alpha, u_\alpha, v_\alpha, w_\alpha, x_\alpha, y_\alpha, z_\alpha, \ldots$ are actual variables of type α of $\mathrm{CTT}_{\mathrm{uqe}}$.

Let $\mathcal{C}$ be a set of typed symbols disjoint from $\mathcal{V}$. A *constant of type* α of $\mathrm{CTT}_{\mathrm{uqe}}$ is a member of $\mathcal{C}$ with subscript α. $\mathcal{C}$ includes the following *logical constants* of $\mathrm{CTT}_{\mathrm{uqe}}$: $=_{\alpha \to \alpha \to o}$, $\iota_{(\beta \to o) \to \beta}$, is-var$_{\epsilon \to o}$, is-var$^\alpha_{\epsilon \to o}$, is-con$_{\epsilon \to o}$, is-con$^\alpha_{\epsilon \to o}$, app$_{\epsilon \to \epsilon \to \epsilon}$, abs$_{\epsilon \to \epsilon \to \epsilon}$, cond$_{\epsilon \to \epsilon \to \epsilon \to \epsilon}$, quo$_{\epsilon \to \epsilon}$, is-expr$^\alpha_{\epsilon \to o}$, $\sqsubset_{\epsilon \to \epsilon \to o}$, and is-free-in$_{\epsilon \to \epsilon \to o}$ for all $\alpha, \beta \in \mathcal{T}$ with $\beta \neq o$. $\mathbf{c}_\alpha, \mathbf{d}_\alpha, \ldots$ are syntactic variables ranging over constants of type α.

An *expression of type* α of $\mathrm{CTT}_{\mathrm{uqe}}$ is a string of symbols defined inductively by the formation rules below. $\mathbf{A}_\alpha, \mathbf{B}_\alpha, \mathbf{C}_\alpha, \ldots$ are syntactic variables ranging over expressions of type α. An expression is *eval-free* if it is constructed using just the first six formation rules.

1. *Variable:* $\mathbf{x}_\alpha$ is an expression of type α.
2. *Constant:* $\mathbf{c}_\alpha$ is an expression of type α.
3. *Function application:* $(\mathbf{F}_{\alpha \to \beta} \, \mathbf{A}_\alpha)$ is an expression of type β.
4. *Function abstraction:* $(\lambda \, \mathbf{x}_\alpha \, . \, \mathbf{B}_\beta)$ is an expression of type $\alpha \to \beta$.
5. *Conditional:* $(\text{if } \mathbf{A}_o \, \mathbf{B}_\alpha \, \mathbf{C}_\alpha)$ is an expression of type α.
6. *Quotation:* $\ulcorner \mathbf{A}_\alpha \urcorner$ is an expression of type ϵ if $\mathbf{A}_\alpha$ is eval-free.
7. *Evaluation:* $\llbracket \mathbf{A}_\epsilon \rrbracket_{\mathbf{B}_\beta}$ is an expression of type β.

The purpose of the second argument $\mathbf{B}_\beta$ in an evaluation $\llbracket \mathbf{A}_\epsilon \rrbracket_{\mathbf{B}_\beta}$ is to establish the type of the evaluation.[3] A *formula* is an expression of type o. A *predicate* is an expression of a type of the form $\alpha \to o$. When there is no loss of meaning, matching pairs of parentheses in expressions may be omitted. We assume that function application formation associates to the left so that an expression of the form $((\mathbf{G}_{\alpha \to \beta \to \gamma} \, \mathbf{A}_\alpha) \, \mathbf{B}_\beta)$ may be written as $\mathbf{G}_{\alpha \to \beta \to \gamma} \, \mathbf{A}_\alpha \, \mathbf{B}_\beta$.

Remark 2.21 (Conditionals). We will see in the next section that $(\text{if } \mathbf{A}_o \, \mathbf{B}_\alpha \, \mathbf{C}_\alpha)$ is a conditional expression that is not strict with respect to undefinedness. For instance, if $\mathbf{A}_o$ is true, then $(\text{if } \mathbf{A}_o \, \mathbf{B}_\alpha \, \mathbf{C}_\alpha)$ denotes the value of $\mathbf{B}_\alpha$ even when $\mathbf{C}_\alpha$ is undefined. We construct conditionals using an expression constructor instead of a constant since constants always denote functions that are effectively strict with respect to undefinedness. We will use conditional expressions to restrict the domain of a function.

An occurrence of a variable $\mathbf{x}_\alpha$ in an eval-free expression $\mathbf{B}_\beta$ is *bound* [*free*] if (1) it is not in a quotation and (2) it is [not] in a subexpression of $\mathbf{B}_\beta$ of the form $\lambda \, \mathbf{x}_\alpha \, . \, \mathbf{C}_\gamma$. An eval-free expression is *closed* if no free variables occur in it.

2.3   Constructions

Let $\mathcal{E}$ be the function mapping eval-free expressions to expressions of type ϵ that is defined inductively as follows:

---

[3] It would be more natural for the second argument of an evaluation to be a type, but that would lead to an infinite family of evaluation operators, one for every type, since type variables are not available in $\mathrm{CTT}_{\mathrm{uqe}}$ (as well as in $\mathrm{CTT}_{\mathrm{qe}}$ and $\mathcal{Q}_0$).

Table 1. Six kinds of eval-free expressions

Kind	Syntax	Syntactic value
Variable	$\mathbf{x}_\alpha$	$\ulcorner \mathbf{x}_\alpha \urcorner$
Constant	$\mathbf{c}_\alpha$	$\ulcorner \mathbf{c}_\alpha \urcorner$
Function application	$\mathbf{F}_{\alpha \to \beta}\, \mathbf{A}_\alpha$	$\mathsf{app}_{\epsilon \to \epsilon \to \epsilon}\, \mathcal{E}(\mathbf{F}_{\alpha \to \beta})\, \mathcal{E}(\mathbf{A}_\alpha)$
Function abstraction	$\lambda\, \mathbf{x}_\alpha\,.\, \mathbf{B}_\beta$	$\mathsf{abs}_{\epsilon \to \epsilon \to \epsilon}\, \mathcal{E}(\mathbf{x}_\alpha)\, \mathcal{E}(\mathbf{B}_\beta)$
Conditional	$(\text{if}\ \mathbf{A}_o\ \mathbf{B}_\alpha\ \mathbf{C}_\alpha)$	$\mathsf{cond}_{\epsilon \to \epsilon \to \epsilon \to \epsilon}\, \mathcal{E}(\mathbf{A}_o)\, \mathcal{E}(\mathbf{B}_\alpha)\, \mathcal{E}(\mathbf{C}_\alpha).$
Quotation	$\ulcorner \mathbf{A}_\alpha \urcorner$	$\mathsf{quo}_{\epsilon \to \epsilon}\, \mathcal{E}(\mathbf{A}_\alpha)$

1. $\mathcal{E}(\mathbf{x}_\alpha) = \ulcorner \mathbf{x}_\alpha \urcorner$.
2. $\mathcal{E}(\mathbf{c}_\alpha) = \ulcorner \mathbf{c}_\alpha \urcorner$.
3. $\mathcal{E}(\mathbf{F}_{\alpha \to \beta}\, \mathbf{A}_\alpha) = \mathsf{app}_{\epsilon \to \epsilon \to \epsilon}\, \mathcal{E}(\mathbf{F}_{\alpha \to \beta})\, \mathcal{E}(\mathbf{A}_\alpha)$.
4. $\mathcal{E}(\lambda\, \mathbf{x}_\alpha\,.\, \mathbf{B}_\beta) = \mathsf{abs}_{\epsilon \to \epsilon \to \epsilon}\, \mathcal{E}(\mathbf{x}_\alpha)\, \mathcal{E}(\mathbf{B}_\beta)$.
5. $\mathcal{E}(\text{if}\ \mathbf{A}_o\ \mathbf{B}_\alpha\ \mathbf{C}_\alpha) = \mathsf{cond}_{\epsilon \to \epsilon \to \epsilon \to \epsilon}\, \mathcal{E}(\mathbf{A}_o)\, \mathcal{E}(\mathbf{B}_\alpha)\, \mathcal{E}(\mathbf{C}_\alpha)$.
6. $\mathcal{E}(\ulcorner \mathbf{A}_\alpha \urcorner) = \mathsf{quo}_{\epsilon \to \epsilon}\, \mathcal{E}(\mathbf{A}_\alpha)$.

A *construction* of $\mathrm{CTT}_{\mathrm{uqe}}$ is an expression in the range of $\mathcal{E}$. $\mathcal{E}$ is clearly injective. When $\mathbf{A}_\alpha$ is eval-free, $\mathcal{E}(\mathbf{A}_\alpha)$ is a construction that represents the syntactic structure of $\mathbf{A}_\alpha$. That is, $\mathcal{E}(\mathbf{A}_\alpha)$ is a syntactic value that represents how $\mathbf{A}_\alpha$ is constructed as an expression. In contrast to $\mathrm{CTT}_{\mathrm{qe}}$, the constructions of $\mathrm{CTT}_{\mathrm{uqe}}$ do not include "improper constructions"—such as $\mathsf{app}_{\epsilon \to \epsilon \to \epsilon}\, \ulcorner \mathbf{x}_\alpha \urcorner \ulcorner \mathbf{x}_\alpha \urcorner$—that do not represent the syntactic structures of eval-free expressions.

The six kinds of eval-free expressions and the syntactic values that represent their syntactic structures are given in Table 1.

2.4 Theories

Let $\mathcal{B}' \subseteq \mathcal{B}$ and $\mathcal{C}' \subseteq \mathcal{C}$. A type α of $\mathrm{CTT}_{\mathrm{uqe}}$ is a $\mathcal{B}'$-*type* if each base type occurring in α is a member of $\mathcal{B}'$. An expression $\mathbf{A}_\alpha$ of $\mathrm{CTT}_{\mathrm{uqe}}$ is a $(\mathcal{B}', \mathcal{C}')$-*expression* if each base type and constant occurring in $\mathbf{A}_\alpha$ is a member of $\mathcal{B}'$ and $\mathcal{C}'$, respectively. A *language* of $\mathrm{CTT}_{\mathrm{uqe}}$ is the set of all $(\mathcal{B}', \mathcal{C}')$-expressions for some $\mathcal{B}' \subseteq \mathcal{B}$ and $\mathcal{C}' \subseteq \mathcal{C}$ such that $\mathcal{B}'$ contains the logical base types of $\mathrm{CTT}_{\mathrm{uqe}}$ (i.e., o and ι) and $\mathcal{C}'$ contains the logical constants of $\mathrm{CTT}_{\mathrm{uqe}}$. A *theory* of $\mathrm{CTT}_{\mathrm{uqe}}$ is a pair $T = (L, \Gamma)$ where L is a language of $\mathrm{CTT}_{\mathrm{uqe}}$ and Γ is a set of formulas in L (called the *axioms* of T). $\mathbf{A}_\alpha$ is an *expression of a theory* T if $\mathbf{A}_\alpha \in L$.

2.5 Definitions and Abbreviations

We will utilize the logical constants and abbreviations defined in [7] as well as those defined in Table 2. $(\mathbf{A}_\alpha \downarrow)$ says that $\mathbf{A}_\alpha$ is defined, and similarly, $(\mathbf{A}_\alpha \uparrow)$ says that $\mathbf{A}_\alpha$ is undefined. $\mathbf{A}_\alpha \simeq \mathbf{B}_\alpha$ says that $\mathbf{A}_\alpha$ and $\mathbf{B}_\alpha$ are *quasi-equal*, i.e., that $\mathbf{A}_\alpha$ and $\mathbf{B}_\alpha$ are either both defined and equal or both undefined. $\mathrm{I}\, \mathbf{x}_\alpha\,.\, \mathbf{A}_o$ is a *definite description*. It denotes the unique $\mathbf{x}_\alpha$ that satisfies $\mathbf{A}_o$. If there is no or more than one such $\mathbf{x}_\alpha$, it is undefined. The defined constant $\perp_\alpha$ is a canonical undefined expression of type α.

Table 2. Definitions and abbreviations

$[\![\mathbf{A}_\epsilon]\!]_\beta$	Stands for $[\![\mathbf{A}_\epsilon]\!]_{\mathbf{B}_\beta}$
$(\mathbf{A}_\alpha\downarrow)$	Stands for $\mathbf{A}_\alpha = \mathbf{A}_\alpha$
$(\mathbf{A}_\alpha\uparrow)$	Stands for $\neg(\mathbf{A}_\alpha\downarrow)$
$(\mathbf{A}_\alpha \simeq \mathbf{B}_\alpha)$	Stands for $(\mathbf{A}_\alpha\downarrow \vee \mathbf{B}_\alpha\downarrow) \supset \mathbf{A}_\alpha = \mathbf{B}_\alpha$
$(\mathrm{I}\mathbf{x}_\alpha \cdot \mathbf{A}_o)$	Stands for $\iota_{(\alpha\to o)\to\alpha}(\lambda\mathbf{x}_\alpha \cdot \mathbf{A}_o)$ where $\alpha \neq o$
$\perp_o$	Stands for F_o
$\perp_\alpha$	Stands for $\mathrm{I}\,x_\alpha \cdot x_\alpha \neq x_\alpha$ where $\alpha \neq o$

3   Semantics

The semantics of $\mathrm{CTT}_{\mathrm{uqe}}$ is the same as the semantics of $\mathrm{CTT}_{\mathrm{qe}}$ except that the former admits undefined expressions in accordance with the traditional approach to undefinedness [4]. Two principal changes are made to the $\mathrm{CTT}_{\mathrm{qe}}$ semantics: (1) The notion of a general model is redefined to include partial functions as well as total functions. (2) The valuation function for expressions is made into a partial function that assigns a value to an expression iff the expression is defined according to the traditional approach.

3.1   Frames

A *frame* of $\mathrm{CTT}_{\mathrm{uqe}}$ is a collection $\{D_\alpha \mid \alpha \in \mathcal{T}\}$ of domains such that:

1. $D_o = \{\mathrm{T}, \mathrm{F}\}$, the set of standard *truth values*.
2. D_ϵ is the set of *constructions* of $\mathrm{CTT}_{\mathrm{uqe}}$.
3. For $\alpha \in \mathcal{B}$ with $\alpha \notin \{o, \epsilon\}$, D_α is a nonempty set of values (called *individuals*).
4. For $\alpha, \beta \in \mathcal{T}$, $D_{\alpha\to\beta}$ is some set of *total* functions from D_α to D_β if $\beta = o$ and some set of *partial and total* functions from D_α to D_β if $\beta \neq o$.

3.2   Interpretations

An *interpretation* of $\mathrm{CTT}_{\mathrm{uqe}}$ is a pair $(\{D_\alpha \mid \alpha \in \mathcal{T}\}, I)$ consisting of a frame and an interpretation function I that maps each constant in $\mathcal{C}$ of type α to an element of D_α such that:

1. For all $\alpha \in \mathcal{T}$, $I(=_{\alpha\to\alpha\to o})$ is the total function $f \in D_{\alpha\to\alpha\to o}$ such that, for all $d_1, d_2 \in D_\alpha$, $f(d_1)(d_2) = \mathrm{T}$ iff $d_1 = d_2$.
2. For all $\alpha \in \mathcal{T}$ with $\alpha \neq o$, $I(\iota_{(\alpha\to o)\to\alpha})$ is the partial function $f \in D_{(\alpha\to o)\to\alpha}$ such that, for all $d \in D_{\alpha\to o}$, if the predicate d represents a singleton $\{d'\} \subseteq D_\alpha$, then $f(d) = d'$, and otherwise $f(d)$ is undefined.
3. $I(\text{is-var}_{\epsilon\to o})$ $[I(\text{is-con}_{\epsilon\to o})]$ is the total function $f \in D_{\epsilon\to o}$ such that, for all constructions $\mathbf{A}_\epsilon \in D_\epsilon$, $f(\mathbf{A}_\epsilon) = \mathrm{T}$ iff $\mathbf{A}_\epsilon$ is some variable $\mathbf{x}_\alpha \in \mathcal{V}$ [constant $\mathbf{c}_\alpha \in \mathcal{C}$] (where α can be any type).

4. For all $\alpha \in \mathcal{T}$, $I(\text{is-var}^\alpha_{\epsilon \to o})$ $[I(\text{is-con}^\alpha_{\epsilon \to o})]$ is the total function $f \in D_{\epsilon \to o}$ such that, for all constructions $\mathbf{A}_\epsilon \in D_\epsilon$, $f(\mathbf{A}_\epsilon) = \mathrm{T}$ iff $\mathbf{A}_\epsilon$ is some variable $\mathbf{x}_\alpha \in \mathcal{V}$ [constant $\mathbf{c}_\alpha \in \mathcal{C}$].

5. $I(\text{app}_{\epsilon \to \epsilon \to \epsilon})$ is the partial function $f \in D_{\epsilon \to \epsilon \to \epsilon}$ such that, for all constructions $\mathbf{A}_\epsilon, \mathbf{B}_\epsilon \in D_\epsilon$, if $\text{app}_{\epsilon \to \epsilon \to \epsilon} \mathbf{A}_\epsilon \mathbf{B}_\epsilon$ is a construction, then $f(\mathbf{A}_\epsilon)(\mathbf{B}_\epsilon) = \text{app}_{\epsilon \to \epsilon \to \epsilon} \mathbf{A}_\epsilon \mathbf{B}_\epsilon$, and otherwise $f(\mathbf{A}_\epsilon)(\mathbf{B}_\epsilon)$ is undefined.

6. $I(\text{abs}_{\epsilon \to \epsilon \to \epsilon})$ is the partial function $f \in D_{\epsilon \to \epsilon \to \epsilon}$ such that, for all constructions $\mathbf{A}_\epsilon, \mathbf{B}_\epsilon \in D_\epsilon$, if $\text{abs}_{\epsilon \to \epsilon \to \epsilon} \mathbf{A}_\epsilon \mathbf{B}_\epsilon$ is a construction, then $f(\mathbf{A}_\epsilon)(\mathbf{B}_\epsilon) = \text{abs}_{\epsilon \to \epsilon \to \epsilon} \mathbf{A}_\epsilon \mathbf{B}_\epsilon$, and otherwise $f(\mathbf{A}_\epsilon)(\mathbf{B}_\epsilon)$ is undefined.

7. $I(\text{cond}_{\epsilon \to \epsilon \to \epsilon \to \epsilon})$ is the partial function $f \in D_{\epsilon \to \epsilon \to \epsilon \to \epsilon}$ such that, for all constructions $\mathbf{A}_\epsilon, \mathbf{B}_\epsilon, \mathbf{C}_\epsilon \in D_\epsilon$, if $\text{cond}_{\epsilon \to \epsilon \to \epsilon \to \epsilon} \mathbf{A}_\epsilon \mathbf{B}_\epsilon \mathbf{C}_\epsilon$ is a construction, then $f(\mathbf{A}_\epsilon)(\mathbf{B}_\epsilon)(\mathbf{C}_\epsilon) = \text{cond}_{\epsilon \to \epsilon \to \epsilon \to \epsilon} \mathbf{A}_\epsilon \mathbf{B}_\epsilon \mathbf{C}_\epsilon$, and otherwise $f(\mathbf{A}_\epsilon)(\mathbf{B}_\epsilon)(\mathbf{C}_\epsilon)$ is undefined.

8. $I(\text{quo}_{\epsilon \to \epsilon})$ is the total function $f \in D_{\epsilon \to \epsilon}$ such that, for all constructions $\mathbf{A}_\epsilon \in D_\epsilon$, $f(\mathbf{A}_\epsilon) = \text{quo}_{\epsilon \to \epsilon} \mathbf{A}_\epsilon$.

9. For all $\alpha \in \mathcal{T}$, $I(\text{is-expr}^\alpha_{\epsilon \to o})$ is the total function $f \in D_{\epsilon \to o}$ such that, for all constructions $\mathbf{A}_\epsilon \in D_\epsilon$, $f(\mathbf{A}_\epsilon) = \mathrm{T}$ iff $\mathbf{A}_\epsilon = \mathcal{E}(\mathbf{B}_\alpha)$ for some (eval-free) expression $\mathbf{B}_\alpha$.

10. $I(\sqsubset_{\epsilon \to \epsilon \to o})$ is the total function $f \in D_{\epsilon \to \epsilon \to \epsilon}$ such that, for all constructions $\mathbf{A}_\epsilon, \mathbf{B}_\epsilon \in D_\epsilon$, $f(\mathbf{A}_\epsilon)(\mathbf{B}_\epsilon) = \mathrm{T}$ iff $\mathbf{A}_\epsilon$ is a proper subexpression of $\mathbf{B}_\epsilon$.

11. $I(\text{is-free-in}_{\epsilon \to \epsilon \to o})$ is the total function $f \in D_{\epsilon \to \epsilon \to \epsilon}$ such that, for all constructions $\mathbf{A}_\epsilon, \mathbf{B}_\epsilon \in D_\epsilon$, $f(\mathbf{A}_\epsilon)(\mathbf{B}_\epsilon) = \mathrm{T}$ iff $\mathbf{A}_\epsilon = \ulcorner \mathbf{x}_\alpha \urcorner$ for some $\mathbf{x}_\alpha \in \mathcal{V}$ and $\mathbf{x}_\alpha$ is free in the expression $\mathbf{C}_\beta$ such that $\mathbf{B}_\epsilon = \mathcal{E}(\mathbf{C}_\beta)$.

An *assignment* into a frame $\{D_\alpha \mid \alpha \in \mathcal{T}\}$ is a function φ whose domain is $\mathcal{V}$ such that $\varphi(\mathbf{x}_\alpha) \in D_\alpha$ for each $\mathbf{x}_\alpha \in \mathcal{V}$. Given an assignment φ, $\mathbf{x}_\alpha \in \mathcal{V}$, and $d \in D_\alpha$, let $\varphi[\mathbf{x}_\alpha \mapsto d]$ be the assignment ψ such that $\psi(\mathbf{x}_\alpha) = d$ and $\psi(\mathbf{y}_\beta) = \varphi(\mathbf{y}_\beta)$ for all variables $\mathbf{y}_\beta$ distinct from $\mathbf{x}_\alpha$. For an interpretation $\mathcal{M} = (\{D_\alpha \mid \alpha \in \mathcal{T}\}, I)$, $\text{assign}(\mathcal{M})$ is the set of assignments into the frame of $\mathcal{M}$.

3.3   General Models

An interpretation $\mathcal{M} = (\{D_\alpha \mid \alpha \in \mathcal{T}\}, I)$ is a *general model* for CTT_{uqe} if there is a partial binary valuation function $V^{\mathcal{M}}$ such that, for all assignments $\varphi \in \text{assign}(\mathcal{M})$ and expressions $\mathbf{D}_\delta$, either $V^{\mathcal{M}}_\varphi(\mathbf{D}_\delta) \in D_\delta$ or $V^{\mathcal{M}}_\varphi(\mathbf{D}_\delta)$ is undefined[4] and each of the following conditions is satisfied:

1. Let $\mathbf{D}_\delta \in \mathcal{V}$. Then $V^{\mathcal{M}}_\varphi(\mathbf{D}_\delta) = \varphi(\mathbf{D}_\delta)$.
2. Let $\mathbf{D}_\delta \in \mathcal{C}$. Then $V^{\mathcal{M}}_\varphi(\mathbf{D}_\delta) = I(\mathbf{D}_\delta)$.
3. Let $\mathbf{D}_\delta$ be $\mathbf{F}_{\alpha \to \beta} \mathbf{A}_\alpha$. If $V^{\mathcal{M}}_\varphi(\mathbf{F}_{\alpha \to \beta})$ is defined, $V^{\mathcal{M}}_\varphi(\mathbf{A}_\alpha)$ is defined, and the function $V^{\mathcal{M}}_\varphi(\mathbf{F}_{\alpha \to \beta})$ is defined at the argument $V^{\mathcal{M}}_\varphi(\mathbf{A}_\alpha)$, then

$$V^{\mathcal{M}}_\varphi(\mathbf{D}_\delta) = V^{\mathcal{M}}_\varphi(\mathbf{F}_{\alpha \to \beta})(V^{\mathcal{M}}_\varphi(\mathbf{A}_\alpha)).$$

Otherwise, $V^{\mathcal{M}}_\varphi(\mathbf{D}_\delta) = \mathrm{F}$ if $\beta = o$ and $V^{\mathcal{M}}_\varphi(\mathbf{D}_\delta)$ is undefined if $\beta \neq o$.

---

[4] We write $V^{\mathcal{M}}_\varphi(\mathbf{D}_\delta)$ instead of $V^{\mathcal{M}}(\varphi, \mathbf{D}_\delta)$.

4. Let $\mathbf{D}_\delta$ be $\lambda\,\mathbf{x}_\alpha$. $\mathbf{B}_\beta$. Then $V_\varphi^{\mathcal{M}}(\mathbf{D}_\delta)$ is the (partial or total) function $f \in D_{\alpha\to\beta}$ such that, for each $d \in D_\alpha$, $f(d) = V_{\varphi[\mathbf{x}_\alpha\mapsto d]}^{\mathcal{M}}(\mathbf{B}_\beta)$ if $V_{\varphi[\mathbf{x}_\alpha\mapsto d]}^{\mathcal{M}}(\mathbf{B}_\beta)$ is defined and $f(d)$ is undefined if $V_{\varphi[\mathbf{x}_\alpha\mapsto d]}^{\mathcal{M}}(\mathbf{B}_\beta)$ is undefined.

5. Let $\mathbf{D}_\delta$ be (if $\mathbf{A}_o$ $\mathbf{B}_\alpha$ $\mathbf{C}_\alpha$). If $V_\varphi^{\mathcal{M}}(\mathbf{A}_o) = \mathrm{T}$ and $V_\varphi^{\mathcal{M}}(\mathbf{B}_\alpha)$ is defined, then $V_\varphi^{\mathcal{M}}(\mathbf{D}_\delta) = V_\varphi^{\mathcal{M}}(\mathbf{B}_\alpha)$. If $V_\varphi^{\mathcal{M}}(\mathbf{A}_o) = \mathrm{F}$ and $V_\varphi^{\mathcal{M}}(\mathbf{C}_\alpha)$ is defined, then $V_\varphi^{\mathcal{M}}(\mathbf{D}_\delta) = V_\varphi^{\mathcal{M}}(\mathbf{C}_\alpha)$. Otherwise, $V_\varphi^{\mathcal{M}}(\mathbf{D}_\delta)$ is undefined.

6. Let $\mathbf{D}_\delta$ be $\ulcorner\mathbf{A}_\alpha\urcorner$. Then $V_\varphi^{\mathcal{M}}(\mathbf{D}_\delta) = \mathcal{E}(\mathbf{A}_\alpha)$.

7. Let $\mathbf{D}_\delta$ be $\llbracket\mathbf{A}_\epsilon\rrbracket_\beta$. If $V_\varphi^{\mathcal{M}}(\text{is-expr}_{\epsilon\to o}^\beta\,\mathbf{A}_\epsilon) = \mathrm{T}$, then

$$V_\varphi^{\mathcal{M}}(\mathbf{D}_\delta) = V_\varphi^{\mathcal{M}}(\mathcal{E}^{-1}(V_\varphi^{\mathcal{M}}(\mathbf{A}_\epsilon))).$$

Otherwise, $V_\varphi^{\mathcal{M}}(\mathbf{D}_\delta) = \mathrm{F}$ if $\beta = o$ and $V_\varphi^{\mathcal{M}}(\mathbf{D}_\delta)$ is undefined if $\beta \neq o$.

Proposition 3.31. *General models for* $\mathrm{CTT}_{\mathrm{uqe}}$ *exist.*

Proof. The proof is similar to the proof of the analogous proposition in [7]. $\square$

Other theorems about the semantics of $\mathrm{CTT}_{\mathrm{uqe}}$ are the same or very similar to the theorems about the semantics of $\mathrm{CTT}_{\mathrm{qe}}$ given in [7].

Let $\mathcal{M}$ be a general model for $\mathrm{CTT}_{\mathrm{uqe}}$. $\mathbf{A}_o$ *is valid in* $\mathcal{M}$, written $\mathcal{M} \vDash \mathbf{A}_o$, if $V_\varphi^{\mathcal{M}}(\mathbf{A}_o) = \mathrm{T}$ for all $\varphi \in \mathsf{assign}(\mathcal{M})$. $\mathbf{A}_o$ is *valid in* $\mathrm{CTT}_{\mathrm{uqe}}$, written $\vDash \mathbf{A}_o$, if $\mathbf{A}_o$ is valid in every general model for $\mathrm{CTT}_{\mathrm{uqe}}$. An expression $\mathbf{B}_\beta$ is *semantically closed* if no variable "is effective in" it, i.e.,

$$\vDash \forall\,\mathbf{y}_\alpha\ .\ ((\lambda\,\mathbf{x}_\alpha\ .\ \mathbf{B}_\beta)\,\mathbf{y}_\alpha = \mathbf{B}_\beta)$$

holds for all variables $\mathbf{x}_\alpha$ (where $\mathbf{y}_\alpha$ is any variable of type α that differs from $\mathbf{x}_\alpha$). It is easy to show that every closed eval-free expression is semantically closed. If $\mathbf{B}_\beta$ is semantically closed, then $V_\varphi^{\mathcal{M}}(\mathbf{B}_\beta)$ does not depend on $\varphi \in \mathsf{assign}(\mathcal{M})$. The notion of "$\mathbf{x}_\alpha$ is effective in $\mathbf{B}_\beta$" is discussed in detail in [7].

Let $T = (L, \Gamma)$ be a theory of $\mathrm{CTT}_{\mathrm{uqe}}$ and $\mathbf{A}_o$ be a formula of T. A *general model for* T is a general model $\mathcal{M}$ for $\mathrm{CTT}_{\mathrm{uqe}}$ such that $\mathcal{M} \vDash \mathbf{A}_o$ for all $\mathbf{A}_o \in \Gamma$. $\mathbf{A}_o$ is *valid in* T, written $T \vDash \mathbf{A}_o$, if $\mathbf{A}_o$ is valid in every general model for T. T is *normal* if each member of Γ is semantically closed.

4   Theory Morphisms

In this section we define a "semantic morphism" of $\mathrm{CTT}_{\mathrm{uqe}}$ that maps the valid semantically closed formulas of one normal theory to the valid semantically closed formulas of another normal theory. Theory morphisms usually map base types to types. By exploiting the support for partial functions in $\mathrm{CTT}_{\mathrm{uqe}}$, we introduce a more general notion of theory morphism that maps base types to semantically closed predicates that represent sets of values of the same type. This requires mapping expressions denoting functions on the base type to expressions denoting functions with domains restricted to the semantically closed predicate.

For $i = 1, 2$, let $T_i = (L_i, \Gamma_i)$ be a normal theory of $\mathrm{CTT_{uqe}}$ where, for some $\mathcal{B}_i \subseteq \mathcal{B}$ and $\mathcal{C}_i \subseteq \mathcal{C}$, L_i is the set of all $(\mathcal{B}_i, \mathcal{C}_i)$-expressions. Also for $i = 1, 2$, let $\mathcal{T}_i$ be the set of all $\mathcal{B}_i$-types and $\mathcal{V}_i$ be the set of all variables in L_i. Finally, let $\mathcal{P}_2$ be the set of all semantically closed predicates in L_2.

4.1 Translations

In this section, we will define a translation from T_1 to T_2 to be a pair (μ, ν) of functions where μ interprets the base types of T_1 and ν interprets the variables and constants of T_1. $\overline{\mu}$ and $\overline{\nu}$ will be canonical extensions of μ and ν to the types and expressions of T_1, respectively.

Define τ to be the function that maps a predicate of type $\alpha \rightarrow o$ to the type α. When $\mathbf{p}_{\alpha \rightarrow o}$ and $\mathbf{q}_{\beta \rightarrow o}$ are semantically closed predicates, let

$$\mathbf{p}_{\alpha \rightarrow o} \rightharpoonup \mathbf{q}_{\beta \rightarrow o}$$

be an abbreviation for the following semantically closed predicate of type $(\alpha \rightarrow \beta) \rightarrow o$:

$$\lambda f_{\alpha \rightarrow \beta} . \forall x_\alpha . (f_{\alpha \rightarrow \beta} x_\alpha \neq \perp_\beta \supset (\mathbf{p}_{\alpha \rightarrow o} x_\alpha \wedge \mathbf{q}_{\beta \rightarrow o} (f_{\alpha \rightarrow \beta} x_\alpha))).$$

If $\beta = o$ $[\beta \neq o]$, $\mathbf{p}_{\alpha \rightarrow o} \rightharpoonup \mathbf{q}_{\beta \rightarrow o}$ represents the set of total [partial and total] functions from the set of values represented by $\mathbf{p}_{\alpha \rightarrow o}$ to the set of values represented by $\mathbf{q}_{\beta \rightarrow o}$. Notice that

$$\tau(\mathbf{p}_{\alpha \rightarrow o} \rightharpoonup \mathbf{q}_{\beta \rightarrow o}) = \alpha \rightarrow \beta = \tau(\mathbf{p}_{\alpha \rightarrow o}) \rightarrow \tau(\mathbf{q}_{\beta \rightarrow o}).$$

Given a total function $\mu : \mathcal{B}_1 \rightarrow \mathcal{P}_2$, let $\overline{\mu} : \mathcal{T}_1 \rightarrow \mathcal{P}_2$ be the canonical extension of μ that is defined inductively as follows:

1. If $\alpha \in \mathcal{B}_1$, $\overline{\mu}(\alpha) = \mu(\alpha)$.
2. If $\alpha \rightarrow \beta \in \mathcal{T}_1$, $\overline{\mu}(\alpha \rightarrow \beta) = \overline{\mu}(\alpha) \rightharpoonup \overline{\mu}(\beta)$.

It is easy to see that $\overline{\mu}$ is well-defined and total.

A *translation from* T_1 *to* T_2 is a pair $\Phi = (\mu, \nu)$, where $\mu : \mathcal{B}_1 \rightarrow \mathcal{P}_2$ is total and $\nu : \mathcal{V}_1 \cup \mathcal{C}_1 \rightarrow \mathcal{V}_2 \cup \mathcal{C}_2$ is total and injective, such that:

1. $\mu(o) = \lambda x_o . T_o$.
2. $\mu(\epsilon) = \lambda x_\epsilon . T_o$.
3. For each $\mathbf{x}_\alpha \in \mathcal{V}_1$, $\nu(\mathbf{x}_\alpha)$ is a variable in $\mathcal{V}_2$ of type $\tau(\overline{\mu}(\alpha))$.
4. For each $\mathbf{c}_\alpha \in \mathcal{C}_1$, $\nu(\mathbf{c}_\alpha)$ is a constant in $\mathcal{C}_2$ of type $\tau(\overline{\mu}(\alpha))$.

Throughout the rest of this section, let $\Phi = (\mu, \nu)$ be a translation from T_1 to T_2. $\overline{\nu} : L_1 \rightarrow L_2$ is the canonical extension of ν defined inductively as follows:

1. If $\mathbf{x}_\alpha \in \mathcal{V}_1$, $\overline{\nu}(\mathbf{x}_\alpha) = \nu(\mathbf{x}_\alpha)$.
2. If $\mathbf{c}_\alpha \in \mathcal{C}_1$, $\overline{\nu}(\mathbf{c}_\alpha) = \nu(\mathbf{c}_\alpha)$.
3. If $\mathbf{F}_{\alpha \rightarrow \beta} \mathbf{A}_\alpha \in L_1$, then $\overline{\nu}(\mathbf{F}_{\alpha \rightarrow \beta} \mathbf{A}_\alpha) = \overline{\nu}(\mathbf{F}_{\alpha \rightarrow \beta}) \overline{\nu}(\mathbf{A}_\alpha)$.

4. If $\lambda \mathbf{x}_\alpha . \mathbf{B}_\beta \in L_1$, then $\overline{\nu}(\lambda \mathbf{x}_\alpha . \mathbf{B}_\beta) =$

$$\lambda \overline{\nu}(\mathbf{x}_\alpha) . (\text{if } (\overline{\mu}(\alpha) \overline{\nu}(\mathbf{x}_\alpha)) \overline{\nu}(\mathbf{B}_\beta) \perp_{\tau(\overline{\mu}(\beta))}).$$

5. If $(\text{if } \mathbf{A}_o \mathbf{B}_\alpha \mathbf{C}_\alpha) \in L_1$, $\overline{\nu}(\text{if } \mathbf{A}_o \mathbf{B}_\alpha \mathbf{C}_\alpha) = (\text{if } \overline{\nu}(\mathbf{A}_o) \overline{\nu}(\mathbf{B}_\alpha) \overline{\nu}(\mathbf{C}_\alpha))$.
6. If $\ulcorner \mathbf{A}_\alpha \urcorner \in L_1$, then $\overline{\nu}(\ulcorner \mathbf{A}_\alpha \urcorner) = \ulcorner \overline{\nu}(\mathbf{A}_\alpha) \urcorner$.
7. If $[\![\mathbf{A}_\epsilon]\!]_{\mathbf{B}_\beta} \in L_1$, then $\overline{\nu}([\![\mathbf{A}_\epsilon]\!]_{\mathbf{B}_\beta}) = [\![\overline{\nu}(\mathbf{A}_\epsilon)]\!]_{\overline{\nu}(\mathbf{B}_\beta)}$.

Lemma 4.11. *1. $\overline{\nu}$ is well-defined, total, and injective.*
2. If $\mathbf{A}_\alpha \in L_1$, then $\overline{\nu}(\mathbf{A}_\alpha)$ is an expression of type $\tau(\overline{\mu}(\alpha))$.

Proof. The two parts of the proposition are easily proved simultaneously by induction on the structure of expressions. □

Remark 4.12. We overcome the Constant Interpretation Problem mentioned in Sect. 1 by requiring ν to injectively map constants to constants which, by Lemma 4.11, implies that $\overline{\nu}$ injectively maps expressions to expressions. We will see in the next section that this requirement comes with a cost.

A formula in L_2 is an *obligation* of Φ if it is one of the following formulas:

1. $\exists x_{\tau(\mu(\alpha))} . \mu(\alpha) x_{\tau(\mu(\alpha))}$ where $\alpha \in \mathcal{B}_1$.
2. $\overline{\mu}(\alpha) \nu(\mathbf{c}_\alpha)$ where $\mathbf{c}_\alpha \in \mathcal{C}_1$.
3. $\nu(=_{\alpha \to \alpha \to o}) = \lambda x_{\alpha'} . \lambda y_{\alpha'} . (\text{if } (\overline{\mu}(\alpha) x_{\alpha'} \wedge \overline{\mu}(\alpha) y_{\alpha'}) (x_{\alpha'} =_{\alpha' \to \alpha' \to o} y_{\alpha'}) \perp_o)$
   where $\alpha \in \mathcal{T}_1$ and $\alpha' = \tau(\overline{\mu}(\alpha))$.
4. $\nu(\iota_{(\alpha \to o) \to \alpha}) = \lambda x_{\alpha' \to o} . (\text{if } (\overline{\mu}(\alpha \to o) x_{\alpha' \to o}) (\iota_{(\alpha' \to o) \to \alpha'} x_{\alpha' \to o}) \perp_{\alpha'})$
   where $\alpha \in \mathcal{T}_1$ with $\alpha \neq o$ and $\alpha' = \tau(\overline{\mu}(\alpha))$.
5. $\nu(\mathbf{c}_\alpha) = \mathbf{c}_\alpha$ where $\mathbf{c}_\alpha$ is $\mathsf{is\text{-}var}_{\epsilon \to o}$, $\mathsf{is\text{-}con}_{\epsilon \to o}$, $\mathsf{app}_{\epsilon \to \epsilon \to \epsilon}$, $\mathsf{abs}_{\epsilon \to \epsilon \to \epsilon}$,
   $\mathsf{cond}_{\epsilon \to \epsilon \to \epsilon \to \epsilon}$ $\mathsf{quo}_{\epsilon \to \epsilon}$, $\ulcorner \urcorner_{\epsilon \to \epsilon \to o}$, or $\mathsf{is\text{-}free\text{-}in}_{\epsilon \to \epsilon \to o}$.
6. $\nu(\mathbf{c}_\alpha^\beta) = \mathbf{c}_\alpha^{\tau(\overline{\mu}(\beta))}$ where $\mathbf{c}_\alpha$ is $\mathsf{is\text{-}var}_{\epsilon \to o}^\beta$, $\mathsf{is\text{-}con}_{\epsilon \to o}^\beta$, or $\mathsf{is\text{-}expr}_{\epsilon \to o}^\beta$ and $\beta \in \mathcal{T}_1$.
7. $\overline{\nu}(\mathbf{A}_o)$ where $\mathbf{A}_o \in \Gamma_1$.

Notice that each obligation of Φ is semantically closed.

4.2   Semantic Morphisms

A *semantic morphism* from T_1 to T_2 is a translation (μ, ν) from T_1 to T_2 such that $T_1 \vDash \mathbf{A}_o$ implies $T_2 \vDash \overline{\nu}(\mathbf{A}_o)$ for all semantically closed formulas $\mathbf{A}_o$ of T_1. (A *syntactic morphism* from T_1 to T_2 would be a translation (μ, ν) from T_1 to T_2 such that $T_1 \vdash_P \mathbf{A}_o$ implies $T_2 \vdash_P \overline{\nu}(\mathbf{A}_o)$ for all semantically closed formulas $\mathbf{A}_o$ of T_1 where P is some proof system for $\mathrm{CTT_{uqe}}$.) We will prove a theorem (called the Semantic Morphism Theorem) that gives a sufficient condition for a translation to be a semantic morphism.

Assume $\mathcal{M}_2 = (\{D_\alpha^2 | \alpha \in \mathcal{T}\}, I_2)$ is a general model for T_2. Under the assumption that the obligations of Φ are valid in T_2, we will extract a general model for T_1 from $\mathcal{M}_2$.

For each $\alpha \in \mathcal{T}_1$, define $\underline{D}^2_{\tau(\overline{\mu}(\alpha))} \subseteq D^2_{\tau(\overline{\mu}(\alpha))}$ as follows:

1. $\underline{D}^2_{\tau(\overline{\mu}(o))} = \underline{D}^2_o = D^2_o = \{\text{T}, \text{F}\}$.
2. $\underline{D}^2_{\tau(\overline{\mu}(\epsilon))} = \underline{D}^2_\epsilon =$

$$\{d \in D^2_\epsilon \mid d = V^{\mathcal{M}_2}_\varphi(\overline{\nu}(\mathbf{A}_\epsilon)) \text{ for some construction } \mathbf{A}_\epsilon \in L_1\}$$

where φ is any member of $\mathsf{assign}(\mathcal{M}_2)$.

3. If $\alpha \in \mathcal{T}_1 \backslash \{o, \epsilon\}$, $\underline{D}^2_{\tau(\overline{\mu}(\alpha))} =$

$$\{d \in D^2_{\tau(\overline{\mu}(\alpha))} \mid V^{\mathcal{M}_2}_\varphi(\overline{\mu}(\alpha))(d) = \text{T}\}$$

where φ is any member of $\mathsf{assign}(\mathcal{M}_2)$.

For each $\alpha \in \mathcal{T}_1$, define $\overline{D}^1_\alpha$ inductively as follows:

1. $\overline{D}^1_o = \{\text{T}, \text{F}\}$.
2. $\overline{D}^1_\epsilon$ is the set of constructions of $\mathrm{CTT}_{\mathsf{uqe}}$.
3. If $\alpha \in \mathcal{B}_1 \backslash \{o, \epsilon\}$, $\overline{D}^1_\alpha = \underline{D}^2_{\tau(\overline{\mu}(\alpha))}$.
4. If $\alpha \rightarrow \beta \in \mathcal{T}_1$, then $\overline{D}^1_{\alpha \rightarrow \beta}$ is the set of all *total* functions from $\overline{D}^1_\alpha$ to $\overline{D}^1_\beta$ if $\beta = o$ and the set of all *partial and total* functions from $\overline{D}^1_\alpha$ to $\overline{D}^1_\beta$ if $\beta \neq o$.

For each $\alpha \in \mathcal{T}_1$, define $\rho_\alpha : \underline{D}^2_{\tau(\overline{\mu}(\alpha))} \rightarrow \overline{D}^1_\alpha$ inductively as follows:

1. If $d \in \underline{D}^2_\epsilon$, $\rho_\epsilon(d)$ is the unique construction $\mathbf{A}_\epsilon$ such that $\overline{\nu}(\mathbf{A}_\epsilon) = d$.
2. If $\alpha \in \mathcal{B}_1 \backslash \{\epsilon\}$ and $d \in \underline{D}^2_{\tau(\overline{\mu}(\alpha))}$, $\rho_\alpha(d) = d$.
3. If $\alpha \rightarrow \beta \in \mathcal{T}_1$ and $f \in \underline{D}^2_{\tau(\overline{\mu}(\alpha \rightarrow \beta))}$, $\rho_{\alpha \rightarrow \beta}(f)$ is the unique function $g \in \overline{D}^1_{\alpha \rightarrow \beta}$ such that, for all $d \in \underline{D}^2_{\tau(\overline{\mu}(\alpha))}$, either $f(d)$ and $g(\rho_\alpha(d))$ are both defined and $\rho_\beta(f(d)) = g(\rho_\alpha(d))$ or they are both undefined.

Lemma 4.21. *If $\alpha \in \mathcal{T}_1$, $\rho_\alpha : \underline{D}^2_{\tau(\overline{\mu}(\alpha))} \rightarrow \overline{D}^1_\alpha$ is well defined, total, and injective.*

Proof. This lemma is proved by induction on $\alpha \in \mathcal{T}_1$. ρ_ϵ is well defined since $V^{\mathcal{M}_2}_\varphi$ is identity function on constructions and $\overline{\nu}$ is injective by Lemma 4.11. $\square$

For each $\alpha \in \mathcal{T}_1$, define $D^1_\alpha \subseteq \overline{D}^1_\alpha$ as follows:

1. If $\alpha \in \mathcal{B}_1$, $D^1_\alpha = \overline{D}^1_\alpha$.
2. If $\alpha \rightarrow \beta \in \mathcal{T}_1$, $D^1_{\alpha \rightarrow \beta}$ is the range of $\rho_{\alpha \rightarrow \beta}$.
3. If $\alpha \in \mathcal{B} \backslash \mathcal{B}_1$, D^1_α is any nonempty set.
4. If $\alpha \rightarrow \beta \in \mathcal{T} \backslash \mathcal{T}_1$, $D^1_{\alpha \rightarrow \beta}$ is the set of all *total* functions from D^1_α to D^1_β if $\beta = o$ and the set of all *partial and total* functions from D^1_α to D^1_β if $\beta \neq o$.

For $\mathbf{c}_\alpha \in C_1$, define $I_1(\mathbf{c}_\alpha) = \rho_\alpha(V_\varphi^{\mathcal{M}_2}(\overline{\nu}(\mathbf{c}_\alpha)))$ where φ is any member of assign$(\mathcal{M}_2)$. Finally, define $\mathcal{M}_1 = (\{\mathcal{D}_\alpha^1 \mid \alpha \in \mathcal{T}\}, I_1)$.

Lemma 4.22. *Suppose each obligation of Φ is valid in $\mathcal{M}_2$. Then $\mathcal{M}_1$ is a general model for T_2.*

Proof. By the first group of obligations of Φ, $\mathcal{D}_\alpha^1$ is nonempty for all $\alpha \in \mathcal{B}_1$, and so $\{\mathcal{D}_\alpha^1 \mid \alpha \in \mathcal{T}\}$ is a frame of $\mathrm{CTT}_\mathrm{uqe}$. By the second to sixth groups of obligations of Φ, $\mathcal{M}_1$ is an interpretation of $\mathrm{CTT}_\mathrm{uqe}$. For all $\mathbf{A}_\alpha \in L_1$ and $\varphi \in$ assign$(\mathcal{M}_1)$, define $V_\varphi^{\mathcal{M}_1}(\mathbf{A}_\alpha)$ as follows:

($\star$) $V_\varphi^{\mathcal{M}_1}(\mathbf{A}_\alpha) = \rho_\alpha(V_{\overline{\nu}(\varphi)}^{\mathcal{M}_2}(\overline{\nu}(\mathbf{A}_\alpha)))$ if $V_{\overline{\nu}(\varphi)}^{\mathcal{M}_2}(\overline{\nu}(\mathbf{A}_\alpha))$ is defined and $V_\varphi^{\mathcal{M}_1}(\mathbf{A}_\alpha)$ is undefined otherwise,

where $\overline{\nu}(\varphi)$ is any $\psi \in$ assign$(\mathcal{M}_2)$ such that, for all $\mathbf{x}_\beta \in \mathcal{V}_1$, $\rho_\beta(\psi(\overline{\nu}(\mathbf{x}_\beta))) = \varphi(\mathbf{x}_\beta)$. This definition of $V_\varphi^{\mathcal{M}_1}$ can be easily extended to a valuation function on all expressions that can be shown, by induction on the structure of expressions, to satisfy the seven clauses of the definition of a general model. Therefore, $\mathcal{M}_1$ is a general model for $\mathrm{CTT}_\mathrm{uqe}$. Then ($\star$) implies

($\star\star$) $\mathcal{M}_1 \vDash \mathbf{A}_o$ iff $\mathcal{M}_2 \vDash \overline{\nu}(\mathbf{A}_o)$

for all semantically closed formulas $\mathbf{A}_o \in L_1$. By the seventh group of obligations of Φ, $\mathcal{M}_2 \vDash \overline{\nu}(\mathbf{A}_o)$ for all $\mathbf{A}_o \in \Gamma_1$, and thus $\mathcal{M}_1$ is a general model for T_1 by ($\star\star$). $\square$

Theorem 4.23 (Semantic Morphism Theorem). *Let T_1 and T_2 be normal theories and Φ be a translation from T_1 to T_2. Suppose each obligation of Φ is valid in T_2. Then Φ is a semantic morphism from T_1 to T_2.*

Proof. Let $\Phi = (\mu, \nu)$ be a translation from T_1 to T_2 and suppose each obligation of Φ is valid in T_2. Let $\mathbf{A}_o \in L_1$ be semantically closed and valid in T_1. We must show that $\overline{\nu}(\mathbf{A}_o)$ is valid in every general model for T_2. Let $\mathcal{M}_2$ be a general model for T_1. (We are done if there are no general models for T_2.) Let $\mathcal{M}_1$ be extracted from $\mathcal{M}_2$ as above. Obviously, each obligation of Φ is valid in $\mathcal{M}_2$, and so $\mathcal{M}_1$ is a general model for T_1 by Lemma 4.22. Therefore, $\mathcal{M}_1 \vDash \mathbf{A}_o$, and so $\mathcal{M}_2 \vDash \overline{\nu}(\mathbf{A}_o)$ by ($\star\star$) in the proof of Lemma 4.22. $\square$

5 Examples

We will illustrate the theory morphism machinery of $\mathrm{CTT}_\mathrm{uqe}$ with two simple examples involving monoids, the first in which two concepts are interpreted as the same concept and second in which a type is interpreted as a subset of its denotation. Let $C_\mathrm{log} \subseteq C$ be the set of logical constants of $\mathrm{CTT}_\mathrm{uqe}$.

5.1 Example 1: Monoid with Left and Right Identity Elements

Define $M = (L_M, \Gamma_M)$ to be the usual theory of an abstract monoid where:

1. $\mathcal{B}_M = \{o, \epsilon, \iota\}$.
2. $\mathcal{C}_M = \mathcal{C}_{\log} \cup \{e_\iota, *_{\iota \to \iota \to \iota}\}$.   ($*_{\iota \to \iota \to \iota}$ is written as an infix operator.)
3. L_M is the set of $(\mathcal{B}_M, \mathcal{C}_M)$ expressions.
4. $\mathcal{V}_M$ is the set of variables in L_M.
5. Γ_M contains the following axioms:

   a. $\forall x_\iota . \forall y_\iota . \forall z_\iota . x_\iota *_{\iota \to \iota \to \iota} (y_\iota *_{\iota \to \iota \to \iota} z_\iota) = (x_\iota *_{\iota \to \iota \to \iota} y_\iota) *_{\iota \to \iota \to \iota} z_\iota$.
   b. $\forall x_\iota . e_\iota *_{\iota \to \iota \to \iota} x_\iota = x_\iota$.
   c. $\forall x_\iota . x_\iota *_{\iota \to \iota \to \iota} e_\iota = x_\iota$.

Define $M' = (L_{M'}, \Gamma_{M'})$ to be the alternate theory of an abstract monoid with left and right identity elements where:

1. $\mathcal{B}_{M'} = \mathcal{B}_M$.
2. $\mathcal{C}_{M'} = \mathcal{C}_{\log} \cup \{e_\iota^{\text{left}}, e_\iota^{\text{right}}, *_{\iota \to \iota \to \iota}\}$.   ($*_{\iota \to \iota \to \iota}$ is written as an infix operator.)
3. $L_{M'}$ is the set of $(\mathcal{B}_{M'}, \mathcal{C}_{M'})$ expressions.
4. $\mathcal{V}_{M'} = \mathcal{V}_M$.
5. $\Gamma_{M'}$ contains the following axioms:

   a. $\forall x_\iota . \forall y_\iota . \forall z_\iota . x_\iota *_{\iota \to \iota \to \iota} (y_\iota *_{\iota \to \iota \to \iota} z_\iota) = (x_\iota *_{\iota \to \iota \to \iota} y_\iota) *_{\iota \to \iota \to \iota} z_\iota$.
   b. $\forall x_\iota . e_\iota^{\text{left}} *_{\iota \to \iota \to \iota} x_\iota = x_\iota$.
   c. $\forall x_\iota . x_\iota *_{\iota \to \iota \to \iota} e_\iota^{\text{right}} = x_\iota$.

We would like to construct a semantic morphism from M' to M that maps the left and right identity elements of M' to the single identity element of M. This is not possible since the mapping ν must be injective to overcome the Constant Interpretation Problem. We need to add a dummy constant to M to facilitate the definition of the semantic morphism. Let $\overline{M}$ be the definitional extension of M that contains the new constant e_ι' and the new axiom $e_\iota' = e_\iota$.[5]
  Let $\Phi = (\mu, \nu)$ to be the translation from M' to $\overline{M}$ such that:

1. $\mu(\iota) = \lambda x_\iota . T_o$.
2. ν is the identity function on $\mathcal{V}_{M'} \cup \mathcal{C}_{\log} \cup \{*_{\iota \to \iota \to \iota}\}$.
3. $\nu(e_\iota^{\text{left}}) = e_\iota$.
4. $\nu(e_\iota^{\text{right}}) = e_\iota'$.

It is easy to see that Φ is a semantic interpretation by Theorem 4.23.

---

[5] Technically, e_ι' is a constant chosen from $\mathcal{C} \backslash \mathcal{C}_M$. There is no harm is assuming that such a constant already exists in $\mathcal{C}$.

5.2   Example 2: Monoid Interpreted as the Trivial Monoid

The identity element of a monoid forms a submonoid of the monoid that is isomorphic with the trivial monoid consisting of a single element. There is a natural morphism from a theory of a monoid to itself in which the type of monoid elements is interpreted by the singleton set containing the identity element. This kind of morphism cannot be directly expressed using a definition of a theory morphism that maps base types to types. However, it can be directly expressed using the notion of a semantic morphism we have defined.

The desired translation interprets the type ι as the set $\{e_\iota\}$ and the constants denoting functions involving ι as functions in which the domain of ι is replaced by $\{e_\iota\}$. This is not possible since the mapping ν must map constants to constants to overcome the Constant Interpretation Problem. We need to add a set of dummy constants to M to facilitate the definition of the semantic morphism.

Define μ are follows:

1. For $\alpha \in \{o, \epsilon\}$, $\mu(\alpha) = \lambda x_\alpha . T_o$.
2. $\mu(\iota) = \lambda x_\iota . x_\iota = e_\iota$.

Let $\overline{M}$ be the definitional extension of M that contains the following the new defined constants:

1. $='_{\alpha \to \alpha \to o} = \lambda x_{\alpha'} . \lambda y_{\alpha'} . (\text{if } (\overline{\mu}(\alpha) \, x_{\alpha'} \wedge \overline{\mu}(\alpha) \, y_{\alpha'}) \, (x_{\alpha'} =_{\alpha' \to \alpha' \to o} y_{\alpha'}) \perp_o)$
   where $\alpha \in \mathcal{T}$ contains ι and $\alpha' = \tau(\overline{\mu}(\alpha))$.
2. $\iota'_{(\alpha \to o) \to \alpha} = \lambda x_{\alpha' \to o} . (\text{if } (\overline{\mu}(\alpha \to o) \, x_{\alpha' \to o}) \, (\iota_{(\alpha' \to o) \to \alpha'} \, x_{\alpha' \to o}) \perp_{\alpha'})$
   where $\alpha \in \mathcal{T}$ contains ι and $\alpha' = \tau(\overline{\mu}(\alpha))$.
3. $*'_{\iota \to \iota \to \iota} = \lambda x_\iota . \lambda y_\iota . (\text{if } (\overline{\mu}(\iota) \, x_\iota \wedge \overline{\mu}(\iota) \, y_\iota) \, (x_\iota *_{\iota \to \iota \to \iota} y_\iota) \perp_\iota).$[6]

Let $\Psi = (\mu, \nu)$ to be the translation from M to $\overline{M}$ such that:

1. μ is defined as above.
2. ν is the identity function on $\mathcal{V}_{M'}$.
3. ν is the identity function on the members of $\mathcal{C}_{\log}$ except for the constants $=_{\alpha \to \alpha \to o}$ and $\iota_{(\alpha \to o) \to \alpha}$ where $\alpha \in \mathcal{T}$ contains ι.
4. $\nu(=_{\alpha \to \alpha \to o}) = \ ='_{\alpha \to \alpha \to o}$ for all $\alpha \in \mathcal{T}$ containing ι.
5. $\nu(\iota_{(\alpha \to o) \to \alpha}) = \iota'_{(\alpha \to o) \to \alpha}$ for all $\alpha \in \mathcal{T}$ containing ι.
6. $\nu(e_\iota) = e_\iota$.
7. $\nu(*_{\iota \to \iota \to \iota}) = *'_{\iota \to \iota \to \iota}$.

It is easy to see that Φ is a semantic interpretation by Theorem 4.23.

---

[6] The definition of $*'_{\iota \to \iota \to \iota}$ can be simplified by noting that $e_\iota *_{\iota \to \iota \to \iota} e_\iota$ equals e_ι.

6 Conclusion

$\mathrm{CTT_{qe}}$ is a version of Church's type theory with quotation and evaluation described in great detail in [7]. In this paper we have (1) presented $\mathrm{CTT_{uqe}}$, a variant of $\mathrm{CTT_{qe}}$ that admits undefined expressions, partial functions, and multiple base types of individuals, (2) defined a notion of a theory morphism in $\mathrm{CTT_{uqe}}$, and (3) given two simple examples that illustrate the use of theory morphisms in $\mathrm{CTT_{uqe}}$. The theory morphisms of $\mathrm{CTT_{uqe}}$ overcome the Constant Interpretation Problem by requiring constants to be injectively mapped to constants. Since $\mathrm{CTT_{uqe}}$ admits partial functions, $\mathrm{CTT_{uqe}}$ theory morphisms are able to map base types to sets of values of the same type—which enables many additional natural meaning-preserving mappings between theories to be directly defined as $\mathrm{CTT_{uqe}}$ theory morphisms. Thus the paper demonstrates how theory morphisms can be defined in a traditional logic with quotation and evaluation and how support for partial functions can be leveraged to obtain a wider class of theory morphisms.

The two examples presented in Sect. 5 show that constructing a translation in $\mathrm{CTT_{uqe}}$ from a theory T_1 to a theory T_2 will often require defining new dummy constants in T_2. This is certainly a significant inconvenience. However, it is an inconvenience that can be greatly ameliorated in an implementation of $\mathrm{CTT_{uqe}}$ by allowing a user to define a "pre-translation" that is automatically transformed into a bona fide translation. A pre-translation from T_1 and T_2 would be a pair (μ, ν) where μ maps base types to either types or semantically closed predicates, ν maps constants to expressions that need not be constants, and ν is not required to be injective. From the pre-translation, the system would automatically extend T_2 to a theory T_2' and then construct a translation from T_1 to T_2'.

Our long-range goal is to implement a system for developing biform theory graphs utilizing logics equipped with quotation and evaluation. The next step in this direction is to implement $\mathrm{CTT_{qe}}$ by extending HOL Light [11], a simple implementation of HOL [10].

Finally, the author thanks the reviewers for their comments and suggestions.

References

1. Andrews, P.B.: An Introduction to Mathematical Logic and Type Theory: To Truth through Proof, 2nd edn. Kluwer, Dordrecht (2002)
2. Carette, J., Farmer, W.M.: High-level theories. In: Autexier, S., Campbell, J., Rubio, J., Sorge, V., Suzuki, M., Wiedijk, F. (eds.) CICM 2008. LNCS, vol. 5144, pp. 232–245. Springer, Heidelberg (2008). doi:10.1007/978-3-540-85110-3_19
3. Farmer, W.M.: Theory interpretation in simple type theory. In: Heering, J., Meinke, K., Möller, B., Nipkow, T. (eds.) HOA 1993. LNCS, vol. 816, pp. 96–123. Springer, Heidelberg (1994). doi:10.1007/3-540-58233-9_6
4. Farmer, W.M.: Formalizing undefinedness arising in calculus. In: Basin, D., Rusinowitch, M. (eds.) IJCAR 2004. LNCS, vol. 3097, pp. 475–489. Springer, Heidelberg (2004). doi:10.1007/978-3-540-25984-8_35

5. Farmer, W.M.: Andrews' type system with undefinedness. In: Benzmüller, C., Brown, C., Siekmann, J., Statman, R. (eds.) Reasoning in Simple Type Theory: Festschrift in Honor of Peter B: Andrews on his 70th Birthday. Studies in Logic, pp. 223–242. College Publications, London (2008)

6. Farmer, W.M.: The formalization of syntax-based mathematical algorithms using quotation and evaluation. In: Carette, J., Aspinall, D., Lange, C., Sojka, P., Windsteiger, W. (eds.) CICM 2013. LNCS, vol. 7961, pp. 35–50. Springer, Heidelberg (2013). doi:10.1007/978-3-642-39320-4_3

7. Farmer, W.M.: Incorporating quotation and evaluation into Church's type theory. Computing Research Repository (CoRR), abs/1612.02785 (2016). 72 pages

8. Farmer, W.M.: Incorporating quotation and evaluation into Church's type theory: syntax and semantics. In: Kohlhase, M., Johansson, M., Miller, B., de Moura, L., Tompa, F. (eds.) CICM 2016. LNCS, vol. 9791, pp. 83–98. Springer, Cham (2016). doi:10.1007/978-3-319-42547-4_7

9. Farmer, W.M., Guttman, J.D., Javier Thayer, F.: Little theories. In: Kapur, D. (ed.) CADE 1992. LNCS, vol. 607, pp. 567–581. Springer, Heidelberg (1992). doi:10.1007/3-540-55602-8_192

10. Gordon, M.J.C., Melham, T.F.: Introduction to HOL: A Theorem Proving Environment for Higher Order Logic. Cambridge University Press, Cambridge (1993)

11. Harrison, J.: HOL light: an overview. In: Berghofer, S., Nipkow, T., Urban, C., Wenzel, M. (eds.) TPHOLs 2009. LNCS, vol. 5674, pp. 60–66. Springer, Heidelberg (2009). doi:10.1007/978-3-642-03359-9_4

12. Kohlhase, M.: Mathematical knowledge management: transcending the one-brain-barrier with theory graphs. Eur. Math. Soc. (EMS) Newsl. 22–27 (2014)

Semantic Representation of General Topology in the Wolfram Language

Ian Ford$^{(\boxtimes)}$

Wolfram|Alpha, Champaign, IL 61820, USA
ianf@wolfram.com

Abstract. The Wolfram Knowledgebase, powered by the entity framework, contains expertly curated data from thousands of diverse domains. We have begun expanding this framework to include mathematical knowledge, making significant strides in the representation of results pertaining to continued fractions, function spaces, and most recently, topology. This paper will focus on our progress in the representation of general topology. We have curated over 700 entities representing concept definitions, theorem statements, and concrete topological spaces, as well as their corresponding properties, including their formal representations as well as references, computed properties, and other metadata. Virtually every formal representation in this project required extensions to the Wolfram Language, mostly for basic set theory. We will outline all of these design choices by way of examples, as well as present additional functionality for querying, usage messages, formatting, and other computations.

Keywords: General topology · Wolfram Language · Mathematica · Entity framework

1 Introduction

The vast majority of mathematical knowledge is written in what Iancu calls *common mathematical language* (CML) [5], a synthesis of natural language and mathematical formulae. The use of computers is still largely limited to electronic storage of documents written in CML and to formal theorem proving, but there is some interest in knowledge management of flexible formality. In this paper, we explore the use of the Wolfram Data Framework (WDF) [13] for mathematical knowledge management. The WDF is already used to symbolically represent real-world knowledge from thousands of domains, and we are expanding that knowledge to include general topology. With a relatively simple syntax and small set of new constructs, we are able to semiformally represent a substantial amount of topology knowledge while retaining a fair deal of computational utility.

© Springer International Publishing AG 2017
H. Geuvers et al. (Eds.): CICM 2017, LNAI 10383, pp. 163–177, 2017.
DOI: 10.1007/978-3-319-62075-6_12

2 The Wolfram Language and the Wolfram Data Framework

Although Mathematica is commonly referred to as a computer algebra system, the Wolfram Language (which Mathematica implements) is a full-fledged, multi-paradigm programming language [15]. The Wolfram Language syntax is very uniform; in fact, all objects in the Wolfram Language are either *atomic expressions* (e.g. strings, integers, images, symbols) or *compound expressions* of the form f[x,y,...], where f is an arbitrary expression called the *head* of the compound expression and x, y, ... are arbitrary expressions referred to variously as the *arguments*, *elements*, *parts*, *operands*, or *contents* of the compound expression [17]. All other syntactic elements of the Wolfram Language are syntactic sugar. For example, {1,2,3} is syntactic sugar for List[1,2,3]. Computations are performed primarily via symbolic pattern matching and replacement rules. In Mathematica, expressions are printed in a two-dimensional form called *standard form*, which sometimes is quite different from its one-dimensional *full form*.

The Wolfram Data Framework is the name for the combination of the Wolfram Language and the Wolfram Knowledgebase [14]. The Wolfram Knowledgebase consists of millions of datasets called *entities* [18]. Entities are represented symbolically in the Wolfram Language as Entity[type,name], where type is a string called the *entity type*, which identifies a broad category of similar entities, and name is a string called the *canonical name*, which together with the entity type uniquely identifies the entity. The Wolfram Language provides extensive functionality for accessing and doing computations with the data stored in these datasets. The website Wolfram|Alpha [20], powered by the Wolfram Language, supports natural language queries of the Knowledgebase.

There are thousands of entity types in the Knowledgebase, representing such real-world entities as countries, cities, chemicals, species, movies, people, etc., as well as more abstract entities like words, scientific formulas, and even mathematical theorems. The data of each entity is a set of property-value pairs, with each entity type having different lists of supported properties. The values of the properties can in principle be any Wolfram Language expression, but are most commonly physical quantities, strings, dates, and even other entities.

3 General Topology Entity Store

We are augmenting the Knowledgebase with general topology knowledge divided into four main entity types: "TopologyConcept", "TopologyTheorem", "TopologicalSpace", and "TopologySource". Since the general topology entities are not yet part of the Knowledgebase, we have made them available as a custom EntityStore [18] which can be loaded from the Wolfram Data Repository [13]. Full lists of each type can be extracted using EntityList[1]:

---

[1] You can see that the standard form for an entity is a box containing a string called the entity's *common name*. The common name is a property that is available for all entities.

```
In[1]:= PrependTo[$EntityStores, ResourceData["General Topology EntityStore"]];

In[2]:= PrependTo[$ContextPath, "GeneralTopology`"];

In[3]:= RandomSample[EntityList["TopologyConcept"], 10]

Out[3]= { left closed right open interval reals , is maximal with respect to finite intersection property , is star refinement of ,
          indexed product space , is path in , indiscrete topology , uniform structure generated by pseudometric ,
          is cluster point of , space with topology of compact convergence , is subcontinuum of }

In[4]:= RandomSample[EntityList["TopologyTheorem"], 10]

Out[4]= { continuous if preimages of subbasis elements are open , indexed product topology subbasis is a subbasis , Peano curve exists ,
          classical Ascoli's Theorem , hyperconnected locally Hausdorff space is degenerate , metrizable implies perfectly normal ,
          degenerate space is indecomposable continuum , discrete iff totally disconnected locally connected ,
          topology of pointwise convergence subbasis is a subbasis , box topology basis is a basis }

In[5]:= RandomSample[EntityList["TopologicalSpace"], 10]

Out[5]= { R with the compact complement topology , Euclidean space , ordered square ,
          [-1, 1] with the either-or topology , Z with the particular point topology , Sorgenfrey plane ,
          R with the indiscrete topology , S¹ , R with the cocountable topology , R*\Z with the deleted integer topology }

In[6]:= EntityList["TopologySource"]

Out[6]= { Munkres 2000 , Steen and Seebach 1978 }
```

We will discuss each of these entity types in detail in the sections to follow.

4   Scope

The scope of the general topology entity store is significantly restricted compared to formal languages developed for the express purpose of representing mathematics. The definitions and theorems in the general topology entity store are semiformal in the sense that they are symbolic expressions in the Wolfram Language, but there is no underlying logic or notion of well-formedness beyond the basic Wolfram Language syntax. As Iancu notes in [5], the main use of systems such as Coq [2], Mizar [1], Isabelle [11], HOL Light [4], et al. is proof verification and interactive theorem proving, and as such, they require full formalization and a choice of logical foundation. This is a hefty task and not the purpose of this project.[2] Rather, the goal is to develop a semiformal language which is natural and easy to use within the Wolfram Language and which allows as much mathematical knowledge to be added to the Knowledgebase as painlessly as possible.

As in Mizar [1], Metamath [8], and much of the natural language mathematical discourse, the basic language is essentially[3] set theory with first-order

---

[2] There is some interest in introducing a symbolic type language within the Wolfram Language suitable for communicating basic information between proof assistants and Mathematica. This could be used, for example, to use Mathematica's computer algebra functionalities to assist these proof assistants (see Lewis [7]).

[3] We say "essentially" because Wolfram Language syntax is very permissive. Syntactically valid expressions can semantically represent statements in a first-order theory, but are not guaranteed to do so in all cases. For example, ForAll, is intended to be used a first-order quantifier, and functions like Resolve use heuristics (such as assuming variables appearing in inequalities are real numbers) to attempt to remove quantifiers, but ForAll is not axiomitized. The argument structure allows for arbitrary expressions to be passed as arguments, in which cases the expression remains in an unevaluated symbolic form.

logic. Kieffer, Avigad, and Friedman argue in [6] that this is the most promising approach to sharing mathematical knowledge. Our system is less formal than the practical set theory that they introduce in [6], but still allows for similar computations such as finding related definitions and automatically generating natural language definitions and statements from the symbolic representations, as we will show in Sects. 6 and 7. As in [6], the bulk of our examples come from Munkres' popular topology textbook *Topology* [10].

We use the Wolfram Language's built-in domain symbols [16] `Reals`, `Booleans`, `Element` ($\in$), and `NotElement` ($\notin$), the Boolean logical operators [19] `And` (`&&`), `Or` (`||`), `Not` (`!`), `Implies` ($\Rightarrow$), `Equivalent` ($\Leftrightarrow$), `Equal` (`==`), `Unequal` (`!=`), `ForAll` ($\forall$), and `Exists` ($\exists$), as well as the formatting symbols `Subset` ($\subset$), `SubsetEqual` ($\subseteq$), `\[EmptySet]` ($\varnothing$), making use of the fact that these functions remain unevaluated on arbitrary symbolic expressions and thus avoiding foundational questions entirely.

We also introduced several undefined symbols to represent various set constructions (e.g. `SetBuilder`, `SetUnion`, `PowerSet`, `Mapping`). These symbols are (for now) purely representational, but we have provided usage messages that detail the semantics of the various argument structures used.

```
In[7]:= Activate[EntityValue["GeneralTopology", "UsageMessages"]];
```

```
In[8]:= ?SetBuilder
```

SetBuilder[{x_1, ..., x_n}] represents the set {x_1, ..., x_n}.
SetBuilder[f[x], x ∈ X] represents the set of all f(x) such that x ∈ X.
SetBuilder[f[x], x ∈ X, p[x]] represents the set of all f(x) such that x ∈ X and x satisfies the property p.
SetBuilder[f[x_1, ..., x_n], {x_1∈X_1, ..., x_n∈X_n}, p[x_1, ..., x_n]] is the same as above, but for multiple arguments.

5   Formal Representations

Using the above constructs, we can symbolically represent propositions in elementary set theory in a quite natural way. For example, the cofinite topology on the reals can be expressed as follows:

```
In[9]:= cofinite = SetBuilder[U, U ⊆ Reals, U == ∅ || IsFiniteSet[SetMinus[Reals, U]]]
```

```
Out[9]= SetBuilder[U, U ⊆ R, U == ∅ || IsFiniteSet[SetMinus[R, U]]]
```

We represent topological spaces as *associations*, also known as *associative arrays*, *maps*, or *dictionaries*. The *keys* in this association are `"Elements"` and `"Topology"`, where the corresponding values are the underlying set of the space and its topology, respectively. Thus the topological space obtained by giving the reals the cofinite topology could be represented as follows:

```
In[10]:= realsWithCofiniteTopology = <|"Elements" → Reals, "Topology" → cofinite|>
```

```
Out[10]= <|Elements → R, Topology → SetBuilder[U, U ⊆ R, U == ∅ || IsFiniteSet[SetMinus[R, U]]]|>
```

The underlying set and the topology of a topological space can be extracted with application:

```
In[11]:= realsWithCofiniteTopology["Elements"]
```

```
Out[11]= R
```

```
In[12]:= realsWithCofiniteTopology["Topology"]
```

```
Out[12]= SetBuilder[U, U ⊆ R, U == ∅ || IsFiniteSet[SetMinus[R, U]]]
```

We use script variables to represent arbitrary topological spaces. Thus if $\mathcal{X}$ is a topological space variable in a concept definition or theorem statement, then its underlying set is $\mathcal{X}$["Elements"] and $\mathcal{X}$["Topology"] is its collection of open sets, as can be seen in the following theorem:

In[13]:= `local formulation of continuity` (topology theorem) ["InputFormSummaryGrid"]

Theorem	LocalFormulationOfContinuity
AlternateNames	"MunkresTheorem18.2(f)"
QualifyingObjects	$\mathcal{X}$, $\mathcal{Y}$, f
Restrictions	Element[$\mathcal{X}$, Category["Top"]["Ob"]]
	Element[$\mathcal{Y}$, Category["Top"]["Ob"]]
	Element[f, Functions[$\mathcal{X}$["Elements"], $\mathcal{Y}$["Elements"]]]
Statement	Implies[
	Exists[C, C ⊆ $\mathcal{X}$["Topology"] && SetUnion[C] == $\mathcal{X}$["Elements"] && ForAll[U, Element[U, C], Element[
	Restriction[f, U], Category["Top"]["Hom"][Math["AsTopologicalSubspaceOf"][U, $\mathcal{X}$], $\mathcal{Y}$]]]],
	Element[f, Category["Top"]["Hom"][$\mathcal{X}$, $\mathcal{Y}$]]]
References	{{"Munkres2000", "Pages" -> {108}}}

6 Computable Formatting

One of the great strengths of this symbolic representation is that it is quite easy to use the Wolfram Language to define formatting rules to convert these symbolic expressions to a human readable form. This is accomplished by defining a series of `MakeBoxes` rules. `MakeBoxes` is the low-level function used to tell the Mathematica front-end how to display an expression. By defining how it behaves on the symbols `SetBuilder`, `IsFiniteSet`, and `SetMinus`, expressions involving those symbols can be automatically typeset in a human-readable form.

```
In[14]:= SetBuilder /: MakeBoxes[SetBuilder[x_, (r : Element | Subset | SubsetEqual)[x_, A_], p_], TraditionalForm] :=
    MakeBoxes[{Row[{"", r[x, A], " | ", p, ""}]}, TraditionalForm]
```

```
In[15]:= IsFiniteSet /: MakeBoxes[IsFiniteSet[A_], TraditionalForm] :=
    MakeBoxes[Row[{A, " is finite"}], TraditionalForm]
```

```
In[16]:= SetMinus /: MakeBoxes[SetMinus[X_, A_], TraditionalForm] :=
    MakeBoxes[PrecedenceForm[Backslash[X, A], 300], TraditionalForm]
```

```
In[17]:= cofinite // TraditionalForm
```

Out[17]//TraditionalForm=
    $\{U \subseteq R \mid U = \emptyset \vee R \setminus U \text{ is finite}\}$

To access and use these and other formatting rules in your Wolfram Language session, evaluate `Activate[EntityValue["GeneralTopology", "FormattingRules"]];`.

7 Topology Concepts

Topology concepts *represent* function definitions of various types. For example, one can think of `is compact` as a predicate on the class of topological spaces; i.e., a function which accepts a topological space and outputs `True` if the space is compact and `False` otherwise. Other concepts represent relations. For example, `is topology on` can be thought of as a function which takes two sets as arguments and outputs whether the first is a topology on the second. Still other concepts represent more general functions or constructions. For example, `path components` can be thought of as taking a topological space and returning its set of path components.

Now although these entities can be thought of as functions in this way, the only sense in which they are *actually* functions is that they may take entity properties as input to output the corresponding property value. To represent a concept entity as a function suitable for formal representations, we use the `Math` head and pass the canonical name as an argument as we will illustrate with the following example:

In[18]:= [**uniform metric reals** (topology concept)] ["Arguments"]

Out[18]= {J}

In[19]:= [**uniform metric reals** (topology concept)] ["Restrictions"]

Out[19]= {J ∈ Sets, J ≠ ∅}

In[20]:= [**uniform metric reals** (topology concept)] ["Notation"]

Out[20]= {d̄ → Math[StandardBoundedMetric][Tuple[R, StandardMetricReals]]}

In[21]:= [**uniform metric reals** (topology concept)] ["Output"]

Out[21]= Mapping[SetProduct[Functions[J, R], Functions[J, R]], R, Tuple[x, y] ↦ Supremum[SetBuilder[d̄[x[j], y[j]], j ∈ J]]]

Thus Math["UniformMetricReals"] takes a nonempty set J as input and outputs the uniform metric on $\mathbb{R}^J$. The elements of [uniform metric reals] ["Notation"] are just replacement rules which can be applied to the other parts of the definition without changing the meaning. In this case, each instance of $\bar{d}$ can be interchanged with Math["StandardBoundedMetric"][Tuple[Reals, StandardMetricReals]]:

In[22]:= ReplaceAll[[**uniform metric reals** (topology concept)] ["Output"], [**uniform metric reals** (topology concept)] ["Notation"]]

Out[22]= Mapping[SetProduct[Functions[J, R], Functions[J, R]], R,
  Tuple[x, y] ↦ Supremum[SetBuilder[Math[StandardBoundedMetric][Tuple[R, StandardMetricReals]][x[j], y[j]], j ∈ J]]]

The use of notation often greatly increases readability and allows argument restrictions and outputs to be expressed closer to how a human would write them.

The type "TopologyConcept" has several other properties containing metadata and computed values. The full list can be accessed with EntityProperties:

In[23]:= EntityProperties["TopologyConcept"]

Out[23]= { [alternate names] , [arguments] , [references] , [input form summary grid] ,
  [label] , [notation] , [output] , [property relations] , [referenced concepts] , [reference citations] ,
  [related concepts] , [related theorems] , [restrictions] , [summary grid] , [topological property] }

To see the source for a concept entity, use [reference citations] (canonical name "References"):

In[24]:= [**is compact** (topology concept)] ["References"]

Out[24]= {{ [Munkres 2000] , Pages → {164} }, { [Steen and Seebach 1978] , Pages → {4, 18} }}

[Munkres 2000] [10] and [Steen and Seebach 1978] [12] are entities of type "TopologySource" and thus have their own properties:

In[25]:= EntityProperties["TopologySource"]

Out[25]= { [ASIN] , [authors] , [DOI] , [ISBN-10] , [ISBN-13] , [label] , [language] , [page count] ,
  [preface page count] , [publication city] , [publication date] , [publication type] , [publisher] , [title] }

The property [references] (canonical name "FormattedReferences") uses this information to compute a textual representation of the reference:

In[26]:= [**is compact** (topology concept)] ["FormattedReferences"]

Out[26]= {James Munkres. *Topology, 2nd ed.* Upper Saddle River: Prentice Hall, p. 164, 2000., Lynn Steen and J. Arthur Seebach, Jr. *Counterexamples in Topology, 2nd ed.* New York City: Springer-Verlag, pp. 4 and 18, 1978.}

The property [alternate names] gives alternative canonical names for some concepts:

In[27]:= [**is Hausdorff** (topology concept)] ["AlternateNames"]

Out[27]= IsT2

The property [label] is used by `EntityStore` to specify the common name of the entity. In most cases, this is just the canonical name converted to lower case and with spaces added between words, but in some cases it is quite different[4]:

In[28]:= **Entity["TopologyConcept", "IsT3.5"]**

Out[28]= is $T_{3\frac{1}{2}}$

The properties [related concepts], [related theorems], and [referenced concepts] are computed from the formalizations in [restrictions], [notation], and [output] using the Wolfram Language's pattern matching capabilities. A *referenced concept* is a concept which shows up in the definition, whereas as a *related concept* or *related theorem* is a concept or theorem which references the concept.

In[29]:= **metric spaces** (topology concept) ["ReferencedConcepts"]

Out[29]= { is metric on }

In[30]:= **metric spaces** (topology concept) ["RelatedConcepts"]

Out[30]= { open ball , closed ball , metric sphere , metric topology basis , metric topology , topological space from metric , is bounded subset of , diameter , standard bounded metric , is metric continuous , converges uniformly to , distance point to set , is uniformly continuous , is Cauchy sequence in , is complete , uniform metric , uniform topology , space with uniform topology , is bounded function , bounded functions , sup metric , is isometric embedding , are isometric , metric closure , is completion of , is totally bounded , is equicontinuous at , is equicontinuous , is pointwise bounded , topology of compact convergence basis element , topology of compact convergence basis , topology of compact convergence , space with topology of compact convergence }

In[31]:= **metric spaces** (topology concept) ["RelatedTheorems"]

Out[31]= { metric topology basis is a basis , standard bounded metric equivalent topology , subspace of metric space is metric space , countable product of metric spaces is metrizable , metric continuous iff continuous , Lebesgue Number Lemma , Uniform Continuity Theorem , complete if every Cauchy sequence has convergent subsequence , uniform metric is a metric , product of complete metric space is complete with uniform metric , set of continuous maps into metric space is closed with uniform metric , set of bounded maps into metric space is closed with uniform metric , sup metric is a metric , metric space isometrically embeds into complete metric space , completions are unique up to isometry , metric space is compact iff complete and totally bounded , totally bounded family of continuous functions with uniform metric is equicontinous , equicontinuous family of continuous functions between compact spaces is totally bounded with uniform metric , equicontinuous family of continuous functions between compact spaces is totally bounded with sup metric , topology of copmact convergence basis is a basis , sequence converges in topology of compact convergence iff converges uniformly on compact subspaces , continuous maps compactly generated to metric space is closed in topology of compact convergence , limit of compact convergent sequence from compactly generated to metric is continuous , comparison of uniform compact convergence pointwise convergence topologies , space with compact-open topology is subspace of space with topology of compact convergence , Ascoli's Theorem , Ascoli's Theorem converse , totally bounded implies bounded }

---

[4] This is accomplished by defining a default function used to calculate the common name from the canonical name, but which can be manually overwritten.

All of the defining properties of a concept can be quickly obtained with input form summary grid :

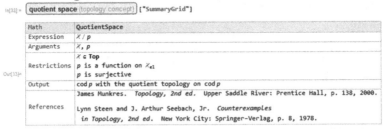

We have defined extensive formatting rules which allow the formal representation of a concept to be automatically converted to a typeset form. These typeset forms are available through summary grid :

In[33]:= quotient space (topology concept) ["SummaryGrid"]

Math	QuotientSpace
Expression	X / p
Arguments	X, p
Restrictions	$X \in$ **Top** p is a function on $X_{\bullet 1}$ p is surjective
Output	cod p with the quotient topology on cod p
References	James Munkres. *Topology, 2nd ed.* Upper Saddle River: Prentice Hall, p. 138, 2000. Lynn Steen and J. Arthur Seebach, Jr. *Counterexamples in Topology, 2nd ed.* New York City: Springer-Verlag, p. 8, 1978.

8   Topology Theorems

Topology theorems share many of the same properties as topology concepts. Rather than having *arguments*, they have *qualifying objects*, and rather than an *output*, they have a *statement*[5]. Other than that, most of the properties are the same as for concepts:

In[34]:= EntityProperties["TopologyTheorem"]

Out[34]= { alternate names , references , input form summary grid , label , notation , property relations , qualifying objects , referenced concepts , reference citations , restrictions , statement , summary grid }

Notice that there is no "RelatedConcepts" or "RelatedTheorems" for "TopologyTheorem", just as there is no "ReferencedTheorems" for "TopologyConcept". This is because we do not have a proof language, and thus theorems are never referenced in our formal representations. While we don't have proofs, we do have theorem statements. Here is a famous metrizability result due to Nagata and Smirnov:

---

[5] One might ask why these properties even have different names from the corresponding concept properties. After all, under the Curry-Howard correspondence, a universally quantified proposition is essentially a function type. For example, $\forall_{x, x \in \text{Reals}} x^2 \geq 0$ can be viewed as a function which takes a real number x and outputs a proof that $x^2 \geq 0$. This is natural and powerful in languages such as Lean [9] which are based on dependent type theory, but as the Wolfram Language does not have a type system, this equivalence is not made.

```
In[35]:= Nagata-Smirnov Metrization Theorem (topology theorem) [{"SummaryGrid", "PropertyRelations"}]
```

Theorem	NagataSmirnovMetrizationTheorem
AlternateNames	MunkresTheorem40.3
QualifyingObjects	X
Restrictions	X ∈ Top
Statement	X is regular and X has a σ-locally finite basis ⇔ X is metrizable
	James Munkres. *Topology*, 2nd ed. Upper Saddle River: Prentice Hall, pp. 250 - 252, 2000.
References	Lynn Steen and J. Arthur Seebach, Jr. *Counterexamples in Topology*, 2nd ed. New York City: Springer-Verlag, p. 37, 1978.

```
{IsMetrizable ⇔ IsRegular && HasSigmaLocallyFiniteBasis}}
```

Notice the property relations property. A *topological property* is a property of a topological space that is preserved under homeomorphisms. Some theorems, such as the Nagata-Smirnov Metrization Theorem, express first order relationships between these topological properties and have simplified forms given in property relations which are suitable for computation. The full list of supported topological properties is available as a property class for the entity type "TopologicalSpace":

```
In[36]:= EntityProperties[EntityPropertyClass["TopologicalSpace", "TopologicalProperties"]]
```

Out[36]= { has σ-locally finite basis , is arc connected , is Baire space , is biconnected , is compact , is compactly generated , is completely Hausdorff , is completely metrizable , is completely normal , is completely regular , is connected , is countable space , is countably compact , is countably infinite space , is countably metacompact , is countably paracompact , is curve , is degenerate space , is disconnected , is discrete , is extremally disconnected Hausdorff , is finite space , is first countable , is fully normal , is fully T_4 , is Hausdorff , is hyperconnected , is indecomposable continuum , is indiscrete , is infinite space , is limit point compact , is Lindelöf , is linear continuum , is locally arc connected , is locally compact , is locally connected , is locally Hausdorff , is locally metrizable , is locally path connected , is manifold , is metacompact , is metrizable , is nondegenerate space , is normal , is paracompact , is path connected , is perfectly normal , is perfectly T_4 , is perfect space , is pseudocompact , is pseudometrizable , is punctiform , is regular , is scattered , is second countable , is semiregular , is separable , is sequentially compact , is σ-compact , is σ-locally compact , is strongly locally compact , is surface , is T_0 , is T_1 , is T_3 , is $T_{3½}$, is T_4 , is T_5 , is topological continuum , is totally disconnected , is totally ordered set , is totally pathwise disconnected , is totally separated , is ultraconnected , is uncountable space , is Urysohn space , is well ordered set , is zero dimensional , satisfies the countable chain condition }

These properties are in one-to-one correspondence with topology concepts with the same name. We can switch between these topological properties and topology concepts effortlessly using the entity framework:

```
In[37]:= compactProperty = EntityProperty["TopologicalSpace", "IsCompact"]
```

Out[37]= is compact

```
In[38]:= compactConcept = Entity["TopologyConcept", "IsCompact"]
```

Out[38]= is compact

```
In[39]:= compactProperty == compactConcept["TopologicalProperty"]
```

Out[39]= True

```
In[40]:= compactConcept == compactProperty["Concept"]
```

Out[40]= True

A topology concept can also have property relations, as you may have noticed earlier. For example:

In[41]:= **is σ-locally compact** (topology concept) [{"SummaryGrid", "PropertyRelations"}]

Out[41]=
Math	IsSigmaLocallyCompact
Expression	x is σ-locally compact
Arguments	x
Restrictions	x is locally compact
Output	x is σ-compact
References	James Munkres. *Topology*, 2nd ed. Upper Saddle River: Prentice Hall, pp. 289 and 316, 2000. Lynn Steen and J. Arthur Seebach, Jr. *Counterexamples in Topology*, 2nd ed. New York City: Springer-Verlag, p. 21, 1978.

{IsSigmaLocallyCompact ⟺ IsLocallyCompact && IsSigmaCompact}

Since a space is defined to be σ-locally compact precisely when it is locally compact and σ-compact, we get the property relation "IsSigmaLocally Compact"⟺"IsLocallyCompact"&&"IsSigmaCompact". Some concepts get property relations based solely on the restrictions property:

In[42]:= **is biconnected** (topology concept) [{"SummaryGrid", "PropertyRelations"}]

Out[42]=
Math	IsBiconnected
Expression	x is biconnected
Arguments	x
Restrictions	x is connected
Output	$\forall_{\{u,v\},u}$ is a connected subspace of x and v is a connected subspace of x $(u_{e1} \cap v_{e1} = \emptyset$ and u is a nondegenerate space and v is a nondegenerate space $\Rightarrow u_{e1} \cup v_{e1} \neq x_{e1})$
References	Lynn Steen and J. Arthur Seebach, Jr. *Counterexamples in Topology*, 2nd ed. New York City: Springer-Verlag, p. 33, 1978.

{IsBiconnected ⟹ IsConnected}

While the output here is definitely a topological property, it is not one that has a name, so the only property relation in this case is "IsBiconnected"⟹"IsConnected". The Wolfram Language and the entity framework make it easy to obtain a list of all curated property relations:

In[43]:= thms = EntityValue[#, "PropertyRelations"] & /@ {"TopologyConcept", "TopologyTheorem"} // Flatten // DeleteMissing

As we alluded to earlier, these Boolean expressions can be symbolically manipulated and transformed. For example, using the theorems Hausdorff implies T₁ and T₁ implies T₀, we should be able to conclude that any Hausdorff space is T_0:

In[44]:= hypothesis =
And @@ Join[{"IsHausdorff"}, Hausdorff implies T₁ (topology theorem) ["PropertyRelations"], T₁ implies T₀ (topology theorem) ["PropertyRelations"]]

Out[44]= IsHausdorff && (IsHausdorff ⟹ IsT1) && (IsT1 ⟹ IsT0)

In[45]:= conclusion = LogicalExpand[hypothesis]

Out[45]= IsHausdorff && IsT0 && IsT1

We can make these kinds of deduction using all of our property relations as assumptions. First, we preprocess each property relation into an equivalent list of simple implications of (conjunctive) clauses. For example, a property relation of the form P ⟹ Q ⟺ R becomes the six relations P&&Q ⟹ R,

P&&R $\Rightarrow$ Q, P&&!Q $\Rightarrow$!R, P&&!R $\Rightarrow$!Q, Q&&!R $\Rightarrow$!P, and !Q&&R $\Rightarrow$!P. Then for some list of input assumptions (e.g. {"IsHausdorff", !"IsCompact"}), we simply scan through the list of these processed property relations, adding to our list of assumptions the right hand side of any relation where the left hand side is a subset of our list of assumptions, then repeat this process until we reach a fixed point. A GUI for making these kinds of deductions is available as EntityValue["GeneralTopology","Graph"]:[6]

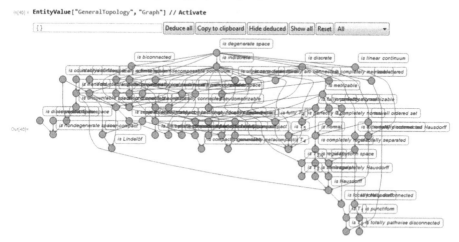

This is the transitive reduction of the graph of the binary relation Implies; i.e., directed edges represent logical implication and the number of edges is minimal among graphs with the same transitive closure. Left-clicking a node adds it to the list of assumptions, while right-clicking a node adds its negation to the list of assumptions. All deduced properties are dynamically highlighted green for True and red for False. Alternatively, you can enter a list of assumptions in the input field and click Deduce all . You can also choose to only display the relationships among properties belonging to one of several property classes:

In[47]:= EntityValue["TopologicalSpace", "PropertyClasses"]

Out[47]= { separation properties , countability properties , compactness properties , metrizability properties ,

connectedness properties , order properties , cardinality properties , topological properties , local properties }

---

[6] The π-Base project [3] uses a similar representation of topological property relations and uses them under the hood to deduce topological properties from the properties asserted of their many example topological spaces, but to our knowledge they do not provide an easy way for users to do their own computations as we do here.

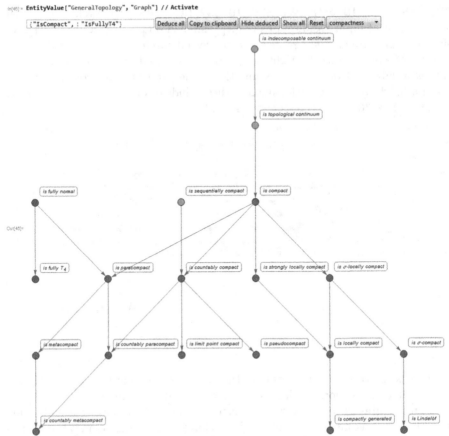

The <kbd>Hide deduced</kbd> button supresses the properties which have already been classified and redraws the graph taking into account the new logical implications that may exist under those assumptions. For example, path connectedness and connectedness are equivalent for a locally path connected space, which we can see by clicking <kbd>is locally path connected</kbd> and then <kbd>Hide deduced</kbd>:

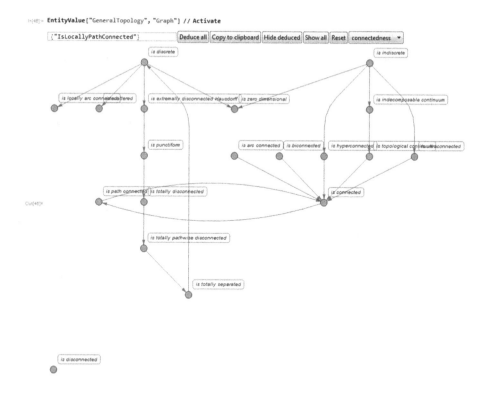

```
In[46]:= EntityValue["GeneralTopology", "Graph"] // Activate
```

9   Topological Spaces

We are in the process of representing specific topological spaces as entities. Topological properties simply become entity properties:

```
In[48]:= R (topological space) ["IsHausdorff"]
Out[48]= True
```

The entity framework makes finding counterexamples easy:

```
In[49]:= EntityList@EntityClass["TopologicalSpace", {"IsConnected" → True, "IsPathConnected" → False}]
Out[49]= { R with the K-topology , topologist's sine curve , Z with the cofinite topology , R with the cocountable topology }
```

There are also properties representing other data associated with a space:

```
In[50]:= R⁺ \ Z with the deleted integer topology (topological space) [{"Elements", "Topology"}] // TraditionalForm
Out[50]//TraditionalForm=
        {{x ∈ R | x > 0 ∧ x ∉ Z}, the topology on {x ∈ R | x > 0 ∧ x ∉ Z} generated by {(n − 1, n) | n ∈ Z ∧ n > 0}}
```

Some entities are parametrized:

```
In[51]:= finite indiscrete space (topological space) ["IsBiconnected"]
Out[51]= Function[n̂, n̂ < 4]
```

In this case the parameter is the cardinality of the space. You can pass parameters to an entity by using `EntityInstance`:

```
In[52]:= EntityInstance[ finite indiscrete space (topological space) , n̂ → 3]["IsBiconnected"]
Out[52]= True
```

You can get more information on the possible parameters with the variables, variable descriptions, and variable constraints properties:

In[53]:= `finite indiscrete space` (topological space) [{"Variables", "VariableDescriptions", "VariableConstraints"}]

Out[58]:= {{ṅ}, {cardinality}, Function[ṅ, ṅ ∈ Z && ṅ > 0]}

Not all properties of a parametrized entity need to depend on the parameter:

In[54]:= `finite indiscrete space` (topological space) ["IsConnected"]

Out[54]= True

Each topological space entity can be represented in a formal statement with head `TopologicalSpace` (much like each concept entity can be represented with the `Math` head):

In[55]:= `closed interval of reals is compact` (topology theorem) ["InputFormSummaryGrid"]

Theorem	ClosedIntervalOfRealsIsCompact
AlternateNames	"MunkresCorollary27.2"
QualifyingObjects	I
Restrictions	Element[I, Math["ClosedIntervals"][Tuple[Reals, StandardOrderReals]]]
Statement	Math["IsCompact"][Math["AsTopologicalSubspaceOf"][I, TopologicalSpace["Reals"]]]
References	{{"Munkres2000", "Pages" -> {173}}}

This, of course, allows formatting rules to be defined for the topological space:

In[56]:= `closed interval of reals is compact` (topology theorem) ["SummaryGrid"]

Theorem	ClosedIntervalOfRealsIsCompact
AlternateNames	MunkresCorollary27.2
QualifyingObjects	I
Restrictions	I is a closed interval of (R, <ₓ)
Statement	I ⊆ R is compact
References	James Munkres. *Topology, 2nd ed.* Upper Saddle River: Prentice Hall, p. 173, 2000.

10   Future Work

As the most recent addition to the entity store, we are still in the process of curating topological spaces for the entity store; however, these examples demonstrate that the entity framework is well-suited as a container for mathematical knowledge. The formalization we used builds on the Wolfram Language in a natural way that makes it quite straightforward to curate knowledge, while still achieving a good degree of computational utility. Potential future improvements to the entity store include continued curation of entities, the curation of grammar rules for natural language queries with Wolfram|Alpha, the development of a proof language, adding our set theory constructs to the Wolfram Language, and perhaps even incorporating a type language that can be reflected to automated theorem provers and proof assistants.

Acknowledgements. I thank CICM, Michael Trott, and Wolfram Research for this opportunity, as well as Stephen Wolfram, Michael Trott, James Mulnix, Eric Weisstein, Robert Lewis, and José Martín-García for their support and great work on pure mathematics in the Wolfram Language.

References

1. Bancerek, G., Byliński, C., Grabowski, A., Korniłowicz, A., Matuszewski, R., Naumowicz, A., Pąk, K., Urban, J.: Mizar: state-of-the-art and beyond. In: Kerber, M., Carette, J., Kaliszyk, C., Rabe, F., Sorge, V. (eds.) CICM 2015. LNCS, vol. 9150, pp. 261–279. Springer, Cham (2015). doi:10.1007/978-3-319-20615-8_17

2. Bertot, Y., Castéran, P.: Interactive Theorem Proving and Program Development - Coq'Art: The Calculus of Inductive Constructions. Texts in Theoretical Computer Science. An EATCS Series. Springer, Heidelberg (2004). https://doi.org/10.1007/978-3-662-07964-5
3. Dabbs, J.: π-Base. https://topology.jdabbs.com/
4. Harrison, J.: HOL light: a tutorial introduction. In: Srivas, M., Camilleri, A. (eds.) FMCAD 1996. LNCS, vol. 1166, pp. 265–269. Springer, Heidelberg (1996). doi:10.1007/BFb0031814
5. Iancu, M.: Towards Flexiformal Mathematics. Ph.D. thesis, Jacobs University (2016)
6. Kieffer, S., Avigad, J., Friedman, H.: A language for mathematical knowledge management, January 2011. https://arxiv.org/abs/0805.1386
7. Lewis, R.Y.: An extensible ad hoc interface between Lean and Mathematica. http://www.andrew.cmu.edu/user/rlewis1/leanmm/leanmm_public_draft.pdf
8. Megill, N.: Metamath: A Computer Language for Pure Mathematics. Lulu Press, Morrisville
9. de Moura, L., Kong, S., Avigad, J., van Doorn, F., von Raumer, J.: The Lean Theorem Prover (system description). https://leanprover.github.io/papers/system.pdf
10. Munkres, J.: Topology, 2nd edn. Prentice Hall, Upper Saddle River (2000)
11. Nipkow, T., Klein, G.: Concrete Semantics - With Isabelle/HOL. Springer, Cham (2014). http://dx.doi.org/10.1007/978-3-319-10542-0
12. Steen, L., Seebach, J.A.: Counterexamples in Topology, 2nd edn. Springer, New York (1978)
13. Wolfram Research Inc.: Wolfram Data Repository. https://datarepository.wolframcloud.com/
14. Wolfram Research Inc.: Wolfram Knowledgebase. https://www.wolfram.com/knowledgebase/
15. Wolfram Research Inc.: The Wolfram Language. https://www.wolfram.com/language/
16. Wolfram Research Inc.: Wolfram Language & System Documentation Center. Assumptions and Domains. http://reference.wolfram.com/language/guide/AssumptionsAndDomains.html
17. Wolfram Research Inc.: Wolfram Language & System Documentation Center. Expressions. https://reference.wolfram.com/language/tutorial/ExpressionsOverview.html
18. Wolfram Research Inc.: Wolfram Language & System Documentation Center. Knowledge Representation & Access. https://reference.wolfram.com/language/guide/KnowledgeRepresentationAndAccess.html
19. Wolfram Research Inc.: Wolfram Language & System Documentation. Logic & Boolean Algebra. https://reference.wolfram.com/language/guide/LogicAndBooleanAlgebra.html
20. Wolfram Research Inc.: Wolfram|Alpha. https://www.wolframalpha.com/

Zeta Types and Tannakian Symbols as a Method for Representing Mathematical Knowledge

Andreas Holmstrom[1,2(✉)] and Torstein Vik[2]

[1] Stockholm University, Stockholm, Sweden
andreas.holmstrom@gmail.com
[2] Fagerlia vgs, Ålesund, Norway
torsteinv64@gmail.com

Abstract. We present two closely related notions called (1) a zeta type and (2) a Tannakian symbol. These are data types for representing information about number-theoretic objects, and we argue that a database built out of zeta types and Tannakian symbols could lead to interesting discoveries, similar to what has been achieved for example by the OEIS, the LMFDB, and other existing databases of mathematical objects. We give several examples illustrating what database records would look like, and we describe a tiny prototype database which has already been used to find and automatically prove new theorems about multiplicative functions.

Keywords: Number theory · Multiplicative functions · Tannakian symbols · Zeta types · Zeta functions · L-functions · Automated conjecture-making · Automated theorem proving

1 Introduction

The aim of this paper is to introduce two new data types, to argue for their usefulness with regards to computer representations of objects studied in modern number theory, and finally to propose a design for a database containing such objects.

We choose to focus in this paper on a specific type of mathematical object called a multiplicative function. Multiplicative functions are ubiquitous in number theory - in addition to classical examples like the Euler function or the Liouville function, there is a multiplicative function associated to any object to which one can assign a *zeta function with Euler product*. The objects falling into this category include motives, Galois representations, automorphic representations, schemes, and certain classes of finitely generated groups. We emphasize however that the scope of this project is much bigger, and we refer to the CICM 2016 work-in progress paper [9] for more details, where the first author made an attempt at formulating these ideas in greater generality, focusing among other things on the *lambda-ring structures* which exist on classes of number-theoretic objects.

H. Geuvers et al. (Eds.): CICM 2017, LNAI 10383, pp. 178–192, 2017.
DOI: 10.1007/978-3-319-62075-6_13

The algebraic theory underlying our computational ideas are also described in a report by Ane Espeseth and the second author [6] and in more depth in the paper [5] which should appear on arXiv soon. The main point to take away from these papers should be that the design choices that we propose here are guided by specific domain knowledge in number theory and related research fields, and this domain knowledge is crucial if we hope to achieve a database that is useful in practice for conjecture-making and automated reasoning about number-theoretic objects.

1.1 Notation

In this paper, a natural number is the same thing as a strictly positive integer, and we write $\mathbb{N}$ for the set of natural numbers. We also use the standard notation $\mathbb{Z}$, $\mathbb{Q}$, $\mathbb{R}$ and $\mathbb{C}$ for the set of integers, the set of rationals, the set of reals, and the set of complex numbers respectively. We write $\mathbb{P}$ for the set of prime numbers, and we use the notation $gcd(a, b)$ for the greatest common divisor of two natural numbers a and b.

2 Zeta Types

We begin by a few definitions, together with several examples of classical multiplicative functions. A general reference for the theory of multiplicative functions is the book of McCarthy [13].

Definition 1. *An* arithmetical function *is a function from* $\mathbb{N}$ *to* $\mathbb{C}$*. An arithmetical function* f *is called a* multiplicative function *if it satisfies the two conditions*

(i) $f(1) = 1$
(ii) $f(mn) = f(m)f(n)$ *for all* m, n *which are coprime.*

A multiplicative function is called completely multiplicative *if the second condition holds for all* m, n *in* $\mathbb{N}$*.*

Definition 2. *A* prime power *is an integer of the form* p^e*, where* p *is a prime number and* e *is a natural number.*

The first few prime powers are 2, 3, 4, 5, 7, 8, 9, 11, 13, 16, 17, 19, ...
    That a function f is multiplicative implies that all function values can be computed if we know the function values for prime power arguments.

Example 1. The Euler totient function is defined by

$\varphi(n)$ = the number of integers x such that $1 \leq x \leq n$ and $gcd(x, n) = 1$

From this explicit definition, we can easily compute values of $\varphi(n)$ for small n. These function values are stored in the Online Encyclopedia of Integer Sequences (OEIS). To be more specific, the first 69 values are stored, and they are:

1, 1, 2, 2, 4, 2, 6, 4, 6, 4, 10, 4, 1, 2, 6, 8, 8, 16, 6, 18, 8, 12, 10, 22, 8, 20, 12, 18, 12, 28, 8, 30, 16, 20, 16, 24, 12, 36, 18, 24, 16, 40, 12, 42, 20, 24, 22, 46, 16, 42, 20, 32, 24, 52, 18, 40, 24, 36, 28, 58, 16, 60, 30, 36, 32, 48, 20, 66, 32, 44.

The fact that the Euler function is multiplicative means that many of these values are redundant; in fact, it would be a good idea to store only the numbers $\varphi(p^e)$ for primes p and exponents e. If we set up a table with these numbers (for small values of p and e, we get Table 1.

Table 1. Bell table of the Euler φ function

$\varphi(p^e)$	$e=1$	$e=2$	$e=3$	$e=4$	$e=5$	$e=6$	$e=7$
$p=2$	1	2	4	8	16	32	64
$p=3$	2	6	18	54	162	486	1458
$p=5$	4	20	100	500	2500	12500	62500
$p=7$	6	42	294	2058	14406	100842	705894
$p=11$	10	110	1210	13310	146410	1610510	17715610
$p=13$	12	156	2028	26364	342732	4455516	57921708

This table has 6 rows and 7 columns, and a small combinatorics argument shows that it gives us access to precisely $(7+1)^6 = 262144$ different values of the Euler function. Clearly this is better than having only 69 values, and we have used approximately the same amount of storage space. But an even bigger advantage is that with the new representation, it is easy to spot patterns in the function values. Looking at the list from OEIS, there is no obvious pattern, beyond perhaps the fact that most of the function values are even. In Table 1 on the other hand, it is easy to see that each row is a geometric sequence, with a very simple formula both for the initial term and for the successive quotient!

This example leads us to the definition of our first new data type.

Definition 3. *We define a zeta type to be a two-dimensional array of numbers, indexed in one direction by the prime numbers, and in the other direction by the natural numbers. More formally, for any commutative ring R, we define an R-valued zeta type to be a partially defined function from $\mathbb{P} \times \mathbb{N}$ to R.*

If we want to specify how many rows and columns we store in the computer, we may speak of a zeta type *truncated after the prime $p = 13$ and the exponent $e = 7$*, or use some other similar description.

In the present article, our focus will be on examples arising from multiplicative functions, but we emphasize that the concept of a zeta type also has many other applications.

Definition 4. *Let f be a multiplicative function. The* Bell table *of f is the array of function values* $f(p^e)$ *for prime numbers p and positive integer exponents e.*

Example 2. The Möbius μ function is stored in the OEIS with the following sequence of function values:

1, −1, −1, 0, −1, 1, −1, 0, 0, 1, −1, 0, −1, 1, 1, 0, −1, 0, −1, 0, 1, 1, −1, 0, 0, 1, 0, 0, −1, −1, −1, 0, 1, 1, 1, 0, −1, 1, 1, 0, −1, −1, −1, 0, 0, 1, −1, 0, 0, 0, 1, 0, −1, 0, 1, 0, 1, 1, −1, 0, −1, 1, 0, 0, 1, −1, −1, 0, 1, −1, −1, 0, −1, 1, 0, 0, 1, −1.

It is very hard to spot any patterns here. But look at Table 2, where the same function is represented by its Bell table.

Table 2. Bell table of the Möbius μ function

$\mu(p^e)$	$e = 1$	$e = 2$	$e = 3$	$e = 4$	$e = 5$	$e = 6$	$e = 7$
$p = 2$	−1	0	0	0	0	0	0
$p = 3$	−1	0	0	0	0	0	0
$p = 5$	−1	0	0	0	0	0	0
$p = 7$	−1	0	0	0	0	0	0
$p = 11$	−1	0	0	0	0	0	0
$p = 13$	−1	0	0	0	0	0	0

We hope that these two examples show the advantages of the zeta type representation over the more traditional "list of function values" representation.

One may ask how many rows and columns should be included in a finite display of a zeta type. This will vary, depending on the situation and the intended applications. As we will see in the next section, the rows of a zeta type typically satisfy some simple recursion formula, and the number of columns displayed should in such cases be large enough to detect what the recursion formula is.

3   Tannakian Symbols

In the previous section we compared the representation of a multiplicative function as a list of function values with its representation as a zeta type. The aim of this section is to construct yet another representation, which is (for many purposes) even better than the zeta type representation.

The construction does not work for all multiplicative functions, only for those which satisfy a property we call rationality. The good news is that the vast majority of all multiplicative functions appearing in the number theory literature satisfy this property.

Definition 5. *Let f be a multiplicative function, and let p be a prime number. The* Bell series *of f at p (see McCarthy [13], p. 60) is the formal power series*

$$f_p(t) = 1 + f(p)\, t + f(p^2)\, t^2 + f(p^3)\, t^3 + \dots$$

Here t is a formal variable, and the series is an element of the formal power series ring $\mathbb{C}[t]$.

Example 3. Looking at the Bell table of the Euler φ function above, we see that the Bell series of φ at the prime number 5 is equal to

$$1 + 4t + 20t^2 + 100t^3 + 500t^4 + 2500t^5 + \dots$$

Definition 6. *A power series is called* rational *if it can be expressed as a quotient $v(t)/u(t)$, where both $u(t)$ and $v(t)$ are polynomials.*

Definition 7. *We say that a multiplicative function is* rational *if for every prime number p, the Bell series $f_p(t)$ is a rational power series.*

Equivalently (see Stanley [17, Theorem 4.1.1]), a multiplicative function is rational if each row in its Bell table is a linearly recursive sequence (where we allow any complex coefficients in the linear recursion relation).

Given a rational multiplicative function f and a prime number p, we want to explain what we mean by the Tannakian symbol of f at the prime p. First of all, recall that the *reciprocal* of a non-zero complex number z is by definition the number $\frac{1}{z}$. Let $u(t)$ and $v(t)$ be two polynomials with no complex roots in common, such that

$$f_p(t) = \frac{v(t)}{u(t)}$$

Such polynomials exist because f is rational, and they are uniquely determined up to a constant factor. Let $\alpha_1, \alpha_2, \dots, \alpha_m$ be the list of all reciprocals of the complex roots of $u(t)$, listed with multiplicity. Similarly, let $\beta_1, \dots, \beta_n$ be the reciprocals of the complex roots of $v(t)$, listed with multiplicity. This definition means precisely that the Bell series of f at the prime p can be expressed by the formula

$$f_p(t) = \frac{\prod(1 - \beta_j t)}{\prod(1 - \alpha_i t)} \tag{1}$$

Definition 8. *Let f be a rational multiplicative function and let p be a prime. We define the* Tannakian symbol *of f at p to be the formal symbol*

$$\frac{\{\alpha_1, \alpha_2, \dots, \alpha_m\}}{\{\beta_1, \dots, \beta_n\}}$$

where the numbers α_i and β_j are taken from the right hand side of Eq. 1.

The elements α_i are referred to as the upstairs elements, and the elements β_j are referred to as the downstairs elements. The object $\{\alpha_1, \alpha_2, \ldots, \alpha_m\}$ (and also the object $\{\beta_1, \ldots, \beta_n\}$) is a multiset of complex numbers (so repeated elements are allowed, and the order of the elements is irrelevant). For the reader who wants a precise mathematical explanation of what type of object a Tannakian symbol is, we can formulate this as follows.

Definition 9. *A Tannakian symbol is an ordered pair of finite disjoint multisets of complex numbers, or (equivalently) a function with finite support from $\mathbb{C}$ to $\mathbb{Z}$.*

To illustrate all this with an example, let us compute the Tannakian symbol of the Möbius function. Every row in the Bell table is the same, so in this example the Tannakian symbol is independent of the chosen prime. The Bell series is

$$1 - 1 \cdot t + 0 \cdot t^2 + 0 \cdot t^3 + 0 \cdot t^4 + \ldots = 1 - t = \frac{1-t}{1}$$

We read off the coefficients of t in the numerator (ignoring the minus sign), and the only such coefficient is 1. In the denominator there are no coefficients at all, so we get an empty set. The Tannakian symbol of the Möbius function therefore equals

$$\frac{\emptyset}{\{1\}}$$

As a second example, we compute the Tannakian symbol of the Euler function at the prime $p = 5$, using the method of adding and subtracting identical terms in order to split the sum into two geometric series.

$$1 + 4t + 20t^2 + 100t^3 + 500t^4 + 2500t^5 + \ldots$$

$$= (1 + 5t + 25t^2 + 125t^3 + \ldots) - (t + 5t^2 + 25t^3 + \ldots)$$

$$= \frac{1}{1-5t} - \frac{t}{1-5t} = \frac{1-t}{1-5t}$$

Now we can read off the Tannakian symbol; it is

$$\frac{\{5\}}{\{1\}}$$

Automation of this procedure (which we have implemented in Sage [16]) relies on the Berlekamp-Massey algorithm (see [3]), which checks a sequence for any possible linear recursion relation and, if it finds such a relation, produces a rational expression for the generating function.

If we are in a situation where we know a formula for function values at prime powers, we don't have to rely on numerical procedures such as Berlekamp-Massey, but we can do an exact symbolic calculation to get a formula for the Tannakian symbol at any prime. For the Euler function, it is well-known that $\varphi(p^e) = p^e - p^{e-1}$, and using this we get

$$f_p(t) = 1 + \sum_{e=1}^{\infty} (p^e - p^{e-1}) t^e = \sum_{e=0}^{\infty} p^e t^e - t \cdot \sum_{e=0}^{\infty} p^e t^e$$

$$= (1-t) \cdot \sum_{e=0}^{\infty} p^e t^e = \frac{1-t}{1-pt}$$

which shows that the Tannakian symbol of the Euler φ function at any prime p is

$$\frac{\{p\}}{\{1\}}$$

Similar calculations for other functions reveal that all functions appearing in classical/elementary number theory have very simple expressions for their symbols.

Example 4. The Liouville function has Tannakian symbol $\frac{\{-1\}}{\emptyset}$ at all primes.

Example 5. The τ function (which gives the number of positive divisors of a number n) has Tannakian symbol $\frac{\{1,1\}}{\emptyset}$ at all primes.

Example 6. The σ function (which gives the sum of all positive divisors of a number) has Tannakian symbol $\frac{\{p,1\}}{\emptyset}$ at all primes. More generally, the k'th divisor function σ_k, which gives the sum of k'th powers of all positive divisors, has Tannakian symbol $\frac{\{p^k,1\}}{\emptyset}$.

Representing a multiplicative function by its Tannakian symbol has two major advantages over the previous two representations. First of all, whenever we can find a closed expression for the symbol as a function of p, we have a *finite* representation which captures *all* function values of the function. Secondly, there is a calculus of Tannakian symbols which means we can easily compute the symbol of a Dirichlet convolution or a product of two multiplicative functions with known symbols. In fact, almost all unary and binary operations on multiplicative functions which appear in the literature have an explicit counterpart in the language of Tannakian symbols; this is the subject of our article in progress with Ane Espeseth [5].

In addition, properties of many mathematical objects can be read directly off their Tannakian symbols. In the case of multiplicative functions, we have for instance:

1. Completely multiplicative (as mentioned in Definition 1) corresponds to the Tannakian symbol having no elements downstairs, and at most one element upstairs, the typical case being $\frac{\{a\}}{\emptyset}$ for some a.
2. Similarly, "specially multiplicative" corresponds to the Tannakian symbol having no elements downstairs and at most *two* elements upstairs, for example being of the form $\frac{\{a,b\}}{\emptyset}$ for some a and b.
3. Finally, a multiplicative function being a "totient" is equivalent to its Tannakian symbol having at most one element upstairs and at most one element downstairs.

4   A Tiny Prototype Database

We want to suggest that a database of zeta types and Tannakian symbols could be a useful tool for researchers in number theory, and if designed in a good way, such a database may even be useful in certain AI-inspired mathematical endeavours, such as automated conjecturing and automated theorem discovery/proving.

We have implemented a very small prototype database of multiplicative functions to illustrate what we have in mind. The database contains approximately 20 classical multiplicative functions, and in addition 5 infinite families of multiplicative function (like the family σ_k of divisor functions, indexed by a positive integer k).

The entire database is contained in a single `json` file, which is displayed below. The reader will recognize the Tannakian symbols for the Möbius function, the Euler φ function, and the other examples from the previous section.

```json
{
    "format": "Edinburgh 1",
    "functions": [
        {
            "name":      "zero",
            "symbol":    "/",
            "latex":     "\\epsilon"
        }, {
            "name":      "one",
            "symbol":    "{1}/",
            "latex":     "1",
            "latex_eval": "1"
        }, {
            "name":      "mu",
            "symbol":    "/{1}",
            "latex":     "\\mu"
        }, {
            "name":      "id",
            "symbol":    "{p}/",
            "latex":     "Id",
            "latex_eval": "{-}"
        }, {
            "name":      "id_2",
            "symbol":    "{p^2}/",
            "latex":     "Id_2",
            "latex_eval": "{\\left(-\\right)}^2"
        }, {
            "name":      "id_3",
            "symbol":    "{p^3}/",
            "latex":     "Id_3",
            "latex_eval": "{\\left(-\\right)}^3"
        }, {
            "name":      "tau",
            "symbol":    "{1, 1}/",
            "latex":     "\\tau"
        }, {
            "name":      "tau_3",
            "symbol":    "{1, 1, 1}/",
            "latex":     "\\tau_3"
        }, {
            "name":      "tau_4",
            "symbol":    "{1, 1, 1, 1}/",
            "latex":     "\\tau_4"
        }, {
            "name":      "sigma",
            "symbol":    "{1, p}/",
            "latex":     "\\sigma"
        }, {
            "name":      "euler_phi",
            "symbol":    "{p}/{1}",
            "latex":     "\\varphi"
        }, {
            "name":      "liouville",
            "symbol":    "{-1}/",
            "latex":     "\\lambda"
        }, {
            "name":      "gamma",
            "symbol":    "{1}/{2}",
            "latex":     "\\gamma"
        }, {
            "name":      "dedekind_psi",
            "symbol":    "{p}/{-1}",
            "latex":     "\\psi"
        }, {
            "name":      "theta",
            "symbol":    "{1}/{-1}",
            "latex":     "\\theta"
        }, {
            "name":      "core",
            "symbol":    "{1}/{1-p}",
            "latex":     "\\text{Core}_1"
        }, {
            "name":      "beta",
            "symbol":    "{p,-1}/",
            "latex":     "\\beta"
        }, {
            "name":      "char_fn_squares",
            "symbol":    "{1, -1}/",
            "latex":     "\\epsilon_2"
        }, {
            "name":      "char_fn_squarefree",
            "symbol":    "/{-1}",
            "latex":     "\\xi"
        }
    ],
    "function-families": [
        {
            "indexed_by": ["k"],
            "name":      "id_$k$",
            "symbol":    "{p^$k$}/",
            "latex":     "Id_{$k$}",
            "latex_eval": "{\\left(-\\right)}^{$k$}"
        }, {
            "indexed_by": ["k"],
            "name":      "sigma_$k$",
            "symbol":    "{p^$k$, 1}/",
            "latex":     "\\sigma_{$k$}"
        }, {
            "indexed_by": ["k"],
            "name":      "jordan_$k$",
            "symbol":    "{p^$k$}/{1}",
            "latex":     "\\jordan_{$k$}"
        }, {
            "indexed_by": ["k"],
```

```
    "name":      "psi_$k$",                    "symbol":    "|$k$ * [1]|",
    "symbol":    "{p^$k$}/{-1}",               "latex":     "\\tau_{$k$}"
    "latex":     "\\psi_{$k$}"             }
}, {
    "indexed_by": ["k"],                  ]
    "name":      "tau_$k$",           }
```

This file and related code are available at the second author's GitHub repository [18]. For specification of the format, we also refer to this repository, more specifically to "Edinburgh 1.md" in the Classical-Multiplicative-Functions folder.

5   An Application to Automated Theorem Generation

5.1   Identities Between Multiplicative Functions

There are many theorems in the number theory literature about how values of different multiplicative functions are related to each other. One of the simplest examples is a well-known statement about the Euler φ function.

The point of this example and the next is to illustrate what typical identities between multiplicative functions look like, and also to illustrate how Tannakian symbols work in actual proofs. For more details on exactly how and why these techniques work, we have to refer to our other papers with Espeseth ([5,6]).

Example 7. Let's look again at a list of function values $\varphi(n)$ for small values of n.

n	1	2	3	4	5	6	7	8	9	10	11	12	...	20
$\varphi(n)$	1	1	2	2	4	2	6	4	6	4	10	4	...	8

We said earlier that it is difficult to spot patterns in these values, but this doesn't mean no patterns exist. In fact, one particular pattern can be found by choosing a number n (let us choose the number 6), and looking at all the function values of *divisors* of 6. The divisors are 1, 2, 3 and 6, and the corresponding function values (circled below) are 1, 1, 2, and 2. Now take the sum of the function values. We get the number 6!

n	1	2	3	4	5	6	7	8	9	10	11	12	...	20
$\varphi(n)$	①	①	②	2	4	②	6	4	6	4	10	4	...	8

Doing the same again, but with the number 20, we get the divisors 1, 2, 4, 5, 10 and 20, and the corresponding function values are 1, 1, 2, 4, 4 and 8. Their sum happens to be precisely 20!

n	1	2	3	4	5	6	7	8	9	10	11	12	...	20
$\varphi(n)$	①	①	2	②	④	2	6	4	6	④	10	4	...	⑧

We are led to believe that there is a general law here, which says that the sum of the values of the Euler function over the divisors of a given integer is precisely that given integer. This statement can be rewritten as an identity:

$$\sum_{d\mid n} \varphi(d) = n \tag{2}$$

There are several ways of proving this identity, but we want to give a proof sketch that illustrates the use of Tannakian symbols. We first note that φ is a multiplicative function whose Tannakian symbol is $\frac{\{p\}}{\{1\}}$, and that the identity function is also multiplicative, with Tannakian symbol $\frac{\{p\}}{\emptyset}$. The right hand side is of course the value of the identity function applied to n. The left hand side is the Dirichlet convolution of φ with the constant function given by $f(n) = 1$, and this constant function has Tannakian symbol $\frac{\{1\}}{\emptyset}$. The identity (2) is therefore equivalent to the statement

$$\frac{\{p\}}{\{1\}} \oplus \frac{\{1\}}{\emptyset} = \frac{\{p\}}{\emptyset} \tag{3}$$

which is obviously true by the general rules for taking Dirichlet convolution of two Tannakian symbols. Hence the original identity is proved.

Example 8. Let us look at a more complicated example. Recall that the τ function counts the number of positive divisors of a positive integer n. For example, the number 10 has four positive divisors (1, 2, 5 and 10), so $\tau(10) = 4$. The table of function values looks like this:

n	1	2	3	4	5	6	7	8	9	10	11	12	..	16	..	25
$\tau(n)$	1	2	2	3	2	4	2	4	3	4	2	6	..	5	..	3

Now take any integer - for example the number 4. Square the number - in our case we get 16. Now let's play a game with the divisors of 16 (which are 1, 2, 4, 8 and 16). Consider the alternating sum

$$\tau(1) \cdot \tau(16) - \tau(2) \cdot \tau(8) + \tau(4) \cdot \tau(4) - \tau(8) \cdot \tau(2) + \tau(16) \cdot \tau(1)$$

If we plug in the values of the τ function here, we see that the sum is equal to $\tau(4)$.

Let's try again. We pick the number 5, and compute

$$\tau(1) \cdot \tau(25) - \tau(5) \cdot \tau(5) + \tau(25) \cdot \tau(1)$$

Now this sum is equal to $\tau(5)$! The pattern we see here can be generalized to any n, providing we take care in the placement of plus and minus signs in the sum. If we denote by $\Omega(n)$ the number of prime factors of n counted with multiplicity (so that $\Omega(4) = \Omega(6) = 2$ and $\Omega(8) = 3$), then the general identity is

$$\sum_{d|n^2} (-1)^{\Omega(d)} \tau(d) \tau\left(\frac{n^2}{d}\right) = \tau(n) \tag{4}$$

Again, let us provide a proof sketch. The τ function is multiplicative, and its Tannakian symbol is $\frac{\{1,1\}}{\emptyset}$. The left hand side is what Redmond and Sivaramakrishnan [15] call the *norm operator* applied to τ, and in our new language, this is an example of an *Adams operation* in a lambda-ring structure on multiplicative functions, and for such Adams operations, we have explicit formulas (in the world of Tannakian symbols). This particular Adams operation acts by squaring all elements of the symbol, so the left hand side of the identity is $\frac{\{1^2,1^2\}}{\emptyset}$ while the right hand side is $\frac{\{1,1\}}{\emptyset}$. Now the identity follows immediately from the elementary fact that $1 \cdot 1 = 1$.

5.2   Automatic Generation of New Identities with Proofs

What we can do using our miniature database is to search for more identities like this. This procedure relies on the algebraic theory of Tannakian symbols, which is illustrated by the examples above, and covered in detail in [5]. The methodology is somewhat similar to Zeilberger's classical work [19] on identities between special functions. Whereas Zeilberger exploits the fact that special functions have finite representations via the theory of holonomic power series, we exploit the fact that many multiplicative functions have finite representations via the theory of Tannakian symbols.

The methodology we follow is:

1. Represent each function in the database by its Tannakian symbol.
2. Generate a list of Tannakian symbol expressions by applying various unary and binary operations to combinations of symbols from the database.
3. Partition the list of expressions using the equivalence relation given by equality after simplification.
4. Any two expressions in the same equivalence class gives an identity between multiplicative functions. This gives a list of new theorems.
5. Discard identities that are trivial, for example of the form $X + Y = Y + X$.

Using this procedure, we find thousands of new identities, many of which seem interesting enough to be publishable in a decent number theory journal. We present a small screenshot of a simplified version of our Sage interface, to give a feeling for what the code and the output looks like.

```
In [73]:  funcs = [phi, id, id_2, tau, sigma, liouville, mu]

          sums = [l + r for l, r in itertools.combinations_with_replacement(funcs, 2)]

          for lhs in sums:
              for rhs in funcs:
                  if lhs == rhs:
                      print html(lhs & rhs)
```

$$\sum_{d_0|n} \varphi(d_0) \cdot \tau\left(\frac{n}{d_0}\right) = \sigma(n)$$

$$\sum_{d_0|n} d_0 \cdot \mu\left(\frac{n}{d_0}\right) = \varphi(n)$$

$$\sum_{d_0|n} \sigma(d_0) \cdot \mu\left(\frac{n}{d_0}\right) = n$$

The reason that these identities (which in many cases were not known before) are theorems and not conjectures is that we have a closed formula for the relevant Tannakian symbols as functions of the prime p. This means that when two expressions evaluate to the same thing (as Tannakian symbols), then all function values of the left and the right hand side of the identity must also be equal.

5.3   A Brief Introduction to Other Operations

With our formalism of Tannakian symbols and zeta types, we can analyze all operations on multiplicative functions that we have been able to find in the number theory literature. There is no space to develop this theory in any depth here, but we can give a brief survey of what the operations are, with references to definitions.

There are four fundamental binary operations on the set of all multiplicative functions. These are:

1. Dirichlet convolution.
2. Tensor product.
3. Unitary convolution.
4. Ordinary product.

The last operation is just the ordinary and elementary operation given by multiplying complex-valued functions. The first and third are defined in the Encyclopedia of Mathematics, in the entry on Dirichlet convolution [4], while the second is defined for general multiplicative functions in [5], and for Tannakian symbols (and hence for all rational multiplicative functions) in [6].

There are four fundamental unary operations, namely:

1. The norm operator of Redmond and Sivaramakrishnan, and various generalizations.
2. Precomposition with a power function.

3. The k'th convolute operator.
4. A certain nameless operation related to base change of varieties over finite fields.

To convey the flavour of what these operations are, let us include here just the definitions of Dirichlet convolution and the norm operator, both of which appeared in the proof sketches above.

Definition 10. *Let f and g be two multiplicative functions. The* Dirichlet convolution *of f and g is the function h defined by the formula*

$$h(n) = \sum_{d|n} f(d)g(n/d)$$

where the sum on the right hand side is taken over all positive divisors d of n.

Definition 11. *The* norm *of a multiplicative function f is the function g defined by*

$$g(n) = \sum_{d|n^2} (-1)^{\Omega(d)} f(n^2/d) f(d)$$

where $\Omega(d)$ is the number of prime factors of d counted with multiplicity. Here the sum is taken over all positive divisors of n^2.

6   Conclusion

We have argued that zeta types and Tannakian symbols are useful tools for a better understanding of multiplicative functions, and we have implemented a small program for automated theorem discovery, which generates identities between such functions. Many of the identities seem to be new and interesting results.

For future work, we propose setting up a much larger database of zeta types and Tannakian symbols, which would make it possible to experiment with automated conjecturing and other computational procedures in even more interesting settings. As a motivating example, we display the zeta type associated to an L-function of one elliptic curve.

	$e = 1$	$e = 2$	$e = 3$	$e = 4$	$e = 5$
$p = 2$	1	-1	-3	-1	5
$p = 3$	0	-3	0	9	0
$p = 5$	-3	4	3	-29	72
$p = 7$	-1	-6	13	29	-120
$p = 11$	-1	1	-1	1	-1

Understanding L-functions like this one is among the greatest challenges of modern number theory. Recent years have seen several major advances in faster algorithms for computing L-functions (i.e. computing the numbers appearing in zeta types like the one above), and the vast amount of data generated this way offers many intriguing challenges to researchers willing to combine a deep mathematical understanding of the objects involved with large-scale computations of various kinds. We refer to the recent work of Brown and Schnetz [1], of Costa and Tschinkel [2], of Harvey [7,8] and of Kedlaya [10] for more details on current research in this field.

When it comes to database content, there would be significant overlap between our database and the already established L-functions and Modular Forms Database (LMFDB) [12], and some limited overlap with the Online Encyclopedia of Integer Sequences (OEIS) [14] but our database would represent the objects in a different way, and it would also contain many objects not directly related to what is currently in the LMFDB or the OEIS.

We have preliminary work in place on json specifications for various types of mathematical objects represented by zeta types and Tannakian symbols. However, we believe that the next step in our process should not be to set up a huge database and fill it with lots and lots of data, but to choose a specific research project and set up a medium-sized database to support this project. Gaining experience this way will lead to better design choices if we at a later stage choose to go ahead with a more ambitious large-scale project.

The projects we have in mind as such a possible first step include:

- Find Tannakian symbol representations for all (or almost all) of the multiplicative functions in the OEIS (currently there is a total of 1459 such sequences) and search for new identities between them.
- Build a database of zeta types associated to L-functions of hypergeometric motives and check various standard conjectures on these objects.
- Try out the recent Sage package of Larson and Van Cleemput [11] which implements Dalmatian heuristics for automated conjecture-making. This is a domain-independent package for producing conjectures about inequalities between combinations of real-valued invariants, and could easily be set up to work on a database of zeta types or Tannakian symbols.
- Set up a database of Tannakian symbol representations for Dirichlet characters, and do computations aiming to elucidate the lambda-ring structure of the lambda-ring generated by all Dirichlet characters.
- Set up a database of Tannakian symbols associated to representations of finite groups, and use this database in a project on the lambda-ring structure of representation rings.

Acknowledgements. Aspects of this work has been presented in various talks, including at CICM 2016, at AITP 2017 (Conference on Artificial Intelligence and Theorem Proving), at the Representation Theory 2016 Conference in Uppsala, and at seminars in Stockholm and in Leicester. We would like to acknowledge the encouragement and many helpful comments received on these occasions, and in particular we thank Michael Kohlhase, Volodymyr Mazorchuk, Frank Neumann, Florian Rabe, Andreas Strömbergsson, and Josef Urban.

(Slides from some of these talks are available on the first author's webpage; andreasholmstrom.org. Together with the other documents mentioned, they may serve as a complement to this paper.)

Finally, we also want to thank Magnus Hellebust Haaland and Olav Hellebust Haaland for implementing the Berlekamp-Massey algorithm for us in Sage; many of the automated procedures for computing with Tannakian symbols rely on this implementation.

References

1. Brown, F., Schnetz, O.: Modular forms in quantum field theory. Commun. Number Theor. Phys. **7**(2), 293–325 (2013)
2. Costa, E., Tschinkel, Y.: Variation of Neron-Severi ranks of reductions of K3 surfaces. Exp. Math. **23**, 475–481 (2014)
3. Encyclopedia of Mathematics: Berlekamp-Massey algorithm. https://www.encyclopediaofmath.org/index.php/Berlekamp-Massey_algorithm
4. Encyclopedia of Mathematics: Dirichlet convolution. https://www.encyclopediaofmath.org/index.php/Dirichlet_convolution
5. Espeseth, A., Holmstrom, A., Vik, T.: New perspectives on multiplicative functions: Lambda-rings and Tannakian symbols. Preprint in preparation (draft version available upon request, but see also [6])
6. Espeseth, A., Vik, T.: Motivic symbols and classical multiplicative functions. Research report, Norwegian Contest for Young Scientists (2016, submitted). http://andreasholmstrom.org/wp-content/2016/05/motivic-symbols-classical-final-version.pdf
7. Harvey, D.: Counting points on hyperelliptic curves in average polynomial time. Ann. of Math. **179**(2), 783–803 (2014)
8. Harvey, D.: Computing zeta functions of arithmetic schemes. Proc. Lond. Math. Soc. **111**(6), 1379–1401 (2015)
9. Holmstrom, A.: Towards automated conjecture-making in higher arithmetic geometry. In: CEUR Workshop Proceedings, vol. 1785, pp. 204–218 (2016)
10. Kedlaya, K.S.: Computing zeta functions via p-Adic cohomology. In: Buell, D. (ed.) ANTS 2004. LNCS, vol. 3076, pp. 1–17. Springer, Heidelberg (2004). doi:10.1007/978-3-540-24847-7_1
11. Larson, C.E., Van Cleemput, N.: Automated conjecturing I: Fajtlowicz's Dalmatian heuristic revisited. Artif. Intell. **231**, 17–38 (2016)
12. The LMFDB Collaboration: The L-functions and modular forms database. http://www.lmfdb.org
13. McCarthy, P.J.: Introduction to Arithmetical Functions. Springer, New York (1986)
14. Online Encyclopedia of Integer Sequences. http://oeis.org/
15. Redmond, D., Sivaramakrishnan, R.: Some properties of specially multiplicative functions. J. Number Theor. **13**(2), 210–227 (1981)
16. The Sage Developers: SageMath, the Sage Mathematics Software System, Version 7.6 (2017). http://www.sagemath.org
17. Stanley, R.: Enumerative Combinatorics, vol. 1, 2nd edn. Cambridge University Press, Cambridge (2014)
18. Vik, T., Classical multiplicative functions. GitHub repository (2017). https://github.com/torstein-vik/zeta-types-smc/blob/master/Classical-Multiplicative-Functions/
19. Zeilberger, D.: A holonomic systems approach to special functions identities. J. Comput. Appl. Math. **32**(3), 321–368 (1990)

Presentation and Manipulation of Mizar Properties in an Isabelle Object Logic

Cezary Kaliszyk[1](✉) and Karol Pąk[2](✉)

[1] Universität Innsbruck, Innsbruck, Austria
cezary.kaliszyk@uibk.ac.at
[2] Uniwersytet w Białymstoku, Białystok, Poland
pakkarol@uwb.edu.pl

Abstract. One of the crucial factors enabling an efficient use of a logical framework is the convenience of entering, manipulating, and presenting object logic constants, statements, and proofs. In this paper, we discuss various elements of the Mizar language and the possible ways how these can be represented in the Isabelle framework in order to allow a suitable way of working in typed set theory. We explain the interpretation of various components declared in each Mizar article environment and create Isabelle attributes and outer syntax that allow simulating them. We further discuss introducing notations for symbols defined in the Mizar Mathematical Library, but also synonyms and redefinitions of such symbols. We also compare the language elements corresponding to the actual proofs, with special care for implicit proof expansions not present in Isabelle. We finally discuss Mizar's hidden arguments and demonstrate that some of them are not necessary in an Isabelle representation.

1 Introduction

Set theory has been the standard foundation used by mathematicians in the past and is still the foundation with which the majority are most familiar today. However, when it comes to formalized mathematics, most proof assistants are based on other foundations. This could be one of the important factors that are hindering a wider adoption of formal proof. Mizar [4] has been the pioneering proof assistant based on classical logic combined with the axioms of set theory. It also offers several unique features commonly used by mathematicians, such as powerful symbol overloading, e.g. the plus symbol can be used to represent more than one hundred different kinds of addition that are recognized based on the types of arguments. Additionally, several kinds of additions can be used simultaneously if arguments of more specific types can be applied to different plus that give the same result for such types. It also features one of the largest libraries of formalized mathematics, the Mizar Mathematical Library (MML) [2]. Unfortunately the complete foundations of Mizar have only been specified in

The paper has been supported by the resources of the Polish National Science Center granted by decision n°DEC-2015/19/D/ST6/01473.

H. Geuvers et al. (Eds.): CICM 2017, LNAI 10383, pp. 193–207, 2017.
DOI: 10.1007/978-3-319-62075-6_14

documentation and by the algorithm implemented by the Mizar system, rather than in a fully formal way.

Furthermore the implementation of Mizar does not have a small core, to which all the proofs could be reduced, as it is in the case of the implementations of many proof assistants [20]. To overcome these limitations, in our previous work [6] we have proposed an Isabelle [19] object logic [13], which implements the core foundations of Mizar. We have expressed most features supported by Mizar logic including the Mizar type system, basic mechanisms for introducing definitions, and we proved the first 32 facts from the MML including theorems, registrations as well as definitions that required Mizar-style justifications. The main motivations for the project are to provide an independent certification of the MML and to provide easy access to MML data from other systems. This can in the long run give an alternative Mizar implementation.

One problem with the emulation of Mizar as an Isabelle object logic was the convenience of entering and manipulating the Mizar objects, statements, and proofs. Many properties that in Mizar could be introduced using concise and convenient notations (such as for example Mizar clusters) would require explicitly specifying existential statements or even meta-logic implications.

In this paper we investigate the features of Mizar which allow convenient input and manipulation of the set theoretic objects and explore the possibilities to provide similar mechanisms in an Isabelle object logic. The main motivation for this particular work is to give notations usable first in the reference implementation of Mizar foundations, with further work allowing to translate the whole MML to the proposed syntax in an automated way.

1.1 Related Work

Many packages and improvements have been introduced in the Isabelle/HOL object logic that allow convenient defining, manipulating, and display of its objects. Default type-classes are assumed, Trueprop[1] is automatically added around HOL propositions, packages allow various ways of introducing definitions and type definitions conveniently. Isabelle and many other logical frameworks (Twelf [17], MMT [16]) allow adding nice notations to object-logic defined functions and other entities.

Some mechanisms of this kind have been also used and developed for Isabelle/ZF [14]. Further improvements of some of its features have been also considered in other systems that implement set theory. ProofPeer [11] allows using the same notation for meta-level application and ZF application and is able to infer the kind of application at each instance [12]. The Atelier B including Rodin [1], as well as Metamath [10] include specific user interface techniques for nicer set theoretic notations. Furthermore, both specific tactic and various general purpose automation techniques have been considered to provide type

---

[1] Trueprop is the HOL object logic constant that turns a higher-order logic boolean into a meta-level proposition.

inference in various Isabelle object logics. Mizar type inference can be to a large extent automated using first-order automated theorem provers [7,18].

There has been a lot of work on improving legibility of proofs, in particular for the Mizar proof language and proof style [9]. The main purpose has been to present the proofs in a concise but readable way [15], whereas in this paper we are trying to focus on the outer and inner syntax for Isabelle/Mizar rather than on the proof structure.

Bancerek [3] has developed a formal theory of Mizar linguistic concepts, which includes quasi-loci, quasi-terms, quasi-adjectives, and quasi-types, which is accompanied by the Mizar article ABCMIZ_0 formalizing the Mizar type system.

1.2   Paper Content and Contributions

After shortly recalling the basics of our Isabelle/Mizar object logic in Sect. 2 and explaning some improvements in its foundations, we propose the mechanisms that allow imitating the notations and the presentation of Mizar objects. In particular:

- We propose a syntax for Mizar-like definitions of all kinds of functors, modes, predicates, and attributes. This includes support for conditional definitions, where the given types are not sufficient to guarantee the soundness of the definitions (Sect. 3).
- We discuss the background information available in Mizar and propose mechanisms that allow extending this information in Isabelle (Sect. 4), in particular environment declarations, properties, and registrations.
- We propose a mechanism that allows hiding certain functor arguments in the Isabelle object logic, that mimics the hidden argument inference present in Mizar. The proposed mechanism allows hiding the arguments that appear neither in the definition body nor in the result type. Moreover, we introduce Mizar-style redefinitions and propose how arguments that do not appear in original definitions can be hidden (Sect. 5).

2   Mizar Object Logic

In this section we shortly remind the basics of the Mizar object logic fully introduced by us in [6] and present the new developments in this foundation.

We start with the Isabelle/FOL object logic. We disable the notations $=$, $\forall$, $\exists$ of the first-order polymorphic equality, and polymorphic quantifiers. We instead introduce the Isabelle types for Mizar sets, Mizar types, and type modifiers and restrict the symbols for equality and quantifiers to the type of Mizar sets. We further introduce new constants with appropriate axiomatizations that allow the introduction of concrete Mizar types and their modifiers, as well as mechanisms that allow establishing such definitions given the proofs of the necessary conditions (definitions are further discussed in the next Sect. 3). Given these foundations, the same axiomatization of set theory as in Mizar (Tarski-Grothendieck) can next be introduced, and can be followed by the same definitions to build up a standard library of set theory.

We have introduced some simplifcations and optimizations in the definition of the foundations since it was proposed [6]. We separated types from type modifiers, with the aim of automating some type inference. We were able to remove the axiom that postulated the existence of functors, if their existence and uniqueness were shown. Instead, the definition body can be converted into a temporary attribute (type modifier), from which global choice can give the attributes. Finally, we separated the type membership operator be from the type modifier membership is, to reduce confusion. We will discuss changes in the definition mechanism in the next Section.

3   Definition Syntax

Many logical foundations include not only inference rules, but also rules that allow extending the actual logic, such as introducing definitions and type definitions in higher-order logic. For a logical framework to fully emulate such logics, it is necessary to adequately enable such extension mechanisms. In our previous work [6] we showed that a number of basic Mizar definitions can be directly emulated in Isabelle. However, we need to introduce a more involved definition mechanism to cover the more advanced Mizar definitions including conditional ones (called *permissive* in Mizar), as well as the definitions of new modes and attributes, which are the focus of this section.

All Mizar logic extensions are introduced in *definition* blocks. A definition block can be made up of (multiple) declarations of the types of definition arguments (referred to as *loci declarations* in Mizar), optional assumptions, and the actual definitions which can use these declarations. The Mizar CHECKER verifies that the argument types employed in the definition block are non-empty. It is possible to apply types for which non-emptiness has not been proved using the optional assumptions. The actual defined object can be of four kinds: meta-level functions and constants (referred to as *functors* in Mizar), Mizar soft types (referred to as *modes* in Mizar), predicates, and type restrictions (*attributes* in Mizar). In all these cases the defined object together with its its list of arguments constitutes the definition pattern, where the arguments are the bound variables introduced inside the current definitional block whose types are non-empty. Note, that not all arguments must be visible in the pattern, hidden arguments will be discussed in Sect. 5.

3.1   Conditional Definitions

Definitions with assumptions explicitly stated in the definition block are very frequent in Mizar [5]. Such definitions are referred to as *permissive definitions* in Mizar literature. The assumptions are often used to express the relations between the arguments in cases where the type (non-empty ones) and attributes is not powerful enough to capture all the definedness conditions. Consider the conditional assumption "polynomial has a root". It can be used to define the type of a root of an arbitrary non-zero degree polynomial over an arbitrary ring (not restricted to algebraically closed fields).

The majority of the conditional definitions contained in the MML are not however there to overcome the non-emptiness problem. Their main role is to provide more freedom in the formulation of reasoning steps, in such a way that they are verified by the Mizar system. This is desired, because of how Mizar identifies which defined object does the current symbol refer to: as the patterns used in the definitions can be overshadowed by subsequent definitions, the Mizar ANALYZER must consider the types of the objects in the argument list. These types are computed based on the explicitly given types of argument variables together with the information contained in the clusters (Sect. 4.2, [4,5]).

Conditional definitions can therefore be used to allow writing terms, which can be correctly identified even given more general argument types, but whose interpretation is only possible with more precise types given in the definition assumptions. Consider the conditional definition of projection introduced in XTUPLE_0 (left) together with its non-conditional variant (right), as well as two formulas that use this functor (we will arrive at this definition in Isabelle/Mizar at the end of this section):

```
definition                              definition
    let x be object;                        let x be pair object;
    assume x is pair;
    func x'1 -> object means                func x'1 -> object means
        x = [y1,y2] implies it = y1;            x = [y1,y2] implies it = y1;
end;                                    end;
```

```
for x be pair object holds x'1 = ...
for x be object st x is pair holds x'1 = ...
```

The conditional definition allows the projection functor in the term x'1 to be correctly identified by Mizar in both formulas. However, in the case of the non-conditional variant, the ANALYZER cannot identify the term: Given the type of x explicitly given as object, the functor '1 with the argument x cannot be substituted in the definition and the unknown functor 103 error is reported.

3.2   Functor Definitions

The functions in Mizar's first-order logic (from the logical framework point of view these are meta-level functions) are referred to as *functors* in Mizar. New functors are defined in a definition block using the keyword func followed by the functor pattern (for example f.x for the image of x under function f), the result type (which must be non-empty) and the actual definition body. There are two types of functor definitions that differ in the form of the body of the definition: definitions by equals and by means.

A definition by equals equates the functor given the arguments to a Mizar term, with the type constraint. Definitions by means allow the define functors indirectly, by giving the intended properties. The properties can use all the parameters introduced in the current definitional block, together with a special variable it, which marks the defined functor. The following abbreviations allows for Mizar-like syntax for introducing the definition in Isabelle, further using λit to bind the currently defined object:

abbreviation (input) equals_prefix
    ("func _ → _ equals _" [10,10] 10)
where "func pat → type equals def ≡
    pat = theM (λit. it be type & it = def)"

abbreviation (input) means_prefix
    ("func _ → _ means _" [0,0] 10)
where " func pat → type means condition ≡
    pat = theM (λit. (it be type & condition(it)))"

Using a definition by means forces the user to prove two correctness conditions (proofs required by the user to ensure the soundness of a definition), existence and uniqueness immediately in the definitional block, i.e., there exists an object that has the result type and fulfills the property, as well as any two objects of the type which satisfy the property must be equal. Mizar uses these correctness conditions to create a definitional theorem from the definition body, which we can formalize once in Isabelle:

lemma means_property:
assumes df: "f = theM(λx. x be D & P(x))"
    and ex: "ex x being D st P (x)"
    and un: "⋀x y. x be D ⟹ y be D ⟹
        P (x) ⟹ P (y) ⟹ x = y"
    shows "f be D & P(f) & (x be D & P(x) implies x = f)"

A definition by equals can be considered as a special case of a definition by means, where the definition body has the form it = ..., where it does not occur on the right-hand side. The correctness conditions can be simplified to the coherence condition, i.e. that the term on the right-hand side has the correct result type. The definitional theorem is also simplified:

lemma equals_property:
assumes df: "f = theM(λx. x be D & x=g)"
    and coherence: "g be D"
    shows "f be D & f = g"

Mizar allows conditional definitions for both definitions by equals and by means. The presence of assumptions in the definition block implies more complex definitional theorems, which include properties of functor definitions both when the variables satisfy the assumptions and when it is not the case. If the assumptions are not satisfied, the only information the Mizar CHECKER has about the term is its result type.

To obtain the same behavior in Isabelle, we introduce the following notation:

abbreviation(input) assume_means_prefix
    ("assume _ func _ → _ means _" [0,0,0,0] 10)
where "assume as func def → type means condition ≡
    def = theM (λit.(it be type & (as implies condition (it))))"

together with an interpretation of the definitional theorem, where $q : Q$ is used for the assumptions:

```
lemma assume_means_property:
assumes df: "f = theM(λx. (x be D & (R implies P (x))))"
   and q: Q
   and assume_ex: "R ⟹ ex x being D st P(x)"
   and assume_un: "⋀x y. R ⟹ x be D ⟹ y be D ⟹
      P (x) ⟹ P (y) ⟹ x = y"
   and mode_ex: "ex x being  D st True"
shows
   "f be D & (R implies P(f) & (x be D & (P (x)) implies x = f))"
```

The conclusion of the theorem corresponds exactly to the information exposed by Mizar to the user. The proof of the theorem proceeds in different ways depending on whether the assumptions are true: If R holds, lemma *means_property* can be immediately used, if it does not, it is only necessary to show the type of the definition which follows from the description operator. The indefinite description operator will be denoted in this paper as theM.

We can finally introduce the conditional definition of projection in Isabelle, that was the motivation for this section, with a syntax that is as convenient as that given by Mizar, which given the same as the Mizar proofs of existence and uniqueness is equivalent to the original one.

```
definition xtuple_0_def_2_prefix (" _ '1" [90] 95) where
   "assume x is pair
   func x '1 → object means
      (λit. for y1,y2 be object st x=[y1,y2] holds it = y1)"
```

3.3   Expandable Modes

The Mizar type system can be extended with new types (referred to as mode in Mizar) in two ways. First, *expandable modes* allow the user to introduce an abbreviation for any Mizar type that can already be expressed as a collection of attributes applied to an already defined radix type (type without attributes). Second, *non-expandable modes* allow the user to introduce a type which is a subtype of an existing type, which additionally satisfies the condition given in the definition body. Just like in the case of defining functors, in both mode cases the pattern occurs with a fixed list of arguments introduced in the current definitional block. For non-expandable modes, additionally the parent type and the definition body must be given, and again it can be used to refer to the mode being defined.

In order to use the defined mode in Mizar, it is necessary to show the existence condition, i.e. that there exist at least one element of the defined type. In case of non-expandable modes, this must be shown in the definition block, whereas for *expandable modes*, Mizar attempts to automatically show it using the defined clusters available in the article's background knowledge (the details on the treatment of background knowledge will be discussed in Sect. 4), and if it is not possible reports the 136 *Non registered cluster* error.

Expandable modes are considered standard abbreviations internally expanded by Mizar into a collection of adjectives associated with a radix type. This expansion is repeated until the radix type in a non-expandable mode. Therefore, we introduce such types as abbreviations in the Isabelle emulation.

```
abbreviation funct_2_def_1 ("Function-of _ , _" 190)
where "Function-of X,Y ≡ (X,Y: quasi-total) || (PartFunc-of X,Y)"
```

3.4 Non-expandable Mode and Attribute Definitions

For non-expandable modes we again introduce two notations that allow introducing new types using definitions without assumptions, as well as conditional ones. Together with the definition interpretation theorems (requiring existence), this allows an Isabelle syntax for introducing types that is equivalent to that given in Mizar. For brevity we present here only the conditional ones.

```
abbreviation (input) assume_mode_prefix
   ("assume _ mode _ → _ means _" [0,0,0,0] 10)
where "assume as mode M → type means cond ≡
   (M ≡ define_mode(λit. it be type & (as implies cond(it))))"

lemma assume_mode_property:
assumes df: "M ≡ define_mode(λx. x be D & (R implies P (x)))"
   and q: Q
   and assume_ex: "R ⟹ ex x being D st P(x)"
   and mode_ex: "ex x being D st True"
shows
   "(x be M iff (x be D & (R implies P(x)))) & Ex (λx. x be M)"
```

Attributes, which allow further restriction of types are treated equivalently: they are implications with more assumptions in the definitions in case of conditional definitions. The attribute definition details can be found in the formalization.

4   Background Knowledge

Mizar *background knowledge* are the facts that do not need to be explicitly given when justifying reasoning steps. Such facts can be associated to objects when the latter are defined. Relevant knowledge available in the article environment is automatically considered in the justification of any step whose statement incorporates objects associated with that knowledge. Mizar allows supplementing background knowledge using *properties* and *registrations*. Here we only introduce the syntax for the background knowledge, it is not implicitly used yet.

4.1 Property

A *property* is a specific characteristic which can be associated with a functor or with a predicate. For unary functors (functors having one visible argument) the properties permitted by Mizar are projectivity ($f(f(x)) = f(x)$) and involutiveness ($f(f(x)) = x$). For a binary functor the properties known to Mizar are commutativity ($g(x,y) = g(y,x)$) and idempotence ($g(x,x) = x$). Finally, for predicates the properties are reflexivity, irreflexivity, symmetry, asymmetry, and connectedness (all binary). Clearly such properties can only be formulated, when the types of the arguments and result as stated in a particular property is valid.

Mizar allows writing such properties with the convenient syntax rather than unfolding such definitions, which additionally makes these properties known to the automation. For convenience we also provide input abbreviations that allow such syntax. Unfortunately apart from the name of the property and the object, we need to explicitly give the type of arguments, which Isabelle cannot infer on the Isar level. The abbreviations are analogous to those presented in the paper already, we show here only a few uses of such notations for brevity. Please consult the formalization for examples of all Mizar properties.

theorem *xboole_0_def_8_asymmetry:*
  "asymmetry set xboole_0_def_8"

theorem *relat_1_def_7_involutiveness:*
    "involutiveness Relation relat_1_def_7"

4.2   Registrations that Facilitate Type Inference

Mizar *registrations* are all features related to the automatic processing of type information. There are three kinds of registrations: clusters which aid the computation of types in the presence of adjectives, reductions which are special kinds of rewrite rules, and identify, which allows resolving conflicts that arise when Mizar attempts to identify objects based on their arguments.

There are three kinds of clusters:

– *existential registrations* used to retain type non-emptiness information. For example funct_1_cl_2 states that there exists a set which is also a relation.
– *conditional registrations* used to extend the list of adjectives assigned to a term, given that particular adjectives have already been established. For example relat_1_cl_0 states that every empty set is a relation. In particular, if the adjectives list is empty, a conditional registration allows establishing adjectives about any terms of given types. For example relset_1_cl_1 establishes that every subset of a Cartesian product is a relation.
– *functorial registrations* used to automatically provide type information for compound terms. For example the singleton pair $\{[a,b]\}$ is both a relation and a function because of the clusters relat_1_cl_7 and funct_1_cl_3.

We introduce the following notations, which allow introducing all three kinds of Mizar clusters in the Isabelle emulations with the same convenient syntax. Each actual cluster becomes an Isabelle lemma, which needs to be explicitly used in type checking.

abbreviation *(input) cluster_prefix_existential*
    ("let _ cluster _ for _" [10,10,10] 10)
where *"let lt cluster attrs for type*
        ≡ (lt ⟹ (Ex (λ X. X be attrs ‖ type)))"

abbreviation *(input) cluster_prefix_conditional*
    ("let _ cluster _ → _ for _" [10,10,10,10] 10)
where *"let lt cluster attrs → attrs2 for type*
        ≡ (lt ⟹ (⋀X. (X be type ∧ X is attrs) ⟹ X is attrs2))"

abbreviation *(input) cluster_prefix_functorial*
    ("let _ cluster _ → _" [10,10,10] 10)
where *"let lt cluster fun → attrs*
        ≡ (lt ⟹ fun is attrs)"

Reductions are another mechanism supported by Mizar in registration blocks used to enhance the capabilities offered by the properties shown in functor definitional blocks. Reductions are similar to rewrite rules that replace a term by its subterm, however Mizar does not perform the replacement, but rather creates an equality between the two terms. This equality can, but does not need to be used as part of the justification. Reductions allow arbitrary terms as left-hand sides, and are therefore more general than properties which are limited to Mizar patterns (functor with variable list). Mizer reductions are further discussed in [8].

Similarly to our emulation of Mizar properties, we rely on the user to state reductions as theorems. We again introduce an abbreviation that allows the convenient Mizar syntax of reductions and show an example of a reduction from the MML:

abbreviation *(input) reduce_prefix*
    ("let _ reduce _ to _" [10,10,10] 10)
where *"let lt reduce term to subterm*
        ≡ (lt implies (term = subterm))"

theorem *relat_1_id_dom:*
    "let X be set reduce dom (id X) to X"

5   Hidden Arguments

As already hinted in Sect. 3, a defined concept does not need to be explicitly applied to all the arguments declared in the definition block. This is possible, when Mizar can infer these arguments based on the types of arguments explicitly given in the pattern. Indeed, given the unique types associated with every term, it is possible to unambiguously infer the list of arguments occurring in this type.

Consider the function composition operation. Its result is clearly a function. We can justify, that the composition p∘f is of the type X↦Z given f:X↦Y and p:Y↦Z. Using a conditional definition, we can reduce the requirements concerning the type of p: namely that its range is a subset of Z and that the image of f is a subset of the domain of p.

The original Mizar definition of typed function composition is presented on the left and the Isabelle counterpart on the right. The Mizar formalization allows the user to omit X, Y, and Z in the term p/*f, as all three can be uniquely determined by types Function of X,Y, Z-valued Function. In a regular Isabelle definition it is not possible to omit any of the three variables, because the type system offered by the Isabelle framework on the Isar level is too weak to allow the inference of such hidden arguments.

```
definition
    let X,Z be set, Y be non empty set;
    let f be Function of X,Y;
    let p be Z-valued Function;
    assume rng f c= dom p;
    func p/*f -> Function of X,Z equals
        p*f;
end;
```

```
definition funct_2_def_11
    (" _ '/*'[_, _] _ " [10,0,0,10] 90)
where
    "assume rng f c= dom p
     func p /*'[X, Z] f →
             Function-of X,Z equals
         p*'f"
```

We have so far avoided introducing ML-level procedures for definitions, which might allow us to reimplement some of Mizar's inference mechanisms. Without this, all variables that appear in the definition body, as well as the result in case of functors, and the mother type in case of modes, must be present in the pattern of the defined object. Thanks to the use of a let construction in the definitional theorem we can hide the variable Y. The variables X, Z must remain visible in the proposed approach.

Even if with the proposed approach some of the Mizar hidden variables remain visible in Isabelle, this does come in particularly useful in Mizar redefinitions. Almost all variables introduced in MML redefinitions are hidden arguments, and the proposed approach will allow keeping them all hidden. The definitions of Mizar objects in MML are often stated with little requirements given to the arguments that are necessary to create an object prototype, as well as a pattern for it. As more is proved about the object, it can be redefined making its type more precise.

Such redefinitions can be used to modify the actual definition, the type of a functor, or the mother type for a mode. Clearly, this is only possible if the modified definition or type can be proved from the more specific arguments. Therefore Mizar requires the user to prove certain correctness conditions appropriate for the kind of redefinition, in order to ensure that the definition is compatible with the original one. For a type redefinition the coherence condition is required, which ensures that the new object has the correct new type. For the modification of the definition body, the compatibility correctness condition is required, which states that the original one and the new one are equivalent under the new assumptions.

To enable redefinitions with the same correctness conditions as those required by Mizar, for each object kind we prove corresponding theorems. We show here only the ones for redefinitions of functors and modes, for the remaining ones refer to the file Mizar_Defs.thy in the formalization.

```
lemma redefine_func_means_property:
assumes lt: "lt"
assumes coherence: "F be M"
assumes compatibility: "⋀ it. it be M ⟹
            ((it = F) ⟷ newCondition(it))"
shows "F be M ∧ newCondition(F)"
    using coherence compatibility lt by auto
```

Note that proving the correctness conditions for a mode requires using the *Set axiom*, namely that objects are sets and that object is the root of the Mizar type hierarchy. A redefinition becomes a regular theorem in Isabelle/Mizar, for example the redefinition of the range **rng** if the input argument is a **Function**:

```
theorem funct_1_def_3:
  "let f be Function
   redefine func rng f → set means
     (λ it. for y being object holds y in it iff
        (ex x being object st x in dom f & y = f . x))"
```

5.1 Hidden Arguments in Redefinitions

Providing redefinitions as theorems also helps in convenient support for new arguments in the redefinitions. Consider the definition of function application (MML article **FUNCT_1**) which given an arbitrary function **f** and object **x** returns the second element of the pair **[x,it]** contained in **f** if **x** belongs to the domain of the function, or the empty set otherwise.

```
definition
    let f be Function; let x be object;
    func f.x -> set means
    [x,it] in f if x in dom f otherwise it = {};
end;
```

The following redefinition performed in Mizar gives a more specific type of function application. Given that **f** is a function from the non-empty set **C** to the set **D**, and that the argument **c** is an element of **C**, the type of the functor can be made more precise, namely it returns an element of **D**. Note the additional arguments with respect to the original definition.

```
definition
    let C be non empty set, D be set;
    let f be Function of C,D;
    let c be Element of C;
    redefine func f.c -> Element of D;
end;
```

We could interpret a redefinition with additional arguments as a definition of a functor by equals, where the pattern contains all the variables present in the block (**C,D,f,c** in the example).

```
definition funct_2_def_5_2 (" _ , _ : _ . _" 190) where
  "func C, D : f . c → (Element-of D) equals f . c"
```

However, the argument **C** is not necessary neither in the functor type **Element of D** nor in the definition body **f.c**. In Mizar, the variable **C** is only used to specify the argument types of **f**. Using the Isabelle counterpart of the Mizar let construction (as we did in the initial experiments [6]) required the use of C in the pattern. By avoiding the let construction and providing the assumptions only in the interpretation of the definitional theorem, it is possible to reduce the arguments only to those present in the function body and result type (for functors) and mother type (for modes). Furthermore, the fact that a redefinition is a regular lemma allows us to finally hide also the variable **D**.

definition `funct_2_def_5_1 (" _ : _ . _" 190)` **where**
  `"func D : f . c → (Element-of D) equals f . c"`

theorem `funct_2_def_5:`
  `"let C be non empty‖set & D be set &`
        `f be (Function-of C,D) & c be Element-of C`
  `redefine func f . c → (Element-of D)"`

5.2   Hidden Arguments in Proofs

An important difference between the Mizar proofs and Isabelle's Isar proofs, is the fact that Isar requires the assumptions and the thesis for any proof block to be fixed in advance, whereas in Mizar various mechanisms (such as automatic unfolding of definitions) allows these to remain open. This means that when translating a reasoning from Mizar to Isabelle/Isar, even for specifying the block assumptions and thesis it is necessary to reconstruct the complete lists of hidden arguments, which would clearly hinder legibility. Most of the cases where this becomes an issue, are the proof blocks in which Mizar automatically unfolds definitions. The following example illustrates the necessary added arguments:

theorem `funct_2_th_50:`
  `"for y be object, X be non empty ‖set holds`
        `for f1,f2 be Function-of X,{y} holds f1=f2"`
proof`(intro ballI)`
  fix `y X f1 f2`
  assume `T0: "y be object" "X be non empty‖set"`
                `"f1 be  Function-of X,{y}" "f2 be  Function-of X,{y}"`
  show `"f1 = f2"`
  proof `(rule  iffD2[OF funct_2_def_7[of X "{y}" f1 f2]])`

   In order to unfold the definition of equality in Isabelle, it is necessary to not only use the redefinition lemma **funct_2_def_7**, but also the complete list of the arguments which appeared in the redefinition block X"{y}" f1 f2.

theorem `funct_2_def_7:`
  `"let A be set & B be set &`
        `f1 be Function-of A,B & f2 be Function-of A,B`
  `redefine pred f1 = f2 means`
        `for a be Element-of A holds f1 . a = f2 . a"`

   By reconstructing the arguments and adding them only in the cases where they are necessary, we can preserve readability while allow Isabelle to verify the proof scripts.

6   Conclusion

We have presented a number of components that make it convenient to use the Mizar object logic developed in Isabelle in a style that is similar to that offered by Mizar.

This includes mechanisms that allow all kinds of definitions available in Mizar, including conditional ones and making sure that the proof obligation required by Isabelle for each kind of definition corresponds to the Mizar's minimal requirements that guarantee the soundness of the defined *object*. We provided the relevant interpretation of the background information available in Mizar that is introduced using registrations and properties. We suggested mechanisms for Mizar's redefinitions, and provided a partial solution for hiding in Isabelle the arguments that are hidden in Mizar. Our work does directly generalize to other logical frameworks. However, as we do focus on Mizar-specific mechanisms, it is not clear whether it can be useful for logics not based on set theory with soft type system.

We tested the provided mechanisms in the process of further development of the Isabelle/Mizar library. We attempted to manually reformalize a number of subsequent articles in the MML. The current state of the Isabelle/Mizar formalization includes 65 Mizar-style definitions including 3 conditional ones, where 28 of them required Mizar-style justifications. In addition, we adopted all 10 properties originally formulated for these definitions in the MML. We further proved also 30 theorems, 26 registrations, 4 schemes, and 2 reductions. The total size of the development is 132 kB, and it is available at: http://cl-informatik.uibk. ac.at/cek/cicm2017/

6.1 Future Work

Mizar is abundant in mechanisms that allow for convenient input and manipulation of mathematical expressions. We have so far not considered imitating the notations used in the Mizar proof style, including the Mizar let and take. The abbreviations introduced focused on the first part of the MML, and we have not introduced any mechanisms for the two features not covered by the foundations and appearing only in later part of the library: Mizar structures and Fraenkel operators. A number of attributes and abbreviations introduced in the paper allow for much nicer manual input, but are not connected with any automation procedure so far. Finally, we have so far focused on using the Isar level as much as possible. Adding new outer syntax on the Isabelle/ML level, for example for definitions, would allow more hidden arguments, and would allow not separating the definition from the defining lemmas.

Acknowledgements. We thank Chad Brown for the discussions on the various set-theoretic foundations. This work has been supported by the ERC grant no. 714034 *SMART* and OeAD Scientific & Technological Cooperation with Poland grant PL 03/2016.

References

1. Abrial, J., Butler, M.J., Hallerstede, S., Hoang, T.S., Mehta, F., Voisin, L.: Rodin: an open toolset for modelling and reasoning in Event-B. STTT **12**(6), 447–466 (2010)

2. Alama, J., Kohlhase, M., Mamane, L., Naumowicz, A., Rudnicki, P., Urban, J.: Licensing the Mizar mathematical library. In: Davenport, J.H., Farmer, W.M., Urban, J., Rabe, F. (eds.) CICM 2011. LNCS, vol. 6824, pp. 149–163. Springer, Heidelberg (2011). doi:10.1007/978-3-642-22673-1_11

3. Bancerek, G.: On the structure of Mizar types. In: Geuvers, H., Kamareddine, F. (eds.) ENTCS, vol. 85, pp. 69–85. Elsevier (2003)

4. Bancerek, G., Byliński, C., Grabowski, A., Korniłowicz, A., Matuszewski, R., Naumowicz, A., Pąk, K., Urban, J.: Mizar: state-of-the-art and beyond. In: Kerber, M., Carette, J., Kaliszyk, C., Rabe, F., Sorge, V. (eds.) CICM 2015. LNCS, vol. 9150, pp. 261–279. Springer, Cham (2015). doi:10.1007/978-3-319-20615-8_17

5. Grabowski, A., Korniłowicz, A., Naumowicz, A.: Four decades of Mizar. J. Autom. Reasoning 55(3), 191–198 (2015)

6. Kaliszyk, C., Pąk, K., Urban, J.: Towards a Mizar environment for Isabelle: foundations and language. In: Avigad, J., Chlipala, A. (eds.) Conference on Certified Programs and Proofs (CPP 2016), pp. 58–65. ACM (2016). doi:10.1145/2854065.2854070

7. Kaliszyk, C., Urban, J.: MizAR 40 for Mizar 40. J. Autom. Reasoning 55(3), 245–256 (2015). doi:10.1007/s10817-015-9330-8

8. Korniłowicz, A.: On rewriting rules in Mizar. J. Autom. Reasoning 50(2), 203–210 (2013)

9. Korniłowicz, A.: Enhancement of MIZAR texts with transitivity property of predicates. In: Kohlhase, M., Johansson, M., Miller, B., de Moura, L., Tompa, F. (eds.) CICM 2016. LNCS, vol. 9791, pp. 157–162. Springer, Cham (2016). doi:10.1007/978-3-319-42547-4_12

10. Megill, N.D.: Metamath: A Computer Language for Pure Mathematics. Lulu Press, Morrisville, North Carolina (2007)

11. Obua, S., Fleuriot, J.D., Scott, P., Aspinall, D.: ProofPeer: Collaborative theorem proving. CoRR, abs/1404.6186 (2014)

12. Obua, S., Fleuriot, J., Scott, P., Aspinall, D.: Type inference for ZFH. In: Kerber, M., Carette, J., Kaliszyk, C., Rabe, F., Sorge, V. (eds.) CICM 2015. LNCS, vol. 9150, pp. 87–101. Springer, Cham (2015). doi:10.1007/978-3-319-20615-8_6

13. Paulson, L.C.: Isabelle: the next 700 theorem provers. In: Odifreddi, P. (ed.) Logic and Computer Science (1990), pp. 361–386 (1990)

14. Paulson, L.C.: Set theory for verification: I. From foundations to functions. J. Autom. Reasoning 11(3), 353–389 (1993)

15. Pąk, K.: Improving legibility of formal proofs based on the close reference principle is NP-hard. J. Autom. Reasoning 55(3), 295–306 (2015)

16. Rabe, F.: A logical framework combining model and proof theory. Math. Struct. Comput. Sci. 23(5), 945–1001 (2013)

17. Schürmann, C.: The Twelf proof assistant. In: Berghofer, S., Nipkow, T., Urban, C., Wenzel, M. (eds.) TPHOLs 2009. LNCS, vol. 5674, pp. 79–83. Springer, Heidelberg (2009). doi:10.1007/978-3-642-03359-9_7

18. Urban, J., Sutcliffe, G.: ATP-based cross-verification of Mizar proofs: method, systems, and first experiments. Math. in Comput. Sci. 2(2), 231–251 (2008)

19. Wenzel, M., Paulson, L.C., Nipkow, T.: The Isabelle framework. In: Mohamed, O.A., Muñoz, C., Tahar, S. (eds.) TPHOLs 2008. LNCS, vol. 5170, pp. 33–38. Springer, Heidelberg (2008). doi:10.1007/978-3-540-71067-7_7

20. Wiedijk, F. (ed.): The Seventeen Provers of the World. LNCS (LNAI), vol. 3600. Springer, Heidelberg (2006). doi:10.1007/11542384

Visual Structure in Mathematical Expressions

Andrea Kohlhase[1], Michael Kohlhase[2(✉)], and Michael Fürsich[1]

[1] Information Management, University of Applied Sciences Neu-Ulm,
Neu-Ulm, Germany
[2] Computer Science, FAU Erlangen-Nürnberg, Erlangen, Germany
michael.kohlhase@fau.de

Abstract. Mathematics uses formulae to express knowledge about objects concisely and economically. Mathematical formulae are at the same time an indispensable tool for the initiated and a formidable barrier to novices. Surprisingly little is known about the cognitive basis of this practice. In this paper we start to rectify this situation with an investigation of how humans read (and understand) mathematical expressions.

A previous exploratory study suggested the interplay of visual patterns and content structure as a key ingredient of decoding and understanding math expressions that differentiates between math-literate and -illiterate subjects. The main contribution of this paper is an eye-tracking study on mathematically trained researchers conducted to verify the mathematical practices suggested by the first study and refine our understanding of the mechanisms.

1 Introduction

The art of expressing mathematical knowledge in math expressions evolved over the last three centuries and has revolutionized the way this is created, stored, and communicated. Given their importance for mathematical practice, surprisingly little is known about the cognitive basis of reading, understanding, and creating formulae.

As math expressions can neither be considered text nor image, it was previously suggested that they form a separate category (see e.g., [Fre]) which humans perceive differently. This perception was coined by ARCAVI "symbol sense", i.e., a *"complex and multifaceted 'feel' for symbols [. . .] a quick or accurate appreciation, understanding, or instinct regarding symbols"* [Arc03, p. 31]. In 2005 W. SCHNOTZ presented a study proving that *"comprehension is highly dependent on what kind of information is presented and how it is presented"* [Sch05, p. 73]. Even though he used only text and image information chunks, it is suspected that math expressions build a category that enables math-oriented persons to understand math in their own way. The "formula shock" [SGM10] effect is well-known, but how exactly do math-oriented people read math expressions differently? If we can get a deeper understanding, then we might get new insights for the design of math software or information systems. Let us summarize:

In [BR14] an eye-tracking study showed that people with a high mathematical expertise related proof items with an according supportive image. They

© Springer International Publishing AG 2017
H. Geuvers et al. (Eds.): CICM 2017, LNAI 10383, pp. 208–223, 2017.
DOI: 10.1007/978-3-319-62075-6_15

found that the participants tend to jump between text and image and it was suggested that relating the different representations enables the relation in different memory stores. Thus, more effective and efficient retrieval and creation of math knowledge is enabled by the use of math expressions. In particular, with their visual and textual aspects they present a sophisticated cognitive tool for mathematicians.

In [KT13] KAMALI AND TOMPA studied the retrieval for content in mathematical documents. Their empirical research also indicates that math expressions are special. They conclude that math expressions should neither be used as conventional document fragments nor with a too exact retrieval algorithm as both result in very poor search results. Instead they showed that algorithms that are based on making use of the Content MathML representation of the document corpus fare much better.

In this paper we report on two eye-tracking studies we have conducted to better understand the reading and understanding of formulae. Eye-tracking is an interesting angle of attack, as there is a demonstrable correlation between what a participant attends to and where she is looking at – see for example [Ray98] for an overview. The "eye-mind hypothesis" [HWH99] even claims a correlation between the cognitive processing of information and the person's gaze at the specific location of the information.

The paper starts off by briefly reporting on our exploratory eye-tracking pilot study in Sect. 2. That identified some potential *mathematical* practices when decoding and understanding math expressions by comparing students with different affinities towards math. For this paper we have conducted a new study with trained math researchers, which we report on in Sect. 3. Section 4 reports on how the new data affects the hypotheses developed in the pilot study. The new data suggests more math practices, which we explore in Sect. 5. In particular, we refine the "Operator Tree Practice" into the "Gestalt Tree Hypothesis", which combines the visual and conceptual sides of formulae. Section 6 concludes the paper.

2   The Math Expressions Pilot Study

To explore and identify idiosyncratic practices with math expressions, we invited 23 participants to look at concrete math expressions, e.g., the expression in the back of Fig. 1 in an eye-tracking study. [KF16] gives a detailed description. The goal of this exploratory study consisted in finding relevant discrepancies within various user groups. The only difference we could make out though was the one between math-oriented and non-math-oriented subjects.

Group	Female	Male
MATH	5	5
¬MATH	7	6

The math expressions were shown to the participants as images on a Tobii t60 Eye Tracking Screen (17″ and 4:3 ratio with 60 Hz). They were asked to think aloud while reading/understanding expressions; audio/video recordings were collected together with the eye-tracking data.

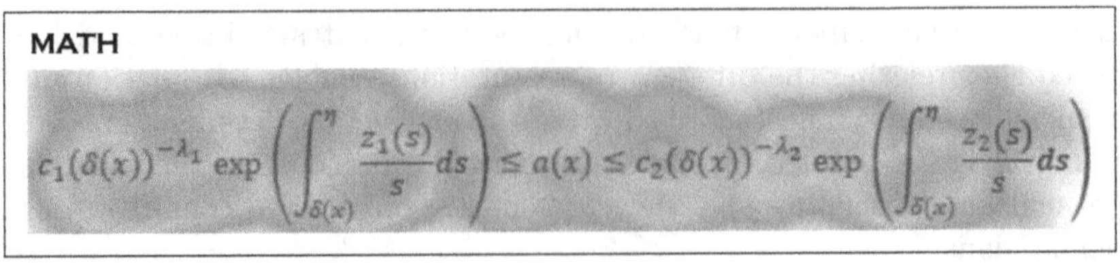

MATH

$$c_1(\delta(x))^{-\lambda_1} \exp\left(\int_{\delta(x)}^{\eta} \frac{z_1(s)}{s} ds\right) \leq a(x) \leq c_2(\delta(x))^{-\lambda_2} \exp\left(\int_{\delta(x)}^{\eta} \frac{z_2(s)}{s} ds\right)$$

Fig. 1. Exemplary math expression with heatmap of math-oriented subjects (Color figure online)

This data was analyzed to establish which practices are particular to mathematically inclined participants. On this basis [KF16] postulated a set of "math practices" which were to be confirmed or rejected by a bigger study focused on mathematicians and more diverse mathematical expressions – the original goal for our main experiment.

We will confirm the following math practices from this pilot study [KF16]:

P-MP1: *"Math-oriented people use <u>visual</u> patterns for math detection".*

P-MP2: *"Simple math expressions can be treated as placeholders for argument positions and therefore as neglectable in the math expression decomposition process".*

P-MP3: *"The decomposition of a math expression is organized along its procedural character".*

P-MP4: *"In the decomposition of a math expression, some symbols carry structural information, which is read independently from its functional information".*

and discuss

P-MP5: *"The decoding of a math expression starts from the left until a first meaningful sub-expression is grasped. Further comprehension is chunked into understanding sub-expressions and their relations".*

Before we venture there, we report yet another conjectured math practice based on the pilot study data: We observed that non-math-oriented participants tended to look over the integral in Fig. 1 in a left-to-right fashion like reading text, while math-oriented subjects seemed to follow on the one hand **P-MP3** and on the other **P-MP5**. A more precise account of the latter is given in Fig. 2, which superimposes the sequence of fixations by an

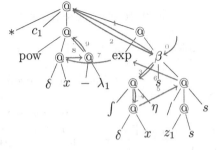

Fig. 2. Math-exploration of expression 3

exemplary math-oriented subject over the (first subexpression of) the Integral represented as an operator tree in content MathML. The first two steps $(1, 2)$ segment the formula: the proband looked at large left bracket for orientation, identified the first factor $c_1(\delta(x))^{-\lambda_1}$ to its left, and then found the matching right bracket. Steps 3, moves to the integral symbol and step 4 fixes the lower bound – the upper limit does not seem to receive much by the MATH group. Finally, step 5 passes to the body of the integral before step 6 discovers that the integral has the exponential function applied to it. Then the attention shifts to the first factor again and explores its base and exponent (steps 7 and 8). This exploration of the left-hand-side of the inequality is followed by an orientation towards the right-hand-side via the two "$\leq$" symbols, and then an exploration of the right hand side that is very similar to the one detailed in Fig. 2. Thus, we suggest the combination of **P-MP3** and **P-MP5** as a stronger and better framed mathematical practice:

> **MP1:** *"Math expressions are decoded in the order of a depth-first traversal of the corresponding operator tree".*

This is somewhat surprising, since the gaze plot is induced by the proband's *process of decoding the mathematical expression*, whereas the operator tree – represented as a content MathML expression in [KF16] – represents the *result* of the decoding process. In particular, one would think that the decoding process would follow "visual patterns" and be driven by "visual cues".

To verify the established set of mathematical practices we conducted the experiment, we report on in the following.

3   The Math Expressions Study with Mathematicians

Group	Female	Male
MATH	1	28
¬MATH	0	0

This eye-tracking study was carried out at the CICM 2016 conference in Bialystok in July 2016. We were able to recruit 29 participants – all not only math-oriented but except one even mathematically highly trained scientists. The set-up was very similar to the one in our pilot study: we used the same Tobii t60 Eye Tracking Screen (17″ and 4:3 ratio with 60 Hz) but in a mobile setup.

We selected three math expressions (see Fig. 3) from CICM talks to use for the study, so that we could assume participants were relatively familiar with them. The study contrasted them with various manually constructed (variations of) "visual patterns" consisting of a subset of the expression structure replaced by blank space or empty boxes like e.g. the extreme case □ = □. Figures 7 and 8 show more examples. Probands were asked to carefully look at the equations from Fig. 3 and then for each of a group of visual patterns to determine if these were *"representations"*[1] of the respective expression. Subjects were encouraged to

---

[1] As expected the term "representation" triggered various philosophical comments concerning its interpretation space and the resulting potentially different correct answers in the questionnaire.

(1)	$\int_{m}^{4m} \left(e^{3x} + e^{x} \right) dx = 100$
(2)	$N(\mu, \sigma) = \frac{1}{\sigma\sqrt{2\pi}} exp \left(-\frac{(x-\mu)^2}{2\sigma^2} \right)$
(3)	$\varepsilon \left(F_{\alpha \to \beta} A_{\alpha} \right) = app_{\varepsilon \to \varepsilon \to \varepsilon} \varepsilon \left(F_{\alpha \to \beta} \right) \varepsilon \left(A_{\alpha} \right)$

Fig. 3. The math expressions of our eye-tracking study

think aloud during the process but to be as fast as possible. The eye-movements, the questionnaire data, and the think-aloud protocol were recorded.

In the study we have gathered data concerning the order of fixations, the specific areas of the fixations, their length and amount of occurrences, and the questionnaire data. As the questions in the questionnaire were all of the same type – a 3-point Likert scale with options "yes", "no", and "I'm not sure" – we use (if at all) the standard mean as simple quantitative measure for the analysis of the questionnaire data. The eye-tracking specific data like data about fixations were analyzed via visual tools.

In particular, to get a better understanding of the order and intensity in which objects in math expressions are looked at, we used the visualization in form of a **gaze plot**, in which eye fixations are represented by dots that are connected, numbered, and accumulated according to their occurrence in a given time frame and whose size indicates the length of the gaze. **Heatmaps** as the one in Fig. 1 are another visual analysis tool. In an eye-tracking study the longest and most fixated areas are the hottest (red), the rarely fixated ones the coldest (green).

The general approach of our analysis of the new data was to inspect gaze plots and heat maps of randomly chosen probands for conspicuous patterns, interpret these, and check the remaining ones for typicality. We integrate the patterns found in [KF16] into this discussion.

4   Result: Math Practices wrt. Math Expression Decoding

In the following we concisely explain the conjectured math practices and argue confirmation or rejection.

Confirming MP1 and P-MP3; Discussing P-MP5. In Sect. 2 we have used an operator tree analysis for the left branch of the expression in Fig. 1 to formulate **MP1** ("*Math expressions are decoded in the order of a depth-first traversal of the corresponding operator tree*").

We studied all gaze plots of the math expressions in Fig. 3 to gain more insight on this. Figure 4 shows the (sequence of) fixations by proband P04 when reading expression (1) in Fig. 3 as a typical example – the corresponding operator

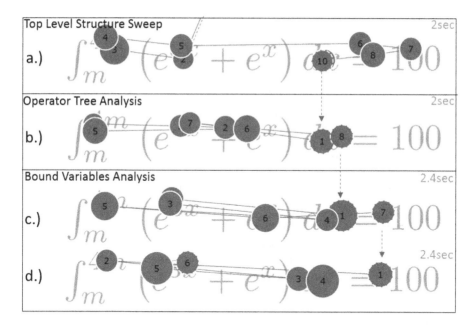

Fig. 4. The gaze plot for P04 on expression (1)

tree on the left of Fig. 11. We distributed all 28 fixations over images (a)–(d) to conserve readability. Generally, the last fixation of the previous box is taken up as the first one ("1") in the following. In the top box we see the very first scan of a formula presented to P04. In particular, the subject doesn't know yet of the tasks to come wrt. this formula. The scan starts roughly in the middle, then fixates all the major components in a left-right-left sweep (fixations "1"-"10") ending on the "dx" followed by an operator analysis according to the operator tree and finishing with some cross-checking with respect to the bound variable.

Our data fully confirms **MP1** and thus the weaker **P-MP3** (*"The decomposition of a math expression is organized along its procedural character"*): we consistently see fixations follow the operator tree in the expressions in Fig. 3. In particular, we verified that 21 out of the 29 participants followed the operator tree for expression (1), 18 for (2) and 21 for (3). Figure 5 shows three data lines for tracing the operator tree which superpose if the values coincide. Note that the conspicuous absence of the blue and red line indicates that most subjects answered consistently.

We could not confirm the unconstrained left-to-right aspect in **P-MP5** ("The decoding of a math expression starts from the left until a first meaningful subexpression is grasped. Further comprehension is chunked into understanding sub-expressions and their relations"): by and large the first fixations are near the center of the formula, and then tend to move into the leftmost argument of the first operator (as is consistent with **MP1**). We now attribute the left-to-right aspect in **P-MP5** to the fact that the equation in Fig. 1 is an inequality

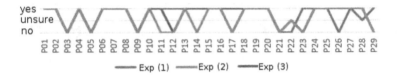

Fig. 5. Operator tree tracing (Color figure online)

chain, whose visual pattern (cf. **P-MP1**, but also see below) probands directly recognize and move into the left-most argument – i.e. all the way left in the expression. The chunking on the other hand could be observed, see Definition 2 for more discussion.

Confirming P-MP2. For **P-MP2** (*"Simple math expressions can be treated as placeholders for argument positions and therefore as neglectable in the math expression decomposition process"*) we have to show more evidence that simple subexpressions in math expressions are ignored by most subjects in our study.

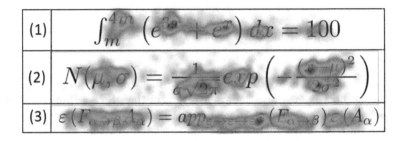

Fig. 6. Detecting top-level structure in formulae

We observed (see Fig. 6) that probands almost consistently did not fixate the lower limit m – a variable – of expression (1), whereas they overwhelmingly fixated the lower bound $\delta(x)$ and neglected the upper limit η in the integral of the exploratory study in Fig. 1. We conclude that probands see single variables in argument positions as "arbitrary" and only return to them if they also appear in more restricting context. So, we confirm **P-MP2**.

We conjecture that the upper limit in expression (1) and the lower in Fig. 1 are used as visual anchors, since they are larger and more complex.

Confirming P-MP1. We can uphold **P-MP1** (*"Math-oriented people use visual patterns for math detection"*) for **detection** – i.e. determining that a text region was "Math": even though we only presented very reduced visual patterns (e.g. $\Box = \Box$, $\Box \leq \Box$) to probands, none of them complained that this is not "Math".

Confirming P-MP4. The mathematical practice **P-MP1** (*"In the decomposition of a math expression, some symbols carry structural information, which is* *read independently from its functional information"*) can be confirmed. In Fig. 6, we can observe that the brackets and the integral are almost never fixated. Even the equation sign and the number on the right hand side of the equation are mostly unfocused. We remark that large (stretchy) operators like brackets and displayed integrals are more salient as structuring operators.

In Fig. 4 we have to assume that the overall structure of the formula has been determined in the very first sweep. Thus, together with **P-MP4** the top-level structure of the expression seems to be visual, so that we conjecture.

MP2: *"Visual patterns are used for detection of top-level structure in expressions".*

---

5   Result: The Gestalt Tree Hypothesis

Once more let us have a closer look at Fig. 4. We already observed that in box (a) P04 essentially conducted a sweep of the expression from left to right to grasp the top-level structure. In the next box (b) the head operator of the body of the integral (the operator "+" in fixation 2) is fixated, then the first summand, the upper integral limit, and the second summand to come back to the "dx". In the last sweep depicted in the lowest box containing (c) and (d) of Fig. 4 the fixations jump between subexpressions and integral limits and seem to concentrate on the bound variable x. One is tempted to interpret the gaze plot as containing three phases. The first one establishes the nature as an integral equation, the second one establishes the operator tree of the integrand, whereas the third pass checks the occurrences of the bound variables.

5.1   Visual Structure and Gestalt in Math Expressions

The above gives us the leading intuition and further evidence strongly suggests that an even stronger version of **MP2** and **MP1** may hold. Before we can analyze and state this, we will have to invest in some terminology that combines concepts from computer vision and formula structure.

Definition 1. The **top-level (visual) structure** (TLVS) of an expression consists of a **segment** S – a set of pixels that is considered a meaningful part of the image – that encompasses the expression, an **operator** O (also called the **head symbol**), and **sub-segments** S_i of S that mark arguments of O.

Example 1. The top-level structure of expression (1) is an "equation", where S is the whole image, O is the symbol "=", and the sub-segments S_i correspond to the left/right hand sides of the equation:

$$\int_{m}^{4m} \left(e^{3x} + e^{x} \right) dx = 100$$

Note that TLVSs can be nested; e.g. the left hand side of (1) is an integral, so here O is the integral operator together with dx. We have three segments for the limits and the body of the integral. This nesting structure induces a tree structure, where the nodes are operators: the operator tree of the expression.

Definition 2. The **visual structure** (VS) of a mathematical expression consists of a hierarchical segmentation S of the expression together with an operator tree T, such that S – seen as a tree given by the nesting structure of segments and T are isomorphic, i.e. tree structure and operators coincide.

Example 2. We obtain the following (two-level to ensure legibility) visual structure for (1), it yields the operator tree on the right:

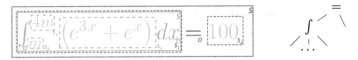

The top-level heat map of expression (1) in Fig. 6 and the initial "sweep phase" of the gaze-plot in Fig. 4 show us an interesting feature wrt. our data: It seems that all of the segmentation of (1) in Example 2 is something the experienced readers can take in at one go. Arguably (1) is an "integral equation", which is a – two-deep – visual structure in the sense of Definition 2.

This 'holistic' phenomenon seems to be closely related with the notion of **"Gestalt"** as defined in [Wag+12, p. 1218]: "*A Gestalt is an integrated, coherent structure or form, a whole that is different from the sum of the parts. Gestalts emerge spontaneously from self-organizational processes in the brain. Gestalts result from global field forces that lead to the simplest possible organization, or minimum solution, given the available stimulation.*". Even though classical Gestalt theory is controversial modern versions are actively debated today [ibid.]. Following these ideas we define.

Definition 3. A **condensed visual structure** of an expression E consists of a segment G that encompasses E, an **operator tree** T, and segments S_i of G, such that the S_i correspond to the leaves of T.

The **Gestalt** of E is a condensed visual structure (G, T, S_i) that can be decoded by human readers holistically.

Example 3. The Gestalt of (1) is that of an "integral equation", i.e.

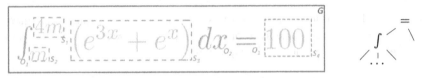

Note that Gestalts can be nested just like TLVS. We call such a nested tree a **Gestalt tree** (GT), and GT naturally induce operator trees a well (trees of trees can be flattened to trees).

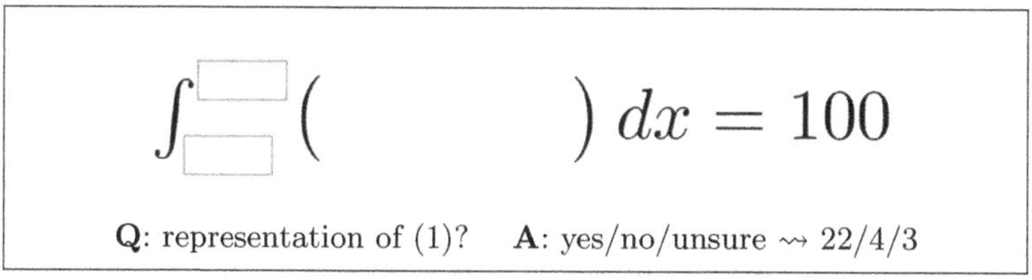

$$\int_{\Box}^{\Box} \left(\qquad\qquad \right) dx = 100$$

Q: representation of (1)?   **A**: yes/no/unsure ⤳ 22/4/3

Fig. 7. Accepting visual patterns

With Definition 3 we can postulate a set of **Gestalt patterns** for mathematicians, i.e. operator tree/segmentation patterns that can be used to decode mathematical expressions – in principle – modulo resource considerations like the size of the argument segments. We conjecture that Gestalt patterns are learned along with the mathematical concepts they correspond to. Thus, the set of Gestalt patterns is particular to a mathematician or mathematical community of practice and defines what she/they can decode easily. Note also that Gestalt patterns are very close to the visual patterns we use for testing in our study.

Using our new concepts, we can reformulate and strengthen **MP2** to

> **MP3:** *"Gestalt patterns are used for decoding structure in math expressions".*

We remark that **MP3** resolves the apparent contradiction in the observation that the gaze plot seems to follow the operator tree of an expression which should be the result of the decoding process: The (instantaneous) recognition of the Gestalt of a formula establishes the inner segmentation, and so it is not surprising that subsequent recursive exploration respects this.

Supporting MP3 in the Eyetracking Data. We observe that all probands respect the segmentation of the Gestalt tree, e.g. in equations the first couple of fixations are all in the left-hand side, and then switch over to the right-hand side, only occasionally fixating the head symbol. Together with **P-MP4** above this strongly supports **MP3**: as the visual cues of the TLVS are not fixated, but the segmentation is obeyed, it must be taken in precognitively – i.e., in one piece.

MP3 is also borne out by probands' answers in Fig. 7, where a majority accepted the visualization of the TLVS of expression (1) in Fig. 3: when asked whether this Fig. 7 is a representation of (1) 23 of 29 answered positively and only 4 negatively. Finally, 28 of 29 probands rejected out of hand that the TLVS visualization in Fig. 8 could be a representation of expression (3). This shows that the operator O is a constitutive part of the TLVS and thus the Gestalt.

5.2 Gestalt in Visual Imagery

The most baffling result of our study is that when confronted with visual patterns that abstracted the equations from Fig. 3, directly after the (full) equations

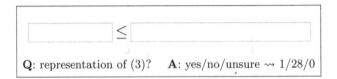

Q: representation of (3)?   **A:** yes/no/unsure ⤳ 1/28/0

Fig. 8. Rejecting visual patterns

themselves, probands fixated the locations where salient parts of the hidden subexpressions had been. Figure 9 shows the situation; note that the fixations are quite similar to those in the second box in Fig. 4, i.e. after the integral equation Gestalt pattern has been decoded. The only real difference are fixations "6", "7", and "9" in Fig. 9, which seem to delimit the body segment of the integral Gestalt.

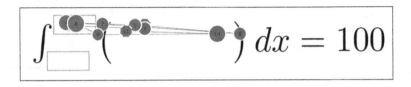

Fig. 9. Visual imagery (P04) for a visual pattern for expression (1)

We can describe this phenomenon in terms of **visual imagery**. The term describes the experience of "seeing with the minds eye" or in other words the human ability of "to conjure up a visual experience in the absence of retinal stimulation" [CHH12]. Whether the mental image is stored in the human brain in a pictoral form, a linguistic descriptive form, or a combination is still a vivid topic of study in cognitive psychology, see [Tye00] for a discussion. Here, we simply use the term for our observation of our subjects' eye movements along mathematical subexpressions that are absent in the image looked at in the study.

Surprisingly, visual imagery was not an isolated phenomenon, but in fact widespread in 28 probands (the eye-tracking recording of one proband was damaged and thus inconclusive) of our study. For expression (1) for instance, 16 clearly used visual imagery, for 9 subjects it was not sure and only 3 probands definitely did not use visual imagery. Figure 10 shows more gaze plots; here we have superimposed the elided parts of the original formula in light blue to show the precision of the visual imagery.

On the other hand visual imagery was much less pronounced in the probabilistic distribution function (2) and the type theory formula (3): For expression (2) the decision whether subjects used visual imagery was much more difficult. We identified 6 as clearly exhibiting visual imagery, with 10 we were not sure and 12 were not. For expression (3) we didn't dare a valid assessment. This

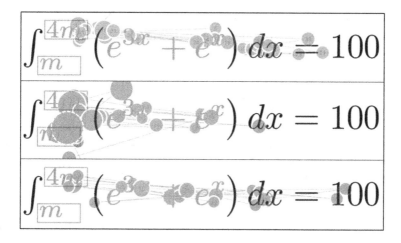

Fig. 10. More visual imagery of P02, P14, and P16 (Color figure online)

difference to (1) may be a consequence of the fact that in subsequent visual patterns the 'box abstraction' became expected and thus only box sizes were taken into account: Instead of visual imagery of formula structures we start to see visual scans of box boundaries or dimensions. We will have to conduct further experiments to distinguish between effects here.

Even though the visual/structural imagery effect diminishes in our study, we interpret it as a strong support for the notion that Gestalt patterns drive the decoding process for mathematical expressions (in trained mathematicians), i.e. **MP3**.

The Formula Understanding Phase. But **MP3** only covers part of the data we observe when probands study formulae. Concretely, it covers the first two sweeps we saw from P04 in the two top boxes in Fig. 4. But many probands of the main study (and most math-oriented of the exploratory one) followed it up with a "cross-checking phase", which consists of fixations that directly access interesting semantical features – e.g. bound variables in various subexpressions, or other variables, literals, or subtrees that occur more than once. We conjecture that this "direct access" is only possible because the Gestalt tree determines the **loci** (i.e. locations in the presentation that correspond to subtrees in the content/operator tree) for them. The few exceptions did consistently cross-check after each of the last phases, which fits as well.

> **MP4:** *"Once the Gestalt tree is established, probands cross-check details across loci in the Gestalt tree".*

We tentatively interpret this "cross-checking phase" we see the eye-tracker data as a semantic understanding phase, where formula readers correlate information from the subexpressions to each other. We conjecture that in this phase readers also correlate subexpressions with expressions from the context. To check this, we would have to conduct experiments, where some of the context is explicitly represented in the document presented to the user. We expect to see fixations on the context expressions in the "cross-checking phase".

The Gestalt Tree Hypothesis: We sum up **MP3** and **MP4** as

---

Gestalt Tree Hypothesis (GTH):
The process of decoding mathematical expressions has two phases
1. recursively establishing the Gestalt tree by matching the formula presentation against Gestalt patterns (the **reading/parsing phase**).
2. cross-checking structural detail across loci in the visual tree (the **understanding phase**).

We formulate this as a hypothesis even though our data supports it quite strongly, since our study was only designed to study the effects of "visual patterns" on the formula decoding process of mathematicians and not particularly the GTH.

Representing the Gestalt Tree: Now that we have identified potential mechanisms used by math-oriented human readers in reading and understanding formulae, let us see how that relates to the representational practices in mathematical knowledge management.

The core intuition behind the Gestalt concept and by homomorphic extension behind Gestalt trees is that they correlate visual patterns and operator structure. This directly maps to the concept of "parallel markup via cross-references" in MathML [Aus+10, Sect. 5.4.2].

Figure 11 shows the content MathML tree of expression (1) on the left and the presentation tree on the right. The cross-references that mark up corresponding subtrees are shown as green dashed lines. The content tree is made up of operator applications (@ and their children) and bindings (β nodes). In our example the binding is the integral where the first child of the β is the binding operator – the integral with its limits, the second is the bound variable x, and the third is the integrand, which is an operator application again. In the layout tree we find layout primitives like rows and sub/superscript patterns.

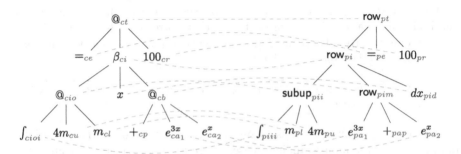

Fig. 11. Content and presentation trees of the integral expression (1) (Color figure online)

If we tease apart layer for layer con- serving the cross-references, we get one- level correspondences like the one shown on the right that correspond directly to TLVS or (more-level) VS, which can be

condensed into Gestalts by backgrounding inner cross-references. Coinciden- tally, these structures directly correspond to the notation definitions for OMDoc [KMR08]. The notation-definition-based parsing process we studied in [TK16] can (after the fact) also be seen as an implementation of the first phase in the Gestalt Tree Hypothesis.

6   Conclusion

In this paper we have tried to shed some light on the processes governing how trained mathematicians read and understand mathematical formulae. After an exploratory study with a mixed group of math-oriented and non-math-oriented students, which revealed cognitive practices particular to math-oriented subjects, we conducted a follow-up study with 28 mathematically highly trained scientists to study these mathematical practices in more detail. Our study is a qualitative data analysis – for which 28 subjects is a very respectable number. In particular, we do not claim a quantitative significance.

Our scientific contribution consists in the confirmation/refinement of several math practices regarding the decoding of math expressions. In a nutshell, we could show that math expressions are decoded in the order of a depth-first traversal of the operator tree, simple ones often only serve as placeholders for argument positions, and visual patterns are used for top-level structure detection in math expressions.

In the eye-tracking data, it became apparent that the structure detection phase of the parsing process is almost instantaneous and "holistic" which led us to coin the concept of a formula Gestalt and hypothesize that Gestalt pat- terns govern the way mathematicians parse formulae. While the Gestalt Tree Hypothesis is strongly supported by the eye-tracking data obtained from our study, the study itself was not designed to test this hypothesis per se. Therefore, more careful studies are needed to prove it in the future.

Moreover, we noticed significant differences between the groups of partici- pants that self-identified as computer scientists vs. mathematicians for gazing at expression (3) in Fig. 3, which is in the domain of type-theory that is more tied to CS than math: The CS group paid significantly more attention to the type components, whereas the true mathematicians seemed more interested in the homomorphic structure at the term level. This suggests that familiarity with the domain affects the way probands read formulae. We leave the investigation of this interesting aspect to future work.

Finally, it would be interesting to compile a catalog of Gestalt patterns com- monly in use in Mathematics. Actually, given that we can represent Gestalt patterns in notation definitions, we can interpret the notation definitions in the

SMGloM terminology base [Koh14] as a start that could be tested for cognitive reality.

References

[Arc03] Arcavi, A.: The role of visual representations in the learning of mathematics. Educ. Stud. Math. **52**(3), 215–241 (2003)

[Aus+10] Ausbrooks, R., et al.: Mathematical Markup Language (MathML) Version 3.0. W3C Recommendation. World Wide Web Consortium (W3C) (2010). http://www.w3.org/TR/MathML3

[BR14] Beitlich, J., Reiss, K.: Das Lesen mathematischer Beweise - Eine Eye Tracking Studie. In: Roth, J., Ames, J. (eds.) Beiträge zum Mathematikunterricht 2014. WTM-Verlag, pp. 157–160 (2014)

[CHH12] Cichy, R.M., Heinzle, J., Haynes, J.D.: Imagery and perception share cortical representations of content and location. Cereb. Cortex **22**(2), 372 (2012)

[Fre] Freudenthal, H.: Didactical Phenomenology of Mathematical Structures. Mathematics Education Library. Springer, Dordrecht (1983). ISBN: 9027715351

[HWH99] Henderson, J.M., Weeks Jr., P.A., Hollingworth, A.: The effects of semantic consistency on eye movements during complex scene viewing. J. Exp. Psychol. Hum. Percept. Perform. **25**(1), 210–228 (1999). http://dx.doi.org/10.1037/0096-1523.25.1.210

[KF16] Kohlhase, A., Fürsich, M.: Understanding mathematical expressions: an eye-tracking study. In: Kohlhase, A., Libbrecht, P. (eds.) Mathematical User Interfaces Workshop, July 2016. http://ceur-ws.org/Vol-1785/M2.pdf

[KL16] Kohlhase, A., Libbrecht, P. (eds.) Mathematical User Interfaces Workshop at CICM, July 2016. http://ceur-ws.org/Vol-1785/

[KMR08] Kohlhase, M., Müller, C., Rabe, F.: Notations for living mathematical documents. In: Autexier, S., Campbell, J., Rubio, J., Sorge, V., Suzuki, M., Wiedijk, F. (eds.) CICM 2008. LNCS, vol. 5144, pp. 504–519. Springer, Heidelberg (2008). doi:10.1007/978-3-540-85110-3_41. http://omdoc.org/pubs/mkm08-notations.pdf

[Koh14] Kohlhase, M.: A data model and encoding for a semantic, multilingual terminology of mathematics. In: Watt, S.M., Davenport, J.H., Sexton, A.P., Sojka, P., Urban, J. (eds.) CICM 2014. LNCS, vol. 8543, pp. 169–183. Springer, Cham (2014). doi:10.1007/978-3-319-08434-3_13. http://kwarc.info/kohlhase/papers/cicm14-smglom.pdf

[KT13] Kamali, S., Tompa, F.W.: Retrieving documents with mathematical content. In: Jones, G.J.F., et al. (eds.) Proceedings of the 36th International ACM SIGIR Conference on Research and Development in Information Retrieval, Dublin, Ireland, pp. 353–362. ACM (2013). ISBN: 978-1-4503-2034-4

[Ray98] Rayner, K.: Eye movements in reading and information processing: 20 years of research. Psychol. Bull. **124**(3), 372–422 (1998). (in English)

[Sch05] Schnotz, W.: An integrated model of text and picture comprehension. In: Mayer, R.E. (ed.) The Cambridge Handbook of Multimedia Learning, pp. 49–69. Cambridge University Press, Cambridge (2005). Reprinted as pp. 72–103 (2014)

[SGM10] Strahl, A., Grobe, J., Müller, R.: Was schreckt bei Formeln ab? - Untersuchung zur Darstellung von Formeln. In: PhyDid B - Didaktik der Physik - Beiträge zur DPG-Frühjahrstagung 0.0 (2010)

[TK16] Toloaca, I., Kohlhase, M.: Notation-based Semantification. In: Kohlhase, A., Libbrecht, P. (eds.) Mathematical User Interfaces Workshop, pp. 73–81, July 2016. http://ceur-ws.org/Vol-1785/M6.pdf

[Tye00] Tye, M.: The Imagery Debate. Representation and Mind series. MIT Press, Cambridge (2000)

[Wag+12] Wagemans, J., et al.: A century of gestalt psychology in visual perception: II. Conceptual and theoretical foundations. Psychol. Bull. **138**, 1218–1252 (2012)

Mathematical Models as Research Data via Flexiformal Theory Graphs

Michael Kohlhase[1]([✉]), Thomas Koprucki[2]([✉]), Dennis Müller[1]([✉]),
and Karsten Tabelow[2]([✉])

[1] Informatik, FAU Erlangen-Nürnberg, Martensstr. 3, 91058 Erlangen, Germany
michael.kohlhase@fau.de, d.mueller@kwarc.info
[2] Weierstrass Institute (WIAS), Mohrenstr. 39, 10117 Berlin, Germany
{thomas.koprucki,karsten.tabelow}@wias-berlin.de

Abstract. Mathematical modeling and simulation (MMS) has now been established as an essential part of the scientific work in many disciplines. It is common to categorize the involved numerical data and to some extent the corresponding scientific software as research data. But both have their origin in mathematical models, therefore any holistic approach to research data in MMS should cover all three aspects: data, software, and models. While the problems of classifying, archiving and making accessible are largely solved for data and first frameworks and systems are emerging for software, the question of how to deal with mathematical models is completely open.

In this paper we propose a solution – to cover all aspects of mathematical models: the underlying mathematical knowledge, the equations, boundary conditions, numeric approximations, and documents in a flexiformal framework, which has enough structure to support the various uses of models in scientific and technology workflows.

Concretely we propose to use the OMDoc/MMT framework to formalize mathematical models and show the adequacy of this approach by modeling a simple, but non-trivial model: van Roosbroeck's drift-diffusion model for one-dimensional devices. This formalization – and future extensions – allows us to support the modeler by e.g., flexibly composing models, visualizing Model Pathway Diagrams, and annotating model equations in documents as induced from the formalized documents by flattening. This directly solves some of the problems in treating mathematical models as "research data" and opens the way towards more MKM services for models.

1 Introduction

Mathematics is a common ground for science and technology: research problems are described using mathematical models, which are then solved either by symbolic derivation or numerical simulation. In the last decade *mathematical modeling and simulation* (MMS) has been established as a primary scientific research method alongside the classical methods of experiment and theory. It is now an essential part of the scientific work in many disciplines and application

© Springer International Publishing AG 2017
H. Geuvers et al. (Eds.): CICM 2017, LNAI 10383, pp. 224–238, 2017.
DOI: 10.1007/978-3-319-62075-6_16

areas. Research in the area of MMS is characterized by *mathematical models, scientific software* for their treatment, and *numerical data* related to computations (input, output, parameters), see [KT16]. There, it was proposed to categorize these three parts as the research data in MMS as they are jointly required to understand and verify research results, or to build upon them.

Specifically, *numerical data* is generally regarded as research data in the usual sense and data repositories and information services such as DataCite [Bra09] or RADAR [RNH14, Kra15] exist or are emerging. Increasingly, *software* is also categorized as research data [For15] and an information service on mathematical software, swMath [GS14], has already been developed.

The representation of mathematical models themselves – the mathematical knowledge they contain and the discipline-specific knowledge they are based on – is far less clear. Current practice is to publish them as mathematical papers with a mixture of mathematical formulae and natural language. This leads to ambiguity, duplication, and incompleteness in presentation and makes the treatment of models as research data impossible. To allow "data repositories" for models we would need a way of automatically identifying and classifying them. Analogously, connecting models to input/output data or to software systems is impossible without such services.

Classically the computer-actionable representation of "models" is the domain of modelling languages like the Universal Modelling Language (UML [UML]), Systems Biology Markup Language (SBML [Huc+03, SBML]), or MODELICA [Mod14], a "modelling language for physical systems". These allow to describe complex software/biological/physical systems in terms of their components and the connections/interactions between them in a machine-actionable way. These languages usually support visualizations of the respective "models" diagrammatically for communication with/among humans and code generation for the computational systems of the domain. Many of them come with large libraries of standardized components that make the assembly of models less tedious.

We claim that these languages only solve part of the description problem for MMS models: They describe large technical or biological systems composed of elementary units and their effective behavior by parametrized and often empirical *compact models*. However, they do not provide a detailed description of the physical (biological or chemical) spatio-temporal processes governing their behavior on the level of fundamental laws and constitutive relations, typically expressed by partial differential equations. This type of mathematical models is important for many disciplines such as the natural and engineering sciences as well as life and environmental sciences, but a machine-understandable representation is missing.

In this paper we restrict our attention to such models: complex models of simple devices. If we can formalize and machine-support them, we can scale them up to complex devices with classical modeling languages. We will perform a case study for the representation of such type of models using the van Roosbroeck system [VR50]. It is the standard model [Sel84, Far+16] to describe the current flow in semiconductor devices ranging from diodes and transistors to LEDs, solar cells, lasers and novel materials such as organic semiconductors. Even its relatively simple one-dimensional stationary version has more than ten non-trivially connected equations.

In this paper we propose a solution to the "models as research data" problem by flexiformalization of all aspects of mathematical models: the underlying mathematical knowledge, the equations, boundary conditions, numeric approximations, and documents in a framework that has enough structure to support the various uses of models in scientific and technology workflows.

Concretely we propose to the OMDoc/MMT framework to model mathematical models and show the adequacy of this approach by modeling a simple, but non-trivial model: van Roosbroeck's drift-diffusion model in one-dimensional devices. To make this paper self-contained we introduce OMDoc/MMT theory graphs in the next section and the mathematics of the van Roosbroeck model in Sect. 3. Then we discuss the flexiformalization in Sect. 5 and the services that can be built on this in Sect. 6. Section 7 concludes the paper.

2   Flexiformal Theory Graphs

OMDoc [Koh06] is a wide-coverage representation language for mathematical knowledge (formal) and documents (informal/narrative). In the last decade development has focused on the formal aspect leading to the OMDoc/MMT instance (Meta-Meta-Theories [RK13, HKR12, Rab14]), which increases expressivity, clarifies the representational primitives and formally defines the semantics of this fragment.

OMDoc/MMT is designed to be foundation-independent and introduces several concepts to maximize modularity and to abstract from and mediate between different foundations, to reuse concepts, tools, and formalizations. The OMDoc/MMT language *integrates successful representational paradigms*

- the logics-as-theories representation from logical frameworks,
- theories and the reuse along theory morphisms from the heterogeneous method,
- the Curry-Howard correspondence from type theoretical foundations,
- URIs as globally unique logical identifiers from OpenMath,
- the standardized XML-based interchange syntax of OMDoc,

and makes them available in a single, coherent representational system for the first time. The combination of these features is based on a small set of carefully chosen, orthogonal primitives in order to obtain a simple and extensible language design.

OMDoc/MMT offers very few primitives, which have turned out to be sufficient for most practical settings. These are

1. *constants* with optional types and definitions,
2. types and definitions of constants are *objects*, which are syntax trees with binding, using previously defined constants as leaves,

3. *theories*, which are lists of constant declarations and
4. *theory morphisms*, that map declarations in a domain theory to expressions built up from declarations in a target theory.

Using these primitives, logical frameworks, logics and theories *within* some logic are all uniformly represented as OMDoc/MMT theories, rendering all of those equally accessible, reusable and extendable. Constants, functions, symbols, theorems, axioms, proof rules etc. are all represented as constant declarations, and all terms which are built up from those are represented as objects.

Theory morphisms represent truth-preserving maps between theories. Examples include theory inclusions, translations/isomorphisms between (sub)theories and models/instantiations (by mapping axioms to theorems that hold within a model), as well as a particular theory inclusion called *meta-theory*, that relates a theory on some meta level to a theory on a higher level on which it depends. This includes the relation between some low level theory (such as the theory of groups) to its underlying foundation (such as first-order logic), and the latter's relation to the logical framework used to define it – e.g. LF; see [Pfe01] for an overview.

All of this naturally gives us the notion of a *theory graph*, which relates theories (represented as nodes) via edges representing theory morphisms (as in Fig. 1), being right at the design core of the OMDoc/MMT language. It is a central advantage of the OMDoc/MMT system that theory mor-

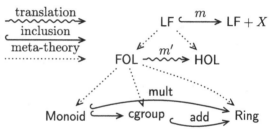

Fig. 1. A theory graph with meta-theories

phisms "transport axioms, definitions, theorems, ..." to new contexts and thus induce knowledge that is not explicitly represented in the graph. Therefore it is a central design invariant of the system that we can name all induced objects with canonical URIs, the MMT URIs, which contain enough information to reconstruct the induced objects themselves – given the graph.

Recently, OMDoc/MMT has been extended to enable handling content of *flexible formality* [Koh13] in a bid to reach full OMDoc coverage. In a nutshell, *informal* parts are modeled as opaque constants, objects or theories [Ian17]. While they can obviously not be formally analyzed with respect to their formal structure, they can still be used in (and be subject to) the various knowledge management services provided by MMT, in particular they can be connected to formal content via theory morphisms. As a result, we believe we can use OMDoc/MMT to represent all kinds of mathematical models and their domains of application in a unified manner, whether they can be fully formalized in some logic or need to be represented informally.

This approach seems to be feasible in view of the general L-concept of physical theories [Sch96], which relies on a formalization of statements on physical objects and their relations also using a formalized mathematical theory.

3 Van Roosbroeck Model

As guiding example for the formalization of models we consider a simplified variant of the van Roosbroeck system [VR50, Sel84, Far+16]. It describes the flow of charge carriers (electrons and holes) in a self-consistent electric field in a semiconductor device using a drift-diffusion approximation. Therefore it is also frequently called the *drift-diffusion model.*

In its unipolar version, that means only considering one charge carrier species, it is suited for the simulation of many devices ranging from simple layered n-doped/intrinsic/n-doped (nin) structures, see Fig. 2, to organic transistors [Kas+16]. Specifically, we will focus in this paper on the one-dimensional unipolar van Roosbroeck system assuming a homogeneous material on an interval $\Omega = [0, L]$ with Ohmic contacts at each end. It consists of two nonlinear ordinary differential equations for the unknown electrostatic potential $\psi(x)$ and the quasi Fermi potentials for electrons $\varphi_n(x)$ as follows:

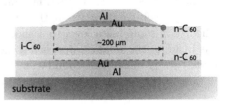

Fig. 2. Schematic structure of a device consisting of n-doped/intrinsic/n-doped layers of the organic semiconductor C_{60}. Reprinted from [Fis+12] with permission from Elsevier.

$$-\frac{d}{dx}\left(\varepsilon_s \frac{d}{dx}\psi\right) = q\left[C - N_c \exp\left(\frac{q(\psi - \varphi_n) - E_c}{k_B T}\right)\right], \tag{1a}$$

$$\frac{d}{dx}\left[-q\mu_n N_c \exp\left(\frac{q(\psi - \varphi_n) - E_c}{k_B T}\right)\frac{d}{dx}\varphi_n\right] = 0. \tag{1b}$$

It links Poisson's Eq. (1a) for the electrostatic potential to the continuity equation for electron density

$$n(\psi, \varphi_n) = N_c \exp\left(\frac{q(\psi - \varphi_n) - E_c}{k_B T}\right). \tag{2}$$

The term in brackets in continuity Eq. (1b) represents the flux of the electron current density j_n. We stress here that we have used the so-called Boltzmann approximation. In general, the exponentials will be replaced by some monotonically increasing *statistical distribution function* $\mathcal{F}$ [Far+16].

The elementary charge q and the Boltzmann constant k_B are universal physical constants. The (absolute) dielectric permittivity $\varepsilon_s = \varepsilon_0 \varepsilon_r$ is given as the product of the vacuum dielectric permittivity ε_0 and the relative permittivity of the semiconductor material ε_r. The electron mobility μ_n, the effective conduction band density of states N_c as well as the conduction band-edge energy E_c are assumed to be constant. The temperature T is also assumed to be constant. The doping profile $C = C(x)$ describes material properties. For a more detailed discussion on the physics behind these different quantities we refer to [Sel84, Far+16].

The system (1) needs to be supplied with boundary conditions at $x = 0$ and $x = L$. For applied external voltages U_1 and U_2, we require the Dirichlet boundary conditions at the *Ohmic contacts*, that is

$$\psi(0) = \psi_0(0) + U_1, \qquad \psi(L) = \psi_0(L) + U_2, \qquad (3a)$$
$$\varphi_n(0) = U_1, \qquad \varphi_n(L) = U_2, \qquad (3b)$$

For a discussion on the meaning and choice of the built-in potentials $\psi_0(0)$, $\psi_0(L)$ see [Far+16].

In the literature, authors frequently use a different set of unknowns for the van Roosbroeck system by replacing the quasi Fermi potential with the electron density n. A formulation based on the electron density involves an alternative expression for electron current entering the continuity equation, namely the classical drift-diffusion form, see [Far+16]. Consequently, the choice of the unknowns introduces an ambiguity of the model equations which a mathematical knowledge management system for its formal representation has to reflect.

Here, we start with the more general formulation using the quasi Fermi potential, see (1), as it naturally appears in the thermodynamic description of the van Roosbroeck system since the negative gradient of the quasi Fermi potential is the driving force of the current [BGH05]. Moreover, it is mathematically even more beautiful as it makes it possible to write the whole van Roosbroeck system in a gradient form [Mie11]. In the following section we will develop a formal representation of this model and demonstrate how the different aspects of the coupled system can be explained therein.

4   Model Pathways Diagrams

As we have seen in the last section, even relatively simple mathematical models – the model only covers the stationary (time-independent) case in one dimension – can be quite intimidating. The central intuition that helps to understand them is that a model makes assertions about measurable quantities in the real world – in our case in the physical world. Concretely, models employ a system of physical laws that assert relations between physical quantities. For instance a "displacement law" asserts a relation between the electric field E, the dielectric permittivity ε_s of a material and the resulting displacement field D accounting for induced polarization due to the bound charges, and can therefore be used to compute the latter from the former. Similarly, a permittivity law can be used to compute the (absolute) permittivity ε_s from the vacuum dielectric permittivity ε_0 and a material parameter ε_r.

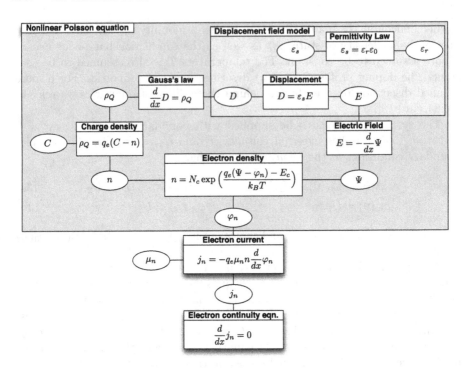

Fig. 3. The Model Pathway Diagram for the van Roosbroeck model, cf. Eqs.(1). Two sub MPDs are highlighted using colored boxes: the displacement field model (red) and the nonlinear Poisson equation (blue). For simplicity the handling of the boundary conditions have been dropped as well as some quantities, e.g. conduction band-edge energy E_c or the temperature T. (Color figure online)

To help understand the inner (physical) structure of mathematical models (and guide formalization) we have developed a special kind of diagrams: **Model Pathway Diagrams** (MPD). These depict physical quantities – see [Wik] for a list – as circles labeled with their physical notations and connect them by physical laws, which we draw as named rectangles which contain the respective equation. In an MPD each law node must be connected to all quantities that appear in the equation by a path. We use undirected edges in MPDs, since mathematically, physical laws are relations only and therefore have no prescribed input/output directions. MPDs may be cyclic, but should be transitively non-redundant. The usefulness of diagrammatic representations for physical phenomena has been proven for example by Feynman diagrams [Fey49] in the perturbation theory for quantum field theory.

Figure 3 shows a MPD for the van Roosbroeck system that teases apart the respective contributions of the various laws and shows the quantities they relate.

Definition 1 (MPD Model). Let $\mathcal{Q}$ denote the set of quantities in an MPD M and $\mathcal{L} \subseteq \mathcal{Q}$ be the set of leaves in the quantities of M. The triple $\mathcal{M} = (M, \mathcal{U}, \mathcal{P})$, is a **MPD model for** a set of **unknown quantities** $\mathcal{U} \subseteq \mathcal{Q}$ **given** the parameters $\mathcal{P} = \mathcal{L} \backslash \mathcal{U}$, if the MPD has at least one quantity leaf, i.e., $\mathcal{L}$ is not empty. An MPD model for $\mathcal{U}$ given $\mathcal{P}$ is **underdetermined** if $|\mathcal{Q}| > |\mathcal{R}| + |\mathcal{U}| + |\mathcal{P}|$, where $\mathcal{R}$ is the set of relations (laws, constitutive relations) in the MPD.

Example 1 (van Roosbroeck model). The MPD in Fig. 3 is an MPD model, the van Roosbroeck model, for the electrostatic potential ψ and the quasi-Fermi potential φ_n given the doping profile C, the relative permittivity ε_r, and the electron mobility μ_n. Thus, $\mathcal{U} = \{\psi, \varphi_n\}$ and $\mathcal{P} = \mathcal{L} = \{C, \varepsilon_r, \mu_n\}$.

Example 2 (Displacement field model). The sub-MPD in Fig. 3 highlighted by the red color is a model for the displacement field D given the electric field E and the relative permittivity ε_r. $\mathcal{U} = \{D\}$ and $\mathcal{P} = \mathcal{L} \backslash \mathcal{U} = \{E, \varepsilon_r\}$. Its flexiformal representation in OMDoc/MMT will be discussed in Sect. 5.

Example 3 (Nonlinear Poisson equation). The sub MPD in Fig. 3 highlighted by the blue color is a model, the nonlinear Poisson equation, for the electrostatic potential ψ given the quasi-Fermi potential φ_n, the doping profile C, and the relative permittivity ε_r. Thus $\mathcal{U} = \{\psi\}$ and $\mathcal{P} = \mathcal{L} = \{C, \varepsilon_r, \varphi_n\}$.

Remark 1 (Physical equivalent sets of unknown quantities). The choice of unknown quantities $\mathcal{U}$, e.g., in the nonlinear Poisson equation, involves some ambiguity: Instead of $\mathcal{U} = \{\psi\}$, one could as well use, e.g., the electric field E or the electron density n. These choices are physically equivalent and the particular selection depends on the specific aspects to be modeled.

Remark 2 (Inverse problems). Furthermore, if we replace $\mathcal{U} = \{\psi\}$ by the doping profile $\mathcal{U} = \{C\}$ the resulting MPD model for the doping profile C is underdetermined and constitutes an inverse problem. In order to enable its solution an additional leaf for a quantity ψ_0 can be added connected to the MPD by a target law $\psi = \psi_0$. Then the solution determines a doping profile, when the target potential ψ_0 is attained.

In the MPD in Fig. 3, we can directly get an overview over the structure of the van Roosbroeck model. We observe the (nonlinear) Poisson equation complex on the top and the carrier transport complex on the bottom, which are coupled by the quantities n (electron density), and Ψ. N.B. the electron density n is physically equivalent to the quasi-Fermi potential in the sense of Remark 1. The corresponding sub-MPDs are directly related to the sub Eqs. (1a) and (1b) of the van Roosbroeck model. Both sub-MPDs possess a distinct topological structure: The nonlinear Poisson equation is characterized by the loop (diamond structure) of the density n, the charge density ρ_Q, the displacement D, the electric field E and the electrostatic potential Ψ. In contrast, the sub-MPD for the carrier transport has a tree-like structure with the root being the quasi-Fermi potential φ_n. These topological structures can be utilized for the mathematical theory of the respective equations. Furthermore, it paves a way for the development of iterative schemes for the numerical solution of the fully coupled system, e.g. the Gummel's (decoupling) method [Gum64, Sel84, Far+16].

5 Flexi-Formalizing a Non-trivial Model, a Case Study

We are currently studying the model introduced in the last section, formalizing the inherent knowledge in OMDoc and augmenting (parts of) [Far+16] into an active document, see [Koh+] for first results.

We base the development on a higher-order logic with records, (predicate) subtypes, and literals [Rab] for basic mathematical objects like real numbers and arithmetics. We use this theory as the meta-language for all theories, but do not show it in our diagrams. Instead we start the development with the Math-in-the-Middle development of elementary maths [Mit] and let the formalization be guided by the MPD in Fig. 3.

We model physical quantities as special theories that introduce a (type) constant which is a SI dimension, see, e.g., the theory for the dielectric permittivity on the right.

$$\mathcal{Q}_{DielectricPermittivity}$$
$$\mathsf{permittivity : type} = \frac{\mathsf{charge}}{\mathsf{voltage \cdot length}}$$

We call these theories **quantity theories**; they directly implement the quantity nodes (circles) in MPDs. Given these basic theories, (and more mathematical and physics background; e.g., SI units), we can implement the physical laws as OMDoc/MMT theories. Figure 4 has e.g. the theory DispLaw, which includes three quantity theories $\mathcal{Q}_{DielectricPermittivity}$, $\mathcal{Q}_{EField}$, and $\mathcal{Q}_{Displ}$ (and some more background material not shown in Fig. 4) and states their relation in a simple equation. Similarly, the theory DPMat corresponds to the Permittivity Law theory in Fig. 4. Figure 5 has the OMDoc/MMT source for the charge law (called "electron current" in Fig. 3).

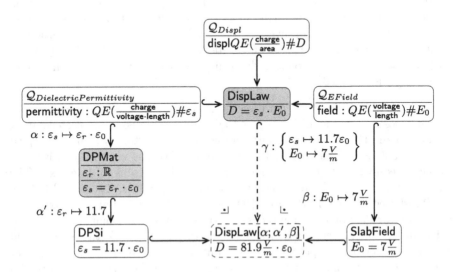

Fig. 4. Application of models

Note that a theory graph $\mathcal{T}$ as the one in Fig. 4 induces an MPD $\mathcal{M}$ in the sense of the last section. In particular it corresponds to the MPD Displacement field model in Fig. 3, see also Example 2. This motivates the following

Definition 2 (Model in a Theory Graph). Let $\mathcal{T}$ be an OMDoc/MMT theory graph, $\mathcal{M}$ a subgraph in $\mathcal{T}$ consisting only of quantity/law theories and inclusions between them, and $\mathcal{D}_{\mathcal{M}} := (N, E)$ where N is the set of nodes of $\mathcal{T}$ labeled with (a) the notation of the quantity symbol for quantity theories and (b) the content of the axioms for the law theories and E is the set of inclusions in $\mathcal{M}$. Then, we call $\mathcal{M}$ a **model** in $\mathcal{T}$, iff $\mathcal{D}_{\mathcal{M}}$ is a MPD model. We define a "model for $\mathcal{U}$ given $\mathcal{P}$" as in Definition 1.

The lower part of Fig. 4 shows the process of instantiating the model in the upper part to concrete values via theory extensions (via the inclusions α' and β) to concrete values – here $\varepsilon_r = 11.7$ for the relative dielectric permittivity of silicon (in theory DPSi) and $E_0 = 7\frac{F}{m}$ for the electric field applied to the silicon slab (in theory SlabField). These together allow to compute the theory DispLaw$[\alpha; \alpha', \beta]$ and inclusion γ (the dashed part of Fig. 4) as the co-limit of DPSi and Slabfield modulo DispLaw. Technically, the co-limit DispLaw$[\alpha; \alpha', \beta]$, which represents the result of the model instantiated to some device that is a silicon slab with an external field of $7\frac{V}{m}$ can be computed as the double pushout along $\alpha; \alpha'$ and β as all the theory morphisms involved are injective. Note that α is a model-internal instantiation that connects the two laws into a model, whereas α' and β are application morphisms that instantiate it to a particular situation description.

In Fig. 4 we have only shown a small part of the van Roosbroeck model, but we have developed the whole OMDoc/MMT theory graph corresponding to Fig. 3.

Figure 5 shows a snippet of our formalization in its original OMDoc/MMT syntax. It shows the law for charge densities as occurring in the van Roosbroeck model as a constant total_charge_law. The equation is stated in the type using

```
theory ChargeLaw : top:?Base =
  include device?DeviceGeometry
  include device?DopingProfile
  include ?PoissonParameters
  include top:/Species?ElectronsAndHoles
  include top:?SpatialChargeDensity

  /T The total charge denoted by $Q$ composed of doping profile $C$ and
  electron and hole densities $n$ and $p$, defined by
  $Q$ = $q$($C$+$p$ - $n$).
  total_charge_density : {x : Ω} ⊢ Q x ≐
    -q · ((C x) + (holes/z · (holes/density x)) + (electrons/z · (electrons/density x))
```

Fig. 5. Excerpt of the OMDoc/MMT formalization (total charge density law)

the Curry-Howard Isomorphism: $\vdash E$ is the type of proofs of E. It relates the total charge $Q(x)$ to various other quantities (such as the doping profile $C(x)$ and the respective densities of the electrons and holes) that are imported via theory inclusions. This modular structure allows for selectively substituting the imported quantities with specific values.

The complete theory graph (not counting the background knowledge in the MitM ontology) contains 38 theories and 63 inclusions. As these theories are exclusively physical quantities and laws, we expect them to be highly reusable.

6   Knowledge Management Services for Models

The most immediate consequence of Definition 2 is that given an overall theory graph $\mathcal{T}_{MMS}$ of quantities, laws, and background knowledge formalizations, we can represent models as sets of MMT URIs – of the theories and inclusions in the model. This allows to build model repositories as envisioned in the introduction.

Another consequence of the correspondence between theory graphs and MPD established by Definition 2 is that we can build a MPD-viewer for models (again given $\mathcal{T}_{MMS}$). All we need is to build a graph viewer that distinguishes between quantity and law theories – we have encoded the necessary information in special MMT metadata in our formalization. Figure 6 shows our formalization of the van Roosbroeck model in our prototype MPD viewer.

The representation of the physical relations between the quantities in the MDP and the corresponding theory graph allows for a quick and easy creation of a zoo of related mathematical models. For example, in the MPD of the van Roosbroeck system in Fig. 3 one can easily replace the exponential Boltzmann law for the electron density by a Fermi-Dirac or Gauss-Fermi statistics for the

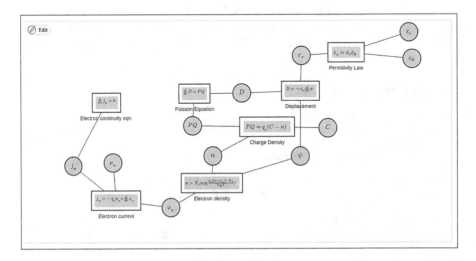

Fig. 6. Screenshot of the MPD Viewer displaying the van Roosbroeck Theory Graph, cf. Fig. 3

description of organic semiconductors. The relationship between these models is given by the sharing of the same structure using different theories for specific relations between quantities. In total this enables the derivation of a classification of mathematical models based on the representing theory graphs or the corresponding MPDs.

The fresh view on mathematical models by MPDs allows us to highlight the complex structure of coupled systems of partial differential equations and supports their development from smaller building blocks. The classical van Roosbroeck system for electrons *and* holes can be constructed from the unipolar version for electrons only, cf. Figure 3 by duplicating the transport complex and introducing a hole density quantity p and a corresponding quasi-Fermi potential φ_p. The expression for the total charge density ρ_Q has to be adjusted accordingly. Furthermore, recombination processes can be added to the model combining electron and hole density on the level of the transport complex. By doing so, the two topological separate sub-MPDs for the electrons and holes couple, see [MPDHub]. This requires a modular structure by parametrizing and thus sharing the formalization of density and current laws for both species, electrons and holes. This can be achieved by standard features (structures; named imports) in OMDoc/MMT.

The elimination of quantities from the MPD or theory graph by incrementally inserting – suitably rewritten versions of the – relations generates a large variety of derived MPDs using fewer quantities and relations increasing their individual complexity and losing semantic details represented by the full graph. This process can be meta-modeled in OMDoc/MMT by adding induced views to the theory graph (outside of the MPD subset) so that the relation reduction corresponds directly to view application. The main advantage for MKM purposes is that the flattened version can be directly written in the form of a MMT URI. Even though it is not explicitly represented in the graph it can be computed by the MMT system given only the represented graph and the MMT URI.

For example, the nonlinear Poisson equation in (1a) represents the fully flattened version of the depicted MPD, cf. Example 3. These more compact versions of the model might have advantages for specific analysis or objectives even though they are semantically less vivid.

7   Conclusion and Future Work

We have developed a knowledge-based meta-modeling approach for mathematical models and a first set of added-value services that make use of the involved representations.

For discovering structure in mathematical models we have introduced *model pathway diagrams* (MPDs). As these constitute an important didactical and structural representation of mathematical models, we have started a collection effort for MPDs at [MPDHub]. On the one hand this can serve as a seed for a future model repository that complements existing research data repositories, on the other hand, MPDs guide formalization, and so provide a valuable first step towards scaling the model formalization effort started in this paper.

We have further formalized a simple, but non-trivial model in a modular OMDoc/MMT theory graph $\mathcal{T}_{vR}$ and have used this representation for associating the equations by their MMT URI. These can be used to explain the mathematical provenance of the "flattened" equations in papers from the physics knowledge in $\mathcal{T}_{vR}$. Future services could include "formula search modulo flattening" via our ♭-search system [KI12] to discover instances of models in the literature or plug-and-play model composition services, where models can be assembled from theories in a "physics theory graph" based on MPD viewer.

The next steps of our further research will focus on the understanding of finite-volume discretization as MPDs, which will provide the connection to the numerical methods for the determination of a specific solution for given parameters and the software implementing those. We will investigate the relation between the MPDs of the continuous model (system of PDEs) and its discretized counterpart. Moreover, a modular concept for spatially multi-dimensional models and its theory graphs has to be developed. Having established a collection of models with deep MPD graphs we will study their refactoring into smaller components. Here, we gained first experience by refactoring the MPD of the bipolar van Roosbroeck system for electrons and holes using parameterized MPDs describing a generic carrier species, see Sect. 6. Additionally, different formulations of the same model might rely on different quantities and different sets of equations. We will study a minimal representation of such alternatives.

The main difference of our approach here to classical modeling languages like MODELICA is that the latter is primarily motivated by modeling *physical systems* that are built up from connected components, whereas we are interested in modeling *the physics of a system* (similar words, but very different meaning). Consequently our models consist of quantities connected by physical laws (or dually: physical laws connected by quantities), not component systems with physical connections. In this sense our work is complementary to classical modeling languages.

The actual model descriptions are similar, since the physical connections are often governed by equations as well, e.g., for the transport of some material flow or electrical current. SBML is similar, only that it models cells or sub-cellular structures as systems of reactants, connected by reactions (which are governed by rules). Even UML is similar, where we have software components which are connected by ports.

The work reported in this paper marks a first step towards treating models with flexiformal methods, which allows them to become research data. While our initial results are very promising, flexiformalization of mathematical knowledge is a high-investment, possibly high-gain endeavor. We hope, that the semantic services we can offer based on the formalization will assist research, improve interdisciplinary communication and increase reproducibility in MMS in the future.

Acknowledgements. We gratefully acknowledge EU funding for the OpenDreamKit project in the Horizon 2020 framework under grant 676541. Our discussions have particularly profited from contributions by Florian Rabe (MMT advice) and Wolfram Sperber (general math background). Finally, Marcel Rupprecht has developed the MPD viewer mentioned in Sect. 4.

References

[BGH05] Bandelow, U., Gajewski, H., Hünlich, R.: Fabry-perot lasers: thermodynamics-based modeling. In: Piprek, J. (ed.) Optoelectronic Devices. Springer, New York (2005)

[Bra09] Brase, J.: DataCite - A global registration agency for research data. In: Fourth International Conference on Cooperation and Promotion of Information Resources in Science and Technology, COINFO 2009, pp. 257–261. IEEE (2009)

[Far+16] Farrell, P., et al.: Numerical methods for drift-diffusion models. In: Piprek, J. (ed.) Handbook of Optoelectronic Device Modeling and Simulation: Lasers, Modulators, Photodetectors, Solar Cells, and Numerical Models, vol. 2. Taylor & Francis, Berlin (2016). (WIAS Preprint No. 2263. To appear, 2017)

[Fey49] Feynman, R.P.: Space-time approach to quantum electrodynamics. Phys. Rev. **76**(6), 769–789 (1949)

[Fis+12] Fischer, A., et al.: Self-heating effects in organic semiconductor crossbar structures with small active area. Org. Electron. **13**(11), 2461–2468 (2012)

[For15] Deutsche Forschungsgemeinschaft. DFG Guidelines on the Handling of Research Data. Adopted by the Senate of the DFG at September 30 (2015)

[GS14] Greuel, G.-M., Sperber, W.: swMATH – an information service for mathematical software. In: Hong, H., Yap, C. (eds.) ICMS 2014. LNCS, vol. 8592, pp. 691–701. Springer, Heidelberg (2014). doi:10.1007/978-3-662-44199-2_103

[Gum64] Gummel, H.K.: A self-consistent iterative scheme for one-dimensional steady state transistor calculations. IEEE Trans. Electron Devices **11**(10), 455–465 (1964)

[HKR12] Horozal, F., Kohlhase, M., Rabe, F.: Extending MKM formats at the statement leveld. In: Jeuring, J., Campbell, J.A., Carette, J., Reis, G., Sojka, P., Wenzel, M., Sorge, V. (eds.) CICM 2012. LNCS, vol. 7362, pp. 65–80. Springer, Heidelberg (2012). doi:10.1007/978-3-642-31374-5_5

[Huc+03] Hucka, M., et al.: The systems biology markup language (SBML): a medium for representation and exchange of biochemical network models. Bioinformatics **19**(4), 524 (2003)

[Ian17] Iancu, M.: Towards flexiformal mathematics. Ph.D. thesis. Jacobs University, Bremen (2017)

[Kas+16] Kaschura, F., et al.: Operation mechanism of high performance organic permeable base transistors with an insulated and perforated base electrode. J. Appl. Phys. **120**(9), 094501 (2016)

[KI12] Kohlhase, M., Iancu, M.: Searching the Space of Mathematical Knowledge. In: Sojka, P., Kohlhase, M. (eds.) DML and MIR 2012. Masaryk University, Brno (2012). http://kwarc.info/kohlhase/papers/mir12.pdf

[Koh+] Kohlhase, M., et al.: A Case study for active documents and formalization in math models: the van Roosbroeck Model. https://mathhub.info/MitM/models. Accessed 5 Feb 2017

[Koh06] Kohlhase, M.: OMDoc – An Open Markup Format for Mathematical Documents [version 1.2]. LNCS (LNAI), vol. 4180. Springer, Heidelberg (2006). http://omdoc.org/pubs/omdoc1.2.pdf

[Koh13] Kohlhase, M.: The flexiformalist manifesto. In: Voxronkov, A., et al. (eds.) 14th International Workshop on Symbolic and Numeric Algorithms for Scientific Computing (SYNASC 2012), pp. 30–36. IEEE Press, Timisoara (2013). http://kwarc.info/kohlhase/papers/synasc13.pdf

[Kra15] Kraft, A.: RADAR-A repository for long tail data. In: Proceedings of the IATUL Conferences. Paper 1 (2015)

[KT16]   Koprucki, T., Tabelow, K.: Mathematical models: a research data category? In: Greuel, G.-M., Koch, T., Paule, P., Sommese, A. (eds.) ICMS 2016. LNCS, vol. 9725, pp. 423–428. Springer, Cham (2016). doi:10.1007/978-3-319-42432-3_53

[Mie11] Mielke, A.: A gradient structure for reaction-diffusion systems and for energy-drift-diffusion systems. Nonlinearity $24(4)$, 1329 (2011)

[Mit]   MitM: The Math-in-the-Middle Ontology. https://mathhub.info/MitM. Accessed 5 Feb 2017

[Mod14] Modelica Association. Modelica-A Unified Object-Oriented Language for Physical Systems Modeling-Language Specification Version 3.3 Revision 1, 2014 (2014). http://www.modelica.org

[MPDHub] MPDHub wiki. https://github.com/WIAS-BERLIN/MPDHub/wiki/. Accessed 22 Mar 2017

[Pfe01] Pfenning, F.: Logical Frameworks. In: Robinson, A., Voronkov, A. (eds.) Handbook of Automated Reasoning, Vol. I and II. Elsevier Science and MIT Press, North Holland (2001)

[Rab]   Rabe, F.: Generic Literals. http://kwarc.info/frabe/Research/rabe_literals_14.pdf

[Rab14] Rabe, F.: How to identify, translate, and combine logics? J. Log. Comput. (2014)

[RK13]   Rabe, F., Kohlhase, M.: A scalable module system. Inf. Comput. **230**, 1–54 (2013). http://kwarc.info/frabe/Research/mmt.pdf

[RNH14] Razum, M., Neumann, J., Hahn, M.: RADAR-Ein Forschungsdaten- repositorium als Dienstleistung für die Wissenschaft. Z. Bibl. Bibliographie **61**(1), 18–27 (2014)

[SBML]   The Systems Biology Markup Language. http://sbml.org. Accessed 17 Mar 2017

[Sch96] Schröter, J.: Zur Meta-Theorie der Physik. Walter de Gruyter GmbH & Co KG, Berlin (1996)

[Sel84] Selberherr, S.: Analysis and Simulation of Semiconductor Devices. Springer, Wien, New York (1984)

[UML]   Unified Modeling Language. http://www.uml.org/. Accessed 13 Sep 2016

[VR50]   Van Roosbroeck, W.: Theory of the flow of electrons and holes in germanium and other semiconductors. Bell Syst. Tech. J. **29**(4), 560–607 (1950)

[Wik]   Wikipedia: List of physical quantities – Wikipedia, The Free Encyclopedia. https://en.wikipedia.org/w/index.php?title=List_of_physical_quantities. Accessed 22 Mar 2017

A Verified Algorithm Enumerating Event Structures

Juliana Bowles⬥ and Marco B. Caminati$^{(\boxtimes)}$⬥

School of Computer Science, University of St Andrews,
Jack Cole Building, North Haugh, St Andrews, KY 16 9SX, UK
{jkfb,mbc8}@st-andrews.ac.uk

Abstract. An event structure is a mathematical abstraction modeling concepts as causality, conflict and concurrency between events.
While many other mathematical structures, including groups, topological
spaces, rings, abound with algorithms and formulas to generate, enumerate and count particular sets of their members, no algorithm or formulas
are known to generate or count all the possible event structures over a
finite set of events. We present an algorithm to generate such a family,
along with a functional implementation verified using Isabelle/HOL. As
byproducts, we obtain a verified enumeration of all possible preorders
and partial orders. While the integer sequences counting preorders and
partial orders are already listed on OEIS (On-line Encyclopedia of Integer Sequences), the one counting event structures is not. We therefore
used our algorithm to submit a formally verified addition, which has been
successfully reviewed and is now part of the OEIS.

Keywords: Formal methods · OEIS · Verified algorithm · Enumeration · Counting · Discrete · Event structures · Isabelle/HOL · Automated
reasoning · Logic

1 Introduction

Event structures [18,19] model distributed systems, representing sequential-
parallel behaviour, concurrency and non-determinism in a natural way. Event
structures feature simple notions, namely, a set of events and binary relations
over events. Amongst the relations we have *causality*, a partial order describing
how the events are causally related, and *conflict* specifying which events are in
conflict. In addition, a natural condition makes sure that conflict propagates
over causality, i.e., events caused by conflicting events are still conflicting. Being
expressed in terms of such basic concepts as partial orders and binary relations,
this model has fruitful connections with combinatorics [2], topology [20], category theory [4], graph theory [2], and other causal models such as Petri nets [20].

   For the same reason, basic problems regarding event structures, such as
checking if a given structure is a valid event structure, whether it can be

---

This research is supported by EPSRC grant EP/M014290/1.

H. Geuvers et al. (Eds.): CICM 2017, LNAI 10383, pp. 239–254, 2017.
DOI: 10.1007/978-3-319-62075-6_17

completed to a valid event structure, and event structure composition can be processed through a variety of computational tools [3,5,6]. However, the generation of all the possible event structures over a finite set of N events is not straightforward. Currently, it is not even known how many distinct event structures there are, given a finite set of events. We will refer to these two problems as *enumeration* and *counting*, respectively. Given that the enumeration of partial orders is a hard problem, and that even the most elaborate of the known techniques for counting partial orders pass through some form of enumeration [15], the counting and enumeration problem for event structures inherit a similar amount of hardness: indeed, we are not aware of any theoretical results to count event structures which would avoid enumerating partial orders. Hence, the counting problem for the event structures motivates the enumeration problem. The naive approach consisting of generating all the possible relations and checking them for compliance to the definition of event structures is prohibitively inefficient, even for very low values of N. This paper presents a novel, recursive enumerating and counting algorithm which does better than that, based on an original theoretical result characterising event structures (Lemma 2); as a further contribution, the paper shows how it can be formalised and proved to be correct in the theorem prover Isabelle. The paper is organised as follows: Sect. 2 presents the definition of event structure, and the problem through a formal description and a simple example. Section 3 describes our algorithm, and the lemma on which it is based. Section 4 introduces the Isabelle formalisation of the involved structures, the Isabelle implementation of the algorithm, and its correctness theorems. Section 5 discusses improvements to the algorithm, and provides performance data and numerical results, while Sect. 6 concludes.

2   Description of the Problem

We recall that a pre-order on a set is a relation which is reflexive on that set and transitive, and that a partial order over a set is an antisymmetric pre-order over that set.

Definition 1. *An event structure is a triple $E = (Ev, \rightarrow^*, \#)$ where Ev is a set of events and $\rightarrow^*, \# \subseteq Ev \times Ev$ are binary relations called* causality *and* conflict, *respectively. Causality $\rightarrow^*$ is a partial order over Ev. Conflict $\#$ is symmetric and irreflexive, and propagates over causality, i.e., $e \# e' \wedge e' \rightarrow^* e'' \Rightarrow e \# e''$ for all $e, e', e'' \in Ev$. An event e may have an immediate successor e' according to the order $\rightarrow^*$: in this case, we can write $e \rightarrow e'$. The relation given by $\rightarrow$ is called* immediate causality.

We will introduce a function `enumerateEs` taking one natural number N as an argument, and returning a list containing, without repetitions, each possible event structure over a set of N distinct events. The events are represented by the first N natural numbers: $0, \ldots, N - 1$. Each entry of the output list is a pair (O, C) of relations over the set $\{0, \ldots, N - 1\}$, the causality and the conflict, respectively. Finally, each relation will be represented by a set of ordered pairs, i.e., elements of the Cartesian product $\{0, \ldots, N-1\} \times \{0, \ldots, N-1\}$, as customarily done in set theory. This implies that, given an event structure $(E, \to^*, \#)$, and two events e_0, e_1, we can write $(e_0, e_1) \in \to^*$ and $(e_0, e_1) \in \#$ in lieu of $e_0 \to^* e_1$ and of $e_0 \# e_1$, respectively.

Based on `enumerateEs`, we also introduce a second function `countEs` taking the same argument, and returning a natural number counting the distinct elements of the list `enumerateEs N`.

As an example, let us illustrate the output of our algorithm for the case $N = 2$: in other words, we only have two events, 0 and 1, and we want to know all the possible valid event structures defined on these two events.

`enumerateEs 2` returns the list

```
"[({(0,0), (0,1), (1,1)}, {}), ({(0,0), (1,0), (1,1)}, {}),
  ({(0,0), (1,1)}, {(0,1), (1,0)}),({(0,0), (1,1)}, {})
]" :: ((nat × nat) set × (nat × nat) set) list.
```

It has four entries (what follows the character] on the last line is not part of the list, but only specifies the type of the list itself), so, naturally, `countEs` returns 4.

Note that the first element of each pair of the list above is a partial order on $\{0, 1\}$, and hence contains at least $(0, 0)$ and $(1, 1)$ due to reflexivity. The first two pairs describe two isomorphic event structures (Fig. 1, on the left): they can be obtained one from the other by swapping the numerical labels of their events. Since in this case the two events are related by causality, no conflict is possible, in light of propagation property in Definition 1: hence, the only possibility is the empty conflict relation, which corresponds to the second element of the first two pairs of the list above being the empty set.

The remaining two pairs of list above describe two event structures (Fig. 1, on the right) with the same causality relation: no event is caused by the other (i.e., each event is in causal relation only with itself); in this situation, the definition of event structure allows only two possibilities. That is, either there are no conflicts, or the two events are mutually in conflict.

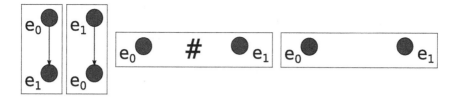

Fig. 1. The event structures over two events (arrows represent immediate causality)

3   Description of the Algorithm

The algorithm has two stages: first, all the possible partial orders on $\{0, \ldots, N-1\}$ (also called *posets*) are computed; then, for each such partial order, a list of all the allowed conflicts for it is computed. By an allowed conflict for a given partial order o, we mean a relation c over $\{0, \ldots, N-1\}$ such that (o, c) is an event structure. Once we have in place procedures to compute these two objects, obtaining our final algorithms `enumerateEs` and `countEs` is easy.

3.1   Computation of Posets

To enumerate all posets over $\{0, \ldots, N-1\}$, we represent them through their *adjacency matrices*. An adjacency matrix A for a relation $\mathcal{R}$ over $\{0, \ldots, N-1\}$ is a square boolean matrix of dimension N such that $A_{i,j} = 1$ if and only if $(i-1)\,\mathcal{R}\,(j-1)$. There is clearly a one-to-one correspondence between such matrices and all the possible relations over $\{0, \ldots, N-1\}$, therefore they can be used to represent such relations. Hence, we will say that a square boolean matrix is reflexive (respectively, transitive) when the corresponding relation is reflexive (respectively, transitive). This representation is useful in our case, because there is a simple result expressing the property that a relation is transitive and reflexive as simple conditions on the rows and columns of its adjacency matrix.

Lemma 1. *Assume a square, boolean matrix B of order $N+1$ is partitioned as follows:*

$$B = \begin{bmatrix} A & \alpha \\ {}^{\tau}\beta & 1 \end{bmatrix},$$

where α and β are column vectors of order N. Then B is reflexive and transitive if and only if A is reflexive and transitive and, $\forall i, j \in \{1, \ldots, N\}$,
1. $(A_{i,j} \wedge \beta_i) \to \beta_j$, and 2. $(\alpha_i \wedge (\neg A_{i,j})) \to \beta_j$, and 3. $(A_{i,j} \wedge \alpha_j) \to \alpha_i$.

We omit the straightforward proof here, and note that Lemma 1 gives a way to compute recursively all transitive and reflexive matrices, by reducing this task to computing all pairs of column vectors (α, β) satisfying the conditions (1), (2) and (3). We will find that those conditions admit a computable functional translation into Isabelle/HOL, thereby allowing the recursive computation of all transitive and reflexive matrices of a given (finite) dimension N. Doing this corresponds to enumerating all the preorders over $\{0, \ldots, N-1\}$, which can be easily used to enumerate all the partial orders over the same set (see Sect. 4.2).

3.2   Computation of Allowed Conflicts

Let P be a partial order, and denote with $F(P)$ the set of all allowed conflicts for P. We introduce a result permitting the recursive computation of F. To be able to proceed, we need some basic definitions: we denote with $P - A$ the sub-relation of P obtained by removing all the pairs of P whose first or second element is in the set A. This can be formally obtained, for example, by writing $P \backslash (A \times \operatorname{ran} P) \backslash (\operatorname{dom} P \backslash A)$, where $\backslash$ is the infix symbol for set-theoretical difference. In the following definitions, we will denote with dom and ran the domain and range of a relation; $\wp$ and $\times$ will denote the powerset operator and the infix operation symbol for Cartesian product, respectively.

Definition 2. $P^\rightarrow$ *is the map* $A \mapsto \{y.\exists x \in A.\,(x, y) \in P\}$. *That is,* $P^\rightarrow(A)$ *is the image of* A *through the relation* P. *We will often omit brackets around* A *when the latter is expressed in braces notation; e.g.* $P^\rightarrow(\{a\})$ *becomes* $P^\rightarrow\{a\}$.

We note that the $^\rightarrow$ operator is defined on any relation and yields a function, hence it can be iterated (e.g., $(P^\rightarrow)^\rightarrow$ always exists). Another widely used notation for $P^\rightarrow(A)$ is $P[A]$.

Definition 3. *Given a finite partial order* P, $\overline{P}$ *is the transitive reduction of* P *(also known as the covering relation of* P*):* $(x, z) \in \overline{P}$ *if and only if* $(x, z) \in P\backslash\{(x, x)\}$ *and* $\forall y.\,(x, y) \in P \wedge (y, z) \in P \rightarrow y = x \vee y = z$.

In other words, the covering relation of P only considers the immediate strict successors according to P; in yet other words, $\overline{P}$ is the smallest relation from which P can be reconstructed by reflexive and transitive closure operations [1].

Definition 4. P^{-1} *is the inverse of the relation* P. *When* P *is a partial order,* $m \in \mathrm{dom}\,P$ *is a minimal element for* P *if* $(x, m) \in P \rightarrow x = m$.

That is, m is minimal when there are no elements smaller than m. We recall that for finite partial orders there is always at least one minimal element. This permits to always apply the following lemma, which is the basis for our algorithm.

Lemma 2. *Let* P *be a finite partial order, and* m *be a minimal element for* P. *Then*

$$F(P) = \bigcup_{c \in F(P - \{m\})} f(P, m, c), \tag{1}$$

where $f(P, m, c)$ *is defined as*

$$\left\{ c \cup (\{m\} \times Y) \cup (Y \times \{m\}) . \right.$$

$$\left. Y \in ((P - \{m\})^\rightarrow)^\rightarrow \left(\wp \left(\mathrm{dom}\,P \backslash \bigcup_{M \in \overline{P}^\rightarrow\{m\}} \mathrm{dom}\,P\backslash c^\rightarrow\{M\} \right) \right) \right\}. \tag{2}$$

Lemma 2 is useful for our purposes because it reduces the computation of $F(P)$ to the evaluation of the function $c \mapsto f(P, m, c)$, with c ranging over $F(P - \{m\})$. Since $P - \{m\}$ is still a finite partial order, and of strictly smaller cardinality than P as soon as $m \in \mathrm{dom}\,P$ (e.g., when m is minimal), we can proceed by recursion. This is also because f is in turn directly computable from its three arguments: it only involves set-theoretical operations, which are straightforward to compute in HOL.

To illustrate how we will exploit the lemma, consider the simple example of an event structure presenting an event having no successors. Then, we can pick this event as the m appearing in Lemma 2: the argument of $\wp$ reduces to dom P, and we assume, since we will build a recursive algorithm, to know all the possible conflicts for the reduced causality $p := P - \{m\}$, i.e., the set $F(p)$. Lemma 2 then instructs us to consider a subset X of dom P, a possible conflict relation $c \in F(p)$, and to extend it to $c \cup (\{m\} \times Y) \cup (Y \times \{m\})$, where $Y := p[X]$: the thesis is that by varying X and c, we obtain all the allowed conflicts for P.

It should also be noted that Lemma 2 holds upon replacing $\overrightarrow{P}\{m\}$ with any X such that $\overrightarrow{P}\{m\} \subseteq X \subseteq P^{\rightarrow}\{m\}$, but fails to hold in general if $X \subset \overrightarrow{P}\{m\}$. Therefore, the lemma gives an optimal set on which to perform the aforementioned recursion.

Proof (of Lemma 2). We prove separately that $F(P) \subseteq \bigcup_{c \in F(P-\{m\})} f(P, m, c)$ and that $F(P) \supseteq \bigcup_{c \in F(P-\{m\})} f(P, m, c)$.

Proof of $F(P) \subseteq \bigcup_{c \in F(P-\{m\})} f(P, m, c)$: assume $C \in F(P)$; then, (P, C) is an event structure, and therefore $(p := P - \{m\}, c := C - \{m\})$ also is, so that $c \in F(p)$. Now, consider $Y := C^{\rightarrow}\{m\}$. Given the identity $C = (C - \{m\}) \cup \{m\} \times C^{\rightarrow}\{m\} \cup (C^{-1})^{\rightarrow}\{m\} \times \{m\}$, which becomes $C = c \cup \{m\} \times Y \cup Y \times \{m\}$ due to symmetry of C, it suffices to show that $Y \in p^{\rightarrow\rightarrow}\left(\wp\left(\text{dom } P \backslash \bigcup_{M \in \overrightarrow{P}\{m\}} \text{dom } P \backslash c^{\rightarrow}\{M\}\right)\right)$. But $P^{\rightarrow}(Y) = p^{\rightarrow}(Y) = Y$ due to the monotonicity of C over P, hence this amounts to showing that

$$Y \subseteq \text{dom } P \backslash \bigcup_{M \in \overrightarrow{P}\{m\}} \text{dom } P \backslash c^{\rightarrow}\{M\}. \tag{3}$$

When $\overrightarrow{P}\{m\} = \emptyset$, this reduces to showing the triviality $Y \subseteq \text{dom } P$. We can therefore assume $\overrightarrow{P}\{m\} \neq \emptyset$, causing (3) to become $Y \subseteq \bigcap_{M \in \overrightarrow{P}\{m\}} c^{\rightarrow}\{M\}$ via De Morgan rules. The latter inclusion is obvious from the propagation property of C.

Proof of $F(P) \supseteq \bigcup_{c \in F(P-\{m\})} f(P, m, c)$: consider $c \in F(P - \{m\})$, and $X \subseteq \text{dom } P \backslash \bigcup_{M \in \overrightarrow{P}\{m\}} \text{dom } P \backslash c^{\rightarrow}\{M\}$. Set $Y := (P - \{m\})^{\rightarrow}(X)$. We need to prove that $C := c \cup \{m\} \times Y \cup Y \times \{m\}$ is a valid conflict for P. The symmetry of C is immediate from that of c and from the symmetry of its definition. The irreflexivity of C follows from that of c and from the fact that $m \notin Y$. It only remains to show that C propagates over P. To this end, consider x_1, x_2, y and assume that both $(x_1, x_2) \in P$ and $(x_1, y) \in C$. We want to prove that $(x_2, y) \in C$. If $x_2 = m$, then $x_1 = x_2$ and the thesis is immediate. If $x_1 = m \neq m_2$, then $y \in Y$ and $X \subseteq \bigcap_{M \in \overrightarrow{P}\{m\}} c^{\rightarrow}\{M\}$. Moreover, there exists $M \in \overrightarrow{P}\{m\}$ such that $(M, x_2) \in P - \{m\}$. Since $(P - \{m\}, c)$ is an event structure, $c^{\rightarrow}\{x_2\} \supseteq c^{\rightarrow}\{M\} \ni y$.

Note that proving $F(P) \subseteq \bigcup_{c \in F(P-\{m\})} f(P, m, c)$ did not require any hypothesis on m.

4   Implementation and Formalisation

The code[1] consists of Isabelle/HOL functions computing the wanted objects (preorders, posets, conflicts and event structures) and of Isabelle/HOL proofs that they compute the right objects.

In the case of event structures, this concretely means that we first introduce formal definitions for each side of Eq. 1: the one for the left-hand side (conflictsFor) is close to the pen-and-paper Definition 1, while the one for the right-hand side (conflictsFor2) is recursive and allows us to compute the wanted results. Afterwards, we prove equality (1) itself. This separation is needed because the pen-and-paper definitions of the mathematical objects we are interested in describe them, but usually do not provide a way of constructing them [8].

In the next subsection, we give the Isabelle/HOL translations of the mathematical definitions about event structures, including conflictsFor; in the following ones, we introduce, respectively, the recursive construction for conflictsFor2 and the Isabelle theorem translating Eq. (1), i.e., the equivalence of conflictsFor and conflictsFor2. We end the section by putting all together into the computable functions enumerateEs and countEs.

4.1   Formalisation of the Notion of Event Structure

The definition of conflictsFor is, as expected, straightforward:

```
definition "conflictsFor Or =
           {C| C. isLes Or C & Field C ⊆ Field Or}",
```

where {C| C. ...} is Isabelle's syntax for set comprehension. We recall that the field of a relation is the union of its domain and range (the domain, range and field of a partial order coincide, anyway). Note that we do not need to specify the set of events appearing in Definition 1 because, since we are encoding relations as set of pairs, and since the partial order is reflexive, the set of events can be always reconstructed by taking the field of it. However, since the conflict relation is not reflexive, we must impose that its field is indeed a subset of the set of events: in fact, one can find examples of valid event structures where the conflict relation field ranges from the empty set to the set of all the events.

isLes is a boolean predicate telling whether two relations form an event structure, and is a likewise straightforward rendition of Definition 1 in Isabelle/HOL:

```
definition "isLes Or C == isMonotonicOver C Or &
            sym C & irrefl C & isPo Or",
```

where isPo Or is true exactly when Or is a partial order, and is merely a shortcut for the three conditions of reflexivity, transitivity and antisymmetry, already present (as symmetry and irreflexivity are) in Isabelle/HOL standard library. The only condition we had to specify, because not already present in Isabelle's library, is isMonotonicOver C Or, telling us whether the propagation condition in

---

[1] About 9.5 KSLOC, available at http://bitbucket.org/caminati/oeises.

Definition 1 is respected; the Isabelle definition is also close to the pen-and-paper version:

```
definition "isMonotonicOver C Or =
            ∀ x y. (x,y) ∈ Or ⟶ C''{x} ⊆ C''{y}",
```

$C``\{x\}$ being Isabelle's syntax for $C^{\rightarrow}(\{x\})$ (see Definition 2).

It is now easy to define all the event structures over a given set X:

```
definition"posOver X={P. Field P=X & isPo P}".
definition "esOver X={(P, C)| P C. P∈posOver X &
                                   C∈ conflictsFor P}".
```

4.2   Construction of Posets

We start by recursively constructing all the possible preorders over $\{0,\ldots,N-1\}$ by applying Lemma 1. This requires expressing conditions (1), (2) and (3) in that lemma into computable equivalents, which is done respectively by cond1Comp, cond2Comp, and cond3Comp defined as follows.

```
definition "cond1Comp matr col =
allSubLists (if (filterpositions id col = []) then
[True. i<-[0..<size (matr!0)]] else
rowAnd (map (nth matr) (filterpositions id col)))"

definition "cond2Comp matr row = ((set o concat)
  (map (filterpositions id)
       (sublist matr (set (filterpositions id row)))))
⊆ (set (filterpositions id row))"

definition "cond3Comp matr col = (set o concat)
  (map (filterpositions id)
       (sublist (List.transpose matr)
                (set (filterpositions id col))))
⊆ (set (filterpositions id col))"
```

Here, filterpositions f l returns a list of all the indices such that the corresponding entries of l satisfy f. allSubLists l returns all the possible boolean lists obtained from l by leaving the Falses fixed and assigning arbitrary values to the other entries. rowAnd A takes the logical "and" of all the rows of the matrix A. sublist l I returns the sublist of l obtained by taking only the entries whose indices are in the set I. We had to construct filterpositions, allSubLists and rowAnd in a computable way, while sublist is pre-defined in Isabelle libraries. concat concatenates a list of lists, while set converts a list to a set.

Now, we refer to Lemma 1 to define a function enumerating all preorders on $\{0,\ldots,N-1\}$, by enumerating all transitive and reflexive square matrices of order N:

```
fun enumeratePreorders where
"enumeratePreorders 0 = [[[]]]" |
```

```
"enumeratePreorders (Suc n) = concat (map (split auxFun)
[(matr,col). matr<-enumeratePreorders n,
   col<-filter (cond3Comp matr)
            (allSubLists [True. n<-[0..<size (matr!0)]])])]" ,
```

where split uncurries its argument, and where list comprehension notation has been used.[2] auxFun is an auxiliary function defined as:

```
definition "auxFun matr col =
map (appendAsColumn (col@[True]))
     (map (  1. matr@[1]) (filter (cond2Comp matr)
                            (cond1Comp matr col)))" ,
```

and making use of cond1Comp and of cond2Comp, along with the function appendAsColumn c A, which appends to the matrix A the column c; filter f l returns the list of entries of l which verify f, while @ is the infix operator for list concatenation. To go from the enumeration of preorders to that of partial orders, we pass through the enumeration of strict preorders and of strict partial orders as intermediate steps. First, we can enumerate strict preorders as follows:

```
definition "enumerateStrictPreorders N =
            map (setDiag False) (enumeratePreorders N)" ,
```

where setDiag a A sets to a all the diagonal entries of the matrix A. Now, we can obtain the enumeration of all strict partial orders:

```
definition "enumerateStrictPOs N = filter
  (  adjMatr. symmetricEntries adjMatr = {})
  (enumerateStrictPreorders N)" ,
```

where symmetricEntries A is a computable function returning the pairs of indices corresponding to the symmetric entries of the matrix A (we omit its definition here). Finally, we can enumerate all partial orders by:

```
definition "enumeratePo N =
  map (adj2PairList o (setDiag True))
      (enumerateStrictPOs N)" ,
```

where adj2PairList converts back from the adjacency matrix to the corresponding order relation, expressed as a list of pairs over the set $\{0, \ldots, N-1\}$.

4.3   Construction of Event Structures

The definition of conflictsFor2

```
function conflictsFor2 where "conflictsFor2 P=
(let (M,p)=ReducedRelation P in if M=None then [{}] else
concat [remdups (generateConflicts (set P) (the M) c).
       c<-conflictsFor2 p])"
```

---

[2] Such a notation has the form, in the simplest but typical case, $[g\ x.\ x<-1,\ Q\ x]$, and intuitively represents the list obtained by applying the generic function g to the entries of a given list l which satisfy a condition Q.

reproduces the right-hand side of Eq. (1) in Isabelle: the union becomes `concat`, f becomes `generateConflicts`, and the quantifier for the union operation is represented by `c<−conflictsFor2 p`. First, `ReducedRelation P` takes care of finding a minimal element m for the partial order `P`, which is needed to build $P - \{m\}$ appearing in (1), and returns both m and $P - \{m\}$ as an ordered pair. This is slightly complicated by the fact that, although we will always use it on partial order arguments, `conflictsFor2` has to always terminate, even when `P` is not necessarily a partial order. And, when `P` is not a partial order, we no longer know what to return as m; to work around this problem, `ReducedRelation` returns a pair (M, p), where M has an `option` type. This means that we can describe the cases when a minimal element for `P` is not defined by assigning to `M` the value `None`, whilst in the other cases we can extract from `M` the actual value m of the minimal element using the operator `the`. Only in this latter case $P - \{m\}$ has a definite value, which gets passed (with the name `p`) to `conflictsFor2` for recursion. Otherwise, the list containing only the empty conflict relation ([{}]) is returned immediately.

   `generateConflicts` is the Isabelle version of the function f appearing in Lemma 2:

```
definition "generateConflicts P m c =
[c∪({m}×Y)∪(Y×{m}). Y <−
  map (Image {z∈P. fst z≠m & snd z≠m})
    (map set (sublists
           (if P''{m}−{m}={}
            then sorted_list_of_set (Domain P)
            else sorted_list_of_set
                   (∩ {c''{M}|M. M ∈ next P {m}})))))]",
```

where `next P {m}` is the set of the immediate successors of `m` and corresponds to $\overrightarrow{P}\ \{m\}$ appearing in expression (2). While Eq. (2) and `generateConflicts`'s definition have the same structure, there are some minor differences. First, `generateConflicts` returns a list of relations, while f returns a set of relations. In general, it is easier to prove theorems about sets than about lists but, on the other hand, it is easier and more efficient to compute using lists, rather than sets. For the same reason, the argument of `conflictsFor2` is a list of pairs representing a relation, while the argument of F appearing in (1) is a set of pairs. Since lists contain more information than the corresponding finite sets, this is not a problem. The Isabelle function `set` goes from a list to a set, while `sorted_list_of_set` goes the other way around. When passing from a set representation of relation to a list-based one, the $\rightarrow$ operator (Definition 2) becomes the `map` operator, the powerset operator $\wp$ becomes `sublists`. Another difference with expression (2) is that it differentiates two cases for computational reasons: when `P"{m}−{m}≠{}` the argument of $\wp$ occurring in (2) can be simplified to the intersection appearing after `sorted_list_of_set`. In Isabelle, `P"A` is the infix notation for `Image P A`, where `Image` is the operator $\rightarrow$ (Definition 2). Now we can construct all the event structures over `N` elements:

```
definition "enumerateEs N=
```

```
concat (map (λ P. (map (λx. (set P, x)) (conflictsFor2 P)))
             (enumeratePo N))",
```

where `enumeratePo` enumerates all the partial orders over $\{0, \dots, N-1\}$.
Counting all the event structures over N is also immediate:

Listing 1.1. Definition of `countEs`

```
definition"countEs N=listsum (map (size o conflictsFor2)
                                   (enumeratePo N))".
```

Note that we chose a combination of `listsum` and `size` instead of directly
applying `size` to a suitable concatenation of list, due to better performance.
However, this slightly complicates the proofs of the results we will see in Sect. 4.4.

4.4   Correctness Proof in Isabelle

Our way of formally verifying the correctness of our algorithm is to
prove Isabelle theorems stating the equivalence between `conflictsFor` and
`conflictsFor2`, between `esOver` and `enumerateEs`, between `card o esOver` and
`countEs`. This spawns a series of intermediate lemmas to be proven, stating that
`enumerateStrictPOs`, `enumeratePo`, `enumeratePreorders` all return the expected
entities. Additionally, all the functions converting from one representation to
another (e.g., from a list of pairs to the corresponding adjacency matrix, and
the other way around) need to be proven correct. Here, we describe the mile-
stones in this chain of proofs.

To prove the correctness of the function `enumeratePreorders` (Sect. 4.2), we
formally proved Lemma 1, and then formally proved the correspondence between
`cond1Comp` and condition (2), between `cond2Comp` and condition (1), and between
`cond3Comp` and condition (3). This allowed us to prove the following theorem:

```
theorem correctnessThm: assumes"N>0"shows
"set (enumeratePreorders N) = {a| a. N=size a &
  isRectangular N a & transMatr a N & reflMatr a N}",
```

which says that the set of matrices obtained via the computable function
`enumeratePreorders` matches the set of all transitive and reflexive matrices. Note
that, since we are encoding a matrix in Isabelle as a list of rows, we have to
make sure that each row has the same size. This is the goal of `isRectangular`.
The theorem above also has a version expressed in the language of list of pairs,
without using matrices:

```
theorem"set (map (set o adj2PairList) (enumeratePreorders N))
       = {r| r. trans r & refl_on {0..<N} r}".
```

The correctness theorem for partial orders generation is:

```
theorem poCorrectness: assumes"N>0"shows
"set (map set (enumeratePo N)) = posOver {0..<N}".
```

The theorem above is the first component of the proof of the correctness for `enumerateEs`. The other component is the correctness proof for `conflictsFor2`; this is attained by formally proving Lemma 2 and then applying it to the recursive definition of `conflictsFor2`. The result is:

```
theorem conflictCorrectness: assumes"trans (set Or)"
"reflex (set Or)""antisym (set Or)"shows
"set (conflictsFor2 Or)=conflictsFor (set Or)".
```

Putting together `conflictCorrectness` and `poCorrectness`, we obtain

```
theorem esCorrectness: assumes"N>(0::nat)"shows
                    "set (enumerateEs N)= (esOver {0..<N})".
```

5   Performance and Results

Since we enumerate, and not only count, all the event structures, we face a fundamental complexity problem: the enumeration of event structures entails that of posets, and the latter has exponential complexity [13].

However, some considerations led us to attain for our algorithm some performance improvements which, although marginal in the general case, turned out to be significant for the computations related to the small values of N that we were able to obtain. Originally, the definition for `conflictsFor2` was more naive than the one we introduced in Sect. 4.1:

```
function conflictsFor2v0 where"conflictsFor2v0 Or=
(let (M,or)=ReducedRelation Or in if M=None then [{}]
else let m=the M in concat [(generateConflicts (set Or) m c).
                            c<-conflictsFor2v0 or])".
```

The key difference is that we did not take care of removing duplicate entries in the recursive generation of the wanted event structures. At a purely mathematical level, this does not matter much since we eventually convert the obtained list to a set: see, e.g., the statement of `esCorrectness`, Sect. 4.4. From an algorithmic point of view, however, this does matter, since keeping duplicate entries represents a computational burden which gets amplified through recursion. It should also be noticed that, with the definition above, the definition of `countEs` needed to be different, since we do not want to count duplicates, and therefore was based on a `card o set` operation, rather than on a combination of `listsum` and of `size`, as in Listing 1.1. The problem coming from duplicates is typical of formal enumerations and counting algorithms [12]. Therefore, a second attempt was tried:

```
function conflictsFor2v1 where"conflictsFor2v1 Or=
(let (M,or)=ReducedRelation Or in if M=None then [{}]
else let m=the M in (remdups o concat)
  [(generateConflicts (set Or) m c).
    c <- conflictsFor2v1 or])",
```

whereby a `remdups` operation was simply added at the end of each recursion to remove duplicate entries. This measure improved the performance of our algorithm; moreover, it eliminated the need of resorting to a `card o set` application when calculating `countEs`. This is because `remdups` guarantees that there are no repetitions, and hence, to count the number of event structures, we can directly count the number of elements of the list returned by `countEs`. However, since `remdups` has quadratic time complexity [14], it pays off to invert the order of `remdups` and `concat`, which leads to the final definition of `conflictsFor2`. It should be noted that implementing this optimisation comes at a price: since it is no longer obvious that the output of `conflictsFor2` has no repetitions, we need to formally prove this; once we do that, we can prove correctness for `countEs`:

```
theorem assumes"N>0"shows"card(esOver{0..<N})=countEs N".
```

Orthogonal to the optimisation coming from a thoughtful placement of `remdups`, there is another one, which we proceed to explain. Lemma 2 holds for any m chosen among the minimal elements of the partial order P; this reflects in the definition of `conflictsFor2`, where `ReducedRelation` performs this choice to compute the recursion step. The selected minimal element, `the M`, is passed to `generateConflicts`, where it is used as a pivot to generate the new conflict relations. While this generation is always correct as long as `the M` is indeed a minimal element, the efficiency of the corresponding computation does vary according the choice of the pivot. Indeed, there is a noticeable difference in performance between choosing the pivot without a criterion and with a reasonable one, as we proceed to illustrate. The final `ReducedRelation` does use a criterion :

```
definition"ReducedRelation P=(let minRel=
 List.filter (λ(x,y). x ∉ (snd'((set P)-{(x,x)}))) P in
 let Minimals=remdups (map fst minRel) in
 let Multiplicities=
  map (λz. (size(Next P [z]),z)) Minimals in
 let suitableVals=Maxs(set (map fst Multiplicities)) in
 let somePivot=optApp snd (List.find (λ(x,y).x∈suitableVals)
                           Multiplicities) in
 (somePivot, filter
   (λ(x,y). x ≠ the somePivot & y ≠ the somePivot) P))".
```

`Next P [z]` computes $\overrightarrow{P}\ \{z\}$, so that `Multiplicities` contains each minimal element of `P` along with the number of its immediate successors. This is used to select (through the function `Maxs`) one minimal element having the highest number of immediate successors (`optApp` and `List.find` break possible ties in case such an element is not unique). Finally, the picked value m (in the form of `the somePivot`) and the reduced relation $P - \{m\}$ are returned as a pair. The idea here is that, since in the definition of `generateConflicts` there is an intersection over all the immediate successors of the pivot, by maximising the number of successors, the resulting intersection will tend to be smaller. And this is desirable, because an expensive operation of powerset will be taken on the resulting intersection. On the other hand, the original implementation of

Table 1. Seconds to compute `countEs 5`

conflictsFor2v0	conflictsFor2v1	conflictsFor2
222	10	2

Table 2. Seconds to compute `countEs 6`

ReducedRelationV0	ReducedRelation
94	79

`ReducedRelation` was the most naive possible with no particular criterion for the selection of the pivot:

```
definition"ReducedRelationV0 P=(let min=
 (List.find (λx. x ∉ (snd'((set P)−{(x,x)}))) (map fst P))
 in (min, filter (λ(x,y). x ≠ the min & y ≠ the min) P))"
```

Table 1 compares how the execution time of `countEs 5` changes when adopting `conflictsFor2v0`, `conflictsFor2v1` and the final `conflictsFor`. Table 2 compares how the execution time of `countEs 6` (using `conflictsFor`) changes when adopting `ReducedRelationV0` and `ReducedRelation`. Times were averaged on three runs, after discarding the first one, and were taken on the same machine (dual core Intel Core 2 @ 2.40 GHz).

Finally, we present in Table 3 the results (for $N \in \{0, \ldots, 7\}$) of counting all the preorders, partial orders and event structures through the verified algorithms we presented. `countEs 7` took about 55 h to compute.

Table 3. Counting results

N	Preorders	Partial orders	Event structures	N	Preorders	Partial orders	Event structures
0	1	1	1	4	355	219	916
1	1	1	1	5	6942	4231	41099
2	4	3	4	6	209527	130023	3528258
3	29	19	41	7	9535241	6129859	561658287

6   Conclusions

We provided an original algorithm to enumerate and count event structures, and formally proved its correctness along with the correctness of its implementation. An immediate application of our work was the realisation that the integer sequence counting the event structures is not listed on the OEIS [16], and has no trivial or immediate link to known sequences; this was confirmed by OEIS' *Super-seeker* service, which "will try hard to find an explanation for your sequence" [16]. We therefore submitted it to the OEIS; it passed the review process and is now published at http://oeis.org/A284276. Although there is existing work on the verified enumeration and counting of mathematical objects [7, 11, 12], this is the first mechanically certified addition to the OEIS we are aware of. Another immediate consequence upon looking at the obtained sequence is that even the counting problem is likely to be as hard as that of counting posets, given the fact that no advanced result permitting to detach the numbering of event structures from that of posets is known, and given the fast growth of the sequence, testified by the last column of Table 3. In the process, we also supplied formal correctness theorems for two existing OEIS sequences (A000798 and A001035).

Furthermore, we not only provided counting, but full enumeration of preorders, posets and event structures; we believe that this can be of interest for further investigations, in a way similar to how the enumeration of structures can be exploited for their classification and further investigations [10,17], as well as for simulations [9].

References

1. Aho, A.V., Garey, M.R., Ullman, J.D.: The transitive reduction of a directed graph. SIAM J. Comput. **1**(2), 131–137 (1972)
2. Assous, M.R., et al.: Finite labelling problem in event structures. Theor. Comput. Sci. **123**(1), 9–19 (1994)
3. Baldan, P., Corradini, A., Montanari, U.: Contextual Petri nets, asymmetric event structures, and processes. Inf. Comput. **171**(1), 1–49 (2001)
4. Bowles, J.K.F.: Decomposing interactions. In: Johnson, M., Vene, V. (eds.) AMAST 2006. LNCS, vol. 4019, pp. 189–203. Springer, Heidelberg (2006). doi:10. 1007/11784180_16
5. Bowles, J.K.F., Caminati, M.B.: Mind the gap: addressing behavioural inconsistencies with formal methods. In: 2016 23rd Asia-Pacific Software Engineering Conference (APSEC). IEEE Computer Society (2016)
6. Bruni, R., Melgratti, H., Montanari, U.: Event structure semantics for nominal calculi. In: Baier, C., Hermanns, H. (eds.) CONCUR 2006. LNCS, vol. 4137, pp. 295–309. Springer, Heidelberg (2006). doi:10.1007/11817949_20
7. Butelle, F., Hivert, F., Mayero, M., Toumazet, F.: Formal proof of SCHUR conjugate function. In: Autexier, S., Calmet, J., Delahaye, D., Ion, P.D.F., Rideau, L., Rioboo, R., Sexton, A.P. (eds.) CICM 2010. LNCS, vol. 6167, pp. 158–171. Springer, Heidelberg (2010). doi:10.1007/978-3-642-14128-7_15
8. Caminati, M.B., et al.: Sound auction specification and implementation. In: Proceedings of the Sixteenth ACM Conference on Economics and Computation, pp. 547–564. ACM (2015)
9. Costa-Gomes, M., et al.: Choice, Deferral and Consistency. Discussion Paper Series, Department of Economics 201416. Department of Economics, University of St. Andrews (2014)
10. Distler, A., Shah, M., Sorge, V.: Enumeration of AG-Groupoids. In: Davenport, J.H., Farmer, W.M., Urban, J., Rabe, F. (eds.) CICM 2011. LNCS, vol. 6824, pp. 1–14. Springer, Heidelberg (2011). doi:10.1007/978-3-642-22673-1_1
11. Genestier, R., Giorgetti, A., Petiot, G.: Sequential generation of structured arrays and its deductive verification. In: Blanchette, J.C., Kosmatov, N. (eds.) TAP 2015. LNCS, vol. 9154, pp. 109–128. Springer, Cham (2015). doi:10.1007/ 978-3-319-21215-9_7
12. Kammüller, F.: Mechanical analysis of finite idempotent relations. Fundamenta Informaticae **107**(1), 43–65 (2011)
13. Kleitman, D.J., Rothschild, B.L.: Asymptotic enumeration of partial orders on a finite set. Trans. Am. Math. Soc. **205**, 205–220 (1975)

14. Lochbihler, A.: Formalising finfuns – generating code for functions as data from Isabelle/HOL. In: Berghofer, S., Nipkow, T., Urban, C., Wenzel, M. (eds.) TPHOLs 2009. LNCS, vol. 5674, pp. 310–326. Springer, Heidelberg (2009). doi:10.1007/978-3-642-03359-9_22

15. Pfeiffer, G.: Counting transitive relations. J. Integer Sequences **7**(2), 3 (2004)

16. Sloane, N.: The on-line Encyclopedia of integer sequences. Ann. Math. Informaticae **41**, 219–234 (2013)

17. Vera-López, A., Arregi, J.: Conjugacy classes in unitriangular matrices. Linear Algebra Appl. **370**, 85–124 (2003)

18. Winskel, G., Nielsen, M.: Models for concurrency. In: Abramsky, S., Gabbay, D.M., Maibaum, T.S.E. (eds.) Handbook of Logic in Computer Science: Semantic Modelling, vol. 4, pp. 1–148. Oxford University Press, Oxford (1995)

19. Winskel, G.: Event structures. In: Brauer, W., Reisig, W., Rozenberg, G. (eds.) ACPN 1986. LNCS, vol. 255, pp. 325–392. Springer, Heidelberg (1987). doi:10.1007/3-540-17906-2_31

20. Winskel, G.: Events, causality and symmetry. Comput. J. **54**(1), 42–57 (2011). https://doi.org/10.1093/comjnl/bxp052

Reasoning with Concept Diagrams About Antipatterns in Ontologies

Zohreh Shams$^{1(\boxtimes)}$, Mateja Jamnik$^{1(\boxtimes)}$, Gem Stapleton^2, and Yuri Sato^2

^{1} Computer Laboratory, University of Cambridge, Cambridge, UK
{zohreh.shams,mateja.jamnik}@cl.cam.ac.uk
^{2} Visual Modelling Group, University of Brighton, Brighton, UK
{g.e.stapleton,y.sato}@brighton.ac.uk

Abstract. Ontologies are notoriously hard to define, express and reason about. Many tools have been developed to ease the ontology debugging and reasoning, however they often lack accessibility and formalisation. A visual representation language, *concept diagrams*, was developed for expressing ontologies, which has been empirically proven to be cognitively more accessible to ontology users. In this paper we answer the question of "How can concept diagrams be used to reason about inconsistencies and incoherence of ontologies?". We do so by formalising a set of inference rules for concept diagrams that enables stepwise verification of the inconsistency and incoherence of a set of ontology axioms. The design of inference rules is driven by empirical evidence that concise (merged) diagrams are easier to comprehend for users than a set of lower level diagrams that are a one-to-one translation from OWL ontology axioms. We prove that our inference rules are sound, and exemplify how they can be used to reason about inconsistencies and incoherence.

1 Introduction

Ontologies are sets of statements that represent individuals, classes and their properties, typically expressed using symbolic notations such as description logics (DL) [3] and OWL [1]. Although ontologies are widely used for knowledge representation in domains involving diverse stakeholders, the languages they are expressed in are often inaccessible to those unfamiliar with mathematical notations. To address this shortcoming some ontology editors, such as Protégé [2], provide visualisation facilities. Instead of using diagrams as an auxiliary tool to aid comprehension and accessibility, like in Protégé, some have taken one step further by using a logic that is fundamentally diagrammatic (e.g., [4,7]). However, these diagrammatic notations are either informal [4] or do not fully exploit the potential of formal diagrammatic notations (e.g., [7]). The design of concept diagrams [14] for expressing ontologies is based on cognitive theories of what makes a diagrammatic notation accessible, in particular to novice users [5].

This research was funded by a Leverhulme Trust Research Project Grant (RPG-2016-082) for the project entitled Accessible Reasoning with Diagrams.

H. Geuvers et al. (Eds.): CICM 2017, LNAI 10383, pp. 255–271, 2017.
DOI: 10.1007/978-3-319-62075-6_18

Concept diagrams are extensions of Euler diagrams and, in addition to closed curves for set representation, they use dots (spiders) and arrows for individuals and properties, respectively.

Similar to traditional logical systems, concept diagrams are equipped with inference rules which are used for specifying, reasoning and evaluating ontologies. Evaluating ontologies involves debugging them of inconsistencies and incoherence [12] before they can be published. These, so-called *antipatterns*, capture the unintended model-instances of an ontology [6,9]. An inconsistent ontology is one that cannot have any model and, so, entails anything [11], whereas an incoherent ontology is one that entails an unsatisfiable (i.e., empty) class or property. In other words, from an incoherent ontology we can infer that there exists a class or a property that is unsatisfiable (i.e., empty).

Empirical evidence proves that for incoherence checking, novice users not only perform significantly better with concept diagrams than with OWL [1] or DL [3], but also that merging concept diagrams (corresponding to each ontology axiom) into a single diagram makes them easier for humans to reason with [13]. This result coincides with cognitive evidence [18] that humans often mentally merge the representations of axioms into one when checking for inconsistency and incoherence.

In this paper, we formalise the use of concept diagrams for reasoning about inconsistencies and incoherence in ontologies by defining inference rules that merge axioms into a concise and cognitively more accessible concept diagram. We base our design of inference rules on empirical evidence that concise (merged) diagrams are easier to comprehend for users than a set of lower level diagrams that express equivalent information [13]. We prove that our concept diagrams inference rules are sound and exemplify how they can be used to spot inconsistency and incoherence.

This paper is organised as follows. In Sect. 2 we give an overview of the syntax and semantics of concept diagrams, followed by Sect. 3 that introduces how concept diagrams are reasoned with. In Sect. 4 we review the related work and finally, we conclude in Sect. 5.

2   Concept Diagrams

This section presents the syntax and semantics of concept diagrams [19]. We start with an example in Fig. 1. This concept diagram has the following syntax and semantic interpretation:

- One dot – called a spider – which represents a named individual, Sara;
- Two *boundary rectangles* (represented by □) each of which represents the universal set.
- Eight curves, representing eight sets, six of which have labels (e.g., People). The two curves without labels represent *anonymous sets*. The spatial relationships between curves and spiders within a boundary rectangle convey semantics. For example, the syntax within the LHS rectangle says that Sara

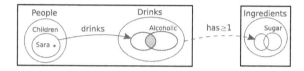

Fig. 1. A concept diagram.

is in the set Children; Children is a subset of People; the sets People and Drinks are disjoint; and Alcoholic drink set is a subset of Drinks.

- Shading (e.g., intersection of Alcoholic and the unlabelled curve inside Drink) which is used to place upper bounds on set cardinality: in a shaded region, all elements are represented by spiders. Since there are no elements in this particular shaded region, the region is empty.
- Two arrows, one of which is *solid* and the other one is *dashed*. Arrows are used to convey semantics about binary relations, using their sources and targets. A solid arrow asserts that things in arrow's source are only related to things in arrow's target under a certain relation (e.g., Children only drink Drinks and only those Drinks that are not Alcoholic.). A dashed arrow asserts that things in arrow's source relate to things in arrow's target amongst other things. The dashed arrow here, is sourced on Drinks and targets an unlabelled curve. This unlabelled curve, say c, represents a subset of Ingredients (which could be Sugar or some other Ingredients) to which members of Drinks are related under has relation. The dashed arrow's annotation, ≥ 1, places a constraint on set Drinks: all elements of Drinks must be related to at least one element of c under has Relation.

2.1   Syntax

When using concept diagrams for ontology representation, ontology classes, individuals in classes, and object properties, are respectively represented by curves, spiders and arrows. These require labels. Therefore, we start by defining three pairwise disjoint sets, $\mathcal{L}_S$ (for identifying particular individuals), $\mathcal{L}_C$ (for particular classes), and $\mathcal{L}_A$ (for object properties), which are, respectively, sets of **names** for spiders, curves and arrows. Informally, in concretely drawn diagrams (as opposed to their sentential abstract representation), spiders and curves are allowed to be unlabelled, as seen in Fig. 1. Formally, however, these unlabelled entities act as variables. As such, we define two further pairwise disjoint, countably infinite sets (also disjoint from the former three), $\mathcal{V}_S$ (for anonymous individuals), $\mathcal{V}_C$ (for anonymous classes) which are **variables** for spiders and curves respectively. In drawn concept diagram, we typically omit labels for variables to avoid clutter. However, if the same anonymous spider or curve appears more than once, so that the variable label is used on more than one spider or curve, then this label must be drawn. Further, we define $\mathcal{L}_A^- = \{op^- : op \in \mathcal{L}_A\}$, allowing us to denote inverse properties.

At the abstract level, concept diagrams include a set of spiders that are chosen from a countably infinite set, S. In a drawn diagram, each spider is a tree whose nodes are placed in distinct zones (i.e., dots connected by lines placed in 'minimal' regions in the diagram). Any two spiders may be joined by $=$, to assert that two individuals are the same. For example, if s in Fig. 1 was joined to, say s' (i.e., $s_{\bullet} = {}_{\bullet}s'$), they would be the same individual. Also, $=$ may be annotated with ? (i.e., $\overset{?}{=}$) to indicate uncertainty about equality: the two spiders may represent either equal or distinct individuals.

Concept diagrams also include closed curves, selected from a countably infinite set, $\mathcal{C}$. The closed curves give rise to zones that are regions inside some or none of the curves. Formally, a zone is a pair of finite, disjoint sets of curves, $(in, C\backslash in)$, where $C \subseteq \mathcal{C}$ is a finite set of curves. Intuitively, $(in, C\backslash in)$ is inside every curve of $in \subseteq C$ and outside every curve of $C\backslash in$. For example, in Fig. 1, both LHS and RHS diagram components have five zones.

Arrows are another component of concept diagrams. At the abstract level, arrows are of the form $(s, t, \circ)$ and all of them are labelled. Here, s is the arrow's source, t is the target and $\circ$ is either $\rightarrow$ or Arrows can be sourced on the boundary rectangle, curves or spiders. Arrow labels can be object properties, or their inverses. Arrows can also be assigned labels that express minimum, maximum and equality cardinality constraints. These labels are written on arrows in diagrams as $\leq n$, $\geq n$ and $= n$; formally they are ordered pairs, such as $(\leq, n)$.

Prior to defining concept diagrams, we define *class and object property diagrams* (Definition 1) that are the main building blocks of concept diagrams, and allow assertions to be made about classes and object properties of an ontology in a universe (i.e., within a boundary rectangle).

Definition 1 (Class and object property diagram). *A **class and object property diagram**, $\chi = (S, C, Z, Z^*, \eta, \tau_=, \tau_?, A, \lambda_s, \lambda_c, \lambda_a, \lambda_\#)$ consists of:*

1. $S \subset \mathcal{S}$ *that is a finite set of spiders;*
2. $C \subset \mathcal{C}$ *that is a finite set of curves;*
3. Z *that is a set of zones such that* $Z \subseteq \{(in, C\backslash in) : in \subseteq C\}$.
4. $Z^* \subseteq Z$ *that is a set of shaded zones;*
5. $\eta : S \rightarrow \mathcal{P}(Z)\backslash\{\emptyset\}$ *that is a function that returns the location of each spider. $\mathcal{P}(Z)$ represents the set of subsets (i.e., powerset) of Z, and since the habitat of a spider has to be a non-empty set of zones, we remove $\emptyset$ from $\mathcal{P}(Z)$);*
6. $\tau_=$ *that is a reflexive, symmetric relation on S that identifies whether two spiders are joined by an equals sign; $(s_1, s_2) \in \tau_=$ means that s_1 is joined to s_2 by $=$ (indicating they are the same);*
7. $\tau_?$ *that is a reflexive, symmetric relation on S, disjoint from $\tau_=$. It identifies if two spiders are joined by $\overset{?}{=}$; $(s_1, s_2) \in \tau_?$ means s_1 is joined to s_2 by $\overset{?}{=}$ (indicating that s_1 and s_2 may or may not be equal);*
8. A *that is a finite multiset of arrows such that for all $(s, t, \circ)$ in A, s and t are in $S \cup C \cup \{\square\}$, where $\square$ is a boundary rectangle;*
9. $\lambda_s : S \rightarrow \mathcal{L}_S \cup \mathcal{V}_S$ *that is a function that maps spiders to spider labels;*
10. $\lambda_c : C \rightarrow \mathcal{L}_C \cup \mathcal{V}_C$ *that is a function that maps curves to curve labels;*

11. $\lambda_a : A \rightarrow \mathcal{L}_\mathcal{A} \cup \mathcal{L}_\mathcal{A}^-$ that is a function that maps arrows to arrow labels or their inverses.
12. $\lambda_\# : A \rightarrow (\leq, =, \geq) \times N$ that is a partial function that maps arrows to cardinality constraints.

We write $S(\chi)$ to denote the set of spiders in χ and so forth for the other sets.

We are now in a position to define concept diagrams. A concept diagram (Definition 2), is a set of class and object property diagrams, possibly with additional arrows that have a source inside one boundary rectangle and a target inside another. Again, the labels for these additional arrows are chosen from $\mathcal{L}_\mathcal{A}$ and they may be annotated with cardinalities.

Definition 2 (Concept Diagram). *Concept diagram* $d = (\mathcal{COP}, A_o, \lambda_o, \lambda_\#)$, *has components defined as follows:*

1. $\mathcal{COP}$ *is a finite set of class and object property diagrams such that for any pair of distinct diagrams,* χ_i *and* χ_j, *in* $\mathcal{COP}$, $S(\chi_i) \cap S(\chi_j) = \emptyset$ *and* $C(\chi_i) \cap C(\chi_j) = \emptyset$.
2. A_o *is a finite multiset of arrows such that for all* $(s, t, \circ)$ *in* A_o,
   (a) $s \in \bigcup_{\chi \in \mathcal{COP}} S(\chi) \cup C(\chi) \cup (\{\Box\} \times \mathcal{COP})$ *and* $t \in \bigcup_{\chi \in \mathcal{COP}} S(\chi) \cup C(\chi) \cup (\{\Box\} \times \mathcal{COP})$, *and*
   (b) *for all diagrams,* χ, *in* $\mathcal{COP}$ *it is not the case that* $s \in S(\chi) \cup C(\chi) \cup \{(\Box, \chi)\}$ *and* $t \in S(\chi) \cup C(\chi) \cup \{(\Box, \chi)\}$,
3. $\lambda_o : A_o \rightarrow \mathcal{L}_\mathcal{A} \cup \mathcal{L}_\mathcal{A}^-$ *is a function that maps arrows to object property and their inverses,*
4. $\lambda_\# : A_o \rightarrow \{\leq, =, \geq\} \times N$ *is a partial function that maps arrows to cardinality constraints.*

Note that, item 2 of this definition guarantees that the set of arrows in A_o have their source and targets in two different rectangles (e.g., has in Fig. 1). In other words, these arrows are different from the set A in class and object property diagrams, when the source and target of the arrows are within the same rectangle (e.g., drinks in Fig. 1).

2.2 Semantics

We take a standard approach to defining the semantics of concept diagrams. First, the vocabulary over which the logic is defined is interpreted appropriately (Definition 3), which is the basis for our definition of a model for a concept diagram (Definition 5).

Definition 3 (Interpretation). *An **interpretation** is a pair,* $I = (U, .^I)$, *where*

- U *is a non-empty set, called the universal set,*
- *for each element* i *in* $\mathcal{L_S}$, i^I *is an element of* U,
- *for each element* c *in* $\mathcal{L_C}$, c^I *is a subset of* U,

– *for each element op in $\mathcal{L}_A$, op^I is a binary relation on U.*

We also need to interpret the variables and zones in class and object property diagrams. To do so, we first extend interpretations to variables.

Definition 4 (Extended Interpretation). *Given an interpretation, $I = (U, .^I)$, an* **extended interpretation** *is a pair, $I' = (U, .^{I'})$, such that*

– *for each element x in $\mathcal{V}_S$, $x^{I'}$ is an element of U, and*
– *for each element X in $\mathcal{V}_C$, $X^{I'}$ is a subset of U.*

Definition 5 (Model).[1] *Let $d = (\mathcal{COP}, A_o, \lambda_o, \lambda_\#)$ be a concept diagram and let $I = (U, .^I)$ be an interpretation. I is a* **model** *for d if there exists an extended interpretation, $I' = (U, .^{I'})$, such that*

1. *for each class and object property diagram χ_i, in $\mathcal{COP}$*
   (a) *the union of the sets represented by the zones in χ is U, that is $\bigcup\limits_{z \in Z(\chi)} z^{I'} = U$, where each zone $z = (in, C \backslash in)$ represents the set $z^{I'} = (\bigcap\limits_{\kappa \in in} \lambda_c(\kappa)^{I'}) \backslash (\bigcup\limits_{\kappa \in C \backslash in} \lambda_c(\kappa)^{I'})$;*
   (b) *each shaded zone in χ represents a set containing only elements mapped to by spiders in χ, that is $z^{I'} \subseteq \bigcup\limits_{\sigma \in S(\chi)} \{\lambda_s(\sigma)^{I'}\}$;*
   (c) *for each spider, σ, in χ, $\lambda_s(\sigma)^{I'}$ is an element in the set denoted by one of the zones in which σ is placed;*
   (d) *any two spiders, σ_1 and σ_2, in χ not joined by $=$ map to distinct elements, that is $\lambda_s(\sigma_1)^{I'} \neq \lambda_s(\sigma_2)^{I'}$;*
   (e) *any two spiders, σ_1 and σ_2, in χ joined by $=$ but not annotated with ? map to the same element, that is $\lambda_s(\sigma_1)^{I'} = \lambda_s(\sigma_2)^{I'}$;*
   (f) *for each solid arrow, a_j, with source s, target t and label op, the image of op^I when the domain is restricted to the set represented by s, equals to the set represented by t;*
   (g) *for each dashed arrow, a_j, with source s, target t and label op, the image of op^I when the domain is restricted to the set represented by s, is a superset of the set represented by t;*
   (h) *if an arrow is annotated with cardinality constraint, $(\diamond, n)$, then each element of the source set is related to $\diamond n$ elements in the target set, and*
2. *for each connecting arrow, a_j, in A_o with source in χ_i and target in χ_j,*
   (a) *if a_j is a solid arrow with source s, target t and label op, the image of op^I when the domain is restricted to the set represented by s, equals to the set represented by t;*
   (b) *if a_j is a dashed arrow with source s, target t and label op, the image of op^I when the domain is restricted to the set represented by s, is a superset of the set represented by t;*

---

[1] For simplicity and succinctness, we treat single elements as singleton sets (e.g. a spider represents an element via its label, but we treat it as a singleton set).

    (c) if a_j is annotated with a cardinality constraint, $(\diamond, n)$, then each element of the source set is related to $\diamond n$ elements in the target set.

Let $\mathcal{D}$ be a set of concept diagrams. Then I is a model for $\mathcal{D}$ if I is a model for each concept diagram in $\mathcal{D}$.

3 Reasoning with Concept Diagrams

Similar to traditional logical systems, concept diagrams are equipped with inference rules. Reasoning with concept diagrams involves using different kinds of inference rules including first-order logic rules (e.g., substitution [5]), pure diagrammatic rules (e.g., Delete Syntax, see Sect. 3.1), and rules that combine information from two diagrams. In what follows, we first mention the existing inference rules for concept diagrams. Next, based on existing rules, we introduce inference rules that are tailored for merging concept diagrams and thus support inconsistency/incoherence checking tasks.

3.1 Existing Inference Rules

Here we briefly mention the set of sound inference rules devised for concept diagrams in the past [5]. They are applicable to the fragment of concept diagrams we characterised in Sect. 2. Figure 2 exemplifies the inference rules we are later on using in the examples in this paper. Rules are displayed in two dimensions, for instance, $\frac{d_1 \quad d_2}{d_3} R$ shows rule R with premises d_1 and d_2 and conclusion d_3.

- Delete Syntax (*del*): this inference rule removes syntax from a diagram.
- Copy Spider (*c*): this rules copies a spider in a curve from diagram d_1 to d_2, where d_2 contains the same curve with no spider.
- Copy Curve 1 (*cc1*): this inference rule copies curve C from diagram d_2 to d_1, where both diagrams contain curve B, while C is a curve containing B only in d_2.
- Copy Curve 2 (*cc2*): this inference rule copies curve B from diagram d_2 to d_1, where both diagrams contain spider s_2 and s_2 is in curve B in d_2 only.

    In addition, concept diagrams are a superclass of spider diagrams [8], thus we inherit all of the inference rules for spider diagrams. Due to space limitation, we refer the readers to [20] for details.

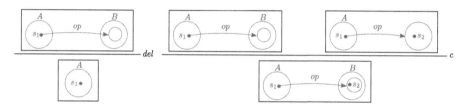

Fig. 2. Inference rules from [5].

3.2   Incoherence and Inconsistency

We begin by defining what it means for D, a set of concept diagrams representing axioms in ontology o, to be incoherent and inconsistent [17].

Definition 6 (Incoherence). *A set of concept diagrams, $\mathcal{D}$, is **incoherent**, if one of the following conditions is met:*

- *there is a label, A, in $\mathcal{L}_C$ such that for all models, $I = (U, .^I)$, for $\mathcal{D}$ $A^I = \emptyset$,*
- *there is a label, op, in $\mathcal{L}_A$ such that for all models, $I = (U, .^I)$, for $\mathcal{D}$ $op^I = \emptyset$,*

*Such empty labels are called **unsatisfiable**.*

To prove that ontology o is incoherent, we have to show that a class or an object property is unsatisfiable (i.e., empty). When using a set of concept diagrams, $\mathcal{D}$, to define o, the task is thus to prove a lemma of the form:

(i) a curve labelled A necessarily represents an empty class, or
(ii) an arrow labelled op necessarily represents an empty object property.

A lemma of type (i) is proved if, carrying out the proof visually, we derive a diagram in Fig. 3a: an entirely shaded region with no spiders represents the empty set in any model. Type (ii) lemmas are proved if the proof derives a diagram in Fig. 3b, in which the target of the arrow is entirely shaded with no spiders: this target represents the empty set, implying the image of op is empty, thus op is an empty relation.

For example, the left inference rules in Fig. 4 spot an incoherence by showing that A is unsatisfiable. We have that the universal image of op is restricted to B, while there is set A such that the partial image of A under op includes C. However, C and B are disjoint. Since the universal image of op is restricted to B, the image of A under p cannot be outside B, which is clearly not the case here. So A is empty. The right inference rule shows that object property op is empty, because the first premise displays the image of op as a subset of intersection of B and C, while the second premise defines B and C as disjoint.

We now define what it means for a set of concept diagrams to be inconsistent. As we proceed, we also adopt $\perp$ as a canonical representation of inconsistency.

Definition 7 (Inconsistency). *A set of concept diagrams, D, is **inconsistent**, if it has no models.*

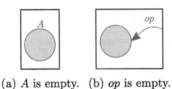

(a) A is empty.   (b) op is empty.

Fig. 3. Representation of incoherence in concept diagrams.

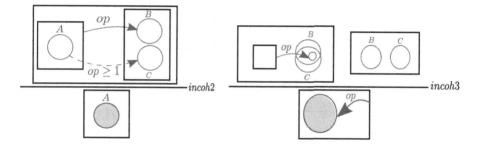

Fig. 4. Incoherence examples.

Note that every inconsistent diagram is also incoherent.

Diagrams in Fig. 5 show antipatterns that lead to inconsistency. In the left rule, we see that A and B are disjoint and then we assert that they have at least one element, s_1, in common. Both classes A and B are inconsistent in this case. The right hand side rule shows an example of an inconsistent object property, where we first have that the image of A under op is restricted to B, then we have that the image is restricted to C, while B and C are disjoint non-empty sets.

3.3   Using Inference Rules to Detect Incoherence and Inconsistency

Having defined incoherence and inconsistency, we now design inference rules that facilitate their detection. We derive proofs for Lemmas 1 and 2 that show that two sets of axioms are incoherent and inconsistent, respectively. To prove these lemmas we design rules that step-by-step take us from the axioms to the goal state in which the lemma is proved. These inference rules are general and can then be used for similar reasoning cases in other ontologies. Our approach to designing inference rules is driven by the requirements of the proof, rather than in isolation from the proof. We believe that proof driven inference rules give rise to more natural proofs. In contrast, the established common approach to designing inference rules in logic is primarily driven by the requirements of the theoretical properties (e.g., soundness and completeness) of the rules.

The following lemma shows that the set of axioms in Fig. 6 is incoherent.

Lemma 1. *Thunder is empty.*

Proof. Figure 7 shows the proof.

In this proof (Fig. 7), we aim to establish that "Thunder" is empty from axioms in Fig. 6. First, Axioms (c) and (d) are merged by using inference rule *cc*. *cc* is one of existing rules for spider diagrams [8] and stands for copy contour (contours in spider diagrams are equivalent to curves in concept diagrams) and is introduced in [20]. Applying *cc* to diagram *d* copies the curve labelled "GodDevice" from diagram (d) to diagram (c), giving diagram (e) as conclusion. In the next step (e) and (a) are merged using *cc* twice in a row. "SuperPower" already

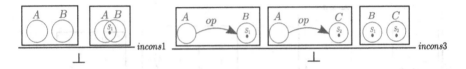

Fig. 5. Inconsistency examples.

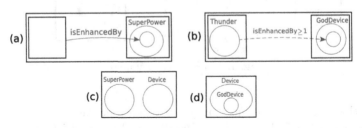

Fig. 6. A set of incoherent axioms.

exists in (a), so the two curves being copied from (e) to (a), are "Device" and "GodDevice". The result of merging (e) and (a) gives (f). Next, (f) and (b) are merged using rule *mrg1*. This rule is formally defined in Definition 8.

Definition 8 (rule *mrg1*). *Let d_1 and d_2 be two concept diagrams, each containing an arrow, a_1 and a_2 respectively, labelled op such that*

1. *a_1 is solid, its source is some boundary rectangle, $\square$, and its target is a curve, c_{1t} in χ_{1t}, which is an object and class property diagram;*
2. *a_2 is dashed or solid and its source and target are curves c_{2s} and c_{2t} in χ_{2s} and χ_{2t}, respectively, while c_{2t} is properly contained in c_3.*

Also let χ_{1t} in d_1 contain curve c_4 disjoint from c_{1t}, such that c_4 has the same label as c_3 in d_2. Now let d_3 be a concept diagram such that d_3 is a copy of d_1 with a new arrow, a_3, and two new curves, c_5, and c_6 as follows:

1. *c_5 is added to the boundary rectangle that is the source of a_1 in d_1,*
2. *c_5 has the same label as c_{2s} in d_2,*
3. *c_6 is added inside c_4 from d_1,*
4. *c_6 has the same label as c_{2t} in d_2,*
5. *a_3 is sourced on c_5 and targets c_6, and*
6. *a_3 has the same shape (dashed or solid), label and cardinality as a_2 in d_2.*

*Then diagrams d_1 and d_2 can be merged to form diagram d_3 using **rule mrg1**.*

mrg1 is exemplified in Fig. 8, where in the left hand premise c_{1t} and c_4 are represented by curves labelled A and B. On the right, c_{2s}, c_3, and c_{2t} are represented by curves labelled C, B, and D. In the conclusion, c_5, and c_6 are represented by curves C and D.

After merging (f) and (b) and deducing (g), the next inference rule used in Fig. 7 is *incoh2*, defined in Definition 9, and exemplified in Fig. 4.

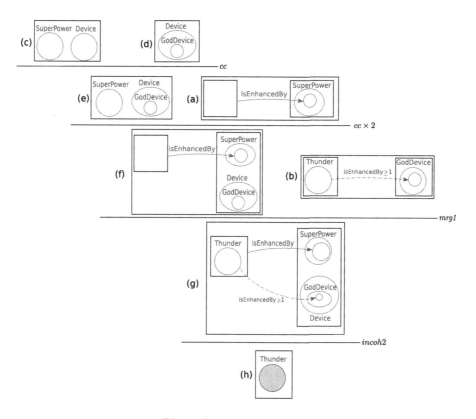

Fig. 7. A proof of Lemma 1.

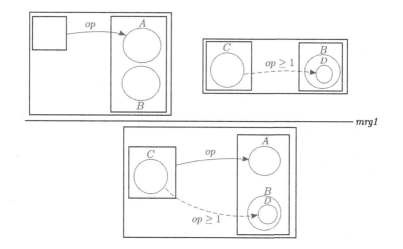

Fig. 8. Inference rule *mrg*1.

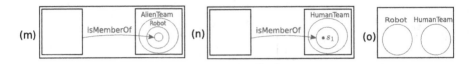

Fig. 9. A set of inconsistent axioms.

Definition 9 (rule *incoh2*). *Let d be a concept diagram with two arrows a_1 and a_2 with the same label op, such that*

1. a_1 *is solid, its source is some boundary rectangle and its target is curve c_{1t} in another boundary rectangle that frames concept and object property diagram χ_t,*
2. a_2 *is dashed or solid, its source is curve c_{2s} whose label is in $\mathcal{L}_C$ and which is in the boundary rectangle that is the source of a_1, its target is curve c_{2t} in χ_t and it is annotated with $(\diamond, n)$ where $\diamond \in \{\geq, =\}$ and $n \geq 1$,*
3. c_{2t} *and c_{1t} are disjoint.*

Applying **rule *incoh2*** *to d gives d', where d', in its boundary rectangle, contains a single curve c_3 that is all shaded, contains no spiders and has the same label as c_{2s} in d.*

Applying rule *incoh2* to (g) gives (h), where "Thunder" is empty and therefore the lemma is proved and the set of axioms in Fig. 6 is incoherent.

We now prove a lemma that shows that the set of axioms in Fig. 9 is inconsistent.

Lemma 2. *Robot is inconsistent.*

Proof. Figure 10 shows the proof.

In the proof, we aim to establish that "Robot" is inconsistent, using axioms presented in Fig. 9. The first inference rule used in Fig. 10 merges Axioms (m) and (n) using *img5*. This inference rule is exemplified in Fig. 11. According to this rule if we have two assertions stating the universal image of property *op* as classes c_{1t} and c_{2t}, then they must represent the same set and therefore, all the spiders in one belong to the other one too. Definition 10 formalises *img5* and the conditions under which it is applicable.

Definition 10 (rule *img5*). *Let d_1 and d_2 be two concept diagrams, each containing a solid arrow a_1 and a_2, labelled op, such that*

(i) a_1 *'s source is some boundary rectangle, and its target is curve c_{1t} in χ_{1t}, where c_{1t} is properly contained by some other curve c_3,*
(ii) a_2 *'s source is some boundary rectangle, and its target is curve c_{2t} in χ_{2t}.*

Let d_3 be a copy of d_2 with an additional curve c_4, such that

(i) c_4 is added to χ_{2t} and it splits each existing zone into two, one inside and one outside c_4 except the zones inside c_{2t}, which are not split but are all inside c_4, and
(ii) the label of c_4 is the same as c_3 in χ_{1t}.

*Diagram d_2 can be merged with curve c_3 from d_1 to form d_3 using **rule img5**.*

By applying *img5* to Axioms (m) and (n), we deduce diagram (q). Next, applying rule *del* to (q) gives (r). *del* is one of the existing rules for concept diagrams that was explained in Sect. 3.1. Merging (r) with Axiom (o) is done using inference rule *incons1* (exemplified in Fig. 5), that is described in Definition 11.

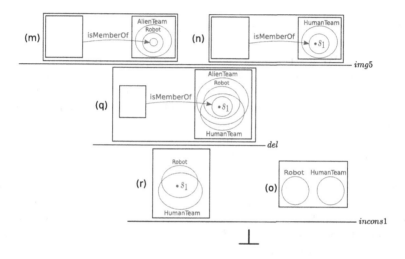

Fig. 10. A proof of Lemma 2.

Definition 11 (rule *incons1*). *Let d_1 and d_2 be two concept diagrams such that there are two curves in d_1, say c_1 and c_2, that are disjoint, while d_2 contains two curves c_3 and c_4 with at least one spider in their intersection. If c_1 and c_2 in d_1 have the same labels as c_3 and c_4 in d_2, respectively, **rule incons1** spots the inconsistency and concludes false ($\perp$).*

By applying *incons1* to r and o, we deduce false, and spot the inconsistency of "Robot" and hence the inconsistency of the set of axioms presented in Fig. 9.

3.4 Correctness

Here, we investigate the soundness and completeness of the inference rules introduced. Rules used in proofs of Lemmas 1 and 2 are *cc*, *mrg1*, *incoh2*, *img5*, *del* and *incons1*. *cc* and *del* are proved sound in [5,20], respectively. Due to space limitation, below we only prove the soundness of rule *incoh2*. Other rules can be proven sound in a similar manner.

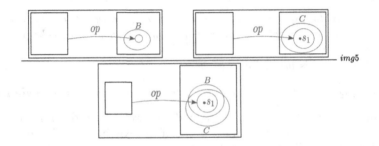

Fig. 11. Inference rule $img5$.

Theorem 1. *Rule incoh2 (Definition 9) is sound.*

Proof (Sketch). We need to show that any model for the premise (d), is also a model for the conclusion (d'). Let $I = (U, .^I)$ be an interpretation such that there exists an extension, $I' = (U, .^{I'})$ that shows I is a model for d. Then for the solid arrow a_1, the image of $op^{I'}$ equals $\lambda_c(c_{1t})^{I'}$. Due to the cardinality constraint, $(\diamond, n)$, on a_2, each element of $\lambda_c(c_{2s})^{I'}$ is related to at least one element of $\lambda_c(c_{2t})^{I'}$ under $op^{I'}$. Suppose, for proof by contradiction, that $\lambda_c(c_{2s})^{I'} \neq \emptyset$. Let $e \in \lambda_c(c_{2s})^{I'}$ and let e' be an element in $\lambda_c(c_{2t})^{I'}$ that e is related to under $op^{I'}$. Then e' is an element of $\lambda_c(c_{1t})^{I'}$. So $\lambda_c(c_{1t})^{I'} \cap \lambda_c(c_{2t})^{I'} \neq \emptyset$. On the other hand, since I is a model for d, and c_{1t} and c_{2t} are disjoint in d, we have $\lambda_c(c_{1t})^{I'} \cap \lambda_c(c_{2t})^{I'} = \emptyset$. Therefore the assumption that $\lambda_c(c_{2s})^{I'} \neq \emptyset$ is false. Consider now the only curve, c_3, in d'. Since $\lambda_c(c)$ is a label in $\mathcal{L_C}$, any extension, I'', of I clearly ensures $\lambda_c(c_3)^{I''} = \emptyset$. Since c_3 is entirely shaded, I satisfies d'. Hence, I is a model for d', as required.

Ensuring completeness in most logical systems is hard. For a diagrammatic logic for ontologies based on concept diagrams, the difficulty is caused by [(i)] the existence of several syntactic elements for concept diagrams (e.g., spiders, curves, shading, etc.); and the constant need to devise new rules to capture the inference required when reasoning about ontologies representing different domains. We conjecture that concept diagrams, as defined here, correspond to a fragment of second-order logic with one and two place predicates. One-place and two-place predicates arise due to the use of labelled curves and arrows respectively. Second-order (existential) quantification occurs through the use of unlabelled curves. Although concept diagrams do not contain quantifiers in their syntax, an equivalent fragment of SOL would need to do so. For instance, two non-overlapping labelled curves, A and B say, give rise to (first-order) universal quantification and express $\forall x \ \neg(A(x) \wedge B(x))$. Due to the restricted way in which second-order quantification arises, finding a complete set of inference rules should be possible. Completeness is a desirable property that we leave for future work (non-trivial). Proving it involves considering and formalising variants of inference rules in all combinations of all syntactic elements of concept diagrams. Consider inference rule $img5$ presented in Fig. 11. The variants of this rule can be defined for other combination of arrows, when the target and source of arrows are various combination of spiders, curves and boundary rectangles.

4   Related Work and Discussion

Debugging ontologies is a challenging task. A variety of tools, in particular visualisation tools [15, 16], have been developed to help ontology engineers with the debugging process. Similar to these efforts, concept diagrams attempt to aid debugging ontologies through visualisations. However, we argue that in addition to having cognitive advantages over DL and OWL [13], concept diagrams are cognitively more accessible than ontology visualisation methods based on node-link diagrams (e.g., SOVA [15] and VOWL [16]). This can naturally be explained by referring to better *well-matchedness* [10] of concept diagrams to ontologies. Well-matchedness of a notation is assessed based on how well its syntax and semantics mirror each other. Concept diagrams use syntactic spatial relationships (e.g., curve containment) to reflect the corresponding semantics (e.g., subset relation). In node-link diagrams classes and properties are represented as nodes, while different arrow-like connectors are used to capture the relation between the nodes. In contrast to concept diagrams, node-link diagrams use topological relations to convey semantics (e.g., subset superset relation is expressed using an arrow with a hollow end). The lack of well-matchedness in tools like [15, 16] suggests that they may not be as cognitively effective as concept diagrams. In addition to cognitive advantages, concept diagrams are fully formalised, which is not the case for several ontology visualisation tools (e.g., UML diagrams [4]). As a formalised logical system, concept diagrams can be used not only as a visualisation tool, but also as a reasoning tool, as it was highlighted in this paper.

Similar to our work, concept diagrams have recently been used for the detection and justification of antipatterns [13]. However, in [13] the focus is on the specification and representation of incoherence using concept diagrams rather than the inference rules and the reasoning mechanism that checks incoherence. In contrast, our goal is to design inference rules for reasoning. Moreover, we use these inference rules for reasoning about both incoherence and inconsistency.

5   Conclusion and Future Work

In this paper we described how to reason about inconsistency and incoherence in ontologies using concept diagrams. Unlike, many visual tools for ontology engineering [15, 16], concept diagrams are designed to be formal, yet accessible, evidenced by empirical studies [13]. There are two alternatives to use concept diagrams as ontology debugging tool, namely (i) to prove a one to one translation of ontology axioms in concept diagrams; and to merge ontology axioms in a single concept diagram. We focused on the latter. This choice was informed by existing cognitive empirical evaluations [13, 18] and resulted in proposing a set of sound inference rules for merging concept diagrams.

We conjecture that concept diagrams used in this paper (Sect. 2) are as expressive as a fragment of second-order logic with one and two place predicates. In the future we will extend the set of inference rules for this fragment with the aim of achieving completeness.

We will use concept diagrams and their inference rules in building the first mechanised reasoning system for concept diagrams and reasoning about ontologies. An exciting aspect of the future work from this perspective is the empirical studies that we have outlined to inform the intuitiveness of the inference rules we are implementing. We believe that the intuitiveness of the inference rules can significantly contribute to a more accessible reasoner for ontology engineering.

References

1. The OWL2 web ontology language. https://www.w3.org/TR/owl2-direct-semantics/, December 2016
2. Protégé: A free, open-source ontology editor. http://protege.stanford.edu, December 2016
3. Baader, F., Horrocks, I., Sattler, U.: Description logics. In: Staab, S., Studer, R. (eds.) Handbook on Ontologies. International Handbooks on Information Systems, pp. 21–43. Springer, Heidelberg (2009)
4. Brockmans, S., Volz, R., Eberhart, A., Löffler, P.: Visual modeling of OWL DL ontologies using UML. In: McIlraith, S.A., Plexousakis, D., Harmelen, F. (eds.) ISWC 2004. LNCS, vol. 3298, pp. 198–213. Springer, Heidelberg (2004). doi:10.1007/978-3-540-30475-3_15
5. Chapman, P., Stapleton, G., Howse, J., Oliver, I.: Deriving sound inference rules for concept diagrams. In: 2011 IEEE Symposium on Visual Languages and Human-Centric Computing, VL/HCC 2011, pp. 87–94. IEEE (2011)
6. Corcho, Ó., Roussey, C., Blázquez, L.M.V., Pérez, I.: Pattern-based OWL ontology debugging guidelines. In: Proceedings of the Workshop on Ontology Patterns (WOP 2009), vol. 516, CEUR Workshop Proceedings. CEUR-WS.org (2009)
7. Dau, F., Eklund, P.W.: A diagrammatic reasoning system for the description logic ACL. J. Vis. Lang. Comput. **19**(5), 539–573 (2008)
8. Gil, J., Howse, J., Kent, S.: Formalizing spider diagrams. In: IEEE Symposium on Visual Languages, pp. 130–137. IEEE Computer Society (1999)
9. Guizzardi, G., Sales, T.P.: Detection, simulation and elimination of semantic anti-patterns in ontology-driven conceptual models. In: Yu, E., Dobbie, G., Jarke, M., Purao, S. (eds.) ER 2014. LNCS, vol. 8824, pp. 363–376. Springer, Cham (2014). doi:10.1007/978-3-319-12206-9_30
10. Gurr, C.: Effective diagrammatic communication: syntactic, semantic and pragmatic issues. J. Vis. Lang. Comput. **10**(4), 317–342 (1999)
11. Horridge, M., Parsia, B., Sattler, U.: Explaining inconsistencies in OWL ontologies. In: Godo, L., Pugliese, A. (eds.) SUM 2009. LNCS, vol. 5785, pp. 124–137. Springer, Heidelberg (2009). doi:10.1007/978-3-642-04388-8_11
12. Horrocks, I., Patel-Schneider, P.F., van Harmelen, F.: From SHIQ and RDF to OWL: the making of a web ontology language. J. Web Semant. **1**(1), 7–26 (2003)
13. Hou, T., Chapman, P., Blake, A.: Antipattern comprehension: an empirical evaluation. In: Formal Ontology in Information Systems. Frontiers in Artificial Intelligence, vol. 283, pp. 211–224. IOS Press (2016)

14. Howse, J., Stapleton, G., Taylor, K., Chapman, P.: Visualizing ontologies: a case study. In: Aroyo, L., Welty, C., Alani, H., Taylor, J., Bernstein, A., Kagal, L., Noy, N., Blomqvist, E. (eds.) ISWC 2011. LNCS, vol. 7031, pp. 257–272. Springer, Heidelberg (2011). doi:10.1007/978-3-642-25073-6_17
15. Itzik, N., Reinhartz-Berger, I.: SOVA - a tool for semantic and ontological variability analysis. In: Joint Proceedings of the CAiSE 2014 Forum and CAiSE 2014 Doctoral Consortium, vol. 1164, pp. 177–184. CEUR-WS.org (2014)
16. Lohmann, S., Negru, S., Haag, F., Ertl, T.: Visualizing ontologies with VOWL. Semant. Web **7**(4), 399–419 (2016)
17. Qi, G., Hunter, A.: Measuring incoherence in description logic-based ontologies. In: Aberer, K., Choi, K.-S., Noy, N., Allemang, D., Lee, K.-I., Nixon, L., Golbeck, J., Mika, P., Maynard, D., Mizoguchi, R., Schreiber, G., Cudré-Mauroux, P. (eds.) ASWC/ISWC -2007. LNCS, vol. 4825, pp. 381–394. Springer, Heidelberg (2007). doi:10.1007/978-3-540-76298-0_28
18. Ragni, M., Khemlani, S., Johnson-Laird, P.N.: The evaluation of the consistency of quantified assertions. Mem. Cogn. **42**(1), 53–66 (2014)
19. Stapleton, G., Howse, J., Chapman, P., Delaney, A., Burton, J., Oliver, I.: Formalizing concept diagrams. In: 19th International Conference on Distributed Multimedia Systems, Visual Languages and Computing, pp. 182–187. Knowledge Systems Institute (2013)
20. Urbas, M., Jamnik, M., Stapleton, G.: Speedith: a reasoner for spider diagrams. J. Logic Lang. Inf. **24**(4), 487–540 (2015)

A Web-Based Toolkit for Mathematical Word Processing Applications with Semantics

Nathan C. Carter[1](✉) [iD] and Kenneth G. Monks[2]

[1] Bentley University, Waltham, MA, USA
ncarter@bentley.edu
[2] University of Scranton, Scranton, PA, USA
monks@scranton.edu

Abstract. *Lurch* is an open-source word processor that can check the steps in students' mathematical proofs. Users write in a natural language, but mark portions of a document as meaningful, so the software can distinguish content for human readers from content it should analyze.

This paper describes the *Lurch Web Platform*, a system of tools the authors have created as part of a project to upgrade *Lurch* from a desktop application to a web application. That system of tools is available on GitHub for other mathematical software developers to use in their own projects. It includes a web editor with mathematical typesetting, an interface for marking up documents with mathematical (or other structured) meaning, OpenMath support, meaning visualization tools, and document dependence and sharing features, among others.

We conclude with design plans for ongoing development of the web version of *Lurch* that will be built on the *Lurch Web Platform*.

1 Introduction

1.1 Background

From 2008–2012, the authors built a proof-checking word processor called *Lurch*. It is quite different from most of the proof checkers with which the reader may be familiar (e.g., Agda [21], Coq [12], HOL [16], Lean [14]) in two ways. First, its engine is not nearly as sophisticated as the engines in those software packages. Second, its user interface is much more natural, and provides a far lower barrier of entry than any of the packages just listed. Both of these differences stem from the fact that the target audience of *Lurch* is students in their first proof-based course.

We share with Isabelle's PIDE [26] and CalcCheck [17] the common goal of checking students' work and giving immediate feedback to help with learning.

Lurch was supported from 2008–2012 in part by the National Science Foundation's Division of Undergraduate Education, in the Course, Curriculum, and Laboratory Improvement program (grant #0736644). Views expressed in this document are not necessarily those of the National Science Foundation.

H. Geuvers et al. (Eds.): CICM 2017, LNAI 10383, pp. 272–291, 2017.
DOI: 10.1007/978-3-319-62075-6_19

But there are important differences. CalcCheck is wedded to a specific mathematical system, whereas *Lurch* attempts to be more general. And both PIDE and CalcCheck require users to learn a language and/or notation other than that of standard mathematics, and enter it in a plain text editor. Thus the student must learn more than just mathematics; they must also learn to read and write a nonstandard encoding of mathematics as plain text.

In contrast, the *Lurch* interface is a basic word processor in which students write in a natural language, with mathematical symbols or typeset mathematical expressions where they choose to insert them. Users highlight sections of text that contain mathematical statements, reasons, or citations of premises, and mark them as such with a few keystrokes or the mouse. The software then pays attention only to the marked sections, ignoring the natural language text just as a compiler ignores comments. Thus the only language students need to learn to use *Lurch* is standard mathematical notation, and the instructor spends less time teaching software, and more time teaching logic and mathematics.

The current version of the software (version 0.8) is for desktop systems (Mac, Windows, Linux) and is free and open source [8]. It has been very helpful to the authors' students when used in their introduction to proof courses over the past several years, but has some limitations that discourage wider adoption. Those limitations are discussed in Sect. 2.2, and relate to efficiency improvements, bug fixes, and interface innovations.

Consequently the authors are currently rewriting it as a web app to remove those limitations. Much of the web-based development is complete, and in a modular way, so that the components of the web-based application can be reused in other projects. Several reusable components are already available on our GitHub repository [10], including a web-based word processor with typesetting for mathematical expressions, a user interface for marking and connecting document content, OpenMath support, background threads for arbitrary processing of document meaning, Dropbox integration, and more. Collectively, we call this set of modules the *Lurch Web Platform*, and it is currently available for use in other open- or closed-source projects.

1.2 Purpose and Contribution

Offering these resources to the community and documenting their capabilities is the main contribution of this paper. Because Sect. 3 discusses them in detail, it is by far the longest. It also describes the kinds of applications that can be built on the *Lurch Web Platform*, and introduces several demo applications that are available on the same GitHub repository. Screenshots and an overview of each appear in that section, with the intent that other developers who wish to use any of our tools can model their code after that in the demo applications.

One purpose for the *Lurch Web Platform* is to allow us to create a web-based version of our desktop application *Lurch*. To distinguish the two, we will call the web version *webLurch*. That application is still under development, and Sect. 4 describes progress to date as well as the design principles we are following as we build it.

We begin with some background on the current release of *Lurch* (version 0.8, a desktop application), in Sect. 2. That section also covers the limitations of the desktop version that motivate porting it to the web.

2   *Lurch* 0.8

2.1   Capabilities

Lurch is a free and open-source word processor that runs on Windows, Mac, and Linux systems. Users write documents that contain mathematical proofs, and *Lurch* checks each step in those proofs and gives feedback on its correctness. Figure 1 shows a portion of a *Lurch* document, with some proof steps correct and some incorrect. A *Lurch* document may contain any amount of text, formatting, and images, plus meaningful and non-meaningful mathematical content, including proofs.

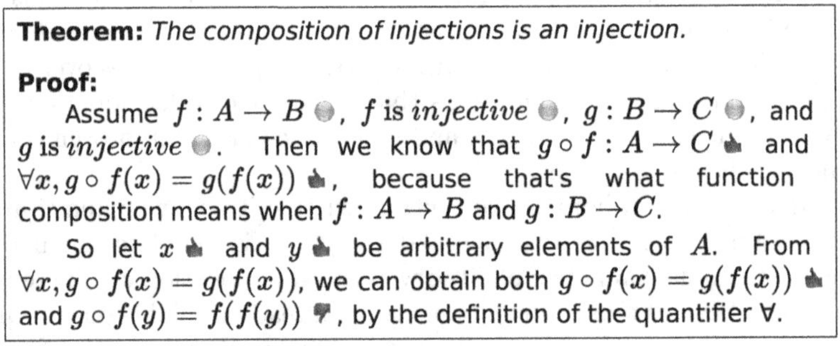

Theorem: *The composition of injections is an injection.*

Proof:
   Assume $f : A \to B$ 🔵, f is *injective* 🔵, $g : B \to C$ 🔵, and g is *injective* 🔵.   Then we know that $g \circ f : A \to C$ 👍 and $\forall x, g \circ f(x) = g(f(x))$ 👍,   because   that's   what   function composition means when $f : A \to B$ and $g : B \to C$.
   So let x 👍 and y 👍 be arbitrary elements of A.   From $\forall x, g \circ f(x) = g(f(x))$, we can obtain both $g \circ f(x) = g(f(x))$ 👍 and $g \circ f(y) = f(f(y))$ 👎, by the definition of the quantifier $\forall$.

Fig. 1. A screenshot of a *Lurch* document in which feedback appears after each step of the user's reasoning. Correct steps are followed by green thumbs-up icons, incorrect steps by red thumbs-down icons, and premises by yellow circles. One error is intentionally included in this proof to show the thumbs-down icon. (Color figure online)

To check the steps of the user's work, *Lurch* needs to know more than a typical word processor does—not just presentation, but semantics. Figure 1 may appear as if the software is reading English, but *Lurch* does not do any natural language processing. Instead, users mark portions of their document (such as mathematical expressions or the names of reasons) as meaningful, and the software pays attention only to those portions when evaluating the user's work.

Figure 2 shows a small portion of a *Lurch* document in which a user has highlighted a mathematical expression and marked it as meaningful. Users can also mark text as a reason (e.g., modus ponens, associativity, etc.) and indicate which meaningful expressions that reason supports. There are a small number of other types of markup not relevant here; see [4] for a full specification.

The red bubble around the expression in Fig. 2 indicates that the user has told *Lurch* to pay attention to the expression's meaning. The label "$\forall$ quantification" indicates that *Lurch* has read the expression and parsed it, and is reporting the main operator (or quantifier) thereof. Bubbles are only shown when the user's

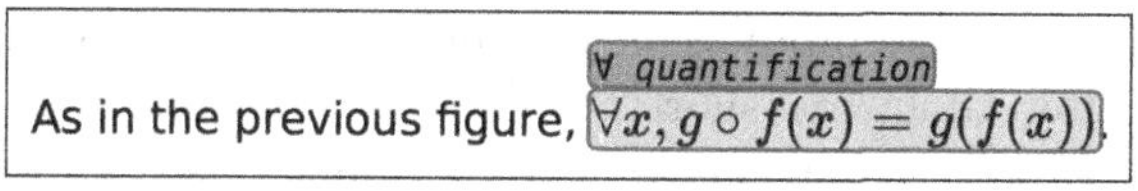

> As in the previous figure, $\forall x, g \circ f(x) = g(f(x))$.
>
> ∀ quantification

Fig. 2. A screenshot of a small fragment of a *Lurch* document showing two features. First, to indicate which text *Lurch* should interpret as meaningful, users highlight the text and click a button to mark it as a meaningful expression, which will be displayed in a red bubble. Second, *Lurch* supports typeset mathematics (via MathJax [11]). (Color figure online)

cursor is inside them, paralleling the behavior of Microsoft *Word*'s equation editor [13] and *LyX*'s math mode [25]. So while Fig. 1 shows no bubbles, that is only because the cursor was not inside any of them when the screenshot was taken. The bubbles exist in the document nonetheless, placed there by its author, one surrounding each step of work.

Authors are thus free to write as much exposition as they like between bubbles, because *Lurch* ignores all text not inside a bubble. This permits both exposition in a natural language and an unambiguous communication of user intentions to the software, with minimal invasiveness on the user's document or workflow.

Lurch is tied to no particular mathematical system. All rules of deduction and axioms are defined (using a hierarchy of bubbles) in *Lurch* documents called *libraries*. Several libraries ship with the software, and users base their own documents on those libraries. Users are free to create new axiom systems or even new logics by writing or modifying libraries. The only hard-coded rules are those for variable scopes and declarations, modeled after the system in [29].

Additional details on the current release of *Lurch* (version 0.8) have been published elsewhere. The project goals and user interface are covered in [6], the data structures and validation routines in [5], the pedagogical aspects in [7], and a detailed specification of system behavior in [4]. The website [8] contains an overview, demo videos, download links, and other details.

2.2 Limitations

While we have had success with version 0.8 in several courses [6,7], it could be improved in several ways. Here are the most important ones.

1. **Interface:** Feedback from users has generated many new user interface ideas and principles that will improve the user experience.
2. **Engine:** *Lurch*'s reasoning system can benefit from a redesign incorporating what we have learned from classroom use and other proof checkers. Implementing that redesign involves significant recoding.
3. **Platform:** Since the current version was first released (2008) web browsers have become much more powerful. Many more applications can now be web-based, and there are many advantages to moving *Lurch* to the web, including ease of accessibility.

4. **Inefficiency:** The more proof steps in a document, the slower *Lurch* validates its content. After about five short proofs, most desktop *Lurch* users need to start a new document to regain the desired application responsiveness. Much of this is due to a single-threaded interpreter on which much of the desktop version was built.

Thus we are in the middle of designing and implementing a web version of the software to address these issues, plus some not listed here. Work in progress can be followed on GitHub at [10].

3 The *Lurch Web Platform*

Having covered *Lurch*'s current capabilities and limitations, we can now move to the heart of this paper. The web version under development is being implemented as a set of modules that include a foundation on which other web-based mathematical software can be built, the *Lurch Web Platform*. Several demo applications illustrating its capabilities exist in the GitHub repository [10]. This section describes those modules and demo applications.

Figure 3 shows the relationships among most of the components in *webLurch*. The set of tools marked as the *Lurch Web Platform* in that figure is the main contribution of the work to date; they are free and open source as part of the *webLurch* project. The subsections that follow each introduce one or more components of the platform and corresponding example applications.

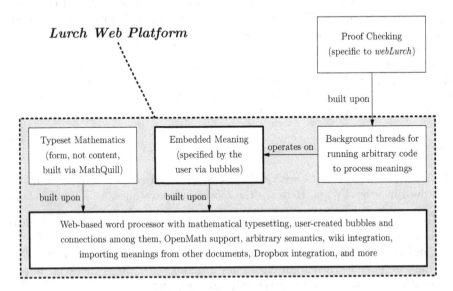

Fig. 3. The relationships among the modules discussed in Sect. 3. The Proof Checking module is specific to the needs of *webLurch*, and is the only module that has not yet been completed; the others are usable in other projects now. The main contribution reported in this paper is the set of modules marked as the *Lurch Web Platform*.

Because our software is to run in a web browser, it must be implemented (eventually) in JavaScript. Our codebase is entirely written in Literate Coffee-Script [1], a variation of Markdown [15] in which all code blocks are interpreted as CoffeeScript, which compiles to JavaScript as part of our build process. GitHub automatically renders Literate CoffeeScript source to attractive HTML so that our source code is self-documenting [10].

JavaScript is one of the most active development ecosystems, due to its broad applicability (front end, back end, desktop, and mobile), and so there are many toolkits one can import into a web application to solve a wide variety of problems. We have imported several into *webLurch*, such as jQuery [24]. But we cover here only the tools we have contributed ourselves, with two exceptions that are too important not to mention.

First, our toolkit is built on the web-based editor TinyMCE [18]. This open source, web-based editor is used by some of the largest web applications, including WordPress, Evernote, and Blackboard. It boasts over 100 million websites to which it has been deployed and over one million hits to its content delivery network per day. Consequently, it is a well-tested and feature-rich foundation on which to build. It can be a simple editor, as shown in Fig. 4, or extended with a variety of available plugins to add new features. Developers can create their own plugins, and several of the components we have developed as part of the *Lurch Web Platform* are TinyMCE plugins. While the figure shows a small editor, it can be configured as a full-screen application, which we do in all of our demo applications.

Second, we add MathQuill [23] to that editor, for WYSIWYG editing of typeset mathematics, using code by a third party, as documented in our codebase [10, **app/eqed** folder]. Thus we do not list it among our accomplishments, but its presence is important to the power of the final product, as well as any tool that others may choose to build on the same foundation.

In the remainder of this section, we discuss the components of *webLurch* that we have built to work with TinyMCE, either as standalone JavaScript libraries

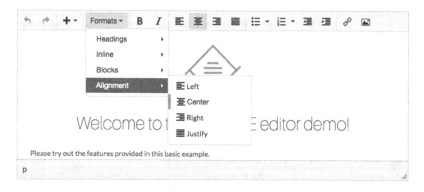

Fig. 4. A screenshot of the TinyMCE editor in a basic configuration, captured from the TinyMCE website [18]

or as TinyMCE plugins. The work completed to date is summarized in Table 1. The following subsections expound on that table.

These features are showcased in the following five demo applications, which have already been built using the *Lurch Web Platform*. They can be used by other developers as starting points (or templates) for their own work.

1. **Simple Example:** The Hello World application of the *Lurch Web Platform*. Includes typesetting of mathematical expressions and visualization of simple semantic markup.
2. **Complex Example:** Defines two types of markup. Illustrates how to create background computations and interface extensions.
3. **Math Evaluator:** Documents can contain mathematical expressions. The application can compute their OpenMath semantics and display or evaluate it.
4. **OMCD Editor:** An OpenMath Content Dictionary editor, generalizable to other XML formats.
5. **Lean UI:** A simple user interface for the theorem proving engine Lean [14].

These five demo applications are usable live on the project website [9], under the Examples and Demos menu. They are explained further in the following sections.

3.1   The Groups and Connections Interface

Bubbles and Groups. Section 2.1 describes the role of "bubbles" in the user interface for the desktop version of *Lurch*, and Fig. 2 shows how bubbles can

Table 1. Components of our work to date on *webLurch*. The Demo app column tells which of our demo applications showcases the component most readily (though often more than one demo app includes it). All demo apps are accessible from the Examples and Demos menu of the project website [9].

	Section	Location in repository [10]	Demo app
Major contributions			
Groups	3.1	app/groupsplugin.litcoffee	Simple Example
Connections	3.1	app/groupsplugin.litcoffee	Lean UI
Overlays	3.1	app/overlayplugin.litcoffee	all
Parser	3.2	src/parsing-duo.litcoffee	Math Evaluator
OpenMath support	3.2	src/openmath-duo.litcoffee	OMCD Editor
Background processing	3.3	src/background.litcoffee	Complex Example
Dependencies	3.4	app/dependenciesplugin.litcoffee	None
Minor contributions			
Suggestions	3.1	app/main-app-proto-groups-solo.litcoffee	Main app only
Matching algorithm	3.3	src/matching-duo.litcoffee	Main app only
Wiki integration	3.4	app/main-app-import-export-solo.litcoffee	Main app only
Embedding	3.4	app/main-app-import-export-solo.litcoffee and app/main-app-sharing-solo.litcoffee	Main app only
Permalinks	3.4	app/main-app-import-export-solo.litcoffee	Main app only

wrap individual mathematical expressions. But bubbles can also be hierarchically nested, a feature currently used when defining new axioms and rules of logic in *Lurch*. Users can impact how *Lurch* computes the meanings of bubbles by editing the properties of each bubble in the hierarchy. Details appear in [4,5].

Thus the bubble interface paradigm is a lightweight way to add to a word processor's documents arbitrary hierarchical information with precise, user-defined meaning. As an example, consider Fig. 5, which comes from the desktop application *Lurch*. It shows an instructor's definition of the function notation $f : A \to B$ in terms of ordered pairs and cartesian products. The software constructs meaning from the bubbled structure in a way specific to *Lurch*, but the meaning-making process could be different in another application with a similar user interface. Examples of several such applications appear later in this paper.

Undecorated:	**function** $f{:}A{\to}B$ if and only if $f{\subseteq}A{\times}B$ and $\forall x, \exists ! y, (x,y) \in f$
Showing bubbles:	**Iff rule:ion** conclusion, $\subseteq$ expression $f{:}A{\to}B$ if and only if $f{\subseteq}A{\times}B$ and $\forall x, \exists ! y, (x,y) \in f$
Showing boundaries:	(**function** > [[$f{:}A{\to}B$] if and only if [$f{\subseteq}A{\times}B$] and [$\forall x, \exists ! y, (x,y) \in f$]]

Fig. 5. A small portion of a *Lurch* document defining the notation $f : A \to B$, shown three times. On top, the content is as it appears in the document naturally. In the middle, the content is as it appears with the cursor inside the expression $f \subseteq A \times B$, thus with all bubbles containing the cursor shown. On the bottom, the content is as it appears when the user has requested the software to display all bubble boundaries. The first line of each image is shown in blue because that is how the original document author chose to format it. The word "function" in the third copy is shown as (function> to indicate that it is a label for the subsequent definition.

Any software system using such an interface can then use its own custom algorithms for interpreting (or otherwise processing) that hierarchical information. We will cover how to process it in Sect. 3.2, but for now we focus on the interface itself. The bubble paradigm enables software to present attractive, editable documents that are readable easily by humans and readable unambiguously by machines, a powerful combination.

We have been using the informal word bubble until now, but let us be more precise. We will use the term *group* to mean any contiguous region of document content that has been marked by the user as meaningful in some way. We use the related term *bubble* to mean the visual representation in the interface of that data structure. The group persists from its creation until the user chooses to delete it, if ever; but the bubble exists only when the user's cursor is inside the group. This avoids unhelpful visual clutter.

Features. As suggested in Sect. 2.1, *Lurch* has different types of groups, including mathematical expressions (as in Fig. 2), reasons, premises, and others. The details (covered in [4,5]) are not relevant here because developers who wish to use our tools to develop their own software will define their own types of groups with their own meanings.

The groups module in *webLurch* supports all of the following features.

1. arbitrarily many types of groups, each with customizable behavior and visual styling
2. functions for reading and writing the group's content and custom data stored invisibly in the group
3. functions for choosing, showing, or hiding the icons shown at the beginning or ending of a group (such as the validation results in Fig. 1 or the boundaries on the bottom of Fig. 5)
4. events triggered when bubbles and their tags are shown (as in Fig. 2), to which developers can attach custom event handlers to customize appearance and behavior
5. events fired for clicks, double clicks, context menus, etc., on groups, their tags, and their boundaries, to which developers can also attach event handlers

Applications. Although bubbles and groups are only the first module we are introducing, there are several types of applications one could build on the *Lurch Web Platform* using them alone. For instance, a bubble-based interface could be used in a word processor for literate programming. Most of the document would be for human consumption, and only blocks grouped as meaningful would receive syntax highlighting and inclusion in compilation or interpretation.

The demo application entitled Simple Example on our project website demonstrates only the groups module. Keep in mind that our choice of language makes the source code human readable directly from the repository, which serves as documentation for the demo applications.

The Simple Example is intended to be minimal, in that it exemplifies only the groups module, and does so trivially. It computes and logs to the browser console basic information about any group the user forms in the document. Developers wishing to create their own applications based on the *Lurch Web Platform* may wish to start with a copy of this example, then incorporate code from more complex demo applications discussed later in the paper, as needed.

Even that simple demo application has a few other features not built into TinyMCE by default. It supports saving and loading documents in the browser's LocalStorage object using *jsfs* [3] and supports WYSIWYG editing of typeset mathematics using MathQuill [23]. Furthermore, the bubbles and their tags are drawn on top of the document using an invisible HTML element layered on top of the editor that is permeable to mouse and keyboard events. That overlay is a separate TinyMCE plugin we created as part of our project, and supports arbitrary drawing on the document (using the HTML Canvas API), not just bubbles and their tags.

Theorem: *The composition of injections is an injection.*

Proof:

Assume $f: A \to B$, f is injective, $g: B \to C$, and g is   *4 assumptions*
injective. Then we know that $g \circ f: A \to C$ and $\forall x, g \circ f(x) =$ ✓
$g(f(x))$, because that's what function composition means when
$f: A \to B$ and $g: B \to C$.

So let x and y be arbitrary elements of A. From   ✓
$\forall x, g \circ f(x) = g(f(x))$, we can obtain both $g \circ f(x) = g(f(x))$ ✓
and $g \circ f(y) = f(f(y))$, by the definition of the quantifier $\forall$.

Wrong use of $\forall$

Fig. 6. A mock-up showing how feedback could be styled to look like hand-written feedback from an instructor. The proof is the same as that in Fig. 1, but with the feedback written in a more human way.

In the future, we plan to use that transparent overlay for more than just bubble drawing. For instance, we can give students feedback in a way that imitates how an instructor writes on a paper assignment. A mock-up of such an interface appears in Fig. 6. Applications built on the *Lurch Web Platform* can use the overlay to decorate a user's document with arbitrary visual information, an idea we will return to in Sect. 4. In fact, the connections described in the next section are also drawn using the same transparent overlay.

Connections. User feedback from the desktop version of *Lurch* caused us to design into *webLurch* the notion of connections among groups. In Fig. 5 we saw a primitive way to connect labels (in that case the word function) to meaningful expressions (in that case the rule being defined). The visual indicator (the angle bracket on the right edge of the word function) connects the label to the subsequent meaningful expression.

A more flexible and attractive means of connecting groups would be an arbitrary directed graph on the groups in a document, so we added that feature to the groups module in the *Lurch Web Platform*. A screenshot appears in Fig. 7.

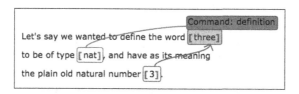

Fig. 7. A portion of a *webLurch* document with three groups and two directed connections among them. This document comes from the Lean UI demo application described at the end of Sect. 3.1 and online at [9].

Just as we made a distinction between groups and bubbles (the former being the data and the latter being its visual representation), we make the same distinction here. A *connection* is the data relating two groups, and persists from when a user creates it until he or she deletes it, if ever. An *arrow* is the visual representation of that connection, shown only when the user's cursor is in one of the bubbles involved in the connection.

As the figure exemplifies, the flexibility of the connections mechanism allows the user to write documents with whatever natural language structure or flow makes the most sense for a human reader, and then to overlay on it indications of the meaning that the software can process in lieu of understanding the natural language. The two major benefits of this flexible interface are complete lack of ambiguity and no limitation to any particular natural language (or set thereof).

To see an application demonstrating the value of the connections paradigm, visit the website [9] and read the tutorial for the Lean UI demo application on the Examples and Demos menu. It integrates a JavaScript version of the engine from Lean [14] into an interface built on the *Lurch Web Platform*. Figure 8 shows an example Lean proof written using that demo application. The cursor is not inside any group, so no bubbles are shown, but positive feedback (in the form of a green check) is shown for each expression, because none gave errors when run through the Lean engine. To see all the groups and connections in the document, refer to the tutorial just mentioned.

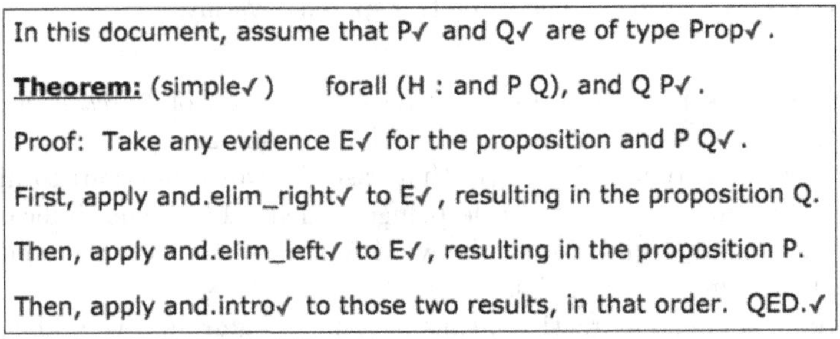

In this document, assume that P✓ and Q✓ are of type Prop✓ .

Theorem: (simple✓)   forall (H : and P Q), and Q P✓ .

Proof: Take any evidence E✓ for the proposition and P Q✓ .

First, apply and.elim_right✓ to E✓ , resulting in the proposition Q.

Then, apply and.elim_left✓ to E✓ , resulting in the proposition P.

Then, apply and.intro✓ to those two results, in that order. QED.✓

Fig. 8. An example proof using the Lean UI demo application in the *webLurch* source code repository. See the end of Sect. 3.1 for a partial explanation, or the website [9] for a full tutorial. (Color figure online)

That application is a proof of concept; the interface is not optimal for a Lean power user, but it shows the type of interface that our tools make possible, which may be more intuitive to students than Lean syntax. It could also be streamlined and enhanced; it is merely a prototype created to showcase the groups and connections features. It also shows some TinyMCE features, such as customizing the toolbars and monitoring user typing to do custom replacements, such as replacing \neq with $\neq$.

3.2 Computing Meaning

From the Document to Semantics. The previous section showed that groups and connections give users great flexibility for how to write documents that can be read and understood easily by both humans and computers. But how does the system make meaning from the groups and connections the user has placed in the document?

Each application built on the *Lurch Web Platform* can define how it processes groups and connections. In the desktop release of *Lurch*, each time a meaningful expression changes, its meaning is recomputed, and each step of reasoning in the document is re-checked to see if it remains valid after the updates to groups' meanings. The meanings themselves depend in part on the contents of the groups (sometimes via a parser) and in part on data not in the document proper (such as the contents of bubble tags, or the types of the groups).

Although *webLurch* is still in development, it behaves very similarly (with some efficiencies not present in the desktop version). But other applications built on the *Lurch Web Platform* need not behave the same way; many of the demo applications differ from one another in this regard.

Toward this end, the *Lurch Web Platform* provides three features. First, developers can install handlers that react to various events generated by groups, including content changes, changes in internal data, and mouse events. Meaning can be computed from any of these sources of data, and stored as internal data in the appropriate group.

Second, a simple implementation of the Earley parsing algorithm is included in the *Lurch Web Platform* for situations in which the meaning-making process will include parsing. Finally, the *Lurch Web Platform* includes a function for converting the typeset mathematical notation used in MathQuill into its most likely or natural meaning, as an OpenMath data structure. Thus for many common mathematical applications, tools are already included for converting standard notation to the desired meaning.

As the previous paragraph suggests, a partial JavaScript implementation of OpenMath is therefore included in the *Lurch Web Platform*. Contributions that complete it (or replace it) are welcome.

Computation. Readers interested in seeing the features described in this section used in a simple demo application should view the Math Evaluator application on the website [9]. Users can input typeset mathematics, wrap it in a group, then use the group's context menu to see the OpenMath XML form of the expression or to evaluate the expression numerically.

Although such an application is hardly exciting to an end user, its purpose is to show how all the features mentioned so far in this section (as well as several from the previous section) appear in code. Developers can use the application as a template to create more complex applications with similar features. Even so, such a demo application illustrates how useful the *Lurch Web Platform* can be as an interface to any of the many computational mathematics software applications in existence.

XML Data Creation. A second demo application using the features in this section is one for authoring OpenMath Content Dictionaries, available at the same website [9], under the heading OMCD Editor. A screenshot appears in Fig. 9, showing how the XML for an OpenMath Content Dictionary can be generated from the human-readable form edited in the application.

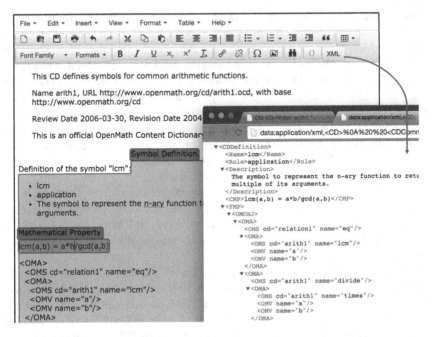

Fig. 9. Screenshot from the OpenMath Content Dictionary Editor demo application on our project website [9]. The red arrow indicates that using the XML button on the toolbar generates XML in a new browser tab, for saving or exporting using the browser. (Color figure online)

That demo application uses an XML Groups module to which the developer must provide a data structure defining the types of nodes in the hierarchy, the rules of which types must/can/cannot be placed inside which others, and what feedback should be shown to the user if constraints are violated.

The XML Groups module can work for many XML formats, of which OpenMath Content Dictionaries are just one example. One could envision a similar editor being created for any XML format, such as MathBook XML [2] or MMT [22]. In fact, for any XML Document Type Definition, one might programmatically convert it to a *Lurch Web Platform*-based application that allows a user to write documents of that form in a user-friendly way, and prevents creation of invalid documents.

3.3 Processing Computed Meaning

Timing. The Lean UI demo application and the OpenMath Content Dictionary demo application introduced in the previous section process the meanings of the groups in a document in the same way: When the user requests it, the application converts the entire document into another format (Lean code in one case, XML in the other), then sends it to some other destination (the Lean engine in one case, and the browser for display in the other). But an application need not wait for a user's action before processing document meaning.

The (incomplete) *webLurch* application monitors the user's document for changes as they happen and updates the meanings of only what groups have changed, then updates the validation results for those same groups and any groups that depend on them. A computational application might be of either of these two types, or something different still, depending on its nature.

Consider an application that, like *webLurch*, must respond efficiently in real time to the user's edits, keeping the feedback shown in the document up-to-date with any changes the user makes (like most spreadsheets do, for example). Three main challenges arise in such a situation.

1. Processing document content may be time consuming, and thus it should be done in a background thread when possible. Since more than one computation may be waiting to be run, multiple background threads should be used to the degree supported by the underlying hardware.
2. Because the result of one background computation may be used as input for another, that dependency graph must be respected by any algorithm that dispatches work to background threads. That algorithm must know when it can process two groups in parallel and when they must be done sequentially.
3. While computations are being run, the user may modify the document. For example, if the user has just edited group X, and the system is computing the consequences of that change by processing group X in some way, before that processing is complete the user may edit group X again, or another group Y that influences X or is influenced by it. The system should be intelligent enough to terminate and then restart the processing of group X in such a situation (rather than continuing to invest resources in processing stale data). This issue is also intertwined with the previous.

The Background Module. We have implemented a system that meets these challenges, as a module in our source code repository (called Background), using the Web Workers feature of modern browsers [28]. Its API permits clients to register arbitrary functions for processing groups and to specify dependencies among such computations. The system then correctly organizes such computations in series or in parallel. It terminates running computations early if their data has become stale, and moves queued computations to the back of the queue if their data depends on the results of other processes waiting in the queue.

A demo application showcasing just the elementary features of this background processing appears on our website with the others [9], and is entitled

Complex Example. It does simple computations, but artificially delays them to take one second each (by repeating the computation constantly until one second has elapsed) in order to test how the background module handles lengthier, processor-intensive computations. The application uses visual indicators to show that background processing is happening, and replaces those indicators with computation results when they become available.

Developers who wish to use this feature can model their code after that of the Complex Example demo application. It also shows how to register more than one type of group, decorate group ending boundaries with visual feedback, modify group contents, and extend the menu shown when the user clicks the tag over a bubble.

3.4   Document Import, Export, and Sharing

Document Storage. The nature of a web editor makes cloud storage of documents essential. The current default storage solution for *webLurch* is the browser's LocalStorage object, which is permanent, but within the browser only.

One can also share *webLurch* documents via permalinks. The entire contents of the document are encoded in the query string of a URL, which is then passed through the Google URL shortener, generating a short link that permanently refers to a specific document. In such a paradigm, the Google URL shortener is a kind of cloud storage platform. This solution is built into the *Lurch Web Platform*, and thus all applications built on it. From the File menu, a user chooses "Share document..." and obtains the dialog box shown in Fig. 10, the top half of which gives the permalink.

Fig. 10. The *webLurch* application dialog for sharing documents via permalinks or HTML code for embedding in web pages. The particular permalink shown in this figure is to an empty document, and only the beginning of the embedding code is visible in the screenshot.

It is also useful to be able to embed small *webLurch* application instances inside other web pages. For instance, a tutorial site on how to use the software (or a particular mathematical system within it) may wish to include an instance of the actual application in the tutorial, with specific content pre-loaded. This solution, too, is implemented by the dialog box in Fig. 10; its bottom half contains the HTML embedding code for the current document. Several pages of the Users' Guide, available from the Authors menu of the project website [9], use this feature.

A simple Dropbox integration is complete, but not a full one, and Google Drive integration is in process. Naturally, contributions to these efforts from other developers are welcome.

Dependencies. Most programming languages contain the notion of importing the data and algorithms defined in one or more other source code files into the current source code file. This notion is important in software like *Lurch*, in which a student's homework might begin by importing all the theorems and axioms the student has been taught at that point in the course. When a document A wishes to import a document B, we say that A *depends on* B, or that B is a *dependency* of A.

To be able to import dependencies requires some kind of publicly accessible cloud storage for *webLurch* documents. Although the permalinks mentioned above could serve this purpose, they would have a significant downside. If an author updates a dependency, then the new version necessarily has a different permalink than the original, and so no document that depends on the original would see the author's updates, unless they were each manually updated to import the new version. It would be more desirable, when a dependency added improvements or fixed errors, that those benefits propagated automatically to all documents using that dependency.

One obstacle to solving this problem are the security measures built into the modern web. Client-side JavaScript loaded from a website cannot typically load resources from a different domain. To permit such loading, the Cross-Origin Request Sharing (CORS) specification was created [27]. Thus if *webLurch* were to distribute documents and dependencies across various websites, each would need to follow the protocol in that specification to explicitly allow access by all the others. In many cases, the user sharing the file may not even have authority to change the CORS permissions for the entire site. We therefore solve this problem a different way, using a wiki.

Wiki Integration. We have created a means for public cloud storage on the same server on which the *webLurch* application itself is running, a wiki with the following properties.

1. It is an instance of MediaWiki [20], extended with per-page permissions and visibility based on user accounts [19].

2. Although the *webLurch* application is not yet near completion, it can already export files directly to such a wiki running on the same server as the application itself, using a command on the File menu. Each such exported file becomes a page in the wiki. Because *webLurch* documents are just HTML, they can be stored and shown in a wiki exactly the same way they appeared in *webLurch* itself, except without the overlaid bubbles and arrows.

3. To support such exporting, *webLurch* lets the user specify their wiki credentials in the *webLurch* settings, so that it can automatically protect their pages with the appropriate permissions. Initially, each such exported file is private to its author only.

4. Users who have created wiki pages by exporting them from *webLurch* documents can choose to make any subset of them public on a page-by-page basis, and share the URL with others. Read and write permissions can be set separately, on a user-by-user basis.

5. Users with read access to a wiki page can simply use the URL for that page as a dependency in the *webLurch* application.

6. Users with write access to a wiki page will find a link in the wiki sidebar for editing the page in *webLurch*. If the user follows that link, then edits the document, *webLurch* tracks the document's origin so that the user can easily push the changes back, updating the wiki page.

7. If such a user attempts to edit an exported *webLurch* document directly in the wiki using the wiki's editor, it shows a warning encouraging the user to use *webLurch* as the editor instead.

These features are implemented and are part of our source code repository, but are not yet deployed on a server that is open to the public, because the main *webLurch* application is still in the early stages of development. The application, without wiki integration enabled, is available for testing on GitHub [9].

Users who wish to try it out should consider walking through the tutorials under the Authors section on that website, which covers the features that have been implemented so far. The initial steps we have completed on the main application can be considered the final demo application covered in this paper, because it includes several features that do not show up in any of the other demo applications, such as the Dropbox integration mentioned earlier.

4   Future Work

The focus of this paper has been on the *Lurch Web Platform*—reusable software tools we have developed as part of our work upgrading and rewriting *Lurch* for the web. This should be useful to anyone who wishes to develop web-based software that involves editing a document with typeset mathematical notation and processing some corresponding mathematical meaning, but of course it is only part of our work. Since we are still at work using these features to complete *webLurch*, this paper would not be complete without sharing briefly our vision for doing so. We do so by describing the main differences we have planned between the desktop and web versions.

As stated in Sect. 2.2, there were some limitations to *Lurch* version 0.8 that motivated a redesign. The nature of those limitations required a full rewrite of the application for the web, which gives us the opportunity to change or improve many other aspects of the software. We describe the most significant improvements in the remainder of this section.

First, *Lurch* version 0.8 contains just one mathematical notation, hard-coded into the software. There is just one parsing algorithm, and each symbol can be used in just one way. Instructors can write whatever axioms they like to govern the meaning of the symbols, and share those axioms with their students, but the notation is fixed. In *webLurch* we are moving to fully user-defined notation. Although this feature exists in other software systems, and is thus nothing new, our goals in *Lurch* include user interface constraints on each user-facing feature. So our design for giving the user the power to create languages cannot require an overly technical interface.

We are prioritizing the design principle that mathematical objects should be first-class citizens, with mathematical terminology foremost in the application. For instance, the terminology of groups, bubbles, connections, and arrows mentioned throughout this paper is language for developers, not end users. Student (and even instructor) users should be thinking only of mathematics, not software. So, for instance, a *Lurch* software tutorial should not use the words group or bubble, but instead refer to the group's meaning to the user, such as a mathematical expression or a premise citation.

In the same spirit, we are aiming for user feedback to be even more similar to what an instructor would give on a paper assignment. Rather than expect student users to learn the lights and thumbs symbols in Fig. 1, we should use the overlay module discussed at the end of Sect. 3.1 to draw on top of the user's document with the same style of positive and negative feedback that an instructor would give when marking up a student's paper homework. We aim to make the *webLurch* user experience similar to mathematical work done without a computer, except with the benefits of frequent and immediate feedback the computer can provide. This should help the user more easily transfer what they learn from *webLurch* to their mathematical work on paper.

Although the bubble user interface is very easy for users to learn and imposes a minimal burden on them, we wish to make it even easier. A user writing a lengthy proof may create as many as 100 groups. Doing so requires first selecting the content to be grouped, by mouse or keyboard actions (or thinking ahead to create the group before typing its content), using a keyboard shortcut or toolbar button to form the group, then an arrow key or mouse click to move the cursor outside the group before typing further. This could clearly be streamlined. We do so in *webLurch* in two ways.

We have recently prototyped a feature in which the software watches what the user is typing and makes reasonable guesses about when the user has typed meaningful mathematical content, and what type of content it is. The software then presents these suggestions in the form of new groups and connections, drawn with dashed lines to show that they do not truly exist yet, but are just suggestions. The user can confirm with a single keystroke, or simply ignore the suggestion. If the user accepts the suggestion, the software places the cursor immediately after the changes so the user can just keep typing.

Additionally, certain specific types of *Lurch* document content have more formalized syntax than others. While the most general form of a document is the largely unstructured, prose-like form shown in Fig. 1, some courses may be teaching formal logical systems with line-numbered proofs, no explanatory text, and a rigid form for citing reasons and premises on each line. In such circumstances, the instructor should be able to specify such a form, and the software would then be able to automatically create all the groups and connections on each line of a proof just by analyzing its syntactic content. The user should not need to do anything other than type the line. This feature, which can be enabled, disabled, and customized on a per-document basis, is also planned for inclusion in *webLurch*, as another way of focusing the end user's work on mathematical content rather than the software in which the mathematics is taking place.

These are a sample of our design ideas for the *webLurch* application, all of which we will implement on the *Lurch Web Platform* described in this paper. They represent significant improvements over the desktop application, and together with the ease of access of web applications, should make it much easier for instructors to adopt *Lurch* into their courses and customize it in a way that will benefit their students the most.

References

1. Ashkenas, J.: Literate CoffeeScript, February 2013. http://coffeescript.org/#literate
2. Beezer, R.A.: MathBook XML Author's Guide, March 2017. http://mathbook.pugetsound.edu/doc/author-guide/mathbook-author-guide.pdf
3. Carter, N.: jsfs: a (small) filesystem stored in the browser's LocalStorage. A free and open source software project, May 2015. http://github.com/nathancarter/jsfs
4. Carter, N., Monks, K.G.: Introduction to Lurch: advanced users guide (2012). http://lurchmath.org/AUG-v1.html
5. Carter, N., Monks, K.G.: Lurch: a word processor built on OpenMath that can check mathematical reasoning. In: Lange, C., et al. (eds.) Workshops and Work in Progress at CICM, EEEE 1010. CEUR Workshop Proceedings (2013)
6. Carter, N., Monks, K.G.: Lurch: a word processor that can grade students' proofs. In: Lange, C., et al. (eds.) Workshops and Work in Progress at CICM, FFFFF 1010. CEUR Workshop Proceedings (2013)
7. Carter, N., Monks, K.G.: From formal to expository: using the proof-checking word processor Lurch to teach proof writing. In: Schwell, R., Franko, J., Steurer, A. (eds.) Beyond Lecture: Resources and Pedagogical Techniques for Enhancing the Teaching of Proof-Writing Across the Curriculum. Mathematical Association of America (2015)
8. Carter, N., Monks, K.G.: Lurch: a word processor that can check your math. A free and open source software project, March 2017. http://lurchmath.org
9. Carter, N., Monks, K.G.: webLurch: a web-based word processor that can check your math. A free and open source software project under development, March 2017. http://nathancarter.github.io/weblurch

10. Carter, N., Monks, K.G.: GitHub repository for the webLurch project (2017). https://github.com/nathancarter/weblurch
11. Cervone, D., et al.: MathJax: beautiful math in all browsers. A free and open source software project (2017). http://mathjax.org
12. The Coq Development Team: The Coq proof assistant reference manual version 0.8 (2004). http://coq.inria.fr
13. Microsoft Corporation: Microsoft office support: write an equation (2017). https://support.office.com/en-us/article/Write-an-equation-88e01bd4-54c5-4cf7-af83-8601084bf919
14. de Moura, L., Kong, S., Avigad, J., van Doorn, F., von Raumer, J.: The lean theorem prover. In: 25th International Conference on Automated Deduction (CADE-25) (2015)
15. Gruber, J.: Markdown, December 2004. https://daringfireball.net/projects/markdown/
16. Harrison, J.: The HOL Light system reference, October 2016. https://github.com/jrh13/hol-light/
17. Kahl, W.: The teaching tool CALCCHECK a proof-checker for Gries and Schneider's "Logical Approach to Discrete Math". In: Jouannaud, J.-P., Shao, Z. (eds.) CPP 2011. LNCS, vol. 7086, pp. 216–230. Springer, Heidelberg (2011). doi:10.1007/978-3-642-25379-9_17
18. TinyMCE, J.L., et al.: JavaScript WYSIWYG editor. A free and open source software project (2017). http://tinymce.com
19. MediaWiki: Extension:articleprotection – MediaWiki, the free wiki engine (2015). https://www.mediawiki.org/w/index.php?title=Extension:ArticleProtection&oldid=1487335
20. MediaWiki: MediaWiki – MediaWiki, the free wiki engine (2016). http://www.mediawiki.org/
21. Norell, U.: Dependently typed programming in Agda. In: Koopman, P., Plasmeijer, R., Swierstra, D. (eds.) AFP 2008. LNCS, vol. 5832, pp. 230–266. Springer, Heidelberg (2009). doi:10.1007/978-3-642-04652-0_5
22. Rabe, F., Kohlhase, M.: A scalable module system. Inf. Comput. **230**, 1–54 (2013)
23. Seoul-Oh, H., Adkisson, J.: MathQuill: WYSIWYG math with only HTML, CSS, and JS. A free and open source software project, February 2017. http://mathquill.com
24. The jQuery Foundation: jQuery API Documentation, June 2016. https://api.jquery.com/
25. The LyX Team: LyX 1.6.1 - The Document Processor [Computer software and manual]. Internet (2009). http://www.lyx.org. Accessed 16 Feb 2009
26. Wenzel, M., Wol, B.: Isabelle/PIDE as platform for educational tools. In: Workshop on Computer Theorem Proving Components for Educational Software (THedu 2011). Electronic Proceedings in Theoretical Computer Science, vol. 79 (2012). doi:10.4204/EPTCS.79.9
27. The World Wide Web Consortium: Cross-origin resource sharing, W3C recommendation 16, January 2014. https://www.w3.org/TR/cors/
28. The World Wide Web Consortium: Web workers, W3C working draft 24, September 2015. https://www.w3.org/TR/2015/WD-workers-20150924/
29. Velleman, D.J.: Variable declarations in natural deduction. Ann. Pure Appl. Logic **144**(1–3), 133–146 (2006). doi:10.1016/j.apal.2006.05.009

ENIGMA: Efficient Learning-Based Inference Guiding Machine

Jan Jakubův[(✉)] and Josef Urban

Czech Technical University in Prague, Prague, Czech Republic
jakubuv@gmail.com, josef.urban@gmail.com

Abstract. ENIGMA is a learning-based method for guiding given clause selection in saturation-based theorem provers. Clauses from many previous proof searches are classified as *positive* and *negative* based on their participation in the proofs. An efficient classification model is trained on this data, classifying a clause as *useful* or *un-useful* for the proof search. This learned classification is used to guide next proof searches prioritizing useful clauses among other generated clauses. The approach is evaluated on the E prover and the CASC 2016 AIM benchmark, showing a large increase of E's performance.

1 Introduction: Theorem Proving and Learning

State-of-the-art resolution/superposition automated theorem provers (ATPs) such as Vampire [16] and E [21] are today's most advanced tools for general reasoning across a variety of mathematical and scientific domains. The stronger the performance of such tools, the more realistic become tasks such as full computer understanding and automated development of complicated mathematical theories, and verification of software, hardware and engineering designs. While performance of ATPs has steadily grown over the past years due to a number of human-designed improvements, it is still on average far behind the performance of trained mathematicians. Their advanced knowledge-based proof finding is an enigma, which is unlikely to be deciphered and programmed completely manually in near future.

On large corpora such as Flyspeck, Mizar and Isabelle, the ATP progress has been mainly due to learning how to select the most relevant knowledge, based on many previous proofs [1,2,10,12]. Learning from many proofs has also recently become a very useful method for an automated finding of parameters of ATP strategies [9,17,20,23], and for a learning of sequences of tactics in interactive theorem provers (ITPs) [7]. Several experiments with the compact leanCoP [19] system have recently shown that directly using a trained machine learner for an internal clause selection can significantly prune the search space and solve additional problems [5,11,25]. An obvious next step is to implement efficient learning-based clause selection also inside the strongest superposition-based ATPs.

In this work, we introduce ENIGMA – *Efficient learNing-based Internal Guidance MAchine* for state-of-the-art saturation-based ATPs. The method applies

© Springer International Publishing AG 2017
H. Geuvers et al. (Eds.): CICM 2017, LNAI 10383, pp. 292–302, 2017.
DOI: 10.1007/978-3-319-62075-6_20

fast machine learning algorithms to a large number of proofs, and uses the trained classifier together with simpler heuristics to evaluate the millions of clauses generated during the resolution/superposition proof search. This way, the theorem prover automatically takes into account thousands of previous successes and failures that it has seen in previous problems, similarly to trained humans. Thanks to a carefully chosen efficient learning/evaluation method and its tight integration with the core ATP (in our case the E prover[1]), the penalty for this ubiquitous knowledge-based internal proof guidance is very low. This in turn very significantly improves the performance of E in terms of the number of solved problems in the CASC 2016 AIM benchmark [22].

2 Preliminaries

We use $\mathbb{N}$ to denote the set of natural numbers including 0. When S is a finite set then $|S|$ denotes its size, and S^n where $n \in \mathbb{N}$ is the n-ary Cartesian product of S, that is, the set of all vectors of size n with members from S. When $\mathbf{x} \in S^n$ then we use notation $\mathbf{x}_{[i]}$ to denote its i-th member, counting indexes from 1. We use $\mathbf{x}^T$ to denote the transposed vector.

A Multiset M over a set S is represented by a total function from S to $\mathbb{N}$, that is, $M(s)$ is the count of $s \in S$ in M. The union $M_1 \cup M_2$ of two multisets M_1 and M_2 over S is the multiset represented by the function $(M_1 \cup M_2)(s) = M_1(s) + M_2(s)$ for all $s \in S$. We use the notation $\{s_1 \mapsto n_1, \ldots, s_k \mapsto n_k\}$ to describe a multiset, omitting the members with count 0.

We assume a fixed first-order theory with stable symbol names, and denote Σ its signature, that is, a set of symbols with assigned arities. We use L to range over the set of all first-order literals (LITERAL), C to range over the set of all first-order clauses (CLAUSE). Finally, we use $\mathbf{C}$ to range over sets of clauses (CLAUSES).

3 Training Clause Classifiers

There are many different machine learning methods, with different function spaces they can explore, different training and evaluation speeds, etc. Based on our previous experiments with premise selection and with guiding leanCoP [11,25], we have decided to choose a very fast and scalable learning method for the first ENIGMA instantiation. While more expressive learning methods usually lead to stronger single-strategy ATP results, very important aspects of our domain are that (i) the learning and proving evolve together in a feedback loop [24] where fast learning is useful, and (ii) combinations of multiple strategies – which can be provided by learning in different ways from different proofs – usually solve much more problems than the best strategy.

After several experiments, we have chosen LIBLINEAR: open source library [4] for large-scale linear classification. This section describes how we use LIBLINEAR

---

[1] We use E Prover 1.9.1 (http://www.eprover.org/).

to train a clause classifier to guide a given clause selection. Section 3.1 describes how training examples can be obtained from ATP runs. Section 3.2 describes how clauses are represented as fixed-length feature vectors. Finally, Sect. 3.3 describes how to use LIBLINEAR to train a clause classifier.

3.1 Extracting Training Examples from ATP Runs

Suppose we run a saturation-based ATP to prove a conjecture φ in theory T. When the ATP successfully terminates with a proof, we can extract training examples from this particular proof search as follows. We collect all the clauses that were selected as given clauses during the proof search. From these clauses, those which appear in the final proof are classified as *positives* while the remaining given clauses as *negative*. This gives us two sets of clauses, positive clauses $\mathbf{C}^{\boxplus}$ and negative clauses $\mathbf{C}^{\boxminus}$.

Re-running the proof search using the information $(\mathbf{C}^{\boxplus}, \mathbf{C}^{\boxminus})$ to prefer clauses from $\mathbf{C}^{\boxplus}$ as given clauses should significantly shorten the proof search. The challenge is to generalize this knowledge to be able to prove new problems which are in some sense similar. To achieve that, the positive and negative clauses extracted from proof runs on many related problems are combined and learned from jointly.

3.2 Encoding Clauses by Features

In order to use LIBLINEAR for linear classification (Sect. 3.3), we need to represent clauses as finite *feature vectors*. For our purposes, a feature vector $\mathbf{x}$ representing a clause C is a fixed-length vector of natural numbers whose i-th member $\mathbf{x}_{[i]}$ specifies how often the i-th feature appears in the clause C.

Several choices of clause features are possible [14], for example sub-terms, their generalizations, or paths in term trees. In this work we use term walks of length 3 as follows. First we construct a feature vector for every literal L in the clause C. We write the literal L as a tree where nodes are labeled by the symbols from Σ. In order to deal with possibly infinite number of variables and Skolem symbols, we substitute all variables and Skolem symbols with special symbols. We count for each triple of symbols $(s_1, s_2, s_3) \in \Sigma^3$, the number of directed node paths of length 3 in the literal tree, provided the trees are oriented from the root. Finally, to construct the feature vector of clause C, we sum the vectors of all literals $L \in C$.

More formally as follows. We consider a fixed theory T, hence we have a fixed signature Σ. We extend Σ with 4 special symbols for variables (⊛), Skolem symbols (⊙), positive literals (⊕), and negative literals (⊖). A *feature* ϕ is a triple of symbols from Σ. The set of all features is denoted FEATURE, that is, FEATURE $= \Sigma^3$. *Clause (or literal) features* Φ is a multiset of features, thus recording for each feature how many times it appears in a literal or a clause. We use Φ to range over literal/clause features and the set of all literal/clause features (that is, feature multisets) is denoted FEATURES. Recall that we represent multisets as total functions from FEATURE to $\mathbb{N}$. Hence every member

$\Phi \in$ FEATURES is a total function of the type "FEATURES $\rightarrow$ N" and we can write $\Phi(\phi)$ to denote the count of ϕ in Φ.

Now it is easy to define function *features* of the type "LITERAL $\rightarrow$ FEATURES" which extracts features Φ from a literal L. For a literal L, we construct a rooted *feature tree* with nodes labeled by the symbols from Σ. The feature tree basically corresponds to the tree representing literal L with the following exceptions. The root node of the tree is labeled by $\oplus$ iff L is a positive literal, otherwise it is labeled by $\ominus$. Furthermore, all variable nodes are labeled by the symbol $\circledast$ and all nodes corresponding to Skolem symbols are labeled by the symbol $\odot$.

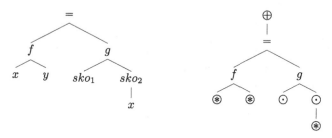

Fig. 1. The tree representing literal L_1 from Example 1 (left) and its corresponding feature tree (right).

Example 1. Consider the following equality literal $L_1 : f(x, y) = g(sko_1, sko_2(x))$ with Skolem symbols sko_1 and sko_2, and with variables x and y. In Fig. 1, the tree representation of L_1 is depicted on the left, while the corresponding feature tree used to collect features is shown on the right. $\qquad \square$

Function *features* constructs the feature tree of a literal L and collects all directed paths of length 3. It returns the result as a feature multiset Φ.

Example 2. For literal $L_2 : P(x)$ we obtain *features*$(L_2) = \{(\oplus, P, \circledast) \mapsto 1\}$. For literal $L_3 : \neg Q(x, y)$ we have *features*$(\neg Q(x, y)) = \{(\ominus, Q, \circledast) \mapsto 2\}$. Finally, for literal L_1 from Example 1 we obtain the following multiset.

$$\{(\oplus, =, f) \mapsto 1 \, , \quad (\oplus, =, g) \mapsto 1 \, , \quad (=, f, \circledast) \mapsto 2 \, , \quad (=, g, \odot) \mapsto 2 \, , \quad (g, \odot, \circledast) \mapsto 1\}$$

$\qquad \square$

Finally, the function *features* is extended to clauses (*features* : CLAUSE $\rightarrow$ FEATURES) by multiset union as *features*$(C) = \bigcup_{L \in C}$ *features*(L).

A Technical Note on Feature Vector Representation. In order to use LIBLINEAR, we transform the feature multiset Φ to a vector of numbers of length |FEATURE|. We assign a natural index to every feature and we construct a vector whose i-th member contains the count $\Phi(\phi)$ where i is the index of feature ϕ. Technically, we construct a bijection *sym* between Σ and $\{0, \ldots, |\Sigma| - 1\}$ which encodes symbols by natural numbers. Then we construct a bijection between

FEATURE and $\{1, \ldots, |\text{FEATURE}|\}$ which encodes features by numbers[2]. Now it is easy to construct a function *vector* which translates Φ to a vector from $\mathbb{N}^{|\text{FEATURE}|}$ as follows:

$$\textit{vector}(\Phi) = \mathbf{x} \text{ such that } \mathbf{x}_{[code(\phi)]} = \Phi(\phi) \text{ for all } \phi \in \text{FEATURE}$$

3.3   Training Clause Classifiers with LIBLINEAR

Once we have the training examples $(\mathbf{C}^{\boxplus}, \mathbf{C}^{\boxminus})$ and encoding of clauses by feature vectors, we can use LIBLINEAR to construct a classification model. LIBLINEAR implements the function *train* of the type "CLAUSES × CLAUSES → MODEL" which takes two sets of clauses (positive and negative examples) and constructs a classification model. Once we have a classification model $\mathcal{M} = \textit{train}(\mathbf{C}_{\boxplus}, \mathbf{C}_{\boxminus})$, LIBLINEAR provides a function *predict* of the type "CLAUSE × MODEL → $\{\boxplus, \boxminus\}$" which can be used to predict clause classification as positive ($\boxplus$) or negative ($\boxminus$).

LIBLINEAR supports several classification methods, but we have so far used only the default solver L2-SVM (L2-regularized L2-loss Support Vector Classification) [3]. Using the functions from the previous section, we can translate the training examples $(\mathbf{C}^{\boxplus}, \mathbf{C}^{\boxminus})$ to the set of instance-label pairs $(\mathbf{x}_i, y_i)$, where $i \in \{1, \ldots, |\mathbf{C}^{\boxplus}| + |\mathbf{C}^{\boxminus}|\}$, $\mathbf{x}_i \in \mathbb{N}^{|\text{FEATURE}|}$, $y_i \in \{\boxplus, \boxminus\}$. A training clause C_i is translated to the feature vector $\mathbf{x}_i = \textit{vector}(\textit{features}(C_i))$ and the corresponding y_i is set to $\boxplus$ if $C_i \in \mathbf{C}^{\boxplus}$ or to $\boxminus$ if $C_i \in \mathbf{C}^{\boxminus}$. Then, LIBLINEAR solves the following optimization problem:

$$\min_{\mathbf{w}} \left(\frac{1}{2} \mathbf{w}^T \mathbf{w} + c \sum_{i=1}^{l} \xi(\mathbf{w}, \mathbf{x_i}, y_i) \right)$$

for $\mathbf{w} \in \mathbb{R}^{|\text{FEATURE}|}$, where $c > 0$ is a penalty parameter and ξ is the following loss function.

$$\xi(\mathbf{w}, \mathbf{x_i}, y_i) = \max(1 - y_i' \mathbf{w}^T \mathbf{x_i}, 0)^2 \text{ where } y_i' = \begin{cases} 1 & \text{iff } y_1 = \boxplus \\ -1 & \text{otherwise} \end{cases}$$

LIBLINEAR implements a coordinate descend method [8] and a trust region Newton method [18].

The model computed by LIBLINEAR is basically the vector $\mathbf{w}$ obtained by solving the above optimization problem. When computing the prediction for a clause C, the clause is translated to the corresponding feature vector $\mathbf{x} = \textit{vector}(\textit{features}(C))$ and LIBLINEAR classifies C as positive ($\boxplus$) iff $\mathbf{w}^T \mathbf{x} > 0$. Hence we see that the prediction can be computed in time $O(\max(|\text{FEATURE}|, \textit{length}(C)))$ where $\textit{length}(C)$ is the length of clause C (number of symbols).

---

[2]   We use $\textit{code}(\phi) = \textit{sym}(\phi_{[1]}) \cdot |\Sigma|^2 + \textit{sym}(\phi_{[2]}) \cdot |\Sigma| + \textit{sym}(\phi_{[3]}) + 1$.

4 Guiding the Proof Search

Once we have a LIBLINEAR model (classifier) $\mathcal{M}$, we construct a clause weight function which can be used inside the ATP given-clause loop to evaluate the generated clauses. As usual, clauses with smaller weight are selected before those with a higher weight. First, we define the function *predict* which assigns a smaller number to positively classified clauses as follows:

$$predict\text{-}weight(C, \mathcal{M}) = \begin{cases} 1 & \text{iff } predict(C, \mathcal{M}) = \boxplus \\ 10 & \text{otherwise} \end{cases}$$

In order to additionally prefer smaller clauses to larger ones, we add the clause length to the above predicted weight. We use $length(C)$ to denote the length of C counted as the number of symbols. Furthermore, we use a real-valued parameter γ to multiply the length as follows.

$$weight(C, \mathcal{M}) = \gamma \cdot length(C) + predict\text{-}weight(C, \mathcal{M})$$

This scheme is designed for the E automated prover which uses *clause evaluation functions* (CEFs) to select the given clause. A clause evaluation function *CEF* is a function which assigns a real weight to a clause. The unprocessed clause with the smallest weight is chosen to be the given clause. E allows combining several CEFs to jointly guide the proof search. This is done by specifying a finite number of CEFs together with their *frequencies* as follows: $(f_1 \star CEF_1, \ldots, f_k \star CEF_k)$. Each frequency f_i denotes how often the corresponding CEF_i is used to select a given clause in this weighted round-robin scheme. We have implemented learning-based guidance as a new CEF given by the above *weight* function. We can either use this new CEF alone or combine it with other CEFs already defined in E.

5 Experimental Evaluation

We use the AIM[3] category of the CASC 2016 competition for evaluation. This benchmark fits our needs as it targets internal guidance in ATPs based on training and testing examples. Before the competition, 1020 training problems were provided for the training of ATPs, while additional 200 problems were used in the competition. Prover9 proofs were provided along with all the training problems. Due to several interesting issues, we have decided not to use the training Prover9 proofs yet and instead find as many proofs as possible by a single E strategy[4].

---

[3] AIM is a long-term and large-scale project [15] in applied automated deduction concerned with proving open algebraic conjectures by Kinyon and Veroff.

[4] Different proof search settings (term orderings, rewriting settings, etc.) may largely change the proof search and make training examples incompatible. That is to say, a classifier trained on proofs produced with some proof search settings should be used only with the same settings. In our case, the proof search settings used to produce competition proofs are not known. Thus we resort to a single E prover strategy and generate compatible training data ourselves.

Using fast preliminary evaluation, we have selected a strong E^5 strategy S_0 (see Appendix A) which can by itself solve 239 training problems with a 30 s time-out. For comparison, E's auto-schedule mode (using optimized strategy scheduling) can solve 261 problems. We train a clause classifier model $\mathcal{M}_0$ (Sect. 3) on the 239 proofs and then run E enhanced with the classifier $\mathcal{M}_0$ in different ways to obtain even more training examples. Either we use the classifier CEF based on $\mathcal{M}_0$ (i.e., function $weight(C, \mathcal{M}_0)$ from Sect. 4) alone, or combine it with the CEFs from S_0 by adding $weight(C, \mathcal{M}_0)$ to S_0 with a grid of frequencies ranging over $\{1,5,6,7,8,9,10,15,20,30,40,50\}$. Furthermore, every combination may be run with a different value of the parameter $\gamma \in \{0, 0.1, 0.2, 0.4, 0.7, 1, 2, 4, 8\}$ of the function $weight(C, \mathcal{M}_0)$. All the methods are run with 30 s time limit, leading to the total of 337 solved training problems. As expected, the numbers of processed clauses and the solving times on the previously solved problems are typically very significantly decreased when using $weight(C, \mathcal{M}_0)$. This is a good sign, however, the ultimate test of ENIGMA's capability to learn and generalize is to evaluate the trained strategies on the testing problems. This is done as follows.

On the 337 solved training problems, we (greedily) find that 4 strategies are needed to cover the whole set. The strongest strategy is our classifier $weight(C, \mathcal{M}_0)$ alone with $\gamma = 0.2$, solving 318 problems. Another 15 problems are added by combining S_0 with the trained classifier $weight(C, \mathcal{M}_0)$ using frequency 50 and $\gamma = 0.2$. Three more new problems are solved by S_0 and two more by the trained classifier alone using $\gamma = 0$. We take these four strategies and use only the proofs they found to train a new enhanced classifier $\mathcal{M}_1$. The proofs yield 6821 positive and 219012 negative examples. Training of $\mathcal{M}_1$ by LIBLINEAR takes about 7 s – 2 s for feature extraction and 5 s for learning. The classifier evaluation on the training examples takes about 6 s and reaches 97.6% accuracy (ratio of the correctly classified clauses).

This means that both the feature generation and the model evaluation times per clause are at the order of 10 s. This is comparable to the speed at which clauses are generated by E on our hardware and evaluated by its built-in heuristics. Our learning-based guidance can thus be quickly trained and used by normal users of E, without expensive training phase or using multiple CPUs or GPUs for clause evaluation.

Then we use the $\mathcal{M}_1$ classifier to attack the 200 competition problems using 180 s time limit as in CASC. We again run several strategies: both $weight(C, \mathcal{M}_1)$ alone and combined with S_0 with different frequencies and parameters γ. All the strategies solve together 52 problems and only 3 of the strategies are needed for this. While S_0 solves only 22 of the competition problems, our strongest strategy solves 41 problems, see Table 1. This strategy combines S_0 with $weight(C, \mathcal{M}_1)$ using frequency 30 and $\gamma = 0.2$. 7 more problems are contributed by $weight(C, \mathcal{M}_1)$ alone with $\gamma = 0.2$ and 4 more problems are added by the E auto-schedule mode. For comparison, Vampire[6] solves 47 problems

---

[5] All the experiments were performed at Intel Xeon 2.3 GHz workstation.

[6] We use Vampire 4.0 in CASC mode.

Table 1. Number of problems from the 200 AIM CASC 2016 competition problems solved by differently parameterized heuristics. Different rows represent different value of γ (0,0.2,8). Columns represent different strategies (auto-schedule is E's default automated mode, 0 stands for S_0 without any Enigma guidance, ∞ stands for $weight(C, \mathcal{M}_1)$ used alone, while other column labeled with f means that $weight(C, \mathcal{M}_1)$ was combined with S_0 with frequency f). Entries with "-" were not run because of time restrictions.

	Auto-schedule	0	1	5	10	15	30	50	∞
0	29	22	-	-	-	-	**18**	17	16
0.2			23	31	32	40	**41**	33	40
8			23	31	31	40	**41**	33	35

(compared to our 52 proofs) with 3*180 s time limit per problem (simulating 3 runs of our best strategies, each with 180 time limit per problem).

5.1 Looping and Boosting

The recent work on the premise-selection task has shown that typically there is not a single optimal way how to guide proof search. Re-learning from new proofs as introduced by MaLARea and combining proofs and learners usually outperforms a single method. Since we are using a very fast classifier here, we can easily experiment with giving it more and different data.

First such experiment is done as follows. We add the proofs obtained on the solved 52 competition problems to the training data obtained from the 337 solved training problems. Instead of immediately re-learning and re-running (as in the MaLARea loop), we however first boost all positive examples (i.e., clauses participating in the proofs) by repeating them ten times in the training data. This way, we inform the learner to more strongly avoid misclassifying the positive examples as negative, than the other way round. The resulting clasifier $\mathcal{M}_2$ has lower overall accuracy on all of the data (93% vs. 98% for the unboosted), however, its accuracy on the relatively rare positive data grows significantly, from 12.5% to 81.8%.

Running the most successful strategy using $\mathcal{M}_2$ instead of $\mathcal{M}_1$ indeed helps. In 180 s, it solves additional 5 problems (4 of them not solved by Vampire), all of them in less than 45 s. This raises ENIGMA's performance on the competition problems to 57 problems (in general in 600 s). Interestingly, the second most useful strategy (now using $\mathcal{M}_2$ instead of $\mathcal{M}_1$) which is much more focused on doing inferences on the positively classified clauses, solves only two of these new problems, but six times faster. It is clear that we can continue experimenting this way with ENIGMA for long time, producing quickly a large number of strategies that have quite different search properties. In total we have proved 16 problems unsolved by Vampire.

6   Conclusions

The first experiments with ENIGMA are extremely encouraging. While the recent work on premise selection and on internal guidance for leanCoP indicated that large improvements are possible, this is the first practical and usable improvement of a state-of-the-art ATP by internal learning-based guidance on a large CASC benchmark. It is clear that a wide range of future improvements are possible: the learning could be dynamically used also during the proof search, training problems selected according to their similarity with the current problem,[7] more sophisticated learning and feature characterization methods could be employed, etc.

The magnitude of the improvement is unusually big for the ATP field, and similar to the improvements obtained with high-level learning in MaLARea 0.5 over E-LTB (sharing the same underlying engine) in CASC 2013 [13]. We believe that this may well mark the arrival of ENIGMAs – efficient learning-based inference guiding machines – to the automated reasoning, as crucial and indispensable technology for building the strongest automated theorem provers.

Acknowledgments. We thank Stephan Schulz for his open and modular implementation of E and its many features that allowed us to do this work. We also thank the Machine Learning Group at National Taiwan University for making LIBLINEAR openly available. This work was supported by the ERC Consolidator grant no. 649043 *AI4REASON*.

A   The E Prover Strategy Used in Experiments

The following fixed E strategy S_0, described by its command line arguments, was used in the experiments:

```
--definitional-cnf=24 --destructive-er-aggressive --destructive-er
--prefer-initial-clauses -F1 --delete-bad-limit=150000000 --forward-context-sr
-winvfreqrank -c1 -Ginvfreq -WSelectComplexG --oriented-simul-paramod -tKBO6
-H(1*ConjectureRelativeSymbolWeight(SimulateSOS,0.5,100,100,100,100,1.5,1.5,1),
   4*ConjectureRelativeSymbolWeight(ConstPrio,0.1,100,100,100,100,1.5,1.5,1.5),
   1*FIFOWeight(PreferProcessed),
   1*ConjectureRelativeSymbolWeight(PreferNonGoals,0.5,100,100,100,100,1.5,1.5,1),
   4*Refinedweight(SimulateSOS,3,2,2,1.5,2))
```

References

1. Blanchette, J.C., Greenaway, D., Kaliszyk, C., Kühlwein, D., Urban, J.: A learning-based fact selector for Isabelle/HOL. J. Autom. Reasoning **57**(3), 219–244 (2016)
2. Blanchette, J.C., Kaliszyk, C., Paulson, L.C., Urban, J.: Hammering towards QED. J. Formalized Reasoning **9**(1), 101–148 (2016)

---

[7] In an initial experiment, a simple nearest-neighbor selection of training problems for the learning further decreases the solving times and proves one more AIM problem unsolved by Prover9.

3. Boser, B.E., Guyon, I., Vapnik, V.: A training algorithm for optimal margin classifiers. In: COLT, pp. 144–152. ACM (1992)
4. Fan, R., Chang, K., Hsieh, C., Wang, X., Lin, C.: LIBLINEAR: A library for large linear classification. J. Mach. Learn. Res. **9**, 1871–1874 (2008)
5. Färber, M., Kaliszyk, C., Urban, J.: Monte Carlo connection prover. CoRR, abs/1611.05990 (2016)
6. Gottlob, G., Sutcliffe, G., Voronkov, A. (eds.) Global Conference on Artificial Intelligence (GCAI 2015), Tbilisi, Georgia. EPiC Series in Computing, EasyChair, vol. 36, 16–19 October 2015
7. Gransden, T., Walkinshaw, N., Raman, R.: SEPIA: search for proofs using inferred automata. In: Felty, A.P., Middeldorp, A. (eds.) CADE 2015. LNCS, vol. 9195, pp. 246–255. Springer, Cham (2015). doi:10.1007/978-3-319-21401-6_16
8. Hsieh, C., Chang, K., Lin, C., Keerthi, S.S., Sundararajan, S.: A dual coordinate descent method for large-scale linear SVM. In: ICML, ACM International Conference Proceeding Series, vol. 307, pp. 408–415. ACM (2008)
9. Jakubuv, J., Urban, J.: BliStrTune: hierarchical invention of theorem proving strategies. In: Bertot, Y., Vafeiadis, V. (eds.) Proceedings of the 6th ACM SIGPLAN Conference on Certified Programs and Proofs (CPP 2017), Paris, France. pp. 43–52. ACM. 16–17 January 2017(2017)
10. Kaliszyk, C., Urban, J.: Learning-assisted automated reasoning with Flyspeck. J. Autom. Reasoning **53**(2), 173–213 (2014)
11. Kaliszyk, C., Urban, J.: FEMaLeCoP: Fairly efficient machine learning connection prover. In: Davis, M., Fehnker, A., McIver, A., Voronkov, A. (eds.) LPAR 2015. LNCS, vol. 9450, pp. 88–96. Springer, Heidelberg (2015). doi:10.1007/978-3-662-48899-7_7
12. Kaliszyk, C., Urban, J.: MizAR 40 for Mizar 40. J. Autom. Reasoning **55**(3), 245–256 (2015)
13. Kaliszyk, C., Urban, J., Vyskočil, J.: Machine learner for automated reasoning 0.4 and 0.5. CoRR, abs/1402.2359, 2014, Accepted to (PAAR 2014)
14. Kaliszyk, C., Urban, J., Vyskočil, J.: Efficient semantic features for automated reasoning over large theories. In: Yang, Q., Wooldridge, M. (eds.) IJCAI 2015, pp. 3084–3090. AAAI Press (2015)
15. Kinyon, M., Veroff, R., Vojtěchovský, P.: Loops with Abelian inner mapping groups: an application of automated deduction. In: Bonacina, M.P., Stickel, M.E. (eds.) Automated Reasoning and Mathematics. LNCS, vol. 7788, pp. 151–164. Springer, Heidelberg (2013). doi:10.1007/978-3-642-36675-8_8
16. Kovács, L., Voronkov, A.: First-order theorem proving and VAMPIRE. In: Sharygina, N., Veith, H. (eds.) CAV 2013. LNCS, vol. 8044, pp. 1–35. Springer, Heidelberg (2013). doi:10.1007/978-3-642-39799-8_1
17. Kühlwein, D., Urban, J.: MaLeS: A framework for automatic tuning of automated theorem provers. J. Autom. Reasoning **55**(2), 91–116 (2015)
18. Lin, C., Weng, R.C., Keerthi, S.S.: Trust region newton method for logistic regression. J. Mach. Learn. Res. **9**, 627–650 (2008)
19. Otten, J., Bibel, W.: leanCoP: lean connection-based theorem proving. J. Symb. Comput. **36**(1–2), 139–161 (2003)
20. Schäfer, S., Schulz, S.: Breeding theorem proving heuristics with genetic algorithms. In: Gottlob et al. [6], pp. 263–274
21. Schulz, S.: E - A Brainiac Theorem Prover. AI Commun. **15**(2–3), 111–126 (2002)
22. Sutcliffe, G.: The 8th IJCAR automated theorem proving system competition - CASC-J8. AI Commun. **29**(5), 607–619 (2016)

23. Urban, J.: BliStr: The Blind Strategymaker. In: Gottlob et al. [6], pp. 312–319
24. Urban, J., Sutcliffe, G., Pudlák, P., Vyskočil, J.: MaLARea SG1 - Machine learner for automated reasoning with semantic guidance. In: Armando, A., Baumgartner, P., Dowek, G. (eds.) IJCAR 2008. LNCS, vol. 5195, pp. 441–456. Springer, Heidelberg (2008). doi:10.1007/978-3-540-71070-7_37
25. Urban, J., Vyskočil, J., Štěpánek, P.: MaLeCoP machine learning connection prover. In: Brünnler, K., Metcalfe, G. (eds.) TABLEAUX 2011. LNCS, vol. 6793, pp. 263–277. Springer, Heidelberg (2011). doi:10.1007/978-3-642-22119-4_21

Proof Mining with Dependent Types

Ekaterina Komendantskaya[1(✉)] and Jónathan Heras[2]

[1] Mathematical and Computer Sciences,
Heriot-Watt University, Edinburgh, UK
ek19@hw.ac.uk
[2] Mathematics and Computer Science,
University of La Rioja, Rioja, Spain
joheras@gmail.com

Abstract. Several approaches exist to data-mining big corpora of formal proofs. Some of these approaches are based on statistical machine learning, and some – on theory exploration. However, most are developed for either untyped or simply-typed theorem provers. In this paper, we present a method that combines statistical data mining and theory exploration in order to analyse and automate proofs in dependently typed language of Coq.

Keywords: Interactive theorem proving · Coq · Dependent types · Tactics · Machine learning · Clustering · Theory exploration

1 Introduction

Interactive Theorem Provers (ITP) are functional programming languages for writing and verifying proofs in type theory. Some of them, like Coq or Agda, feature dependent and higher-order inductive types. The ITP community has developed several methods to improve automation, e.g. special tactic languages (*Ltac* in Coq [4]) or special libraries (e.g. SSReflect [7]). Some provers are hybrid between automated theorem proving and ITP, e.g. ACL2 [19]. The Isabelle/HOL community pioneered methods of direct interfacing of interactive provers with third-party automated provers [3], which can also work for a subset of Coq [5].

The large volume of proof data coupled with growing popularity of machine-learning tools inspired an alternative approach to improving automation in ITP. Machine-learning can be used to learn proof strategies from existing proof corpora. This approach has been tested in different ITPs: in Isabelle/HOL via its connection with Sledgehammer [3] or via the library Flyspeck [18], in ACL2 [14] and in Mizar [24]. For Coq, however, only partial solutions have been suggested [8,9,12,20].

Several challenges arise when data mining proofs in Coq:

C1. Unlike e.g. ACL2 or Mizar, Coq's types play a role in proof construction and the proposed machine-learning methods should account for that.

The work was supported by EPSRC grants EP/J014222/1 and EP/K031864/1.

H. Geuvers et al. (Eds.): CICM 2017, LNAI 10383, pp. 303–318, 2017.
DOI: 10.1007/978-3-319-62075-6_21

C2. Unlike e.g. Isabelle/HOL, Coq has *dependent types*, thus separation between proof term and type level syntax is impossible. Any machine-learning method for Coq should reflect the dependency between terms and types.

C3. Coq additionally has a tactic language *Ltac* introduced to facilitate interactive proof construction. This feature being popular with users, it also needs to be captured in our machine-learning tools.

Challenge C3 was tackled in [8,9,12,20], but we are not aware of any existing solutions to challenges C1-2. It was shown in ML4PG [12,20] that clustering algorithms can analyse similarity between *Ltac* proofs and group them into clusters. Generally, this knowledge can be used either to aid the programmer in proof analysis [12], or as part of heuristics for construction of new similar proofs [14]. This paper enhances ML4PG's clustering methods with the analysis of proof-term structure, which takes into consideration mutual dependencies between terms and types, as well as the recursive nature of the proofs. The novel method thus addresses challenges C1-2. To complete the picture, we also propose a new premiss selection algorithm for Coq that generates new proof tactics in the *Ltac* language based upon the clustering output, thus addressing C3 in a new way.

Together, the proposed proof clustering and the premiss selection methods offer a novel approach to proof automation with dependent types: *"Data mine proof terms, generate proof tactics"*. This allows to access and analyse the maximum of information at the data mining stage, and then reduce the search space by working with a simpler tactic language at the proof generation stage.

2   Bird's Eye View of the Approach and Leading Example

1. Data mining Coq proof terms. In Coq, to prove that a theorem A follows from a theory (or current proof context) Γ, we would need to *construct* an inhabitant p of type A, which is a proof p of A in context Γ; denoted by $\Gamma \vdash p : A$. Sometimes, p is also called the *proof term* for A. A type checking problem $(\Gamma \vdash p : A?)$ asks to verify whether p is indeed a proof for A, a type inference problem $(\Gamma \vdash p :?)$ asks to verify whether the alleged proof is a proof at all; and a type inhabitation problem $(\Gamma \vdash? : A)$ asks to verify whether A is provable. Type inhabitation problem is undecidable in Coq, and the special tactic language *Ltac* is used to aid the programmer in constructing the proof term p.

We illustrate the interplay of Coq's syntax and the *Ltac* tactic language syntax in the following example. Consider the following proof of associativity of append that uses *Ltac* tactics:

```
Theorem app_assoc: forall l m n:list A, l ++ m ++ n = (l++m)++ n.
Proof.
intros l m n; induction l; simpl; trivial.
rewrite IHl; trivial.
Qed.
```

What we see as a theorem statement above is in fact the type of that proof, and the tactics merely help us to construct the proof term that inhabits this type, which we can inspect by using `Print app_assoc.` command:

```
app_assoc = fun l m n : list A =>
list_ind (fun l0 : list A => l0 ++ m ++ n = (l0 ++ m) ++ n)
    eq_refl
(fun (a : A) (l0 : list A) (IHl : l0 ++ m ++ n = (l0 ++ m) ++ n)
    =>
eq_ind_r (fun l1 : list A => a :: l1 = a :: (l0 ++ m) ++ n)
    eq_refl IHl) l
    : forall l m n : list A, l ++ m ++ n = (l ++ m) ++ n
```

Because Coq is a dependently typed language, proof terms and types may share the signature. Context Γ above is given by the List library defining, among other things, the two list constructors and operation of append.

The first methodological decision we make here is to data mine proof terms, rather than Ltac tactics.

2. Capturing the structural properties of proofs by using term trees. *The second decision we make when analysing the Coq syntax is to view both proof term and type associated with a Coq's object as a tree.* This makes structural properties of proofs apparent.

To use an example with a smaller tree, consider the Coq Lemma `forall (n : nat)(H : even n), odd (n + 1)`. Its term tree is depicted in Fig. 1.

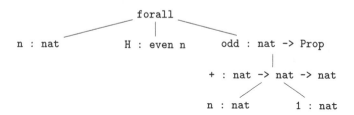

Fig. 1. *Coq term tree for the pCIC term forall (n : nat) (H : even n), odd (n + 1).*

3. Clustering term trees. *We next decide on a suitable machine learning approach to analyse Coq proofs, and settle on unsupervised learning. Clustering algorithms* [2] *have become a standard tool for finding patterns in large data sets.* We use the term *data object* to refer to an individual element within a data set. In our case, the data set is given by Coq libraries, and the data objects are given by term trees obtained from Coq terms and types. Theorem `app_assoc` is one object in the List library.

Clustering algorithms divide data objects into similar groups (clusters), based on (numeric) vector representation of the objects' properties. The process of extracting such properties from data is called *feature extraction* [2]. *Features* are parameters chosen to represent all objects in the data set. *Feature values* are usually given by numbers that instantiate the features for every given object. If n features are chosen to represent all objects, the features form *feature vectors* of length n; and clustering is conducted in an n-dimensional space.

3.1. Converting tree structures to feature matrices.

We now need to decide how to convert each proof tree into a feature vector. A variety of methods exists to represent trees as matrices, for instance using adjacency or incidence matrices. The adjacency matrix method shares the following common properties with various previous methods of feature extraction for proofs [17,21]: different library symbols are represented by distinct features, and the feature values are binary. For large libraries and growing syntax, such feature vectors grow very large (up to 10^6 in some experiments).

We propose an alternative method that can characterise a large (potentially unlimited) number of Coq terms by a finite number of features and a (potentially unlimited) number of feature values. The features that determine the rows and columns of the matrices are given by the term tree depth and the level index of nodes. In addition, given a Coq term, its features must differentiate its term and type components. As a result, in our encoding each tree node is reflected by three features that represent the term component and the type component of the given node, as well as the level index of its parent node in the term tree, cf. Table 1 (in which td refers to "tree depth").

Table 1. Term tree matrix for $forall$ $(n$ $:$ $nat)$ $(H$ $:$ $even$ $n)$, odd $(n+1)$.

	Level index 0	Level index 1	Level index 2
td0	$([\texttt{forall}]_{Gallina}, -1, -1)$	$(0,0,0)$	$(0,0,0)$
td1	$([\texttt{n}]_{term},[\texttt{nat}]_{type},0)$	$([\texttt{H}]_{term},[\texttt{even n}]_{type},0)$	$([\texttt{odd}]_{term},[\texttt{nat} \to \texttt{Prop}]_{type},0)$
td2	$([\texttt{+}]_{term},[\texttt{nat} \to \texttt{nat} \to \texttt{nat}]_{type},2)$	$(0,0,0)$	$(0,0,0)$
td3	$([\texttt{n}]_{term},[\texttt{nat}]_{type},0)$	$([\texttt{1}]_{term},[\texttt{nat}]_{type},0)$	$(0,0,0)$

3.2. Populating feature matrices with feature values.

Feature matrices give a skeleton for extracting proof properties. Next, it is important to have an intelligent algorithm to populate the feature matrices with rational numbers – i.e. *feature values*. Consider the associativity of the operation of list append given in Theorem `app_assoc`. Associativity is a property common to many other operations. For example, addition on natural numbers is associative:

```
Theorem plus_assoc: forall l m n: nat, l + (m + n) = (l + m) + n.
Proof.
intros l m n; induction l; simpl; trivial.
rewrite IHl; trivial.
Qed.
```

The corresponding proof term is as follows:

```
plus_assoc = fun l m n : nat =>
nat_ind (fun l0 : nat => l0 + (m + n) = l0 + m + n) eq_refl
  (fun (l0 : nat) (IH1 : l0 + (m + n) = l0 + m + n) =>
   eq_ind_r (fun n0 : nat => S n0 = S (l0 + m + n)) eq_refl IH1) l
   : forall l m n : nat, l + (m + n) = l + m + n
```

We would like our clustering tools to group theorems `app_assoc` and `plus_assoc` together. It is easy to see that the term tree structures of the theorems `app_assoc` and `plus_assoc` are similar, and so will be the structure of their feature matrices. However, the feature matrix cells are populated by feature values. If values assigned to `list` and `nat` as well as to `++` and `+` are very different, then these two theorems may not be grouped into the same cluster.

To give an example of a bad feature value assignment, suppose we define functions $[.]_{term}$ and $[.]_{type}$ to blindly assign a new natural number to every new object defined in the library. Suppose further that we defined natural numbers at the start of the file of 1000 objects, and lists – at the end of the file, then we may have an assignment $[\mathtt{nat}]_{type} = 0, [\mathtt{+}]_{term} = 1, [\mathtt{list}]_{type} = 999, [\mathtt{++}]_{term} = 1000$. This assignment would suggest to treat functions `+` and `++` as very distant. If these values populate the feature matrices for our two theorems `app_assoc` and `plus_assoc`, the corresponding feature vectors will lie in distant regions of the n-dimensional plane. This may lead the clustering algorithm to group these theorems in different clusters.

Seeing that the definitions of `list` and `nat` are structurally similar, and so are `++` and `+`, we would rather characterise their similarity by close feature values, irrespective of where in the files they occur. But then our algorithm needs to be intelligent enough to calculate how similar or dissimilar these terms are. For this, we need to cluster all objects in the chosen libraries, find that `list` and `nat` are clustered together, and `++` and `+` are clustered together, and assign close values to objects from the same cluster. In this example, definitions of `list`, `nat`, `++` and `+` do not rely on any other definitions (just Coq primitives), and we can extract their feature matrices and values directly (after manually assigning values to a small fixed number of Coq primitives). In the general case, it may take more than one iteration to reach the primitive symbols.

We call this method of mutual clustering and feature extraction *recurrent clustering*. It is extremely efficient in analysis of dependently-typed syntax, in which inductive definitions and recursion play a big role. It also works uniformly to capture the entire Coq syntax: not just proofs of theorems and lemmas in *Ltac* like in early versions of ML4PG, but also all the type and function definitions.

4. Using clusters to improve proof automation. Suppose now we have the output of the clustering algorithm, in which all Coq objects of interest are grouped into n clusters. All objects in each cluster share some structural similarity, like `app_assoc` and `plus_assoc`. Suppose we introduce a new lemma L for which we do not have a proof but which is clustered together with `app_assoc` and `plus_assoc`. We then can re-adjust the sequences of *Ltac* tactics used in proofs of `app_assoc` and `plus_assoc` and prove L.

Our running example so far was simple, and the tactics used in the proofs did not refer to other lemmas. The new recurrent clustering method is most helpful when proofs actually call some other auxiliary lemmas. Simple recombination of proof tactics does not work well in such cases: our new lemma L clustered with other finished proofs in cluster C may require similar, but not exactly the same auxiliary lemmas.

Take for example lemma `maxnACA` that states the inner commutativity of the maximum of two natural numbers in the SSReflect library ssrnat:

```
Lemma maxnACA : interchange maxn maxn.
```

ML4PG clusters `maxnACA` together with already proven lemmas $\{$`addnACA, minnACA, mulnACA`$\}$ — these three lemmas state the inner commutativity of addition, multiplication and the minimum of two naturals, respectively. We will try to construct the proof for `maxnACA` by analogy with the proofs of $\{$`addnACA, minnACA, mulnACA`$\}$. Consider the proof of the lemma `addnACA` in that cluster: it is proven using the sequence of tactics by `move=> m n p q; rewrite -!addnA (addnCA n)`. That is, it mainly relies on auxiliary lemmas `addnA` and `addnCA`. The proof of `addnACA` fails to apply to `maxnACA` directly. In particular, the auxiliary lemmas `addnA` and `addnCA` do not apply in the proof of `maxnACA`. But similar lemmas would apply! And here the clustering method we have just described comes to the rescue. If we cluster all auxiliary lemmas used in the proofs of $\{$`addnACA, minnACA, mulnACA`$\}$ with the rest of the lemmas of the ssrnat library we find the cluster $\{$`minnA, mulnA, maxnA, addnA`$\}$ and the cluster $\{$`minnAC, mulnAC, maxnAC, addnCA`$\}$. These two clusters give us candidate auxiliary lemmas to try in our proof of `maxnACA`, in places where `addnA` and `addnCA` were used in `addnACA`. As it turns out, the lemmas `maxnA` and `maxnAC` will successfully apply as auxiliary lemmas in `maxnACA`, and the sequence of tactics by `move=> m n p q; rewrite -!maxnA (maxnCA n)` proves the lemma `maxnACA`.

Paper overview. The rest of the paper is organised as follows. Section 3 introduces some of the background concepts. In Sect. 4, we define the algorithm for automatically extracting features matrices from Coq terms and types. In Sect. 5, we define a second algorithm, which automatically computes feature values to populate the feature matrices. These two methods are new, and have never been presented before. In Sect. 6, we propose the new method of premiss selection and tactic generation for Coq based on clustering. Finally, in Sect. 7 we survey related work and conclude the paper.

3   Background

The underlying formal language of Coq is known as the *Predicative Calculus of (Co)Inductive Constructions* (pCIC) [4].

Definition 1 (pCIC term).

- *The sorts* Set, Prop, Type(i) *(i ∈ ℕ) are terms.*
- *The global names of the environment are terms.*
- *Variables are terms.*
- *If x is a variable and T, U are terms, then* forall x:T,U *is a term. If x does not occur in U, then* forall x:T,U *will be written as* T -> U. *A term of the form* forall x1:T1, forall x2:T2, ..., forall xn:Tn, U *will be written as* forall (x1:T1)(x2:T2)...(xn:Tn), U.
- *If x is a variable and T, U are terms, then* fun x:T => U *is a term. A term of the form* fun x1:T1 => fun x2:T2 => ... => fun xn:Tn => U *will be written as* fun (x1:T1)(x2:T2)...(xn:Tn)=> U.
- *If T and U are terms, then* (T U) *is a term – we use an uncurried notation* ((T U1 U2 ... Un)) *for nested applications* ((((T U1)U2)... Un)).
- *If x is a variable, and T, U are terms, then* (let x:=T in U) *is a term.*

The syntax of Coq [4] includes some terms that do not appear in Definition 1; e.g. given a variable x, and terms T and U, fix name (x:T):= U is a Coq term used to declare a recursive definition. The notion of a term in Coq covers a very general syntactic category in the Gallina specification language. However, for the purpose of concise exposition, we will restrict our notion of a term to Definition 1, giving the full treatment of the whole Coq syntax in the actual ML4PG implementation.

Clustering. A detailed study of performance of different well-known clustering algorithms in proof-mining in ML4PG can be found in [20]. In this paper we use the k-means clustering algorithm throughout as it gave the best evaluation results in [20] and is rather fast (we use an implementation in Weka [10]).

The chosen clustering algorithm relies on a user-supplied parameter k that identifies the number of clusters to form. Throughout this paper, we will use the following heuristic method [14, 20] to determine k:

$$k = \left\lfloor \frac{\text{objects to cluster}}{10 - g} \right\rfloor,$$

where g is a user-supplied granularity value from 1 to 5. Lower granularity (1–2) indicates the general preference for a smaller number of clusters of larger size, and higher granularity (3–5) suggests a larger number of clusters of smaller size. In this setting, g is supplied by the user, via the ML4PG interface, as an indicator of a general intent.

4   Feature Extraction, Stage-1: Extracting Feature Matrices from pCIC Terms

We first introduce a suitable tree representation of pCIC terms. We refer to Sect. 2 for examples supporting the definitions below.

Definition 2 (pCIC term tree). *Given a pCIC term C, we define its associated pCIC term tree as follows:*

- *If C is one of the sorts* Set, Prop *or* Type(i)*, then the pCIC term tree of C consists of one single node, labelled respectively by* Set:Type(0), Prop:Type(0) *or* Type(i):Type(i+1)*.*
- *If C is a name or a variable, then the pCIC term tree of C consists of one single node, labelled by the name or the variable itself together with its type.*
- *If C is a pCIC term of the form* forall (x1:T1)(x2:T2)...(xn:Tn), U *(analogously for)* fun (x1:T1)(x2:T2)...(xn:Tn)=> U; *then, the term tree of C is the tree with the root node labelled by* forall *(respectively)* fun *and its immediate subtrees given by the trees representing* x1:T1, x2:T2, xn:Tn *and U.*
- *If C is a pCIC term of the form* let x:=T in U*, then the pCIC tree of C is the tree with the root node labelled by* let*, having three subtrees given by the trees corresponding to* x, T *and U.*
- *If C is a pCIC term of the form* T -> U*, then the pCIC term tree of C is represented by the tree with the root node labelled by* ->*, and its immediate subtrees given by the trees representing* T *and U.*
- *If C is a pCIC term of the form* (T U1 ... Un)*, then we have two cases. If T is a name, the pCIC term tree of C is represented by the tree with the root node labelled by T together with its type, and its immediate subtrees given by the trees representing* U1,..., Un*. If T is not a name, the pCIC term tree of C is the tree with the root node labelled by* @*, and its immediate subtrees given by the trees representing* T, U1,...,Un*.*

Note that pCIC term trees extracted from any given Coq files consist of two kinds of nodes: *Gallina* and *term-type* nodes. Gallina is a specification language of Coq, it contains keywords and special tokens such as forall, fun, let or -> (from now on, we will call them Gallina tokens). The term-type nodes are given by expressions of the form t1:t2 where t1 is a sort, a variable or a name, and t2 is the type of t1.

We now convert pCIC term trees into feature matrices:

Definition 3 (pCIC Term tree depth level and level index). *Given a pCIC term tree T, the depth of the node t in T, denoted by depth(t), is defined as follows:*

- *depth(t) = 0, if t is a root node;*
- *depth(t) = n + 1, where n is the depth of the parent node of t.*

The nth level of T is the ordered sequence of nodes of depth n. As is standard, the order of the sequence is given by visiting the nodes of depth n from left to right. We will say that the size of this sequence is the width *of the tree at depth n. The width of T is given by the largest width of its levels. The level index of a node with depth n is the position of the node in the nth level of T. We denote by $T(i,j)$ the node of T with depth i and index level j.*

We use the notation $M[\mathbb{Q}]_{n \times m}$ to denote the set of matrices of size $n \times m$ with rational coefficients.

Definition 4 (pCIC term tree feature matrix). *Given a pCIC term t, its corresponding pCIC term tree T_t with the depth n and the width m, and three injective functions $[.]_{term} : pCIC$ terms $\rightarrow \mathbb{Q}^+$, $[.]_{type} : pCIC$ terms $\rightarrow \mathbb{Q}^+$ and $[.]_{Gallina} : Gallina$ tokens $\rightarrow \mathbb{Q}^-$, the feature extraction function $[.]_M = \langle [.]_{term}, [.]_{type}, [.]_{Gallina} \rangle : pCIC$ terms $\rightarrow M[\mathbb{Q}]_{n \times 3m}$ builds the term tree matrix of t, $[t]_M$, where the (i,j)-th entry of $[t]_M$ captures information from the node $T_t(i,j)$ as follows:*

- *if $T_t(i,j)$ is a Gallina node g, then the (i,j)th entry of $[t]_M$ is a triple $([g]_{Gallina}, -1, p)$ where p is the level index of the parent of g.*
- *if $T_t(i,j)$ is a term : type node $t1:t2$, then the (i,j)th entry of $[t]_M$ is a triple $([t1]_{term}, [t2]_{type}, p)$ where p is the level index of the parent of the node.*

One example of a term tree feature matrix for the term tree of `forall (n : nat)(H : even n), odd (n + 1)` is given in Table 1. Since the depth of the tree is 4, and its width is 3, it takes the matrix of the size 4×9 to represent that tree. Generally, if the largest pCIC term tree in the given Coq library has the size $n \times m$, we take feature matrices of size $n \times 3m$ for all feature extraction purposes. The resulting feature vectors have an average density ratio of 60%. It has much smaller feature vector size, and much higher density than in sparse approaches [17,21]. It helps to obtain more accurate clustering results.

In Definition 4, we specify the functions $[.]_{Gallina}, [.]_{term}$ and $[.]_{type}$ just by their signature. The function $[.]_{Gallina}$ is a predefined function. The number of Gallina tokens is fixed and cannot be expanded by the Coq user. Therefore, we know in advance all the Gallina tokens that can appear in a development, and we can assign a concrete value to each of them. The function $[.]_{Gallina} : Gallina$ tokens $\rightarrow \mathbb{Q}^-$ is an injective function defined to assign close values to similar Gallina tokens and more distant numbers to unrelated tokens.

The functions $[.]_{term}$ and $[.]_{type}$ are dynamically re-defined for every library and every given proof stage, as the next section will explain.

5 Feature Extraction Stage-2: Assigning Feature Values via Recurrent Clustering

When defining the functions $[.]_{term}$ and $[.]_{type}$, we must ensure that these functions are sensitive to the structure of terms, assigning close values to similar terms, and more distant values to dissimilar terms.

Starting with the primitives, $[.]_{term}$ and $[.]_{type}$ will always assign fixed values to the pre-defined sorts in Coq (cf. item (1) in Definition 5). Next, suppose t is the nth object of the given Coq library. For variables $x_1, \ldots, x_n$ occurring in a term t, $[x_i]_{term} = i$ and $[x_j]_{type} = j$, using a method resembling de Brujn indices (cf. item (2)). Item (3) defines $[.]_{term}$ and $[.]_{type}$ for the recursive calls. The most interesting (recurrent) case occurs when $[.]_{term}$ and $[.]_{type}$ need to be defined for subterms of t that are defined elsewhere in the library. In such cases, we use output of recurrent clustering of the first $n - 1$ object of the library. When the first $n - 1$ Coq objects are clustered, each cluster is automatically assigned a unique integer number. Clustering algorithms additionally assign a *proximity value* (ranging from 0 to 1) to every object in a cluster to indicate the proximity of the cluster centroid, or in other terms, the certainty of the given example belonging to the cluster. The definitions of $[.]_{term}$ and $[.]_{type}$ below use the cluster number and the proximity value to compute feature values:

Definition 5. *Given a Coq library, its nth object given by a pCIC term t, the corresponding pCIC term tree T_t, and a node $s = T_t(k, l)$, the functions $[.]_{term}$ and $[.]_{type}$ are defined respectively for the term component $t1$ and the type component $t2$ of s as follows:*

1. *(Base case) If $t1$ (or $t2$) is the ith element of the set $\{\texttt{Set}, \texttt{Prop}, \texttt{Type(0)}, \texttt{Type(1)}, \texttt{Type(2)}\ldots\}$ then its value $[t1]_{term}$ (or $[t2]_{type}$) is given by $100 + \sum_{j=1}^{i} \frac{1}{10 \times 2^{j-1}}$.*
2. *(Base case) If $t1$ (or $t2$) is the ith distinct variable in t, then $[t1]_{term}$ (or $[t2]_{type}$) is assigned the value i.*
3. *(Base case) If $t1 = t$, i.e. $t1$ is a recursive call (or $t2 = t$, i.e. t is an inductive type definition), we assign a designated constant to $t1$ (or $t2$, respectively).*
4. *(Recurrent case) If $t1$ or $t2$ is an mth object of the given Coq libraries, where $m < n$, then cluster the first $n-1$ objects of that library and take into account the clustering output as follows.*
   If $t1$ (or $t2$) belongs to a cluster C_j with associated proximity value p, then $[t1]_{term}$ (or $[t2]_{type}$, respectively) is assigned the value $200 + 2 \times j + p$.
5. *(Recurrent case) If $t1:t2$ is a local assumption or hypothesis, then cluster this object against the first $n - 1$ objects of the given libraries and take into account the clustering output as follows. If $t1$ (or $t2$) belongs to a cluster C_j with associated proximity value p, then $[t1]_{term}$ (or $[t2]_{type}$, respectively) is assigned the value $200 + 2 \times j + p$.*

In the formula for sorts (item 1), the component $\sum_{j=1}^{i} \frac{1}{10 \times 2^{j-1}}$ produces small fractions to reflect the similarity of all sorts, and 100 is added in order to distinguish sorts from variables and names. The formula $200 + 2 \times j + p$ used elsewhere assigns $[t]$ a value within $[200+2 \times j, 200+2 \times j+1]$ depending on the proximity value of t in cluster j. Thus, elements of the same cluster have closer values compared to the values assigned to elements of other clusters. For example, using the three clusters shown below, $[\texttt{eqn}]_{term} = 200 + 2 \times 1 + 0.5 = 202.5$, where 0.5 is the proximity value of $\texttt{eqn}$ in Cluster 1. By contrast, $[\texttt{drop}]_{term} = 200 + 2 \times 2 + 0.7 = 204.7$, where 0.7 is a proximity value of $\texttt{drop}$ in Cluster 2.

The Algorithm at Work: Examples

We finish this section with some examples of clusters discovered in the basic infrastructure of the SSReflect library [7]. We include here 3 of the 91 clusters discovered by our method automatically after processing 457 objects (across 12 standard files), within 5–10 s.

– Cluster 1:

```
Fixpoint eqn (m n : nat) :=
  match m, n with
  | 0, 0 => true | m'.+1, n'.+1 => eqn m' n'
  | _, _ => false end.
Fixpoint eqseq (s1 s2 : seq T) :=
  match s1, s2 with
  | [::], [::] => true | x1 :: s1', x2 :: s2' => (x1 == x2) && eqseq
    s1' s2'
  | _, _ => false end.
```

– Cluster 2:

```
Fixpoint drop n s := match s, n with | _ :: s', n'.+1 => drop n' s' |
  _, _ => s end.
Fixpoint take n s := match s, n with | x :: s', n'.+1 => x :: take n'
  s' | _, _ => :: end.
```

– Cluster 3:

```
Definition flatten := foldr cat (Nil T).
Definition sumn := foldr addn 0.
```

The first cluster contains the definitions of equality for natural numbers and lists—showing that the clustering method can spot structural similarities across different libraries. The second cluster discovers similarity between take (takes the first n elements of a list) and drop (drops the first n elements of a list). The last pattern is less trivial of the three, as it depends on other definitions, like foldr, cat (concatenation of lists) and addn (sum of natural numbers). Recurrent term clustering handles such dependencies well: it assigns close values to cat and addn, since they have been discovered to belong to the same cluster. Note the precision of the recurrent clustering. Among 457 terms it considered, 15 used foldr, however, Cluster 3 contains only 2 definitions, excluding e.g. Definition allpairs s t:=foldr (fun x => cat (map (f x)t))[::] s; Definition divisors n:=foldr add_divisors [:: 1] (prime_decomp n) or Definition Poly:=foldr cons_poly 0. This precision is due to the recurrent clustering process with its deep analysis of the term and type structure, including analysis of any auxiliary functions. This is how it discovers that functions add_divisors or cons_poly are structurally different from auxiliary functions cat and addn, and hence definitions allpairs, divisors and Poly are not included in Cluster 3.

This deep analysis of term structure via recurrent clustering improves accuracy and will play a role in the next section.

6 Applications of Recurrent Proof Clustering. A Premiss Selection Method

Several premiss selection methods have been proposed for Isabelle, HOL, as well as several other provers: [18,24]. Relying on Coq's tactic language, and the clustering results of the previous section, we can formulate the problem of **premiss selection for Coq** as follows: *Given a cluster C of pCIC objects from a Coq library L and an arbitrary theorem/lemma T in this cluster, can we recombine sequences of proof tactics used to prove other theorems/lemmas in C in such a way as to obtain a proof for T? In particular, if the proof of T requires the use of auxiliary Lemmas from L, can we use the outputs of the recurrent clustering to make valid suggestions of auxiliary lemmas?*

The algorithm below answers these questions in the positive. To answer the second question, we suggest to automatically examine all auxiliary lemmas $A_1, \ldots, A_m$ used in proofs that belong to the cluster C, and look up the clusters to which $A_1, \ldots, A_m$ belong in order to suggest auxiliary lemmas for T. This is the essence of the clustering-based premiss selection method we propose here (see especially the item 4(b) and Algorithm 1 below). As Sect. 2 has illustrated, often a combination of auxiliary lemmas is required in order to complete a given proof, and the below algorithm caters for such cases.

Premise Selection Method 1. *Given the statement of a theorem T and a set of lemmas L, find a proof for T as follows:*

1. *Using the recurrent clustering and $T \cup L$ as dataset, obtain the cluster C that contains the theorem T (possibly alongside other lemmas $L'_1, L'_2, \ldots L'_n$).*
2. *Obtain the sequence of tactics $\{T_1^j, \ldots, T_{n_i}^j\}_j$ that are used to prove each lemma L'_j in C.*
3. *Try to prove T using $T_1^j, \ldots, T_{n_j}^j$, for each $j \in \{1, \ldots n\}$.*
4. *If no such sequence of tactics proves T, then infer new arguments for each tactic T_k^j as follows:*
   - *(a) If the argument of T_k^j is an internal hypothesis from the context of a proof, try all the internal hypothesis from the context of the current proof.*
   - *(b) If the argument of T_k^j is an external lemma E, use the recurrent clustering and L as dataset to determine which lemmas are in a cluster with E and try all those lemmas in turn as arguments of T_k^j.*
   - **** This can be naturally extended to tactics with several arguments, as Algorithm 1 shows.*

The heart of the above procedure is the process of Lemma selection (item 4(b)), which we state more formally as Algorithm 1.

Algorithm 1. Premiss selection method based on clustering (item 4(b) of Method 1)

Require: S – a set of lemmas and theorems contained in the given Coq libraries $\mathcal{L}_1, \ldots, \mathcal{L}_s$.
Require: $T(L_1, \ldots, L_k)$ – an Ltac tactic T with arguments containing $L_1, \ldots, L_k \in S$.
Require: S/C_n partition of the set S into n clusters $C_1, \ldots, C_n$.
1: Denote by $L^j_{C_i}$ the jth lemma of cluster C_i.
2: The algorithm returns a list of suggested lemmas in place of each $L_l \in (L_1, \ldots, L_k)$.
3: **for** $l = 1, \ldots, k$ **do**
4:    **for** $i = 1, \ldots, n$ **do**
5:      **if** $L_l \in C_i$ **then**
6:        **for** $j = 1, \ldots \|C_i\|$ **do**
7:          $L_k := [L_k::L^j_{C_i}]$
8:        **end for**
9:      **end if**
10:    **end for**
11:    **return** (L_k)
12: **end for**

Evaluation

Using five Coq libraries of varied sizes, we perform an empirical evaluation of the premiss selection method, and thereby testify the accuracy of the proposed recurrent clustering. Our test data consists of the basic infrastructure of the SSReflect library [7], the formalisation of Java-like bytecode presented in [12], the formalisation of persistent homology [11], the Paths library of the HoTT development [22], and the formalisation of the Nash Equilibrium [23].

Table 2. Percentage of proofs discovered by analogy with similar proofs in the given library, for bigger ($g = 1$) and smaller ($g = 5$) clusters.

Library	Language	Granularity $g = 1$	Granularity $g = 3$	Granularity $g = 5$	Library size (No of Theorems)
SSReflect library	SSReflect	36%	35%	28%	1389
JVM	SSReflect	56%	58%	65%	49
Persistent homology	SSReflect	0%	10%	12%	306
Paths (HoTT)	Coq	92%	91%	94%	80
Nash equilibrium	Coq	40%	37%	36%	145

The results of our experiments are given in Table 2. The success rate of the premiss selection method depends on how similar the proofs of theorems in a given library are. Additionally, and unlike all other premiss selection methods [18,24], we now have to factor in the fact that Coq's proofs as given by the tactics in *Ltac* language may require a sophisticated combination of tactics for which our premiss selection method does not cater. Indeed, some proofs may not call auxiliary lemmas at all and incorporate all the reasoning within one proof. This explains the high success rate in the *Paths (HoTT)* library, where most of the lemmas are proven in the same style, and using auxiliary lemmas in the same well-organised way, and the low rate in the *Persistent Homology* library, where just a few lemmas have similar proofs with auxiliary lemmas. The granularity value does not have a big impact in the performance of our experiments, and almost the same number of lemmas is proven with different granularity values. In some cases, like in the Nash equilibrium library, a small granularity value generates bigger clusters that increase the exploration space allowing to prove more lemmas. However, reducing the granularity value can also have a negative impact; for instance, in the JVM library the number of clusters is reduced and this leads to a reduction in the number of the proven theorems.

7   Conclusions and Related Work

The presented hybrid method of proof mining combines statistical machine learning and premiss selection, Coq's proof terms and *Ltac* tactics. It is specifically designed to cater for a dependently typed language such as that of Coq. The *recurrent clustering* analyses tree structures of proof terms and types, and groups all Coq objects (definitions, lemmas, theorems, ...) into n sets, depending on their dependencies and structural similarity with the given libraries. Previous versions of ML4PG could only analyse tactics, rather than proof terms or definitions.

The output of the clustering algorithm can be used to directly explore the similarity of lemmas and definitions, and ML4PG includes a graphical interface to do that. In this paper we presented a novel method of premiss selection that allows to use the output of clustering algorithms for analogy-based premiss selection. We use the *Ltac* language to automatically generate candidate tactics from clusters. *Ltac*'s language gives a much simpler syntax to explore compared with a possible alternative – a direct generation of Coq term trees.

Evaluation of the method shows that it bears promise, especially in the libraries where the proofs are given in a uniform style, and auxiliary lemmas are used consistently. Capturing the role of auxiliary lemmas in proofs is known to be a hard problem in proof mining, and recurrent clustering gives a good solution to this problem. Other existing methods, like [8,9] address limitations of our premiss selection method, and suggest more sophisticated algorithms for tactic recombination. Integration of these methods with ML4PG is under way.

The recurrent clustering method is embedded into ML4PG: http://www.macs.hw.ac.uk/~ek19/ML4PG/. The integration of the Premiss Selection method into ML4PG or directly into Coq's *Ltac* is still future work.

Related work

Statistical machine learning for automation of proofs: premiss selection. The method of statistical proof-premise selection [17,18,21,24] is applied in several theorem provers. The method we presented in Sect. 6 is an alternative method of premiss selection, due to its reliance on the novel algorithm of recurrent clustering. Also, this paper presents the first premiss selection method that takes into consideration the structure of proof terms in a dependently typed language.

Automated solvers in Coq. In [5], the standard *"hammer"* approach was adopted, where a fragment of Coq syntax was translated into FOL, and then the translated lemma and theorem statements (without proof terms) were proven using existing first-order solvers. By contrast, our approach puts emphasis on mining proof terms that inhabit the lemmas and theorems in Coq. Our method does not rely on any third party first-order solvers. Results of clustering of the Coq libraries are directly used to reconstruct Coq proofs, by analogy with other proofs in the library. Thus, the process of (often unsound and inevitably incomplete) translation [5] from the higher-order dependently typed language of Coq into FOL becomes redundant.

Theory exploration: models from tactic sequences. While statistical methods focus on extracting information from existing large libraries, *symbolic methods* are instead concerned with automating the discovery of lemmas in new theories [8,9,13,15,16], relying on existing proof strategies, e.g. proof-planning and rippling [1,6]. The method of tactic synthesis given in Sect. 6 belongs to that group of methods.

The method developed in this paper differs from the cited papers in that it allows to reason deeper than the surface of the tactic language. I.e., statistical analysis of pCIC proof terms and types as presented in Sect. 4 is employed before the tactics in the *Ltac* language are generated.

Combination of Statistical and Symbolic Machine Learning Methods in theorem proving. Statistical machine learning was used to support auxiliary lemma formulation by analogy in the setting of ACL2, see [14]. In this paper, we extended that approach in several ways: we included types, proof terms and the tactic language – all crucial building blocks of Coq proofs as opposed to first-order untyped proofs of ACL2.

References

1. Basin, D., et al.: Rippling: Meta-Level Guidance for Mathematical Reasoning. Cambridge University Press, New York (2005)
2. Bishop, C.: Pattern Recognition and Machine Learning. Springer, Heidelberg (2006)
3. Blanchette, J., et al.: Hammering towards QED. J. Formalized Reasoning **9**(1), 101–148 (2016)
4. Coq development team. The Coq Proof Assistant Reference Manual, version 8.4pl3. Technical report (2013)
5. Czajka, L., Kaliszyk, C.: Goal translation for a Hammer for Coq. In: Proceeding of Hammers for Type Theories, EPTCS. vol. 210 , pp. 13-20 (2016)

6. Duncan, H.: The use of Data-Mining for the Automatic Formation of Tactics. Ph.D. thesis, University of Edinburgh (2002)
7. Gonthier, G., Mahboubi, A.: An introduction to small scale reflection. J. Formalized Reasoning **3**(2), 95–152 (2010)
8. Gransden, T., Walkinshaw, N., Raman, R.: Mining state-based models from proof corpora. In: Watt, S.M., Davenport, J.H., Sexton, A.P., Sojka, P., Urban, J. (eds.) CICM 2014. LNCS, vol. 8543, pp. 282–297. Springer, Cham (2014). doi:10.1007/978-3-319-08434-3_21
9. Gransden, T., Walkinshaw, N., Raman, R.: SEPIA: Search for proofs using inferred automata. In: Felty, A.P., Middeldorp, A. (eds.) CADE 2015. LNCS, vol. 9195, pp. 246–255. Springer, Cham (2015). doi:10.1007/978-3-319-21401-6_16
10. Hall, M., et al.: The WEKA data mining software: an update. SIGKDD Explor. **11**(1), 10–18 (2009)
11. Heras, J., et al.: Computing persistent homology within Coq/SSReflect. ACM Trans. Comput. Logic **14**(4), 26:1–26:16 (2013)
12. Heras, J., Komendantskaya, E.: Recycling proof patterns in Coq: case studies. J. Math. Comput. Sci. **8**(1), 99–116 (2014)
13. Hetzl, S., Leitsch, A., Weller, D.: Towards algorithmic cut-introduction. In: Bjørner, N., Voronkov, A. (eds.) LPAR 2012. LNCS, vol. 7180, pp. 228–242. Springer, Heidelberg (2012). doi:10.1007/978-3-642-28717-6_19
14. Heras, J., Komendantskaya, E., Johansson, M., Maclean, E.: Proof-pattern recognition and lemma discovery in ACL2. In: McMillan, K., Middeldorp, A., Voronkov, A. (eds.) LPAR 2013. LNCS, vol. 8312, pp. 389–406. Springer, Heidelberg (2013). doi:10.1007/978-3-642-45221-5_27
15. Johansson, M., et al.: Conjecture synthesis for inductive theories. J. Autom. Reasoning **47**(3), 251–289 (2011)
16. Johansson, M., Rosén, D., Smallbone, N., Claessen, K.: Hipster: integrating theory exploration in a proof assistant. In: Watt, S.M., Davenport, J.H., Sexton, A.P., Sojka, P., Urban, J. (eds.) CICM 2014. LNCS, vol. 8543, pp. 108–122. Springer, Cham (2014). doi:10.1007/978-3-319-08434-3_9
17. Kaliszyk, C., Urban, J.: Lemma mining over HOL Light. In: McMillan, K., Middeldorp, A., Voronkov, A. (eds.) LPAR 2013. LNCS, vol. 8312, pp. 503–517. Springer, Heidelberg (2013). doi:10.1007/978-3-642-45221-5_34
18. Kaliszyk, C., Urban, J.: Learning-assisted theorem proving with millions of lemmas. J. Symb. Comput. **69**, 109–128 (2015)
19. Kaufmann, M., Manolios, P., Moore, P. (eds.): Computer-Aided Reasoning: An Approach. Kluwer Academic Publishers, Boston (2000)
20. Komendantskaya, E., et al.: Machine learning for proof general: interfacing interfaces. Electron. Proc. Theor. Comput. Sci. **118**, 15–41 (2013)
21. Kühlwein, D., Blanchette, J.C., Kaliszyk, C., Urban, J.: MaSh: machine learning for sledgehammer. In: Blazy, S., Paulin-Mohring, C., Pichardie, D. (eds.) ITP 2013. LNCS, vol. 7998, pp. 35–50. Springer, Heidelberg (2013). doi:10.1007/978-3-642-39634-2_6
22. The Univalent Foundations Program. Homotopy Type Theory. Institute for Advanced Study. https://github.com/HoTT/HoTT/wiki (2013)
23. Roux, S.: Acyclic preferences and existence of sequential nash equilibria: a formal and constructive equivalence. In: Berghofer, S., Nipkow, T., Urban, C., Wenzel, M. (eds.) TPHOLs 2009. LNCS, vol. 5674, pp. 293–309. Springer, Heidelberg (2009). doi:10.1007/978-3-642-03359-9_21
24. Urban, J., et al.: ATP and presentation service for Mizar formalizations. J. Autom. Reasoning **50**(2), 229–241 (2013)

Formalization of Transform Methods Using HOL Light

Adnan Rashid$^{(\boxtimes)}$ and Osman Hasan

School of Electrical Engineering and Computer Science (SEECS)
National University of Sciences and Technology (NUST), Islamabad, Pakistan
{adnan.rashid,osman.hasan}@seecs.nust.edu.pk,
http://save.seecs.nust.edu.pk/projects/tm.html

Abstract. Transform methods, like Laplace and Fourier, are frequently used for analyzing the dynamical behaviour of engineering and physical systems, based on their transfer function, and frequency response or the solutions of their corresponding differential equations. In this paper, we present an ongoing project, which focuses on the higher-order logic formalization of transform methods using HOL Light theorem prover. In particular, we present the motivation of the formalization, which is followed by the related work. Next, we present the task completed so far while highlighting some of the challenges faced during the formalization. Finally, we present a roadmap to achieve our objectives, the current status and the future goals for this project.

Keywords: Laplace transform · Fourier transform · Interactive theorem proving · HOL Light

1 Introduction

Differential equations are indispensable for modeling the dynamical behaviour of continuous-time engineering and physical systems. Transform methods, which include the Laplace and Fourier transform, have been widely used for the differential equation based dynamical analysis of these systems. These transform methods are the integral based methods, which convert a time varying function into its corresponding s or ω-domain representations based on Laplace and Fourier transform, respectively. Moreover, this transformation converts the differential and integral operators in the time domain to their corresponding algebraic operators, namely, multiplication and division, in Laplace (s) or Frequency (ω) domain and thus the arithmetic manipulation of the resulting equations involving these operators becomes easier. These equivalent representations of the differential equations can further be used for the transfer function and frequency response analysis of these continuous-time systems. Laplace transform is used for the analysis of the systems with causal input, whereas, in the case of non-causal input systems, Fourier transform is used. This analysis varies in its complexity depending on the size, design parameters, constraints and the nature

© Springer International Publishing AG 2017
H. Geuvers et al. (Eds.): CICM 2017, LNAI 10383, pp. 319–332, 2017.
DOI: 10.1007/978-3-319-62075-6_22

of the input and output signals. The Laplace and Fourier transform methods have been widely used for the analysis of many continuous-time systems, as shown in Table 1.

Table 1. Applications of transform methods

Laplace transform	Fourier transform
	Analog circuits [42, 47]
Control systems [4, 14, 17, 34, 35]	Signal processing [11, 13, 21, 37]
Analog circuits [47]	Image processing [15]
Power electronics [1, 40]	Biomedical imaging [13]
Astronomy [3, 6, 28]	Communication systems [9, 16, 32, 48]
Mechanical systems [4, 36]	Mechanical systems [36]
Nuclear physics [33, 43]	Optics [20, 44]
	Electromechanics [12, 29, 31]

Traditionally, the transform methods based analysis is done using paper-and-pencil proof and computer simulation methods, such as symbolic and numerical methods. However, due to the human-error proneness of paper-and-pencil proof methods and the presence of unverified symbolic algorithms, discretization errors and numerical errors in the simulations methods, the accuracy of the analysis cannot be ascertained. This in turn can lead to compromising performance and efficiency of the underlying system. Interactive theorem proving [27] allows us to overcome these limitations by providing support for logic-based modeling of the system and its intended behaviour and verifying their relationship based on deductive reasoning within the sound core of a theorem prover. With the same motivation, the Laplace [45] and Fourier [39] transforms have been formalized in higher-order logic. In the paper, we mainly describe the past, ongoing and the planned activities for this project[1], which was started in System Analysis and Verification (SAVe) lab[2] in 2012. The formalization of Laplace [45] and Fourier [39] transforms has been developed using the multivariate calculus theories of HOL Light [24]. These formalizations also include the formal verification of some of the classical properties, such as, existence, linearity, frequency shifting, modulation, time reversal, differentiation and integration in time-domain. We choose HOL Light theorem prover for the transform methods based analysis due to the presence of the multivariate calculus theories [24], which contain an extensive reasoning support for differential, integral, transcendental and topology theories.

The rest of the paper is organised as follows: Sect. 2 presents the related work. The proposed approach for the transform methods based analysis is presented

---

[1] http://save.seecs.nust.edu.pk/projects/tm.html.

[2] http://save.seecs.nust.edu.pk.

in Sect. 3. We present the mathematical and formal definitions of transform methods, some of their formally verified classical properties and their mutual relationship in Sect. 4. Section 5 provides the detail about the tasks that have been completed so far, the challenges faced during the formalization of transform methods, the current status and the future goals in this project. We present some of the case studies to illustrate the usefulness of the formal transform based analysis in Sect. 6. Finally, Sect. 7 concludes the paper.

2   Related Work

Fast Fourier transform (FFT) is used for the computation of discrete Fourier transform (DFT), which is used for the analysis of the systems with the discrete-time input. Theorem provers, such as ACL2, HOL and PVS have been used for the verification of different FFT algorithms. Gamboa [18,19] mechanically verified the correctness of FFT using a simple proof of FFT proposed by Misra using the ACL2 theorem prover. This proof utilizes the powerlist data structures, which enable the modeling of FFT using recursive functions in an efficient way and can handle the verification of many complex FFT algorithms. Similarly, Capretta [8] formalized the FFT and inverse Fourier transform (iFT) in Coq. The author used structural recursion to formalize the FFT. Whereas, the iFT is formalized using a different data type to facilitate formal reasoning about the summation operation. Moreover, isomorphism is used to link both of these data types. Similarly, Akbarpour et al. [2] used the HOL theorem prover for the formal specification and verification of a generic FFT algorithm. The authors used real, complex, IEEE floating point and fixed-point arithmetic theories of HOL to perform the error analysis of the FFT algorithms at real, floating-point and fixed-point levels.

Harrison [23] formalized the Fourier series for a real-valued function in the HOL Light theorem prover. The formalization includes the formal definition of Fourier series and formal verification of some of its properties. Similarly, Chau et al. [10] formalized the Fourier coefficient formulas and their properties in ACL2(r). Fourier series and their formalizations presented in HOL Light and ACL2(r) can only cater for the systems with inputs represented as periodic functions. Recently, Z-transform [41] has also been formalized in the HOL Light theorem prover. However, Z-transform can only be utilized for the analysis of the systems with discrete-time input functions and cannot cater for the continuous-time systems, which is the main focus of the current paper.

3   Proposed Approach

Figure 1 depicts the proposed approach for the transform methods based analysis of the continuous-time systems using the HOL Light theorem prover. The user provides the differential equation that models the dynamics of the system, which needs to be analyzed, and the corresponding input to the system. This differential equation is modeled in higher-order logic using the multivariate calculus theories

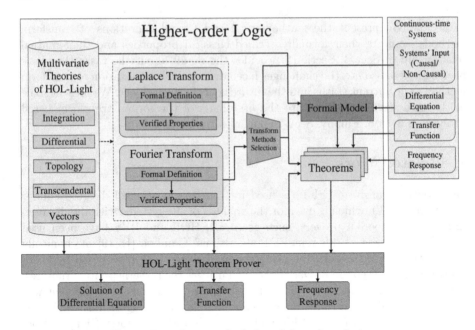

Fig. 1. Transform methods based formal analysis

of HOL Light. In the next step, we need to verify the corresponding properties, such as transfer function, frequency response or the solution of the corresponding differential equations. Our formalization of the Laplace and Fourier transform methods is used to develop the formal reasoning related to this verification. Our formal approach allows the user to perform the analysis of a continuous-time system by selecting the suitable transform method (Laplace or Fourier) depending on the type of the system's input, i.e., if the input to the system is a causal function, then the Laplace transform is used. Similarly, in the case of the non-causal input, Fourier transform can be used.

4   Results and Discussions

In this section, we present the existing formal definitions and some of the formally verified classical properties of the Laplace and Fourier transforms. We also give some suggestions that can improve these definitions in terms of reasoning effort required to verify their properties.

4.1   Laplace Transform

Laplace transform of a function $f(t) : \mathbb{R}^1 \to \mathbb{C}$ is mathematically expressed as the following Eq. [3]:

$$\mathcal{L}[f(t)] = (\mathcal{L}f)(s) = F(s) = \int_0^\infty f(t)e^{-st}dt, \ s \ \epsilon \ \mathbb{C} \tag{1}$$

where s is a complex variable. The limit of integration is from 0 to ∞. The above equation can alternatively represented as:

$$F(s) = \lim_{b \to \infty} \int_0^b f(t)e^{-st}dt \qquad (2)$$

We formalize Eq. 1 using its alternate representation (Eq. 2), as follows [45]:

Definition 1 Laplace Transform.
```
⊢ ∀ s f. laplace f s =
    lim at_posinfinity (λb. integral (interval [lift (&0), lift b])
                            (λt. cexp (--(s * Cx (drop t))) * f t))
```

In the above definition, `integral` represents the vector integral. It takes the integrand function $f : \mathbb{R}^N \to \mathbb{R}^M$, and a vector-space $i : \mathbb{R}^N \to \mathbb{B}$, which defines the region of convergence, and returns the integral of `f` on `i` as a vector $\mathbb{R}^M$ [25]. The function `lim` in Definition 1 takes a vector function $f : A \to \mathbb{R}^M$ and `net : A` and returns `l` of data-type $\mathbb{R}^M$, i.e., the value to which `f` converges at the given `net`. The function `lift` accepts a variable of type $\mathbb{R}$ and maps it to a 1-dimensional vector with the input variable as its single component. Similarly, `drop` takes a 1-dimensional vector and returns its single element as a real number [26].

The Laplace transform of a function f exists, if the function `f` is piecewise smooth and of exponential order on the positive real line [3]. The existence of the Laplace transform is formally defined as follows [45]:

Definition 2 Laplace Exists.
```
⊢ ∀ s f. laplace_exists f s ⇔
    (∀ b. f piecewise_differentiable_on interval [lift (&0), lift b]) ∧
    (∃ M a. Re s > drop a ∧ exp_order f M a)
```

The function `exp_order` in the above definition is formally defined as [45]:

Definition 3 Exponential Order Function.
```
⊢ ∀ f M a. exp_order f M a ⇔ &0 < M ∧
    (∀ t. &0 <= t ⇒ norm (f (lift t)) <= M * exp (drop a * t))
```

We used Definitions 1, 2 and 3 to formally verify some of the classical properties of the Laplace transform, given in Table 2, which mainly include the linearity, frequency shifting, differentiation and integration in the time domain. The formalization of the Laplace transform took around 5000 lines of code and approximately 450 man-hours.

The formal definition of the Laplace transform presented as Definition 1 is modeled using the notion of the limit. However, the HOL Light definition of the integral function (`integral`) implicitly encompasses infinite limits of integration, so we do not require to include another limiting process in its definition. Moreover, the region of integration (the positive real line) given in Eq. 1 can be modeled using the notion of set. So the mathematical definition of the Laplace transform, given by Eq. 1, can alternatively be modeled in HOL Light as:

Table 2. Properties of Laplace transform

Mathematical Form	Formalized Form
Limit Existence of Integral of Laplace Transform	
$\exists l. \left(\int_0^\infty f(t)e^{-st} \to l \right)$	⊢ ∀ f s. laplace_exists f s ⇒ (∃1. ((λb. integral (interval [lift (&0),lift b]) (λt. cexp (--(s * Cx (drop t))) * f t)) → 1) at_posinfinity)
Linearity	
$\mathcal{L}[\alpha f(t) + \beta g(t)] =$ $\alpha F(s) + \beta G(s)$	⊢ ∀ f g s a b. laplace_exists f s ∧ laplace_exists g s ⇒ laplace (λt. a * f t + b * g t) s = a * laplace f s + b * laplace g s
Frequency Shifting	
$\mathcal{L}[e^{s_0 t} f(t)] =$ $F(s - s_0)$	⊢ ∀ f s s0. laplace_exists f s ⇒ laplace (λt. cexp (s0 * Cx (drop t)) * f t) s = laplace f (s - s0)
First-order Differentiation	
$\mathcal{L}\left[\dfrac{d}{dt} f(t) \right] =$ $sF(s) - f(0)$	⊢ ∀ f s. laplace_exists f s ∧ (∀t. f differentiable at t) ∧ laplace_exists (λt. vector_derivative f (at t)) s ⇒ laplace (λt. vector_derivative f (at t)) s = s * laplace f s - f (lift (&0))
Higher-order Differentiation	
$\mathcal{L}[\dfrac{d^n}{dt^n} f(t)] = s^n F(s)$ $- \sum_{k=1}^n s^{k-1} \dfrac{d^{n-k} f(0)}{dx^{n-k}}$	⊢ ∀ f s n. laplace_exists_higher_deriv n f s ∧ (∀t. higher_derivative_differentiable n f t) ⇒ laplace (λt. higher_vector_derivative n f t) s = s pow n * laplace f s - vsum (1..n) (λk. s pow (k - 1) * higher_vector_derivative (n - k) f (lift (&0)))
Integration in Time Domain	
$\mathcal{L}\left[\int_0^t f(\tau)d\tau \right] = \dfrac{1}{s}F(s)$	⊢ ∀ f s. &0 < Re s ∧ laplace_exists f s ∧ laplace_exists (λx. integral (interval [lift (&0),x]) f) s ∧ (∀x. f continuous_on interval [lift (&0),x]) ⇒ laplace (λx. integral (interval [lift (&0),x]) f) s = inv s * laplace f s

⊢ ∀ s f. laplace_transform f s =
    integral {t| &0 <= drop t} (λt. cexp (--(s * Cx (drop t))) * f t)

In the above definition, the region of integration, i.e., $[0, \infty)$ is modeled as {t | &0 <= drop t} and this definition is equivalent to Definition 1. Moreover, this revised definition considerably simplifies the reasoning process in the verification of the properties of the Laplace transform since it does not involve the notion of limit.

4.2   Fourier Transform

The Fourier transform of a function $f(t) : \mathbb{R}^1 \to \mathbb{C}$ is mathematically defined as:

$$\mathcal{F}[f(t)] = (\mathcal{F}f)(\omega) = F(\omega) = \int_{-\infty}^{+\infty} f(t)e^{-i\omega t}dt, \ \omega \in \mathbb{R} \tag{3}$$

where ω is a real variable. The limit of integration is from $-\infty$ to $+\infty$. We formalize Eq. (3) as the following HOL Light function [39]:

Definition 4 Fourier Transform.
⊢ ∀ w f. fourier f w =
        integral UNIV (λt. cexp (--((ii * Cx w) * Cx (drop t))) * f t)

The Fourier transform of a function f exists, i.e., the integrand of Eq. 3 is integrable, and the integral has some converging limit value, if f is piecewise smooth and is absolutely integrable on the whole real line [3,39]. The Fourier existence condition can thus be formalized in HOL Light as follows:

Definition 5 Fourier Exists.
⊢ ∀ f. fourier_exists f =
        (∀ a b. f piecewise_differentiable_on interval [lift a, lift b]) ∧
        f absolutely_integrable_on {x | &0 <= drop x} ∧
        f absolutely_integrable_on {x | drop x <= &0}

In the above function, the first conjunct expresses the piecewise smoothness condition for the function f. Whereas, the next two conjuncts represent the condition that the function f is absolutely integrable on the whole real line.

We used Definitions 4 and 5 to verify some of the classical properties of Fourier transform, given in Table 3, such as existence, linearity, frequency shifting, modulation, time reversal and differentiation in time-domain. The formalization took around 3000 lines of code and approximately 250 man-hours.

The absolute integrability condition in Definition 5 is modeled using two conjuncts, i.e., the absolute integrability on the positive and negative real line, respectively. This condition can alternatively be modeled as:

    f absolutely_integrable_on UNIV

The function UNIV in the above condition presents the whole real line and is a composite modeling of the positive and negative real lines. Thus, this revised condition can better model the integrability condition and its equivalence to the earlier condition can be easily verified using some properties of the integrals.

4.3   Relationship Between Laplace and Fourier Transforms

By restricting the complex-valued function $f(t) : \mathbb{R}^1 \rightarrow \mathbb{C}$ and the Laplace variable $s : \mathbb{R}^2$, we can find a very important relationship between Laplace and Fourier transforms. If the function f is causal, i.e., $f(t) = 0$ for all $t < 0$ and the real part of the Laplace variable $s : \mathbb{R}^2$ is zero, i.e., $Re\ s = 0$, then the Laplace transform of function f is equal to Fourier transform [47]:

Table 3. Properties of Fourier Transform

Mathematical Form	Formalized Form
Integrability	
$f(t)e^{-i\omega t}$ *integrable* *on* $(-\infty, \infty)$	$\vdash \forall$ f w. fourier_exists f s $\Rightarrow$ (λt. cexp (--((ii * Cx w) * Cx (drop t))) * f t) integrable_on UNIV
Linearity	
$\mathcal{F}[\alpha f(t) + \beta g(t)] =$ $\alpha F(\omega) + \beta G(\omega)$	$\vdash \forall$ f g w a b. fourier_exists f $\wedge$ fourier_exists g $\Rightarrow$ fourier (λt. a * f t + b * g t) w = a * fourier f w + b * fourier g w
Frequency Shifting	
$\mathcal{F}[e^{i\omega_0 t} f(t)] = F(\omega - \omega_0)$	$\vdash \forall$ f w w0. fourier_exists f $\Rightarrow$ fourier (λt. cexp ((ii * Cx w0) * Cx (drop t)) * f t) w = fourier f (w - w0)
Modulation (Cosine and Sine Based Modulation)	
$\mathcal{F}[cos(\omega_0 t) f(t)] =$ $\dfrac{F(\omega - \omega_0) + F(\omega + \omega_0)}{2}$	$\vdash \forall$ f w w0. fourier_exists f $\Rightarrow$ fourier (λt. ccos (Cx w0 * Cx (drop t)) * f t) w = $\dfrac{\text{fourier f (w} - \text{w0)} + \text{fourier f (w} + \text{w0)}}{\text{Cx (\&2)}}$
$\mathcal{F}[sin(\omega_0 t) f(t)] =$ $\dfrac{F(\omega - \omega_0) - F(\omega + \omega_0)}{2i}$	$\vdash \forall$ f w w0. fourier_exists f $\Rightarrow$ fourier (λt. csin (Cx w0 * Cx (drop t)) * f t) w = $\dfrac{\text{fourier f (w} - \text{w0)} - \text{fourier f (w} + \text{w0)}}{\text{Cx (\&2) * ii}}$
Time Reversal	
$\mathcal{F}[f(-t)] = F(-\omega)$	$\vdash \forall$ f w. fourier_exists f $\Rightarrow$ fourier (λt. f (--t)) w = fourier f (--w)
First-order Differentiation	
$\mathcal{F}[\dfrac{d}{dt} f(t)] = i\omega F(\omega)$	$\vdash \forall$ f w. fourier_exists f $\wedge$ fourier_exists (λt. vector_derivative f (at t)) $\wedge$ ($\forall$t. f differentiable at t) $\wedge$ ((λt. f (lift t)) $\rightarrow$ vec 0) at_posinfinity $\wedge$ ((λt. f (lift t)) $\rightarrow$ vec 0) at_neginfinity $\Rightarrow$ fourier (λt. vector_derivative f (at t)) w = ii * Cx w * fourier f w
Higher-order Differentiation	
$\mathcal{F}[\dfrac{d^n}{dt^n} f(t)] = (i\omega)^n F(\omega)$	$\vdash \forall$ f w n. fourier_exists_higher_deriv n f $\wedge$ ($\forall$t. differentiable_higher_derivative n f t) $\wedge$ ($\forall$p. p < n $\Rightarrow$ ((λt. higher_vector_derivative p f (lift t)) $\rightarrow$ vec 0) at_posinfinity) $\wedge$ ($\forall$p. p < n $\Rightarrow$ ((λt. higher_vector_derivative p f (lift t)) $\rightarrow$ vec 0) at_neginfinity) $\Rightarrow$ fourier (λt. higher_vector_derivative n f t) w = (ii * Cx w) pow n * fourier f w

$$(\mathcal{L}f)(s) \,|_{Re\ s\ =\ 0} = \ (\mathcal{F}f)(Im\ s)$$

The above relationship can be verified in HOL Light as follow:

```
⊢ ∀ f s. laplace_exists f s ∧
    (∀t. t IN {t | drop t <= &0} ⇒ f t = vec 0) ∧ (∀t. Re s = &0)
                        ⇒ laplace_transform f s = fourier_transform f (Im s)
```

This relationship is very crucial in a sense, if the function is causal, then the Laplace transform can be used in the analysis, rather than the Fourier transform.

5   Achieved Goals, Current Status and Future Plans

The project started with the formalization of the Laplace transform and one of the major challenge faced during its formalization was that we were not very familiar with multivariable calculus theories of HOL Light and thus reasoning about theorems involving integration, differentiation and limits of the real and vector functions was very tedious for us as novice users of the system. Moreover, we found that many basic properties required to reason about transform methods were not available in the multivariable theories in HOL Light and thus we ended up verifying many classical properties related to integration, differentiation and limit, including *Comparison test for improper integrals, Integration by substitution, Integration by parts* and the *Relationship between derivative of a real and vector functions* [45]. The other major difficulty faced during these formalizations was the unavailability of detailed proofs for the properties of transform methods in literature. The available paper-and-pencil based proofs were found to be very abstract and we had to build the formal reasoning, at our own, for their verification. Moreover, some of the assumptions of the properties of the Fourier transform were not explicitly mentioned in the literature, which we have extracted during the verification of these properties. The foundational formalization of the Laplace and Fourier transform took about 8000 lines of HOL Light code and 700 man hours. The main benefit of this formalization was found in the ability to conduct formal transform method based analysis of many systems, including linear transfer converter [45], which is widely used component in power electronics, the first and second-order Sallen-Key low-pass filters [46] and the automobile suspension system [39]. The foundational formalization of Laplace and Fourier transforms was found to be quite useful in this context and the analysis of these applications was found to be very straightforward and took only 1600 lines of HOL Light code and 8 man hours only.

The distinguishing feature of the transform methods based formal analysis, compared to traditional analysis methods, is the generic nature of the formally verified theorems. All the variables and functions are universally quantified and thus can be specialized to obtain the results for any given values. Moreover, all of the required assumptions are guaranteed to be explicitly mentioned along with a formally verified theorem due to the inherent soundness of the theorem proving approach. Moreover, the high expressiveness of the higher-order logic enables us to model the differential equation and the corresponding transfer function and frequency response in their true continuous form, whereas, in model checking, they are mostly discretized and modeled using a state-transition system, which may compromise the completeness of the analysis. A comparison of different analysis techniques for the transform methods is presented in Table 4. The evaluation of these techniques is performed based on various parameters, such as expressiveness, accuracy and automation. For example, in model checking, we cannot truly model the integration and differentiation, and their discretization results into an abstracted model, which makes it less expressive. Moreover, in theorem proving, the verification is done interactively due to the undecidable nature of higher-order logic. We are mainly working on facilitating the user in this interactive verification part by providing formal reasoning support for Laplace and Fourier transforms.

Table 4. Comparison of analysis techniques for transform methods

	Paper-and-pencil proof	Simulation	Computer algebra system	Model checking	Theorem proving
Expressiveness	✓	✓	✓		✓
Accuracy	✓ (?)			✓	✓
Automation		✓	✓	✓	

We are currently focussing on the following three tasks:

- Formalization of inverse Laplace and Fourier transforms: We have formally verified the uniqueness property of the Laplace transform and are working on verifying it for the Fourier Transform. These properties would enable us to verify the analytical solutions of linear differential equations.
- Automation of the transform methods based formal analysis: We are in the process of developing some tactics to automate the transform methods based formal analysis of the continuous-time systems. These tactics would only require the differential equation, modeling the dynamics of the systems, and expressions for the corresponding transfer functions and frequency responses and would automatically verify the relationships between them. This would allow non-experts in theorem proving to benefit from our formal approach for the analysis of the systems.
- Formalization of Vectorial Laplace transform: The current formalization of the Laplace transform can only be used for the formal analysis of the single-input single-output (SISO) control systems. We are working on extending the reasoning support for the normal Laplace transform to complex vectors. The resulting formalization would help us to formally verify the transfer function of the multiple-input multiple output (MIMO) control systems, which are modeled using the state space representations.

To further extend the scope of transform methods based formal analysis of systems, we plan to work on the following two tasks in the future:

Table 5. Applications of Transform Methods

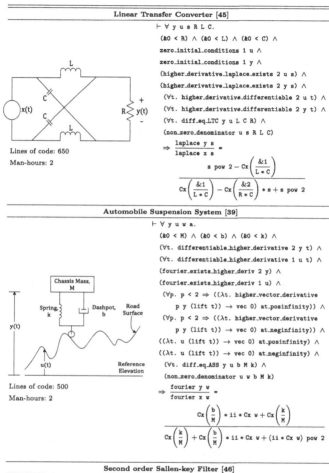

Linear Transfer Converter [45]

$\vdash \forall\ y\ u\ s\ R\ L\ C.$

$(\&0 < R) \land (\&0 < L) \land (\&0 < C) \land$

zero_initial_conditions 1 u $\land$

zero_initial_conditions 1 y $\land$

(higher_derivative_laplace_exists 2 u s) $\land$

(higher_derivative_laplace_exists 2 y s) $\land$

$(\forall t.\ $higher_derivative_differentiable 2 u t$) \land$

$(\forall t.\ $higher_derivative_differentiable 2 y t$) \land$

$(\forall t.\ $diff_eq_LTC y u L C R$) \land$

(non_zero_denominator u s R L C)

Lines of code: 650

Man-hours: 2

$$\Rightarrow \frac{\text{laplace y s}}{\text{laplace x s}} = \frac{s\ \text{pow}\ 2 - Cx\left(\frac{\&1}{L*C}\right)}{Cx\left(\frac{\&1}{L*C}\right) - Cx\left(\frac{\&2}{R*C}\right) * s + s\ \text{pow}\ 2}$$

Automobile Suspension System [39]

$\vdash \forall\ y\ u\ w\ a.$

$(\&0 < M) \land (\&0 < b) \land (\&0 < k) \land$

$(\forall t.\ $differentiable_higher_derivative 2 y t$) \land$

$(\forall t.\ $differentiable_higher_derivative 1 u t$) \land$

(fourier_exists_higher_deriv 2 y) $\land$

(fourier_exists_higher_deriv 1 u) $\land$

$(\forall p.\ p < 2 \Rightarrow ((\lambda t.\ $higher_vector_derivative

p y (lift t)$) \to$ vec 0) at_posinfinity$)) \land$

$(\forall p.\ p < 2 \Rightarrow ((\lambda t.\ $higher_vector_derivative

p y (lift t)$) \to$ vec 0) at_neginfinity$)) \land$

$((\lambda t.\ $u (lift t)$) \to$ vec 0) at_posinfinity$) \land$

$((\lambda t.\ $u (lift t)$) \to$ vec 0) at_neginfinity$) \land$

$(\forall t.\ $diff_eq_ASS y u b M k$) \land$

(non_zero_denominator u w b M k)

Lines of code: 500

Man-hours: 2

$$\Rightarrow \frac{\text{fourier y w}}{\text{fourier x w}} = \frac{Cx\left(\frac{b}{M}\right) * ii * Cx\ w + Cx\left(\frac{k}{M}\right)}{Cx\left(\frac{k}{M}\right) + Cx\left(\frac{b}{M}\right) * ii * Cx\ w + (ii * Cx\ w)\ \text{pow}\ 2}$$

Second order Sallen-key Filter [46]

$\vdash \forall\ $R1 R2 C1 C2 Vin Vout s. $(\&0 < $R1$) \land$

$(\&0 < $C1$) \land (\&0 < $C1$) \land (\&0 < $C2$) \land$

zero_initial_conditions Vin Vout Va $\land$

(laplace_exists_higher_deriv 2 Vout s) $\land$

(laplace_exists_higher_deriv 2 Vin s) $\land$

$(\forall t.\ $differentiable_higher_derivative 2 Vout t$) \land$

$(\forall t.\ $differentiable_higher_derivative 2 Vin t$) \land$

$(\forall t.\ $differentiable_higher_derivative 2 Va t$) \land$

(non_zero_denom Vin s R1 R2 C1 C2) $\land$

$(\forall t.\ $SKF_behav Vin Vout R1 R2 C1 C2$)$

Lines of code: 250

Man-hours: 2

$$\Rightarrow \frac{\text{laplace Vout s}}{\text{laplace Vin s}} = \frac{Cx(\&1)}{Cx\left(R1 * C1 * R2 * C2\right) * s\ \text{pow}\ 2 + Cx\left(C2 * (R1 + R2)\right) * s + Cx(\&1)}$$

- Linking the formal library of the Laplace transform with the formalization of Z-transform [41]: This linkage will enable us to perform the formal analysis of the hybrid (exhibiting continuous and discrete behaviour) systems.
- Formalization of two-dimensional Fourier transform: This requires the formalization of double integral and its properties, which, to the best of our knowledge, have not been formalized in the current multivariable calculus theories of HOL Light. The two-dimensional Fourier transform would build upon this theory of double integration. This formalization will enable us to perform the formal analysis of many electromagnetic (e.g., [7,30]) and the optical systems (e.g., [5,7]). Moreover, this formalization of double integral can also be used for the formal analysis of some other applications in physics, such as, quantum [22] and mechanics [38].

6   Impact

Our foundational formalization of the Laplace [45] and the Fourier [39] transforms has been used for the formal analysis of the various systems and some of them are presented in Table 5. Due to the availability of the higher-order-logic formalization of transform methods, the analysis of these applications was very straightforward. It can be seen that these analyses took very few lines of code and very less manual effort, which clearly illustrates the effectiveness of our foundational formalization. These formalizations of the Laplace and Fourier transform can be further used for the analysis of the many other applications, including control systems, power electronics, signal processing and communication systems.

7   Conclusion

This paper provides a synthetic presentation of our ongoing project on the formalization of transform methods using the HOL Light theorem prover. We present the proposed approach for the transform methods based formal analysis of the continuous-time systems along with the foundational formal definitions of the Laplace and Fourier transform. The paper highlights the main objectives of the project that have been achieved so far, the challenges faced during this formalization, and the ongoing tasks and the future goals for this project. Once all the planned formalization tasks are accomplished, then these foundations can be used for the formal analysis of many safety-critical systems, such as control systems, power electronics, signal processing, electromagnetics and optical systems.

Acknowledgements. This work was supported by the National Research Program for Universities grant (number 1543) of Higher Education Commission (HEC), Pakistan.

References

1. Abad, G.: Power Electronics and Electric Drives for Traction Applications. Wiley, Hoboken (2016)
2. Akbarpour, B., Tahar, S.: A methodology for the formal verification of FFT algorithms in HOL. In: Hu, A.J., Martin, A.K. (eds.) FMCAD 2004. LNCS, vol. 3312, pp. 37–51. Springer, Heidelberg (2004). doi:10.1007/978-3-540-30494-4_4
3. Beerends, R.J., Morsche, H.G., Van den Berg, J.C., Van de Vrie, E.M.: Fourier and Laplace Transforms. Cambridge University Press, Cambridge (2003)
4. Bogart, T.F.: Laplace Transforms and Control Systems Theory for Technology: Including Microprocessor-Based Control Systems. Wiley, New York (1982)
5. Born, M., Wolf, E.: Principles of Optics: Electromagnetic Theory of Propagation, Interference and Diffraction of Light. Elsevier, Amsterdam (1980)
6. Boyce, W.E., DiPrima, R.C., Haines, C.W.: Elementary Differential Equations and Boundary Value Problems, vol. 9. Wiley, New York (1969)
7. Bracewell, R.N.: The Fourier Transform and its Applications. McGraw-Hill, New York (1978)
8. Capretta, V.: Certifying the fast fourier transform with Coq. In: Boulton, R.J., Jackson, P.B. (eds.) TPHOLs 2001. LNCS, vol. 2152, pp. 154–168. Springer, Heidelberg (2001). doi:10.1007/3-540-44755-5_12
9. Chapin, L.: Communication Systems (1978)
10. Chau, C.K., Kaufmann, M., Hunt Jr., W.A.: Fourier Series Formalization in ACL2 (r). arXiv preprint arXiv:1509.06087 (2015)
11. Chu, E.: Discrete and Continuous Fourier Transforms: Analysis, Applications and Fast Algorithms. CRC Press, Boca Raton (2008)
12. Davidson, D.B.: Computational Electromagnetics for RF and Microwave Engineering. Cambridge University Press, Cambridge (2005)
13. Devasahayam, S.R.: Signals and Systems in Biomedical Engineering: Signal Processing and Physiological Systems Modeling. Springer Science & Business Media, New York (2012)
14. Dorf, R.C., Bishop, R.H.: Modern Control Systems. Prentice Hall, Eindhoven (1998)
15. Dougherty, G.: Digital Image Processing for Medical Applications. Cambridge University Press, Cambridge (2009)
16. Du, K.L., Swamy, M.N.S.: Wireless Communication Systems: From RF Subsystems to 4G Enabling Technologies. Cambridge University Press, Cambridge (2010)
17. Fortmann, T.E., Hitz, K.L.: An introduction to linear control systems. CRC Press, Boca Raton (1977)
18. Gamboa, R.A.: Mechanically verifying the correctness of the fast fourier transform in ACL2. In: Rolim, J. (ed.) IPPS 1998. LNCS, vol. 1388, pp. 796–806. Springer, Heidelberg (1998). doi:10.1007/3-540-64359-1_743
19. Gamboa, R.A.: The correctness of the fast fourier transform: a structured proof in ACL2. Formal Methods Syst. Des. **20**(1), 91–106 (2002)
20. Gaskill, J.D.: Linear Systems, Fourier Transforms, and Optics, 1st edn. Wiley, New York (1978)
21. Gaydecki, P.: Foundations of Digital Signal Processing: Theory, Algorithms and Hardware Design. Institution of Engineering and Technology, Stevenage (2004)
22. Gorini, V., Frigerio, A.: Fundamental Aspects of Quantum Theory, vol. 144. Springer Science & Business Media, USA (2012)

23. Harrison, J.: Fourier Series (2015). http://github.com/jrh13/hol-light/blob/master/100/fourier.ml
24. Harrison, J.: HOL Light Multivariate Calculus (2017). https://github.com/jrh13/hol-light/tree/master/Multivariate
25. Harrison, J.: Integration Theory in HOL Light (2017). https://github.com/jrh13/hol-light/blob/master/Multivariate/integration.ml
26. Harrison, J.: Real Vectors in Euclidean Space (2017). http://github.com/jrh13/hol-light/blob/master/Multivariate/vectors.ml
27. Hasan, O., Tahar, S.: Formal Verification Methods. Encyclopedia of Information Science and Technology, pp. 7162–7170. IGI Global Pub., Hershey (2015)
28. Hilbe, J.M.: Astrostatistical Challenges for the New Astronomy, vol. 1. Springer Science & Business Media, New York (2012)
29. Jancewicz, B.: Trivector fourier transformation and electromagnetic field. J. Math. Phys. **31**(8), 1847–1852 (1990)
30. Jin, J.M.: Theory and Computation of Electromagnetic Fields. Wiley, Hoboken (2011)
31. Kriezis, E.E., Chrissoulidis, D., Papagiannakis, A.: Electromagnetics and Optics. World Scientific, Singapore (1992)
32. Madhow, U.: Introduction to Communication Systems. Cambridge University Press, Cambridge (2014)
33. McLachlan, N.W.: Laplace Transforms and their Applications to Differential Equations. Courier Corporation, Cedar City (2014)
34. Nise, N.S.: Control Systems Engineering. Wiley, New York (2007)
35. Ogata, K., Yang, Y.: Modern Control Engineering. Prentice-Hall, Englewood Cliffs (1970)
36. Oppenheim, A.V., Willsky, A.S., Hamid Nawab, S.: Signals and Systems. Prentice Hall Processing Series, 2nd edn. Prentice Hall Inc., Upper Saddle River (1996)
37. Papoulis, A.: Signal Analysis, vol. 2. McGraw-Hill, New York (1977)
38. Pytel, A., Kiusalaas, J.: Engineering Mechanics: Dynamics. Nelson Education, Scarborough (2016)
39. Rashid, A., Hasan, O.: On the formalization of fourier transform in higher-order logic. In: Blanchette, J.C., Merz, S. (eds.) ITP 2016. LNCS, vol. 9807, pp. 483–490. Springer, Cham (2016). doi:10.1007/978-3-319-43144-4_31
40. Rashid, M.H.: Power Electronics: Circuits, Devices, and Applications. Pearson Education India, Delhi (2009)
41. Siddique, U., Mahmoud, M.Y., Tahar, S.: On the formalization of Z-transform in HOL. In: Klein, G., Gamboa, R. (eds.) ITP 2014. LNCS, vol. 8558, pp. 483–498. Springer, Cham (2014). doi:10.1007/978-3-319-08970-6_31
42. Siebert, W.M.: Circuits, Signals, and Systems, vol. 2. MIT press, Cambridge (1986)
43. Stacey, W.M.: Nuclear Reactor Physics. Wiley, New York (2007)
44. Stark, H.: Application of Optical Fourier Transforms. Elsevier, Burlington (2012)
45. Taqdees, S.H., Hasan, O.: Formalization of laplace transform using the multivariable calculus theory of HOL-light. In: McMillan, K., Middeldorp, A., Voronkov, A. (eds.) LPAR 2013. LNCS, vol. 8312, pp. 744–758. Springer, Heidelberg (2013). doi:10.1007/978-3-642-45221-5_50
46. Taqdees, S.H., Hasan, O.: Formally verifying transfer functions of linear analog circuits. IEEE Des. Test (2017). http://save.seecs.nust.edu.pk/pubs/2017/DTnA_2017.pdf
47. Thomas, R.E., Rosa, A.J., Toussaint, G.J.: The Analysis and Design of Linear Circuits, Binder Ready Version. Wiley, New York (2016)
48. Ziemer, R., Tranter, W.H.: Principles of Communications: System Modulation and Noise. Wiley, Chichester (2006)

Combining Refinement and Signal-Temporal Logic for Biological Systems

Usman Sanwal[1]([✉]) and Umair Siddique[2]

[1] Computational Biomodeling Laboratory, Department of Computer Science,
Åbo Akademi University, Turku Centre for Computer Science, 20500 Turku, Finland
msanwal@abo.fi
[2] Department of Computing and Software, McMaster University, Hamilton, Canada

Abstract. System-level modeling and analysis of biological phenomena have become an important research topic amongst different fields including mathematics, computer science, electrical and system engineering. This is a consequence of the recent development in these fields which can be utilized to understand the dynamics of complex biological organisms such as cancer, malaria and diabetes, etc. However, the concept of model refinement (i.e., the transformation of an abstract models into a detailed model) is largely unexplored in biology. In this paper, we describe our ongoing project which aims at combining the concept of model refinement and temporal logic for the analysis of a wide class of biological systems.

Keywords: Biomodeling · Refinement · Event-B · Signal-Temporal Logic

1 Introduction

In the last two decades, significant progress has been made towards the system-level modeling of biological systems and diseases such as cell signaling pathways, metabolic networks, diabetes and cancer. The concept of *abstraction* provides a convenient method to model complex systems at various levels of detail. The main idea is to build a simple model of the system and progressively add details which ultimately allow us to consider a suitable model for a specific study. Recent research in this direction includes differential equations based modeling [9], Petri nets [8], guarded command languages [7] and rule-based modeling [4]. The main focus of this research project is twofold:

- modeling of biological systems in Event-B [2], a formal method for stepwise development and refinement of complex models. To the best of our knowledge, this is the first time that Event-B is used for describing biological systems. One of the main strengths of refinement in Event-B is the formal relation amongst different abstract models, which is established through gluing invariants. However, establishing such a relation is difficult in other approaches, e.g., models based on ordinary differential equations, continuous time Markov chains and Petri nets.

© Springer International Publishing AG 2017
H. Geuvers et al. (Eds.): CICM 2017, LNAI 10383, pp. 333–339, 2017.
DOI: 10.1007/978-3-319-62075-6_23

- transforming Event-B models into a suitable form (e.g., a systems of differential equations) for quantitative analysis using the Signal-Temporal Logic (STL), a temporal logic capable of reasoning about continuous functions. Consequently, we can quantitatively evaluate interesting biological behaviors such as *oscillations, stabilization* and *interdependence* of different biological entities in the model. For example, we can describe the following property in STL: *"if the concentration of entity x goes above some threshold θ_1 then within $t \in [T_1, T_2]$ time the concentration of entity y drops below θ_2".*

Organization: Sects. 2 and 3 provide an overview of Event-B and STL, respectively. In Sect. 4, we describe our proposed framework and current status of the project along with the description of ongoing and future tasks. Finally, Sect. 5 concludes the paper.

2 Event-B

Event-B [2] is a formal method widely used for modeling and reasoning about complex computing systems. The core concept and design of Event-B are inspired by B-Method [1]. In Event-B, we can progressively add details in the underlying model (i.e., introduction of new system variables) through refinement. Event-B model is composed of two components: Machine and Context. The machine is the dynamic part of the Event-B model and consists of variables, invariants and events whereas context is the static part of the Event-B model and it includes axioms, constants and theorems.

Example 1: Metabolic networks describe the physiological and biochemical properties of biological cells. Every species is modelled by a variable of type $\mathbb{N}$ (natural numbers) denoting the current number of that species. The state of the system is modelled by the species interacting with each other and the reactions become events in Event-B. Assume we have two reactions:

$$2X \rightarrow Y \tag{1}$$

$$X + Y \rightarrow Z \tag{2}$$

An Event-B model for these reactions consists of 3 variables, corresponding to the three species:

$$\boxed{\begin{array}{c} \textbf{VARIABLES} \\ x, y, z \end{array}}$$

The types of these variables are specified as invariants $x \in \mathbb{N}$, $y \in \mathbb{N}$ and $z \in \mathbb{N}$ and their initial values are described by an Initialisation event. For modelling these two reactions, we define two events. To model the event guard, we need the precondition necessary for the event to happen. In our case, this is ensured by having enough reactants to consume. Thus, the guard of the first event will be $x \geq 2$ (we can conserve two x quantities) and the guard of the second event will be $x \geq 1$ and $y \geq 1$. The actions of the event model the updates in the species involved in the reaction, including both the reactants and the products. Thus, as in the first reaction we consume $2x$ and produce y, this is modelled in the actions: $x := x - 2$ and $y := y + 1$. In the second reaction, we produce z and consume for this x and y, hence the corresponding actions are $x := x - 1$, $y := y - 1$ and $z := z + 1$. *Proof obligations* of these events are discharged automatically. In Event-B, these two events have the following form:

```
FirstEvent
WHERE
    @grd1 x ≥ 2
THEN
    @act1 x := x − 2
    @act2 y := y + 1
END
```

```
SecondEvent
WHERE
    @grd1 x ≥ 1
    @grd1 y ≥ 1
THEN
    @act1 x := x − 1
    @act2 y := y − 1
    @act2 z := z + 1
END
```

3   Signal-Temporal Logic (STL)

Temporal logic provides a mechanism to specify evolution of a system behaviour over time. Traditionally, temporal logic has been used to specify the properties of software and hardware systems over discrete state-space. However, *Metric Interval Temporal Logic* (MITL) [3] uses the notion of dense-time and allows to model continuous evolution of system variables. Our work is based on *Signal Temporal Logic* (STL) [10] which strengthens MITL by incorporating predicates on the real-valued variables.

STL Syntax: A formula φ in STL is constructed from atomic predicates which describe the instantaneous behaviour of systems variables, combined using Boolean and temporal operators. Formally, a formula is constructed using the following grammar:

$$\varphi ::= \mu \mid \neg\varphi \mid \varphi \vee \varphi \mid \varphi\, \mathbf{U}_{[a,b)}\, \varphi \mid \Diamond_{[a,b]}\, \varphi \mid \Box_{[a,b]}\, \varphi$$

where μ, $\mathbf{U}$, $\Diamond$ and $\Box$ represent, a predicate, 'until', 'eventually' and 'always' operators, respectively. Formally, μ describes a generic constraint applied to a trajectory ζ defined as a function of time instant τ. For example, such a constraint (corresponding to example in the Introduction) is $\mu : (x(\tau) - \theta_1 > 0)$. Temporal formula $\Diamond_{[0,5]}\, \mu$ describes that the constraint μ has to be true at least once within 5 time units, whereas $\Box_{[0,5]}\, \mu$ specifies that the constraint μ must be true all time during the 5 time units. Whereas temporal formula $\phi_1\, \mathbf{U}_{[0,5]}\, \phi_2$ is satisfied if ϕ_1 holds continuously until some time within 5 time units when ϕ_2 becomes true.

STL Semantics: The semantics of STL has been defined for both qualitative (Boolean) [10] and quantitative [6] evaluation. The Boolean semantics of STL decides whether the trajectory ζ satisfies the formula φ at time τ by structural induction on the STL formula. The quantitative semantics of STL is defined in terms of a function Υ which takes the trajectory ζ, time τ and formula φ and returns a real-valued number $\Upsilon(\varphi, \zeta, \tau)$ quantifying the degree of satisfaction of φ by ζ at time τ.

Breach [5] is a MATLAB/C++ toolbox which provides an efficient framework to formally model hybrid dynamical systems and analyze their properties specified in STL. Some important features of Breach include simulation and plotting of continuous signals, qualitative and quantitative monitoring of STL properties and parameter synthesis of STL specifications.

Example 2: The biological reaction described in Eq. (2) can be transformed into a differential equations based model and consequently specified in Breach as follows:

$$\begin{cases} \frac{dx(t)}{dt} = -\alpha x(t)y(t) \\ \frac{dy(t)}{dt} = -\alpha x(t)y(t) \\ \frac{dz(t)}{dt} = \alpha x(t)y(t) \\ x(0) = p_1, \ y(0) = p_1 \ and \ z(0) = p_3 \quad (intial \ conditions) \end{cases} \quad (3)$$

where α represents the rate of reaction, and variables $x(t)$, $y(t)$ and $z(t)$ represent the concentration of X, Y and Z at time t, respectively. We can now formalize several interesting biological behaviours in STL. For example:

– $z(t)$ will become more than 10 within 5 s: $\Diamond_{[0,5]}(z(t) \geq 10)$
– $z(t)$ remains low until $x(t)$ stabilizes within 10 s:
  $z(t) < 1 \, \mathbf{U}_{[0,10]} \, (\Box(\|\frac{dx(t)}{dt}\| < 0.0000001))$

Notice that $\Box$ without a (subscripted) time interval represents $\Box_{[0,\infty]}$.

4   Framework for Biomodeling and Analysis

The proposed framework, given in Fig. 1, outlines the main idea behind our bio-modeling and analyzing a wide range of biological systems. Our modeling starts from the available literature of a biological network (e.g., metabolic network, cancer or malaria, etc.). As a first step, we build an abstract model $\mathcal{M}^1$ in Event-B. At this point, we have two targets:

– transform the abstract model ($\mathcal{M}^1$) into an equivalent differential equations based model $\mathcal{D}^1$;
– build a refined model $\mathcal{M}^2$ depending upon the availability of additional information.

In biology, it is common to find underlying networks with various levels of details. For example, it can be a consequence of different studies by different research groups or discovery of new biological entities through experimental observations (e.g., imaging, laser scanning, etc.). Following these steps, we can

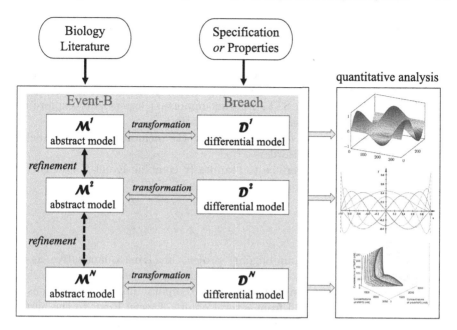

Fig. 1. Proposed framework for biomodeling and refinement

build N refined models $(\mathcal{M}^1 - \mathcal{M}^N)$ through successive refinements and N differential models $(\mathcal{D}^1 - \mathcal{D}^N)$ through transformation for each refined model ($\mathcal{M}^i$ to $\mathcal{D}^i$). During the course of this development, we can perform quantitative analysis for each model ($\mathcal{D}^i$) for a given biological property specified as an STL formula. Indeed, we perform quantitative analysis in Breach toolbox and can visually inspect (through various plots) interesting behaviours. Note that our framework provides two novel advantages as compared to other approaches: Firstly, each refined model is formally linked and serves for bookkeeping purposes in a formal language. Secondly, we can perform quantitative analysis in various steps which can greatly reduce computational cost. In fact, analysis of some properties might take huge computational resources or might not terminate for some cases. However, it might be sufficient to analyse certain properties at a higher-level of abstraction thus reducing the size of the model.

As a proof-of concept, the molecular model for heat shock response introduced in [11] was formally modeled in Event-B in [12]. The model was first introduced in a simplified presentation, after which details were added to it through 5 consecutive refinements in Event-B. As a result of this refinement, model expands from 10 species and 17 irreversible reactions to 20 species and 55 irreversible reactions. Our ongoing and future work includes the following tasks:

– Formalize the rules for transforming the model $\mathcal{M}^i$ to $\mathcal{D}^i$. Indeed transformation rules are based on the Law of Mass Action which provides ODEs for the concentrations of the species involved in the bio-(chemical) reactions. We plan to formalize this transformation in HOL Light[1] proof assistant and formally prove its soundness.

- Develop a template for frequently used STL properties (e.g., oscillations, stabilization, steady state, etc.). Potentially, we would like to generate them from plain text, so that our framework can be used by biologists without prior knowledge of Event-B and STL. Another important aspect is to explore the parameter synthesis capabilities of Breach toolbox.
- Build an extensive library of biological networks including cancers, diabetes, heart diseases and brain disorders.
- Build a graphical user interface to seamlessly combine Event-B and Breach toolbox through verified transformation rules.

5   Conclusion

We describe in this paper our ongoing project involving quantitative model refinement as an approach to stepwise construction of a biological network in Event-B and quantitative analysis of Signal-Temporal Logic specifications in Breach toolbox. This is useful from several points of view: First, to the best of our knowledge, there is no work available related to implementation of biological models in Event-B, except the proof of concept model of the heat shock response in [12]. Second, formally refined models can serve as a library of reusable biological models. Third, parametric Signal-Temporal Logic specifications for each refined model can be used for parameter synthesis. Such parameters can provide some useful indications for future drug designs for infectious diseases.

References

1. Abrial, J.-R.: The B-book: Assigning Programs to Meanings. Cambridge University Press, New York, NY, USA (1996)
2. Abrial, J.-R.: Modeling in Event-B: System and Software Engineering, 1st edn. Cambridge University Press, New York, NY, USA (2010)
3. Alur, R., Feder, T., Henzinger, T.A.: The benefits of relaxing punctuality. J. ACM **43**(1), 116–146 (1996)
4. Danos, V., Feret, J., Fontana, W., Harmer, R., Krivine, J.: Rule-based modelling and model perturbation. In: Priami, C., Back, R.-J., Petre, I. (eds.) Transactions on Computational Systems Biology XI. LNCS, vol. 5750, pp. 116–137. Springer, Heidelberg (2009). doi:10.1007/978-3-642-04186-0_6
5. Donzé, A.: Breach, a toolbox for verification and parameter synthesis of hybrid systems. In: Touili, T., Cook, B., Jackson, P. (eds.) CAV 2010. LNCS, vol. 6174, pp. 167–170. Springer, Heidelberg (2010). doi:10.1007/978-3-642-14295-6_17
6. Donzé, A., Maler, O.: Robust satisfaction of temporal logic over real-valued signals. In: Chatterjee, K., Henzinger, T.A. (eds.) FORMATS 2010. LNCS, vol. 6246, pp. 92–106. Springer, Heidelberg (2010). doi:10.1007/978-3-642-15297-9_9

---

[1] http://www.cl.cam.ac.uk/~jrh13/hol-light/.

7. Gratie, D.E., Iancu, B., Azimi, S., Petre, I.: Quantitative model refinement in four different frameworks, with applications to the heat shock response. In: Petre, L., Sekerinski, E. (eds.) From Action Systems to Distributed Systems, pp. 201–214. Taylor & Francis, Boca Raton (2016)
8. Gratie, D.E., and Petre, I.: Hiding the combinatorial state space explosion of bio-models through colored petri nets. Annals of University of Bucharest, LXI, pp. 23–41 (2014)
9. Iancu, B., Czeizler, E., Czeizler, E., Petre, I.: Quantitative refinement of reaction models. Int. J. Unconventional Comput. 8(5–6), 529–550 (2012)
10. Maler, O., Nickovic, D., Pnueli, A.: Checking temporal properties of discrete, timed and continuous behaviors. In: Avron, A., Dershowitz, N., Rabinovich, A. (eds.) Pillars of Computer Science. LNCS, vol. 4800, pp. 475–505. Springer, Heidelberg (2008). doi:10.1007/978-3-540-78127-1_26
11. Petre, I., Mizera, A., Hyder, C.L., Meinander, A., Mikhailov, A., Morimoto, R.I., Sistonen, L., Eriksson, J.E., Back, R.-J.: A simple mass-action model for the eukaryotic heat shock response and its mathematical validation. Nat. Comput. 10(1), 595–612 (2011)
12. Sanwal, U., Petre, L., and Petre, I.: Stepwise construction of a metabolic network in Event-B: the heat shock response. TUCS Technical reports, (1160) (2016)

VMEXT: A Visualization Tool for Mathematical Expression Trees

Moritz Schubotz[1](✉), Norman Meuschke[1](✉), Thomas Hepp[1](✉),
Howard S. Cohl[2](✉), and Bela Gipp[1](✉)

[1] Department of Computer and Information Science,
University of Konstanz, Box 76, 78457 Konstanz, Germany
{moritz.schubotz,norman.meuschke,thomas.hepp,bela.gipp}@uni-konstanz.de
[2] Applied and Computational Mathematics Division, National Institute of Standards
and Technology, Gaithersburg, MD 20899-8910, USA
howard.cohl@nist.gov
http://www.isg.uni-konstanz.de
http://www.nist.gov/people/howard-cohl

Abstract. Mathematical expressions can be represented as a tree consisting of terminal symbols, such as identifiers or numbers (leaf nodes), and functions or operators (non-leaf nodes). Expression trees are an important mechanism for storing and processing mathematical expressions as well as the most frequently used visualization of the structure of mathematical expressions. Typically, researchers and practitioners manually visualize expression trees using general-purpose tools. This approach is laborious, redundant, and error-prone. Manual visualizations represents a user's notion of what the markup of an expression should be, but not necessarily what the actual markup is. This paper presents VMEXT – a free and open source tool to directly visualize expression trees from parallel MathML. VMEXT simultaneously visualizes the presentation elements and the semantic structure of mathematical expressions to enable users to quickly spot deficiencies in the Content MathML markup that does not affect the presentation of the expression. Identifying such discrepancies previously required reading the verbose and complex MathML markup. VMEXT also allows one to visualize similar and identical elements of two expressions. Visualizing expression similarity can support developers in designing retrieval approaches and enable improved interaction concepts for users of mathematical information retrieval systems. We demonstrate VMEXT's visualizations in two web-based applications. The first application presents the visualizations alone. The second application shows a possible integration of the visualizations in systems for mathematical knowledge management and mathematical information retrieval. The application converts LaTeX input to parallel MathML, computes basic similarity measures for mathematical expressions, and visualizes the results using VMEXT.

Keywords: Mathematical information retrieval · Expression tree · LaTeX · MathML · Visualization

© Springer International Publishing AG 2017
H. Geuvers et al. (Eds.): CICM 2017, LNAI 10383, pp. 340–355, 2017.
DOI: 10.1007/978-3-319-62075-6_24

1 Introduction

Mathematical notation strives to have a well-defined vocabulary, syntax, and semantics. Similar to sentences in natural language or constructs in a programming language, mathematical expressions consist of constituents that have a coherent meaning, such as terms or functions. We consider a mathematical expression to be any sequence of mathematical symbols that can be evaluated, e.g., typically formulae. The syntactic rules of mathematical notation, such as operator precedence and function scope, determine a hierarchical structure for mathematical expressions, which can be understood, represented, and processed as a tree. *Mathematical expression trees* consist of functions or operators and their arguments. Experiments by Jansen, Marriott, and Yelland suggest that mathematicians use some notion of mathematical expression trees as a mental representation to perform mathematical tasks [JMY00].

Describing and processing mathematical content using expression trees is established practice in mathematics and computer science as our review of related work in Sect. 2 shows. However, no standard for the content of nodes, or the structure and visual representation of such trees has yet emerged. Additionally, we did not find tools that support generating expression tree visualizations from mathematical markup. All of the visualizations that we were able to glean from the literature were manually created using general purpose tools.

With this paper, we seek to contribute to the establishment of an openly available, widely accepted, visualization of mathematical expression trees, encoded using the MATHML standard. For this purpose, we propose a tree visualization that operates on parallel MATHML markup and provides the visualization as a free and open source tool. We structure the presentation of our contributions as follows. Section 2.1 presents details of the MATHML standard that serves as the data structure for our visualization approach. Section 2.2 reviews the strength and weaknesses of existing approaches for visualizing mathematical expression trees to derive our visualization concept. Section 3 present our visualization tool VMEXT. Section 3.3 describes a demo application that shows how the visualization can be integrated into other applications. Section 3.4 explains how end users and developers can apply and obtain VMEXT. Section 4 concludes the paper by discussing our plans for further extending and improving VMEXT.

2 Related Work

As briefly motivated in the previous section, we seek to reduce the effort for researchers and practitioners to generate expression tree visualizations for mathematical content. Additionally, we hope to contribute to establishing a standardized representation of mathematical expression trees. In Sect. 2.1, we present the MATHML standard and explain why we see it as a promising data format to achieve this goal. In Sect. 2.2, we review existing approaches for visualizing mathematical expression trees to explain how we derived the major building blocks of our visualization approach.

2.1 MathML

Mathematical Markup Language (MATHML) is a W3C[1] and ISO standard (ISO/IEC DIS 40314) for representing mathematical content using XML syntax. MATHML is part of HTML5 and enables one to serve, receive, and process mathematical content on the World Wide Web. MATHML allows users to describe the notation and/or the meaning of mathematical content using two vocabularies: Presentation MATHML (PMML) and Content MATHML (CMML). The vocabularies can be used independently of each other or in conjunction.

Presentation MATHML focuses on describing the visual layout of mathematical content. The PMML vocabulary contains elements for basic mathematical symbols and structures. Each element specifies the role of the presentation element, e.g., the element `<mi>` represents identifiers and the element `<mo>` represents operators. The structure of PMML markup reflects the two-dimensional layout of the mathematical expression. Elements that form semantic units are encapsulated in `<mrow>` elements, which are comparable to `<div>` elements in HTML. Listing 1.1 exemplifies PMML markup for the expression $f(a + b)$.

Content MATHML focuses on explicitly encoding the semantic structure and the meaning of mathematical content using expression trees. In other words, the CMML vocabulary seeks to specify the frequently ambiguous mapping from the presentation of mathematical content to its meaning. For example, the presentation of the expression $f(a + b)$ represents two possible syntactic structures: e.g., f could represent either an identifier or a function. CMML uses `<apply>` elements to make explicit which elements represent functions. Subordinate elements represent the arguments of the functions. Listing 1.2 illustrates CMML markup for the expression $f(a + b)$.

```
1  <math xmlns="http://www.w3.org/1998/Math/MathML">
2    <semantics>
3      <mrow id="r1">
4        <mi id="i1">f</mi>
5        <mo id="o1">(</mo>
6        <mrow id="r2">
7          <mi id="i2">a</mi>
8          <mo id="o2">+</mo>
9          <mi id="i3">b</mi>
10       </mrow>
11       <mo id="o3">)</mi>
12     </mrow>
```

Listing 1.1. Presentation MATHML encoding of the expression $f(a + b)$ [Sch17]

Content MATHML offers two subsets of elements to specify function types: Pragmatic Content MATHML and Strict Content MATHML. Pragmatic Content MATHML uses a large set of predefined functions encoded as empty elements, e.g., `<plus/>`, as used in Line 17 in Listing 1.2, or `<log/>` for the logarithm.

---

[1] www.w3.org/Math/.

```
13    <annotation−xml encoding="MathML−Content">
14      <apply xref="r1">
15        <ci xref="b">f</ci>
16        <apply xref="r2">
17          <plus xref="o2"/><!-- <csymbol cd="arith1">plus
                </csymbol> in strict encoding -->
18          <ci xref="i2">a</ci>
19          <ci xref="i3">b</ci>
20        </apply>
21      </apply>
22    </annotation−xml>
```

Listing 1.2. Content MATHML encoding of the expression $f(a + b)$ [Sch17]

Strict Content MATHML uses a minimal set of elements, which are further specified by referencing extensible content dictionaries. For example, the plus operator $(+)$ is defined in the content dictionary **arith1**. Using Strict CMML, the operator is encoded using the element for symbols <csymbol>, and declaring that the specification of the symbol is available under the term **plus** in the content dictionary **arith1**. Line 17 in Listing 1.2 shows this option of specifying the plus operator as a comment (green font color).

As described above, the PMML and CMML vocabularies can be used individually and independent of each other. For example, PMML is frequently used without content markup to display mathematical content on websites. CMML without presentation markup can, for instance, be used to exchange data between computer algebra systems. However, PMML and CMML markup can also be used in conjunction to simultaneously describe the presentation, structure, and semantics of mathematical expressions. The combined use of PMML and CMML is commonly referred to as parallel MATHML.

In parallel MATHML markup, presentation and content elements are mutually interlinked by including **xref** arguments that point to the corresponding element in the other vocabulary. The PMML and CMML markup in Listings 1.1 and 1.2 respectively contain **xref**-links to create parallel MATHML.

2.2 Expression Tree Visualizations

Researchers, especially in math information retrieval (MIR), have employed several use-case-specific tree visualizations for mathematical expressions. All visualizations appear to have been created manually to illustrate research in publications. The content and structure of the visualizations vary significantly. Figures 1 and 2 give an overview of the visualizations, which we describe hereafter.

Youssef and Shatnawi use simple ASCII graphics to visualize expression trees. Their visualization resembles binary expression trees. Leaf nodes represent identifiers or numbers; inner nodes represent operators, functions, or brackets [YS06].

In later work, Shatnawi and Youssef replace the ASCII graphics with an equivalent chart. Altamimi and Youssef further improve their visualization by marking subexpression groups with dashed lines (see Fig. 1b) [AY08].

Miner and Munavalli use a different tree to illustrate their research on math search. They render the full expression in the root of the tree and create subnodes for each sub-expression (see Fig. 1c) [MM07]. Sojka and Líška use a similar visualization to illustrate the tokenization and indexing process of their math search system.

Hashimoto, Hijikata, and Nishida use a tree layout that represents the DOM structure of Presentation MATHML markup to illustrate the author's research on MATHML indexing [HHN08]. In this layout, inner nodes represent MATHML elements depicted as circles and leaf nodes represent the content of elements depicted as squares (see Fig. 1d). We assume the authors manually created the visualization, since the focus of their paper is on math search and does not mention an automated visualization approach.

Kamali and Tompa [KT09] and Kamali and Tompa [KT10] use a similar tree representation of the Presentation MATHML structure in their works on math similarity and retrieval. Their visualization does not distinguish between inner nodes and leaf nodes, but depicts all nodes as circles (see Fig. 1a). Two things are notable about this visualization. First, the layout corresponds to the data structure of the mathematical expressions. Second, Kamali and Tompa introduce the notion of defining and visualizing the similarity of mathematical expressions in terms of the structural similarity of sub-trees. The authors visually indicate similar sub-trees by enclosing the respective sub-tree in a dashed line (see Fig. 1a). In subsequent work, Kamali and Tompa [KT13] use a horizontal layout to visualize the same tree. The tree uses boxes instead of circles and directed instead of undirected edges. Kamali and Tompa exclusively consider PMML and do not present an automated approach to create their visualization of the structure and similarity of PMML expressions.

Yokoi and Aizawa consider Content MATHML markup for their research on math similarity search and devise a visualization of the CMML tree [YA09]. Their work introduces apply-free content markup, i.e., omitting the first $<$ apply $>$ element in the CMML markup, since it provides little information on the applied function. Instead, their markup uses the first child of an $<$apply$>$ element. Their manually created visualization also omits $<$apply$>$ elements (see Fig. 2a). We consider this approach valuable, since it reduces the number of nodes to visualize and facilitates the recognition of function types.

Hagino and Saito also consider apply-free Content MATHML markup for their research on partial match retrieval in math search [HS13]. To illustrate their research, they use a tree that depicts the CMML element names in the case of inner nodes and the CMML element names in combination with the elements' content in the case of leaf nodes (see Fig. 2b).

In their review of approaches for math recognition and retrieval, Zanibbi and Blostein point out that building a symbol layout tree is important for math recognition tasks [ZB12]. Symbol layout trees represent horizontally adjacent

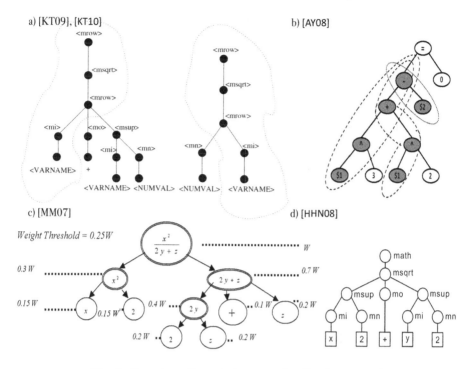

Fig. 1. Overview of expression tree visualizations part 1

symbols that share a writing line and indicate subscript, superscript, above, below, and containment relationships. The authors present a horizontal illustration of the symbol layout tree and a simplified expression tree using a vertical layout (see Fig. 2d). Pattaniyil and Zanibbi uses a similar horizontal illustration of the symbol layout tree (see Fig. 2e) [PZ14].

Zhang and Youssef use Strict Content MATHML for their research [ZY14]. In their visualizations of the CMML tree, they omit the element names for <ci> and <cn> elements, but include <apply> elements. They replace the names of CMML elements with shorter symbols. For instance, they replace <apply> with @ and <power> with ^.

2.3   Summary of Related Work and Research Gap

From our review of the literature, we draw the following conclusions. First, representing mathematical expressions as trees is essential for performing many tasks in mathematical knowledge management (MKM) and mathematical information retrieval (MIR). Expression trees, in which leaf nodes represent terminal symbols and inner nodes represent operators, functions, or brackets are widely used as a data representation. The MATHML standard is a well-established data format for representing the presentation, structure, and semantics of mathematical

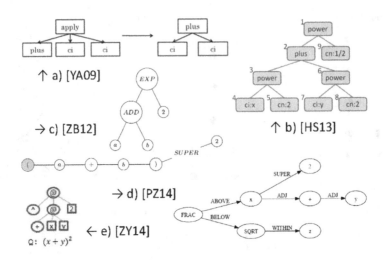

Fig. 2. Overview of expression tree visualizations part 2

content using the expression tree concept. Many researcher rely on MATHML encoded content for MIR and MKM tasks.

Second, researchers frequently employ expression tree visualizations to illustrate their math-related research. While some visualizations reflect the information extracted from mathematical markup, such as MATHML, other visualizations illustrate abstract mathematical expressions. The elements included in the visualizations, their spatial arrangement, and visual appearance varies greatly. Depending on the use case, visualizations may include presentation elements, content elements, or combinations thereof. Especially in the MIR domain, researchers frequently need to visualize similarity of operator (sub-)trees.

Third, although the expression tree concept is at the heart of MATHML and visualizations of MATHML markup are widely used for analysis and presentation purposes, we found no tool that generates such visualizations from MATHML markup. Researchers typically create expression tree visualizations manually using general-purpose tools. This approach results in much manual and redundant effort, diverse visual representations of identical markup, and the danger of creating a visualization that does not reflect the underlying data. To reduce the effort for creating expression tree visualizations and to contribute towards establishing a more canonical design of expression trees, we present the VMEXT system, which we describe in the following section.

3   VMEXT System

VMEXT is an acronym for Visualizing Mathematical Expression Trees. This tool seeks to visually support researchers and practitioners in two well-defined use cases:

1. curating semantically enriched mathematical content, e.g., for use in digital repositories or systems for mathematical knowledge management;
2. examining similarities of two mathematical expressions, e.g., for developing mathematical information retrieval approaches or for examining and interacting with the results of MIR systems.

VMEXT addresses the use cases with two visualizations available as widgets that can easily be integrated into any web application. We present the widgets in Sects. 3.1 and 3.2. Both widgets are available as a demo system at: http://vmext.formulasearchengine.com/. Section 3.3 presents a demo application that exemplifies the possible use of the widgets as part of MKM and MIR systems. Section 3.4 describes how interested parties may use VMEXT's visualizations; integrate the visualizations as widgets or via an API into their own applications; and how to adapt and extend the code.

3.1 Curating Semantically-Enriched Mathematical Content

Making mathematical knowledge accessible through recognition, retrieval, and management systems is a task that has attracted many contributions by researchers and practitioners. (Guidi and Sacerdoti Coen [GS16] and Zanibbi and Blostein [ZB12] present comprehensive reviews on the topic). The MATHML standard (see Sect. 2.1) has been widely adopted to expose both the presentation and semantics of mathematical content for such systems.

However, the MATHML syntax is verbose, complex and therefore not easy to grasp for humans. Furthermore, creating parallel MATHML markup is complicated and error-prone. This is true, especially for the creation of parallel MATHML by converting other formats, such as LATEX, and often results in ambiguous or erroneous markup. Typically, Presentation MATHML elements are less frequently affected by errors than their respective Content MATHML elements. This leads to a situation, in which the visual representation of an expression is correct, yet its semantics are wrong.

VMEXT supports users in quickly checking and improving parallel MATHML by providing an interactive expression tree visualization that simultaneously illustrates the semantic structure (as well as the presentation elements) encoded in the markup.

VMEXT visualizes the structure of the tree as encoded in the Content MATHML markup. However, the labels for each node render the Presentation MATHML elements linked to the respective content elements. VMEXT uses the apply-free CMML notation introduced in [YA09]. In other words, our parser renders the first child of each <apply> element, not the <apply> itself, as an operator or function. All following children are considered as arguments of the function. For a clear layout, VMEXT renders the complete PMML element for the first child, even if the first child is itself an <apply> element. To reduce the size of the individual edges, we replace some CMML elements with shorthand symbols, e.g., we replace <power> with $\wedge$ as can be seen in Fig. 3 (cf. [ZY14], see also Sect. 2).

To facilitate human inspection, VMEXT follows the information seeking mantra proposed by Shneiderman [Shn96]: *overview first, zoom and filter, then details-on-demand.* The nodes in VMEXT can be interactively *filtered* by expanding or collapsing nodes either one at a time or all at once using the expand button. The view-port is adjustable using *pan* and *zoom* interactions to enable focusing on specific parts of the tree. The resize button resets the zoom level. User *navigation* is supported through an overview infix expression rendered at the top of the screen. Hovering over parts of the infix expression or nodes in the tree, highlights the corresponding parts in the tree and the infix expression. Subsection 3.2 shows how hovering over the divide operator highlights the respective sub-tree in light blue. The user can *export* the chosen (sub-)tree rendering, including all manipulations performed through filtering and zooming, as a high-resolution png image, e.g., for use in publications.

To demonstrate how VMEXT's expression tree visualization can aid in curating semantically enriched MATHML markup, we use the integral representation of the Euler gamma function [Olv+, (5.2.1)] as an example

$$\Gamma(z) = \int_0^\infty e^{-t} t^{z-1} \, \mathrm{d}t. \tag{1}$$

Figure 3a–c show VMEXT's rendering for three markup variants of the Euler gamma function. All variants have identical PMML markup, i.e., produce identical visual output as shown in Eq. 1. However, the CMML differs, because we generated the MATHML using LATEXML [Mil15] using different LATEX input (shown in the captions of the figures). Note, that these different LATEX versions encode more or less semantics.

The trees in Fig. 3 a and b show that VMEXT allows an arbitrary number of child nodes, as opposed to the binary expression tree concept we briefly described in Sect. 1. The conversion of generic LATEX input (a), misinterpreted some invisible operators, such as the invisible operator between Γ and (z) that was interpreted as times rather than a function application. Additionally, LATEXML marked some CMML elements as ambiguous, i.e., could not establish a one-to-one relation to a PMML element. For ambiguous nodes, VMEXT renders all PMML elements enclosed by the ambiguous CMML element in a node with dashed borders to emphasize the defective markup for the user. For example, the node for e^{-t} in Fig. 3 was marked as ambiguous.

The LATEX representation using DLMF macros (b) resolves the problem of invisible operators by using the @ symbol to make such operators explicit. However, this representation still results in ambiguous nodes. Representing the Euler gamma function using DLMF and DRMF macros [Coh+14, Coh+15] results in correct CMML markup. In (c), we specify the integral using the semantic macro \Int rather than the generic \int command. We have required that all occurrences of the ∧-operator must denote the power operator. Note that, in order to make this workable, one must create beneficial custom semantic macros for all other uses of the ∧-operator. These include matrix operations ($A^\dagger$), labeling (x^*), function spaces (C^k), norms (L^p), sums ($\sum_{n=0}^\infty$), products ($\prod_{n=0}^\infty$), derivatives ($f^{(2)}(x)$), etc.

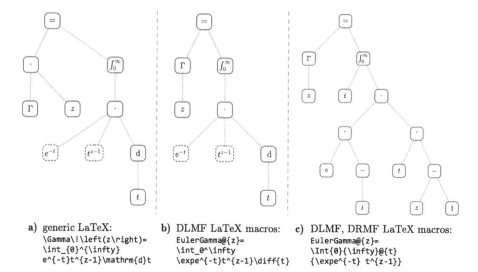

a) generic LaTeX:
```
\Gamma\!\left(z\right)=
\int_{0}^{\infty}
e^{-t}t^{z-1}\mathrm{d}t
```

b) DLMF LaTeX macros:
```
EulerGamma@{z}=
\int_0^\infty
\expe^{-t}t^{z-1}\diff{t}
```

c) DLMF, DRMF LaTeX macros:
```
EulerGamma@{z}=
\Int{0}{\infty}@{t}
{\expe^{-t} t^{z-1}}
```

Fig. 3. Expression trees rendered for MATHML input obtained from converting different LaTeX input. The Presentation MATHML is identical for all three cases, yet the Content MATHML differs.

By rendering the expression tree as encoded by the CMML markup, VMEXT enables users to quickly spot markup deficiencies and illuminates the effects of using different conversions or manually changing markup.

3.2 Examining Similarities of Mathematical Expressions

Our review of MIR literature (see Sect. 2.2) shows that researchers often seek to visualize the similarity of two mathematical expressions, e.g., the similarity between a query expression and a retrieval candidate. To facilitate this task, VMEXT includes a specialized visualization shown in Subsect. 3.2. The presented example compares two notations of the measure Mean Reciprocal Rank.

The widget accepts CMML input for the expressions to compare. Similar elements can be specified by stating the IDs of the similar CMML elements in both trees using JSON. Currently, VMEXT allows one to specify that elements are either similar or identical. The two types of similarity are rendered differently. Since VMEXT is designed to be a visualization tool, it includes no functionality to compute similarities. We demonstrate the integration of the widgets with a basic application that computes similarities in Sect. 3.3.

The center view renders the trees (including the infix overview) for both expressions and visually distinguishes the trees using different background colors. The visualizations offer the same interaction features as the expression tree widget (see Sect. 3.1). In the lower part of the center view, VMEXT renders a combined expression tree. The combined tree includes all nodes from both trees color-coded with the background color of the tree from which they originate. Unique, i.e., dissimilar, sub-trees of both trees are collapsed to direct the user's attention to the similar parts of the trees. For elements marked as similar, VMEXT renders the nodes from both trees and highlights them as exemplified by the nodes MRR and MMR. Nodes that are marked as identical are rendered only once and are highlighted as exemplified by the node $\sum_{i=1}^{|Q|} \frac{1}{r}$.

The integrated visualization of the two expression trees and the combined tree, allows users to quickly inspect the full structure of both expressions and similar sub-trees. The highlight on hover feature helps users to look up the corresponding subtrees for nodes marked as similar in the combined tree.

A specific application that benefits from visualizing the similarity of mathematical expressions is our prototype of a hybrid plagiarism detection system CitePlag[2] [MGB12, Gip+13]. Forms of academic plagiarism vary greatly in their degree of obfuscation ranging from blatant copying to strongly disguised idea plagiarism [MG13]. Our research indicates that not a single, but combined PD approaches are most promising to reliably detect the wide range of plagiarism forms [GMB14, Gip+14, Gip14]. Combined approaches accumulate evidence on potentially suspicious similarity using heterogeneous features, such as literally matching text, similarities in the citations used, and similarity of mathematical content [MG14]. CitePlag is the first system to implement such an integrated analysis and uses the VMEXT framework to visualize the similarity of mathematical content.

3.3   Demo Application

To showcase a possible integration of VMEXT's widgets into MIR and MKM applications, we developed a Java application for input conversion and similarity computation. The demo provides a basic web frontend available at: http:// vmext-demo.formulasearchengine.com and offers two main features.

First, it converts LaTeX input to parallel MathML. The backend of the demo application offers two alternative converters. The first converter employs LaTeXML, whose configuration can be customized via input fields included in the web frontend. The second converter passes the LaTeX input to the Mathoid system[3] [SW14], which employs the speech rule engine[4] [CKS15] to generate Presentation MathML with **CDATA** annotations. These annotations give hints on the possible semantic meaning of expressions. Using a simple XSLT stylesheet, the demo application converts this non-standard-conforming markup to standard parallel MathML markup. The application enables users to quickly run different LaTeX to MathML conversions and immediately examines the effects on the conversion quality using the VMEXT visualizations described in Sects. 3.1 and 3.2.

Second, the demo application computes basic similarity measures for two expressions (Fig. 4). The most basic measure identifies identical nodes. A second measure uses the idea of taxonomic distance of expressions proposed in [ZY14]. Our implementation uses content dictionaries to model the taxonomic distance

---

[2] http://www.citeplag.org.

[3] https://www.mediawiki.org/wiki/Mathoid.

[4] https://github.com/zorkow/speech-rule-engine.

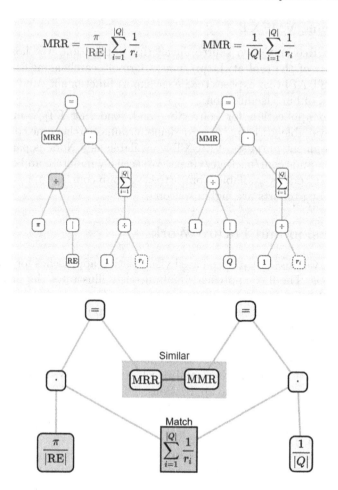

Fig. 4. VMEXT expression tree similarity widget

and builds upon the content dictionary abstraction as introduced in [Sch+14]. The system converts the CMML markup of the expression to Strict CMML to guarantee that the XML encodings of all symbols explicitly state from which content dictionary the symbols originate. All symbols originating from the same content dictionary, like plus and minus, or sine and cosine, are considered similar. Symbols from different content dictionaries, e.g., plus and cosine, are considered dissimilar. The objective of the similarity computation is to provide users with test data to explore the visualization approaches, and not to be meaningful from an analytical perspective.

3.4   Obtaining VMEXT

VMEXT is a free and open source JavaScript application. We host a ready-to-use instance of the tool at: http://vmext.formulasearchengine.com. We also provide a REST API that exposes the image export functionality and the internal representation of our visualization.

The demo application for converting and rendering LaTeX markup (see Sect. 3.3) is available at: http://vmext-demo.formulasearchengine.com.

For development purposes, VMEXT is available as a Node.js package from: https://www.npmjs.com/package/vmext. We actively maintain and enhance the tool; the latest code is available from https://github.com/ag-gipp/vmext. Pull requests and bug reports are highly welcome.

4   Conclusion and Future Work

In this paper, we present two tree-based visualization approaches for mathematical expressions. The first approach simultaneously illustrates the presentation, structure, and semantics of individual expressions. The second approach visualizes the structural and semantic similarity of two expressions. Both approaches operate on parallel MATHML markup and incorporate key elements of expression tree visualizations proposed in the MIR literature.

We implemented the two approaches as part of VMEXT, a system we provide free and open source for end users and developers (see Sect. 3.4). Additionally, we provide two web-based demo applications. The first application[5] presents the visualization widgets alone. The second application[6] demonstrates a possible integration of the widgets in systems for mathematical knowledge management and mathematical information retrieval.

In our future work, we plan to extend VMEXT's functionality beyond exclusively visualizing MATHML markup towards visually assisting markup creation and editing by humans. MATHML shows great promise for enabling unprecedented access to mathematical knowledge. However, converting existing mathematical knowledge to semantic markup formats will require some human interaction. The complexity and verbosity of MATHML makes direct interaction with MATHML markup laborious and time-consuming. We see visual editors as a possible solution to this problem. Enabling users to create and manipulate mathematical notation and MATHML markup via visual support tools would be valuable for increasing the digital accessibility of mathematical knowledge [CS17,Sch+16]. Another possible extension is the consideration of proof structures and the visualization of the directed acyclic graphs, which might occur, if the MATHML <share /> element is used.

Acknowledgements. We thank Ludwig Goohsen and Stefan Kaufhold for their support in developing VMEXT. Furthermore, we thank the Wikimedia Foundation for providing a server to run the VMEXT demo.

---

[5] http://vmext.formulasearchengine.com.
[6] http://vmext-demo.formulasearchengine.com.

References

[AY08]   Altamimi, M.E., Youssef, A.S.: A math query language with an expanded set of wildcards. Math. Comput. Sci. 305–331 (2008). doi:10.1007/s11786-008-0056-4

[CKS15] Cervone, D., Krautzberger, P., Sorge, V.: Towards meaningful visual abstraction of mathematical notation. In: Proceedings CICM (2015)

[Coh+14] Cohl, H.S., McClain, M.A., Saunders, B.V., Schubotz, M., Williams, J.C.: Digital repository of mathematical formulae. In: Watt, S.M., Davenport, J.H., Sexton, A.P., Sojka, P., Urban, J. (eds.) CICM 2014. LNCS (LNAI), vol. 8543, pp. 419–422. Springer, Cham (2014). doi:10.1007/978-3-319-08434-3_30

[Coh+15] Cohl, H.S., Schubotz, M., McClain, M.A., Saunders, B.V., Zou, C.Y., Mohammed, A.S., Danoff, A.A.: Growing the digital repository of mathematical formulae with generic LATEX sources. In: Kerber, M., Carette, J., Kaliszyk, C., Rabe, F., Sorge, V. (eds.) CICM 2015. LNCS, vol. 9150, pp. 280–287. Springer, Cham (2015). doi:10.1007/978-3-319-20615-8_18

[CS17]   Corneli, J., Schubotz, M.: math.wikipedia.org: A vision for a collaborative semi-formal, language independent math(s) encyclopedia. In: Proceedings CAITP (2017)

[Gip+13] Gipp, B., et al.: Demonstration of the first citation-based plagiarism detection prototype. In: Proceedings SIGIR, pp. 1119–1120 (2013). doi:10.1145/2484028.2484214

[Gip+14] Gipp, B., et al.: Web-based demonstration of semantic similarity detection using citation pattern visualization for a cross language plagiarism case. In: Proceedings of International Conference on Enterprise Information Systems, pp. 677–683 (2014). doi:10.5220/0004985406770683

[Gip14] Gipp, B.: Citation-Based Plagiarism Detection - Detecting Disguised and Cross-Language Plagiarism Using Citation Pattern Analysis. Springer, Wiesbaden (2014)

[GMB14] Gipp, B., Meuschke, N., Breitinger, C.: Detection, citation-based plagiarism: practicability on a large-scale scientific corpus. JASIST **65**, 1527–1540 (2014). doi:10.1002/asi.23228

[GS16]   Guidi, F., Sacerdoti Coen, C.: A survey on retrieval of mathematical knowledge. Math. Comput. Sci. 409–427 (2016). doi:10.1007/s11786-016-0274-0

[HHN08] Hashimoto, H., Hijikata, Y., Nishida, S.: Incorporating breadth first search for indexing MathML objects. In: Proceedings SMC, pp. 3519–3523. IEEE (2008). doi:10.1109/ICSMC.2008.4811843

[HS13]   Hagino, H., Saito, H.: Partial-match retrieval with structure-reflected indices at the NTCIR-10 MathTask. In: Proceedings NTCIR-10. National Institute of Informatics (2013)

[JMY00] Jansen, A.R., Marriott, K., Yelland, G.W.: Constituent structure in mathematical expressions. In: CogSci, vol. 22 (2000)

[KT09]   Kamali, S., Tompa, F.W.: Improving mathematics retrieval. In: Proceedings DML, pp. 37–48 (2009)

[KT10]   Kamali, S., Tompa, F.W.: A new mathematics retrieval system. In: Proceedings CIKM, pp. 1413–1416. ACM (2010). doi:10.1145/1871437.1871635

[KT13]   Kamali, S., Tompa, F.W.: Structural similarity search for mathematics retrieval. In: Carette, J., Aspinall, D., Lange, C., Sojka, P., Windsteiger, W. (eds.) CICM 2013. LNCS (LNAI), vol. 7961, pp. 246–262. Springer, Heidelberg (2013). doi:10.1007/978-3-642-39320-4_16

[MG13] Meuschke, N., Gipp, B.: State of the art in detecting academic plagiarism. Int. J. Educ. Integrity **9**, 50–71 (2013)

[MG14] Meuschke, N., Gipp, B.: Reducing computational effort for plagiarism detection by using citation characteristics to limit retrieval space. In: Proceedings JCDL, pp. 197–200 (2014). doi:10.1109/JCDL.2014.6970168

[MGB12] Meuschke, N., Gipp, B., Breitinger, C.: CitePlag: a citation-based plagiarism detection system prototype. In: Proceedings International Plagiarism Conference (2012)

[Mil15] Miller, B.R.: Strategies for parallel markup. In: Kerber, M., Carette, J., Kaliszyk, C., Rabe, F., Sorge, V. (eds.) CICM 2015. LNCS, vol. 9150, pp. 203–210. Springer, Cham (2015). doi:10.1007/978-3-319-20615-8_13

[MM07] Miner, R., Munavalli, R.: An approach to mathematical search through query formulation and data normalization. In: Kauers, M., Kerber, M., Miner, R., Windsteiger, W. (eds.) Calculemus/MKM -2007. LNCS, vol. 4573, pp. 342–355. Springer, Heidelberg (2007). doi:10.1007/978-3-540-73086-6_27

[Olv+] Olver, F.W.J., Olde Daalhuis, A.B., Lozier, D.W., Schneider, B.I., Boisvert, R.F., Clark, C.W., Miller, B.R., Saunders, B.V. (eds.) NIST Digital Library of Mathematical Functions. http://dlmf.nist.gov/. Release 1.0.15 of 2017-06-01

[PZ14] Pattaniyil, N., Zanibbi, R.: Combining TF-IDF text retrieval with an inverted index over symbol pairs in math expressions: the tangent math search engine. In: Proceedings NTCIR-11. National Institute of Informatics (2014)

[Sch+14] Schubotz, M., et al.: Evaluation of similarity-measure factors for formulae based on the NTCIR-11 math task. In: Proceedings NTCIR-11. National Institute of Informatics (2014)

[Sch+16] Schubotz, M., et al.: Semantification of identifiers in mathematics for better math information retrieval. In: Proceedings SIGIR, pp. 135–144. ACM (2016). doi:10.1145/2911451.2911503

[Sch17] Schubotz, M.: Augmenting Mathematical Formulae for More Effective Querying & Effcient Presentation. Epubli Verlag, Berlin (2017, to appear)

[Shn96] Shneiderman, B.: The eyes have it: a task by data type taxonomy for information visualizations. In: Proceedings Visual Languages, pp. 336–343 (1996). doi:10.1109/VL.1996.545307

[SL11] Sojka, P., Líška, M.: The art of mathematics retrieval. In: Proceedings DocEng, pp. 57–60. ACM (2011). doi:10.1145/2034691.2034703

[SW14] Schubotz, M., Wicke, G.: Mathoid: robust, scalable, fast and accessible math rendering for wikipedia. In: Watt, S.M., Davenport, J.H., Sexton, A.P., Sojka, P., Urban, J. (eds.) CICM 2014. LNCS, vol. 8543, pp. 224–235. Springer, Cham (2014). doi:10.1007/978-3-319-08434-3_17

[SY07] Shatnawi, M., Youssef, A.: Equivalence detection using parse-tree normalization for math search. In: Proceedings ICDIM, pp. 643–648. IEEE (2007). doi:10.1109/ICDIM.2007.4444297

[YA09] Yokoi, K., Aizawa, A.: An approach to similarity search for mathematical expressions using MathML. In: Proceedings DML, pp. 27–35. Masaryk University Press, Brno (2009)

[YS06] Youssef, A., Shatnawi, M.: Math search with equivalence detection using parse-tree normalization. In: Proceedings CoSIT (2006)

[ZB12] Zanibbi, R., Blostein, D.: Recognition and retrieval of mathematical expressions. Proc. IJDAR 331–357 (2012). doi:10.1007/s10032-011-0174-4

[ZY14] Zhang, Q., Youssef, A.: An approach to math-similarity search. In: Watt, S.M., Davenport, J.H., Sexton, A.P., Sojka, P., Urban, J. (eds.) CICM 2014. LNCS (LNAI), vol. 8543, pp. 404–418. Springer, Cham (2014). doi:10.1007/978-3-319-08434-3_29

Part-of-Math Tagging and Applications

Abdou Youssef[1,2]([✉])

[1] The George Washington University, Washington DC 20052, USA
ayoussef@gwu.edu
[2] Applied and Computational Mathematics Division, NIST, Gaithersburg, MD, USA

Abstract. Nearly all of the recent mathematical literature, and much of the old literature, are online and mostly in natural-language form. Therefore, math content processing presents some of the same challenges faced in natural language processing (NLP), such as math disambiguation and math semantics determination. These challenges must be surmounted to enable more effective math knowledge management, math knowledge discovery, automated presentation-to-computation (P2C) conversion, and automated math reasoning. To meet this goal, considerable math language processing (MLP) technology is needed.

This project aims to advance MLP by developing (1) a sophisticated part-of-math (POM) tagger, (2) math-sense disambiguation techniques along with supporting Machine-Learning (ML) based MLP algorithms, and (3) semantics extraction from, and enrichment of, math expressions. Specifically, the project first created an evolving tagset for math terms and expressions, and is developing a general-purpose POM tagger. The tagger works in several scans and interacts with other MLP algorithms that will be developed in this project. In the first scan of an input math document, each math term and some sub-expressions are tagged with two kinds of tags. The 1st kind consists of definite tags (such as *operation, relation, numerator*, etc.) that the tagger is certain of. The 2nd kind consists of alternative, tentative features (including alternative roles and meanings) drawn from a knowledge base that has been developed for this project. The 2nd and 3rd scan will, in conjunction with some NLP/ML-based algorithms, select the right features from among those alternative features, disambiguate the terms, group subsequences of terms into unambiguous sub-expressions and tag them, and thus derive definite unambiguous semantics of math terms and expressions. The NLP/ML-based algorithms needed for this work will be another part of this project. These include math topic modeling, math context modeling, math document classification (into various standard areas of math), and definition-harvesting algorithms.

The project will create significant new concepts and techniques that will advance knowledge in two respects. First, the tagger, math disambiguation techniques, and NLP/ML-based algorithms, though they correspond to NLP and ML counterparts, will be quite novel because math expressions are radically different from natural language. Second, the project outcomes will enable the development of new advanced applications such as: (1) techniques for computer-aided semantic enrichment of digital math libraries; (2) automated P2C conversion of math

© Springer International Publishing AG 2017
H. Geuvers et al. (Eds.): CICM 2017, LNAI 10383, pp. 356–374, 2017.
DOI: 10.1007/978-3-319-62075-6_25

expressions from natural form to (i) a machine-computable form and (ii) a formal form suitable for automated reasoning; (3) math question-answering capabilities at the manuscript level and collection level; (4) richer math UIs; and (5) more accurate math optical character recognition.

1 Introduction

Much of the mathematical literature, old and new, is now online [4,18,19,24, 33,45,73], mainly in natural language form, mostly in LaTeX and PDF, and to a lesser extent in presentation-MathML. Therefore, math content processing faces some of the same challenges found in natural language processing (NLP) [41], such as disambiguation and semantics determination. These challenges must be surmounted to enable more effective math knowledge management (MKM), math knowledge discovery (MKD), automated *presentation-to-computation* (P2C) conversion, and automated math reasoning. To meet this goal, considerable math language processing (MLP) technology is needed.

This project aims to advance this field by developing (1) a sophisticated *part-of-math (POM) tagger*, similar to the part-of-speech taggers in NLP [43,52], (2) *math-sense disambiguation* techniques and algorithms that will be integrated with the tagger, and (3) *semantics extraction* from, and enrichment of, math expressions and math documents. These three modules will interact and integrate for maximum synergistic performance.

The first step in creating a tagger is to define a relevant tagset for math terms and expressions, akin to NLP tagsets [52], and then develop a robust general-purpose POM tagger. The tagger will work in several iterations, called *scans*, and interact with other MLP algorithms to be developed in this project for achieving more sophisticated tagging.

In the *first scan*, each math term and some math sub-expressions of the input will be tagged with two kinds of tags. The first consists of definite tags (such as *operation, relation, function, subscript, numerator, integral*, etc.) that the tagger is certain of. The second kind of tags consists of alternative, <u>tentative</u> values of some named features (including alternative roles and meanings) drawn from a knowledge base that has been developed for this project.

The *second and third scans* will, in cooperation with additional algorithms described below, examine the alternative features computed in the 1st scan, determine which of the alternatives are right, disambiguate the terms, group sub-sequences of terms into unambiguous math sub-expressions and tag them, and thus derive definite unambiguous semantics of math terms and math expressions.

To tag and disambiguate effectively, additional algorithms will have to be created. Specifically, to narrow down the role/meaning of a math term, it helps to know which area of mathematics the input document is in. This calls for a *math-document classifier*. Furthermore, knowing the topic, which is more specific than the area of the document, will shed even more light on the math terms. Even more targeted is the notion of *context* which, if properly formulated, will take the tagger a long way in narrowing down the tag choices. A new notion of a math-term's context will be defined, which will involve several components, such as the area and topic of the term's document, the document-provided definitions, the topic model and theme class of the term's *neighborhood* (*e.g.*, (sub)section) in the document, and the actual math expression containing the term as well as a small number of natural language sentences surrounding the math expression. This new notion of context will be formulated into a *context model*, and algorithms for computing and tracking the context model will be developed. Parts of the context are the textual definitions and explanations of terms and notations, which when explicitly present in a document, can be either nearby and consolidated, or far away and scattered. Either way, they need to be *harvested*, by first identifying them, and then determining which definition or explanation matches which math term. Design, development, analysis and optimization of those various algorithms will be another major focus of this project, both in their own right, and in combination with the tagger.

Finally, considerable testing and evaluation of the developed techniques will be done, using available math libraries and archives. One digital library is the DLMF[1] [33], whose contents are in both LaTeX and XHTML/MathML, and are "labeled" in that all the tags of the math terms are known, and thus serve as a good data set for testing and, where needed, for training of the learning algorithms. Another digital repository is the arXiv[2], where the papers are already categorized by math area, and are thus a good data set for training and testing math-document classifiers.

The software resulting from this project will be documented and made available to the public.

The techniques and software products of this project can have many applications, such as:

- More accurate math optical character recognition (math-OCR);
- Techniques for computer-aided semantic enrichment of digital math libraries [17];
- More accurate math search, due to semantic enrichment and term tagging;
- Better math user interfaces: When displaying math on the screen, tagging can provide behind-the-scene annotations for math terms, and build hyperlink connections between various math entities in the document. Those can be displayed on demand;
- Authoring aid: An author can run the tagger in the document being authored, to obtain a list of undefined terms and multi-defined terms, and take remedial actions;
- Automated P2C conversion of math expressions from natural form, like LaTeX or PDF or presentation MathML, to: (i) an unambiguous machine-computable form for computer algebra systems, (ii) Content MathML, and/or (iii) a formal form suitable for use in automated reasoning systems and proof assistants;

---

[1] http://dlmf.nist.gov/.

[2] https://arxiv.org/.

- Math-anaphora resolution: This refers to resolving references to earlier or later items in a discourse; in math, an item may be referred to at times by a math symbol, and at times by its textual name. With the tagger and the harvester, connections between math terms and textual definitions/explanations will be drawn, thus helping resolve anaphoras;
- Math question-answering per manuscript/collection.

This project is expected to have strong impact. It will provide the math processing research community a fundamental and powerful tool that will enable the development of considerably more advanced math processing capabilities, for the benefit of mathematicians, scientists, and general users of mathematics. Sophisticated tagging and semantification (T&S) will lead to better knowledge discovery and automated reasoning capabilities, which are two areas where historically every significant breakthrough has led to great advancement of technology and betterment of human life. For example, by providing *in situ* descriptions of math terms that save a user from scrolling up and down to look up or recall a definition in a math text, T&S can be a convenient and time-saving tool for STEM educators and students. Also, when coupled with a math reader app, it can greatly help visually impaired STEM students and practitioners. Finally, the resulting techniques and tools will enhance the infrastructure for STEM research and education by helping the MLP community create more advanced useful applications.

2 Objectives of the Project

The main objective of this project is to develop a theoretical base and technology infrastructure for extracting implicit semantics from math contents, for the purpose of enabling further innovations and applications in research and technology.

To achieve this overarching objective, the project has the following principal aims:

- To advance the theory and develop novel techniques for appropriately parsing math expressions and equations embedded in math manuscripts and Web pages, and tagging the math terms therein. The resulting system will be termed a *part-of-math tagger* (or simply *POM tagger*), akin to (but algorithmically different from) part-of-speech (POS) taggers for natural languages. The tagger is expected to play the same foundational and stimulating role in math language processing (MLP) as the POS taggers have done in NLP.
- To formulate a fairly comprehensive list of math language ambiguities, and develop *disambiguation techniques* for them, using the tagger and other specific algorithms indicated next.
- To develop and optimize a *math-document classifier*, using standard taxonomies of mathematical subjects (*e.g.*, the MSC[3]), and applying high-accuracy classification methods.

---

[3] http://www.msc2010.org.

- To develop a *math-topic modeler* at different levels of granularity.
- To formulate and model a new notion of math context, and develop algorithms for computing and updating the context. Unlike the simple notion of a term's context being just a few terms surrounding the term, the new notion of a term's context involves the following major components: (1) the math area/class of the term's document, (2) the document-provided definitions, (3) a topic model and theme class of the most immediate (sub)section containing the term, (4) the math expression/formula containing the term, and (5) the 2–4 natural language sentences surrounding the latter math expression.
- To develop a *harvester* that (1) identifies in a given math manuscript the various definitions and notations, often given in a combination of natural language and math language, and (2) tie those definitions and notations to specific math terms in expressions and equations throughout the manuscript. While harvesting algorithms have started to emerge [50,54], our harvester will interact with the tagger and the other modules mentioned above to deliver a superior synergistic performance.
- Optimize the interactions between, and integration of, the tagger, the disambiguation algorithms, the math-document classifier, the math-topic modeler, the math-context modeler, and the harvester, to optimize the individual and collective performance of those modules.

3   Related Work

This project touches upon, and draws from, several important areas, most notably (1) math processing, especially math language processing (MLP) and math knowledge management (MKM), (2) natural language processing (NLP), especially POS tagging, word-sense disambiguation, and general lexical/syntactic/semantic NLP foundational concepts and techniques, and (3) machine learning, especially classification and topic modeling.

In MLP, considerable work has been done in several areas, which are relevant to this project both motivationally and from the perspective of research methods and findings.

One area is math character recognition and formula recognition [13,60,67,72] in: (1) scanned documents [5,21,47], and (2) machine-readable PDF documents [11,12,70]. Our tagger works currently from TeX/LaTeX sources, but can be expanded to work from PDF sources using math term/expression recognition techniques as a very important preprocessing step.

Another related MLP area is the conversion tools such as the LaTeXML tool that converts from TeX/LaTeX to XML/HTML/MathML [44,55]. Some of the parsing techniques developed and used in LaTeXML are directly applicable in our tagging work. The main limitation of the current conversion tools, however, is that they convert to presentational math, with little or no semantics extraction or disambiguation capabilities. Therefore, conversion tools can be prime users of the findings and techniques that will result from this project.

Mathematical knowledge management, more broadly, covers the activities of not only collecting, organizing, and representing math knowledge, but also developing systems and techniques for searching [2,26,32,38,40,68,69,72,74], semantifying/annotating [36,54,63], and managing and making use of such knowledge [35]. Math digital libraries can greatly benefit their users from semantic enrichment of their contents: for cognitive use of semantic annotations, for more effective math search and retrieval, and/or for more effective math text mining and math reasoning based applications. Therefore, the MKM needs and goals will guide this project, and will in turn benefit from the techniques and findings of the project.

NLP is a well-established field that bears direct relevance to MLP and this project. POS tagging [23,42,52,58] and word-sense disambiguation [1,48] are two very mature areas and have had great impact on the NLP field and industry. This project will utilize POS tagging and disambiguation techniques to a great extent. It must be noted, however, that the work in this project is different from NLP in several fundamental respects:

- The parts of math are entirely different from the parts of speech, and therefore, the math tagsets and the corresponding tagging algorithms will have to be different.
- The (implicit) grammar underlying math expressions is different from the grammars of natural languages. Also, the wealth of knowledge related to natural language grammars, theoretical and computational linguistics, and the many resources available to NLP such as machine-readable lexicons[4], thesauri, collocations, etc., have no counterpart in the math language arena.

  Some researchers have started to look into math language from that computational linguistics perspective [57,59,61,64], studying [20,22,29,39,49,57, 65,66] and relying on math-notation practices [3,14] and underlying math grammars (*e.g.*, combinatory categorical grammar [22]). We will make use of the math linguistics work that is emerging, to help with the tagging and disambiguation, by giving higher probabilities to math roles/senses/meanings that the notational practices and "subconscious" grammars seem to favor. We will also make use of the burgeoning work on using NLP techniques of processing the text (as opposed to the math formulas) in math documents to shed light on the semantics of math terms in formulas [16,25,27,34]. The interplay between tagging+disambiguation and such techniques is expected to open up new possibilities: to inform better POM tagging, and conversely, to advance MLP in ways that would be hard, if not impossible, without tagging.
- In natural language, (nearly) every term is a word in the dictionary, and thus the dictionary definitions form a good starting point for tagging, disambiguation, and ensuing syntactic and semantic processing. In math, however, while some terms have standard meanings/roles/uses, many terms are rather abstract, have no prior agreed-upon meaning/role, or worse yet, are assigned new (and shifting) meanings that overwrite their common meanings. This complicates tagging, disambiguation, and semantic determination in MLP, and thus calls for fresh new approaches to be created and studied.

---

[4] http://wordnet.princeton.edu/wordnet/download/current-version/.

Fundamental to this project is classification, whether document-level classification, context modeling, or term-sense disambiguation. Therefore, this project will use well-established machine learning techniques for classification [6,30,46,62], as well as deep learning (deep neural networks) [8,31] which has begun to be used in NLP [10,56]. The goal here is to determine the best performing classifier for the purposes of this project, rather than advance classification and learning techniques in general.

Regarding math-document classification *per se*, a taxonomy of math areas will be needed. Fortunately, there are several taxonomies that can be used. They include *Mathematics Subject Classification*[5] (MSC2010) by the American Mathematical Sociert (AMS), the arXiv's *Categories within Mathematics*[6] taxonomy, and Wikipedia's math taxonomy[7]. In this project, the arXiv's taxonomy will be used due to the wide availability of labeled data (*i.e.*, math papers that are classified and have keywords), which are useful for training and testing classifiers. Also, if enough labeled data is found for the MSC2010, it will be used as well for the math-document classification work in this project.

There have been some promising efforts in math-document classification. Schoneberg and Sperber [53] used POS tagging of the text portions of math documents to identify noun phrases and in turn shed semantic light on math terms in formulas. Then, using POS tags, they developed a document classifier (on math abstracts and reviews), and showed an improvement in performance over non-tagged document classification. This demonstrates the promise of tagging for document classification, and is reason to expect that sophisticated POM tagging (alone or in addition to POS tagging) can improve document classification to a greater extent.

The project will need to develop topic models and context models. Topic modeling is now well understood and the standard techniques [7,9] developed for topic modeling will be adapted to math-topic modeling and also applied for the context modeling work that is planned in this project. Also, some work has been done on math context and its uses in math search [71], including resolving references between formulas, use of textual context around formulas, and topic modeling to identify subjects in math documents.

Finally, public domain software will be used in this project wherever possible, such as the Stanford CoreNLP [43] and the WEKA data mining software [28], to name a few.

4   Elements of the Projects

This section outlines the elements, concepts and constructs of the project.

---

[5] http://www.msc2010.org.

[6] https://arxiv.org/.

[7] https://en.wikipedia.org/wiki/Areas_of_mathematics.

4.1   Math Tokenization, Parts of Math, Tagset and Feature Sets

Clearly, as the tagger is at the core of the project, two fundamental parts must be addressed: (1) categories of math tokens, and (2) parts of math of the various token categories.

Much like in natural language we have the fundamental linguistic parts like nouns, verbs, etc., in math expressions and formulas we have fundamental notions of operations, relations, variables, functions, objects (like sets, groups, vector spaces), and so on. After a close examination of the literature, math authoring tools like LaTeX, and Unicode symbols for math, the author has delineated certain categories of math tokens, and specified (1) a fairly comprehensive set of parts of math, (2) a corresponding tagset, and (3) relevant features for the various parts of math. The tokens and parts of math are briefly presented in Table 1, where the tagset is very much the rightmost column (supplemented with the bold items of the middle column wherever indicated). In addition to the tags in the tagset, important features have been defined and will be computed by the tagger for the sake of disambiguation and richer semantic annotations; those features are specified in Subsect. 4.2.

Note about Math Fonts: Math letters, both Latin and Greek, and sometimes even numbers, are used in a variety of typefaces, font weights (bold vs. plain), font styles (italics vs. upright), and font sizes. The typefaces commonly used in math are: Computer Modern, Roman, Sans serif, Calligraphic, Blackboard, Fraktur, Typewriter, etc. Math is sensitive to typeface, font weight & style, and sometimes size. The same letter, say R, can be used simultaneously in different fonts (*e.g.*, $R, \mathrm{R}, \mathsf{R}, \mathcal{R}, \mathbb{R}, \mathfrak{R}, \mathrm{R}, \mathbf{R}$) to designate different entities in the same context. Therefore, the tagger also tags math letters with regard to typeface, font weight & style, and possibly size.

In addition to *tags*, the tagger will compute *features* for each term. These features provide additional semantics (per term/expression) and will help the later scans of the tagger to disambiguate the terms and sub-expressions. The initial set of features to be computed is presented in Subsect. 4.2. Note that some features will not be computed in the first scan (*e.g.*, *accent-function* and *accent-purpose*) due to inadequate information at that stage, but will be computed in the disambiguation scans. Note also that, as the project progresses, and the software is put in the public domain and used, the tagset and features will likely change and evolve to better meet the needs of the community.

4.2   Features to be Computed by the POM Tagger

The tagger will compute for each math token (and some math phrases) several features of different types. This subsection presents those features, grouping them into subclasses of features.

Fundamental features:

- **Category/Role:** The value of this feature can be *operation, operator, relation, function, variable, parameter, argument, constant, quantifier, separator,*

Table 1. Math tokens and various parts of math.

Tokens	Explanations and examples	Part of math
Numbers	12, −10.5, etc	*Numeric quantity; index; reference*
Letters, Alphabetic strings	We will focus on the three most widely used alphabets in math: Roman, Greek (upper and lower case), Hebrew	*Function; variable; argument; index; parameter; identifier*
Operators, operations	- **Unary operations** and **unary operators**	*Operator*, *operation* of the right arities
	- **Binary operations**	
	- **Multi-ary operations**	
Relations	- **Equality/definition, approximation, similarity, equivalence, congruence**	*Relation* (of various kinds as indicated in the left box in bold)
	- **Inequalities**	
	- **Set-theoretic relations**	
	- **Logic relations**	
	- **Turnstile relations** (used in logic, category theory, model theory, proof theory, etc.)	
	- **Triangle-shaped inequalities** (used in abstract algebra)	
	- **Geometry/linear-algebra relations**	
	- **Negated binary relations**	
	- **Miscellaneous:** proportional ($\propto$), divides ($\mid$), etc.	
Fence symbols	- **Delimiters:** ( ) [ ] { } ⌊ ⌋ ⌈ ⌉	etc.	*Left-delimiter; right-delimiter; constructor; distributed multi-glyph operator*
	- **Constructors:** for creating/denoting sets, vectors, intervals	
	- **Distributional multi-glyph (DMG) operators:** $\mid.\mid$, $\|.\|$, $\langle.,.\rangle$, $\mid.\rangle$, etc	
Logic tokens	**Quantifiers:** $\forall, \exists, \exists!, \nexists, \Box, \Diamond$ etc	*Quantifier; proof token*
	Proof tokens	
Punctuations	",", ";", ".", ":", "|", "\\", "/". They can be simple **punctuations, separators** between elements/arguments, **implied conjunctions** and **conditionals**, glyphs in **distributed multi-glyph operators**, etc.	The designations in the left box (in bold)
Math accents	- **Diacritics:** bars, underlines, hats, tildes, dots, rings, arrows/harpoons, primes, etc.	*Accent* (of various types)
	- **Grouping accents:** over/under horizontal braces/brackets/parentheses etc.	
	- **Extensible accents:** adding symbols above and/or below the accents	
Arrows	Of various orientations, directions, valences, head and tail shapes, line type and shape	*Arrow* of various types
Various shapes	**Harpoons, smiles, frowns, spoons, pitchforks, angles**	The designations in the left box (in bold)
Ellipses	Triple dots of various orientations	*Ellipsis* with its orientation
Literals, constants	**Standard sets, empty set,** standard **functions** (*e.g.*, sin), standard **math constants** (*e.g.*, π, e), etc.	The designations in the left box (in bold)
"Other"	Any symbol not covered in the above categories	*Symbol*

punctuation, abbreviation, acronym, delimiter, left-delimiter, right-delimiter, constructor, accent, etc.

- **Subcategory:** This specifies further the category of the token, e.g., for "$<$", the category is "relation" and the subcategory is "order". Values can be *subscript, superscript, numerator, denominator, lower-limit* (of an integral), *constraint/condition, definition,* etc.
- **Meaning:** Such as "scalar addition", "the cosine function", etc.
- **Description:** This is lexical/syntactic description that can help disambiguate the token in the 2nd scan.
- **Areas:** This specifies the math area(s) where the symbol is used in the ascribed role/meaning.
- **Notational-status:** This specifies whether the math is *generic, standard* (i.e., as commonly understood), or *defined* (in the manuscript).

<u>Signature features</u> (for functions and operators): Those features specify the number and type of the arguments, which arguments are variables and which are parameters, the morphology of the function name (e.g., if it has subscripts/superscripts/prescripts), and the return data type:

- **Argument-structure**
- **Argument-datatype**
- **Return-datatype**
- **Presubscript-structure**
- **Presubscript-datatype**
- **Presubscript-value**

- **Subscript-structure**
- **Subscript-datatype**
- **Subscript-value**
- **Superscript-structure**
- **Superscript-datatype**
- **Superscript-value**

<u>Font features</u> and <u>Accent features</u>: Font features specify the font characteristics of the math term, and accent features specify the characteristics of the accent (the meaning of the latter will become clear in the next subsection):

Font Features

- **Typeface**
- **Font-style**
- **Font-weight**

Accent Features

- **Accent-purpose**
- **Accent-function**
- **Accent-position**

<u>Other features:</u>

- **Definitional-Mode** (for functions): This describes how a function is defined. Some functions are defined directly (e.g., by giving the value of the function as an algebraic expression in terms of the variables, or as a series), or indirectly through a variety of ways such as a differential equation, an integral equation, a transform, etc.
- **Arity** (for operations, operators, and even relations): It can be *unary, binary,* or N-*ary*

- **Affixity** (for operations and operators): It can be *prefix, infix, postfix,* or *other* (*e.g.,* $|\cdot|$, $\lfloor\cdot\rfloor$, $\lceil\cdot\rceil$)
- **Data-type:**
    - For numbers and variables: It can be *natural, integer, real, complex, set, group,* etc.
    - For operations and relations: This feature describes the data type of the operands. Furthermore, in the case of operations, it describes the data type of the answer.
- **Number-format** (for numbers)
- **Dimension** (for vector variables)

The tagset and feature set may seem unnecessarily too large. For annotation applications, users can use whatever relevant subsets of those tags/features. For classification tasks (e.g., disambiguation, document classification, etc.), some feature selection will take place in the project to narrow down the features (by selection and/or abstraction) to a small, highly relevant set.

4.3   Math Disambiguation

The second and third scan of the tagger will primarily disambiguate between alternative features, and narrow down the general tagging done in the first scan. This section identifies the ambiguities that will be addressed in this project, and presents a brief summary of the disambiguation methods to be used.

4.3.1   Math Ambiguities
In the course of this project, the following math ambiguities have been identified:

1. **Superscript ambiguity:** A superscript can be an exponent (as in x^2), index (*e.g.,* x_i^j), order of differentiation (*e.g.,* $y^{(2)}$ as the 2nd derivative of y), or a unary operator (*e.g.,* the "+" in $\mathbb{R}^+$ restricts $\mathbb{R}$ to the set of non-negative real numbers, the "c" in A^c complements the set A, and the "t" in A^t transposes the matrix A).
2. **Missing-operator ambiguity:** A missing operator can be any of the following:
    - the application of a function at the token/expression that follows, *e.g.,* $a(t+1)$ can be the acceleration function applied at time $(t+1)$;
    - the product of two quantities, *e.g.,* $a(t+1)$ can be the product of a with $(t+1)$;
    - differentiation, as in "dy" standing for the differentiation of y as opposed to the product of some quantities "d" and y;
    - The concatenation of tokens to produce a single token;
3. **Scope ambiguity** (or **missing-delimiters ambiguity**): Sometimes, delimiters are left out and assumed to be implied. For example, some standard functions (like trigonometric ones, as well as "exp" and "log") are applied without the use of parentheses, such as "$\sin x$", and even "$\sin 2\pi x$" standing for "$\sin(2\pi x)$", whereas an expression like "$\sin 2\pi x + 5$" means "$\sin(2\pi x) + 5$".

Similarly, in some simple inline fractions, the numerator and/or denominator can be more than one single token, as in $1/2\pi$ (intended to be $\frac{1}{2\pi}$). Knowing the intended locations of implicit delimiters is a major math ambiguity to resolve.

4. **Definition-overload ambiguity:** Many math symbols have well-known meanings, and yet are sometimes redefined (e.g., π is 3.1415... but is often redefined as something else). Nearly all the Latin and Greek letters have the same polysemy problem.

5. **Role ambiguities:** The different subclasses of such ambiguities are briefly discussed next:

   (a) **Function vs. variable vs. parameter vs. object ambiguities:** Often, a generic math symbol can be in any of these roles. For a tagger to be useful, it must be able to distinguish and disambiguate between those four parts of math.

   (b) **Operation vs. relation vs. object ambiguities:** Some math symbols (e.g., $\perp$) can be in any of those three roles and must be disambiguated.

   (c) **Operation vs. relation vs. punctuation ambiguities:** Similarly, some math symbols (e.g., "$|$" and "$\|$") can be in any of those three roles and must be disambiguated.

   (d) **Punctuation marks ambiguities:** Commas and semicolons can serve as normal punctuation, or as separators between arguments of a function or elements of a sequence, or as connectors between different components of a formula/definition. In the latter case, a comma can be the equivalent of (1) a conjunctive connector ("and") between several (sub)formulas, or (2) a conditional (like "if", "when") joining a formula and its constraint(s). Similarly, a symbol like "$|$" can play the connector role of conditional, or the role of a "such-that" in a definition (of a set), and so on. Disambiguating between these competing roles is of great importance.

   (e) **Fence ambiguities:** A fence (*aka* delimiters, *e.g.*, braces, brackets or angle brackets) can play different roles: as a delimiter, as a math-object constructor, as a distributed multi-glyph (DMG) operator, or even as a relation (as in the case of "$<$" and "$>$").

A DMG operator is one that consists of multiple symbols separated by the argument(s) of the operator. For example, "$|.|$" is an operator denoted with two matching single vertical bars separated by the argument, and can stand for absolute value, matrix determinant, set cardinality, etc.; the bra "$\langle.|$" and ket "$|.\rangle$" operators consist each of two distinct glyphs separated by the argument; and the inner product is often denoted as "$\langle\cdot,\cdot\rangle$" or "$\langle\cdot|\cdot\rangle$". When encountering such symbols, it is indispensable to determine whether each symbol is a relation, a separator, or a glyph (part) of a DMG operator.

Fence symbols, such as parentheses, brackets, and braces, can serve as not only as scope-marking delimiters, but also as constructors of certain mathematical objects. For example, parentheses around comma-separated lists make (ordered) sequences/tuples/vectors; curly braces around the same make sets, and brackets around the same may refer to lists/vectors and sometimes intervals. In such situations, the parentheses/brackets/braces effectively serve as *constructors* rather than scope-marking *delimiters*.

Disambiguating between these different roles should be of obvious utility.

(f) **Accent ambiguities:** Primes ($'$), over-lines, over-dots, hats, and other accents placed next to, above, or sometimes below individual symbols, can be an integral accent (a morphological part of the name), or an operator applied on the symbol, such as:

  i. differentiation of a function (e.g., y' and $\dot{v}$ designate derivatives)
  ii. Boolean complementation of variables (e.g., x' and $\bar{x}$ as complement of x)
  iii. conjugation (e.g., $\bar{z}$ as the conjugate of complex number z)
  iv. statistical mean (e.g., $\bar{x}$ as the mean of some random variable x)
  v. statistical estimator of a parameter (e.g., $\hat{\theta}$ denotes an estimator of parameter θ).

(g) **Type resolution:** Even after a token has been determined to be a variable, a parameter, an object, an operation or a relation, such tokens have data types that would be desirable to determine for more specific semantics. Also, in the case of relations, the subclass of the relation is important semantics as well.

(h) **Arity resolution:** Operations and even relations have arities (e.g., unary, binary, etc.), and must be determined for full semantics.

(i) **Signature resolution:** Mathematical function have signatures, *i.e.*, number and data types of arguments, and number and data types of "returned" values. Function signature need to be determined since it forms a key component of function semantics.

4.3.2   Disambiguation Methods

The tagger, in scan 2 and 3, will address these ambiguities. The disambiguation techniques that will be developed will employ standard feature-based statistical classification methods [6,10,30,46,56,62] as well as deep learning [8,31]. The features to be used are (1) the alternative feature sets produced in the 1st scan, and (2) the elements of the context model that is produced by the context modeler using the document classifier, topic modeler, and harvester, defined earlier, and discussed briefly in the next subsection. Also, *type inferencing* will be used for disambiguation. For example, if the document defines a token L as $L = \Delta + x^2$, and earlier tagging determines that Δ is the Laplacian operator, it will be concluded that L is an operator. More broadly, Combinatory categorical Grammars (CCGs) have been found to help with type inferencing [22], and therefore, they are likely to be useful for part-of-math inferencing and disambiguation. CCGs will be explored in this research for this purpose. It should be noted, however, that those techniques and others (syntactic and statistical) will be initially explored on a tentative basis, individually and in combination;

afterwards, naturally, the more promising ones will be further pursued, while less promising ones abandoned.

4.4 Document Classifiers, Topic and Context Modeler, and Harvester

The math-document classifier will be based on standard classification techniques [6,8,10,30,31,46,56,62], and the taxonomies of classes used will be that of the arXiv[8], and also the American Mathematical Society's MSC2010[9].

The Latent Dirichlet Allocation based method [9] will be used for topic modeling. The input to the topic modeler will include: (1) the textual terms in the math document (when modeling the topic of a document) or in a math term's neighborhood (when helping model a context), and (2) the math term's tags and alternative features produced by the 1st scan of the tagger.

The harvester will construct a graph where the nodes represent mathematical objects, and the edges represent references between objects. To build the harvester, we will rely on (1) POM tagging of the math, (2) POS tagging of the text in the document, and (3) special keywords and phrases that are commonly used by math authors when introducing definitions and notations. POS tagging and special keywords have been used for harvesting; what will be different in this project is the exploitation of POM tagging, with the expectation that the synergistic performance of the harvester (and the rest) will be superior.

5 Current State of the Project

The first scan of the POM tagger: The first scan of the tagger has been completed (10 K lines of Java code). This scan recognizes all the lexical math terms, and some of the math phrases (e.g., fractions, radicals, binomial coefficients, subscripts, superscripts, etc.). For each math term, the 1st scan computes and attaches not only a primary tag (the math-lexical class of the term), but also a number of alternative, tentative feature sets (with tentative values) that will feed into scans 2 & 3. As indicated earlier, those feature sets capture alternative math-syntactical and math-semantic features (including mathematical roles/categories and possible meanings) for the term. Resolving between those alternatives will be performed in Scans 2 and 3 of the tagger.

The Knowledge Base: The alternative feature sets are obtained from a knowledge base (KB) that was built for this project. The KB already has over 2800 entries so far, one entry per math term/symbol that could be used by math authors, including all the LaTeX encoded math symbols [37], all the math symbols in the Unicode [51], etc. Each entry specifies the math term, and one or more alternative feature-sets for the term (up to 18 sets at this time). The feature sets range in size, from 2 to 14 features. What distinguish one alternative feature-set

---

[8] https://arxiv.org/archive/math.

[9] http://www.msc2010.org.

from another are: the math domain where the term is used, the role/category of the term, the meaning of the term, and/or lexical and syntactic considerations. For example, the symbol Γ can stand for the *Gamma* (probability) *distribution* of two parameters, or the the *gamma function* (a special function) of one complex variable, or the *incomplete gamma function* of two complex variables, or the *p-adic gamma function* of one integer variable in Number Theory, etc. For each of those uses, there is a separate feature set in the entry of Γ in the KB, specifying the math domain (e.g., special functions, probability theory, or number theory), the role (e.g., function), the name/meaning (e.g., the p-adic gamma function), the number and data type of the arguments, and so on.

Preliminary Math-doc Classification and Definition-Harvesting: The author, along with collaborators, has done work in semantification of math documents [54], especially the identifier-definition extraction. Using both the natural language portion and the math expressions in an input math document, and especially the math domain of the document, we were able to infer the actual meaning of a math identifier and improve the performance of automated identifier-definition extraction. The contribution of the document's math domain was mainly in the identification of the *namespace* of the employed mathematical notation. To determine the domain, we developed preliminary math-document classification using clustering and mapping of clusters to standard subject classification schemata. This recent work justifies: (1) adding the math domain as one of the features in alternative features in the KB, and (2) the need for further development of document classification. The results obtained in that work will serve as: (1) a base to build on and improve, especially with the help of the tagging that was not available when that work was performed, and (2) a baseline against which to compare the improvements in performance of the planned document classifier and harvester.

6   Future Stages of the Projects

The project, expected to take about 3–4 years and involving the author and about two graduate students, will be carried out in several stages outlined below. All implementations will be in Java. Note that the envisioned applications, mentioned earlier, will constitute separate projects; some will be done in parallel, while other applications will be carried out after the current project, and most of them will involve collaboration with other researchers (e.g., [15]).

Stage 1: Thoroughly test and refine *the first scan of the tagger*, which is already implemented.

Stage 2: Design, implement, and optimize the *math-topic modeler*, *math-document classifier*, and *harvester*.

Stage 3: Design and develop the *second scan of the tagger*, so it disambiguates math terms and symbols, using (1) the tags and alternative feature sets of the math terms, produced by the first scan, (2) the models produced by the topic modeler, context modeler, and document classifier, and (3) the output of the harvester.

Stage 4: Design and develop the *third scan*, so it groups subsequences of tagged math terms into "mathematical phrases" such as (1) functions applied at arguments, (2) derivatives of functions/expressions, (3) implicit fractions, etc. This stage involves a high degree of disambiguation of the connections or "relations" between adjacent terms in a math expression.

Stage 5: Iteratively refine the three scans, the topic modeler, context modeler, document classifier, and harvester, to improve the individual and synergistic performance of the modules.

Stage 6: Document all the modules and put them and their documentations in the public domain (GitHub and the project Web site) for general use.

References

1. Agirre, E., Lopez de Lacalle, A., Soroa, A.: Knowledge-based WSD on specific domains: performing better than generic supervised WSD. In: IJCAI, pp. 1501–1506 (2009)
2. Anca, S.: Natural language and mathematics processing for applicable theorem search. Master's thesis, Jacobs University Bremen (2009)
3. Anderson, R.H.: Two-dimensional mathematical notation. In: Fu, K.S. (ed.) Syntactic Pattern Recognition, Applications, pp. 174–177. Springer, New York (1977)
4. arXiv.org: https://arxiv.org/
5. Alvaro, F., Sanchez, J.-A., Benedi, J.-M.: Recognition of printed mathematical expressions using two-dimensional context-free grammars. In: International Conference on Document Analysis and Recognition, Beijing, China, pp. 1225–1229 (2011)
6. Bishop, C.: Pattern Recognition and Machine Learning. Springer, New York (2006)
7. Blei, D.: Introduction to probabilistic topic models. Commun. ACM **55**(4), 77–84 (2012)
8. Bengio, Y., LeCun, Y., Hinton, G.: Deep learning. Nature **521**, 436–444 (2015)
9. Blei, D., Ng, A., Jordan, M., Lafferty, J.: Latent Dirichlet allocation. J. Mach. Learn. Res. **3**, 993–1022 (2003)
10. Bowman, S., Potts, C., Manning, C.: Learning distributed word representations for natural logic reasoning. In: The AAAI Spring Symposium on Knowledge Representation and Reasoning (2015)
11. Baker, J.B., Sexton, A.P., Sorge, V.: A linear grammar approach to mathematical formula recognition from PDF. In: Carette, J., Dixon, L., Coen, C.S., Watt, S.M. (eds.) CICM 2009. LNCS, vol. 5625, pp. 201–216. Springer, Heidelberg (2009). doi:10.1007/978-3-642-02614-0_19
12. Baker, J.B., Sexton, A.P., Sorge, V.: Faithful mathematical formula recognition from PDF documents. In: International Workshop on Document Analysis Systems, Boston, USA, pp. 485–492 (2010)
13. Chan, K.-F., Yeung, D.-Y.: Mathematical expression recognition - a survey. Int. J. Doc. Anal. Recogn. **3**, 3–15 (2000)
14. Cajori, F.: A History of Mathematical Notations, vol. 2. Open Court Publishing Company, Chicago (1929)

15. Cohl, H., Schubotz, M., Youssef, A., Greiner-Petter, A., Gerhard, J., Saunders, B.V., McClain, M.A., Bang, J., Chen, K.: Semantic preserving bijective mappings of mathematical formulae between word processors and computer algebra systems. In: CICM 2017, Edingburgh, Scotland (2017)
16. Cramer, M., Fisseni, B., Koepke, P., Kühlwein, D., Schröder, B., Veldman, J.: The naproche project controlled natural language proof checking of mathematical texts. In: Fuchs, N.E. (ed.) CNL 2009. LNCS, vol. 5972, pp. 170–186. Springer, Heidelberg (2010). doi:10.1007/978-3-642-14418-9_11
17. Cohl, H.S., McClain, M.A., Saunders, B.V., Schubotz, M., Williams, J.C.: Digital repository of mathematical formulae. In: Watt, S.M., Davenport, J.H., Sexton, A.P., Sojka, P., Urban, J. (eds.) CICM 2014. LNCS, vol. 8543, pp. 419–422. Springer, Cham (2014). doi:10.1007/978-3-319-08434-3_30
18. (World) Digital Mathematics Library: https://www.math.uni-bielefeld.de/~rehmann/DML/dml_links.html
19. The European Digital Mathematics Library: https://eudml.org/
20. Ganesalingam, M.: The Language of Mathematics. Ph.D. thesis, Cambridge University (2009)
21. Garain, U.: Identification of mathematical expressions in document images. In: International Conference on Document Analysis and Recognition, Barcelona, Spain, pp. 1340–1344 (2009)
22. Ginev, D.: The Structure of Mathematical Expressions. Master thesis, Jacobs University Bremen, Bremen, Germany (2011)
23. Goldwater, S., Griffiths, T.: A fully Bayesian approach to unsupervised part-of-speech tagging. In: Association for Computational Linguistics (2007)
24. Göttinger Digitalisierungszentrum: http://gdz.sub.uni-goettingen.de/gdz/
25. Grigore, M.: Knowledge-poor Interpretation of Mathematical Expressions in Context. Master thesis, Jacobs University Bremen, Bremen, Germany (2010)
26. Guidi, F., Coen, S.C.: A survey on retrieval of mathematical knowledge. In: Kerber, M., Carette, J., Kaliszyk, C., Rabe, F., Sorge, V. (eds.) CICM 2015. LNCS, vol. 9150, pp. 296–315. Springer, Cham (2015). doi:10.1007/978-3-319-20615-8_20
27. Grigore, M., Wolska, M., Kohlhase, M.: Towards context-based disambiguation of mathematical expressions. In: The Joint Conference of ASCM 2009 and MACIS 2009, Math-for-Industry, Fukuoka, Japan (2009)
28. Hall, M., Frank, F., Holmes, G., Pfahringer, B., Reutemann, P., Witten, I.: The WEKA data mining software: an update. SIGKDD Explor. Newslett. **11**(1), 10–18 (2009)
29. O'Halloran, K.L.: Mathematical Discourse: Language, Symbolism and Visual Images. Continuum, New York (2005)
30. Hastie, T., Tibshirani, R., Friedman, J.: The Elements of Statistical Learning: Data Mining, Inference, and Prediction, 2nd edn. Springer, New York (2013)
31. Hinton, G., Salakhutdinov, R.: A better way to pretrain deep Boltzmann machines. Adv. Neural Inf. Process. Syst. **3**, 1–9 (2012)
32. Hambasan, R., Kohlhase, M., Prodescu, C.: MathWebSearch at NTCIR-11. In: 10th NTCIR Conference, pp. 114–119, Tokyo, Japan (2014)
33. Olver, F.W.J., Olde Daalhuis, A.B., Lozier, D.W., Schneider, B.I., Boisvert, R.F., Clark, C.W., Miller, B.R., Saunders, B.V., (eds.) NIST Digital Library of Mathematical Functions. http://dlmf.nist.gov/. Release 1.0.14 of 2016-12-21
34. Kofler, K., Neumaier, A.: DynGenPar – a dynamic generalized parser for common mathematical language. In: Jeuring, J., Campbell, J.A., Carette, J., Reis, G., Sojka, P., Wenzel, M., Sorge, V. (eds.) CICM 2012. LNCS, vol. 7362, pp. 386–401. Springer, Heidelberg (2012). doi:10.1007/978-3-642-31374-5_26

35. Kohlhase, A.: Search interfaces for mathematicians. In: Watt, S.M., Davenport, J.H., Sexton, A.P., Sojka, P., Urban, J. (eds.) CICM 2014. LNCS, vol. 8543, pp. 153–168. Springer, Cham (2014). doi:10.1007/978-3-319-08434-3_12

36. Kohlhase, M.: Semantic Markup for Mathematical Statements. Version v1.2 (2016)

37. Kottwitz, S.: LaTeX Beginner's Guide. PACKT Publishing, Birmingham (2001)

38. Libbrecht, P., Melis, E.: Methods to access and retrieve mathematical content in ACTIVEMATH. In: Iglesias, A., Takayama, N. (eds.) ICMS 2006. LNCS, vol. 4151, pp. 331–342. Springer, Heidelberg (2006). doi:10.1007/11832225_33

39. Libbrecht, P.: Notations around the world: census and exploitation. In: Autexier, S., Calmet, J., Delahaye, D., Ion, P.D.F., Rideau, L., Rioboo, R., Sexton, A.P. (eds.) CICM 2010. LNCS, vol. 6167, pp. 398–410. Springer, Heidelberg (2010). doi:10.1007/978-3-642-14128-7_34

40. Liska, M., Sojka, P., Ruzicka, M.: Similarity search for mathematics: Masaryk University team at the NTCIT-10 math task. In: 10th NTCIR Conference, Tokyo, Japan, pp. 686–691 (2013)

41. Manning, C.D., Schutze, H.: Foundations of Statistical Natural Language Processing. MIT Press, Boston (1999)

42. Manning, C.D.: Part-of-speech tagging from 97% to 100%: is it time for some linguistics? In: Gelbukh, A.F. (ed.) CICLing 2011. LNCS, vol. 6608, pp. 171–189. Springer, Heidelberg (2011). doi:10.1007/978-3-642-19400-9_14

43. Manning, C.D., Surdeanu, M., Bauer, J., Finkel, J., Bethard, S.J., McClosky, D.: The Stanford CoreNLP natural language processing tootlkit. In: ACL (2014)

44. Miller, B.: LaTeXML: A LaTeX to XML/HTML/MathML Converter. http://dlmf.nist.gov/LaTeXML/

45. The database MathSciNet: http://www.ams.org/mathscinet/

46. Murphy, K.P.: Machine Learning: A Probabilistic Perspective. MIT Press, London (2012)

47. Malon, C.D., Uchida, S., Suzuki, M.: Mathematical symbol recognition with support vector machines. Pattern Recogn. Lett. **29**, 1326–1332 (2008)

48. Navigli, R.: Word sense disambiguation: a survey. ACM Comput. Surv. **41**(2), 1–69 (2009)

49. Neumaier, A., Schodl, P.: A framework for representing and processing arbitrary mathematics. In: The International Conference on Knowledge Engineering and Ontology Development, pp. 476–479 (2010)

50. Nghiem, M.-Q., Yokoi, K., Matsubayashi, Y., Aizawa, A.: Mining coreference relations between formulas and text using Wikipedia. In: Second Workshop on NLP Challenges in the Information Explosion Era, Beijing, China, pp. 69–74 (2010)

51. Robertson, W.: Every Symbol (most Symbols) Defined by Unicode-Math (2015)

52. Santorini, B.: Part-of-speech tagging guidelines for the Penn treebank project. 3rd Revision, University of Pennsylvania (1990)

53. Schöneberg, U., Sperber, W.: POS tagging and its applications for mathematics. In: Watt, S.M., Davenport, J.H., Sexton, A.P., Sojka, P., Urban, J. (eds.) CICM 2014. LNCS, vol. 8543, pp. 213–223. Springer, Cham (2014). doi:10.1007/978-3-319-08434-3_16

54. Schubotz, M., Grigorev, A., Leich, M., Cohl, H.S., Meuschke, N., Gippx, B., Youssef, A., Markl, V.: Semantification of identifiers in mathematics for better math information retrieval. In: The 39th Annual ACM SIGIR Conference (SIGIR 2016), Pisa, Italy, pp. 135–144 (2016)

55. Stamerjohanns, H., Kohlhase, M., Ginev, D., David, C., Miller, B.: Transforming large collections of scientific publications to XML. Math. Comput. Sci. **3**(3), 299–307 (2010). Birkhäuser

56. Socher, R., Lin, C., Ng, A.Y., Manning, C.D.: Parsing natural scenes and natural language with recursive neural networks. In: ICML (2011)
57. Smirnova, E., Watt, S.M.: Notation selection in mathematical computing environments. In: Transgressive Computing 2006: A conference in honor of Jean Della Dora (TC 2006), Granada, Spain, pp. 339–355 (2006)
58. Søgaard, A.: Simple semi-supervised training of part-of-speech taggers. In: The ACL Conference Short Papers, pp. 205–208 (2010)
59. So, C.M., Watt, S.M.: Determining empirical characteristics of mathematical expression use. In: Kohlhase, M. (ed.) MKM 2005. LNCS, vol. 3863, pp. 361–375. Springer, Heidelberg (2006). doi:10.1007/11618027_24
60. Suzuki, M., Tamari, F., Fukuda, R., Uchida, S., Kanahori, T.: INFTY: an integrated OCR system for mathematical documents. In: ACM Symposium on Document Engineering, Grenoble, France, pp. 95–104 (2003)
61. Uchida, S., Nomura, A., Suzuki, M.: Quantitative analysis of mathematical documents. Int. J. Doc. Anal. Recogn. 7(4), 211–218 (2005)
62. Vapnik, V.N.: The Nature of Statistical Machine Learning, 2nd edn. Springer, Heidelberg (2000)
63. Watt, S.M.: Exploiting implicit mathematical semantics in conversion between TEX and MathML. TUGBoat 23(1), 108 (2002)
64. Watt, S.M.: An empirical measure on the set of symbols occurring in engineering mathematics texts. In: International Workshop on Document Analysis Systems, Nara, Japan, pp. 557–564 (2008)
65. Wolska, M., Grigore, M.: Symbol declarations in mathematical writing: a corpus study. In: Towards Digital Mathematics Library, DML workshop, pp. 119–127. Masaryk University, Brno (2010)
66. Wolska, M., Grigore, M., Kohlhase, M.: Using discourse context to interpret object-denoting mathematical expressions. In: Towards Digital Mathematics Library, DML workshop, pp. 85–101. Masaryk University, Brno (2011)
67. Yang, M., Fateman, R.: Extracting mathematical expressions from postscript documents. In: ISSAC 2004, pp. 305–311. ACM Press (2004)
68. Youssef, A.: Roles of math search in mathematics. In: Borwein, J.M., Farmer, W.M. (eds.) MKM 2006. LNCS, vol. 4108, pp. 2–16. Springer, Heidelberg (2006). doi:10.1007/11812289_2
69. Youssef, A.: Relevance ranking and hit description in math search. Math. Comput. Sci. 2(2), 333–353 (2008)
70. Yu, B., Tian, X., Luo, W.: Extracting mathematical components directly from pdf documents for mathematical expression recognition and retrieval. In: Tan, Y., Shi, Y., Coello, C.A.C. (eds.) ICSI 2014. LNCS, vol. 8795, pp. 170–179. Springer, Cham (2014). doi:10.1007/978-3-319-11897-0_20
71. Zanibbi, R., Aizawa, A., Kohlhase, M., Ounis, I., Topic, G., Davila, K.: NTCIR-12 MathIR task overview. In: NTCIR-12, Tokyo, Japan (2016)
72. Zanibbi, R., Blostein, D.: Recognition and retrieval of mathematical expressions. Int. J. Doc. Anal. Recogn. 15(4), 331–357 (2012)
73. The database zbMATH: http://www.zentralblatt-math.org/zbmath/
74. Zhang, Q., Youssef, A.: Performance evaluation and optimization of math-similarity search. In: Kerber, M., Carette, J., Kaliszyk, C., Rabe, F., Sorge, V. (eds.) CICM 2015. LNCS, vol. 9150, pp. 243–257. Springer, Cham (2015). doi:10.1007/978-3-319-20615-8_16

Author Index

Printed in the United States
By Bookmasters